Black Submariners in
the United States Navy,
1940–1975

ALSO BY GLENN A. KNOBLOCK
AND FROM McFARLAND

*Historic Iron and Steel Bridges in Maine,
New Hampshire and Vermont* (2011)

*African American World War II
Casualties and Decorations in the Navy,
Coast Guard and Merchant Marine* (2009)

*"Strong and Brave Fellows":
New Hampshire's Black Soldiers and Sailors
of the American Revolution, 1775–1784* (2003)

Black Submariners in the United States Navy, 1940–1975

Glenn A. Knoblock

*Foreword by Melvin G. Williams, Jr.,
Rear Admiral, United States Navy (Ret.)*

McFarland & Company, Inc., Publishers
Jefferson, North Carolina, and London

The present work is a reprint of the illustrated case bound edition of Black Submariners in the United States Navy, 1940–1975, *first published in 2005 by McFarland.*

LIBRARY OF CONGRESS CATALOGUING-IN-PUBLICATION DATA

Knoblock, Glenn A.
Black submariners in the United States Navy, 1940–1975 / Glenn A. Knoblock ;
foreword by Melvin G. Williams, Jr.
p.   cm.
Includes bibliographical references and index.

IBSN 978-0-7864-6430-2
softcover : 50# alkaline paper ∞

1. United States. Navy — African Americans — History — 20th century.
2. United States. Navy — Submarine forces — History — 20th century.   I. Title.
VB324.A47K56 2011   359.9'3'092396073 — dc22   2005000888

BRITISH LIBRARY CATALOGUING DATA ARE AVAILABLE

© 2005 Glenn A. Knoblock. All rights reserved

No part of this book may be reproduced or transmitted in any form or by any means, electronic or mechanical, including photocopying or recording, or by any information storage and retrieval system, without permission in writing from the publisher.

Cover photograph © 2011 Brand X Pictures

Manufactured in the United States of America

*McFarland & Company, Inc., Publishers
Box 611, Jefferson, North Carolina 28640
www.mcfarlandpub.com*

In memory of Paul F. Hensing

He was always about giving people the proper recognition for the deeds that they performed. He would have liked the men in this book.

Dedicated to

Arthur Brown
USS *Narwhal*
1942–1945

Anderson Peter Royal
USS *Silversides*, USS *Dragonet*
1942–1945

Carl Eugene Kimmons
USS *Plunger*, USS *Parche*
1942–1944

Sam Wesley Wallace
USS *Mingo*
1943–1945

Many men have been lucky to call these men shipmates.
I am proud to call them my friends.

Table of Contents

*Foreword by Melvin G. Williams, Jr.,
Rear Admiral, United States Navy (Ret.)*   1
Acknowledgments   3
Preface   7

I. Black Sailors and the Evolution of the Steward's Branch in the United States Navy from 1775 to 1939   9

II. Overview of the Steward's Branch of the United States Navy During World War II   13

III. Becoming a Steward   18
Joining the Navy: Voluntary Enlistment   18
Joining the Navy via the Draft   21
The Navy Boot Camp Experience   22
Black Sailors and the Navy's Rating System During the War   28

IV. Becoming a Submariner   33
From Boot Camp to Submarines   33
From the Surface Navy to the Silent Service   39
Transfer from a Tender, Relief Crew, or Shore Duty   42

V. Life as a Wartime Submariner   45
The Daily Routine of a Submarine Steward   45
Qualifying as a Submariner   53

Battle-Station Action   60
The Men of the O-, R-, and S-Class Boats   77
Other Shipboard Activities   81
Crew Relations Aboard the Boat   94
Rest and Relaxation Ashore   121
Leaving the Boat   137
At War's End   144

VI. The Submarine Navy During the Postwar Years   161
The End of the 1940s and President Truman's Desegregation Order   162
The 1950s: Enter the Nuclear Age   179
The 1960s: Boomers and Fast Attacks   210
1970–1975: An End and a Beginning   239

VII. Histories of Black Submariners   257

Carroll Louden Allen 258	Russell Donan 287
Jesse Allen 260	Donald Fenner 288
William Allison 261	LC Fisher 290
Bruce Anderson 263	Robert Goens 290
Dave Ball 264	John Gray 293
George Bracey 266	William Green 293
Arthur Brown 266	Harold Hale 294
Mack Butler 269	Alfred Hall 296
Wallace Coleman 271	Leslie Hamilton 297
Robert Coley 272	L.T. Hammond 298
David Collier 273	John Harris 299
Clark Cooper 274	Arthur Haynes 300
Tyree Cornish 276	Curtis Hill 300
Joseph Cross 277	Lonnie Jackson 302
Earnest Danford 278	Zedell Jackson 303
Alonza Davis 279	Willie James 303
Everett Davis 280	Isaac Johnson 305
Lewis Davis 282	Woodrow Wilson Jones 307
Shirley Day 283	Carl Kimmons 308
Jesse Debro 285	William Knight 314
Nathan Dogan 286	Richard Lucas 315

George Washington Lytle   316
Sammie Major   317
Elvin Mayo   318
Hosey Mays   319
Edward McNair   321
Bert Minor   323
Eugene Mosley, Jr.   324
R.D. Mosley   325
William Murray   326
Edward Neely   329
Killraine Newton   330
Claude Palmer, Jr.   332
Walter Patrick   333
Roscoe Pennington   337
William Perry   338
John Phillips   340
Paul Ragland   340
Charles Richardson   342
Anderson Royal   343
Albert Rozar   351
Leonard Rozar   352
Harry Senior   354
Spaulding Settle   354
Mason Smith   355
Albert Soles   357
Jake Spurlock   359
Jim Stallings   360
Lacey Stevenson   361
Ezell "Tommy" Strong   362
O'Neal Thaxton   362
Hadwick Thompson   363
Otha Toler   364
Magnus Wade   366
Sam Wallace   368
Strauther Wallace   373
James Washington   373
Rufus Weaver   374
Carl White   378
John Wesley Whitehead   379
Walter Wilson   380

Appendix A. The Steward Rating System, 1939–1974   383
Appendix B. Black Submarine Stewards Killed or Lost During World War II   385
Appendix C. Top Stewards During World War II by Number of War Patrols   388
Appendix D. Black Stewards of World War II   392

Bibliography   467
Published Works   467
Internet Sources   469
Unpublished Personal Manuscripts, Documents, and Letters   469
Unpublished Government Documents, Citations, and Commendations   470
Personal Accounts   470
National Archives Source Material   473

Index   475

Foreword

Melvin G. Williams, Jr.,
Rear Admiral, United States Navy (Ret.)

This is a book in which the author, in my view, adeptly provides two key themes for readers. First, this book provides historical visibility to Black sailors who served in the United States Submarine Force ("the silent service") during the period 1939–1975. The author's research reveals that the majority of the Black sailors who served during this period were primarily restricted to the mess attendant and steward's mate fields. This is despite their education levels and individual competencies which could have qualified them for other fields. The story of their challenges and contributions is not too often told. Second, the book provides a success story of how an organization, the United States Navy, experienced positive cultural change. The reader can follow the culture change within the U.S. Navy to one in which the special skills and talents of each individual were permitted to flourish. Thus, unbridled individual contributions toward the efforts of the team became the cultural norm which, in my experience, has been a force multiplier toward mission accomplishment and organizational effectiveness. It is my opinion that although the U.S. Navy's record today is not perfect in the area of workforce diversity, the navy's modern-day record of equal opportunity and the commitment of its leaders to improve workforce diversity is truly a success story. Both themes are germane to leaders and organizations which endeavor to embrace the value of each individual in a diverse twenty-first-century workforce.

The author, Glenn Knoblock, expressed to me that he has no military background and that, "though I am white and was raised in a predominantly white area, my parents are good people and always taught us to judge someone by what they did—not how they looked." Glenn Knoblock, through expert research, exhaustive interviewing, and a genuine egalitarian approach, has done an exquisite job.

I am a career naval officer and submariner who is fortunate to have benefited from the dedicated contributions made by the mess attendants, navy stewards, and others noted by Knoblock, as well as a beneficiary of the aforementioned positive cultural change within the United States Navy. I personally know several of the individuals cited by the author. I am also familiar with the now disestablished Bainbridge Naval Training Center (near Port Deposit, Maryland). Knoblock indicates that it was at Bainbridge where the majority of the navy's steward's mates received their training during the last years of World War II. It is interesting that it was at this Bainbridge facility that I was privileged to attend the United States Naval Academy Preparatory School in 1973–1974.

As noted by the author, my father, Master Chief Steward Melvin Williams (a submariner), crafted the elements of the navy's present-day mess management specialist (MS) enlisted rating from his kitchen table at home while I was in Bainbridge at the U.S. Naval Academy Preparatory School. My father's recommendations led to the merger of the steward rating and the commissaryman rating, and, as the author says, "ended the era of the steward in the United States Navy." Also, Master Chief Steward Archie Denson (a submariner) was in charge of the navy stewards who served as midshipmen at the U.S. Naval Academy during the period in which I was privileged to attend (1974–1978).

It is with great honor and humility that I continue to serve our nation and navy today. So I encourage you to read this book and recognize the seldom-told challenges and contributions of dedicated individuals, and follow the success of an organization — the United States Navy.

M.G.W., Jr., February 2005

Acknowledgments

Sometimes it is hard for a writer to pinpoint the exact time when the idea for a book came to mind. That is not the case for this book. It was about my fifteenth birthday or so when submarines and submarine warfare from the World War II era became what would be a lifelong interest for me. I read almost anything I could find in the local library on the subject. Yes, the submarines themselves were interesting ships, but for me the real fascination was with the men who operated them. Almost overnight, skippers like Sam Dealey (my favorite) and Dudley Morton became my boyhood heroes. One older book, a beat-up old thing that somehow caught my eye at the library, was titled *Silversides*, by Robert Trumbull. This book, written 1942–1943 but not released until 1945 due to wartime censorship, was unusual in that it told of the everyday men that crewed the boat *Silversides*, not just the skipper and his exec. This was good reading! By far the most interesting man in the book, at least for me, was the Black mess attendant Anderson Peter Royal. So I guess you could say that I've known A.P. Royal for a long time. However, it was not until the year 2002 that I rediscovered him, when I chanced upon a copy of Trumbull's *Silversides* at an old book store and bought it as quickly as I could. I read it again, but this time I wondered not only about Royal, but others like him. Just what did Black men do in the Submarine Force during the war, and what was it like for them? The idea for this book was conceived, and you now hold in your hands the final result. While the most exciting part of researching and writing this book has been talking directly with the submariners themselves, few thrills could match that experienced when I found that A.P. Royal was alive and well and was happy to have his entire story be a part of this book.

In a book such as this, there are so many people to thank that one hardly knows where to begin. First and foremost, I must thank all the Black submariners who agreed to be interviewed for the book and have their stories told. I have found them, almost to a man, cooperative, friendly, and very patient in dealing with the constant questions that come from someone who has never been on a submarine. Of all the men involved, my biggest thanks go to Carl Kimmons, who carefully read through the entire manuscript and offered constructive criticism and praise whenever it was warranted. He was also invaluable in digging up information about other Black submariners, both deceased and living, and in several cases acting as a go-between for me with some families that had important information to share. My thanks also go to Sam Wallace, who has an incredible memory when it comes to names and who helped me out numerous times. Finally, A.P. Royal also read a portion of the manuscript and offered up his own suggestions. The encouragement all these men gave to me in this endeavor to give the submarine stewards of World War II their just due helped to sustain me even when it seemed as if the book would never be finished.

I would be remiss if I did not mention the many submarine wives and family members who also helped me out greatly. Women such as Moyna Richardson, Viola Wilson, Mae Donan, Dorothy Wade, Lily Thompson, Florence Wilson, and Doris Majors patiently and pleasantly answered my inquiries about their late husbands and provided photographs from the men's submarine days. Doing the same were family members of many submariners that are now either very ill or deceased or were otherwise unable to be interviewed, including Mildred Davis, Lawrence and Mark Coleman, Carrie Grooms-Davis, Jim Holloman, Charlene Green, Michael Owens, Ruby Whitehead, Jerry and Sanfuel Jones, Frankie Young, June Perry, and Genevieve McCoy.

Others who have been of great help include Gibson Bell Smith of the National Archives at College Park, Maryland; Brian Gunn for his timely and enthusiastic research on my behalf at the National Archives; retired submarine stewards Donald Wilson and Rufus Weaver, both of whom provided me with the names of and information regarding other Black submariners; Ms. Wendy Gully at the Submarine Force Library in Groton, Connecticut; and Nicole Valerio for her great help in preparing Appendix D. Thanks also to the following individuals who provided information about the vessels: Craig McDonald, for all things related to the *Puffer;* Glen Milhorn, *Gurnard;* Peter Sasgen and Alex Drury, *Rasher;* Howard and Keith Jameson, *Icefish;* William Whelan, *Brill;* Charles Rush, *Carbonero* and *Billfish;* Harry Hall, *Queenfish;* Captain Maurice Rindskopf, *Drum;* Bill Hagendorn, *Growler* and *Tang;* Bruce Broseker, *Thresher;* Dean Brown, *Trout;* Kelly Faino, *Silversides;* Pat Barron, *Stickleback;* Mike Geletka, *Harder;* Les Hewitt, *Pargo;* Kane Kelly, *Hardhead;* Admiral John Maurer, *Atule;* Captain Carl Dwyer, *Puffer;* Captain Slade Cutter, *Seahorse;* John Fakan, *Cod;* Floyd Erickson, *Whale;* Peter Nalle, *Whale;* Bob Devore, *Pogy;* Dave Hussey, *Parche;* Jim Lewis, *S-28* and *Searaven;* Gerald Pilger, *Jallao;* Bill Thisen, curator, Wisconsin Maritime Museum. Since this list cannot possibly cover everyone that I spoke to during this project, to all those individuals who have gone unnamed, I also extend my thanks. Despite all the help I have received, all errors that may have crept into this work are entirely my own doing.

During the writing of this book, which I will equate to a war patrol for our purposes, I had a great crew working with me. Acting as she always does in support of my endeavors, my wife, Terry, was a perfect executive officer and helped keep me on course. My children, John and Anna, patient as always when their Dad is at work, were first-class seaman. Doing signal duty as yeomen were my mother, Ceil Knoblock, and brother-in-law, Dave Wemmer. They did outstanding work transcribing submarine crew records during several trips to the National Archives. Dave also did double duty, serving as damage control officer whenever computer problems threatened. To all the rest of my family, I extend my thanks, as always, for your great support and encouragement.

Finally, some may wonder about this book and why submarine stewards from the Philippines and Guam have not been included. This work was originally conceived as a history of Black men that served in the Submarine Force, not of the men of the steward's branch per se. However, I quickly realized that the two were inextricably linked — one could not be discussed without the other. To keep the focus of the book intact, however, I made the decision to focus solely on Black submarine stewards (and later, Black men in all rates) and to highlight their struggles and accomplishments within the framework of segregated America as it then existed. This does not in any way diminish the accomplishments of the men from the Philippines and Guam that served as stewards in the Submarine Force. They, too, served competently and bravely and sacrificed their lives in the war with Japan. Peter Sococco, a wartime veteran with sixteen war patrols to his credit on *Stingray* who now resides in Norfolk, Virginia, is just one of many such men. *However*, I am forced to leave it to a future writer, one with greater resources and a proper understanding of their unique cultural background, to give them their full due.

Finally, while I have attempted to contact all the living wartime stewards that I could possibly find to record their stories, there are probably some men that I have missed for one reason for another. If you are one of these men yourself, or are acquainted with a Black submariner of World War II, please contact me through the publisher so that I may record that history before it is lost.

Wolfeboro Falls, New Hampshire
Spring 2005

Preface

Like small islands in a vast sea, these once-great defenders of liberty, the submarines of the United States Navy, are scattered throughout America. In Alabama and Texas to the south are *Drum* and *Cavalla*. In the north, in Illinois and Wisconsin, are *Silversides* and *Cobia*. In the east, at Baltimore and Philadelphia, are *Torsk* and *Becuna*, while in the midwest and west, in Oklahoma and California, are *Batfish* and *Pampanito*. Still on patrol as museum ships and war memorials, these submarines, and several others like them, serve as silent yet powerful reminders of a time when the world was on fire. It was a time when the United States Navy performed signal service, acting as firefighters to extinguish the blaze of the rising sun of the Japanese empire that swept the Pacific. Through museums and memorials such as these, we have learned much about the men and machines that helped win the war. But we don't know everything. What about the Black men that helped to man such ships of war, men such as George Lytle, Jim Stallings, Carl Kimmons, and Anderson Royal? What do we know about them? Who among us has ever heard the names of men like Joe Cross, Howard Walker, Donald Fenner, and many more who paid the ultimate price while serving their country? An old submarine phrase that has now entered common usage perhaps states it best: sometimes things just "slip under our radar" and go undetected. Such is the case with America's Black submariners. Despite the fact that Black men have served valiantly in the Submarine Force during World War II and beyond into the age of nuclear submarines, and continue to do so to this day, their accomplishments have gone largely unnoticed. It is now time to get them back onto the radar screen of history.

This work covers the service of America's Black submariners during a thirty-five year span from 1940 to 1975. Based largely on the personal histories of men who served on submarines during this important time in history, this work details their great contributions to the war effort from 1941 to 1945, the postwar years from 1946 to 1947 before desegregation, and the beginning stages of desegregation in the navy from 1948 to 1954. Coverage continues with firsthand accounts from the Black submariners, some of them World War II veterans, who served in the world's first nuclear ships. With the commissioning of the world's first nuclear ship, the submarine *Nautilus*, in 1954, there began a brief but exciting time in which America's first "nuke" boats made fantastic voyages of scientific exploration and discovery. Commencing with the Arctic voyages of *Nautilus* and *Skate*, they reached their zenith in 1960 with *Triton*'s voyage around the world submerged, and came to a close in 1962 with the rendezvous of *Seadragon* and *Skate* at the North Pole. Voyages to the Arctic, especially in waters along the Russian coast, by American submarines would continue on a regular basis every year after this, and still continue even today. Now, however, from 1962 to 1975, they were a part of our nation's cold war activities and were conducted in strict secrecy. Only recently have veteran Black submariners of this era been willing to disclose some details of their service due to the secrecy oath they were sworn to uphold forty years ago. Fittingly, this study includes the personal account of the Black submariner who forced the navy to come to terms with the problem of racial integration within its ranks and made sweeping changes to help eliminate racial bias when the steward rating was abolished in 1975.

That first nuclear submarine, the *Nautilus*, serves today as a museum ship in Groton, Connecticut. Though she is not a war veteran, she is, perhaps, the survivor of an even greater struggle ... the struggle of change. So, too, are America's Black submariners. They fought to win the war and then continued in the service of their country through the cold war era. By doing so in a most capable, competent, and, at times, heroic manner in the most difficult of conditions, they quietly helped to reestablish the rightful place of the Black sailor within the ranks of the United States Navy, where promotion and recognition are based not on a man's skin color, but on his leadership and fighting abilities. This book is their story.

I

Black Sailors and the Evolution of the Steward's Branch in the United States Navy from 1775 to 1939

Black sailors were an important part of the United States Navy long before the advent of the submarine. Prior to discussing the service of Black submariners in World War II, it is only proper that we should briefly examine the tradition of service established by men that came before them.

During the colonial era, Black sailors had already played an important part in manning merchant vessels. Whether slave or free, Black sailors served in a variety of capacities, including as cabin boys (usually slave youths owned by the captain), cooks, or as ordinary or able seamen serving right alongside their white counterparts. When the American Revolution began in 1775, the Continental Navy was established by the newly united colonies. Who would man such ships but the same men that manned the colonies' merchant vessels before the war? This included a large number of Black sailors, both free and slave, who were eager to serve their country in the quest for liberty from the British, despite the fact that their own personal liberty as Black men and slaves was not so certain.

The War of 1812, too, saw the service of many Black sailors. Commodore Oliver Hazard Perry had among his crew fifty Black sailors during the battle of Put-in-Bay on Lake Erie. While Perry objected to the "motley set" (Foner, p. 22) of sailors assigned to his fleet, his commander stated about the Black sailors that "many of them are among my best men" (*ibid.*). After winning his victory against the British fleet on September 10, 1813, Perry, having seen what such men could do, called his Black sailors as being "among my best men" (*ibid.*).

Nearly 30,000 Blacks served in the Union Navy during the Civil War from 1861 to 1864 and performed admirably. Joachim Pease was awarded the Navy Medal of Honor as loader of gun number one on the Union frigate *Kearsarge* during her historic battle with the Confederate raider *Alabama*. The *Kearsarge*'s acting master stated that Pease had "qualities even higher than courage or fortitude" and that he "fully sustained his reputation as one of the best men on the ship" (Quarles, p. 231). Other Black men that received the Navy Medal of Honor during the war were Robert Blake, an ex-slave who served as a powder handler on the USS *Marblehead* during a battle with the Confederates at Stono River, South Carolina; John Lawson, who served on the gunboat *Hartford* at the battle of Mobile Bay; and Aaron Anderson, a crewman on the *Wyandank* during an expedition to clear Mattox Creek, Virginia.

Following the end of the Civil War, the service of Black sailors in the United States Navy continued. While reduced in number, Blacks were still enlisted "on a fully integrated basis" (Foner, p. 67) and could qualify to serve in such ratings as gunners, gunner's mates, and bosuns. Though they could not rise to the rank of officers, they could become chief petty officers and lived, unsegregated, with their fellow crewmen who were white. This is not to say that the picture was all bright and that racial harmony prevailed. As it was on land, so it was on sea, and Black sailors often felt a measure of prejudice. Black sailors that "broke the rules" were often punished more harshly than their white counterparts, while white shipmates, especially those not native to America, often grumbled about sharing duty and quarters with Black sailors (*ibid.*).

While the United States Navy tried to maintain its liberal policies at sea, matters of race relations on land took a turn for the worse. A new age of freedom had dawned for the country's newly freed Black population after the Civil War, but it would not last long. Sponsored by Massachusetts senator Charles Sumner, Congress passed a civil rights bill that became law in 1875. It stated that the United States should "mete out equal and exact justice to all, of whatever nativity, race, ..." (Davis, p. 46). Despite the fact that this law was the "most far-reaching civil rights bill that was to be considered by Congress until 1964" (*ibid.*), it was a failure because it was never enforced. The bill was overturned by the Supreme Court just eight years later, in 1883, when it was challenged by cases that involved segregated railroad cars for Blacks in Tennessee (often cited as the first ever jim crow law), as well as those involving the use of public facilities in Missouri, California, Kentucky, and New York. In their pathetic ruling that declared the law of 1875 unconstitutional, the court held that "Congress could enact legislation to meet ... state action adverse to the rights of citizens ... but Congress could not properly cover the whole domain of rights appertaining to life, liberty, and property" (*ibid.*). With this ruling, the full impact of Jim Crow legislation and its resulting segregation would soon gain a stranglehold on Black "citizens" in the south. The light that had dawned so brightly after the Civil War was soon snuffed out, and by 1910 Blacks were entirely disenfranchised in Mississippi, South Carolina, Louisiana, Virginia, Georgia, North Carolina, Alabama, and Oklahoma (*ibid.*, p. 50).

With all that was happening on land in regard to race relations, it was inevitable that the United States Navy, though operating on the high seas, would soon be affected. The attack on Black sailors in the navy would, inevitably, come from the south. Indeed, an attempt in 1842 by John C. Calhoun, South Carolina's powerful senator, to restrict

Blacks in the navy to service as cooks, servants, and stewards was passed by the Senate but died in the House. It is not surprising that the attempt to infringe on Black sailor's rights in the navy would emanate from the south. After all, many of the Navy's largest home ports were found in southern waters at such places as Charleston, South Carolina, and Norfolk, Virginia, and a large contingent of the branch's leading officers, as well as enlisted seamen, were also from the south.

The move to segregate Blacks in the navy formally began on April 1, 1893, when the messmen's branch of the United States Navy was established "by verbal instructions to the recruiting service rather than by written orders" (Foner, p. 103). Henceforth, new Black recruits were to serve only as messmen, stewards, or cooks. One historian states that these verbal instructions were a "gentlemen's agreement" of sorts, and that Black sailors who served in other ratings, such as bosun's or gunner's mates, would gradually be mustered out of the service (Wright, p. 7). However, if this was the intended immediate result, it was not to be, and "it would appear that those naval officers who possessed crack Negro ratings simply ignored the order" (*ibid.*). This is not surprising, as commanding officers of any era knew that a good chief petty officer, be he Black or white, is worth his weight in gold when it comes to the efficient operation of a ship of war.

With the advent of the Spanish-American War in 1898, just five years after the establishment of the messmen's branch, Black sailors in the United States Navy were still holding their own. Two thousand Black sailors served during the war, including John Jordan, the chief gunner's mate on Admiral George Dewey's flagship the USS *Olympia*, and Robert Penn. Jordan fired the first shot at the battle of Manila Bay, during which the Spanish fleet was decimated, while Penn earned the Congressional Medal of Honor for saving a shipmate's life while the fleet was off the coast of Cuba (Foner, p. 83). After the war, the navy had approximately 500 Black sailors within its enlisted ranks. Despite being praised as "excellent sailors," one man remarked that, though they had demonstrated their loyalty and skills in the recent war, "promotion to higher rates depends entirely upon the recommendation of officers through whose veins, in most cases, runs the poisonous blood of Negrophobia, with a baleful effect unimaginable" (*ibid.*).

Following the Spanish-American War, it was widely rumored that the Navy would halt Black enlistment altogether, but this was not the case. Instead, its operational policy was to gradually phase out Black sailors in all ratings of shipboard service except for those in the messmen's branch. A giant step in this direction was taken in 1907–1908 when, in preparation for the ironically named Great White Fleet's journey around the world, it was decided to discharge all Japanese stewards. This was done because of tension between the Japanese and American governments at the time, and it was thought that the Japanese stewards would act as spies. In their place they were replaced wholesale by Black recruits who "resented their assignments as waiters and busboys" having "joined the Navy in good faith" (Foner, p. 105). To add insult to injury, when the Great White Fleet returned to the states in 1909, all Black petty officers were transferred to shore duty. One of these men, Charles Parnell, later wrote that "We knew that the end of a colored man being anything in the Navy except a flunkey had arrived" (*ibid.*).

In the ensuing years, the restrictions on Black sailors became tighter and tighter. Despite charges of discrimination from Black leaders in New York in 1913, the rear admiral in charge of the "investigation" found such accusations "unwarranted as there is no evidence of discrimination," conceding that the only Blacks in the navy were messmen, but that white men also served in this branch (*ibid.*, p. 106). The final blow came in 1919, when Black enlistment in the navy was halted altogether. While those Black sailors already in the service remained, they were limited to menial functions. Those sailors with general ratings were allowed to retain them, but as they retired or left the service, they were not replaced by Blacks.

It is unclear how many Black submariners there were during this early period of the existence of the Submarine Force from 1901 to 1920, but the number was probably rather small. This is due not only to the fact that the submarine crews of the early A to K classes of boats were small, ranging from seven to twenty-eight men total, including officers, but also because the L boats, first commissioned in 1916, were the first to even have a ship's cook as part of their crew. With the addition of a cook to the crews of the larger O-, R-, and S-class boats (see Chapter V), it wouldn't be long before Black stewards entered the Submarine Force.

One of the many Black men that served in the navy during this time as a steward was submariner John Calvin Harris. A native Virginian, he enlisted into the navy on January 2, 1914, at Norfolk, Virginia, and by October 1917 was in New London, Connecticut, as a mess attendant 1st class on the submarine tender *Fulton*. In September 1923 he went to submarine duty, serving on the *S-1* as an officer's cook under Captain Ralph Christie. It was Christie who would later command a significant part of the Submarine Force in Australia during World War II. During Harris's time aboard *S-1*, the boat was involved in a navy study testing the feasibility of submarine-carried scout aircraft. Just as Harris came aboard, the boat was being modified with the addition of a pod on deck that could carry a small collapsible seaplane. The long-serving Harris would serve in the navy for twenty-five years before retiring in 1939, only to return to active duty in 1942 at New London for another three years. Despite the navy's overall attempts to limit and discourage its number of Black men from 1919 to 1932, John Harris was one man that would keep on serving.

The policy of totally restricting Black enlistment would remain in force for thirteen years, until December 1932, when Black enlistment as mess attendants was reopened. This was only done out of sheer necessity, as the navy was then experiencing a shortage of mess attendants due to a lack of Filipinos that normally filled this position. Seven years later, in June 1939, on the eve of World War II, the Navy had 2,807 Black men in its ranks. As one historian so aptly states, "the American armed forces faithfully reflected the worst racist excesses of American society" (*ibid.*, p. 132).

II

Overview of the Steward's Branch of the United States Navy During World War II

When the United States officially entered World War II after the attack on Pearl Harbor on December 7, 1941, the Black men that filled the rating of mess attendant in the United States Navy were also drawn into the war. Despite the fact that the nation needed all the manpower it could muster to fight the two-front war in Europe and the vast Pacific, the armed forces of the United States collectively dug its heels in and stubbornly resisted the use of Blacks as fighting men as long as was possible. It was only through the strong efforts of Black civic leaders, organizations, and the Black media that Black men were grudgingly accepted as fighting men. However, despite the fact that Black men were accepted for volunteer service beginning in April of 1942, it would be some time before they actually reached the front in all branches of the armed forces. The Tuskegee airmen in the Army Air Corp, operating in the 99th Pursuit Squadron and the 332nd Fighter Group, fought in Africa and Europe from mid–1942 onward and established a fine record. Black marines did not see combat in the Pacific until December 1943, and Black army units were not sent to combat in Europe until mid–1944. In contrast, it was the navy's "fighting mess attendants" that led the way. Despite restrictions on the type of jobs they could perform, it was these men who served in every single naval engagement of the war, from December 7, 1941, to the surrender of Japan in August 1945. Later designated as steward's mates, with promotion available to steward or officer's cook, men of this branch of the United States Navy performed capably and, in many cases, heroically.

Because of official navy policy that was adhered to throughout the war, only Black men in the steward's branch saw combat and, as one historian has written, "it fell to the steward's branch to dispel the mythology surrounding the combat capacity or incapacity of the Black man. That the Steward did so is a matter of history" (Wright, p. 28). Indeed, it was a Mess Attendant 2nd Class named Dorie Miller who *earned* this country's first citation during the war when, on December 7, 1941, he served with distinction aboard the battleship *West Virginia*. During the course of the Japanese onslaught, Miller helped remove wounded men from the decks of the ship to safety, after which he manned a machine gun and, with no prior training, shot down four enemy aircraft. For his actions that day, this Black mess attendant was eventually awarded the Navy Cross. Miller subsequently performed recruiting duty for the navy but was unhappy doing so and requested a return to sea duty. This request was granted, and Miller continued to serve as a mess attendant and saw action in the Pacific. He was one of 644 men lost on November 24, 1943, when his ship, the light-aircraft carrier *Liscome Bay* was sunk off the Gilbert Islands by a Japanese submarine.

Indeed, it is rather ironic that while navy policy excluded Blacks from gun crews and battle stations (Foner, p. 167), in actual wartime conditions such thinking was often abandoned. Instead, during battle conditions, stewards served in a variety of key positions and contributed mightily to the war effort, acting as ammunition passers, serving on gun crews, standing lookout duty, manning communication phones, helping in torpedo reload gangs, as well as assisting with damage control operations and tending to the wounded. In surface ships in particular, the Stewards were put to work below decks as ammunition passers. Working in compartments that were sealed to maintain their ship's water-tight integrity, these men seldom survived when their ship was sunk during enemy action. Aboard submarines, stewards, too, acted as ammunition passers and, more commonly than on surface ships, were *assigned* to gun crews. In addition, unlike on surface ships, men assigned as stewards aboard submarines also helped to maneuver their boat by occasionally manning the important positions of helmsman and bow or stern planesman.

While the men of the steward's branch "were unheralded, and too often, went unappreciated," they "performed their duties as a group of professionals" (Wright, p. 35) and, in many cases, became well accepted as part of the crew. This was especially so among the tight-knit submarine crews. As in the two previous wars, no Black sailor was awarded the Medal of Honor, our country's highest decoration. However, a number of men in the steward's branch during the war were recognized for their heroic service and devotion to duty. Some were recognized by individual citations for their actions, while others were recognized in official reports by superior officers or were crew members of outstanding navy ships that earned the Presidential Unit Citation or the Navy Unit Commendation. The following names will suffice as examples of just a few such men:

- Leonard Roy Harmon, mess attendant 1st class, who gave his life to protect a shipmate aboard the cruiser *San Francisco* during action in the Solomon Islands, was awarded the Navy Cross.

- Lonnie David Jackson, mess attendant 1st class, and Stewart Alexander DeHosnery, mess attendant 2nd class, were awarded the army Silver Star for their service aboard the submarine *Trout* during the evacuation of gold bars from banks in the Philippine Islands.

- William Pinckney, cook 3rd class, who earned the Navy Cross for saving a shipmate's life aboard the carrier *Enterprise* when a bomb exploded.

- Elbert Oliver, steward's mate 1st class, earned a Bronze Star for taking over for a wounded gunner on the carrier *Intrepid* and continuing to maintain accurate fire against enemy torpedo planes despite being wounded himself.
- George Washington Lytle, cook 1st class, earned the Bronze Star for his service during six consecutive war patrols of the submarine *Drum* and for his outstanding performance as "petty-officer" in charge of the forward battery compartment and as first loader of the deck gun.
- Joseph Cross, steward 3rd class, who earned the Bronze Star while serving aboard the submarine *Halibut*. Known as an outstanding lookout, Cross saved the submarine from certain destruction by spotting an incoming Japanese plane.
- Charles Jackson French, mess attendant 2nd class, helped rescue fifteen of his crewmembers when their ship, the carrier *Lexington*, was lost during the battle of the Coral Sea. French swam continuously for two hours and pulled a raft with other survivors to safety. He was commended for his valor by Admiral William Halsey.
- Alonza Crawford, Jr., mess attendant 1st class, who served on the destroyer *Benham* for "wonderful work ... in taking care of wounded ... all the first night and ... almost continuously the first day" (Roscoe, p. 126) from the destroyer *Hamman* after she was torpedoed and sunk during the Battle of Midway.
- Carl E. Clark, steward 1st class, received the Purple Heart for wounds he received on the destroyer *Aaron Ward* during a kamikaze attack on May 3, 1945, off the island of Okinawa. Acting as a radar picket ship, the destroyer was hit by six suicide planes and through the heroic efforts of her crew, remained afloat and made it back to port. Clark helped in damage control and "stayed with the fire" (Clark, p. 102) on deck until it was extinguished. The *Aaron Ward* and her men also received a Presidential Unit Citation for their super-human efforts to save their stricken ship.
- Carl E. Kimmons, officer's cook 3rd class, was awarded the Navy Commendation Medal for action aboard the submarine *Parche* and was a member of the crew that earned that boat the Presidential Unit Citation. On his first boat, the *Plunger*, he was a member of a crew that earned the boat the Unit Commendation for her second, third, and fourth war patrols.

While the men above are just a few of the many Black sailors in the steward's branch that did signal service during the war, it also must be remembered that, though restricted in rating, they faced the same dangers and hazards that were experienced by all men of the United States Navy, no matter what their skin color. Nowhere was the possibility of danger and death aboard a man of war greater than for those men that served in the Submarine Force. Eighteen percent of all U.S. submarines, fifty-two in number, were lost during the war. Lost with them were more than 3,100 enlisted men and 374 officers. Thirty-nine of the United States submarines lost during the war had no survivors. Lost with these submarines were ninety-seven men from the steward's branch, an average of nearly two men per boat. Seventy-four of these men were Black, while most of the remainder were either from the Philippines or the island of Guam. Three lost submarines, *Albacore*, *Tang*, and *Trout* had three Black men aboard, while one submarine, the big *Argonaut*, had seven men from the steward's branch lost when she was sunk, two of whom were Black. The first Black submariner lost during the war was Mess Attendant 1st Class Nathaniel Johnson, who was lost on the *S-26* when she sank in the Gulf of Panama on January 24, 1942, after colliding with an escort vessel. The last Black submariners to lose their lives in World War II were Hubert Hackett, steward's mate 2nd class, and Percy Johnson, Jr., steward's mate 1st class. They died when their boat, the *Bullhead*, was sunk on August 6, 1945, by enemy aircraft, just eight days before Japan surrendered to end the war.

While Black sailors in the steward's branch conducted themselves with skill and honor in combat, their situation at home and how their service was perceived in the public arena was a constant source of irritation, at best, and, at worst, one of degradation. In an attempt to gain wider opportunities for Black men in the navy outside of its steward's branch, it was this very branch that was ridiculed and protested against by Black leaders, the Black press, and Black civic organizations. As one historian states, The steward's branch of the navy "was brought under intense fire by Negro leaders" and became "pawns in the game of Negro equality vs. white status quo and tradition," becoming "targets of scorn by our own people, fellow Negroes" (Wright, p. 18).

The United States Navy started to actively recruit Black men for duty in June 1942. This was in direct response to President Franklin Roosevelt's Executive Order #8802 "which forbade racial and religious discrimination in war industries, government training programs and government industries" (*ibid.*, p. 19). This order was issued by Roosevelt due to extreme political pressure brought to bear by the nation's Black leaders, among them A. Phillip Randolph and Walter White, and the threat of 100,000 Blacks marching on Washington, D.C., in support of racial equality. While the navy would continue to use Black men in the steward's branch, they also set up segregated training facilities where new Black recruits who qualified received training as technical specialists. These men were trained either at the camps of the Great Lakes Naval Training Center in Illinois or at the Hampton Institute in Virginia. Once they completed their training, they were rated in such positions as gunner's mates, carpenters, soundmen, electrician's mates, motor machinists, aviation mechanics, radiomen, yeomen, signalmen, storekeepers, cooks, and quartermaster (Reddick, pp. 208–09). These were ratings that had not been open to Black sailors for over fifty-years. While these new Black sailors of the United States Navy helped to break the color barrier, they were still assigned to segregated duty as construction workers and stevedores at ammunition and supply depots. Because of the navy's adherence to its segregationist policies, none of these newly rated Black sailors were sent into combat and were instead either stationed stateside for the duration of the war or to navy bases in Hawaii or the island of Guam. As one historian has written, it was "bitterly observed that Blacks in the navy had swapped the waiter's apron for the stevedore's hook" (Foner, p. 168).

This understandable bitterness by Black sailors outside the steward's branch manifested itself in several ways during the later stages of the war. The most serious was the well-known Port Chicago mutiny. This occurred following a disastrous explosion at the Port Chicago ammunition depot in California, where 320 seamen, 202 of whom were Black, who worked in loading ships were killed and 390 wounded (National Park Service, p. 2). In the weeks following, the men were ordered back to work at loading ammunition, but a group of 258 Black sailors refused, citing a lack of proper training and safety precautions. Ultimately, all but fifty of the men returned to work. Those who refused to do so were subsequently tried and convicted of mutiny, with the result that they were dishonorably discharged and given stiff prison sentences. While these men were eventually released and restored to duty in 1946 upon appeal, it was not until fifty-three years later, in December 1999, that President William Clinton officially pardoned one of the survivors.

With such facts in mind, it is no wonder that even within the navy itself, there was some degree of discord among these two distinct groups of Black sailors: those men in the steward's branch and those that entered the navy after June 1942 and were allowed to qualify for technical ratings. Frustrations were high on both sides. For the new breed of Black sailors, it was due to their continued segregation and the failure of the navy to utilize them properly. For those in the steward's branch, men that voluntarily enlisted before 1942, their frustrations were the result of several factors. Because of the continued segregationist policies of the navy, they were frozen in their position as stewards and were not allowed to change their rating to that of, say, yeoman or gunner's mate, or any other position. Those who wanted to do so would have to wait until several years after the war for this to become a reality.

This difference between men of the steward's branch and the newly rated Black sailors was fostered by the navy itself and was even reflected in the uniform insignia that were worn on each sailors uniform. The "new Negro dudes" (Wright, p. 20) were entitled to wear regular rating badges on their uniform that included the symbolic American eagle with chevron bars below to signify class, the same as white sailors. In contrast, men that served as stewards wore a rating badge that consisted of a simple crescent, or *C*, with one to four straight bars beneath to signify class. This badge was often referred to derisively by the stewards themselves as a moon and "loaves of bread," and it was not until late in the war that men in the steward's branch of the navy were finally allowed to wear the American eagle and chevron bars on their rating badge. As one former Steward wrote, "we were quasi-members of the Navy and wore a quasi-military badge" (*ibid.*). Because of such differences between these two groups of Black sailors, men in the steward's branch were often "objects of ridicule by our own ... fellow Negroes, who failed to understand our victimization, and by white shipmates as well. We punched it out with Negro Seamen in the streets of Washington, Baltimore, San Francisco, and San Diego, fought our own 'red-neck' shipmates on the docks and fought the enemy at sea" (*ibid.*).

That the men of the steward's branch of the United States Navy had to fight at all different levels, not just the enemy but the perceptions of both Black and white society in America, to gain respect is now readily apparent. No more can such terms as "lowly mess attendants" or "just a steward" be honestly applied to men who fought and died for their country with just as much patriotism and valor as any white soldier or sailor. Dorie Miller was the first in a long line of such men. His fighting spirit would be replicated many times over by the men that served as stewards and officer's cooks in the Submarine Force.

III

Becoming a Steward

JOINING THE NAVY: VOLUNTARY ENLISTMENT

Black men who joined the United States Navy did so either voluntarily or through the process of being drafted via the selective service system. For those men that voluntarily joined the navy, their reasons for doing so and resulting experiences as new recruits varied depending on the time frame when they enlisted.

Men who volunteered well before war began on December 7, 1941, were motivated for several different reasons. Probably first and foremost of these was that of economics. During a period of economic depression in the United States, especially in the south, the navy was an attractive option for those who qualified, offering steady pay, three square meals a day, and a safe place to live. With meals and housing provided, many new recruits were able to send their paychecks back home to help out struggling family members — a wife and children, or parents, grandparents, and brothers and sisters. One such example of this is Jim Stallings, a 1939 navy recruit from Starkville, Mississippi. He faithfully sent his paycheck home every month during the war years to the grandmother that lovingly raised him. Another reason that Blacks enlisted was to get away and to see and experience the wider world away from home. Just as it is today, military service was often attractive to young men for this very reason. Finally, some Black men enlisted because other members of their family had once served in the military. Attracted by a career that offered a uniform, travel, some measure of stability, and regular pay, Black men entered the military for one or all of these reasons.

For those men that voluntarily enlisted after the war began, all of the above reasons were still factors in their decision. However, the patriotism and outrage generated by the attack on Pearl Harbor was an added factor that weighed heavily in their decision to enlist. Often it was a powerful one, and not one that could be swayed by mothers and fathers. Despite the fact that Blacks were treated in their own land, at best, as second-class citizens, the desire of Black men to fight for their country was as strong as that of any white man. For some future submariners, the decision to enlist was motivated by an even more personal kind of patriotism. Future nuclear submariner Donald

Wilson, a native of Columbus, Ohio, enlisted in the navy in September 1945 because he had heard that an older childhood friend from Louisiana, Ulysses Grant Reed, had been killed. Reed had enlisted in the navy in 1942 and soon joined the Submarine Force, making six war patrols on *Haddo*. However, the report of his death was incorrect, and he survived the war. Just as many white men enlisted in the war to follow in the footsteps of older brothers, cousins, or friends who had gone off to war, so, too, did many Black men.

Once a Black man decided to enlist, there was still the matter of being accepted into the navy by local recruiters. In comparison to whites who enlisted, this was no easy task. Prior to the war, a Black man, as one former steward has written, "had to acquire character references that would do honor to today's Naval Academy candidates" (Wright, p. 16). All had to have two letters of recommendation to be considered for induction. However, even if these letters were satisfactory, there was still the matter of passing a medical exam. Black candidates for the navy were often rejected for dental and medical conditions that were both real and imagined. Admittedly, the standards of healthcare that were available for Blacks in many areas were lower than that of whites, resulting in real health issues that would make some men ineligible to join the service. However, there were also many times where Blacks were rejected on this basis when, in fact, there was no problem. Such rejections were more likely based on the fact that a medical officer or recruiter, both of whom were white, did not like the look of a potential recruit, no matter what recommendations he may have possessed.

Recommendations as to the acceptance of a given Black recruit were also based on a quota system. Before the war began, the navy only wanted a relatively small number of Black recruits to fill a set position, that of mess attendant. This is aptly demonstrated by the experiences of Carl Kimmons, from Hamilton, Ohio. He first tried to enlist in the navy in early 1940. After failing the medical exam, the medical officer examining Kimmons remarked to the recruiter, "This one didn't pass. Get me another darkie" (Kimmons). Clearly, this was an attempt by this recruiting station to fill a quota. Undeterred, Kimmons successfully joined the navy two months later, in June 1940.

In regard to the navy's quota for Black men, it was also rumored during this time that the navy "preferred to get Black recruits from the South" and that they wanted "good southern boys" (*ibid.* and Wright, p. 17). While there is no official documentation to support this contention, enough anecdotal evidence exists to suggest that such rumors may have indeed been true. Potential recruit Chester Wright of Hope, Arkansas, enlisted in July 1940. Despite having all the necessary recommendations, he was at first turned down because, as the white recruiting yeoman told him, "You talks too good and you look white men in the eye. This could cause you trouble. You simply don't ack lak a nigger enough" (Wright, p. 16). When Wright got new recommendations from people who stressed his obedience, rather than his intelligence, and played the part of a typical "southern-darkie" in front of the chief recruiter, he "passed with flying colors" and was accepted into the navy (*ibid.*, p. 17).

Did the navy, as Wright states, really discourage the recruitment of "uppity Northern Niggers" (*ibid.*, p. 16)? While many of the navy's Black recruits came from such northern urban centers as Philadelphia, Cleveland, and Chicago, the fact remains that most Black recruits came from the south because that is where the overwhelming majority of Blacks in America lived. According to the 1940 census, 77 percent of the nation's

Black population lived in the south (Davis, p. 102). The added fact that many of the navy's officers came from the south may seem to lend credence to Wright's statement, but we must be careful here. While many officers commanding ships of the United States Navy were most certainly prejudiced and often preferred Filipino mess attendants and stewards over Blacks altogether, many other such officers can be found who treated the Black members of their crew with the respect they deserved. Nowhere was this probably more true than in the Submarine Force.

For those men who wanted to enlist in the navy after the bombing of Pearl Harbor, restrictions were somewhat eased. However, despite the fact that the navy segregated and limited Blacks in all areas, it still had a far better reputation than the army. Will Royal, the father of future recruit Anderson Peter Royal was a World War I veteran from Tulsa, Oklahoma, who had served in the army. With firsthand knowledge of how that branch of the service treated Black men, he advised his son to join the navy. Likewise, Leonard Rozar of Dublin, Georgia, joined the navy because he had "heard devious things about the Army" (Rozar, Leonard). This is not surprising, as the army base at Fort Benning, Georgia, was located only a short distance away, and it is very likely that stories about how the army treated its Black soldiers became common knowledge.

Finally, one area that Black recruits had in common with whites was the matter of age upon enlistment. It was then, as now, the policy of all the branches of the United States Armed Forces that new recruits be of the legal age of eighteen. It is ironic that in this day and age, the right to vote at age eighteen is symbolically linked, at least for young men, to registering for the selective service draft system. However, the statement in our day, "If you're old enough to vote, you're old enough to fight for your country," did not apply to young Black men during the era of World War II. While they were allowed, in a limited capacity, to fight for their country, most Blacks could not vote due to jim crow laws that still prevailed. Still, during this era the two rights were not inexorably linked as they are today, and young Black men were eager to join in the fight. Just as many young white men falsified their birth date to join the navy and go off to war, so too did many Black men. Typical of such men were Sammie Major of Fort Pierce, Florida. He joined the navy when he turned seventeen years of age but used his older sister's birth date to get into the navy without his parents' permission. The discrepancy about his age was not discovered by family and friends until after his death. While many men exaggerated their age to join the navy, many under-aged Black men were able to join with their parents' permission. Arthur Brown of Valdosta, Georgia, enlisted at age sixteen with the aid of his family — he "wanted to help win the war" — while his parents "wanted to make me happy" (Brown, Arthur). Richard Lucas of Rocky Mount, North Carolina, joined the navy at age seventeen. Though drafted, he wanted to join the navy. His parents allowed him to go for simple economic reasons. He was one of twelve children and already had three brothers in the army. The added income his navy service would generate would be a great help to his family during such trying times.

All in all, the experience of a young Black man joining the navy during this time in our nation's history was much like that of the overall Black experience in America. Despite the fact that these young men were ready, willing, and able to fight for their country, it was often a struggle to be given the opportunity to do so.

Joining the Navy via the Draft

Just like their white counterparts, not all Black men were eager to join the armed forces of the United States once the war began. In addition to the standard reasons for not wanting to do so — the necessary family separation or loss of a good job — Black men often had the added reason of knowing that not only was their service as a fighting man only grudgingly accepted, but once they did join they would be relegated to the lowest position available.

In regard to the United States Navy, it "met its manpower needs without the draft" (Foner, p. 143) until 1943. Once the draft was used, here, as in most others areas where the interests of Blacks and whites were intertwined, discrepancies arose. Not only was their little or no Black representation on local draft boards, where "life and death decisions" were made, but Blacks also received only a small share of the draft deferments and exemptions (*ibid.*, p. 142). As an example, of all the deferments issued for defense employment, Blacks constituted less than 5 percent. For ministerial deferments, Black deferment was only slightly higher at 7 percent. In contrast to this, however, the selective service system also had racial quotas that prohibited the drafting of large numbers of eligible Black men, at the expense of white fathers and married men. As one historian states, "instead of asking a local draft board for the first 124 men available for induction ... Selective Service asked for the first 120 eligible white men and first four eligible Blacks" (*ibid.*, p. 143). As in all other matters regarding race, the Black man was at a disadvantage and the selective service system was no different.

Many of the men who were drafted and would soon become submariners did not voluntarily join because they had good jobs and did not want to go off to war. Killraine Newton, of Virginia, had worked at a CCC (Civilian Conservation Corp) camp prior to the war. Newton was subsequently drafted "kicking and screaming" in 1943 while working as a supply clerk at the Yorktown Naval Mine Depot in Virginia. Despite his initial objections, Killraine Newton would go on to have an outstanding naval career and achieve the rank of lieutenant commander.

Other future submariners, too, had jobs that provided a suitable living, making it unnecessary for them to join the military. Arthur Haynes and C.V. Cooper were working at packing plants in their respective home states of Kansas and Texas, while Hosey Mays, a Colorado native, was working for the Union Pacific Railroad. Alfred Hall was working on a riveting gang at the Electric Boat Company in New London, Connecticut, helping to build submarines. One can't help but wonder that if Hall were white, whether he would have been deferred from the draft due to his job in the defense industry. The same can be asked, perhaps, of both John Whitehead, of Chicago, and David Collier of Steubenville, Ohio. Whitehead had moved from Chicago to work at a California shipyard in hope of not being drafted. He was drafted anyway in early 1943, being among the navy's earliest Black draftees. Similarly, David Collier was both going to school and working in the area's steel mills when drafted in 1944. Another interesting example is that of Ernest Danford. A native of Waycross, Georgia, he was enrolled in Georgia Normal Agriculture College when he was drafted in 1944. However, the fact that he wasn't attending classes at the time prevented him from being granted a deferment.

Once a Black man was drafted and sent to the local induction center, it was here that he would learn what branch of the service he would join, based on a quota system. Likely typical is the experience of Walter Patrick, a Virginia native living in Orange, New Jersey, when drafted in 1943. His induction occurred at the end of the working day, and Patrick was excited about joining the marines. However, he was told that their quota was already met for the day. Then he inquired about the army and was told that their quota, too, had been met. When Patrick then asked about the coast guard, he was told "son, we need you in the navy" (Patrick), and so it was.

No matter what their situation was when drafted, these future submariners accepted their country's call to serve and did so, in most cases, in exemplary fashion. Some of these draftees even stayed in the service after the war and became career navy men, serving their country for twenty years or more.

THE NAVY BOOT CAMP EXPERIENCE

Once a new recruit was selected for navy service, he was sent to an induction center for processing. These induction centers were usually located in the larger cities in a given state, and it was here where new recruits from the area were sent to have the necessary paperwork completed and were given a final physical examination. Upon acceptance, recruits were formally enlisted and subsequently transported to navy boot camp for training and an introduction to navy life. The following advice was given to the recruits via a form letter that advised each applicant when and where to report for enlistment:

> It is suggested you bring, on the above mentioned date, only toilet articles and sufficient change of clothing to last until your arrival at the Training Station. You are requested to dress as neatly as possible in order that you may make a good impression while enroute to the Training Station. Upon arrival at the Training Station, you will be given the opportunity to send home, at your own expense, your civilian clothing.
> It is advisable to have only sufficient funds to last until you receive your first pay, a matter of two weeks or less. As recruits are not permitted to wear or keep jewelry while under training, leave such articles as watches, pins, rings, etc., at home and avoid the possibility of their loss while being expressed with your clothes from the Training Station to your home [Fenner, "NRB Form No. 53"].

During the war, the navy had three principal centers where training for Black recruits was conducted. The first, and oldest of these facilities, was located at Norfolk, Virginia. First known as Unit K West and later replaced by Unit B East, it was established in 1932 and was used solely to train new Black recruits in a segregated environment for their duties as mess attendants. This facility was used into 1943 but was subsequently taken over for use as a center to train the navy's destroyermen. To take its place, a new segregated facility, Bainbridge Naval Training Center, was set up for Black recruits near Port Deposit, Maryland. This was where the majority of the navy's steward's mates (formerly called mess attendants) received their training during the last years of the war. A third facility was also used, that being the Great Lakes Naval Training Center, near North Chicago, Illinois, on Lake Michigan.

III. Becoming a Steward

Boot camp recruits at Bainbridge, Maryland, in early 1945. Future submariner William Green is at the far right (third from bottom). By late 1945, Green was in the Pacific but arrived too late to make a war patrol. (Photograph courtesy of the Green family.)

For many of the men, their journey to boot camp was their first substantial trip away from home and was an adventure in and of itself. It was also the first time that some of these men experienced southern segregation at its fullest. Often it began when the train or bus transporting the new Black recruits crossed the old Mason-Dixon line, dividing the north and south. Carl Kimmons, coming from Cincinnati, Ohio, remembered his train transport stopping at Wheeling, West Virginia, so that the conductor could move all the Black recruits into a segregated car for the remainder of the journey to Norfolk, Virginia. While men from the south were used to such segregation, having lived with it all their lives, for men from other locales in the United States it was, at best, an unpleasant surprise. For Hosey Mays, coming by train from Denver, Colorado, the segregation he experienced at Norfolk was a "deep cultural shock" (Mays). Another man sent to Norfolk, John Whitehead, didn't expect the segregation he encountered and was struck by the signs posted all around that stated "For Whites Only." One sign that was particularly offensive and "left a bad taste in my mouth" was the one around the training camp that stated "Sailors and Dogs Not Allowed" (Whitehead). Clearly pointed at Black recruits, this sign was a certain indication to Whitehead of how the Navy regarded its Black servicemen. Of course, for those men that came from the south, social conditions in Norfolk came as no surprise. During this time, all sailors in Norfolk referred to it as "Shit City." As one man relates,

> It was that bad. There were signs on the lawns saying "Dogs and Sailors Keep Off." For African Americans it was worse. Segregation was at its height. In taking the ferry from Norfolk to Portsmouth, African Americans had to remain in their designated segregated areas. The street cars were the same. Street cars ran from the naval base to downtown Norfolk, and African Americans had their designated seats in the rear [Kimmons].

Those men who were sent to the newly established naval training center at Bainbridge, Maryland, found things were no different. Bruce Anderson, a new recruit from Williamsport, Pennsylvania, remembered it as "a big change" and had never run into "out-and-out segregation" until it hit him at Bainbridge "full blast" (Anderson, Bruce). Isaac Johnson, from Texarkana, Arkansas, felt that the new Black recruits were "tolerated" at best, and "were not welcomed with open arms" (Johnson). Donald Wilson, coming from Columbus, Ohio, remembered the shock he felt when they got off the train at Baltimore. Finding a restaurant there to dine in, Wilson was forced to eat behind the restaurant, as Blacks were not allowed in the regular dining area.

However, despite the segregated training conditions at both training centers for Black navy recruits, it must be stated that not all men found the experience disagreeable. Arthur Haynes, from Kansas City, remembered it as being "nothing different" from what he was used to, while Carl Kimmons recalled that "that was the times" and that "anticipated problems never occurred" (Kimmons). Even for some men from the north, the segregated training was little dwelt upon. Gilbert Lomax, of Bryn Mawr, Pennsylvania, recalled that he was "immersed in my own way" and had "no time to think about it" (Lomax). Ernest Danford, a recruit from Georgia, probably stated it best when he called it a "two sides of the track situation" (Danforth). Indeed, it was that type of situation at both Norfolk and Bainbridge. New white recruits were trained nearby at both locations, but the way they were trained and treated, and the quality of their facilities was markedly better.

The naval training center at Norfolk, Virginia, consisted of several different parts. That for Black recruits, known as Unit K West and Unit B East, was a rather simple complex. It consisted of several wooden barracks, unheated with no seating or bunks of any kind, and an administration building known as the "glass house." This was where

New enlistee Carl Eugene Kimmons at boot camp, NTC Norfolk, Virginia, in June 1940. The men were required at times to stand guard over the training compound of Unit K West–B East and wore this outfit, complete with rifle, bayonet, and leggings. Kimmons recalls that when the boot recruits had liberty in town, they used to pretend that they were experienced sailors, but their wrinkled pants below the knees, where the leggings had been, was a dead giveaway. (Photograph courtesy of C. Kimmons.)

the camp's commander, usually a lieutenant junior grade, conducted his affairs. Adjacent to these buildings was a rocky training field, and the whole was surrounded by a tall barbed-wire fence. Decorating the compound area were old cannonballs painted white that lined the walkways. The entrance was usually patrolled by an upper-class recruit who carried an unloaded rifle. In contrast, the white recruits had "nice brick barracks" that had individual bunks and in a heated building, and their portion of the camp was unfenced, allowing them to "come and go as they pleased" (Clark, p. 51). The training ground they drilled on was fully paved.

During their time of instruction here, usually lasting four to six weeks, Black recruits were continually drilled and taught how to march. While a white officer was in overall charge of the camp, the actual training was conducted by an experienced steward who might be a Filipino or African-American. Much time was also spent in swimming exercises. For many Black recruits, this was a new and terrifying experience because they did not know how to swim. This was particularly true of many men from the south, and for a simple reason: unless they grew up in an area with access to a swimming place of their own, many Blacks did not know how to swim because they were not allowed to visit their local public swimming pools due to segregationist policies then in force. As to weapons training, there was little of this going on as Black sailors were not, by official navy policy, part of any gun crews. However, a few men do remember some brief small arms training. Finally, probably the most useful and practical training a Black recruit received was that regarding his duties as a mess attendant (later steward's mate). This included instruction on how to set an officer's table, the proper types of knives and forks to be used during mealtimes, and the proper way to serve an officer. For those who might serve as an officer's cook, there might also be some instruction in basic navy cooking techniques. The length and usefulness of this type of training that actually related to their future duties seems to have varied widely from class to class. Some men remember receiving useful training, while others relate that almost no training was given and that they had to learn as they went along after gaining their first assignments upon graduation. Since there were no proficiency tests and no written training manuals (these did not appear until 1946), a new recruit's training depended heavily on the established stewards that taught them.

At the end of the day's training, recruits were housed in barracks, each of which contained large stanchions from which the men's hammocks were slung at night for sleeping. In the morning, the hammocks were taken down and stowed away for the day. After the recruits left the barracks for another day of training in the morning, the barracks were inspected by an upper class recruit. Any personal belongings or clothes that were found laying about were taken to a small room called the "lucky bag," where they could be claimed by their owner. In return for this transgression, a recruit, in order to get his item back, had to do extra duty or suffer some kind of mild punishment (Clark, p. 52). One of these punishments consisted of a recruit carrying a heavy cannon ball for a designated period of time (Kimmons). Another form of punishment, practiced at Bainbridge, was the dubious task of standing guard over the camp's trashcans (Lomax).

While training of the new recruits was the priority, there was also time reserved for entertainment. This often consisted of athletic competition among the men, of which boxing was probably the most popular. Another popular diversion was going to the movies. However, this was not always a pleasant experience. One man recalls that, after being marched to the movie house in a group, the men were segregated and forced to sit in the balcony, which made it difficult to see the movie screen. Of course, white recruits always had preference — if there were not enough seats for them, the Black recruits were made to leave and were marched back to their barracks (Clark, p. 52). On Sunday, all hands were marched to church to sit in a designated area, and afterward were marched back to camp (Kimmons). Another place of recreation was the small base post exchange (PX) for Black recruits. This was a small room attached to the main base PX for whites and was the only place in camp that Black recruits could go independently. While the portion for white recruits had a soda fountain, jukebox, pool tables, and a small store, the part for Black recruits only had one "raggedy" pool table. There was a window that connected both parts of the PX and was accessible by ringing a bell if a Black recruit needed something from the other side. Most of the time their requests were ignored (Clark, pp. 51–52). In addition to these sanctioned forms of entertainment there was, as in any military encampment of any era,

Mess Attendant Wallace Coleman as a boxer while at boot camp in Norfolk, Virginia, in 1940. He would still do a bit of boxing while in the navy in Australia during the war. (Photograph courtesy of the Coleman family.)

many other diversions among the men, including card playing, gambling, and lively conversation. As a result of their close quarters and common experience, many men, no matter where they came from, formed long-lasting friendships.

While the previously described experiences relate to the naval training center at Norfolk, the situation was essentially the same at Bainbridge, which operated from 1943 onward. While the training facilities there were new compared to those at Norfolk, the conditions of segregation, both within and outside the camp, were the same at both places. It is interesting to note that here, as at Norfolk, white recruits were also trained in a separate camp. They even had a camp newspaper, the Bainbridge *Mainsheet*, that reported on camp events, helpful information, and notable achievements of recruits. No such newspaper was printed for the Black recruits at Bainbridge. One man who attended Bainbridge, Bruce Anderson, remembered that the white recruits from the "other side" were often brought over to watch their Black counterparts during drill and marching activities, not for entertainment, but as an example of how a well-drilled company should look.

In regard to the training at the Great Lakes Naval Training Center in Illinois, again the training here for Black recruits was wholly segregated. On this issue the navy refused to change until late in the war. However, being located in the north, there was no segregation outside the training grounds.

Upon completion of their training period at boot camp, the new recruit now held the rank of mess attendant 3rd class, later steward's mate 3rd class. They were now ready for their first assigned duty station. However, after they "broke boot," each man was given a small period of leave, usually lasting for a week or two. This was a time that the men could return home to visit family and friends before heading off for duty with the navy. Resplendent in their newly earned uniforms and imbued with a sense of military pride, the men were quite a sight to see and were warmly and proudly received by their loved ones. However, the men would often receive a rude awakening when they reentered the public world that was the segregated south at that time. The experience of Walter Patrick is typical, and best told in his own words.

> So after I had spent a few days in Amelia, Virginia, I started back to my home in New Jersey. I had to take the Greyhound bus. That trip was a very upsetting experience for me. When I boarded the bus there were several seats vacant in front next to the driver. I guess you could say after being in New Jersey and in the U.S. Navy uniform I had forgotten my place, so to speak; so I sat in a seat up front. The bus driver turned to me and scolded me "Boy get out of that seat and go to the back of the bus." So I obeyed — and went to the back of the bus to stand up while there were seats in front. Here I'm on my way to fight for a country, to put my life in jeopardy for a country where I had no rights, even in the United States Navy uniform [Patrick].

BLACK SAILORS AND THE NAVY'S RATING SYSTEM DURING THE WAR

Now that we are nearly at the point of a new recruit's entrance to the ranks of the Submarine Force, it will, at this point, be appropriate to study the facts regarding Black sailors and their place in the navy's rating system, the uniform and insignia they were required to wear, and the authority they could wield. While submariners are the specific topic of study, it should be understood that the information in this section applies to all Black navy personnel during this time unless otherwise stated.

When war began in 1941, the men of the steward's branch of the United States Navy, according to one historian, "were, at best an adjunct to the Navy rating structure — an auxiliary group of servants carried along to feed and berth the navy's officer's corp. At worst they were the lowest rung of the Navy's pecking order" (Wright, p. 69). The word "adjunct" in this case is most appropriate, as the ratings system for Black sailors was different from that for whites and were more restricted. From 1932 to 1943, Black sailors in the steward's branch were formally called mess attendants, while informally they were called either the captain's "boy" or a "mess boy" (*ibid.*, p. 70). After completing boot camp, a new Black recruit achieved the official rating of mess attendant 3rd class (MAtt 3/c). He could subsequently receive advancement to the rate of mess attendant 2nd class (MAtt 2/c) and mess attendant 1st class (MAtt 1/c) based on either time in service or for meritorious service. Once the rating of mess attendant first class was achieved, no further advancement was possible.

In contrast, a white recruit's first three ratings were designated as seaman 3rd class on up to seaman 1st class (pay grade E1–E3). Upon reaching this level, a seaman would then go into his specialty area and be rated as, say, a gunner's mate, or boatswain's mate. He would subsequently be eligible (based on merit) to advance three more grades before attaining the rank of a petty officer (E-6) and achieve full status in his specialty as a full rated gunner, boatswain, or whatever his chosen specialty, with the "mate" designation being dropped. With even more time in service, and outstanding performance, a white enlisted man could rise even further as a petty officer, achieving the rank of chief petty officer (E-7). The pay grades of E-8 and E-9 (master chief petty officer) did not yet exist and were not established until December 1959.

Along with the rating discrimination that Black sailors were subject to, there was also the issue of pay. In 1940, a mess attendant 3rd class (E-1) who had joined the navy and was attending boot camp was paid $19 a month. After four months, this pay was automatically raised to $21, about 20 percent less than that of white counterparts who were rated as seaman 3rd class. The same held true upon advancement to mess attendant 2nd class, where the pay was increased to $30 a month, while whites received $36. It was only when the rating of mess attendant 1st class (E-3) was achieved that the pay difference between Blacks and whites in the navy was equalized at $54 monthly.

For submariners, their bimonthly pay was increased substantially with hazardous duty pay. This was a major factor that attracted many stewards to submarine duty. By the end of the war, the pay of stewards was nearly double that before the war began. In 1946, a regular steward's mate 3rd class (E-1) received $50 monthly, while the same man in submarine service made $90. This pay went up to $78 and $140, respectively, for a steward or officer's cook 3rd class, a vast increase from the war years. In addition to their pay, men of the steward's branch could also purchase life insurance up to the amount of $10,000. However, at the cost of one dollar a thousand, many new stewards could not afford to purchase the full amount, and it is likely that many opted not to purchase insurance at all. With men who had family at home to help support, it was the here and now that counted, and $21 a month afforded little extra for such luxuries as life insurance (Kimmons).

The discrimination that Black sailors experienced also extended to the uniform that they wore; the navy making no attempt to hide the fact that men of the stewards branch were of a distinct and lower order. Unlike white sailors, who wore different colors of stripes depending on their place within the navy, Black sailors wore a crescent insignia with bars beneath to denote their rating. When white sailors became rated, they were then allowed to wear chevrons and a badge that depicted their rating insignia and a likeness of the American eagle. It would not be until 1944 that rated Black stewards or officers' cooks were allowed to wear chevrons and the rating badge with an eagle. While stewards often accepted this discriminating rating system in a humorous fashion, referring to the crescent and bars insignia they were forced to wear as a "moon" with "loaves of bread" below, the fact was not lost on them that they were fighting for

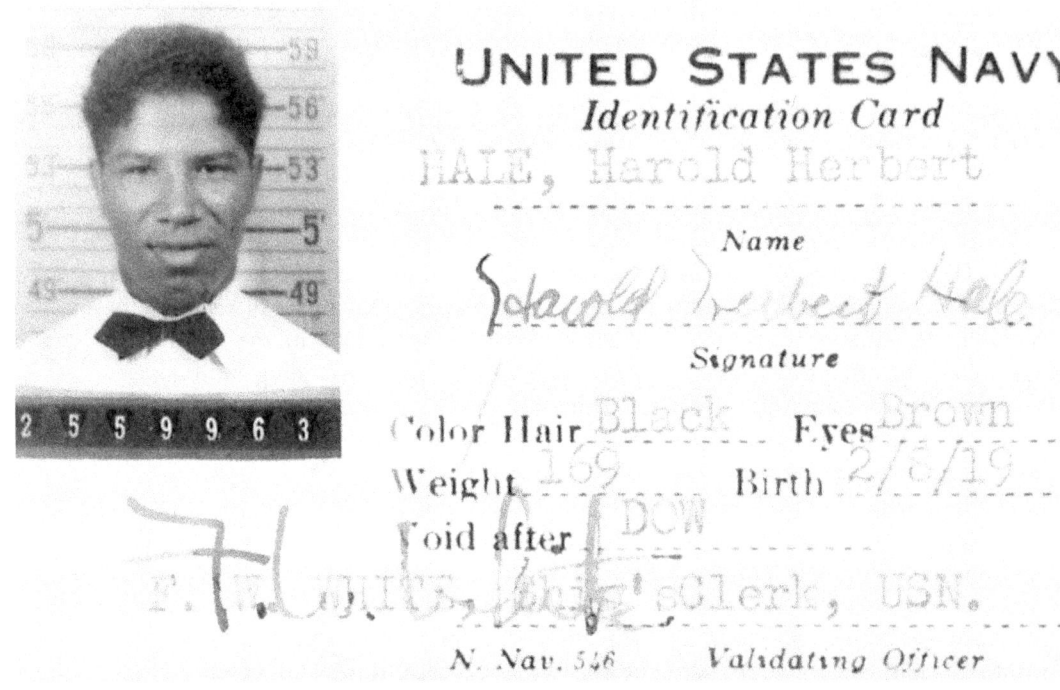

The identification card of Mess Attendant Harold Herbert Hale circa 1939. Hale first served aboard the battleship *Mississippi* before going to submarine duty on *Tunny* in 1942. Note the mess attendant white dress jacket and bow tie worn by stewards on surface craft. Such formal dress was rarely required on submarines. (Photograph courtesy of H. Hale.)

a country that would not even allow them the honor to wear its national symbol (the eagle) on their own uniform (Wright, pp. 69–74).

In 1943 the United States Navy expanded the ratings system for its steward's branch, resulting in a change of terminology as well. The change was a result of not only the greater amount of men in the stewards branch and the practical need for expanded ranks but also due to pressure from outside groups for more equality and opportunity more on par with that of white sailors. From mid-1943 onward, the designation of mess attendant was discontinued and was replaced by the term steward's mate (StM). Thus, a new recruit fresh out of boot camp at Bainbridge was now referred to as a steward's mate 3rd class (StM 3/c), with promotion available to steward's mate 1st class (StM 1/c).

With the newly expanded rating system, the next step in line for a Black sailor was to either that of an officer's cook (Ck) or steward (St). This choice was optional and up to each man when the time for advancement was at hand. (The different duties performed by stewards and officer's cooks is described later.) Thus, a Black sailor could advance from steward's mate 1st class (E-3) to steward or officer's cook 3rd class (E-4). By doing so, he became fully rated in his position and was now a petty officer. Subsequent advancement to steward or officer's cook 2nd and 1st class (pay grades E-5 and E-6), was followed by that of chief steward or chief cook (E-7). During World War II few Black submarines sailors were advanced to chief. However, one of those men who did rise to the rate of chief officer's cook was Jim Stallings, of Starkville, Mississippi. He did so in a rather spectacular fashion, having made twelve war patrols on *Haddock*. His rise from officer's cook 3rd class at the beginning of the war to chief officer's cook in February 1945 took less than four years and, at that time, Stallings' rise to chief was probably the fastest ever within the steward's branch of the navy.

As usual, when it came to matters of race and policy within the military, there were seeming contradictions and limitations. First the uniform. By achieving the rank of steward or officer's cook 3rd class (E-4), a Black sailor was now entitled to drop the traditional white sailor hat and bell-bottom pants and could now wear the white shirts and visored caps reserved for petty officers. In contrast, a white sailor could not wear the uniform of a petty officer until he reached the rating level of E-7. This apparent reverse discrimination against white sailors resulted in jealous whites referring to steward's uniforms as "monkey suits" and even resulted in physical violence against Black stewards who had earned the right, according to the rules of the navy, to wear a petty officer's uniform (*ibid.*, p. 70). However, a closer look at these uniforms will show that they were not equal to that of white petty officers. For example, steward's uniforms had black plastic buttons with anchors on them instead of the traditional brass buttons with the American eagle worn by whites. Incredibly, the brass buttons on the chinstrap of the visored cap for stewards had to be covered so that no brass could show. Even more incredible was the difference in insignia on the cap. White petty officers wore on their visored cap the distinctive "fouled anchor" insignia with the initials *USN*, while the cap of Black petty officers had only the initials *USN* without the anchor insignia (*ibid.*). If it is true that clothes really do "make the man," then it was readily apparent to most Black sailors that the United States Navy was making every attempt, even at the lowest level, to make them less of a sailor than their white counterparts.

If any good came out of this change in uniform for the men in the steward's branch, it was in the matter of the tie. Prior to the war, and into late 1943, stewards were made to wear a bow tie that can only be described as being like that worn by a maître d' in a fancy restaurant. Many stewards did not like the distinctly unmilitary tie and refused to wear it whenever the occasion arose. Steward Hosey Mays of Denver remembers well being picked up by the military police (MPs) while on shore leave for not wearing his bow tie. He was made to buy one within the presence of the MPs and, though he promised to do so, refused to put it on after they left (Mays). With the change in uniform, men of the steward's branch could now wear the traditional "four-in-hand" tie worn by regular Petty Officers (Wright, p. 76).

Along with matters of rank and uniform, there also arises the question of power within the navy hierarchy. It was no secret that the lowest rated man in the United States Navy during this time was the mess attendant (later steward's mate) 3rd class. But what about his position as he arose within the ranks of the steward's branch? What power, say, could a steward's mate 1st class or a steward 1st class have over his fellow sailors, both Black and white? The matter is quite simple. Men in the steward's branch, no matter what their rate, had no authority whatsoever over any white sailor. Thus, both "formally and legally" (Wright, p. 69), a steward 1st class, the highest rate that could be achieved by a Black sailor, had no authority over the lowest rated white sailor, a seaman 3rd class. Put in even simpler terms, a Black petty officer with, say, five years in the navy who had reached the highest rating allowed could not give an order to a lowly white seaman 3rd class with only sixty days in the navy — under any circumstances. As historian Chester Wright states, the stewards and officers cooks "were not allowed to wear the chevrons and the eagle-type rating badge ... which indicated authority," and thus they had none (Wright, p. 69).

IV

Becoming a Submariner

From Boot Camp to Submarines

The process of joining that branch of the United States Navy known as the Submarine Force was a widely varied one for Black sailors and involved many different sets of circumstances. In strictest terms, submarine duty was never mandatory but was sought after on a voluntary basis. Because of the extra hazards of submarine duty, extra pay was allocated to those who served in submarines. Many men joined the submarine service while in boot camp. For some men, like Richard Lucas and many others, this was often a result of the extra pay incentive involved for submarine duty. Others, like Lewis Hammond of Sheffield, Alabama, volunteered because they thought they'd just try it out. As the war progressed and more and more men were needed for submarine duty, experienced submarine stewards with war patrols to their credit were sent to boot camps to recruit for the Submarine Force. Dressed in their best dress uniforms, complete with dolphins and the submarine combat pin with stars that signified the number of successful patrols they had made, these veterans were able to inspire others to join their ranks. One man so inspired was 1944 enlistee Isaac Johnson, from Texarkana, Arkansas. As he recalls, "A steward named Gray [John Gray from *Tautog*] came to us and said 'subs are the place to go.' I looked at all his ribbons, and that's where I wanted to go too" (Johnson). Arthur Haynes, who also volunteered for submarine duty at Bainbridge, had the added incentive that he knew Leroy Toombs, another submarine steward that did recruiting duty. Inspiring patriotism, too, often played a part. Claude Palmer, Jr., of Phenix City, Alabama, volunteered for submarine duty after seeing the movie *Destination Tokyo* while in boot camp at Bainbridge. This movie, about a submarine with a mission to land agents right in the heart of the enemy mainland, starred Cary Grant as the submarine commander; it no doubt inspired many future submariners. Finally, peer pressure was often a determining factor. As Walter Patrick recalls,

> [I] wanted no part of submarine duty, [but my] friends derided me to no end, calling me chicken, yellow-belly, and scarety cat. At that time I had no thought

Steward's Mate L.T. Hammonds of *Batfish* circa 1943. Hammonds, a native of Alabama, made all of his boat's war patrols and was her only Black steward during the war, the rest being Filipinos. He would end the war as an officer's cook 2nd class before returning to civilian life. (Photograph courtesy of L.T. Hammonds.)

that I would pass the tests for submarine; being sickly, small frame, about 126 pounds, and had suffered from a gastric condition for years ... so in my mind I knew that I would not pass the tests. Was I in for a surprise! Out of all six of us that volunteered, I was the only one that passed every test. All my buddies failed the tests [Patrick].

Once a man had made the decision to become a submariner during boot camp, there were different ways in which he might get his start at earning his "dolphins." Probably the most common method for Black sailors joining their boat for the first time during the war was the process of being assigned to a submarine that was being overhauled, under construction, or newly commissioned into service and being readied for its journey to the war zone. There were six locations in the United States where sailors might be sent to join the crew of such a submarine. These were the United States Submarine Base at Groton, Connecticut, just a short distance from the Electric Boat Shipyard in Groton; the Portsmouth Naval Shipyard at Portsmouth, New Hampshire; the Mare Island Naval Shipyard in Vallejo, California; the Manitowoc Shipbuilding Company, at Manitowoc, Wisconsin; the Cramp Shipbuilding Company yard in Philadelphia, Pennsylvania, close to the Philadelphia Navy Yard; and the Boston Naval Shipyard in Boston, Massachusetts. Three of these shipyards, those at Portsmouth, Mare Island, and Boston, were government owned, while the others were privately owned companies with government contracts to build submarines.

The most important of all these submarine builders was the Electric Boat Company in Connecticut. Located close to the Submarine Force headquarters in Groton, it launched sixty-two submarines during the war and was, in fact, the nation's premiere builder of submarines even before war began. Next in importance were the government-owned yards at Portsmouth and Mare Island. The Portsmouth Navy Yard launched more submarines, seventy-two in number, than any other shipyard during the war. The Mare Island yard in California was equally important, but for a different reason. While only seventeen submarines were launched there during the war, a large number of submarines were sent there for overhaul and refit after having made a number of war patrols. Conveniently located on the west coast, submarines could be overhauled and quickly sent back to the Pacific war zone from Mare Island. Thus it was that many new Black submariners were sent from boot camp to serve as replacement crew on a boat being overhauled at Mare Island.

Another important yard was that in Manitowoc, Wisconsin. Twenty-eight submarines were launched from this location, which was the result of a cooperative venture with the Electric Boat Company. Last in importance were the Cramp Shipbuilding Company yard in Philadelphia and the Boston Naval Shipyard. During the war, only twelve submarines were launched by Cramp, four of which were completed at the Boston Naval Shipyard. As a result, few Black submariners got their start at these locales.

Those Black sailors who entered the Submarine Force by way of first being assigned to the submarine base at New London, Connecticut, probably received more training than if they had been sent elsewhere. However, there was no set training phase for the men in the steward's branch who volunteered for submarine duty. This is in distinct contrast to the amount of training received by whites. White men who joined the Submarine Force, no matter what their specialty, be they baker or radioman, usually had to take a grueling two-week course at submarine training school to test their suitability for service in submarines followed by a period of study on all aspects of submarine operations. The master-at-arms of the submarine base during the war was Chief Torpedoman Charlie Spritz, "a former Bronx policeman ... and the navy's version of the marine master sergeant" (McKenzie, p. 1). He could make or break any new submarine recruit and could be intimidating or fatherly, depending on how a prospective submariner performed under his watchful eye. During the first phase of testing, used to determine who would be physically and mentally fit for the submarine service, approximately 25–30 percent of the men that volunteered were rejected. Once the physical portion of the testing phase was passed, volunteers then underwent rigorous coursework and testing that covered every aspect of submarine operations, including "more than thirty electrical, mechanical, and pneumatic systems in the boats" (*ibid.*, p. 2). Prospective submariners took weekly tests, and those who failed two or more of them were washed out of school and returned for duty elsewhere. Those men who graduated from this second phase of testing were now members of "Spritz's Navy" and were ready for submarine duty.

For Black men who volunteered for the Submarine Force, their training was starkly different and, perhaps, reflective of the bottom rung of the ladder that the steward's branch occupied in the navy hierarchy during that time period. At best, the training for Black submariners can be described as random, with some men going through Spritz's course, while many received no formalized training whatsoever. As a result, few Black submariners interviewed ever attended submarine school, and many who joined the navy during the war did not receive training under the guidance of Spritz. New recruit Lewis Hammond recalled that he was given a swimming test only but attended no submarine school; Hosey Mays remembered going to sub school for one day and then being assigned to Building 16, the officer's mess to work under a Filipino chief steward. Bert Minor's experience was similar. As he recalls, "at New London I learned the basics of stewardship, not seamanship" (Minor). Likewise, Elvin Mayo was sent to New London but not to submarine school. For him, it was "like throwin a rabbit into a briar patch" (Mayo). The same was true, too, for Sam Wallace, who was given a pencil and a notebook to take notes but received no formal training while in New London.

However, just as there were some white sailors who never went to submarine school, so were there some Black submariners that *did* attend submarine training school and graduated with flying colors to become full-fledged members of Spritz's Navy. Richard Lucas remembers vividly the psychological screening process and the many tests he had to take before he became a submariner. One man who well recalls the screening process was South Carolinian William Murray. Based on his experiences in this area, one must wonder about how the entire process worked. Murray was drafted in 1943 and volunteered for submarine duty. As he recalls,

> During the course of this so-called psychological evaluation, the psychologist asked me what was the difference between the king of England and the president of the United States. After thinking for a while, the only answer I had for him was that the king was in England and the president was in the United States. Based on his body language, it was quite apparent the answer I gave was unacceptable because he shook his head and wrote something down on a piece of paper, placed it in a folder, handed the folder to me, and instructed me to take it to the inner office. Seething in curiosity as to what he had written, I

utilized the time between offices to peek in the folder — curiosity was my major concern as to what caused his negative body language in response to the answer I gave. I zeroed in on the specific text referencing my response ... and, while to this very date I cannot comprehend how he reached such a disconnected conclusion ... this is what he wrote: "This man is not too bright but God he is patriotic." I wondered to myself, "Now where did he get that from?" [Murray].

An excellent account of what the physical testing was like for a prospective Black submariner, especially one who was a non-swimmer, comes from Walter Patrick:

> I reported to the sub base at Groton, Connecticut, and began my training. I will never forget the diving tower experience. While I was still afraid of being in the water. When I went down in the diving bell to the 12-foot level, strapped on the Momsen Lung and stepped out into the water, I panicked because I did not know how to use the instrument. I kept inhaling and not blowing the air back into the tube. All at once I turned the cable loose and shot up to the top where the chief was waiting. Boy did I get a tongue lashing! He called me every name but a child of God. "Stupid fool, if you were down 100 feet the pressure would have ripped your damn guts out! Get your gear and go with the rest of the men to the 50-foot level." I thought sure that I would die going in at the 50-foot level, but all of a sudden I thought of my mother, who was deceased — she would always tell me to pray. So, I prayed every step down to the 50-foot level. When it was time for me to exit into the water tower, I was not afraid anymore [Patrick].

Steward's Mate Walter Patrick of *Bluegill* in early 1944. The Virginia native made two war patrols on this high-scoring boat under Captain Barr before leaving due to a racial conflict. He would subsequently do tender duty and rose to steward 3rd class before leaving the navy for good in 1946. (Photograph courtesy of W. Patrick.)

For those Blacks who did go through some formalized training at New London, not only did they have to prove to themselves and the navy that they were suitable for submarine duty, but they also had to carry the burden of their race. When a white prospective submariner failed to make the grade, it was simply because of the fact that he, and he alone, was not physically suited for such duty. Race was not an issue. However, many Black men undergoing this testing knew that their success or failure would, in some way, shape, or form, reflect on the perceived suitability of Blacks overall for

Mess Attendant 2nd Class Arthur Brown of *Narwhal*. He joined his boat after arriving in San Diego fresh out of boot camp at Norfolk. Expecting battleship duty, he was sent aboard *Narwhal* as she was departing for the Alaskan campaign in 1942. (Photograph courtesy of A. Brown.)

submarine duty, and they were steeled in their resolve to prove their worthiness. One such man was the aforementioned William Murray. While undergoing training in the escape tank, problems developed, and he began to bleed through the nose. As the bleeding became worse, Murray knew that "All other eyes in the chamber were on me.... At that point, I looked at the faces of all the individuals in the chamber and inwardly declared my determination that I was not going to be the one to say let me out. After all, there were about seven people in the chamber, and as the only Black person, I was not going to be the one to abort that escape process" (Murray). Indeed, Murray did not abort the exercise, and he would pass all the tests necessary to become a submariner.

There are no historical records that exist to document how many Black sailors were given the opportunity to complete the full training program at the submarine school during the war. However, interviews with surviving Black submarine veterans regarding their training experiences would seem to be a general, though by no means scientific, indicator. Based on these accounts, it seems likely that the number of stewards who received training on par with that of white sailors was somewhere between 10 and 20 percent. This means that, at best, no more than two out of ten of the stewards that volunteered for submarine duty ever received training before they even boarded a submarine. That some of this was due to wartime conditions is understandable, but the indifference of the navy when it came to the training of submarine stewards was an even larger factor. The father of future submariner Killraine Newton probably said it best when he advised his son that he would have to be twice as good as any white man to succeed. What was probably implicit in that advice for Newton was the fact that he would also have to do more with less training. For many, the records show that they did, indeed, do just that.

Despite the fact that few Black sailors who were sent to New London received full training before ever stepping foot on a submarine, those who went elsewhere to join their boat often received even less. Since the navy had no dedicated and formalized training course established at the other locations, both government owned and private, where submarines were launched, Black men sent to a submarine undergoing overhaul at Mare Island or a submarine under new construction at Manitowoc, Portsmouth, Philadelphia, or Boston usually had to learn through on-the-job experience after their assignment to a submarine crew. In a few cases, some of these men were sent to Groton for training before gaining their submarine assignment. However, most were sent straight to the yard where the submarine that needed them was being worked on. One minor exception to this was the many submarines launched at Portsmouth, New Hampshire. Because of the close proximity, within a few hours' travel, of Portsmouth to Groton, Black sailors sometimes received some form of training at the submarine base before being sent up the coast to Portsmouth or, if the timing was right, they received training at Groton and were able to join their newly launched boat after she came down to the submarine base from Portsmouth to conduct sea trials before heading off to war. Those men who joined their boat at the builder's yard gained their submarine education by working on the boat as part of her commissioning crew, usually under the guidance of an experienced steward who had already made war patrols.

Finally, despite the fact that submarine duty was supposed to be voluntary, the exigencies of war sometimes took precedence. This resulted in some men being assigned to submarine duty without being given much of a choice. Arthur Brown, from Valdosta, Georgia, was one of these men. Upon completion of boot camp at Norfolk in 1943, he was sent to the destroyer base at San Diego. While he wanted to serve aboard a prestigious battleship, he was instead sent to the submarine *Narwhal* on the day she sailed to take part in the invasion of Attu and Kiska in the Aleutian Islands. When Brown found out he was going on a submarine, he spoke up and said that was not the duty he wanted. The reply he got was typical navy: "It's too damn late, the orders have been cut" (Brown, Arthur). Likewise, Edward Neely of Houston, Texas, was ordered, not asked, to report for submarine duty at Portsmouth, New Hampshire, in 1943 after completing boot camp and helped put the *Billfish* into commission. In cases like these, it would appear that the needs of the war effort were the overriding concern at certain times, and when men were needed to complete a submarine crew, they were ordered to go. And go they did, seldom looking back.

From the Surface Navy to the Silent Service

For those future submariners who "broke boot" without having joined the Submarine Force, they would later do so in a variety of ways. Many of them served on all types of surface ships, from destroyers to aircraft carriers, before putting in for submarine duty. They did so for a variety of reasons. Some wanted more action than could be had on surface ships, while others were unhappy with their treatment aboard surface ships and sought a change.

A number of men who served in destroyers later volunteered for submarine duty. Among them were Magnus Wade, of Columbia, South Carolina; Carl Kimmons; and

Anderson Peter Royal, of Tulsa, Oklahoma. Kimmons and Royal served together on an old four-stack destroyer, the *McFarland*, that was converted to a seaplane tender. Kimmons, with a great mind for detail and organization, spent much of his time in the yeoman's shack helping him out with his work. His call to submarine service came inadvertently when he noticed an unposted communication from the Navy Bureau of Personnel (BUPERS) which stated that the Submarine Force would now admit more Black men for service. Kimmons, upon seeing this information, was immediately interested and shared the information with his friend Royal. Both subsequently volunteered for submarine duty. Kimmons was accepted for service and was sent to the *Plunger*, while Royal had to stay on *McFarland*, as she was already shorthanded. In speaking of his decision to volunteer for submarine duty, Carl Kimmons relates that "When one is young and stupid, he thinks that it will be the other fellow who will get killed — not him. No one asked me to volunteer for submarine duty, I just wanted to do so" (Kimmons). Anderson Royal would later get his chance to serve in submarines. After being aboard *McFarland* during operations in the Marshall and Gilbert islands, and at the battles of Coral Sea and Midway, he got his wish and was sent to the *Silversides*. To this day, Royal believes that if his friend, Carl Kimmons, had not discovered the unposted memo from BUPERS, neither man may have had the outstanding navy careers that they later developed.

Mess Attendant Carl Eugene Kimmons circa 1941. Kimmons, a native of Ohio, first did destroyer duty before going to submarine duty on *Plunger* in 1942. He made seven war patrols during the war on *Plunger* and *Parche* from 1942 to 1944. (Photograph courtesy of C. Kimmons.)

Other men, too, saw service in either surface ships or naval air station units before requesting to be transferred to submarine duty. Charles Williams, of Keatchie, Louisiana, first served in the heavy cruiser *Baltimore* before going to submarines, while South Carolina native James Washington had served on the cruiser *Raleigh*. Harold Hale, of Algoma, West Virginia, had served for some time on the large battleship *Mississippi*

A letter from Mess Attendant Donald Fenner of the battleship *Tennessee* to his mother, Cousy Fenner, circa early 1941. As is clearly evident by this letter, Fenner was unhappy with the treatment of Blacks in the surface navy and wanted out of the navy at all costs. He would, however, persevere and soon volunteered for submarine duty, making war patrols on *Snapper* in 1942. Unfortunately, though he may have found better racial conditions on submarines, he would not survive the war. (Letter courtesy of F. Young.)

prior to the start of the war before going to submarines, while Donald Fenner of Halifax, North Carolina, served quite unhappily on the battleship *Tennessee* before going to a submarine relief crew.

Stewards who served aboard battleships may have had it rougher than those who served aboard other ships in the surface navy. Battleships were the most prestigious ships in the United States Navy and, as such, were usually commanded by its most experienced officers. These were usually older men that were steeped in the grandest traditions of the navy, including ones that, at best, had little regard for African Americans and much preferred Filipinos as stewards. As a result, the treatment that mess attendants such as Donald Fenner received was often unbearable. He wrote to his mother from the *Tennessee*:

> Dear Mother:
>
> I am in Honolulu I am not getting along so well Its real hot out here and I am having some trouble with some officers I'll be out here for six months and when I come bact to the U.S. I am coming out of the Navy It no place for Colored Write the Navy Department for my discharge when I first came in I thought I would like it but thangs have change all the Colored boys are getting

out. Write and let me know whether you can get it or not so I'll know what to doo the wort [work] isn't so hard but I can't get along with the people. Write and see if you could [get] an honorable or Ordinary discharge. If you can not I will have to get a dishonorable one and by the [way] Clearance Hargrove address was wrong he didn't live there. I don't have much to tell every body Hello don't let anyone know about it I'll be seen you'll soon.

    Your son
    Don
I am Saving money to come home with

On the other hand, Harold Hale disliked his battleship for the simple reason that he seldom had shore liberty. Because the transport to be taken ashore for shore liberty was based on one's rating, mess attendants were always at the bottom of the list. As a result, sometimes their wait to go ashore on a given day was in vain, and they would have to wait until the next time or maybe even the time after that. Treatment such as this that African American stewards received aboard larger ships was often intolerable.

Other reasons abounded for transferring to the Submarine Force. One man, John Whitehead of Chicago, had a simple, yet chilling reason for volunteering for submarine duty. After serving on an aircraft carrier for one week, he requested submarine duty with the reasoning that "I didn't want to be beat up or badly wounded. I wanted to die quickly, or come back home" (Whitehead, John). The story of Willie Knight is an extraordinary one. Perhaps blessed with a sort of sixth sense, he served on an aircraft carrier and two cruisers, all of which were sunk in battle after he was transferred off (Reynolds, p. 43). He subsequently volunteered for submarine duty. Likewise, Dave Ball of Little Rock, Arkansas, served in the doomed heavy cruiser *Indianapolis* for over three years from 1936 to 1940 before volunteering for submarine duty. The ship on which he rose to mess attendant 1st class would later be sunk by a Japanese submarine in July 1945 with heavy loss of life. Sam Wallace, also from Little Rock, was assigned to the Norfolk Naval Air Station in Virginia before the war. He was asked to transfer to submarines, trading plane rides for submarine dives. Likewise, Jim Stallings of Starkville, Mississippi, was stationed at San Diego, assigned to Aviation Squadron VP-12 before his transfer to a submarine relief crew at Pearl Harbor. No doubt he liked what he saw, as six months later he volunteered for submarine duty just ten months before the war began. He would stay in submarines until his retirement from the navy twenty-eight years later in 1969.

Transfer from a Tender, Relief Crew, or Shore Duty

Another very common way for a Black sailor to become a submariner after he had left boot camp was through his work on a submarine tender, a submarine relief crew, or shore duty. Many stewards worked aboard the large tenders that served as mother ships for the submarine fleet. Not only did the tenders reprovision an incoming submarine with food, fuel, and other needed items, they also, at times, provided replacement crewmembers. Once a submarine came into port from patrol, her regular crew was given shore liberty for a period lasting anywhere from two weeks to a month.

During this time, the submarine was manned by a relief crew whose job was to repair, overhaul, and perform needed maintenance. Black sailors, serving as stewards and cooks, served aboard the tenders and as part of these relief crews. In addition, they also served as stewards in shore-based installations where high-ranking command personnel and staff officers worked, ate, and slept. Like other men, the men in the steward's branch in these three areas of operational support also often took the place of submarine crew members who were routinely rotated off the boat after each patrol and assigned to other duty. Thus, a steward or officer's cook from a tender, relief crew, or officer's mess ashore, with no prior submarine service at sea, would often take the place of his counterpart on a submarine that was getting ready to head back out on patrol. Sometimes this was done to relieve boredom or an urge to get in on the action at sea, despite the dangers it entailed. For these men, most of whom had never attended submarine school or made a war patrol, almost all of their training would come aboard the boat by way of doing their job. In some cases, they would be given a small amount of preparation by being tested in a decompression chamber aboard a submarine tender or given instruction in emergency drills from an escape trunk.

These men, unlike the men that came to the Submarine Force from boot camp or surface ships, did have one crucial advantage: Since they both worked closely with the men of incoming submarines just off war patrol and socialized with them, they had firsthand knowledge of a particular submarine and her commander and crew and could gauge what type of situation they might get into if they volunteered for submarine duty. Like most ships in the navy, certain submarines could have a good reputation while others did not. This was often based on the officers that commanded them and what kind of men they were, both personally and in combat. Those officers that ran a "happy" and productive ship were obviously preferred to those boats where the crew was not treated as well and where, for a variety of reasons, the submarine in question had little success while on patrol. Situations such as this often resulted in low crew morale, making it necessary to change commanders. Oftentimes, too, a particular submarine was avoided because her commander was seen as being too "gung ho," or reckless, taking too many chances that might result in the loss of the boat and its crew. For as long as sailors have been serving on ships, "scuttlebutt," the seafaring term for gossip, has reigned supreme, and any submarine sailor with his ear to the ground knew what boats to avoid serving on and what captains they should steer clear of. Understandably, at this late date with many of the World War II submarine commanders now deceased, few Black submariners are willing to name those captains that they avoided serving under. However, there is no hesitation when it comes to naming the men that they were honored to serve under. Such men include Frank Latta (*Narwhal*), Lawson Ramage (*Parche*), Creed Burlingame (*Silversides*), George Street (*Tirante*), and a host of others. All were highly successful commanders who were highly decorated and, more importantly, were held in high regard by their crew.

Perhaps the best example of a man choosing his boat is the experience of Elvin Mayo. Serving aboard the tender *Griffin* at Pearl Harbor, he was anxious to "get me a submarine" and watched as the various boats came in from patrol. One boat in particular, the *Jack*, commanded by Tommy Dykers, caught his eye. After watching the *Jack* come in from patrol a second time, Mayo decided he liked the look of her. She seemed to be a well-run ship, and Mayo knew that it was the submarine he wanted to serve on. When the time was right, Mayo met Captain Dykers and asked to serve on *Jack*. The details of Elvin Mayo's memorable conversation with Captain Dykers of the *Jack* can be found in Elvin Mayo's history in the last chapter. The end result was that Mayo got to serve aboard the submarine he wanted all along.

V

Life as a Wartime Submariner

The Daily Routine of a Submarine Steward

Once a Black sailor received orders for his submarine and was mustered on board, it was now his responsibility to learn the daily routine of a submarine steward and all the duties that it entailed. Being new to the service, he would work under a lead steward who may have already had at least one war patrol, and maybe many more, to his credit. Most submarines during the war normally operated with two stewards at all times. However, there were some exceptions. *Scamp*, *Seawolf*, and *Gudgeon* each had only one steward aboard when they were lost, while the big boat *Argonaut* had seven stewards in a crew of 105 men. The lead steward on board a submarine probably had a higher rating than the new steward coming aboard, but this was not always the case. In this case, even if the two stewards held the same rating, the more-experienced submariner was still recognized as the lead steward. After all, he had, in all likelihood, war patrols under his belt, knew the crew, and was probably qualified throughout at least part, if not the entire boat.

Depending on the nationality of the lead steward, the bond between stewards, no matter what their rank, was sometimes a strong one. This could be true if the lead steward were Filipino or Guamanian, but was especially true if both were African Americans. In this case, a mutual friendship and spirit of cooperation usually developed out of necessity, and it was only natural for a good lead steward to act as teacher and protector for his junior charge when they were the only Black men in a crew of sixty or more men. While this same situation was found on surface ships, it was on a much larger scale. For submariners, whether Black or white, it was even more true. Because relatively few men, sixty to ninety in number on average, manned a submarine in the tightest imaginable quarters, a spirit of teamwork was essential to its successful operation. Whether due to poor attitude, poor training, or a combination of both, one man's failure to do his job properly aboard a submarine, no matter what his rate, could affect

Mail call for the crew of *Argonaut* after her Makin Island mission in August 1942. The men are sitting in front of the boat's huge six-inch deck gun, the largest deck gun carried by any submarine. Sadly, it would do the men of *Argonaut* no good, as she was sunk with all hands by Japanese destroyers on January 10, 1943, near Rabaul during her third war patrol. The steward depicted in this photograph, wearing the chief's hat (third from left, in front), is unidentified but is likely Steward 2nd Class Percy Olds or Steward 2nd Class Willie Thomas. Both men were lost with their boat. (Photograph courtesy of Michael Geletka.)

the entire crew. Because of this, many submarine crewmembers developed a close friendship that went beyond the confines of the boat. Again, this was especially true for men in the steward's branch. However, just as was the case with white crew members, there were times when personalities clashed and some stewards did not get along with each other. In cases such as these when a situation developed where men, whether white or Black, of the same rate failed to work together peacefully, word often got back to the executive officer or captain. Then, usually, the man deemed to be the source of trouble was transferred off the boat.

Examples abound of close personal friendships that developed between submarine stewards from the same boat. A few of these include Albert Rozar and Alonza Davis on *Pargo*, Sam Wallace and Mason Smith on *Mingo*, and Hosey Mays and Tim-

The crew of *Batfish* circa 1945. The boat's only Black crewmember during the entire war was Officer's Cook L.T. Hammonds (third row back, fifth from left), while the other steward was a Filipino (second man to the right of Hammond). *Batfish* and her crew became known as champion sub killers after sinking three Japanese submarines February 9–12, 1945, under Captain John Fyfe. (Photograph courtesy of L.T. Hammonds.)

othy Pennyman on *Crevalle*. In some cases, such as that of Lewis Hammond on *Batfish*, no such bond developed because the boat only had one Black steward. In a few rare cases, there was barely concealed animosity between two stewards on a submarine. Sometimes, as was the experience encountered by Walter Patrick on *Bluegill*, this was due to racism against whites. When Patrick went aboard his first submarine, the lead steward, a native of Alabama, had an intense hatred of whites and could barely conceal his contempt for them while aboard *Bluegill*. As a result, the lead steward often made Patrick's job difficult when he tried to do those little extra things for the crew that a steward often does — an unsolicited cup of coffee here, an extra sandwich there. No doubt as a result of this attitude, the lead steward was transferred off *Bluegill* after her first war patrol. The submarine war was difficult enough without having a war within the boat.

The daily duties of submarine stewards were fairly standard throughout the service. Prior to a submarine's departure for sea, they would be active with other crewmembers in helping to load provisions aboard the boat for a patrol that might last anywhere from thirty to sixty days and sometimes longer. Always at the start of a patrol, foodstuffs

The commissary crew of *Baya* in 1945. Steward's Mate Earnest Danford is at rear (second from left), and at center (rear) is Steward 3rd Class Thomas West, Jr. (Photograph courtesy of E. Danford.)

could be found crammed throughout the boat. Fresh food was always used up first, with resort then being made to canned or powdered foods. Unlike other branches of the United States Armed Forces, submarines were always renowned for the fare they provided their crew, and much of the credit is due to men of the steward's branch.

Once at sea, the traditional duties of a steward were performed like clockwork, usually interrupted only when a submarine made contact with the enemy and went into battle station conditions or when operations were curtailed by harsh weather or mechanical breakdowns. Whether they were a mess attendant (later, steward's mate), steward, or officer's cook, the day would begin with the preparation of a light breakfast for the officers in the morning. This would include traditional fare such as eggs and toast, fresh fruit, and oatmeal or cereal. Sometimes, when a submarine had surfaced, the steward would find a few "flying fish conked out on the deck" (Stempf letter). These were considered good eating, so to speak, and were a welcome change from months-old eggs after the boat had been at sea for a time. Naval tradition dictated that these were always saved for the captain, but, on occasion, stewards were known to sneak them to favored junior officers or enlisted men. Once the breakfast dishes were cleared and washed, the steward's next job was to clean the officer's rooms and make their beds. Later in the day, there would be preparations for cooking and serving the noon meal for the officers.

Officer's Cook Willie James on *Whale*. A veteran submariner with prior service on *Drum* and *Wahoo*, James made a number of war patrols on *Whale* and was well known for his culinary talents. His dress in this photograph, with navy-issue dungarees and forage cap, is typical of the informal atmosphere normally found on submarines. (Photograph courtesy of P. Nalle.)

This fare might include a soup or salad, followed by a meat and vegetable course with rolls. Often the meal ended with a light dessert. As with all other meals, coffee was usually the main beverage consumed. Once this meal was finished, it was the responsibility of the steward, as after all meals, to clean up the wardroom and galley (Wallace).

The traditional duties of a steward and that of an officer's cook in a surface ship were usually adhered to on a regular basis. On such craft, the steward was responsible for setting the tableware, serving the prepared food to the officers, providing service during the meal, and cleaning up afterward. The only food that a steward prepared was the salad that preceded the main course. In contrast, the officer's cook would actually cook and prepare meals for the officers. This was not the case aboard submarines, where stewards and officer's cooks performed the same functions (*ibid.*).

Submarine officers normally ate the same food that was prepared by the white ship's cook for the enlisted men. The only difference might be in its presentation and appearance. Served on china dishes reserved for the officer's mess only, many officer's cooks and stewards knew the tricks of the trade when it came to style and appearance. This might mean an added bit of garnish or mashed potatoes whipped to a smooth and creamy consistency, without the lumps often present in the enlisted man's version of the same dish (Lomax). As was the case on surface craft, during meal times the steward or officer's cook who served the meal wore a white mess jacket that looked much like that worn by waiters in a fancy restaurant ashore (Kimmons).

While an officer's cook might perform the role of a steward, and vice versa, there were a number of officer's cooks who were renowned in the Submarine Force for their cooking abilities. It is, indeed, almost humorous at times to discover what a veteran submariner of World War II retains in his memory. While few officers remember much about the officer's cooks and stewards that served them, many recall the memorable meals and desserts they prepared. The legendary Dave Ball on *Rasher* was rumored to have once been a cook at a fancy Washington, D.C., restaurant and at the White House. *Rasher*'s executive officer Bill Norrington well remembers to this day the baked Alaska dessert that Ball concocted. Willie James, too, while on the *Whale*, was "fabled" for his cooking abilities. In an effort to impress a visiting British submarine commander, James was told to "really put it down" for their visitor on *Whale*. James was equal to the challenge, starting off the meal with vichyssoise, followed by a fish in piquant sauce dish "that Willie had invented," followed by a roast beef served with potatoes au gratin, French peas served with bacon, and a salad. After dinner, James served a dessert of crepes Suzette, followed by the exotic Creole beverage of coffee and brandy called Cafe Brulot. When the British commander complimented the *Whale*'s commander on such a fine meal, the commander stated innocently: "Why, these are our normal rations" (Reynolds, p. 43).

While such fancy fare as this was by no means the normal fare for a submariner at sea, stewards could and did work magic in the kitchen even while on war patrol. The executive officer (later commanding officer) of *Drum* during the war, Maurice Rindskopf, well remembers George Lytle, the boat's officer's cook. Lytle was a "well liked" individual and he "crossed swords" with *Drum*'s commander, Robert Rice, only once during the three war patrols they made together. This came about when Lytle was in the habit of baking two cakes every other day while on patrol, one being white with chocolate frosting, the other chocolate with white frosting. One of these cakes was usually for the officers, while the other was distributed to the enlisted men. However, Rice and Rindskopf soon found out that during this patrol, they had each gained ten pounds. Such a situation was very unusual, as men usually lost weight while at sea for a long period of time. Indeed, it was the only time in Rindskopf's submarine career that he ever put on weight while at sea. Once Rice had figured out the reason for his weight gain, the cake baking was halted, much to the chagrin of both Lytle and the rest of the crew (Rindskopf).

In addition to preparing such desserts, stewards also helped to procure more unusual fare to help keep the shipboard diet varied. While undergoing a refit at Freemantle, Australia, nearly 200 rabbits were procured inexpensively for consumption aboard *Bowfin* (Hoyt, p. 24), while Officer's Cook 3rd Class Paul Ragland on *Barb* won five "langoustas" while gambling that were later "offered up as lobster newburg" (Fluckey, p. 77). While the enlisted men on *Bowfin* undoubtedly had rabbit in their diet, it is doubtful that anyone but officers got a taste of lobster on *Barb*.

Steward Anderson Peter Royal on the deck of *Silversides* in 1942. (Photograph courtesy of A.P. Royal.)

In between mealtimes, and, indeed, at most times throughout the day and night, the steward always kept a pot of fresh coffee on hand and, as such, were often kept busy bringing coffee to the officers in the control room, conning tower and, when surfaced, on the bridge. With rare exceptions, coffee was truly the lifeblood of the Submarine Force, and a good steward was instrumental in keeping it in good supply at all times. The amount of coffee consumed by submariners was quite large. Steward's Mate Jesse Debro of the *Queenfish* remembered serving anywhere from thirty to forty cups of coffee a day to officers alone (Debro). The lead steward on the boat, William Boulet, probably served a like amount, meaning that a group of approximately six or seven officers may have each had ten or more cups of coffee a day.

The stories about stewards handling coffee are one of the staples in the yarns of World War II submariners. When Anderson Peter Royal first went to submarines on the *Silversides*, he was told that he couldn't qualify until he could carry three cups of coffee at one time from the pantry to the bridge. Royal practiced doing so for quite some time and became very proficient at it (Trumbull, p. 97). The most difficult part of getting coffee topside was negotiating the long and narrow ladder that ran from the conning tower to the bridge. Naturally, submariners were quite proficient at getting topside, but add to that the task of carrying a cup of steaming hot coffee and the steward's job became more difficult. In a calm sea, this might not be so bad, but during heavy seas, when the boat rocked on the ocean like a floating cork, carrying hot coffee to the men standing lookout on the bridge was an extremely difficult task. One submarine captain always marveled at how his steward could do this, and one day he got his answer when he chanced to see his steward at the bottom of the ladder. As the story goes, he observed the steward take a huge gulp of coffee from the cup without swallowing it and ascend the ladder to the bridge. Once up top, he quickly spat the coffee back into the cup and gave it to one of the men (Schratz, p. 56). One can assume that the captain put a stop to this practice as no mention is made of any disciplinary action being taken against this resourceful, if not quite sanitary, submarine steward. However, the veracity of this story, humorous though it may be, must be questioned. The likelihood of being able to take a gulp of steaming hot coffee seems a bit beyond belief, and it is more likely that the steward in question was quite skilled at his job and received some good-natured ribbing from his officers about how he got their coffee topside.

Following the noontime repast, many boats, based on the captain's preference, also had a light meal served in between lunch and dinner. This would often consist of soup with a side dish of bread and butter and was served somewhere around 3:00 P.M. The final scheduled meal of the day was the evening meal, usually served around 7 P.M. This would normally be a full meal, complete with soup, crackers, and bread and butter before a main course of meat, potatoes, and a vegetable. This main course was often followed by a salad with dressing and a dessert afterward. Though such hearty fare would seem unusual, especially in wartime and in such cramped conditions as a submarine, this was, in fact the norm. This was true for desserts as well. Like many a serviceman, submarine sailors valued their sweets and often went to great lengths to have them. This is well evidenced by the regular baking of cakes and other treats by stewards and officer's cooks such as George Lytle, as well as the involvement of many of the crew, especially engineering personnel, in the creative procurement and operation of shipboard ice cream makers.

When not preparing for meals or cleaning up after them, the steward might perform a variety of functions. Regular duties included cleaning the boat's coffee urns, keeping the galley clean, and performing regular maintenance chores, such as defrosting the refrigerator on an as-needed basis. The trash that accumulated aboard the boat during a patrol also needed to be dealt with, and it was usually the job of the steward to lug it topside when the boat was surfaced, often at night, and throw it overboard. The foulness of this job was sometimes offset by the fact that the steward to whom the task fell was compensated with exposure to fresh air and a starry or sunlit sky.

Stewards performed other duties, too. They might help to show a movie and make popcorn for the officers and crew if such an activity were planned. Even in off-hours, when no meal was planned, many stewards kept a plate of sandwiches at the ready to feed hungry men at all hours of the night.

While stewards were on board, in theory, to serve the officers, they also catered to the needs of the enlisted men when time and circumstances permitted. With such close quarters as those that were found aboard submarines, this was inevitable, and whether this was in the form of an unsolicited cup of coffee, the baking of treats, a favorite sandwich during the midnight watch, or a like activity, these actions not only served to keep morale high throughout the entire boat but also fostered a close-knit spirit of teamwork that was the hallmark of Submarine Force crews during the war. When not on duty, the stewards usually rested, hung out with other crewmembers or, like many a sailor, participated in a never-ending game of cards.

While stewards and officer's cooks performed a variety of functions for both their officers and the crew, there were limitations to what tasks they would perform. These limitations were not set by the navy but by the men of the steward's branch themselves and the traditions and customs that were passed down among its members. While they varied greatly, these traditions resulted in what might best be referred to as an informal code of conduct. For example, steward personnel did not normally perform laundry functions nor were they normally asked to do so. One common area of dispute between stewards and officers was that of shoe care. It was not uncommon for an officer to ask a steward to shine his shoes while still on his feet. Understandably so, this type of job was considered demeaning by stewards. A compromise was often reached by the steward when he persuaded the officer in question to remove his shoes from his feet so that a better job could be done. Most officers complied with this request. Just as in many professions, there were fine lines that could be crossed that resulted in some men being regarded unfavorably by their fellow stewards. Those stewards that fawned over an officer or group of officers, played the stereotypical role of a Black servant, or went out of their way to ingratiate themselves with officers and members of the crew by going well above and beyond their normal functions were looked upon disdainfully and referred to as "ear bangers" or "brown-nosers" (Kimmons). Every group in the United States Armed Forces had, and still does have, such overachievers and the steward's branch was no exception.

Qualifying as a Submariner

Just like other branches of the United States Armed Forces, such as the army's rangers and paratroopers, the men of the Submarine Force were a breed apart in their branch of the service. As such, not only was their service for such dangerous work voluntary, it also required a degree of specialized training that was both rigorous, at times, and ongoing. To volunteer for submarine duty, and even to attend and pass submarine school was not enough to make a man a true submariner and allow him to wear the silver dolphins that were the insignia of a Submarine Force crewmember. No, to earn his dolphins a submariner, be he Black or white, had to serve aboard a submarine and receive training in the boat itself. By going systematically through the boat and learning how its various systems operated, and by being able to operate them properly on his own, a man would earn his dolphins. This hands-on learning process was, and still is, referred to in the Submarine Force as "qualifying," and once a man became qualified in submarines and had proved himself so to the chief petty officers in charge of each area of operations and to the boat's commanding officers, then, and only then, was he allowed the privilege of wearing the silver dolphins (qualified officer personnel wear gold dolphins).

The process of qualifying applied to all personnel aboard a given submarine, no matter what their rating. Thus it was that a new lieutenant junior grade, fresh out of the Naval Academy, had to qualify for submarine service, going through the same process as would a ship's cook, motor machinist, torpedoman, radioman, or any other man. This also applied to men in the steward's branch but, as we will see, there were some notable differences. For those who have never served aboard a submarine, the question as to why a man, any man, would have to learn the operations of an entire submarine might be raised. After all, a man serving in surface craft, say a destroyer or cruiser, was not forced to learn all aspects of that ship's operations. Why is a submarine any different?

First and foremost to be remembered is the size of a submarine and her crew. Where a destroyer might have a crew ranging in size from 200 to nearly 400 men, a submarine's complement of men ranged in size from 60 to 90 men, only rarely exceeding this number. Because of this small complement, it was essential for submariners to receive cross training in all areas of operations. A submarine only carried limited numbers of men in each rating. Therefore, if, say, a radioman or electrician was wounded, sick, or otherwise incapacitated, it would be necessary for another man to take over his duties. By having all submariners qualify throughout the boat, it was certain that when a situation arose, another man could be counted on to perform the needed duties.

A secondary, yet related, reason, was the nature of submarine warfare in general and how it related to the size of the boat. The diesel submarine of World War II was a tightly cramped vessel, with an amazing amount of operational systems crammed throughout the boat. The men serving on board submarines had to pass through a variety of different compartments on a daily basis, whether to go to their quarters for sleep, the crew mess for dinner, or even the control room and conning tower if they were designated to stand watch on the bridge. When out on patrol, anything at any time might happen to send a submarine and her crew into action: an enemy aircraft might dive out of the sun to attack a surfaced submarine; a submarine might spot an enemy convoy on the horizon, or, as sometimes occurred, they might be stalked by an enemy submarine. In any of these situations, and numerous others that might arise, a submarine crewmember had to know what actions to take and be able to capably respond to orders from his officers. The qualifying process helped ensure that a man, any man, no matter where he was at the time, no matter what his rate, would be able to do so. Unlike any other craft in the United States Navy, the failure of just one man to do his job in a critical situation, whether he be a commanding officer who makes a mistake in judgement or an enlisted man who fails to properly close off a compartment, could mean the loss of the entire boat. Not only was this a possibility, it was highly probable. Of the fifty-two United States submarines lost during World War II, forty-four of them were lost with their entire crew. Conversely, when a submarine was in dire circumstances, those who made it through the emergency and back to base could often attribute their survival to the skill and tenacity of their crew in working together to save the boat. On no other naval vessel is the adage "all for one and one for all" more appropriate than on submarines during wartime. In speaking about submarine crews in general, and specifically the men of the steward's branch, Glenn Milhorn may have said it best. A

The qualification training card for submariner Steve Shelby. Though this card dates from 1959, the systems detailed on this card that Shelby had to learn throughout the boat were essentially the same for those stewards who qualified throughout their boats during World War II. (Photograph courtesy of S. Shelby.)

Steward's Mate Walter Patrick (right) getting his dolphins on the deck of *Bluegill* in early 1944. Like some stewards, he qualified in all ares of the boat to earn his silver dolphins and become a full-fledged submariner. (Photograph courtesy of W. Patrick.)

former torpedoman electrician on *Gurnard* for eight war patrols, he succinctly states that "on a submarine everyone is important" (Milhorn).

Just as a steward's training for submarines varied widely, both within the steward's branch and compared to white submariners, so too did the qualifying process. Three different scenarios are found among stewards that served aboard submarines: stewards that either never qualified or did so after an extended amount of time in submarines, those that qualified in just part of the boat, and those stewards that qualified, like white sailors did, throughout the entire boat. Unfortunately, submarine muster rolls and individual service records from this period do not usually identify which men were fully qualified and those that were only part qualified or not at all. Based on this author's research, it appears that most stewards qualified throughout a part of the boat only, with a lesser number of men qualifying in full. Whatever the case for these two scenarios, once these men had received their qualification training, either in part or full, and passed the necessary tests, they were allowed to wear the dolphin insignia that identified them as a submariner.

Just as the style of operations aboard each submarine varied with each individual commander, so too did the qualifying process aboard each boat often differ. For those boats where the commander was indifferent to men in the steward's branch, there was likely to be little encouragement from him and his officers for stewards to learn the entire boat. In this case, usually the bare essentials for a submarine steward's training were the rule. However, in other cases, stewards were either encouraged by the officers they served to get fully qualified throughout the boat or were motivated on their own to do so. In these cases, it would appear that these commanders were able to look beyond a man's rating and likely sought to have his entire crew, without regard to color, fully trained so that his boat was in the best fighting trim possible. It was very rare for a Black submariner not to qualify, and where this was the case, it was often due to unusual circumstances.

Most submarine stewards during the war qualified in the forward part of the boat only. This included the forward battery compartment, the officer's wardroom and sleeping quarters, the galley, and sometimes the control room and the forward torpedo compartment. The rationale for this was quite simple. These were, for the most part, the only compartments in the entire boat where a steward or officer's cook worked and lived. Seldom, if ever, did a steward have cause to be in the after compartments of the boat. Sam Wallace of *Mingo* remembers one extended patrol when his boat was at sea for 87 days, and he had shipmates that he had not seen in two months. When on duty, the steward's station was in and around officers' country. Thus, it was essential that he qualify in these areas and know how to use the communication phones in the forward battery area and how to properly operate the watertight doors that separated them when an emergency arose. Many submarine stewards were also qualified to work in the forward torpedo room because this is where they bunked and slept when not on duty, so it was important that they know the area well. Indeed, many submarine stewards, had they been allowed, could easily have been rated as torpedomen, as will be shown later in this study.

The importance of knowing how each compartment operated, and what to do in an emergency is starkly illustrated by the experiences of Anderson Peter Royal on *Dragonet*. His boat ran aground off Japan on December 15, 1944, causing the whole forward torpedo compartment to flood. Acting quickly, the men stationed there, including Royal, sealed off the compartment and, under the cool guidance of Captain Jack Lewis, brought things under control and emptied the compartment of water. Badly damaged, *Dragonet* headed back to base at Midway Island, travelling thousands of miles through enemy waters on the surface. It was due to the high level of training and courage of such men as Royal and the forward torpedo crew that *Dragonet*'s crew survived the ordeal and, as one historian has noted, she "was the only submarine in the war to completely flood her forward torpedo room and survive" (Blair, p. 806). Despite this example, few stewards were encouraged to qualify throughout the entire boat. As Carl Kimmons states; "Enthusiastic stewards might have wanted to qualify throughout the boat but no one was interested in having them do it. I had drawings of all the ship, but no one was interested — after I learned how to blow the officer's head, I was in" (Kimmons).

For those stewards that did qualify throughout the entire boat, their experiences were generally encouraging ones. Steward's Mate 2nd class Mack Butler, while serving on *Dace*, earned his dolphins and the record notes that he "qualified in all respects (in excess)" (National Archives, reel 1279). Likewise, Walter Patrick qualified fully aboard his boat, *Bluegill*. He states,

When I completed my examination the officer that examined me told the Captain, Lt. Commander Eric L. Barr, Jr., that Steward's Mate Patrick passed the test with a 4.0 grade. Captain Barr said, "Give him 3.9. No man is perfect" [Patrick].

Another man who was fully qualified throughout his boat was the aforementioned Anderson Peter Royal while aboard *Silversides*, his first submarine. Hesitant at first about the qualifying process, Royal soon gave it his all and thoroughly learned all he could with the encouragement of *Silversides'* captain, Creed Burlingame, as well as her executive officer, Roy Davenport. Blessed with a keen intellect and eager to learn all that he could, Royal soon learned more tasks than were required of a steward. One of the things that Royal learned early on, while aboard the destroyer *McFarland*, was the use of signal flags that were used to communicate between two ships at sea. While signal lamps were often used for this purpose, signal flags required more skill to master. Royal's skills in this area made him particularly useful when *Silversides* was entering port at the end of a patrol or on departure for war patrol and worked with surface escort vessels.

Another man who qualified throughout the entire boat was David Collier on *Hake* in 1945. While working in the maneuvering room, however, Collier was given a difficult time by an electrician's mate who told him not to work on qualifying while on his watch. However, once the captain and other officers were notified of the problem by Collier, the situation was resolved, and he proceeded through the rest of his qualifying without incident. Other men that qualified throughout the boats they served on include James Washington on *Cuttlefish*, Bert Minor on *Crevalle*, Jesse Allen on *Devilfish*, and Killraine Newton on *Sailfish*.

Finally, when it came to qualifying and earning the submariner's dolphins, there were some stewards and officer's cooks who served on submarines during the war but never became qualified. This occurred for a variety of reasons, but in most cases this situation applied to those men that served aboard submarines for only a brief time before leaving the Submarine Force for good. One such case was William Allison from Charlotte, North Carolina. He made one war patrol on *Grampus* in May of 1942 but, prior to the boat's departure for her third war patrol, became ill and was replaced by another steward. Subsequently assigned to a submarine tender and a patrol craft, Allison never again served in submarines. While Allison's short stay in submarines was the result, not of a lack of ability, but due to both illness and navy bureaucracy, there are other stewards who served briefly but were quickly replaced because they were found unsuitable in one way or another. The submarine *Bluefish* had two steward's mates that were disqualified from service in January 1945, after less than a month's service, due to chronic seasickness, while the *Finback* had a mess attendant who was court-martialed and received an undesirable discharge from the navy in March 1942 after only four months of service. Of course, men such as these never qualified due to their short time in submarines. However, there are isolated cases where some stewards served aboard submarines for an extended time during the war, yet never qualified to wear the dolphin insignia of the Submarine Force during that time. One such man was George Bracey, from Jackson, Mississippi. He made seven war patrols on *Pargo* from August 1943 to June 1945, yet did not qualify in submarines until after the war ended. The reason for this circumstance is unknown but was certainly not due to any lack of ability on Bracey's part, as he went on to have a long career in submarines before his death in 1963 while serving aboard the nuclear submarine *Thresher*.

When the war began in 1941, qualified Black stewards were to be found in nearly all the types of boats that composed the strength of the Submarine Force. This not only included the newer fleet boats of the *Tambor* class but also those of the slightly older *Salmon* class, as well as their predecessors, the P and V boats, including the giants of the later class, *Argonaut*, *Narwhal*, and *Nautilus*. Even the older S-class and the ancient R- and O-class boats were manned by some Black stewards.

However, there was a limit as to the geographical areas where Black submarine stewards were generally stationed. Those submarines based in the Atlantic and operating from either stateside or Panamanian bases commonly had Black stewards. The same holds true for those submarines, no matter what their class, that were stationed at Pearl Harbor in the Pacific. Of the eleven boats that conducted the first war patrols from Pearl Harbor in December of 1941, all but three, *Pollack*, *Tautog*, and *Thresher*, had Black stewards. In contrast, Black stewards were seldom seen in boats that operated with the Asiatic fleet based out of Manila in the Phillipines. Of the twenty-eight boats that made war patrols from Manila in December of 1941, nearly all had Filipino stewards. While some boats had Chinese stewards, a rarity by this time in the steward's branch, only three boats were manned by Black stewards. Aboard *Spearfish* were mess atendants J.P. Buttrill and Arthur McAdoo, aboard *Sculpin* were Cleo Boyd and A.L. Newton, while *Sturgeon* had William Grandy

Steward's Mate Bert Minor of *Crevalle* in 1945. A native of Denver, Minor's uniform shows his silver dolphins, with submarine combat insignia above and campaign bars below. (Photograph courtesy of B. Minor.)

and Eddie Jackson as mess attendants. These six men were the only Black stewards in the entire submarine fleet in Asian waters. On one hand, given the fact that Manila was their base of operations, it is not surprising that more Filipino stewards were employed in these boats that were based in their homeland. However, it is also known that in prewar days, Black stewards were generally discouraged from entering the Submarine Force, while those Black stewards already in submarine duty were sometimes transferred from boat to boat by commanders who favored stewards of another race. From 1937 to 1939, Boley, Oklahoma, native Curtis Fitchpatrick served in the submarines *Bass* and *S-22* until he was transferred to the mine layer *Gamble* and out of submarines for good. As he recalls, he was "thrown out of sub duty" by an officer who was a "hateful man" that attempted to transfer all the Black stewards out of his squadron (Fitchpatrick).

While there were few Black stewards found in the boats of the Asiatic fleet in 1941, things would change by late 1943, when most submarines in the Pacific would be entirely manned by Black stewards. This was due not only to the fall of the Phillipines to the Japanese, effectively cutting off the supply of stewards from that area, but also because of the many Black men, either enlisted or drafted, that volunteered to join the rapidly expanding Submarine Force fleet. With so many new submarines coming into service, it was soon realized that Black stewards would be needed to man them.

BATTLE-STATION ACTION

Like any other member of a submarine crew, the stewards and officer's cooks had a job to do based on the rating they held. As their rating title made clear, the purpose of such men was to serve the captain and his junior officers and see to their needs, just as it was the everyday duty of a motor machinist to tend to the boats engines and like equipment to keep them in good operating condition at all times. This was part of the everyday routine on board a submarine at sea. However, a submarine during World War II had two modes of operation. During those times when a submarine was heading off on war patrol from friendly waters or was heading back home at the end of a war patrol, and at various times in-between, the normal routine prevailed. However, whenever the enemy was encountered or a dangerous situation developed, the job of the submarine steward, and all men aboard the boat, changed in an instant to that of battle station conditions. At times such as these, the ultimate situation for which the submarine was designed and utilized, then each man aboard the boat had a battle station assignment that was sometimes, especially in the case of stewards and officer's cooks, vastly different than that of their normal duties.

Battle station assignments for men serving on fleet boats during the war took place in two different conditions. Battle station submerged conditions occurred when the boat was engaging or stalking the enemy while submerged. This condition might include attacks on unsuspecting enemy surface vessels, either merchant or naval, or even an attack on an unsuspecting enemy submarine that might have strayed into their area of operations. Battle station submerged conditions were also in force when a submarine was attempting to evade enemy counterattack methods from naval or merchant vessels, either during the course of an attack or in the aftermath of an attack on enemy shipping.

Since a submarine did most of her damage to the enemy while submerged, the situation of battle station submerged was very common during a war patrol and, at times, a daily occurrence.

The most common battle station submerged for a steward or officer's cook was that of phone talker in either the forward battery area or in the forward torpedo room. In these areas, they would man the XJA phones and relay orders that came from the officers in the conning tower or control room during an attack or its aftermath. Another common battle station submerged position for the men of the steward's branch was that of working on the torpedo reload gangs in the forward torpedo room. Because the stewards' bunks were located in this compartment, directly above a pair of unarmed torpedoes, many of them became well-versed in the operations that were carried out there. As part of the torpedo reload gangs, they would help operate the machinery that moved the torpedoes from the racks in which they were stored to the torpedo tubes from which they would be fired at the enemy at the appropriate signal from the conning tower. Due to the size of each torpedo, weighing on average close to 3,000 pounds and 14 feet long, it was back-breaking work, even with the use of rollers and chainfalls, to move the "tin fish" into place for quick firing. Steward's Mate William Rapier on *Tunny* is well remembered by Chief of the Boat Hugh Latham, who recalls that Rapier "was so strong he could load torpedoes almost by himself" (Latham). Among those other stewards that served on torpedo reload gangs were Jesse Debro on *Queenfish*, Herbert Odom on *Silversides*, Napoleon Finley on *Sterlet*, Spaulding Settle on *Tinosa*, Sammy Colston on *Lionfish*, Jesse Allen on *Devilfish*, Richard Lucas on *Raton*, Robert Goens on *Icefish*, Hosey Mays on *Crevalle*, Edward Neely on *Bowfin*, Carl Kimmons on *Plunger*, and likely many more.

The description of Herbert Odom in action on *Silversides* is probably indicative of both the enthusiasm and competence that men of the steward's branch displayed while manning their battle stations. When the call came out over the boat's loudspeakers, calling the captain to the conning tower and ordering "two torpedoes ready forward,"

> [Odom, who was in the wardroom about to serve a meal to Captain Creed Burlingame,] dropped the plate as if it had burned him and whirled out of the wardroom. In the forward torpedo room the crew was preparing No. 3 tube. Odom went to work on No. 4 and had it ready by himself by the time the others completed the first tube. The crew was amazed. This wasn't Odom's job, but he had learned by watching. [When the order to fire came from Captain Burlingame,] Odom was grinning broadly. The tube he had prepared had been fired first. Then the shock of two violent explosions flung his big body back among the bunks [Trumbull, pp. 68–69].

Not long afterward, Captain Burlingame remarked that "We can put this one down as sunk, all right" (*ibid.*).

In addition to the just described duties that stewards had during battle station submerged conditions, there were several other jobs that some of them performed. Ernest Danford's battle station submerged position on *Baya* was in the conning tower. Acting as "scopeman," he helped operate the periscope, the optical apparatus that acts as the eyes of a submarine while she is underwater. One man, William Murray on *Plunger*,

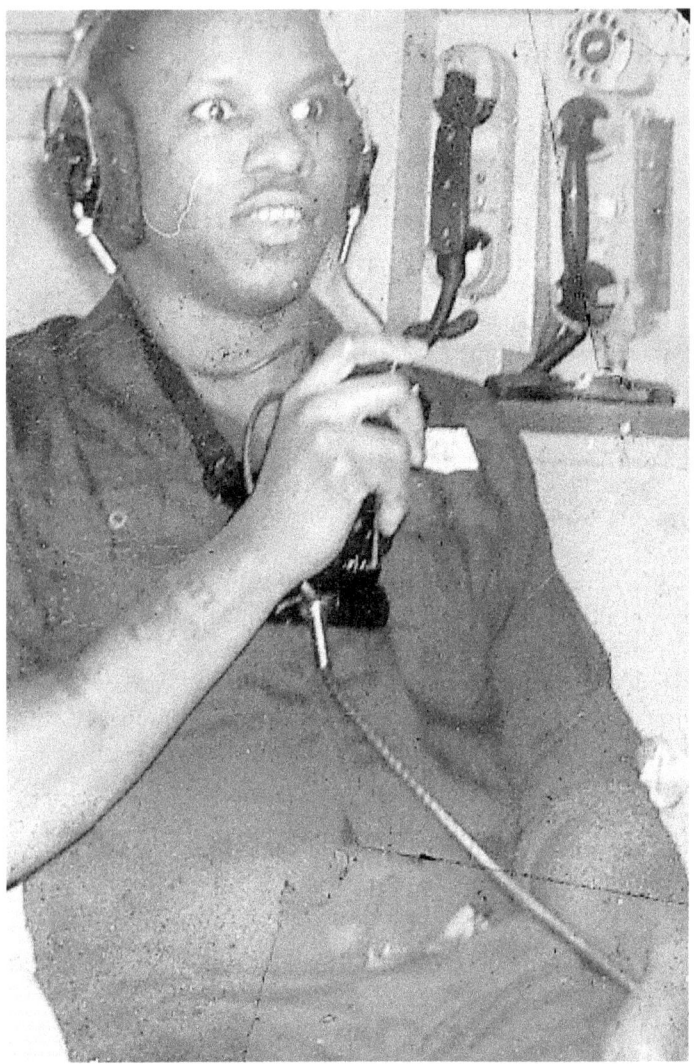

Steward's Mate Archie Denson manning the wardroom phones during battle station submerged on *Besugo* in the early 1950s. This was a traditional post manned by stewards in the Submarine Force dating back to pre–World War II days. (Photograph courtesy of A. Denson.)

acted as a bow planesman and remembered that, on his first war patrol, "I performed this duty under the watchful eyes of a skilled bow planesman who had many ... war patrols under his belt" (Murray). Another unusual position held was that of Leonard Rozar aboard *Tuna*. Having received prior training in the boat's sonar gear, he sometimes acted as a standby soundman when he wasn't manning the phones in the forward battery area.

While all of the preceding battle station submerged positions often involved fast-paced action and excitement, there were other times when men were at their battle station poised for action but with little to do. This was usually the case when the boat was rigged for silent running in order to evade an attack or counterattack from enemy naval vessels. When rigged for silent running, all unnecessary equipment that made sound of any kind was turned off, such as the boat's air conditioning units, and silence reigned throughout the boat. Japanese sonar was sophisticated enough that it could detect a submerged submarine's whereabouts should someone speak too loudly or even if a something inadvertently fell and hit the deck inside the submarine being stalked. At times such as these, which could last anywhere from mere minutes to many hours, tension was high and conditions in the boat could become unbearable. With many systems shut down, the temperature inside the boat rose rapidly, and air quality decreased as time passed on. Despite this, the men had to remain at the ready to spring into action if conditions changed.

During this time, the only sound heard by the crew of a submarine, other than the whispers of their shipmates, was the crash of depth charges that were dropped by the enemy. These were explosive charges dropped from the stern of Japanese destroyers or other patrol craft. Nicknamed "ashcans" by the Americans, they were set to explode at certain prescribed depths. If the enemy's guess was right, and they exploded close enough to a submarine, it usually meant the destruction of the boat and loss of her entire crew. Otherwise, a depth charge that was off the mark might cause damage to the boat, the severity of which depended on its proximity. For the inexperienced submariner, even those depth charges that were too far off to cause damage could be quite nerve wracking. However, not all new submariners fully grasped the reality of a depth-charge attack. Avery Willis on *Tunny* recalls the time that his boat took a pounding, and he was stationed in the after-torpedo room. The boat's newest steward, Steward's Mate 2nd Class James Turner on his first patrol, heard the explosions and remarked to Willis, "We sure are giving them hell, huh?" Willis, impressed by the man's "sheer innocence," told him that, "no, they're trying to sink us," whereupon "the look on his face went from jubilation to sheer despair," as he finally realized that "we could get killed" (Willis).

While many new submariners had experienced a depth charging during training in simulated attack exercises administered by American navy destroyers, they could not compare to the real thing. Regarding these attacks, Harold Hale, a steward that served on *Tunny*, states that "anyboby that says they weren't afraid, they're a liar" (Hale, Harold H.). Perhaps the steward's mate on *Seahorse*, J.C. Crawford, said it best, albeit unwittingly. After the boat's first war patrol, during which they had received a severe depth charging, Crawford came to Executive Officer Slade Cutter and said, "Mr. Cutter, I want to get off the ship." When Cutter asked the likeable steward's mate why, Crawford replied, "Because of them death charges." A bemused Cutter explained that they were "depth" charges, not "death" charges, and asked the young steward's mate to stay on *Seahorse* (Cutter). Crawford agreed, staying on board for a year and another three war patrols.

One of the biggest problems that men faced during a depth charging was its psychological impact. Forced to stay at their duty station, yet inactive and helpless to do anything, men could hear the creaking and groaning of the submarine and the sound of the dreaded ashcans in the water above them. One way to combat such a situation and relieve the tension was found by Officer's Cook 1st Class George Lytle on *Drum*. He was manning the phones in the forward battery during her eighth war patrol when the boat underwent a severe depth-charging. With nothing to do, Lytle kept count of the number of depth charges dropped on *Drum*, "Keeping score on Betty Grable's rear end on the wardroom calendar ... his count was used officially for the patrol report" (Stempf letter).

Finally, on the subject of depth charging, the men that served aboard the *Puffer* should be recognized for their performance under duress. On her first war patrol in October 1943, while patrolling the Makassar Strait, *Puffer* attacked a Japanese merchant vessel but failed to sink her. Six minutes later, the first depth charges were dropped by the wounded ship's escort, a Chidori-class submarine chaser. Twenty minutes later, six depth charges exploded close aboard *Puffer*, causing considerable damage. Thus began a sustained and prolonged attack that held the unlucky submarine down for 38 hours. Damaged and making noise, the battered *Puffer* barely survived the ordeal, "the

longest hold down of an American submarine during the war" (McDonald, p. 1). As the hours went by, some men succumbed to the pressure and some, maybe even the captain himself, gave up all hope of escape. However, there were many men who refused to give up and acquitted themselves honorably during this trying time. Two such men were Steward's Mate 2nd Class John Alden Pruitt and Officer's Cook 2nd Class James Woodley Patton, Jr. While there is no record of the specific actions of Patton during this time, he is well remembered by surviving crewmembers today. One *Puffer* crewmember, however, has a vivid recollection of John Pruitt. Chief Motor Machinist Ladislaus Topor states that Pruitt "should have received a medal for his actions and words" (Topor). While a bucket brigade was organized to help control the flooding in the after torpedo room, Pruitt, likely under the guidance of Pharmacist's Mate 1st Class Robert Spaulding, distributed salt pills to the men at work along with pitchers of lemonade to help prevent dehydration. Pruitt also exhorted the men, telling them "We're gonna be alright. The Lord doesn't want us; it's not our time yet" (*ibid*.). The fact that both men continued on *Puffer* after this harrowing incident is indicative of their performance. While the boat's captain was relieved of his command, Pruitt went on to serve during two more war patrols, while Patton stayed on *Puffer* through the end of the war, making all nine of her war patrols (McDonald, p. 30). This is surely an indicator of the regard in which he was held by both officers and and his fellow enlisted men.

While American submarines did most of their damage to the enemy in undersea operations during the war, they also used surface attack procedures on various occasions when the situation was warranted. In this instance, submariners operated in battle station surface mode. Such operations usually involved attacks on small fishing vessels and other coastal craft that were not large or valuable enough targets to merit expending a torpedo. In this case, such craft were often sunk by a variety of methods, including gunfire from the submarine's 4- or 5-inch deck gun or the smaller 40mm gun or 20mm cannon that was mounted on her cigarette deck.

Some enemy craft were even destroyed by individual crewmen who, under the protection of the submarine and her deck guns, boarded the craft after her crew was killed or subdued and searched her thoroughly in hope of gaining valuable information. After being boarded, the craft was sometimes destroyed by the placement of demolition charges. While many submarine captains relished these types of action early on, it was highly dangerous work, and one for which the submarine was not primarily designed. Possessed of a thin skin, a well-placed burst of gunfire from even a small enemy vessel could spell the doom of a submarine. Even if her pressurized hull was damaged just enough to prevent her from submerging, a submarine stuck on the surface was a sitting duck for any enemy naval vessel or aircraft that might easily detect her.

If gunfire didn't work, smaller enemy vessels also sometimes resorted to ramming a submarine to sink or disable it. The deadly nature of surface submarine warfare is demonstrated by that which involved the *Growler* and her captain, Howard Gilmore. While making a surface attack on a small enemy vessel on the night of February 7, 1943,

Opposite: The crew of *Seahorse* stateside in late 1944. Steward's Mate 1st Class Samuel Sharp is in the second row (center), and Officer's Cook 3rd Class Culasket Adams, Jr., is in the row behind him to the right, wearing the hat of a chief petty officer. (Photograph courtesy of Dick Clower.)

the enemy ship unexpectedly changed course and rammed *Growler*. Upon impact, the Japanese ship fired on the bridge of the submarine, wounding Gilmore and killing two men. "Above the roar of machine gun fire," Gilmore shouted "Clear the bridge" and, minutes later, yelled "Take her down" (Blair, p. 374). By this heroic action, Gilmore saved his boat at the expense of his own life and was awarded the Medal of Honor. While his final words, "Take her down," became legendary in the Submarine Force, they were also a stark reminder of the dangers of surface action.

Other circumstances in which submarines operated in battle station surface mode include surface torpedo attacks on enemy vessels, usually under the cover of darkness; gun attacks on small shore installations or in support of shore-based guerilla operations; lifeguard duty in rescuing downed American aviators; and in situations when forced to engage enemy aircraft. In all of these situations of surface action, the men of the steward's branch, too, had their assigned stations. While many stewards in surface action worked in the positions of phone talker and torpedo reloading, just as they did in battle station submerged mode, many of these men had additional duties to which they were assigned. One of these was to man the submarine's large deck gun, or smaller 40mm gun. Gun crews on submarines were usually comprised of four or five men, including a gunner, a loader or two, a sighter, and a man to handle spent cartridges. In these positions, Black and white submariners worked together as a team in combat situations. Just a few of these men include Arthur Haynes, a loader on the 5-inch deck gun of *Chub*; R..D. Mosely, too, served as a loader on the deck gun of *Pargo*, as did James Patton and Carroll Allen on *Puffer*, Hosey Mays on *Crevalle*, Willie James on *Whale*, and Robert Coley on *Tambor,* while George Washington Lytle served as a first loader on *Drum*'s deck gun. Other men that served in gun crews include Harold Hale on *Tunny*'s 20mm gun; James Sims, a loader on *Scabbardfish*'s 40mm gun; Alfred Hall, who served as a sighter on the gun crew of *Pomfret*; Robert Goens, who served as "kickman" on *Icefish*'s 40mm gun; Al Rozar, who worked on *Pargo*'s 40mm gun crew; and Spaulding Settle, who manned the 40mm gun of *Tinosa*.

Isaac Johnson, who served as second loader on the 5-inch gun crew on *Sennet* well recalls the daily drills that took place on his boat as it headed off to the war zone:

> From the warmer waters of the Carolinas down to Panama, we had deck gun drills two or three times a day, every day. I don't know how heavy exactly those shells were, but by the time we got to Panama, they seemed as heavy as toothpicks [Johnson].

The gunnery service of Rozar and Settle is interesting, as both received formal training in this area. Rozar, the younger brother of submariner Leonard Rozar, went to gunnery school at Mare Island in California in 1941 prior to making his first war patrol as a steward on *Gudgeon*, while Settle gained his gun crew position after attending gunnery school in Hawaii in late 1943. How many other stewards received formal gunnery training is unknown but likely increased in number as the war went on.

Probably the best account of a steward's performance in battle-surface action, from ammunition passer to manning the deck gun, is that offered by former wartime submarine intelligence officer "Jasper" Holmes. As he recounts, on May 10, 1943, while the boat attempted to finish off a damaged Japanese cargo ship she had previously torpedoed,

Plunger continued to fire until she had expended all her ammunition (180 rounds including one round of target practice ammunition). This was quite a feat of strength, requiring relief of all the exhausted ammunition passers except James McGuire, the muscular Negro cook, who stuck it out all the way through, working his way up from the magazine as the others dropped out until he was finally serving the gun [Holmes, p. 229].

It is likely for this reason that McGuire was promoted to officer's cook 2nd class upon the completion of *Plunger*'s sixth war patrol in June 1943.

While gun crews were important, the one thing they needed to get their job done were the shells that were stored below decks in the ammunition magazine. It was difficult work in a submarine passing the 105-pound shells up one at a time through the narrow confines of the hatchway leading to the conning tower and bridge, and a chain of men were needed to get it done quickly. Stewards routinely served alongside their white shipmates as ammunition passers to hoist the shells topside. Among the many stewards who performed this task were Killraine Newton on *Sailfish*, Robert Moore on *Harder*, Jesse Allen on *Devilfish*, Leslie Hamilton on *Brill*, Arthur Brown on *Narwhal*, Louis Jones on *Lionfish*, David Collier on *Hake*, and Walter Patrick on *Bluegill*. Another man that served in this capacity was Benjamin Brown on *Hardhead*. Brown originally had no battle station surface assignment but went to Captain Fitzhugh McMaster asking for one and was assigned to the task of ammunition passer (Kelley). Like most men during the war, Black or white, Brown was no doubt anxious to get his chance at the enemy any way he could.

The service of men of the steward's branch in gunnery positions in the submarine service was a small but significant step in their overall acceptance as fighting men, especially when it is remembered that, prior to World War II, it was official navy policy

Officer's Cook 1st Class Albert Rozar in 1945. Being a steward was not his preference, but he "did it without fuss" and ended up having a thirty-year navy career as a submariner. (Photograph courtesy of A. Rozar.)

to exclude Blacks from such positions. Not only did such service prove that stewards had the skills to perform such duty but also had the trust of their fellow crewmembers to assume such a role. One small example of the how the stewards proved their worth as members of the gun crews to their white shipmates is told by Arkansas native Thomas Metz, a seaman on *Puffer* during her eighth war patrol in May–June 1945. In describing the boat's 5-inch gun action off Bali, he recalls:

> While the gunnery action was proceeding ... there must have been forty men topside that day. When the first Jap shell hit near us, the captain sounded the diving alarm. The boys that stood watches topside knew we would be completely submerged in 50 seconds.... I knew it was going to take some time for all of them to get below, so I dropped through the hatch with two other men, dropped on down to the control room and right onto the forward torpedo room. There was an officer's steward by the name of James Patton on the 5-inch gun crew. There is an ammunition locker topside in front of the conning tower near the 5-inch mount that holds five 5-inch shells worth about $200 each. All of the white men had left the deck, but the one Black man topside did notice this ammunition locker open and stopped to close it and save the $1,000 worth of shells. I've often thought of this in the past thirty years, especially when the people of the south were trying to tell everybody how no-account Black people were [Metz quoted in an email to author from Craig McDonald].

A veteran by now of seven complete war patrols, James Patton was probably not just thinking about doing things correctly and saving the navy money in this instance, but he also likely knew that the boat's fighting ability could be compromised if those shells were lost. Had *Puffer* needed to surface and resort to deck gun action in a hurry, precious time would have been lost in getting more ammunition hoisted from below.

The trust among submariners, no matter what their race, was crucial to the successful operation of the boat as a fighting unit, and was also the reason that many stewards found such duty eminently preferable to that of surface ships. Probably typical of many of the younger submarine commanders during the war was Frederick Gunn, captain of the newly commissioned *Scabbardfish* in April 1944. When assembling the gun crew for his new command, Gunn interviewed each man under consideration, including Steward's Mate 2nd Class James Sims. His concern likely had nothing to do with color but whether the men of his gun crew could be counted on to do their duty as ordered, even if it meant shooting enemy sailors and soldiers in the water after their ship was sunk. This subject was always a controversial one in the Submarine Force, and one in which no official policy was formulated. Thus, each commander was left to make his own decisions in this area. Gunn apparently believed in killing enemy combatants whenever and wherever the opportunity arose and wanted to make sure his men could do so if ordered. Based on his acceptance as a gun crew member, it is evident

Opposite: Steward's Mates Anderson Royal (left) and William Rapier (right) by the deck gun of *Silversides* in late 1942. The two men made one war patrol together before Rapier was transferred and later did duty on *Tunny*. Royal stayed on the boat for four war patrols before going to new construction and *Dragonet*. Like Royal, Rapier was popular with the crew of *Silversides*, and maybe too much so. It was said of him that he may have been transferred off the boat by her captain because he spent too much time with the crew rather than serving the officers. (Photograph courtesy of A.P. Royal.)

that Sims was thought to be trustworthy and reliable by his captain, even if difficult situations should arise (Jackson, William).

Whether conducted on the surface or below, the business of submarine warfare was a dangerous one with potentially dangerous results. Of the 52 American submarines lost during the war, 44 suffered casualties while operating in enemy waters. Most, but not all, were lost with all hands. Of those that had survivors, two, *Flier* and *Robalo*, sank after hitting a mine. *Flier* had seven survivors, none of whom were stewards, while *Robalo* had four men that survived the sinking but died as prisoners of war. Two other boats lost in enemy waters had a higher number of survivors: *Perch* was lost when she was scuttled by her commander after receiving a severe depth-charging that forced her to the surface. Sixty-four men survived as prisoners of war, including both her Filipino stewards. *Grenadier* was lost in a similar manner, being scuttled after receiving damage from an air attack. Luckily, of her 76 man crew, all but four survived as Japanese captives. One of these men was Mess Attendant 1st Class Thomas Trigg who, like *Grenadier*'s other crewmen, survived 29 months as a prisoner of war. The boat's other steward, Mess Attendant 1st Class Justiniano Guico, a Filipino, died in Fukuoka prison camp.

However, no story may be more dramatic than that of the loss of *Tang*. She is the only submarine actually sunk during enemy action that had survivors who lived to tell the tale. All of the other boats previously mentioned were lost while on the surface, with men escaping while their submarine was still afloat. Not so with *Tang*. The end of this renowned boat, skippered by Commander Richard O'Kane, came during the course of her fifth war patrol northeast of Formosa. During the course of an attack on the evening of October 24, 1944, *Tang* fired two torpedoes at her intended target. The first went off without a hitch, but the second torpedo curved sharply, broached, and headed back toward the submarine from which it had come.

The officers of *Tang* saw what was happening and took emergency measures but could not react quickly enough to prevent a torpedo hit. When the explosion came, Commander O'Kane and the men on the bridge were blown into the water. Three would survive, including O'Kane. Another officer, Lieutenant Lawrence Savadkin, was trapped in the flooded conning tower but managed to escape. The boat, hit in the stern area, was fatally damaged and plunged to the bottom, 180 feet down, at a steep angle.

The men stationed in the after torpedo room and engine rooms were probably killed almost instantly, while those trapped in the after battery area gingerly made their way toward the control room amidships, delayed by exploding depth charges dropped by the Japanese escort above that started electrical fires on board. Once in the control room, the survivors from aft tried to blow the boat to the surface, only to find out that the tanks were ruptured and the air used in the attempt was wasted. It was then decided that the men would make their way to the forward torpedo room, where the forward hatch was located. This would be their only means of escape. As one survivor recalled, "Before entering the forward torpedo room, it was decided to burn all the secret documents. The papers were set ablaze in the forward battery room, then the men quickly moved out, closing the hatch behind them" (Hagendorn, p. 7). However, the forward torpedo room was already so crowded with men, including the boat's three stewards, that it was decided "that a part of the group could return to the control room to make good their escape" (*ibid.*) through the conning tower. One of the men that helped to open the hatch to the forward battery room, where the secret papers had been set on fire, was Officer's Cook 3rd Class Rubin Raiford. Described as "a big fellow" (Carter), the strong South Carolinian slowly undogged the hatch, only to have it blown into his face from the pressure that had built up. Raiford's face was "smashed" (Hagendorn, p. 9), but he was alive and still able to function.

However, new problems soon developed. The air, already fouled because of so many men present, was made worse by the smoke and fumes from the fire in the forward battery that were released when the hatch was opened. Despite Raiford's efforts, it was decided that the hatch had to be closed. However, "the damage had already been done. The men began to choke and an uncontrollable cough struck every man. Momsen Lungs were hurriedly donned, but normal breathing was impossible" (Hagendorn, p. 7). In addition, the lighting began to dim and, with *Tang*'s batteries dying one by one, the forward torpedo room went dark except for the ghostly dim of the battle lanterns. As if this wasn't bad enough, the heat generated by the fire in the forward battery contined to rise, becoming "so intense that the paint on the bulkhead was scorching, melting, and running down" (U.S. Navy, *United States Submarine Losses*, p. 117).

With the end of *Tang* drawing near, her life support systems nearly gone, men decided to make their escape through the forward escape hatch. As survivor Motor Machinist Mate 3rd Class Jesse DaSilva recalled, the men entered the hatch four at a time.

> [T]he hatch was closed and the flood valve was opened. The sea water began filling the tiny cramped cubicle. The Momsen Lungs were strapped into place. When they spoke above the noise level their voices came out in strange squeaky sounds. As the water began to compress the trapped air against the overhead, it became noticeably hotter and breathing became very difficult. Men were forced to pant rather than breathe. Sharp pains began to develop in their ears and they held their noses to blow against the pressure ... with their bodies tightly pressed together they waited for the chamber to fill with water which then would equalize the pressure inside to that outside. Only then could the side hatch be opened ... the escape line was secured and the float went to the surface [Hagendorn, p. 8].

Once in the water, the men attempting to escape had to grab the ascent line and go slowly to the surface. Going too fast might mean a case of the bends and a painful death. After DaSilva's group left *Tang* for the last time, they were followed by the final crewmen to leave the boat: Chief Pharmacist's Mate Paul Larson and Officer's Cook 3rd Class Rubin Raiford. Larson made it to the surface in bad shape and had to be held by other survivors to prevent him from drowning. Despite the fact that he was picked up with the other nine survivors, his fate was sealed when the Japanese abused him and eventually murdered him. Raiford nearly made it. However, he "had lost his grip on the ascent line and he surfaced about fifty feet from the small group of survivors" (*ibid.*). Jesse DaSilva went to his aid, but before he could reach Raiford, his arms began to flail and he slipped underwater, drifting away with the tide. What happened to Raiford can only be speculated upon. Maybe he came to the surface too quickly and had the bends, or maybe his facial injuries were just too serious and caused him to be disoriented. It is even likely that Raiford, like many sailors, could not swim. In any case, despite a valiant attempt, he was gone. Jesse DaSilva would be the last man out of *Tang* to survive.

What of the other men that remained below? With the air quality steadily deteriorating, it is likely that they died by asphyxiation. No doubt some men, if not all, that chose to stay in *Tang* knew what their fate would be and were resigned to the final outcome. Perhaps Steward's Mate 2nd Class Ralph Adams was one of these men, but no one can recall his fate. Steward's Mate 1st Class Howard Walker *was* one of those men who accepted his fate quietly and with fortitude. Survivors last remember Walker, an inveterate gambler in happier times, sitting in the forward torpedo room calmly taking in the scene (Caverly, Floyd). Apparently making no attempt at escape, he seems to have accepted the hand that fate had dealt him.

While we know what happened aboard *Tang* in her final moments of life, one can only speculate as to what may have happened aboard those boats that were lost with all on board. No doubt there were many like instances of heroism by officers and crew, stewards included, that ultimately went unrecorded. The actions of Raiford, as well as DaSilva and the boat's other survivors on *Tang* are proof of this.

In addition to the battle station surface positions described previously, there were likely a number of other positions filled by stewards that cannot be documented. However, one man's unusual position in battle station action that is well documented is that of Walter Pye Wilson. Wilson joined *Trigger* on her commissioning at Mare Island in early 1942 and rode her nearly all the way through the war, making eleven official war patrols in all. After he left *Trigger*, she was lost with all hands on her twelfth war patrol. One of *Trigger*'s junior officers, and later executive officer, during Wilson's time aboard was Edward L. Beach. Beach not only had a notable navy career as a submariner, which started on *Trigger*, but also wrote a number of popular and highly regarded books on submarine and naval history. In his 1999 memoir entitled *Salt and Steel: Reflections of a Submariner*, Beach pays tribute to Wilson, his chief steward during the war years, and recounts his action in battle as follows:

> [A]ll was tensely quiet, and the voice of Walter Pye Wilson, our chief wardroom steward, assigned to steer the boat at battle stations, came up sonorously through the hatch. "Watertight doors shut below! Boat's secured for collision!" At battle stations, Black, heavyset Wilson, an old-time submariner, one of the steadiest men aboard as well as one of the most popular, was assigned to steer the ship. He has always been a proverbial tower of strength at his multitudinous duties; from wardroom galley to handling mooring lines to battle station helmsman, he was never at a loss, his cool voice under stress helping to keep the rest of us cool too. The big chrome-plated steering wheel was just beneath the hatch at our feet, so it was logical that whoever was steering should also function as a link in the communication chain. Wilson was a natural for this job [Beach, *Salt and Steel*, p. 133].

Walter Wilson was indeed the right choice for this job, as further details of his wartime service, found in his biography later on in these pages, will amply demonstrate.

In addition to all the battle station assignments described previously that were performed by stewards, there were various other weapons duties that they performed that were equally important. Aboard *Gunnel*, Officer's Cook Magnus Wade "manned a 50-caliber machine gun and took great pride in this. He was an expert gunner" (Vasey). Another such duty was that of BAR man. This was the man assigned to operate the Browning automatic rifle that many submarines carried and used in battle station surface action. Two stewards are remembered as being their boat's BAR man, Steward's Mate 2nd Class Alphonse Floyd on *Thresher* and an unknown steward on *Sterlet*. Interestingly enough, these weapons were assigned to the men without any prior training, and their first practice firings resulted in less-than-perfect results. Floyd was not firmly set with the BAR when he began his test firing on *Thresher*, and the automatic weapon swung in a horizontal arc to the right. The six men on the after cigarette deck had to hit the deck to avoid being hit, and Floyd was stopped in his tracks by a nearby gunner's mate (Barnes, "USS *Thresher*"). Likewise, when the steward fired the BAR for his first time on *Sterlet*, its barrel climbed upward until he was shooting straight up at the sky. The boat's captain laconically informed the steward that they were not aiming at aircraft today but at the towed target (Olmstead). While it is certain that these stewards received a bit of good-natured ribbing for their work with the BAR that day, we can also be sure that they were given the further training they needed to make them proficient in its use.

Another job performed by the men of the steward's branch was duty as lookouts. Whenever a submarine was on the surface, whether on patrol or to rest and recharge her batteries, men always had to be stationed topside on the bridge to keep a sharp lookout. Armed with binoculars and scanning the sea and sky for hours at a time in all types of weather, these men were the first line of defense for the surfaced submarine, their job being to warn the officers on duty of any approaching aircraft or surface vessels. Any time an American submarine was surfaced while on patrol in enemy waters, danger could present itself in an instant, and the closer a submarine was to Japanese home waters, the greater the danger became. This same was also true for the many small straits that were patrolled by submarines in the South Pacific and the Celebes Sea off Indonesia. Two particularly dangerous areas to transit were the Makassar and Lombok straits. In dangerous waters such as these, a lookout who failed to do his job could cause the loss of the entire crew. Of particular danger were enemy aircraft. These could zoom out of the clouds at any time and would have the element of surprise in their favor. One well-placed bomb could destroy a submarine, and, in fact, ten submarines and nearly all of their crews were lost in this manner during the war. On only one boat lost in this manner, *Grenadier*, were there any survivors. The other nine, *Amberjack*, *Cisco*, *Wahoo*, *Grayback*, *Gudgeon*, *Scamp*, *Barbel*, *Trigger*, and *Bullhead*, were lost with all hands.

Stewards were often given preference in lookout duty right from the start of the war, not because they were neccesarily the most trusted men on board, but due to "the widespread navy belief that Blacks had superior night vision" (Blair, p. 109n). Stories abound among wartime submariners about the discussions that commanding officers had with their stewards before sending them off on lookout duty. One example is that between Captain Sam Dealey of *Harder* and his steward, Robert "Alabama" Moore, which is supposed to have gone something like this:

> "Don't take this extra duty lightly, Alabama," admonished Sam.
> "No, Captain, indeed I won't."

V. Life as a Wartime Submariner   75

Officer's Cook Robert Moore in the wardroom of *Harder*, serving coffee to Executive Officer Frank Lynch. Note the mess attendant's white jacket worn by Moore, who made all of *Harder*'s war patrols before he was lost with Captain Sam Dealey and the rest of her crew on August 24, 1944. (Photograph courtesy of M. Geletka.)

"There are many reasons why you must take it very seriously," continued the Skipper. "First, there's the ship. It cost Uncle Sam seven and a half million dollars."

Bob nodded in agreement.

"Then there are your shipmates. If you fail to keep a sharp lookout, they may die."

Again Bob nodded his understanding. Then, as Sam seemed to have reached the end of his point-by-point review, Alabama added: "But, Cap'n, there is one more!"

"Yeah?" asked Sam. "Who?"

"There's me," explained Alabama [Lockwood and Adamson, p. 169].

Whether or not this conversation really took place is doubtful, as, at best, it has a rather patronizing tone that sounds somewhat contrived. At worst, it can be construed

Opposite: The happy crew of *Thresher* in 1945. In the front row, left of center, is Steward's Mate Eddie Robinson holding the boat's mascot. At far left, third row from the bottom, is Steward's Mate Alphonse Floyd, who learned to operate the boat's Browning automatic rifle (BAR). (Photograph courtesy of J. Barnes.)

as the type of navy racism that perpetuated the stereotype of the Black steward as less intelligent than his fellow white shipmates. Whatever its tone, however, there can be no doubt that Dealey really did talk to Moore about his duty as a lookout in one manner or another before giving him the assignment. A similiar conversation is also recorded as having taken place on *Sturgeon* between her captain, "Bull" Wright and "one of his mess boys"(Grider, p. 167), either Mess Attendant 1st Class Eddie Jackson or Mess Attendant 2nd Class William Grandy. As the story goes, the mess attendant, "an excellent lookout," had come up for his watch and "began a sweep of the horizon, and when he saw [the Japanese island of] Honshu, it was clear he was a trifle unnerved" (*ibid*.).

While many stewards performed the job of lookout during the war, few probably had as harrowing of an ordeal and lived to tell about it as James Washington on *Cuttlefish*. While his boat was patrolling off the Japanese island of Honshu, Washington was serving lookout duty when an enemy plane zoomed out of nowhere. It was so close that he could even see the face of its pilot. When he turned to sound the alarm, he found out that he was the only lookout left topside — all the others had cleared the bridge. Washington quickly made it below before *Cuttlefish* made her crash dive and, luckily, avoided the bombs the plane had dropped. Perhaps the most legendary lookout during the war was Steward's Mate 1st Class Joseph Cross on *Halibut*. Fellow shipmate John Perkins, Jr., remembered that Cross had "eyes like a cat" and that his timely spotting of aircraft while on patrol "saved our neck" on more than one occasion. Cross was recognized for his service and was awarded the Bronze Star, one of just a handful of Black submariners so honored during the war. Another interesting example of a steward's lookout service is that of Robert Goens on *Icefish*. As he recalls:

> I was interested in being out in the air, and while I did some baking initially, I wanted to be a lookout. I practiced down the ladder from the lookout area to the deck and through the hatch and got that down to five seconds. An officer had been observing this and reported to the skipper, who called me to his room. He made me chief of lookouts. This caused some resentment among other crew members who thought a person of mixed race was not appropriate for this type of position. On one occasion the weather was stormy with heavy wind and rain, and I was unable to hear the horn indicating the sub was going to dive. Then I observed the water was coming over the bow, and I did not have time to go down to the deck in the usual manner, so I jumped [Goens].

Many other shipboard duties were performed and watch stations manned by stewards in other than battle station action on submarines. These were not so glamorous, but vital nonetheless. They included raising the jackstaff, handling the mooring lines when leaving or coming into port, and various other mundane maintenance chores. Types of watches might include sonar watch and even manning the helm. Aboard the *Tunny*, one steward even trained another at manning the helm during peaceful conditions. Steward Isaac Collins was instructing Steward 1st Class Harold Hale on how to handle the boat's big four-foot wheel and keep the submarine on her proper course when the two started talking and the submarine strayed off course. An officer noted this, remarking to the men that "Hell, you're taking us back to Frisco," and got them back on course (Hale, Harold H.).

One of the most unusual, and dangerous, of the maintenance jobs performed by a steward was the fuel-ballast tank conversions that were done periodically. This involved "crawling around in the superstructure at night with the knowledge that, if a plane snuck up on the boat, it would dive" (Stempf letter), drowning the man doing the conversion. George Lytle on *Drum* did all of these conversions on his boat, "a stack of repeated acts any one of which, if done in an emergency, would have been worth a medal" (*ibid.*). In fact, Lytle did receive a medal, the Bronze Star, but not for the dangerous maintenance tasks he performed. His citation from Secretary of the Navy James Forrestal reads, in part, as follows;

Officer's Cook 1st Class George Washington Lytle. He made ten war patrols on *Drum* and would earn a Bronze Star for his outstanding service both as a steward and as a member of the deck gun crew. (Photograph courtesy of H. Washington, via the Submarine Force Museum and Library.)

> For heroic service as a Member of the Crew on board the U.S.S. *Drum* during the course of six consecutive War Patrols in enemy waters. By his outstanding performance of duty as petty officer-in-charge of the forward battery compartment and as first loader of the deck gun, *Lytle* rendered material assistance to his commanding officer…. His cool courage and devotion to duty in the face of vigorous and persistent depth-charge attacks enhanced the aggressive fighting spirit of the entire crew and were in keeping with the highest traditions of the United States Naval Service [Lytle, "Citation"].

George Lytle was an outstanding submariner, and it is fortunate that he was so recognized for his devotion to duty. Though their service and deeds may differ in time and place, the words used to describe Lytle's character in the citation can also be attributed to many other submarine stewards during the war who fought at their battle stations with equal performance and courage.

THE MEN OF THE O-, R-, AND S-CLASS BOATS

While the main focus of this book is on those Black stewards that made war patrols in the South Pacific theater of operations, it is appropriate to also take a brief look at those other areas where Black submariners were stationed, the types of boats they served on, and the operations in which they participated. In most cases, these activities were a prelude to the real wartime action they would later experience.

Upon volunteering or being assigned to the Submarine Force, many stewards saw brief service aboard the O-class boats that operated out of New London. These boats, a mere 629 tons in size and manned by about 30 men, were the antiques of the force, having been commissioned in 1918. Their role was to give the new submarine recruits their first taste of undersea life for short periods of time. Most, if not all, new submarine recruits that passed through New London at the beginning of the war rode an O-boat at one time or another. One of these men was Mess Attendant Sam Wallace, who called the *O-6* that he served on nothing more than a "rust bucket" (Wallace). While Wallace would later see action on *Mingo*, the steward he replaced on *O-6*, Dave Ball, was sent to *Rasher* as part of her commissioning crew in Wisconsin. Among the crew of *O-4* in 1943 were Steward's Mates 1st Class Andrew Hines and John Singleton. Hines would later serve on *Lizardfish* in the war zone. Another O-boat veteran was Charles Orr, who would later see action in the Pacific on *Lapon*. While service aboard the O-boats was generally routine, the dangers of utilizing such antiquated craft were sadly demonstrated on June 20, 1941, when the *O-9* sank off the coast of New Hampshire with the loss of her 33-man crew. Among those lost was Mess Attendant 3rd Class John Edwards.

Another type of boat that many submarine stewards served on were the R-class boats. These boats were the successors to the O-class, being slightly larger in size and carrying a crew of about sixty men. Like the O-boats, they were used for training submarine crews in the states. However, early in the war a small number were put to active use, making war patrols in the Atlantic. Their job was to look for German U-boats and surface raiders and to guard the Panama Canal Zone but contacts were scarce, and these patrols, usually of about two weeks duration, produced no confirmed sinkings of enemy vessels. Only one boat of this type, the *R-12*, was lost during the war, and this was due to an accident. Among those lost on the *R-12* when she foundered in deep water off Key West, Florida, on June 12, 1943, was Steward's Mate 2nd Class Willie Young. Serving on the *R-14* was Steward's Mate 2nd Class William Bynum. He would later see action in the Pacific on *Burrfish*.

Other submarines that made Atlantic war patrols include the two experimental coastal defense submarines *Mackerel* and *Marlin*. These small boats of 1,179 tons, both newly commissioned in 1941, were also stationed stateside and made several patrols each in the Atlantic. Among the stewards that served on these boats were Tommy Strong (*Mackerel*), and O'Neal Thaxton (*Marlin*). Thaxton would later serve in the Pacific, making one war patrol on *Cero* in 1945. While these boats achieved no officially credited sinkings, legend has it that *Mackerel* and *Marlin*, operating in tandem, were responsible for sinking the Free French submarine *Surcouf* after catching her on the surface refueling a German U-boat in February 1942 (Winslow, p. 82). No proof, however, exists to support this bit of speculation.

Of greater importance are those stewards that served on the S-class boats. These boats, too, were outdated, compared to the more modern fleet boats, but were more serviceable than the O- and R-boats. Because of a shortage of submarines early in the war, the S-boats were put to use early on before being retired from war service in late

1943. After this time, the S-boats operated in the Atlantic, being primarily utilized as training and coastal defense vessels. The S-boats that operated in the South Pacific with the Asiatic fleet through 1943 had few Black stewards. However, there were two notable exceptions. One was the *S-42*. Aboard for all four of that boat's war patrols from Brisbane, Australia, were Mess Attendants 1st Class Masca Anthony and Archie Freeman. The *S-42* has the distinction of being the first Brisbane-based S-boat to sink an enemy vessel. This occurred on May 11, 1942, when she sank a 4,400-ton minelayer off the coast of New Ireland. While Anthony would leave *S-42* after her Australian patrols, Freeman would stay aboard and serve for another three war patrols in Alaskan waters in 1943. However, the most successful of all the S-boats during the war, in terms of enemy ships sunk, was the *S-44*. She, too, was manned by Black stewards, they being Officer's Cook 2nd Class Curtis Glenn and Mess Attendant 1st Class Stanley Jones. Glenn and Jones made all four of *S-44*'s Brisbane-based war patrols in 1942 under Commander John R. Moore. During this time, the boat sank three Japanese ships, including the heavy cruiser *Kako*.

Those S-boats that operated in the Atlantic, as well as in the North Pacific in the Alaska and Aleutian Islands area, had many Black stewards but also employed some Filipinos. Relations between the Black stewards and the rest of the crew were, as in the fleet boats, generally harmonious. As Torpedoman 3rd Class Richard Harris on the *S-12* recalls, "Steward Dallas Jackson and I served together through most of 1944. Nice guy, and ... I didn't consider him different. We had our bunks in the forward torpedo room and got along famously" (Harris). The patrols from both these locations were of a shorter duration than that of the newer fleet boats in the South Pacific, usually lasting about thirty days, and were accompanied by problems unique to this older type of submarine. Besides the many mechanical difficulties that arose due to their age, the S-boats also had one major disadvantage — they had no air conditioning. For those men on patrol in the Caribbean Sea off Panama or in the warm waters off the coast of Florida, the temperatures inside the boats were often well over 100 degrees for long periods of time.

Even worse, however, were the patrols in Alaskan waters from the submarine base at Dutch Harbor. The patrols from this base worked the frigid waters of the Bering Sea and the Sea of Okhotsk, covering the Aleutian and Kurile Island chains. More inhospitable weather for a submarine on war patrol could scarcely be imagined, yet the men of the Submarine Force did the job. As if the operating conditions weren't bad enough, conditions ashore when an S-boat was between patrols weren't much better. The cold and dreary weather left little for the men to do but stay cooped up in the Quonset huts that served as their quarters and drink and talk. Rest, if it can be called that, was often interrupted by Japanese bombing attacks that forced the men to take cover in foxholes outside or run for their boat (Lewis). The submariners based at Dutch Harbor were, indeed, a long way from the comforts of the Royal Hawaiian Hotel at Pearl Harbor.

All in all, the efforts of the S-boat submariners have largely been forgotten, overshadowed by the exploits of the more modern fleet boats. Even less known is the fact that these boats were manned by Black stewards. Probably the champion in terms of S-boat war patrols among the men of the steward's branch is Officer's Cook 1st Class Lee Montgomery Jackson. He made all eight of *S-30*'s war patrols, five of which were

Part of the crew of *S-28* at Attu, Alaska, in 1943. Officer's Cook Jake Spurlock is in the back row, center, wearing the chief's hat. Mess Attendant Levi Bolton stands in front of him. Spurlock, and maybe Bolton, were later lost when *S-28* sank off Pearl Harbor in 1944. (Photograph courtesy of Jim Lewis.)

conducted in Alaskan waters. Jackson is closely followed by the aforementioned Archie Freeman, who made seven war patrols on *S-42*. Another outstanding S-boat steward was Levi Bolton, who made six Alaskan war patrols, three each on *S-30* and *S-28*. Other notable stewards that made S-boat war patrols include Charles Campbell (five on *S-31*), James Wade (five on *S-35*), Joseph Alexander (five on *S-30*), Curtis Glenn (five on *S-44*), Joe Caesar Evans (four on *S-32*), and Bennie Brown (four on *S-28*).

The contribution of the S-boat fleet and the stewards that manned them, however, came at a price. Of the six S-boats lost during the war, three had no loss of life and three had most of their crew lost with them. *S-26* was lost in a collision with an escort vessel in the Gulf of Panama in January 1942. Among those lost was Mess Attendant 1st Class Nathaniel Johnson. *S-44* was the only S-boat with loss of life as a direct result of enemy action. Commanded by Lieutenant Commander Francis Brown, she was sunk during a surface attack on a Japanese destroyer on October 7, 1943, in the Kurile Islands. Lost with her entire crew, save for two survivors, were Officer's Cook 2nd Class Curtis Glenn, a veteran patroller, and Steward's Mate 2nd Class Herman Mitchell, making his first war patrol.

The last S-boat lost during the war was the *S-28*. After making seven Alaskan war patrols, this boat was transferred to Pearl Harbor. On June 20, 1944, she sank for reasons unknown during routine training exercises. Her entire crew was lost, including Officer's Cook 2nd Class Jake Spurlock, who made two Alaskan war patrols. Another steward who is listed as being lost on *S-28* is Steward's Mate 1st Class Levi Bolton. There is, however, some mystery surrounding the fate of this veteran of the Alaskan campaign. Crew muster rolls for *S-28* show that Bolton was to have been transferred off to Submarine Division 41 for duty on July 4, 1944 (National Archives, reel 6587). Levi Bolton appears in the records a year later, listed as being a crew member on *Rasher* in the final months of the war. Perhaps Bolton did not make the training run because his transfer was imminent, and he missed the fateful, final dive of *S-28*, or maybe this is just a record mix-up by the navy's Bureau of Personnel (BUPERS). Interestingly enough, Bolton's name, unlike that of Spurlock, is not listed on the monument in Honolulu, Hawaii, dedicated to American servicemen killed in action in the Pacific during World War II. Research in Social Security records also shows that there was a man named Levi Bolton, of a similar age, who lived for many years after the war ended. Whether this man and the Levi Bolton who served on the *S-28* are one and the same individual has not yet been established.

OTHER SHIPBOARD ACTIVITIES

Having fully examined the regular and battle-station duties of stewards, it is appropriate to examine their other activities while at sea. A war patrol could often last upwards of two months and sometimes longer. Stewards, as well as their white shipmates, had a fair amount of "free" time during certain times while on patrol. The activities of a submarine sailor during such periods can be loosely categorized into three different types: personal care, entertainment, and assumed duties that were not part of the regular routine.

The personal care habits of a submariner are unique to the type of vessel they served on and were virtually the same for all men aboard. Despite the watery environment in which she operated, water itself was a scarce commodity aboard the boats and was heavily conserved while on patrol. Restrictions were usually only lifted as the boat was heading back to her home port at the end of a patrol. Later boats had distillers aboard to convert salt water to fresh water, allowing for a shower or two on a weekly basis, as with Mess Attendant Anderson Royal on *Silversides*. However, this was not the norm early on. Indeed, there was no such thing as running water for regular bathing and dental hygiene on any boat. Instead, water was sparingly used, doled out in small bowls for personal use. When asked about showering on a submarine, one former steward had this to say

> I think the question should be "What's a shower?" The shower stalls on my subs were packed with food for the trip. When the food was used up, the shower was just another empty space! Showers were a no-no. Even for the food handlers. We took "French baths"—water in a face bowl—and washed everything with that. Maybe just before arrival back at port there would be enough condensation water for a quickie—but that would be a luxury. When everyone smells the same, you get used to it [Kimmons].

Since everyone was in the same boat, so to speak, when it came to hygiene, there does not seem to have been any racial problems in this area among the submariners, both Black and white, interviewed. In fact, in some cases men went out of their way to make living in such close quarters agreeable. In recalling Steward's Mate 2nd Class Earl Singer on *Caiman*, one white shipmate remembers him saying, "he knew Black perspiration was offensive and for that reason, he washed his arm pits and crotch twice a day," and held Singer in "high esteem" for his considerate actions (Thomas).

Another aspect of personal care aboard submarines that was complicated was the task of bodily elimination. The toilets on board submarines were in a compartment known as "the head" and were about the size of a telephone booth.

> Inside the compartment was a commode that was flushed just like a commode in a house. The contents were flushed into a sanitary tank which is like a septic tank for a home. It doesn't take a genius to flush a toilet. However, to empty the sanitary tank required a little knowledge [Kimmons].

It was a complicated mechanism with valves that had to be operated in just the right sequence in order to "blow the head" and empty the tank of its contents. It often took new submariners several tries to learn this procedure. For the man that failed to blow the head properly, his "reward" was the unpleasant result of the contents of the tank being blown back into the head and all over himself.

There were three heads in the boat, two for enlisted crew in the after battery area, and one for officers only, located close to the wardroom and officer's staterooms. This often posed a problem for men of the steward's branch. Because their work placed them in officers' country, the head closest to them was technically off-limits, and they were forced to traverse the longer distance to the enlisted head. Many stewards, however, did not do this and clandestinely used the officers' head, hoping they would not be caught doing so. For those who were caught, it usually meant a dressing down from the captain. Despite this prohibition against using the officers' head, stewards that knew how to properly blow the head were often used by officers to perform this task on their behalf. The task of blowing the officers' head was usually assigned to a torpedoman in the forward torpedo room or a steward and, being a task somewhat akin to scraping or painting the ship, was just not something officers did. More often than not the task fell to someone in the steward's branch.

Finally, two activities that fall into the category of personal care on submarines are eating and sleeping. Stewards always slept in the forward torpedo room, close to the officer's wardroom, in bunks suspended from the ceiling over several torpedoes. These bunks were sometimes known as the "bridal suite" and accommodated two stewards. On a boat that had more than two stewards, the third steward was probably given another bunk located in the same compartment or may have been forced to "hot bunk" with another steward. This meant that two stewards would share one bunk throughout an entire patrol on an alternating basis, with one man on duty while the other was sleeping. Other bunks in the forward torpedo area included those for the torpedomen assigned to that compartment and one for the boat's yeoman, whose duty station, the yeoman's "shack," was located in the forward battery area.

One effect of the location of the steward's quarters was an inability, at times, to get away from his duty station. While an off-duty radioman, as an example, could sleep soundly (as far as was possible in a submarine) in the regular crew's quarters with little prospect of being called to duty, except in an emergency, such was not the case for stewards. With their bunks located adjacent to officers' country, their duty station was always close at hand, and many was the time that an off-duty steward was called upon by his officers to serve up a cup of coffee or perform some other chore.

Mealtimes, too, could pose problems for stewards. In many cases, it seems that stewards dined with their fellow enlisted shipmates in the crew mess without problem. However, in some cases racial difficulties arose. Once again, this is not surprising, as in many locales in the United States, restaurants did not allow Black patrons to eat with those who were white. In the South, Blacks could not eat in the regular dining room of a white restaurant and were instead relegated to take-out service, being forced to go to the back door of a restaurant and request food that had to be eaten elsewhere. Because submarine crews were composed of men from all over the country, including southerners, there can be no doubt that some men resented the presence of a Black steward in the same mess and made their opinions known. Again, while this does not appear to have been the norm, just such an incident did occur on *Scabbardfish* which will be related later in these pages. While the crew mess was sometimes a dining area for stewards, it was not the only one. Because of their service in officers' country, many stewards took their meals either alone or with a fellow steward, sitting on a stool or trashcan in the small pantry area adjacent to the officers' wardroom.

A second area of "free" time activity aboard the boats involved a surprising variety of entertainment options. Some of these were done in solitary, such as reading, just plain relaxing in one's bunk, or perusing letters from home. Others liked to listen to music. Some boats had portable phonograph record players, but just as often off-duty men hung around the "radio shack" where the boat's radioman worked. Here, music broadcast all the way from the United States could sometimes be heard, the sounds of the "big band" era drifting over the airways. Even if music direct from the states could not be received, there was always the music played by Japanese radio authorities. Even though this brand of listening meant the men had to suffer the chatter of propagandist Tokyo Rose and her dire (and usually inaccurate) reports on the condition of American servicemen, she was always good for a laugh and played popular American music. Many stewards liked to hang out in the "radio shack" in their off hours, and the radioman on duty enjoyed their company. With the exception of the torpedomen who bunked in the fore torpedo room with them, stewards probably got to know the radiomen the best of all the white enlisted crewmen on the boat.

Three such stewards were Officer's Cook 3rd Class Arthur Brown on *Narwhal*, Steward 2nd Class Stewart DeHosnery on *Trout*, and Steward's Mate 1st Class Walter Jonkins on *Pompon*. It was on *Narwhal* that young Arthur Brown listened to the big band sounds of Glen Miller and where he got his first taste of classical music. His love of such music, developed aboard ship, would lead him later in life to the capital of classical music a continent away. According to fellow shipmate Dean Brown, Stewart DeHosnery on *Trout* also spent time in the boat's "radio shack." DeHosnery was apparently a licensed radio operator before the war, so it was only natural that he spend his off hours here. On *Pompon*, Radioman 1st Class Nathan Henderson well remembers Jonkins, stating that

> Walter stands out in my mind especially.... He spent many hours in the radio shack with me on patrol — even tried to learn the Morse code. He was naturally curious — and naturally very intelligent. Believe he only had a third grade education — but he compensated with his natural intelligence [Henderson].

In addition to the previously mentioned peaceable activities, some men even made a few dollars by performing services for fellow crewmen. These might include acting as a barber or other like activities. One man, Steward's Mate 2nd Class Arthur Ellis on *Atule*, was a watchmaker by trade and always carried his tool kit with him to fix his shipmates' watches as needed.

However, the most popular activity for submarine sailors in their off hours was that of card playing. Endless hours were spent playing such card games as acey-deucy, whist, and, the most popular of all, poker. When it came to card games, it seems that racial barriers were momentarily forgotten. and Black stewards were always welcome participants. A white crewman on *Sterlet*, Radioman 3rd Class Elmer Olmstead, well remembers the steward on his boat and the card games they played. As he states,

> We played poker in the forward torpedo room. It was a perpetual game that would start as soon as we put to sea and would not end until we returned to port unless we were rudely interrupted by the Japs or some other minor happening. We would have someone from most other departments on the ship. Lots of money was won and lost at this game [Olmstead].

Many stewards were accomplished gamblers and not only gained quite a reputation but lots of winnings as well. Officer's Cook 3rd Class Paul Ragland on *Barb* was referred to by his captain as an "ever gambling steward" (Fluckey, p. 77), while *Tang*'s commander Richard O'Kane recalled that "in any ship's company there is always at least one adept gambler. *Tang*'s was Steward's Mate [Howard] Walker, apparently equally at home with cards or bones" (O'Kane, p. 150).

Card games were not the only type of gambling practiced on board the boats during the war. Many stewards were expert handlers of the dice, the constant rolling of which could be heard during the many games of craps that went on aboard the boats. Steward's Mate Jesse Debro on *Queenfish* was one such man who was known as a "crap shooter par excellence" (Hall, Harry). Some boats even managed, under the influence of their captain, to acquire their own slot machines, the proceeds from which were often used to fund ship's parties for the crew when they made home port. However, the chances of a payout were low. As Mess Attendant Carl Kimmons observed, "When I saw the chief of the boat could fix the payout on the slot machines on our boat, I decided right then never to play against those odds" (Kimmons).

In addition to games of chance, there were other games played aboard the boats. Checkers and cribbage were common, and one boat, *Pollack,* even conducted a chess tournament. *Pollack*'s new executive officer, George Grider, was astounded to learn that the victor in this tournament was Steward's Mate 1st Class Hadwick Thompson.

The youthful-looking Hadwick Thompson was a veteran patroller on *Pollack* during World War II. The intelligent steward's mate surprised his officers by winning an on-board chess tournament on *Pollack*, thereby proving that stewards were limited on their duties not by their intelligence and ability but by racist navy policies. (Photograph courtesy of L. Thompson.)

Sometimes, despite difficult conditions, sports were even practiced on the boats. Steward Dave Ball on *Rasher* was a legend in the navy when it came to boxing. As fellow shipmate Jim Ward recalls

> I remember Dave Ball very much, for he bloodied my nose teaching me how to box. This episode happened in the forward engine room — while we were submerged somewhere north of Lombok Strait in January 44. Dave was an "older" guy and had been an exceptional navy boxer, and I was just a raw "assed" recruit" [Ward, James].

Incredibly, the preceding were not the limit when it came to entertainment aboard the boats while at sea. Movies, too, were a popular form of entertainment when they could be had, and were sometimes shown in the forward torpedo room where the stewards bunked. It was during such times as this that stewards often conversed with their white shipmates about personal matters at home. *Puffer* crewman Frank Golay well recalled the conversation he had with Steward's Mate Carroll Louden Allen on one occasion, during which Allen related how he had been apprenticed to a mason at the age of 13, and would build a fireplace for Golay after the war was over. Allen also talked about his family back home, the good marks his children were making in school, and how they were proud of their father's silver dolphins (McDonald). It was at such times as this that submarine shipmates were indeed equals and racial differences were momentarily forgotten.

Other activities included the various contests often held among both the crew and officers, such as one in which an election was held to determine the most popular pin-up girl among the ship's crew. It is interesting to note that white female movie stars such as Betty Grable were not the only pin-up favorites on the boats. The Black singer Lena Horne was also a favorite, especially among the stewards. Steward's Mate Carroll Louden Allen on *Puffer* had numerous photos of Horne taped to the pantry (McDonald), and his white shipmates certainly had no objections.

One other traditional activity, fun at least for those experienced mariners, was the age-old nautical ceremony that was held when a submarine (or any ship) "crossed the

Steward's Mate Carroll Louden Allen of Brunson, South Carolina. This photograph was likely taken in 1942 after Allen completed boot camp. He later volunteered for submarine duty and made six war patrols on *Puffer*. (Photograph courtesy of the Allen family.)

line" (the equator), usually enroute to the submarine base at Pearl Harbor. When time and circumstances permitted, this ceremony was held as an initiation rite to those new mariners who never before had crossed the equator. Such men, whether he be a steward on his first patrol or an ensign fresh from the States, were made to strip to their skivvies, had their head hair forcibly shaved off, and were often coated from head to toe with lard or grease. These novices were then forced to pay homage to King Neptune and other traditional denizens of the deep, played by those experienced "shellbacks" aboard the boat who dressed up in makeshift costumes. Once the novices paid homage to King Neptune, often by kissing his belly, they were then usually forced to run a gauntlet and were doused with salt water. This procedure could take place on a submarine while submerged or on the surface. If a boat were surfaced, the novices were usually thrown overboard into the sea to complete the bizarre ritual. Once this ceremony was complete, the former novice was now declared a shellback by King Neptune. Both Blacks and white participated in this rite of passage at sea, and all were treated the same, regardless of rate or rank. Many stewards well remember their initiation by King Neptune. Steward's Mate Ingram Gentry, serving on the submarine tender *Howard W. Gilmore*, nearly reenlisted in the navy in 1946 just so he could cross the line again and participate in the ritual as a shellback. Walter Patrick, the young steward's mate on *Bluegill*, remembers his initiation. The captain informed the novices that they would all be thrown overboard while crossing the line at the Galapagos Islands. However, Patrick was "scared speechless" as he had never learned to swim, even though he was reassured that "some of the best swimmers in the navy would be out on the bow planes to save us." Luckily for him, a school of sharks was spotted in the area, "so other ways of initiation were used" (Patrick). Since that time, Patrick has always believed that "God sent that school of sharks as an answer to my prayers" (*ibid.*).

Another type of activity that sometimes kept a steward busy, even when he was off duty, was the task of dealing with nonsubmariners that were taken aboard the boat in various situations. These "passengers" can be divided into three different categories: army personnel being transported on special missions, refugees evacuated from enemy-held islands, and aviators rescued at sea. American submarines accomplished a surprising variety of missions during the war besides attacking enemy shipping, and, despite the fact that they were not designed for such missions, it is a tribute to their captains and crew that these missions were so successful. Those missions that involved carrying "passengers" were often stressful, as it made the cramped quarters found on a submarine even tighter. In regard to carrying army personnel, the big boats *Argonaut*, *Nautilus*, and *Narwhal* were the champions. In August 1942, *Argonaut* carried 121 marines for the Makin Island raid, while *Nautilus* carried 90 such men. In May 1943, *Nautilus* carried 109 army scouts, and *Narwhal* 105, for the raid on Attu in the Aleutian Islands. In the case of all three submarines, stewards would have been taxed to the limit in helping to care for and feed these extra men.

Another taxing situation for stewards was the transportation of refugees evacuated from enemy-held islands. This work may have been more difficult, as oftentimes women, children, and infants were among the number of those evacuated. The care and feeding of these individuals often posed additional problems that were not normally found on submarines. After *Crevalle* took 48 people, including 28 women and children, off the island of Negros in the Phillipines in May 1944, Steward Willie Gregory was taxed to the limit, being forced to deal with sand crabs in the wardroom and clogged heads resulting from female refugees flushing their feminine hygiene pads. The clogged head he refused to clear, stating that "he didn't understand things like this" (Ruhe, p. 220). Once again, it was one of the big boats, *Narwhal*, that was tops in the Submarine Force when it came to evacuating personnel. On eight different missions from late 1943 to the end of the war, she rescued over 193 men, women, and children from enemy-held territory, mainly the Phillipine Islands. The largest number evacuated at one time was 81 POW survivors and one doctor from Mindanao in late September 1944. On three different occasions in 1944 *Narwhal* evacuated 27 or more men, women, and children, all from the island of Negros in the Phillipines. In one instance, six of those rescued were prospective mess boys, while one was a steward's mate (all presumably Filipino). Indeed, it might be said that no submarine steward in World War II aided more refugees than Arthur Brown. He made twelve war patrols on *Narwhal*, participating in all eight of her missions to evacuate refugees from enemy-held islands, and well remembers the extra passengers his boat carried. Evidently they remembered Brown, too, for in 2002 he received a phone call of thanks from a man who was a young child when he and his family were rescued by *Narwhal* nearly sixty years before.

No more graphic description of life aboard a submarine packed with a large number of refugees can probably be found than that of the situation on *Angler* in March 1944, skippered by Commander Robert Olsen. There can be no doubt that Officer's Cook 2nd Class Marvin Hearn and Steward's Mate 2nd Class Elijah Strother had their hands full on their boat's second war patrol when she picked up 58 American refugees off the island of Panay in the Phillipines. As Commander Olsen later reported,

> The entire ship's company was berthed in the after battery compartment, except for torpedo watch standers ... men and boys lived in [the] after torpedo room, women and children in [the] forward torpedo room, C.P.O. quarters were inhabited by one woman with a two-month-old baby, one pregnant women, one seriously ill girl, and two elderly women. Ship was immediately infected with cockroaches, body lice, and hair lice. A large percentage of the passengers had tropical ulcers plus an odor that was unique in its intensity. All passengers showed signs of prolonged undernourishment. All passengers were suffering from lacerated feet due to the long march to the embarkation point without footgear. One male passenger was temporarily insane, requiring a twenty-four-hour watch. Two meals a day with soup ... was put into effect at once since it was apparent the ship did not have enough food aboard for a full three meals a day.... Habitability forward of the control room resembled the "Black Hole" of Calcutta, a condition which resulted from children urinating and spitting on the decks, body odors and forty-seven persons sleeping forward of the control room. In spite of a constant watch at the head, it proved impossible to teach our passengers the proper use of this article after two years in the hills [Cope and Karig, pp.35–36].

A final group of passengers that stewards had to care for were those aviators who had been shot down or had crash landed in the ocean and were rescued by submarines. This type of duty, called "lifeguarding," was a valuable service provided by the Submarine Force. During the course of the war in the Pacific, 504 aviators were rescued by 86 different submarines (Roscoe, p. 474, 1954). Not only was this a truly lifesaving service, preserving lives in very dangerous situations, but it also saved the army and navy the expense of training new aviators to replace those who might otherwise have been lost at sea. In fact, one of those men saved by submarines during the war was navy aviator George H. Bush, our nation's future president. Bush was shot down off the Bonin Islands on September 2, 1944, and rescued by *Finback* while making her tenth war patrol. Among the stewards that attended to him were Officer's Cook 3rd Class Elijah Dawson, Jr., and Steward's Mate 2nd Class John Robinson, Jr.

Among the outstanding rescues of the war in this situation were those by *Tang*, to the number of 22, off Truk Atoll in April 1944. There can be no doubt that Steward's Mate 1st Class Howard Walker and Steward 3rd Class Lester Madison had a full workload on this run. While *Tigrone* was tops in this category during the war, rescuing 31 aviators in all, other boats also did their share when called upon. Among those was *Mingo*, which rescued 16 aviators in a daring operation off Balikpapan in October 1944. The harrowing experience under which the rescue was conducted, and the hectic conditions aboard the boat afterward, are well remembered by Officer's Cook Sam Wallace, but these difficulties were mitigated by the satisfaction in knowing that American lives were saved. Another submarine that rescued a large number of aviators late in the war was *Whale*. She picked up 15 aviators during her last patrol and it is well remembered by one of her men that Officer's Cook Willie James "had a good and unobtrusive way of herding the junior officers and all the aviators we picked up" (Nalle). Indeed, handling such aviators required a great deal of both skill and patience. Most of those men rescued were officers, so they shared the captain's mess. However, they were not submariners by any means, and it took many "fly boys" some time getting used to life, if only for a brief time, on the boats. Those aviators who experienced a submarine attack and a depth-charge counterattack were usually only too happy to make it back to land and had a new-found appreciation and camaraderie with their undersea compatriots. In many cases, fast friendships developed between submariners and the grateful aviators they rescued. One example of this is the bond between former steward Arthur Haynes and Morris Perkins. As a steward on *Chub*, Haynes helped to aid several aviators his boat had picked up while on patrol in 1944, including Perkins. Haynes subsequently helped to care for Perkins and his fellow aviators by talking with them, providing them with hot coffee and food, and getting them settled aboard the boat. It was a kindness that Morris Perkins has not forgotten to this day.

Not only American aviators, but also downed Japanese flyers, were rescued from enemy waters by American submarines. This was a rarer occasion, as many Japanese pilots who could have been rescued usually resisted such attempts, believing that they might be tortured by their captors or that it was considered dishonorable to surrender. Among the boats that rescued Japanese aviators was *Tunny*. Helping to perform one of these dangerous operations was Steward's Mate William Rapier who, by his sheer strength, pulled aboard a Japanese aviator who was sunburned and had suffered from exposure. The prisoner of war, who stayed aboard *Tunny* during the rest of her patrol, soon found out how POWs were treated by Americans, probably in contrast to the propaganda he had received, and by the end of the patrol was saddened at having to leave the boat for a prison camp (Latham).

Finally, while service on a submarine might sound from some of the above like fun and games, moments of relaxation and entertainment were usually fleeting at best.

Steward Arthur Haynes, right, of *Chub*, and Morris Perkins, left, a downed aviator picked up by *Chub* during the war. The two men have been friends ever since the war brought them face to face. (Photograph courtesy of Arthur Haynes.)

Once a submarine was operating in the war zone, there were many more times where the atmosphere was one of tense action and danger, resulting in a high level of stress. Add to this the fact that the crew of a submarine operated in a "sardine can" environment and suffered the effects of a lack of natural sunlight for upwards of sixty days, and it is no wonder that submariners found imaginative ways to spend their off-time. However, solace was not always sought in entertainment. Religion, too, played its part on the boats to help men deal with their stressful service. Unlike larger ships of war, submarines did not carry a navy chaplain aboard as part of their complement. As one captain recalled, "On some of the subs, the captains conducted regular religious services, but most skippers felt unqualified" (Grider, p. 215). In cases such as this, it sometimes fell to a member of the crew to conduct services, if regular worship services were desired. In many cases, this task was attended to by the men of the steward's branch, and their services in this area are not only well remembered by their white shipmates but also were highly appreciated.

One of the best known of such stewards who conducted religious services was Steward's Mate Napoleon Finley on *Sterlet*. Finley was an ordained minister residing in Florida when the war began. Upon looking through Finley's file, the captain of *Sterlet* discovered his peacetime occupation and told Finley he wanted him to perform Sunday services. Finley was at odds with himself— despite his ministering abilities, he really just "wanted to be one of the guys" (Lester). A white shipmate and friend, Machinist Mate 1st Class Doyle Lester, advised Finley to go ahead and perform the services, and Finley agreed. These services were held in the forward torpedo room and soon grew in popularity. As Lester recalls,

> The first Sunday, a few guys attended. The second Sunday, everyone not on watch attended. By the third Sunday, everyone wanted to go and many guys tried swapping watches so they could go. You couldn't have asked for a better person, and Finley even tried to get a portable organ [*ibid.*].

"Chaplain" Napoleon Finley is remembered fondly by his shipmates nearly sixty years later for the inspiration he provided. *Sterlet*'s executive officer and later author, the late Paul Schratz, recalled him thusly:

> Frequently I think of Finley holding church services in the forward torpedo room. The picture is always the same. The brightly polished torpedo tubes are behind him. A goodly portion of shipmates are seated on anything they can find as they listed to the morning sermon. Finley stands with his feet slightly apart, his open Bible in his left hand as he steadies himself against the roll and pitch of the boat with his right hand resting lightly on a torpedo war-head.... His homilies displayed wisdom, warmth, and wondrous understanding of the human condition.... Truly an inspiring picture [Schratz, pp. 102, 115].

Napoleon Finley was not the only steward to either conduct religious services or at least provide for their introduction on board their boat. Steward's Mate Clarence Page was responsible, albeit unknowingly, for the introduction of religious services aboard *Flasher*, commanded by George Grider. As Grider remembers, he was commenting on the boat's "dull" meals to his commissary officer, and joked that they reminded him of the Bible verse Hebrews 13:8. When his commissary officer asked what it was, Grider told him to look it up himself, whereupon the commissary officer asked Page for a Bible. The young steward's mate responded eagerly. As Grider further recalls:

> He was back with it in a minute, and one glance at him made me feel thoroughly ashamed. Page was a devout man, and as he smiled at me it was clear what he was thinking: this was Sunday night, and the new captain of the *Flasher* had directed that the Bible be brought in for devotions.... The next Sunday evening, after we had gathered in the wardroom for the evening meal, Page appeared. He had the Bible in his hands.... "I knew you'd want it, sir," he said.... I forgot about it during the week that followed, but on the next Sunday, Page was back again. "A lot to praise the Lord for this week, Captain," he said. After he was gone, we talked it over and decided Page was right. We *did* have a lot to praise the Lord for. From then on, we never let a Sunday go by without reading the Scriptures, with all the reverant attention Page could wish [Grider, pp. 216–17].

For many stewards, even if they did not lead established religious services aboard their boat, they were still a source of inspiration, hope, and comfort to their fellow

Steward's Mate Henry Smith, known as "Smitty" to the crew of *Gurnard*, at a cookout for the crew in 1943. (Photograph courtesy of Glen Milhorn.)

shipmates. Steward's Mate Jesse Debro on *Queenfish* was a devout Christian and was a deacon at his church in Tennessee. He prayed frequently and is remembered fondly by his shipmates today. Even in the most difficult of circumstances, such as a severe depth-charging, many was the time that white shipmates found in their Black stewards a cool sense of comfort and hope, even when all seemed lost. The most extreme of these examples, so far as is known, has already been told, that of James Alden Pruitt on *Puffer*, but there are many more such stories, ranging from the humorous to the inspirational. Charles Rush was awarded the Navy Cross for his actions as chief engineer and diving officer on *Billfish* in November 1943. During this, her second war patrol, the boat was severely depth-charged in the Makassar Strait by three enemy destroyers. The captain was incapacitated, and most men thought they were going to die. While Rush was fighting to save the boat, it was noticed that one of her stewards, probably Officer's Cook 1st Class Leslie Hamilton, was calmly reading the Bible upside down. When asked why, he replied "The Lord knows I believe" (Rush). Likewise, when *Bluegill* was receiving a working over from a Japanese destroyer after sinking the light cruiser *Yubari* on April 27, 1944, one of Steward's Mate Walter Patrick's white shipmates sought him out, declaring "I want to be near you if we're hit or killed" (Patrick). The young steward, nicknamed "Pat," was a daily reader of the New Testament on this, his first war patrol, and after the war became a Baptist minister. It would seem his ministering career and gift of giving comfort through God's word had already begun, even if unintentionally, aboard *Bluegill*.

Humor, too, played a big part in reducing the tension that could build up on a boat out on patrol in enemy waters. You had to have a sense of humor most times just to serve in submarines, otherwise you might be driven crazy. It would seem that many stewards were blessed with the gift of wit and sarcasm and could come up just the right comment or action that fit the dire situation at hand. Indeed, humor had its place on the boats right from the start. When *Plunger* was on her first war patrol in January 1942, in Kii Suido, the northern entrance to the Sea of Japan, she was attacked by a Japanese destroyer with amazing ferocity. During the time that *Plunger* was being jolted by 24 depth charges close on, Mess Attendant 3rd Class John Allen was delivering coffee to the captain. As another depth charge exploded, Allen turned to the captain and said, "We sure are giving them hell, aren't we. How many more of those things have we got?" (Andrews). Despite the gravity of the situation, the captain and crew could not help but be amused. The story, by one account, was later sent stateside for publication in a national magazine.

Another humorous take on a serious incident occurred on *Gurnard* in June 1943, when she was off the Palau Islands on her second war patrol. While submerged and playing "cat and mouse" (Blair, p. 440) with enemy destroyers protecting a convoy, *Gurnard* took two bomb hits which exploded under her and blew the boat upward through the water. With her electricity out and her stern planes jammed in the hard-dive position, the submarine was out of control and in serious trouble. Her skipper, Herb Andrews, ordered all available men to run to the forward torpedo room to keep the boat from continuing its upward momentum from the blast. Had she broached the surface, the Japanese destroyers waiting there would have easily finished her off. The maneuver, however, worked, but now *Gurnard* was heading downward at a swift rate, approaching 500 feet or more. In order to correct the boat's dive angle, Andrews ordered the men in the forward torpedo room to run aft to the torpedo room there as fast as they could. This maneuver worked and, along with some smart work by the boat's chief electrician, *Gurnard* was stabilized and survived the ordeal. One of the men that was sprinting fore and aft to save *Gurnard* was Mess Attendant 1st Class Henry Smith. As one man recalls, afterward "Smitty, as we called him, sat down on a bunk and said a prayer: 'Oh Lord, let's knock off dis ole shit.' It must have gotten to the Man, as we got control and limped back to Pearl" (Milhorn). Bob Ward, *Gurnard*'s executive officer, would later say of his men, stewards included, that "Everybody did the right thing" (Blair, p. 442).

A final example of the men of the steward's branch and their coolness and humor under pressure is that of Officer's Cook 3rd Class Steve Mosley and Steward's Mate 1st Class Joseph Anderson on *Bowfin*. The two stewards made quite a pair and helped keep morale high on the boat as she headed out on her first war patrol in August 1943. They carried on a week-long joke, starting when Mosley proclaimed that he would be the king of Mindanao, the island off which they would be patrolling, while Anderson would be his aide. As one historian records, "Mosley would dress up in shorts, spats, and a stovepipe hat, Anderson would carry an umbrella over his head and shout "Here come de king, here come de King" (Hoyt, p. 27). When the boat's captain observed that the pair might get their throat cut, Anderson replied "Not me, Cap'n ... I got my razor and I'll take care of them" (*ibid.*). Joseph Anderson, now an officer's cook 3rd class, would continue on *Bowfin* through the end of 1943 and into 1944. On her third patrol, Anderson had been told by Commander Walter Griffith to defrost the small refrigerator in the officer's pantry. Twice Anderson was told to get the job done but failed to do so. The third time that Griffith told Anderson to do the job "he grew a little testy" (Hoyt, p. 93). Soon after, *Bowfin* attacked an enemy convoy and, in return, received a depth-charging from the Japanese escorts. As the story goes,

> As the bombardment of depth charges slowed for a bit, Griffith went into the wardroom for a snack and there on the floor with the refrigerator door wide open lay Steward Anderson.
> "What in the hell are you doing, Anderson?" the captain demanded in a voice that his junior officers noted was very testy indeed.
> "Defrostin' the ice box, Cap'n. Defrosting the ice box."
> Even the captain had to laugh. The tension building in the boat decreased a little [*ibid.*].

These are just a few examples of probably many more events involving stewards and their use of religion and humor that have gone unrecorded. They serve to underscore one small, yet important, fact. Black stewards may have occupied the bottom rung in the official navy hierarchy of ratings, but on many boats they were often a leader when it came to the crew's spiritual well-being and high state of morale. This unique type of leadership, seemingly small in nature, was yet another factor that contributed to the high performance turned in by the men of the Submarine Force during World War II.

CREW RELATIONS ABOARD THE BOAT

Now that we have examined the many duties of a submarine steward, it is time to look at how they got along socially with their fellow crewmembers. That they performed the duty of steward admirably has been proven, as has been their battle-station service. What about their social interaction with the crew? How did the men of the steward's branch perceive social and racial conditions aboard the boats of the Submarine Force, and how did their white shipmates view them?

First and foremost to be remembered is that service in the Submarine Force was voluntary. No man was forced to join, for the most part, nor was any man forced to

The commissioning crew of *Bowfin* lined up for inspection at Portsmouth, New Hampshire, on May 1, 1943. Officer's Cook 2nd Class Steve Mosley is in the center, fourth from the right. (Official U.S. Navy photograph.)

stay. All one had to do, in most cases, was to ask off the boat, and his transfer was usually arranged as expediently as possible. This action, of course, had to be taken while in port, as, once at sea on war patrol, he had to finish the cruise. It was only in dire circumstances, usually severe mechanical failure, that a submarine aborted a wartime cruise. Given these facts, can it be said that those wartime stewards who stayed in the Submarine Force for any length of time found their experiences aboard the boats positive and free from serious racial incidents? For the most part, the answer to this question is two-fold. All but two of the 34 stewards or officer's cooks that made war patrols interviewed for this book, admittedly a small number, described their submarine experience as positive overall and, in many cases, even enjoyable. Almost to a man, these veteran Black submariners talked about how their fellow shipmates treated them as submarine sailors first, with no regard for their color. However, many of these same men had a slightly different view when racial conditions in the navy overall were discussed and, important for this study, how they interacted with fellow submariners while on liberty or shore leave. For this reason, we will examine in separate chapters the social conditions of wartime stewards both on and off their boats.

As has been stated at various times in this work, teamwork and a close-knit crew was vital to the successful operation of a submarine. If a crew could not live and work

Crewmembers of *Thresher* displaying the boat's battle-flag in 1945. At far right is Steward's Mate Eddie Robinson. The other crewmembers, from left, are B.F. Lemon, R. Ayres, and John Barnes. (Photograph courtesy of J. Barnes.)

together under such cramped and confined conditions while at sea for sixty days or longer as those found on submarines, the chances were much less that they could successfully meet the enemy. True submariners held true to this ideal and practiced what was preached for the most part, according to most stewards. Perhaps more than any other member of the crew, a steward had to walk a fine line and get along with both enlisted men and officer personnel. Yet he was equal to neither group. Though men of the steward's branch were enlisted men, their position in the navy rating hierarchy was distinctly separate and considered inferior in all regards. No matter what his rate, no steward, even a chief steward, had any formal authority over even the lowest rated white sailor. On the other hand, though the stewards were on board to serve the officer cadre, they were by no means their equals. And, yet, because of their close, everyday relationship with these officers, a steward often developed a close bond with his captain and other officers and got to know them, in many cases, more than any enlisted man ever could.

Steward Relations with Enlisted Personnel

In regards to relations with their fellow enlisted crew members, the stewards were usually treated in a very respectable fashion. Leonard Rozar called the men on *Tuna* "a heck of a crew" (Rozar, Leonard), while Richard Lucas on *Raton* "found submariners to be liberal minded" (Lucas). Some men went even further in describing the attributes of their fellow shipmates. Alfred Hall on *Pomfret* stated that his crew was "like a family" (Hall, Alfred), while Jesse Allen called the men on *Devilfish* "an outstanding crew" (Allen, Jesse). Why were submarine crews so good to serve with? There are several possible explanations for this. First is the fact that many submariners, and certainly more white than Black candidates, were psychologically screened before being accepted for submarine duty. Thus, those men that had characteristics demonstrating a lack of tolerance, disruptive behavior, or an inability to get along well with others were often rejected and subsequently served on surface ships. While such screening did not involve an individual's view on race relations specifically, it may have tended to weed out those with more overt racist tendencies.

Another reason that stewards were usually treated well in the Submarine Force was simply by virtue of their proven service. Submariners were a highly dedicated and professional group that had a unique camaraderie. Though a steward may not have been initially accepted by submariners, once he demonstrated that he, too, had the attributes of a real submariner, then the race issue often faded into the background (it never went away), and he then became "one of their own." This was especially true of those stewards that served aboard their boat for extended periods of time and made multiple war patrols. Men like Jim Stallings (12 patrols on *Haddock*), Walter Wilson (13 patrols on *Trigger*), George Lytle (10 patrols on *Drum*), James Patton, Jr. (9 patrols on *Puffer*), Stewart DeHosnery (9 patrols on *Trout*), John Prophet (8 war patrols on *Growler*), Luther Bryant (7 patrols on *Haddo*), Lonnie Jackson (7 patrols on *Trout*), Mack Butler (7 patrols on *Dace*), and many others like them earned the respect and admiration of the entire crew and were looked upon with some degree of awe by "greenhorns" making their first war patrol. Not only did such men earn the respect they so richly deserved, they also became trusted leaders among many of the enlisted men who still remember them to this day.

Finally, for those stewards that had served on surface craft, the contrast between such service and that aboard submarines was a marked and welcome change. Donald Fenner, having served on the battleship *Tennessee*, was ready to quit the navy before going into submarines. In contrast, after a long career in submarines, Leonard Rozar did postwar duty on the cruiser *Little Rock* and was quite unhappy. As previously alluded to, stewards were more segregated in the larger ships of the surface navy. Though the number of stewards on each ship was greater than that on board submarines, the treatment they received was usually more degrading. In contrast, then, though there were usually no more than two Black stewards (and sometimes only one, the others being Guamanian or Filipino) on submarines, the treatment they received was usually more professional and courteous.

In many cases, the men of the steward's branch did a job they didn't like and didn't ask for, but they performed well nonetheless. Albert Rozar was not happy about being a steward but "did it without fuss" (Rozar, Albert). Mason B. Smith just "went along with the flow ... you just did it. Sometimes I was churning inside, but was calm on the outside" (Smith, Mason B.). While there were many small instances of discrimination aboard the boats, these were often ignored by the men of the steward's branch, and they went on with their work. Jack Higgins, a white crewman on *Dentuda*, did not remember any such discrimination but states that other crew "indicated there might have been a bit but not heavy" (Higgins).

The crew of *Puffer* in 1944. The man in the chief's hat at far left (fourth row) is Officer's Cook James Woodley Patton. He was part of the commissioning crew of *Puffer* at Wisconsin in 1943 and made all nine of her war patrols. Crew remembrances leave little doubt that Patton was a valued crewmember and well-respected submariner. (Photograph courtesy of C. McDonald.)

Ironically, some instances of prejudice rearing its ugly head are better remembered by white crewmembers than the stewards themselves. One example of this occurred on *Scabbardfish*. Steward's Mate James Sims was a well-liked individual who sometimes ate with the enlisted crew in the mess room aft. On one such occasion, an enlisted man from the south objected to Sims' presence, calling him a "nigger." Without comment, Sims left and ate his dinner alone in the officers' galley. However, his fellow shipmates and friends were upset at how Sims was treated and, when the same man that insulted Sims showed up for breakfast the next day, all of the men in the mess got up and left, leaving him to eat alone. Captain Gunn soon got wind of the incident and had the southerner transferred off the boat before the next run (Jackson).

Another example of racism aboard the boats is recalled by Russell Tidd on *Puffer*. He remembers one man in the crew who had been a part-time police officer in Florida before the war and was a "horse's ass, pure and simple a bully; a vicious guy" who thought nothing of shoving the Black men (and others as well) for no reason, and was always willing to "shoot niggers," as he called them (McDonald, Craig).

Yet another example of how racism was dealt with by a commanding officer also occurred on *Puffer*. Steward's Mate Carroll Louden Allen, like most submarine veterans, was usually rather quiet about his experiences during the war. However, he did relate to his son on several occasions the time, probably on *Puffer*'s sixth war patrol in December 1944, when he was the subject of some racist remarks by a fellow enlisted man who was white. The captain, Commander Carl Dwyer, dealt with the offender by sending him topside to toss the boat's garbage overboard, a job normally performed by stewards. While the man was topside, the hatch behind him was shut, and *Puffer* started to submerge, giving the man a scare (HLM). Whether or not this cured the man of his racist tendencies is unknown, but at least it probably taught him to keep his comments to himself.

Given the nature of race relations in America at the time, it is likely that every submarine had at least one man aboard who may have harbored racist feelings toward the men of the steward's branch. Luckily, incidents like those described seem to have been the exception rather than the norm when it came to the outward display of racist attitudes. What is most interesting is the fact that many white crewmembers got to know the stewards they served with, not just as Black men, but as people, and came to the full realization of how society in general, and the navy in particular, put heavy restrictions on their dreams and aspirations at nearly every level. In thinking about the steward he served with on *Peto* during the war, Mike Walsh saw a "very bright young man" in Officer's Cook 3rd Class Carlos Tuttle but wondered "Is this the best the navy can do for this young man" (Walsh). Many stewards themselves probably thought the very same thing. All in all, many stewards were well appreciated by their white shipmates, both for the kind of individuals they were on a personal level and for doing the naval duty that was expected of them. Quartermaster Gerald Pilger on *Jallao* remembers that both of that boat's stewards were "terrific guys," and is quick to point out that "they qualified just like we did" (Pilger). Chief Steward Charles Bivens is recalled as "articulate" and "very professional," while Steward's Mate 1st Class Willie Adams, "funny as hell," spent his off time in the after-battery socializing with the rest of the crew (*ibid.*). Motor Machinist Steve Mocio on *Lionfish* may have said it best, referring to stewards Sammy Colston and Louis Jones, when he called them "good shipmates and good people" (Mochio).

While some white crewmembers recall incidents of prejudice and poor treatment of stewards aboard their boats, many stewards, too, can recall such incidents. Many were able to take these things in stride, but not all. John Wesley Whitehead served admirably aboard *Flying Fish* for three war patrols but was very unhappy. While he liked the officers he served under, the way he felt he was treated by the enlisted crew has left him bitter to this day. In his words, his white shipmates "didn't want any kind of friendship at all" and, when passing by shipmates within the narrow confines of the submarine, white crewmen acted like they were "meeting a dog" and acted as though they were afraid to even come in contact with him. As a result of these problems, Whitehead left *Flying Fish* with the mutual consent of his officers. While such problems as those encountered by John Whitehead were probably atypical in the Submarine Force, they do point to the fact that some boats had happier and more tightly knit crews than others during the war. While it is impossible as this late date to determine with any degree of accuracy whether *Flying Fish* was an unhappy boat, research presented later

Steward's Mate John Wesley Whitehead of *Flying Fish* being honored dockside at Mare Island for his three war patrols. A shipyard worker at Mare Island before the war, Whitehead found duty as a steward distasteful and later transferred to shore duty. He would subsequently return to the shipyard, changing his rate to that of a metalsmith. (Photograph courtesy of R. Whitehead.)

in these pages gives some indication that stewards serving on board her, at least in the early part of the war, were an unhappy lot. In concluding this section on relations with enlisted crew, Robert Coley, who made war patrols on *Tambor* and *Bugara*, probably said it best when he stated that "99 percent of the crew was good" (Coley).

Finally, while we have discussed the relationships between Black stewards and white enlisted men, there is also the matter of how Black stewards got along with each other. In many cases, perhaps most cases, two Black stewards on any given boat usually got along together without serious trouble. As with white crewmen, stewards had their share of personality differences which sometimes resulted in temporary conflict but was usually quickly resolved. Sometimes conflicts were the result of an age difference between two stewards, with the younger of the two displaying a less than mature attitude or disposition. Again, nothing unusual here.

Perhaps one of the biggest sources of conflicts between stewards was the difference in the regions of the United States from which they came. There is some evidence that suggests that some Blacks from the north considered themselves superior to those Blacks who lived in the south, and from this attitude conflicts sometimes arose. While several instances of this type of conflict between northern and southern stewards have been hinted at, one of the most unusual of these conflicts to have been documented occurred aboard *Plunger* in October 1943. Coming aboard that boat in September 1943 were Steward's Mates 2nd Class Albert Lewis and William Murray. Both had joined the navy within three days of each other in May 1943, with Murray coming from South Carolina while Lewis came from Virginia. Although Murray and Lewis were both Black,

Lewis's "features were more Puerto-Rican than Afro-American, or a mixture of Asian Afro-American" (Murray). As Murray later recalls,

> Within the first two to three weeks of our becoming shipmates, an incident occurred which made me positively certain that this was one person whom I had absolutely no desire to go on a War patrol with.... My being a native South Carolinian, and I supposed because of my accent, I was sometimes referred to in a denigrating manner ... as that "Geechee." It appeared that the "Geechee" expressions were used mostly by Blacks, who were not from the south, in a cruel attempt to distinguish them as being superior to Blacks who acknowledged being a southerner.... I didn't even know what the word "Geechee" represented, I often pretended to laugh ... or just remained silent when addressed in that manner, even though I sometimes found the characterization to be offensive. However, on the last occasion of Lewis calling me a so-and-so "damn Geechee," I chose not to remain silent. In fact, I responded by calling him "a Japanese-looking S.O.B." [*ibid.*].

With this comment, Albert Lewis flew into a rage and attacked Murray with a butcher knife. Had it not been for the officers that restrained Lewis, Murray's "naval career would have been a chopped-up, short one" (*ibid.*). The two men were separated, and Murray was sent off *Plunger* and went to the base until things calmed down. While Murray was off his own submarine, Albert Clark, the captain of *Trout*, tied up at a nearby pier, asked Murray to come aboard for lunch and asked if he might transfer to his boat, as there was some doubt if his second steward would be available for their next sailing. As Murray states,

> That suited me fine.... So, when I returned to my sub later that day, I went to my commanding officer and asked him to transfer me.... The Captain took me into his stateroom and sat me down and told me that he wasn't going to grant me a transfer. He wanted me to go to sea with him. He said that he was going to transfer Lewis and would do it that day [*ibid.*].

Despite pleading for a transfer from *Plunger*, Commander Raymond Bass refused, and William Murray stayed on the boat through the war's end. It was a decision that would save Murray's life. Steward's Mate 2nd Class Albert Lewis was indeed transferred off *Plunger* on October 27, 1943, and subsequently served in Submarine Division 43 for two months before joining *Trout* in January 1944 for her eleventh war patrol — the patrol that Murray hoped he would be on. *Trout*, with Lewis and her entire crew, was lost one month later. When she failed to return and the fate of Lewis was realized, William Murray "experienced severe ... sadness" over the event, but was also "provided convincing evidence ... that my destiny was under complete control of some one upstairs" (*ibid.*).

Steward Relations with Officer Personnel

The other group of men that submarine stewards had to interact with and, indeed, the very reason for their presence on board the boat to begin with, was the officer cadre. There were usually about five officers aboard a submarine, consisting of the boat's commander (always called "captain" by navy tradition, no matter what his actual rank), an executive officer who was the second in command, and three other junior men that might serve as gunnery or fire control officer, an engineer and diving officer, and a commissary officer. From time to time, other officers rode the boats, including prospective commanding officers (P.C.O.), wolf-pack commanders, and, on rare occasions, even an admiral or someone of flag rank. No matter what their rank, it was the job of the men of the steward's branch to serve them as needed.

Of course, the most important of these men was the boat's captain, and it is no surprise that many of them are remembered by veteran stewards to this day. Most of them, though not all, are remembered quite fondly. R.D. Mosely on *Pargo* recalls Captain David Bell as "a lifesaver"(Mosely, R.D.), while Alfred Hall on *Pomfret* called Captain John Hess "a great skipper" (Hall, Alfred L.). Likewise Jesse Debro on *Queenfish,* who called Captain Charles Loughlin "a swell guy" (Debro), and Harold Hale on *Tunny,* who said that Captain John Scott and junior officers Gordon Underwood (later commander of *Spadefish*) and Jack Titus (later commander of *Narwhal*) were men that "made you feel good" (Hale, Harold H.). Isaac Johnson on *Sennet* called Captain George Porter "a beautiful skipper, a warrior who prepared us for a time of war" (Johnson). Johnson goes even further, stating that "Porter told me he wanted to involve Blacks in the war" (*ibid.*) and wanted the stewards to be fighting men first. Other captains, too, made a good impression on their stewards. Captain Frank Latta of *Narwhal* is remembered emphatically to this day by Steward 3rd Class Arthur Brown as "a good man" (Brown, Arthur), while C.V. Cooper on *Tuna* calls captains James Hardin and Edward Steffanides "my kind of people ... both were religious and both wanted to come home" (Cooper). On *Plunger*, Steward William Murray had this to say about his captain, Commander Raymond "Benny" Bass:

> The mind set in those days was that a Black would not be treated as well by officers of southern heritage — my experiences tend to completely shatter such myth. Yes, Commander Bass was from Arkansas. But, for three war patrols, he did all he promised me he would. He protected me, and treated me as well as he treated any other person aboard that sub. I shall always remember him as a man of high ideals and fair minded [Murray].

Walter Patrick on *Bluegill* is equally respectful of Captain Eric Barr, Jr., stating that "while under his command I considered him to be a courageous captain with a dare-devil spirit. I've never felt that he had an indifference toward the Blacks in his command" (Patrick). Perhaps the greatest compliment paid to a captain by his steward comes from Robert Goens on *Icefish*. Despite the fact that Captain Richard Peterson had a reputation as being somewhat of a disciplinarian and strictly adhered to navy regulations, Goens fondly remembers Peterson as "a beautiful skipper," and states that "I'd died for that bastard" (Goens). Just a few of the other captains that were rated well by their stewards include Robert Ward on *Sailfish*, Ian Eddy on *Pargo*, John Madison and J.J. Staley on *Mingo*, Hank Munson on *Crevalle*, Lawson Ramage on *Parche,* George Street on *Tirante*, Gus Gugliotta on *Raton*, Thomas Dykers on *Jack*, Eric Barr, Jr., on *Bluegill*, Jim Dempsey on *Cod*, E.C. Hawk and Stephen Gimber on *Pompon*, and Creed Burlingame on *Silversides*.

However, not all submarine captains were as highly regarded. While Steward James

Washington liked his first captain on *Cuttlefish*, Martin "Spike" Hottel, when questioned about his second captain, Elliot Marshal, no reply other than a terse "no comment" was given. Other stewards were more outspoken about their former captains. In speaking of the first captain on *Tuna*, John De Tar, Leonard Rozar referred to him as "a badass with no submarine talent" (Rozar, Leonard). While this assessment by Rozar may seem harsh, it seems to be right on the mark. One historian refers to De Tar as "an odd and controversial character" and one who "believed some crewmen were carrying out acts of sabotage" on *Tuna* (Blair, p. 208). After two war patrols, De Tar was relieved of command and, later in the war, commanded a submarine tender. Ironically, one steward who later served with De Tar out of submarines remembered him as a good skipper.

Another submarine captain disliked by the steward that served him was Edward Hutchinson on *Grampus*. While Hutchinson is well remembered for the outstanding first war patrol of *Rasher* later in the war, Mess Attendant 3rd Class William Allison "hated his guts" while he commanded *Grampus* in 1942. Allison thought Hutchinson was a bit tough on his executive officer, P.D. Quirk, and disliked the way "he let everyone know that he was the boss" (Allison). Once again, a steward's dislike of his commanding officer may have been an indicator of a submarine commander's overall performance. Hutchinson was relieved of command in *Grampus* after three patrols due to poor performance but later redeemed himself in *Rasher* and went on to command a submarine division.

As some of the comments indicate, the attitude of a steward toward the officers he served often had more to do with the way in which the boat was operated rather than the personality of the captain himself. More than perhaps any other enlisted man, the men of the steward's branch had daily opportunities to see a captain and his officers at work in both routine and combat situations. Forced to work with people rather than specialize in machinery, many stewards were astute observers, and it didn't require an education at Annapolis to soon figure out which submarine commanders had what it took to be a good captain and those who didn't. Taken even a step further, many stewards could also gauge what their chances of survival were when riding with a particular captain, and could tell by close observation whether he might be cautious, reckless, or somewhere in-between when operating against the enemy. Captains like Lawson Ramage (*Parche*), George Street (*Tirante*), and Hank Munson (*Crevalle*) made hard-hitting patrols against the enemy that resulted in such distinguished awards as the Medal of Honor (Ramage and Street) or the Navy Cross (Munson) and were highly respected by their crews, especially the men in the steward's branch. Not only did they achieve success against the enemy, but they also treated their crews well and had the skill (and a degree of luck) to bring their men home safely.

Not all submarine commanders possessed these combinations of skills. Some were perceived as being reckless, resulting in the feeling among some crewmembers that they might not make it home alive, while others were overly cautious, achieving little success and causing morale in the boat to drop to a low level. Stewards and other men on the boat wanted the whole package — a captain who could achieve sinkings yet give his crew the confidence that he would bring them back alive. Officer's Cook 3rd Class Edward Neely, who served on *Bowfin* for three war patrols in 1944, may have stated it best when he said that the officers on that boat, especially captains Walter Griffith and John Corbus, were "the best because they knew what they were doing" (Neely).

Any good submarine captain fully understood that his success was dependant on the enlisted men that served under him, stewards included. Once such man whose actions demonstrated this ideal was Captain Carl Dwyer on *Puffer*. When he was awarded the Navy Cross after his boat's sixth war patrol, he gave a commendation to every enlisted man aboard, including Officer's Cook 1st Class James Woodley Patton and Steward's Mate Carroll Louden Allen. Dwyer had his picture taken individually with every enlisted man, and at the top of each man's commendation was his name and an image of the Navy Cross. Many of the men, including Steward's Mate Carroll Allen, cherished this document from Dwyer years after their days on submarines were over, and it was as if they themselves had been awarded the Navy Cross. In a way, they were, at least according to their thankful captain.

While stewards often judged the capability of the officers that they served, their immediate job was more pleasant if they established a good raport with these same officers. Depending on the personality of a commanding officer, sometimes this was possible, and many stewards can fondly recall incidents of friendly exchanges with their captains. Sam Wallace, an officer's cook on *Mingo*, recalls the many friendly bets he had with Captain John Madison, while Anderson Royal on *Silversides* got along famously with Captain Creed Burlingame and Executive Officer Roy Davenport. One commander that appreciated what his stewards did for him was Captain William Holman on *Narwhal*. Steward's Mate 1st Class Arthur Brown recalls that the captain really liked apple pie and told him that he would make him a petty officer if he baked him one. Fortunately, while Arthur Brown was no baker, the ship's baker, "a white guy from Brooklyn" (Brown, Arthur), made the pie for Brown. Sure enough, when Brown presented the pie to Holman, he held true to his word, and Brown was promoted to officer's cook 3rd class on November 1, 1944, after *Narwhal*'s fifteenth and final war patrol.

One misconception among white submariners of World War II is that of the "captain's boy." Many of these men believe that the stewards were the "captain's boy" and followed him from boat to boat during the war, thereby making stewards the personal servant of an individual commander. In fact, the records do not prove this to be true. It is true that some stewards, a relatively small number, did follow a commander from one submarine to another. Timothy Pennyman, a steward's mate 2nd class on *Crevalle*, did follow Commander Hank Munson from that boat to his next command, *Rasher*, as did Officer's Cook 3rd Class Woodrow Wilson Jones, going with Commander Louis McGregor from *Pike* to *Redfish*, but this was not the norm. Nor is this indicative that Pennyman or Jones were their respective commander's personal stewards. Whenever a commander transferred from one boat to another, it was not uncommon for him to have other members of his crew, be he steward, torpedoman, or yeoman, go with him. Oft times this was at the request of the crewmembers themselves or of the captain, but just as often it was the result of the normal shakeup that occurred among the crew after each war patrol. Since about 25 percent of the enlisted crew was transferred off a submarine after every war patrol, it meant that the average number of war patrols made by a steward on board any given submarine was usually three or four. This generally holds true for the men of the steward's branch, but the myth of the "captain's boy" is easily shattered when the records are examined more closely. Walter Wilson served three different skippers on *Trigger*, as did James Patton, Jr., on *Puffer*, Mack Butler and James

Gaylor on *Dace*, Elvin Mayo on *Jack*, George Lytle and Claude McKay on *Drum*, and Sam Wallace on *Mingo*, to name just a few. An even higher number of men served two successive commanders on one submarine during their time as a steward. If anything, in many cases a steward "belonged" more to an individual submarine — staying aboard long after other men had come and gone — than any individual captain.

Probably the most difficult aspect of a steward's relationship with his officers was dealing with those junior officers that were relatively fresh out of the Naval Academy at Annapolis, Maryland. The majority of World War II submarine commanders and their executive officers, the most-senior men on the boat in terms of rank, had graduated from Annapolis anywhere from eight to fourteen years before the war began and were usually settled in their style of command. Not only that, but it is also true that traditional naval protocol was often less strictly adhered to in the Submarine Force. With sixty or more men operating in close contact with each other in cramped quarters for an extended period of time, the relationship between officers and their crew was conducted in a much more relaxed atmosphere than that usually found on surface ships and on shore. However, this routine was sometimes upset with the appearance of a young officer, perhaps an ensign or a lieutenant junior grade who, in the not too distant past, had graduated from the Naval Academy. In general, many of these men are remembered by the stewards as being more "sticklers" (or worse) when it came to navy protocol and tradition and more difficult to deal with. While these recent graduates may have had the appropriate classroom training in navy operations, they often lacked experience when it came to dealing with people.

This "people" experience may have been even more sadly lacking when it came to dealing with the men of the steward's branch. Prior to his shipboard experience, a recent graduate of Annapolis dealt with stewards under totally different circumstances than those found on a submarine. The midshipmen at Annapolis were served by approximately 200 stewards who, having completed boot camp at Norfolk, were assigned there as a regular duty station. In keeping with the worst traditions of jim crow in the south, these men, when not on duty, were kept wholly segregated and had no meaningful interaction with the midshipmen. It is even reported that during the 1940s, and probably earlier, stewards were forced to go out the back door of Bancroft Hall when visitors came to see navy football games so that they would remain unseen by visitors (Wright, p. 69). In effect, stewards were servants first, not crewmembers. In contrast, when recent Annapolis graduates were sent aboard submarines, they found Black stewards that were a vital part of the boat's crew. Not only did they eat and sleep in close proximity to the rest of the crew, but the men of the steward's branch also had important battle station duties. Because of this wide disparity, it often took some time for these newer officers to change their attitudes toward stewards.

Two incidents recalled by several wartime submariners will serve to demonstrate the wide range of attitudes held by some of these most-junior officers, ranging from the ridiculous to that of a more disturbing nature. The first of these involved Hosey Mays, a steward's mate on *Crevalle* and, later, a steward on *Bowfin*. While he greatly enjoyed his submarine service, the one thing that has always stayed with him was the fact that "these young ensigns" could never get coffee themselves, but always had to have a steward do it for them. While regular crew, and some officers, would get their own coffee at times when a steward was not on duty and was sleeping in his bunk, the "ensigns never hesitated to use the buzzer" to rouse the stewards. An even more annoying occurrence was when the young officer would travel the short distance from the wardroom to the fore torpedo room and bang on the steward's bunk while he was sleeping, asking to be served (Mays). In contrast to this is the more disturbing incident involving William Knight and Willie James, both officer's cooks on *Whale* in 1943. Former Chief Pharmacist's Mate Floyd "Doc" Erickson well recalls the time when a junior officer on *Whale* came down with a case of "the crabs." This officer was convinced that his "crabs" were a result of stewards Knight or James using the officer's head and passing on their own supposed case of infestation. As such, he ordered that William Knight and Willie James be thoroughly examined by Erickson. This did, indeed, occur, and both men endured the examination with no outward sign of ill-will or rancor. James in particular "kind of laughed" about the episode, and, in speaking about crabs, told Erickson, "It's not a sin to have them, but it is a sin to keep them" (Erikson). Of course, upon examination Knight and James were given a clean bill of health, and the officer involved had to lay blame elsewhere. While we have no record of what the two stewards really thought about this incident, the humiliation that these two highly regarded stewards were subjected to has remained a vivid and bothersome memory for Floyd Erickson all these years later.

While newly commissioned officers, as a class, were looked upon by their stewards at times somewhat unfavorably, the men of the steward's branch had a way of dealing with them. As Isaac Johnson recalls, "It was up to us [stewards] to break them in. We had our way of dealing with them" (Johnson). This might be in the form of a meal that wasn't quite prepared right, a cold cup of coffee, or no cup of coffee at all. But, as Johnson further states, "99 percent of them [junior officers] were good men" (Johnson), and it must be remembered that among this group there were many good men who not only treated the stewards with respect (despite the example set at the Naval Academy) but held them in high regard for their valued service. One of these men was Lieutenant Lawrence Savadkin on *Tang*. He was new to this high-scoring boat commanded by Richard O'Kane when she headed out for her fifth war patrol, as were Officer's Cook 2nd Class Rubin Raiford and Steward's Mate 1st Class Ralph Adams. Also aboard was Steward's Mate 1st Class Howard Walker, who had made all of *Tang*'s prior patrols. Though Savadkin had never before been in submarines, and never had a chance to get to know his stewards, he soon recognized them not only as "nice fellows" but also "competent submariners" (Savadkin). Sadly, Savadkin would never get the chance to know his stewards, nor many of *Tang*'s other crewmen for that matter, due to her loss toward the end of her patrol.

Another junior officer that appreciated his steward was Peter Nalle, a young "Ensign fresh out of Sub School in the fall of 1944" (Nalle). His steward on *Whale* was Willie James, a man that was "an excellent cook ... well liked by the crew ... unflappable and always cheerful" (*ibid.*).

Finally, in regard to steward-officer relations, we might wonder what the captains themselves might have to say. The late Edward Beach, long-time executive officer on *Trigger* during the war, and later commander of *Piper*, remained close friends with Walter Wilson, his chief steward on *Trigger*, until Wilson's death in 1978. He offered high praise for his abilities and character in his writings. The late Richard O'Kane also wrote about his wartime steward, Howard Walker. While in command of *Tang*, O'Kane remembered that Walker, a steward's mate 1st class, probably "had a standing call every time I was called" and that this "would account for his promptness in many things and on numerous occasions" (O'Kane, p. 434). O'Kane thought briefly about the situation but then decided to leave things as they were for his steward. After all, "why inquire about a good thing and maybe spoil it" (*ibid.*).

While many submarine captains of World War II have now passed away, a few are still left to give their direct impressions of the men of the steward's branch. When asked about the stewards that served under their command during the war, their reactions were varied. Retired Rear Admiral Eugene Fluckey, a Medal of Honor winner on *Barb*, had little recollection of the stewards that served him and showed no interest in talking about them when contacted. However, one of his stewards on *Barb*, the late Paul Ragland, always spoke highly of Fluckey and considered him a great skipper.

One commander, however, Captain Slade Cutter, renowned for his exploits on *Seahorse*, remembered his stewards well. While serving as the executive officer on *Pompano* in late 1941 and early 1942, Cutter vividly recalled his Black steward as a "very popular" guy and that one of his duties was to stand lookout. On two successive patrols, though, aircraft got through and gave *Pompano* a good working over, resulting in damage. Feeling that his lookouts, both white and Black, were not doing their job, Cutter "gathered all the lookouts for a talk and told them how their country depended on them and that we only had 52 subs and couldn't afford to lose any" (Cutter). Cutter also recalled his steward on *Seahorse* and spoke of him highly, calling Steward's Mate 1st Class J.C. Crawford "a darn good steward who was liked by everyone" (*ibid.*). Likewise, retired Rear Admiral Maurice Rindskopf, the executive officer and later commander of *Drum*, spoke highly of Officer's Cook George Lytle and supplied several remembrances of Lytle's service on that boat. Yet another commander who well-recalls his stewards is Captain Carl Dwyer from *Puffer*. In speaking about his men, Officer's Cook James Patton and Steward's Mate Carroll Louden Allen, he states that "They were nice guys, and served us officers well. We couldn't have lived without them. They were very popular with the crew" (Dwyer). However, as was typical of the navy at the time, even a skipper as thoughtful of his men as Dwyer looked at his stewards as a group apart. He further comments, "They qualified, yes, but weren't part of the regular crew; they were in the wardroom" (*ibid.*).

Two men who probably state the captain-steward relationship the best from opposite sides are retired Rear Admiral John Maurer and former steward Anderson Royal. Maurer served as executive officer on *Harder* during the war and later rose to command of *Atule*. When questioned about his stewards aboard both boats, he was forthright and thoughtful. He called the service of the men of the steward's branch "most commendable" and remembered those that served him as being "all nice guys," even if he could not recall them by name. Upon further reflection, he also stated that "in retrospect, I should have gotten to know them better, but I was more interested in being a skipper" (Maurer). Anderson Royal expressed a similar attitude, though stated more directly. He served as a mess attendant/steward on *Silversides* and *Dragonet* during the war and was "realistic minded about the race question" that confronted the navy during the war. His attitude was that "winning the war was the number one objective" and that "we would deal with the color issue afterwards" (Royal). No doubt many submarine commanders felt the same way.

DISCIPLINARY ACTION WITHIN THE STEWARD'S BRANCH

Another way to gauge how stewards got along with their fellow crew and officers aboard submarines during the war is to look at the records that document what types of disciplinary action they may have received while serving. Since the undertaking of such research for every submarine that served during World War II was outside the immediate scope of this work, fifty-two submarines were chosen at random, and their crew muster rolls examined. The results of this sample study show that men of the steward's branch were, for the most part, model submariners and rarely were the subject of disciplinary action. The records examined were enlisted-man muster rolls, which were prepared by shipboard personnel on an approximate monthly basis for each submarine. The frequency of updated muster rolls usually depended on how long a submarine's war patrols might last and, upon return, how long she was in port for a refit. The muster rolls not only record the transfer and addition of all enlisted personnel to the boat but also changes in rating for enlisted men as well as any meritorious or disciplinary action that may have been handed out. Before discussing the disciplinary actions against submarine stewards, it will be helpful to discuss the "legal system," if you will, as it existed on board ships in the United States Navy.

As in days of old, the captain on board any unit, including submarines, in the navy had almost absolute power. All things that happened aboard his boat were his responsibility, including how the ship was run and how it functioned on a daily basis as well as in cases of dispute or misconduct, how justice was handed out. However, while a captain had the power to discipline his crew for most infractions, he did have to operate within the articles and regulations that were established by the navy and dictated how ships in the fleet were to be governed.

Captains were in charge of meting out justice in many cases but not all. Crimes of a more serious nature that may have happened on or off the boat, such as substantial theft of government or personal property, rape, assault, or murder, to name a few, were outside the captain's authority, and men accused of such offenses were sent ashore to be handled by the navy's legal office or someone from the judge advocate general's office. Cases such as this of a serious nature were less common but not unknown, even among submariners. Most unusual were two serious cases that involved crewmen from *Puffer*. Both occurred after that boat's third war patrol in Australia in April 1944. The details of one of these incidents are not fully known but involved a white enlisted man, a motor machinist mate, who had killed someone while on rest and relaxation leave ashore. Anecdotal evidence suggests that some of his fellow crewmembers testified at his trial, and he was found guilty. He subsequently did a 20-year prison sentence at the Portsmouth Naval Prison in New Hampshire (CM).

During this same time, another *Puffer* crewman, Steward's Mate 1st Class John Alden Pruitt, was also judged to have committed a serious crime. In regard to this case, the full details are available and are very interesting. Steward's Mate John Pruitt was part of the commissioning crew of *Puffer* at Manitowoc and served on that boat's first three war patrols. Many details of his service during this time have already been recounted. When the boat came into Fremantle, Australia, after her third patrol in early April 1944, Pruitt was among a number of men that were rotated off the boat, including Executive Officer Franklin Hess. Pruitt subsequently was sent to Submarine

Division 161 for duty, serving in its training allowance aboard the submarine tender *Orion*. He continued his duties here until May 9, 1944, when he went on liberty for the day and was involved in an incident that would end his career as a submariner and send him to jail.

While on liberty, Pruitt left his ship at about 3:00 P.M. and took a cab with some other sailors to downtown Perth. Here, he got out at the King Edward Hotel, and spent the next few hours drinking at various bars in the area. He then met a fellow steward by the name of Goode, and they went into a nearby alleyway to share a bottle of gin.

It is at this point that the several accounts of the succeeding events diverge. Pruitt claims to have left his friend Goode in the alleyway to get something to go with their gin. When he started to return, he encountered Goode, who looked to have been in a fight. Moreover, Goode was missing his sailor's hat and wanted it back, so he returned to the scene of the earlier fight, with Pruitt and several other stewards belatedly following along. When Pruitt and the stewards arrived back at the scene in the alleyway, Goode was fighting with an old man. Pruitt, with submarine stewards Ulysses Grant Reed, Charles Cox, Jr., and Eddie Gordelle trailing behind, jumped into the fray and pulled Goode off the old man, who was bleeding profusely from a knife wound. Together they left the area to avoid the Shore Patrol police and went back to their ships, Goode to the tender *Pelias*, and Pruitt to the *Orion*. This is Pruitt's version of the events of that evening, but the Judge Advocate argued otherwise.

Their charge was that Pruitt was the only man in the alleyway on that night, and that he assaulted and verbally abused one Robert Wells, a boatswain's mate 1st class in the navy, and his girlfriend, Lavinia Mestichelli, as they were leaving to go to the movies. It was further alledged that Pruitt was the aggressor and knocked down Wells and was in the process of striking him with an axe when Ms. Mestichelli stopped Pruitt from doing so, and he fled. Minutes later, it is argued, Pruitt came back to the scene and assaulted Angelo Mestichelli, the young lady's father, by stabbing him several times while fighting with him in the alleyway.

So there you have it, two contradicting stories. The prosecution brought forward seventeen witnesses to bolster the case against Pruitt, while the defense only had two witnesses besides Pruitt himself. One witness that may have helped Pruitt, Ulysses Grant Reed, was unavailable, and no apparent attempt was ever made to question him on the matter. The senior patrol officer investigating the incident for the navy simply states, when asked about Reed, that "Ulysses Grant Reed is aboard a submarine skippered by Lieutenant Commander Nimitz, and I do not know where this vessel is at the present time" (Pruitt Court Martial-Document 128932, p. 65). The only steward to support Pruitt's claim of innocence was Eddie Gordelle, a veteran of two war patrols on *Raton*. Even the testimomy of Pruitt's old executive officer on *Puffer*, Franklin Hess, would do him little good. Despite his testimony that Pruitt "was well liked by his shipmates" and that Hess "never had reason to doubt anything that he [Pruitt] has said" (*ibid.*, p. 105), his testimony was apparently little regarded as it applied, according to the Judge Advocate, only to Pruitt's character while aboard the boat and not ashore. When Hess was further reminded of Pruitt's fight ashore "with the other mess attendant aboard" (*ibid.*, p. 106), Hess told the court that this incident had happened while the boat was being commissioned and that no other incidents had taken place. Further questioning by Pruitt's defense team brought out the fact that Pruitt's qualities and

Steward's Mate 1st Class Johnnie Green on *Narwhal* in 1945. Prior to his war patrol on *Narwhal*, Green did relief crew duty in Fremantle-Perth, Australia, and was a witness at the court martial against Steward's Mate John Pruitt in June 1944. (Photograph courtesy of A. Brown.)

character after the boat's first two war patrols, along with that of other crew members, was discussed, and each time he was kept aboard.

As for the Judge Advocate's case against Pruitt, looked at in modern terms, it was decidedly weak. Of the people who were directly involved in the fighting that supposedly involved Pruitt, sailor Robert Wells could only identify Pruitt in a procedure that even the Judge Advocate states "I am willing to submit that it was poorly done" (*ibid.*, p. 171), while the Mestichellis could not identify Pruitt at all as the assailant. Of the other stewards that testified for the prosecution, none could name Pruitt as the assailant, just that he was involved and on the scene. Two of these men were submarine stewards Charles Cox, Jr., a veteran of one war patrol on *Flasher*, and Johnnie Green, who would make three war patrols on *Narwhal* late in 1944. Cox saw Pruitt on the scene and involved with the old man but could not state for certain that no one else was present. Green was at the general scene of the crime but too far away to identify the antagonists.

What about the man named Goode, who it was claimed by both Pruitt and Gordelle was the real man involved? No effort, apparently, was ever made to find this man, and the Judge Advocate states that "the selection of the name will indicate anything other than guilt" and "It is not the truth, gentlemen. I say it is the dream of a genious" (*ibid.*, pp. 172–3). But, was it really a lie, and was the story of "the mystery man" (*ibid.*) Goode really made up by Pruitt to save his own skin? At first glance, one might believe that this was a made-up story by Pruitt, as in his earliest statements to investigators he makes no mention of Goode. It was only later, when a court martial was ordered that this story came out. When questioned about this inconsistency, and it was a damning one, Pruitt simply states that "Well, in the first place Goode was my "Cobber." I knew those people didn't know him, and I thought they couldn't get anything on me. But I was intending to tell my story at mast, but the Captain told me I was being recommended for a general court martial and any further statement would be held against me, so I didn't" (*ibid.*, p. 96). "Cobber" is an Australian term for friend or buddy, so Pruitt did not tell of his involvement until it was too late, and unintentionally sealed his own fate. Though no effort was ever made to find a man named Goode that was serving on the tender *Pelias* in Fremantle, Pruitt was not lying. Steward's Mate 2nd Class Claude Goode made three war patrols on *Gar* from June 1942 to January 1943 before going to duty on *Pelias*. If we are to believe John Pruitt, this was the man that got in a fight, and he was just lying to protect his friend.

In the end, the seven-man court found John Alden Pruitt guilty of "with intent to do bodily harm, and without just cause or excuse, assault with a dangerous weapon, to wit, a knife, one Angelo Mestichelli, a civilian" (*ibid.*, p. 2). Ironically, he was found not guilty of assaulting sailor Robert Wells, the only man who came even close to identifying Pruitt as the man involved. Pruitt was subsequently sentenced to be reduced to steward's mate 3rd class and was ordered to prison for five years, presumably at the navy prison in Portsmouth, New Hampshire. He would then be dishorably discharged from the navy. It is not known if Pruitt served out his full term or what became of him afterward. However, his was a case, perhaps, of flawed justice, and one that ended an otherwise honorable wartime career. Sadly enough, when *Puffer* was being cleaned out after the war, an emotional letter from Pruitt's mother back home was found in the forward torpedo room that brought back memories of this tragic case to the men that knew John Alden Pruitt (CM).

In getting back to lesser disciplinary matters within the navy, the captain was usually the one to make a determination in the case. After hearing the circumstances of each case and from the parties involved, he made his decision on guilt and, if required, what sentence was to be handed down. Such cases might run the gamut from drunk and disorderly conduct while ashore, being AOL (absent over leave), failure to stand a watch, or even refusal to obey orders. In each case, the captain heard the case during an informal procedure known as "captain's mast." Harkening back to the old days of the sailing navy, this procedure was held at a time set aside each week, or sooner if the need arose, where the captain heard the "charges" against an enlisted man who may have committed an infraction. This proceeding was very informal — there was no record made of what was stated, there was no jury of peers, and no lawyers were involved. It just involved the captain, the junior officer(s) involved, and the man who committed the offense. Unfortunately, because of this informality only a small amount of information about these cases is found in the muster rolls, and often none at all excepting the punishment that was given. However, we do have the details of one such proceeding from a man who was the subject of a captain's mast, William Murray, while aboard *Plunger*, and the incident that precipitated the event. What is most incredible about the proceeding Murray was made to suffer through was the triviality of the "offense" he committed, as well as the intimidation tactics used against him prior to, and at the captain's mast itself. Here is his story:

> Within two weeks of Lt. Commander Fahy assuming command, he ordered me not to serve breakfast in the wardroom to anyone after 0830. All of the officers were acutely aware of the instructions the new Skipper had given me. Those orders were routinely carried out without complaint from officers. So, when Ljg. Pearson, one morning after spending a drunken night in Brisbane, instructed me, at 0953, to prepare him breakfast.... I first thought he was kidding.

Therefore, I told him in a nonchalant manner we would be serving lunch in less than an hour and a half. When he retorted that he was giving me fifteen minutes to get the breakfast on the table, I suddenly realized he was not kidding. So, I told him that I would be starting to make the salad for lunch in about that time period. So, he again asserted that he was giving me fifteen minutes to get the breakfast on the table. At that point I, perhaps, based on twenty-twenty hindsight, became more testy than I should have, when I adamantly retorted that he could give me fifteen years to get it out there and I wouldn't do it under the prevailing circumstances. So, I was not overly surprised when he returned to the pantry ... and informed me that I was on report. Later on that day I was told that I was restricted to the sub. I was still not overly concerned because I was of the impression that I was under the protection of the commanding officer's instruction to me. Well, I soon learned the falseness of my impression.

On the day following the incident the executive officer took me topside for — what he termed — a friendly chat. At the beginning of what turned out to be a conversation of considerable length, he asked me if I was aware that my deliberate refusal to obey a direct order of a commissioned officer, during a time of war, was punishable by death in front of a firing squad. "You need not worry about that," he hastily asserted, because he would never let that happen to me. "All you needed to do," he said, "is to go to Ljg. Pearson and tell him you are sorry for the way you acted.... I just want this thing to go away." Then, very non-chalantly, he (the XO) said, "You know sometimes the craziest things can happen — like slipping off the bow of a sub, and a lost at sea incident report has to be written."

Well, even as green as I was in the navy at that time, I was not so naive as not to recognize that he was subtley trying to intimidate me. When the XO placed his arm on my shoulder and told me they didn't want to do anything to me that would interfere with my allotment going to my wife and my 18-month-old little child, whom I had not yet seen, I was absolutely certain that he was indeed trying to intimidate me.... When the intimidating tactics failed, a captain's mast date was assigned.

At the appointed hour of the captain's mast hearing, I was ushered into the ward room. It did not look like the same room in which I performed my duties on a daily basis. It had been transformed into an awesome looking, unfriendly, ugly place.... The table ... was draped with a dark green cloth that projected an eerie image of a coffin.... The Captain was occupying the chair in which it was his normal custom to sit. Glaring at me across the length of the eerie looking table ... he suddenly took on an appearance that I can best describe as the image of Neptune, the god of the sea, or perhaps it was the image of the devil.... His glaring words convinced me that I was in big trouble. As I stood at attention ... his first utterances were insulting to the good character of my deceased mother ... and slanderous to my legitimacy. The tirade of character assassination occurred within the first thirty seconds ... of my standing before him. His first words, at an almost screaming pitch were: "You bur-head son of a bitch. Who the hell do you think you are? People are trying to help you, and you consider yourself too big to beg Ljg. Pearson for forgiveness?"

The Captain's ferocious attack left me so ... traumatized by fear that I didn't know whether I should run out of the ward room and scream for somebody to help me or stand there and faint — as I felt I was going to do. As it turned out, I did neither. Instead, I found myself attempting to remind the captain about the instruction he had given me ... not to serve breakfast after 0830.

Before I could complete the full verbalization ... he ... severely rebuked me by retorting: "Shut your damn mouth you bur-headed bastard! Don't tell me what I told you! You disobeyed the direct order of a naval commission officer during a time of war, and I am assigning a court-martial officer to deal with this matter. Now get the hell out of here.

I did not move. I was not deliberately refusing to leave! What he did not know was that I was so petrified with fear that I could not ... walk out of that room. So, as though in a trance ... I heard myself speaking: "Captain, I am young, I am green and inexperienced, but I know enough to be certain that this is not the manner in which you should dismiss me." I fought back the tears. But, I stood there for what appeared to have been an eternity.

First, he (the captain) glared at me and appeared to have made a slight motion as though he was coming across the table to attack me. But, instead, he slowly roused from the chair and in an agitated voice said: "Murray, you are dismissed."

He put his hand in salute fashion, so I saluted him. Immediately, my limbs were unfrozen, and I turned and walked out of that ward room. Two hours later, I was serving the same man, sitting in that same chair — lunch! A few days later the court-martial trial was convened, and a few days after that I was given the result.... I was found guilty as charged. As punishments, I was reduced in rating from STM 1 to STM 2 and suffered a reduction in pay of $4.00 per month for three months. That night ... I crawled into my bunk and turned my face towards the torpedo by which I slept, and I wept" [Murray].

For those men who committed offenses, it was often the time spent waiting for captain's mast that was more stressful than the actual event itself. Many of the men, stewards included, knew that their actions went against navy discipline or regulations and were anxious about how they might be punished by the captain. Three types of punishment were usually meted out at captain's mast. These include a monetary fine taken from a sailor's monthly pay for a period of months, a reduction in rating (in effect, a fine, as this meant a man's base pay was also reduced to correspond to his lower rate), or a transfer off the boat for confinement in the brig for a short time and then new duty elsewhere. Sometimes the sentence at captain's mast was a combination of the above, as in Murray's case, and sometimes no sentence was given, just perhaps a warning if a man had a plausible explanation for his actions.

While captain's mast was usually a serious proceeding, this was not always the case. As one story goes, an ensign fresh out of Annapolis came aboard his assigned boat for the first time and, while heading toward officer country, encountered one of the boat's Black stewards. When the ensign asked the steward's name, the reply was "Knight." (Submariners always go by last names and seldom know a man's first name.) Continuing on, the ensign spotted the boat's other Black steward and asked his name. He was told it was "Day." Thinking he was being played by a couple of insubordinate stewards, he had them brought to captain's mast for disciplinary action. When the proceedings started, the captain inquired of his young officer what were the charges against each man. After he told the story of Knight and Day, the captain, somewhat laconically, told his ensign that those, indeed, were their names, and the proceeding was abruptly ended (Gauthwaite). Whether or not this event actually took place is unknown, but two well-known wartime stewards were indeed named William Knight and Shirley Day.

It should also be noted that captain's masts could also be convened for reasons other than handling disciplinary cases. While the overwhelming majority of captain's masts were held for this reason, meritorious mast or commendatory mast, while rare, were also held by a captain to give awards or commendations to men that had earned them. The crew records for *Trout* indicate that on March 23, 1942, Mess Attendant 1st Class Lonnie Jackson was promoted to Officer's Cook 3rd Class for meritorious service. This was due to his service on the boat's second war patrol when she went on a special mission to Corregidor to deliver antiaircraft ammunition to the beleaguered island garrison. After *Trout* was loaded with torpedoes for the rest of her patrol, it was discovered that extra ballast was needed. As a result, the boat also loaded an unusual cargo — 20 tons of gold and silver bars that were removed from banks in Manilla to prevent them from falling into Japanese hands. On *Trout*'s return to Pearl Harbor, the mission made "uplifting newspaper copy" (Blair, p. 207) and the entire crew was awarded an Army Silver Star medal.

Few stewards were officially recognized for outstanding service during the war in the same fashion as Lonnie Jackson. The first ever to be so recognized was Mess Attendant 1st Class Melton Evans on *Gudgeon*. After completing that boat's first war patrol in Japanese waters, Evans was promoted to officer's cook 3rd class "for meritorious conduct" (National Archives, reel 1795). Another man that was noted in this manner and received a "meritorious advancement in rating" (National Archives, reel 7591) to chief officer's cook after participating in all of that boat's ten war patrols to date was Walter Wilson on *Trigger*. Finally, yet another procedure that was held on some boats was Request Mast, where a submarine's executive officer set time aside at certain intervals to hear requests from the crew (Kimmons).

In examining the crew muster rolls for men of the steward's branch from 52 submarines, some interesting facts have been gathered. For these boats, the entries for 387 Black stewards, both regular and replacement crew, were examined. For 35 of the 52 boats whose records were examined, there were no incidents of disciplinary action recorded. This alone bears out the fact that the men of the steward's branch performed good service aboard submarines. For the remaining 17 boats, records show that 23 men were subject to some form of disciplinary action, while another six men were likely subject to such action, though this was not definitely stated. For only 14 of these 29 men was it noted in the records what their offense entailed, while for the others only their sentence is given, with no hint of what infraction they committed.

One of the most common offenses committed by these stewards, and, indeed, among all sailors, was that of being absent over leave (AOL), absent with out leave (AWOL), or being declared a "straggler." Out of the 387 men involved in this study, 8 were designated in these categories. These were all like offenses but under slightly different circumstances.

A man who went AOL was one who failed to return from his authorized leave on time, usually by a number of hours. Sailors on leave usually had an extended time away from the boat, lasting on average from one to three weeks. However, they had to be back on board their boat at a stated time or trouble might result. This happened to young Arthur Brown while he was on *Narwhal*. The boat was in Australia for a refit, and Brown was on authorized leave. However, he did not make it back to the boat on time due to a delay in train service. Once his officers heard the reason for his delayed arrival, Brown was let off with only a warning and was not disciplined.

Being AWOL, on the other hand, was much more serious, involving someone who was away from the boat without being authorized to do so. Not infrequently, a man started out as being AOL, but the longer he was away from the boat and it seemed apparent he might not come back, then the charge was upgraded to that of being AWOL.

The final category, that of a "straggler," usually referred to a man who failed to return from liberty on time. Liberty was a shorter period of time allowed away from the boat, usually no more than a day or two, and often less. Failure to return from liberty was also a common occurrence among sailors of all colors, and being so designated did not always mean one would be punished. Of the three men declared a "straggler" in our 52-boat study, none are recorded as having received punishment. For one of these men, Steward's Mate 1st Class Herman Stone on *Archerfish*, the records state that he did not return from liberty while the boat was in Panama preparing to transit the Canal Zone on its way to Pearl Harbor. Just like men who were AOL, some men who were at first recorded as being a "straggler" later were declared AOL when they were gone for extended periods of time.

One such man who was at first declared a "straggler" and was later charged with being AOL was Walter Ramsey on *Seal*. Gone for seven days, he later pled guilty and suffered an indeterminate loss of pay and confinement in July 1945. Another steward who was charged with being AOL was Jones Patterson on *Bowfin*. However, instead of being absent for a period of days, records show that he was AOL for only two-and-a-half hours. For this seemingly minor infraction, Jones was transferred off the boat and given solitary confinement for ten days and restricted to a bread and water diet. The difference in sentences handed out for Ramsey and Patterson seems harsh, but lacking knowledge of the full facts in each case, it is impossible to determine why Patterson's sentence was so harsh for such a short time being AOL. Another man that went AOL was Officer's Cook 2nd Class Daniel McCormick on *Bonefish* in mid-1943. He was gone for 11 hours and 34 minutes, according to records, and was reduced in rating to officer's cook 3rd class. McCormick's case is interesting, as he was an old hand by 1943, having enlisted in 1936 and had made other war patrols, including two on *Gar* during the first months of the war. He would go on to serve on *Bonefish* for five war patrols and, apparently mending his ways, rose in rating to officer's cook 1st class. However, he was sent off *Bonefish* in August 1944 for disciplinary action for unknown offenses.

Another offense that was noted among several stewards in our sampling was that of theft. Steward's Mate 1st Class George Cooper made the final war patrol on *Seal* before the boat was retired from war service and sent stateside. While back in New London, Cooper was charged with theft of government property and theft of personal property and was sent off the boat within a week or two to be dealt with by the Judge Advocate General's office at the submarine base. The disposition of his case is unknown. Another man charged with a similar offense was Steward's Mate 1st Class Clarence Page on *Flasher*. In May 1945, after having made four war patrols on *Flasher*, Page was charged with being AOL for 22 hours and 50 minutes and the theft of a .45 automatic weapon and ammunition clip. For this seemingly serious action, Page was only reduced in rating to a steward's mate 2nd class. Once again, without the specifics of each case, it is difficult to understand the full extent of what took place. Interestingly enough, both these offenses were committed when the war was winding down and men were anxious to get home. As previously mentioned, Page was a likeable crewmember and was known as a devout Christian on *Flasher*. Perhaps he just wanted a wartime souvenir to take home when he took the .45 automatic. The same reasoning might be made of Cooper when it came to his theft of government property but is more difficult to reconcile with the charge of stealing personal property, possibly that of his fellow shipmates. In either case, both men made poor decisions and were forced to pay the consequences.

Other Black stewards, too, did not always act according to navy regulations. John Sanders made two war patrols on *Pollack* in 1944 before being charged with a failure to stand watch on *Pollack*'s eleventh patrol of the war in August 1944. Sanders was reduced in rating to steward's mate 2nd class and transferred off the boat before her next run. Whether Sanders was due to be rotated off *Pollack* or whether he was transferred off because of his failure to stand watch is unknown.

One of the most interesting disciplinary cases involving a man from the steward's branch is that involving Washington Peeples, Jr., on *Finback*. Peeples enlisted in the navy from Cincinnati, Ohio, in August 1941 and went to submarines straight from boot camp. Rated as mess attendant 3rd class, he was transferred to *Finback*, commanded by Lieutenant Commander Jesse Hull, on February 4, 1942, four days after she was commissioned. Just 32 days later, while still at Portsmouth, New Hampshire, Peeples was summarily court martialed for conduct prejudicial to good order and discipline. He was sentenced to be confined on bread and water for 15 days and was transferred to the marine brig at the Portsmouth Navy Yard on March 19, 1942. Nine days later, presumably after his sentence was finished, Peeples was declared unfit and given an undesirable discharge from the navy. As in most cases of disciplinary action, we have no details of this case. Was Peeples a difficult case because of his personality, or is it a case where Peeples refused to accept the only role a Black man could have in the fighting navy during this era? Maybe his conduct was a combination of both these factors, but if it were the latter, perhaps he was doing all that he could to get out of the navy as quickly as possible, no matter what the cost. If so, he succeeded.

Finally, of the 14 men in this study whose offense is known, two of them were disciplined under circumstances which might have some bearing on the steward-captain relationship. Mess Attendant 3rd Class Roscoe Yates, Jr., enlisted in the navy at New York City on December 16, 1941, probably inspired by the events at Pearl Harbor less than two weeks before. After a brief boot camp, he was sent to Portsmouth, New Hampshire, as part of the crew of a new boat *Flying Fish* and was her only Black steward as she headed out on her first war patrol. During a 51-day patrol that lasted from June through July 1942, Yates was brought to captain's mast on June 30 to face the charge of directly disobeying orders. Unfortunately, just what those orders were and what Yates's sentence was is unknown. However, Roscoe Yates was soon off *Flying Fish*, being transferred off the boat while she was at Midway lagoon on August 7, 1942. His replacement steward was Mess Attendant 2nd Class Leroy Cox, who had enlisted in the navy on August 22, 1940, at Macon, Georgia. Cox joined *Flying Fish* at Midway on August 13 as Yates's replacement and, in less than a month, on September 10, was also subjected to a captains mast for directly disobeying orders. Cox was fined $10 a month for two months but appealed his sentence, the result of which is unknown. Unlike Yates, who was transferred off the boat very quickly, Leroy Cox went on to serve for five war patrols on *Flying Fish* and was promoted to officer's cook 3rd class by the time he left her. *Flying Fish* is the only submarine, as far as is known, where two stewards were disciplined for failing to obey orders. While this may, at first, seem unusual, it is less surprising given the character of *Flying Fish*'s first commanding officer, Glynn R. Donaho. One historian refers to Lieutenant Commander Donaho as a "strange and difficult character" and a man who was "bad at handling people" (Blair, p. 253). Though Glynn Donaho would soon prove himself to be an outstanding submarine skipper in terms of tonnage sunk, he does not seem to be one of those captains that endeared himself, at least early on, to the men of the steward's branch that served him. However, in all fairness to Donaho, it must be remembered that people sometimes change. Leroy Cox served a total of four war patrols under Donaho without further difficulties, while Steward John Wesley Whitehead served with him during Donaho's second tenure as commander of *Flying Fish* without trouble. In all likelihood, this was a case where the stewards of *Flying Fish* figured out how best to deal with their "difficult" captain in order to get the job done.

For those other men in this study whose offense is unknown, the majority received a reduction in rating as the penalty for their misconduct, while several were transferred off their boat for disciplinary action and future duty. This second action is not surprising as submarines were small and cramped, and the last thing a commander wanted on a war patrol that might last two months was a disgruntled or disruptive crewman.

How then, are we to view this unruly group of stewards, and how does their conduct reflect upon the men of the steward's branch as a whole? First and foremost to be remembered is the fact that 94 percent of the men in our sample study were not subject to any discipline whatsoever. Despite being forced to do a job that few would have chosen on their own, the vast majority performed as capable and, in many cases, model sailors. Secondly, let us remember the nature of sailors, any sailor, no matter what his color. Confined on shipboard for extended periods of time, they worked hard and, even when off duty, were, by the nature of their service, always in a navy "environment." When given liberty or leave on land, away from their ships, sailors enjoyed their absence to the fullest. Many took the opportunity to drink to excess as a way to "get away from it all," and disorderly behavior in the form of bar brawls was a frequent occurrence. In general, sailors on leave are notorious for their poor time-management skills and have been since time immemorial. The frequency of men subject to disciplinary action for being AOL or AWOL certainly bears this out.

Often it was that some of a commander's most experienced and reliable petty officers on the boat were disciplinary problems when not on war patrol. One such man may have been Officer's Cook 1st Class Daniel McCormick. A seasoned submariner, by 1944 McCormick had two hash marks on his sleeve and had made seven war patrols, five of which were on *Bonefish*. Even before he made his first war patrol on *Bonefish*, McCormick had gone AOL and, as a result, was busted from officer's cook 2nd class to officer's cook 3rd class and yet remained on the boat. His captain, Lieutenant

Commander Thomas Hogan, must have judged him a reliable submariner, and no doubt he was. Within six months of being reduced in rating, McCormick was back to officer's cook 2nd class, and just five months after that, in May 1944, was promoted to officer's cook 1st class. This was no mean feat as *Bonefish* was considered "a very special boat" (Blair, p. 496) by Admiral Ralph Christie and was chosen by him as his flagship. After the boat's first war patrol, Christie even made a surprise visit to the boat to award Hogan a Navy Cross and pronounced the boat "clean and fit" (*ibid.*). There can be no doubt that had McCormick, who likely served Admiral Christie himself, not done his job, his stay on *Bonefish* would have been short lived. While McCormick was sent off the boat in August 1944 for yet another incident of disciplinary action, this turned out to be a blessing in disguise. *Bonefish* was sunk three patrols later, in June 1945, and was lost with all hands.

In conclusion, for the majority of stewards that were disciplined, let us not judge them too harshly. Just like white sailors that got into trouble, they were held accountable for their errant behavior, suffered the consequences of their actions, and then returned to the service of their country. Little more could be asked for during a time of war.

Unusual Circumstances

While there has been some discussion in this chapter about instances of racial discrimination by white crewmen versus Black stewards on submarines during the war, there is one aspect of racial discrimination that still needs to be touched upon. This is the issue of so-called "reverse" discrimination, where a Black steward displayed prejudice or hatred against fellow crewmembers because they were white. Understandably so, there is little information, except that of an anecdotal nature that touches on this aspect of race relations aboard the boats. A steward who had a barely concealed hatred for his white shipmates could get by in the surface navy. Segregated to a large extent aboard these much larger ships of war, there was safety in numbers. For example, an aircraft carrier that carried a total crew of several thousand would often include in that complement more than 100 stewards. Not so in a submarine, where, at most, there may have been three Black stewards on a boat, usually only two, and sometimes just one. Because submarine stewards worked so closely with both officers and enlisted crew at nearly every hour of the day, one that demonstrated racist tendencies toward whites in general would seldom last longer than one or two war patrols, if any at all, before being transferred off the boat. His stay in the Submarine Force would, indeed, probably be a short one.

For stewards of this nature that did make war patrols, their racist attitudes sometimes had more of an impact on their fellow stewards than on those white shipmates who were the object of their hatred. It was written earlier that stewards walked a fine line — officially he was an enlisted man, but the navy designated him separate and inferior, both from the officers he served and his fellow white enlisted men. This could be bearable when a steward's treatment aboard his boat was satisfactory and when he had as a shipmate a fellow Black steward who could provide friendship, guidance, and understanding. But this was not always the case.

Sometimes the personalities of two stewards might not mesh. This was unavoidable at times, but when two stewards could not co-exist because of discriminatory attitudes, this might leave one of the stewards in no-man's land. Unsupported by his fellow steward, and fearful of retaliation from white crewmembers, he might have to resort to drastic measure as a means of self-preservation. While instances of this type of situation were certainly rare, they did occur. One instance of this type of case happened aboard *Bluegill*, during her first war patrol in 1944. It is only now, nearly sixty years later, that then Steward's Mate 1st Class Walter Patrick, now a retired Baptist minister, has been able to talk about the events that made him leave submarines for good. His story is as follows:

> [There was] a racial issue on board our sub between our steward and some of the white shipmates. Our steward, a native of Alabama, carried a chip on his shoulder. He told me how the whites had treated many members of his family and friends; he had witnessed terrible beatings by the white men — some member, a close relative, had been hanged on a tree; some dragged by mules, sharecroppers cheated by the farmers they worked with, the story goes on and on. So, it was hard to be in close quarters with the whites. He held a terrible feeling inside. I could tell by the way he would grimace when speaking of those terrible atrocities that he had witnessed and heard of during his childhood days. So, most of the time he would go around with a chip on his shoulder, with an expression that said "I dare anyone to knock it off."
>
> One day he was given a chance to show his inner feelings toward the whites. It happened at the shower. Steward was taking his shower while two of us were standing in line. There was this Italian shipmate from Boston in front of me next to the shower. Steward was taking his time soaping and rinsing, the Italian got tired of waiting and decided to speak out.
>
> He said to steward, "What are you trying to do, wash all of the Black off of you?"
>
> Steward rinsed the soap off his hand and shot a fist right into the Italian's face. He went down.... When [the Italian] got to his feet, he looked to me and asked "Why did he do that"? I simply said, "Just say what you just said to him again."
>
> He did not. He had the message.
>
> But this war between steward and whites did not stop then.... One day steward caught me doing what I called a little act of kindness to an enlisted man, giving him some coffee the officers did not want. Steward saw me pouring this coffee in one of the white mates' cups, snatched the pot out of my hand, and poured it down the sink and left the man with his empty cup.
>
> You must understand where I stood.... Here was my superior calling me an Uncle Tom.... I would have tried to solve the problem in a more democratic way and not try to penalize those men for something their foreparents did, but things of this racial problem between steward and the whites got worse.
>
> One day while I was laying in my bunk, which was one of the top bunks, half asleep, I heard some whispering. So I feigned to be asleep and listened. I overheard enough from this group to save steward. Here's what the plot was that I overheard: This was the steward's night to take out the garbage, so let us meet him topside and we will give him the deep six. So, I told steward, and told him to keep it to himself, that I would take his turn taking out the garbage. I felt that I had a better chance than he did, even though I was a little scared. Every

other night we would take turns taking out the garbage. Sure as they had planned, when I went topside with the garbage there were six of those men standing topside, some smoking, and just talking.

One asked me, "Where is your buddy tonight? Didn't you take out the trash last night?"

I said, "Yes, he's sick tonight...."

For many nights on my off night a group of men were there on deck until we were almost in the port of Freemantle. Steward put in for a transfer, and I later left the boat. I'd rather face a court martial and be killed with a gun in my hand than to be fish bait, because I felt that they would soon turn on me. I never again heard of steward" [Patrick].

After this first war patrol on *Bluegill,* young Patrick was both confused and scared. Because of this state of mind, he recalls little today of his second war patrol. Who could he turn to for help? If he reported the white crewmen that were involved in the plot against the lead steward, would he even be believed? In any case, might those same shipmates then try to retaliate against him? Unwilling to take this chance and unwilling to go back to *Bluegill,* Walter Patrick did the only thing he could do — he went AWOL before the boat's next war patrol. He was busted one grade at captain's mast for this action and never told his officers why he went AWOL. He just "took it on myself" and remained silent. Walter Patrick subsequently served in Australia at the Darwin Submarine House and later on the submarine tender *Eurayle,* where he ended the war as a steward 3rd class.

It is interesting to note that the plan by men on *Bluegill* to get rid of a steward they didn't like by tossing him overboard when he came topside at night to dispose of the boat's garbage was an almost perfect one. Black and white submarine veterans agree that this could easily have happened without the perpetrators being discovered, and the incident would have likely been labeled an "accident." Had not Walter Patrick overheard what was going on, the loss of *Bluegill*'s lead steward would probably have been deemed an accident and nothing more. Luckily, such events seldom occurred. We have already read of the intimidating tactics used against William Murray on *Plunger,* and how he was warned that "accidents" like this sometimes happened on submarines. In examining the muster rolls for submarines during the war, only one steward, Steward's Mate 1st Class Louis Jones on *Herring,* was lost in this manner. Jones reported aboard the boat on January 22, 1944, as she was heading out for her seventh war patrol and fell overboard and drowned in the "line of duty" (National Archives, reel 1931) just four days later. His remains were buried at sea.

While there is nothing to suggest foul play in this incident, *Herring* does not seem to have been a good-luck boat for stewards. In addition to the death of Jones, another steward, Mess Attendant 3rd Class Lewis Scott, went AWOL and deserted, while Steward's Mate 1st Class Issiah Thomas was twice disciplined at captain's mast. However, Scott and Thomas, both off the boat, were lucky. *Herring* was lost on her eighth war patrol when sunk by Japanese shore batteries off the Kurile Islands on June 1, 1944. Her entire crew was lost, including veteran patroller, Officer's Cook 1st Class Timothy Burkett, and Jones's replacement, Steward's Mate 2nd Class Nathaniel Campbell.

Crew relations between Blacks and whites on the boats were usually good, and they were nearly always better than those found on surface ships. This is a fact, and one in which the Submarine Force may take pride. However, the experiences of Walter Patrick demonstrate that the role of a submarine steward was, indeed, often a tightrope act in which stewards walked a very thin line, one that bridged the wide chasm that separated Black and white in America in the 1940s.

Rest and Relaxation Ashore

The great Black scholar and writer W.E.B. DuBois once wrote about being a Black man in America that "One ever feels his two-ness — an American, a Negro; two souls, two thoughts, two unreconciled strivings; two warring ideals in one dark body, whose dogged strength alone keeps it from being torn asunder" (DuBois, p. 2). While this passage was penned at a time (1903) when the Submarine Force was in its infancy, it seems particularly appropriate when applied to the men of the steward's branch and how they were treated in the navy during World War II. While aboard the boats, Black sailors serving as stewards were allowed to wear a uniform representative of their country, of being an American, and were treated, for the most part, like any other crewmember. While the fact that these men were Black was not forgotten (nor could it ever be as long as they could only serve as stewards), it was most often a secondary consideration in how they were judged in the small and confined world that defined life aboard a submarine. As long as a steward performed well in his regular and battle-station duties, he was known as a submariner first to his shipmates, and the fact that he was Black had little bearing on how he was regarded. However, the moment he stepped off the boat, his world usually changed — drastically. Now, he was no longer an American submariner first and foremost, but a Black man, and he was treated as such with little regard for his accomplishments at sea. Two "warring ideals" indeed.

The experiences of Black submariners ashore can be divided into four different types, based primarily on geographical location. These are as follows: in the continental United States, in Hawaii, in Australia, and at the several submarine advance bases located at Midway, Guam, Milne Bay, New Guinea, and elsewhere. In each of these places, life ashore for Black submariners, though relatively brief in duration (as it was for any submariner, unless he was ashore for good), was usually different from both that of other locations and, in some cases, the experiences of white shipmates in the same place and at the same time.

Life ashore in the United States was fairly predictable for Black submariners, who were there either to put a new boat into commission at one of the submarine construction yards already mentioned or for a brief period of respite while their boat was back in the states for an overhaul. With the existing racial conditions that then prevailed in the states, there was little surprise for Black stewards on leave, especially those from the south. Thus it was that most stewards knew that freedom in their off-time was dictated by whether or not they were above or below the Mason-Dixon line. Black sailors in Norfolk, Virginia, knew that jim crow laws prevailed there and that it did not matter what kind of military service you had done for your country. If you were Black and expected to ride on a bus, you were forced to sit in the back, even if there were no other passengers. When it came time for drinking and carousing, a popular pastime for many sailors, Black sailors knew they had to stick to their side of town,

Chief stewards on leave in San Diego, circa 1947. Otha Toler is in the center and Sam Wallace is on the right. Both were veteran patrollers of World War II. The other steward at left is unknown. (Photograph courtesy of S. Wallace.)

while whites stayed on their side, and seldom did the twain meet. Wrong as it was, that's just the way it was. In the north, things were somewhat more relaxed, and those stewards who were assigned to boats building in such locales as Boston; Groton, Connecticut; Portsmouth, New Hampshire; and Manitowoc, Wisconsin, had a bit more freedom to go where they pleased without fear of harassment. However, even in the north, problems caused by racial prejudice were not uncommon. Torpedoman William Whelen on *Brill* well recalls the time, while the boat was being finished at the Electric Boat Yard in Groton, Connecticut, that a group of men had liberty and went to the nearby city of Bridgeport. Among the men in this group was Steward's Mate 2nd Class George Bryant. One local bar, however, refused to let Bryant in due to his color, and trouble quickly resulted. Coming to their shipmate's defense, the men of *Brill* took action by barricading the doors to the bar. Patrons inside who wished to leave were allowed to do so, but no one else was allowed in the bar until Bryant was served. Soon, Bryant and his shipmates got the service they had wanted all along.

Many sailors, including stewards, found one source of relief and pleasure in the many houses of prostitution that could be found wherever sailors were found in numbers. Every seafaring town had their well known ladies of the evening. There was

"Battleship" Margaret in Norfolk, while Portsmouth had "Hungry" Helen and "One-Eyed" Mary (Wallace). However, despite this, there was still one taboo between Black and white sailors that could not usually be broken without consequences. This involved Black sailors dating white women. Even in such liberal-minded places as Manitowoc, Wisconsin, it was frowned upon by sailors. Black sailors sometimes even policed themselves on this issue. When *Puffer* was being built, many of her new crewmembers found local girlfriends to spend their off-hours with. Steward's Mate John Alden Pruitt was one of these men. The only problem was that his girl was white. Fellow steward James Patton, Jr., advised Pruitt that this would not go over well with his white shipmates and asked him to desist from such relations. Pruitt refused to do so until forcibly confronted by Patton. As the story goes, once Patton, a former Gold Gloves boxer, administered a whipping to Pruitt, then Pruitt saw the error of his ways and refrained from dating white women (McDonald).

Probably the most popular locale for submarine sailors in port was the area of San Diego, California. Here, there were many well-known bars, such as the Black and Tan and the Creole Palace, that Black sailors had frequented for years. While racial prejudice could be found nationwide, the prejudice that existed in California was of a somewhat mild nature. However, even here problems were not uncommon. San Diego, in particular, was a very racially divided city, and Black servicemen could run into trouble if they were in the wrong place at the wrong time. Veteran Steward Walter Wilson of *Trigger* would never forget the time when he was walking alone in the city in his dress uniform and a white man strode up to him and slapped him in the face without the slightest provocation. Controlling his anger, the mild-mannered Wilson questioned the man about what he was doing and was promptly told that a Black man such as himself had no right to wear a uniform (Wilson, Viola).

Probably the biggest racial contrast was found when Black servicemen traveled across country from one base or port to another. Some Black submariners well remember the train rides that they took across the country to and from different naval bases. As former Mess Attendant Carl Kimmons recalls,

> The train made lengthy stops at various stations en route. At these various stops the local civilians would have coffee and doughnut stands set up to give to the military on the train. Priority was given to the white sailors — if there was anything left, the African American sailors could have them.... African American guards were used to ensure the safe passage of German prisoners of war to camps in the United States. At the train stops, the German prisoners — who had previously been trying to kill American soldiers — were permitted to eat in the restaurants along the way. Their African American guards were not! [Kimmons].

Despite the strong regional prejudice that existed in the United States, many white sailors were sympathetic to the Black stewards that were their shipmates and stood up for them when trouble occurred. Steward's Mate Robert Goens on *Icefish*, a native of Indiana, was little used to the racial conditions he found in New Orleans after his boat transited the Mississippi River from Manitowoc to the Gulf of Mexico. As he recalls

> There were water fountains and restrooms labeled for whites only and colored only. We took these signs down and threw them in the water. My friend that

The crew of *Sailfish* at Sloppy Joe's Bar in Havana, Cuba, in 1944. Steward Killraine Newton is at the center, rear, while the Black man in the front, right, was the group's driver. Unlike many areas in southern waters, Cuba was fun for sailors of all colors. (Photograph courtesy of Ray Bunt.)

was with me, who was white, was targeted by a person on shore pointing at him and saying that if he did not dive in the water and get those signs, he would be thrown in the water. Instead, my friend threw him in the water [Goens].

It is also interesting to note that such prejudices as those found in the south were found in even more southerly locations outside this country in which the United States government operated. When the *Parche* shipped through the Panama Canal Zone in late 1943, former steward Carl Kimmons remembers that he had his "first encounter with segregated water fountains labeled 'gold' and 'silver.' I took a drink from both of them. The water tasted the same" (Kimmons).

Even the British island of Bermuda, which was sometimes a stopping-off place, had its restrictions. Here, as Carl Kimmons relates, another "steward and I went ashore and went to the USO. After a short time there, we were politely advised that there was another USO for Black sailors. We left and took one look at the less-than-substantial Black USO and were very disappointed. We didn't stay there very long" (Kimmons).

One exception to that prejudice found in southern regions was the island of Cuba. When heading off to the war zone, many crewmembers had a brief period of liberty just before their boat transited the Canal Zone. Many sailors, stewards included, made the short trip to Cuba, enjoying the exotic clubs and bars found in the capital city of Havana. In many bars, one of the most popular being Sloppy Joe's, Blacks and whites could drink together without the same racial atmosphere as that found in the southern United States. All in all, the war years saw only a slight change in race relations in the United States, and it little mattered that Blacks, like their white countrymen, had donned a uniform and fought against the Axis powers. The "back of the bus" mentality still prevailed.

A second area where Black submariners spent a fair amount of time ashore was in Hawaii, on the island of Oahu, near Honolulu, where the United States Navy's Pacific headquarters were based at Pearl Harbor. This tropical paradise would seem to have been an ideal haven for submariners on rest and relaxation leave, and so it was for white submariners. However, this was not the case for Black sailors, many of whom have called the prejudicial conditions that existed there worse than that found in any southern city in the continental United States. Why was there such a disparity? Given their racial makeup and their easy-going and friendly attitude, native islanders were not the problem. Steward's Mate Mason Smith, a native of Georgia, probably said it best when he commented that "The United States Navy had a way of transporting their prejudices worldwide" (Smith, Mason B.). This was especially true in Hawaii, where the military had a large presence during the war and still does today. Indeed, it would seem that, when it came to such a presence, the military had a penchant for adopting the jim crow attitude of the south, rather than the more liberal-minded attitudes found in the north. However, this is not surprising, as the military establishment in the United States was conservative by nature, and had many southerners in positions of leadership, including Tennessean Frank Knox as Secretary of the Navy.

The island of Oahu was ideally suited for all sailors on leave, especially submariners. Not only was the climate idyllic, but there were also plenty of bars and houses of prostitution that catered to sailors. In addition, the navy recognized early on that a place was needed for submariners coming off patrol to stay and unwind in a relaxed atmosphere. To that end, the navy confiscated the Royal Hawaiian Hotel on the beach at Waikiki, a bright pink building that was reserved for submariners. Here, the men could stay free of charge for several weeks while they were on leave before reporting back to their boat. All submariners could have a room at the Royal Hawaiian, Black or white, without any segregation. In many cases, Black and white shipmates shared a room together. Because of the famous Royal Hawaiian Hotel (now a National Historic Landmark), many white submariners recall Hawaii as a place without prejudice. Sadly, this was not the case. Once a Black submariner set foot outside of the Royal Hawaiian, only one side of Honolulu was open for him to safely go — the Black side of town. As Carl Kimmons states,

> Hawaii, the land of paradise was not a paradise for African Americans. There was a great deal of animosity between white sailors and African American sailors

in Hawaii. Not on the ships, but when ashore. When ashore, they each had their own sections of town and nightclubs to visit. If one happened to be in the wrong place at the wrong time, a confrontation would probably occur [Kimmons].

Richard Lucas, a steward's mate on *Raton*, stated it more succinctly when he said, "When ashore, we went our way, they [white shipmates] went theirs" (Lucas).

In order to keep sailors out of trouble, all guests at the Royal Hawaiian were not only registered but received a return pass every day they were there so that they could return that evening. The Royal Hawaiian was guarded by the military police, and curfew was at 10:00 P.M., though many sailors did not make it back on time. For those who did not make the curfew, it meant a night's stay in the brig. Few problems seem to have occurred at the Royal Hawaiian itself, and stewards were usually treated by their white shipmates there just as respectfully as they were on the boats. However, prejudice did rear its ugly head from time to time. Dave Veder, a seaman on *Wahoo*, remembers the time that that boat's steward, the affable Willie James, was harassed, and James and his white antagonist came to blows. The powerful James soon put the man in his place by force, and no further troubles resulted (Veder). While Veder cannot recall the nature of the harassment against James, it seems more than likely that it was race related, especially when it is remembered that back in the states in many locations Blacks and whites did not share the same hotels. Still, good times were usually had at the Royal Hawaiian. Sam Wallace of *Mingo* well recalls one time that he and other men staying at the hotel were restricted inside due to some type of epidemic that had broken out in Honolulu. In spite of this, Wallace remembers that "We did have a good time" (Wallace).

In addition to drinking, prostitution was a major source of "entertainment" for the men. The most "infamous" red light district in Honolulu was located on Hotel Street. This street "contained one after another of houses of prostitution. Just about every day the lines to spend two dollars ran from the door, down the hall, down the steps, and down the sidewalk on the street. And not just one place, but several. This was a common sight on Hotel Street during the war" (Kimmons). It was rather ironic that segregation existed in the night clubs, but not in the red light district. In the "very long lines that ran down the stairsteps, ... the lines contained both white and Black sailors, and there were very few disagreements. The prostitutes didn't mind. The only color they cared about was green" (Kimmons).

However, it must not be thought that all submariners engaged in such activities. Indeed, Walter Wilson, an older crewman and chief steward on *Trigger* was always discouraged at the many young prostitutes that met submarine sailors on their return from patrol. Many such men in the navy, like Wilson, were older, married or family men, nondrinkers, religiously inclined, or all of the above, and they sought more wholesome forms of entertainment. There were many such activities that fell into this category, including sightseeing at the island's many historical attractions or simply resting and relaxing in the hotel lobby or on the beach. Incredibly enough, there was even a skating rink that attracted many sailors. Admission and skate rental only cost fifty cents (Kimmons). Oftentimes, too, baseball or softball games were arranged between men from different submarines, and stewards were welcome participants. Another sporting form of entertainment was the boxing matches that were arranged between men from different boats. Many stewards were accomplished boxers and were the pride of their boat. One such man was *Atule*'s Steward's Mate 2nd Class Monroe Griffith of Chicago, Illinois. He was reputed to be a Golden Gloves boxer and, as one man recalls, was "our ace in the hole" in boxing matches with other boats (HC).

For those men that wanted the company of nice girls for the evening, there was always the USO club and canteen. Here, Black entertainers from the states came to give performances for Black servicemen, and the nights were often filled with the sounds of both jazz and big band music. On these evenings, Black servicemen could dance with the USO girls and, in between times, spend the time in conversation while being served refreshments. Just as in the states, USO activities were strictly segregated, with separate USO clubs (and performers) for Black and for white servicemen. Another place that was similar to this was one that had a small snack and ice cream bar with a dime-a-dance place on the second floor (Kimmons).

Finally, it is also worth noting that the same difficulties between Black and white servicemen that existed in the states when it came to women was also found in Hawaii, and Black sailors who dated either white women or native women were likely to get into trouble with white sailors, whether shipmate or not. With the segregationist policies then in effect in Hawaii, spurred on by the military establishment, troubles between Black and white sailors were bound to result. Luckily, these seem to have been minor in nature, with no large-scale problems such as those that occurred in Guam or back in the states (the Port Chicago incident) late in the war. Still, the tropical island of Hawaii that was a paradise for white servicemen during the war was somewhat less so for the men of the steward's branch.

A third area that submariners often spent time ashore in was Australia. Submarine facilities were set up in this country, beginning with those in Darwin on the north coast in late 1941 after the fall of the Phillipine Islands. While this base was a small refit station, more extensive bases were soon set up at Perth-Fremantle on the southwest coast and at Brisbane on the east coast. The submarine base at Perth-Fremantle was established beginning in March 1942 after the fall of Java, while the smaller base at Brisbane was established a month later. When these bases were established in early 1942, the submarines that operated from them were the only naval force in the area at the time. In order to accommodate submariners who were on leave from patrol, the navy leased two facilities, the King Edward Hotel in downtown Perth and the Ocean Beach Hotel on the seashore near the port of Fremantle. Among the many establishments that were frequented by Black sailors in Perth were the Westralia Café, the China Café, the All-Night Restaurant, and the bar in the Newcastle Hotel.

While Hawaii was a paradise for white sailors, it was Australia that was a paradise for Black sailors, particularly submariners. In fact, every Black submariner interviewed for this work that had spent time in that country had nothing but fond remembrances of life ashore there and nothing but praise for the people of Australia for their lack of prejudice and friendly attitude. Most men agree that any prejudice that was encountered in Australia was purely the result of the United States Navy and its own segregationist policies. Steward's Mate Hosey Mays on *Crevalle* remembers being told by his officers when going into Fremantle that there would be a $2,000 fine for fraternizing with Aborigines, and that stewards were the only men on board that were so warned. Mess Attendant 3rd Class William Allison of *Grampus*, and later a crewman on the submarine tender *Otus*, recalls that the Black stewards on the tender *Holland* were all restricted to the ship while it was in port at Albany after one steward "had had an involvement with a white Australian woman" there (Allison).

While Black American servicemen encountered few problems in Australia, the country had a deplorable track record of dealing with its native Aborigine population. Treated as "wards of the state," the Aborigines "were not citizens; they had no vote, and it was an offense for a white Australian to sell them liquor or to cohabit with them" (Huxley, pp. 22–22). However, the vast majority of full-blooded Aborignes lived in the remote interior of Australia, far from the large urban centers such as Perth and Brisbane. Most of the nonwhite Australians that lived in these cities, apart from a very few Aborignes, were of mixed descent, including Caucasian, Aborigne, or Polynesian backgrounds. Though these individuals were dark skinned, they were not treated as Aborignes and, as such, were not generally discriminated against by their own countryman. Though of mixed Aborigne descent, these individuals did not follow the traditional nomadic lifestyle of the Aborignes in the interior and, instead, lived, went to school, and worked under the same conditions as white Australians with few problems (Richardson). Some Australian people of mixed Aborigne descent believe that problems for them regarding race only came about when the American armed forces arrived early in the war (*ibid.*). Given the track record of the American military establishment in other places, such as Hawaii, this was certainly possible. It is also likely that military administrators, when establishing rules prohibiting serviceman from fraternizing with Aborignes, considered all dark-skinned Australians as being Aborignes, whether or not they were considered as such by their own countrymen. However, despite Australia's dismal record when it came to dealing with the Aborigne population, America's Black servicemen stationed there were held in a separate, and much higher regard.

As in the United States, problems for Black sailors in Australia were often the result of their white counterparts. One way that white servicemen tried to disparage Black sailors was by telling the local people, especially Australian women, that Blacks had tails. This sort of storytelling was not a new tactic by white servicemen, as the same sort of thing went on in England, and it seems to have had the opposite effect than that intended. Far from being repelled, many Australian women were curious about the stories, and "this "tale" only made African Americans seem more interesting" (Kimmons). Still, this type of racial slur caused "many confrontations" (*ibid.*) and resulted in many a brawl between Black and white sailors. Robert Goens, a steward's mate on *Icefish*, well recalls one night while at a bar in Perth when "a big Black serviceman jumped up on the bar and dropped his pants. He said 'See, we do not grow tails at midnight'" (Goens).

Both Brisbane and Perth were great places for Black submariners on leave. Hosey Mays, a steward's mate on *Crevalle*, remembers that many of the stewards stuck together and found their own housing while on leave instead of using the hotels leased by the navy. Many times, the stewards were able to get excess "chow" that was left over from boats returning from war patrol, and endless hours were spent drinking, playing cards, listening to music and, of course, chasing women (Mays). Officer's Cook Sam Wallace of *Mingo* well recalls the small rest camp in the little country village of Coolangatta, about seventy-five miles south of Brisbane, where he and other stewards stayed, stating that "we had a blast" (Wallace). Another such rest camp was the one located north of Brisbane at Toowoomba.

For those men that wanted a different type of experience, local residents were more than willing to help. Citizens of both Perth and Brisbane opened their homes and churches to the American servicemen stationed in their country without regard to color. Walter Patrick from *Bluegill* attended a Methodist church in Perth that accepted him "wholeheartedly," and one of the congregation's white families invited him to their home for lunch (Patrick). One family that did such entertaining was the Davidsons of Brisbane. Considered Black by American standards, the Davidsons were actually of mixed Aborigne and Polynesian descent. Their daughter, Moyna, well recalls that

> During the war years in Brisbane I had a chance to meet a lot of the Black servicemen who served on subs. Our house was a place they could come to and feel free to be themselves. We would play cards or go to the movies or the USO club [Richardson].

The USO club referred to was called the George Washington Carver club and was for Blacks only. White sailors, as in Hawaii, had their own USO clubs. While parts of Brisbane and Perth were "off-limits" (*ibid.*) to Black sailors, this color line was established by the United States Navy and had little or no bearing on how the Australian people viewed Black sailors. Indeed, it is likely that Black American sailors were welcome in Australia because of past experiences. The Davidson family of Brisbane had memories dating back over thirty years to the time when America's Great White Fleet of naval vessels visited Australia during its visit to the Far East and many men of the steward's branch stayed with local families during their time ashore. The repeat of this experience during the years of World War II would be equally successful. One man that was a frequent visitor to the Davidson house in Brisbane was Officer's Cook 3rd Class Charles Richardson of *Kingfish*, starting in 1943. As the story goes, Richardson "was liked by my relatives and friends. My mother was crazy about him" (*ibid.*). Mrs. Davidson was not the only person that was "crazy" about Richardson. So, too, was her daughter Moyna. At war's end, following a brief waiting period, Moyna Davidson and Charles Richardson were married in Honolulu in June 1947. The new Mrs. Richardson entered the United States under the provisions of the War Bride Act. Ironically, despite her Aborigne background, it was not until Moyna Richardson moved to the United States that she ever experienced any racism or discrimination (*ibid.*).

Charles Richardson was not the only steward to come home with an "Aussie" war bride. Also stationed in Australia was Officer's Cook 2nd Class Wallace Coleman. He first served in Brisbane with Naval Repair Unit 89 in August 1943 before joining the crew of *Pollack*. While serving in a submarine relief crew, he met young Emma Beryl Martin, also of mixed descent, who was a hostess at the USO club, and the two soon began a whirlwind courtship. On October 3, 1944, after gaining the required permission from his commanding officer, Wallace Coleman and Emma Martin were married at St. Stephen's Cathedral in Brisbane. How many other stewards married Australian war brides is unknown, but such marriages are, nevertheless, an indication of the high degree of racial tolerance found in that country.

As in Hawaii, Australia was also a place where submariners on leave played sports. That most traditional of American games, baseball (and its variant, softball) was played

The wedding photograph of Australian native Emma Martin and Officer's Cook 2nd Class Wallace Coleman in Brisbane, Australia, in 1944. Life for the Colemans would be vastly different in the United States, where race relations were still a vexing problem. (Photograph courtesy of the Coleman family.)

wherever American serviceman gathered. Boxing, too, was a popular sport. New Orleans native Wallace Coleman was a boxer while in the navy overseas, and it may even be that one of the ways he won his Australian bride was by his athletic prowess. Coleman was a strong boxer, "solid as a rock" some said, and though he boxed as a lightweight, he defeated an Australian heavyweight in one match (Coleman). However, the most renowned of all the navy boxers during this era was Chief Steward Dave Ball. After making four war patrols on *Rasher* in 1944 and winning the Bronze Star, Ball served in Submarine Division 121 in Australia. He was persuaded to fight for Australia's boxing middleweight championship in 1944 and was the victor. He would later lose this title, but only because he was transferred back to the United States and could not return to defend it. However, Ball was still regarded by Nat Fischer's *Ring* magazine as one of the top ten contenders in the world for the middleweight crown (*Submarine Base Gazette*, 7/2/1948, p. 4). Ironically, the athletic achievements of Dave Ball were not a source of inspiration and pride just to the men of the steward's branch (many of whom knew him personally) but also the entire Submarine Force. Many white submariners that did not know Ball personally were well aware of his achievements and were proud of how they represented the entire United States Navy, and the Submarine Force in particular.

All in all, Australia was just about as good as it could get for Black submariners on leave. True, they did not have all the comforts of home, nor did they have their loved ones close by (excepting the new-found loves of Richardson and Coleman), but the one thing they did have was the respect of the people whose country they were sent to help defend. That has never been forgotten by the men of the steward's branch.

The final areas under consideration in which Black submariners spent time when not on patrol were in the several advance bases used for submarine refits and refueling located on Midway and Johnston Islands; Milne Bay, New Guinea; Majuro Atoll in the Marshall Islands; and Saipan and Guam in the Marianas Islands. While rest camps were set up in these areas, they did not have the same comforts and attractions as those found in Hawaii and Australia.

The first of these advance bases to be established was those on Midway Island and Johnston Island in June 1942. This occurred after the decisive Battle of Midway, in which the United States Navy dealt the attacking Japanese force a crushing blow by sinking all four of her aircraft carriers. With Midway Island now secure, it was immediately utilized as a forward base for submariners. As its name implies, this small atoll is ideally located in the central Pacific Ocean, and it cut down the travel for submarines on war patrol from Pearl Harbor to Japanese waters by nearly 2,000 miles. Here and on Johnston Island, submarines on their way to and from patrol could top off with fuel, make last-minute repairs, and get stores, medical aid, and crew replacements as the need arose. To that end, there was always a small group of submarine relief crewmen stationed there as part of the submarine divisions that used Midway as their home base. Submarine crew, stewards included, who were either stationed on Midway Island or on leave, stayed at the small "hotel" called Gooneyville Lodge. It was named for the many gooney birds that made the island its home. In addition to the hotel, there were several beer and mess halls set up for the sailors to use in their off hours, provided they had the appropriate pass. Midway was described by one steward as being "lots of sun, gooney birds, and playing Ping-Pong. It was a small island with nothing much to do" (Kimmons). This, indeed, was true, and for most stewards on leave time was spent just relaxing, drinking, or playing sports. As in other places, Midway had its own baseball diamond, and a small newspaper was even published on the island which gave the results from these games and other news items of interest concerning the war. The island's gooney birds were also a source of amusement, at least for some, and many men enjoyed watching these large, awkward birds strut about.

Johnston Island seems to have had even less entertainment, as most stewards recall, than Midway. Still, there was plenty of socializing going on whenever sailors got together, and the men of the steward's branch were no exception. Steward's Mate Alonza Davis was renowned aboard *Pargo* for his habit of missing the boat at sailing time. He had already done so back in the states and did it again when *Pargo* set out on patrol from Johnston Island. As he recalls, "I was just jiving with my friends and missed the boat!" (Davis, Alonza).

One thing that was lacking on both islands was women, no doubt a disappointment for many sailors. There was no native population of girls to choose from, and the island's only inhabitants were the men of the United States Navy. As difficult as this was for some sailors, it was probably just as well when it came to the men of the steward's branch. Because this one source of conflict was lacking, there seems to have been little or no conflict between Black and white sailors on Johnston or Midway Islands. Like any small tropical island, sailors on leave or in-between boat assignments enjoyed their stay at first but soon became bored and were glad to leave.

The next advance base to be established was that at Milne Bay in New Guinea. This base was established In October 1943 after General Douglas MacArthur's forces had defeated the Japanese on New Guinea in a campaign that lasted from June through September. Now that the island was secure, the submarine tender *Fulton* was sent to Milne Bay in October 1943, and submarines from Brisbane began to use it as a forward base for refitting and refueling purposes. As at Midway, submarines were now over a thousand miles closer to their operating area along the equator. While replacement crew members for submarines were stationed here, they seem to have been few in number. Few stewards that made shore at Milne Bay have much recollection of the area, either good or bad. For most, their time in New Guinea was rather short, so no lasting impression was formed. William Allison, formerly of *Grampus* and subsequently aboard *PC 479*, remembers that "the only recreation we had in New Guinea was to go ashore and drink hot beer" (Allison). Like Midway, New Guinea does not seem to have had much to recommend itself to submarine sailors. Whether sailors off duty, either Black or white, had relations there with native women is unknown.

A third area that acted as a submarine advance base and rest camp was Majuro Atoll in the Marshall Islands. Though Majuro Atoll was unoccupied by the Japanese, it was not until the other islands in the Marshall group were liberated in early 1944 that the fine anchorage there could be utilized. With the establishment of a base there, submarines were yet another 2,000 miles closer to Japan. By February 1944, a rest camp was set up for submariners on the small neighboring island of Enimonetto, renamed Myrna Island by the Americans. While no submarine stewards could be found who remembered a stay at this rest facility, its location and size made it comparable with those rest facilities on Midway Island.

The fourth, and final group of islands that had major advance bases established for submarines, as well as rest facilities, were in the Marianas Islands on Saipan and

The crew of *Silversides* at Camp Dealey on Guam in 1945. Steward William Brown is at far left. This group looks akin to the crew of pirate ships of olden days! (Photograph courtesy of Joe Allison.)

Guam. While Saipan was primarily a refit and refueling base, Guam was used for this same purpose but also had a rest camp for submariners. Both islands were occupied by the Japanese during the war until liberation by United States forces in August 1944. The battles to capture these important islands were among the bloodiest in the Pacific war, and casualties were high. Once these islands were "secure," their use as a forward base by the Submarine Force was almost immediately placed into effect. Their use effectively cut in half the distance submarines had to travel from either Australia or Milne Bay, New Guinea, to Japanese home waters and soon resulted in the closing of the submarine bases at Fremantle-Perth and Brisbane.

In October 1944 a rest camp on Guam was established and named "Camp Dealey" in memory of "destroyer killer" Commander Sam Dealey. As the captain of *Harder*, Dealey had achieved outstanding success on five war patrols before his loss and that of his entire crew on August 24, 1944. In addition to having a rest camp named after him, Dealey was also posthumously awarded the Congressional Medal of Honor. Life at Camp Dealey on Guam was much like it was on other islands with rest camps. The hours were mostly spent relaxing on the beach, drinking, and playing sports. The men on Guam stayed in small huts that were rather more primitive than the facilities in other island rest camps like Midway.

However, there was one dangerous element to life on Guam that would have tragic consequences for submariners. While the island was under U.S. control, there were still small pockets of fanatical Japanese soldiers that refused to surrender and hid out in the jungle. As long as U.S. servicemen stayed in the secure areas, they were relatively safe. Even so, each hut had "a .30 cal carbine and a .45 cal pistol" and, as one sailor facetiously stated it was "some way to spend a rest" (Anderson, p. 7). The danger inherent in this jungle rest camp became painfully clear in February 1945 when seven enlisted men on leave from *Sea Fox* hired a guide to take them into the jungle on a "strictly forbidden souvenir hunt" (Blair, p. 835). The group was ambushed by a group of Japanese soldiers, and five of the crew were killed, as was their guide. Not long after this, while the crew of *Sea Fox* were still on "rest," several Japanese soldiers broke into a supply area and one was caught behind the mess hall. Even this late in the war, a submariner spending his rest and relaxation time on Guam must have been a little nervous, and probably happy to get back aboard the boat and out on patrol.

As in Hawaii and Australia, Black sailors on leave on Guam also had to contend with the issue of relations with native woman on the island. Once again, the problem was not with the native islanders themselves but with the white servicemen who were also on the island. In particular, some white members of the marines stationed on the island were upset by the fact that Black servicemen were involved with native women, specifically those "in the village of Agana and about the island" (Peters, p. 13). Whether these marines were upset by the very fact that Black sailors were even dating native women or because they were an added source of competition for the affections of the native girls is unknown. Whatever the cause, it resulted, as one historian states, in "frequent unprovoked annoyances and assaults by White Marines based on the island" against "Negro naval personnel," resulting in "numerous instances of violence" (*ibid.*).

This was not the only problem that Black sailors experienced on the island. Other complaints involved a lack of promotions, a failure to place the men in jobs for which they had been trained, and the fact that, despite the island's location in the war zone, only white servicemen were allowed to carry weapons. While these complaints involved Black sailors that were stationed on the island, it is likely that they had some spill-over effect with the submarine stewards that spent time ashore on Guam, especially in the area of relations with native women. The situation came to a head on the evening of December 24, 1944, when a group of white marines fired on some Black sailors in Agana "because of their attention to local Guamanian girls" (Peters, p. 14). Later that evening, a group of white marines invaded the segregated camp of the Black sailors, claiming that one of their own had been hit by a rock thrown by the Black sailors. Rumors circulated that night and into Christmas Day, including those that reported one Black sailor dead and another wounded. As a result, on Christmas night, a group of forty Black sailors left their camp without permission, confiscating three unauthorized vehicles for transportation. The men were subsequently apprehended by members of the Marine Military Police and were later charged with rioting, unauthorized use of government property, and like offenses. Thus ended a series of incidents that have since been termed the "Guam disorders." The Black sailors that were involved all received sentences ranging from four months to four years in prison but, thanks to vigorous efforts by such groups back in the states as the National Association for the Advancement of Colored Peoples (NAACP), the navy reconsidered the sentences, and all the

Black sailors involved were released by February 1946. Not surprisingly, none of the marines involved were punished. How these "disorders" directly affected Black submariners on leave is unknown, since those men interviewed for this work have few memories about Guam. However, the Guam disorders are certainly indicative of the racial climate that would have been experienced by those submarine stewards on leave that traveled about the island. If the stewards stuck close to camp and did not pursue native women, then their stay on Guam and at Camp Dealey was probably uneventful.

A final area that must be considered in regard to the men of the steward's branch and their time ashore is that of official ship functions. Once a submariner was ashore and on rest leave, his time was his own to do with as he pleased. Whether he chose to stay in his room, say, at the Royal Hawaiian Hotel and read and relax or go out to a given locale's bars and restaurants was not only his decision but at his own expense (except for free lodging). As long as a submarine sailor on leave, whether Black or white, made it back to his boat in time for the next patrol, he was free and on his own. However, during his time ashore, there were occasions when official ship functions were organized, and the whole crew was encouraged to attend. These functions were usually in the form of ship's parties, organized by officers and crew perhaps to celebrate an outstanding war patrol or the ship's "birthday" or some other important occasion. Most of the time, these were considered "official" navy functions and, as such, all expenses for food, drink, etc., were generally paid for by the navy or from a general fund established on the boat for such a purpose. One might surmise that such parties, being official events, were open to all members of the crew, but this was not always true when it came to the men of the steward's branch. Depending on where such parties were held, stewards were prohibited from attending based on their color. Sometimes this prohibition was in the form of direct verbal orders stating that they could not attend, while at other times stewards were merely discouraged from attending. This unwritten policy of excluding stewards from ship's parties was a wide and long-standing practice in the United States Navy and was by no means limited to the boats of the Submarine Force.

Ship's parties were usually first held back in the United States when the boat was commissioned during the war. To celebrate this accomplishment, the formal addition of another unit to the Submarine Force, a party was often organized and attended by officers and enlisted crewman. Not only did this celebrate the men's hard work in getting the boat in operation but it was also a way to help the new crew bond and get to know each other. These celebrations were usually held on land where the new submarine was built and launched, such as Groton, Portsmouth, or Manitowoc. Judging by the group photos that were taken at these events, often showing the men in party hats and with their girlfriends in attendance, stewards were warmly welcomed at these parties. The color line often found ashore was temporarily forgotten, and the men could have an evening of fun and entertainment. Steward's Mate 2nd Class George Bryant, a "wild one" from New York, was a popular shipmate at *Brill*'s Halloween-time commissioning party in Groton in October 1944 and is remembered for the hilarious "skeleton dance" he performed on stage (Whelan).

Subsequent ship's parties that may have been held while a boat was in the war zone were, however, often a different story. At Pearl Harbor and in Australia such events often excluded Black stewards. Sometimes, this was done by direct order of the captain

The ship's party for *Brill* in Perth, Australia, April 1945. Veteran patroller Officer's Cook 1st Class Leslie Hamilton is in the back row, raising his glass in a toast. A seasoned submariner with prior war patrols on *Thresher* and *Billfish*, it was men like Hamilton that gave stability and experience to the crews that manned the new boats that joined the war effort. (Photograph courtesy of W. Whelan.)

of the ship in question. In this case, where a ship's party was held that stewards were not allowed to attend, the stewards as a group were often given money by the officers to have their own get together. Such action was clearly an extension of navy racism and prejudice. Most other units of the United States Navy had similar practices when it came to excluding Black stewards from ship's parties. Even before mess attendants Carl Kimmons and Anderson Royal volunteered for submarine duty, they experienced firsthand such practices while aboard the destroyer *McFarland*. Two other stewards that were affected by this exclusionary policy were Robert Goens and John Ellis on *Icefish*. When that boat was in Perth, Australia, in July 1945 and had a ship's party, both men were excluded because of their race. However, fellow shipmate Howard Jameson recalls that Goens was anxious to go and asked his shipmates if they would help him pass as a dark-skinned Caucasian, asking that they "let me be white tonight" (Jameson, Howard). The light-complexioned Goens was well liked on *Icefish* and made all of her war patrols, so his white shipmates agreed to help him out, and he went to the party. While Goens is shown in the photo that was taken at the party, his fellow steward, Ellis is not. He was too Black to attend. With all the teamwork and camaraderie that existed on board submarines, it is hard to believe that stewards could ever be expressly prohibited from attending such events. The fact that they were excluded in some cases only serves to reinforce the fact that once a steward was ashore, he was a Black man, which was the overriding factor on which he was judged.

In addition to being directly excluded from such social events, there was another way in which Black stewards were kept from attending. As Steward's Mate Hosey Mays on *Crevalle* remembers, stewards were often kept in the dark about such events and "didn't hear about such things, and we weren't always invited" (Mays). Because of this underhanded tactic, many stewards did not attend these events, and their failure to appear was often interpreted by their white shipmates as a sign that they did not want to attend such affairs. While the exclusion of Black stewards from ship's parties and other events was widely practiced, there were no specific rules about such events, and it must be said that many boats did the right thing by including their stewards in whatever events were organized. It is also true that, in many cases, their fellow white shipmates, such as those on *Icefish*, were sympathetic to the men of the steward's branch and welcomed their attendance at these functions, even if it meant breaking the rules.

LEAVING THE BOAT

For all submariners the time always came when they left the boat on which they were serving. This came about in two ways: either a crew member was ordered off the boat, whether or not he wanted to go, or he asked to be transferred on his own. Each of these situations could have both positive and negative aspects that were, in many ways, unique to the all volunteer Submarine Force.

For those men ordered off the boat, this was done for a variety of reasons. The most common of these was the regular crew rotation that occurred after each war patrol, when approximately 25 percent of the crew was transferred off for other assignments. This was done so that submarine crews would always be comprised of a mixture of veteran patrollers and newer crewmembers who could learn from them. Seasoned veterans that were transferred off the boat were usually transferred to another submarine, sent back to the United States to "new construction," or sent to a submarine tender for duty in a submarine relief crew. Being sent stateside for "new construction" meant that he would be part of a boat that was then building and would soon be commissioned. Once the boat was commissioned and her crew had gone through a short period of training, it was time to go back to the war zone. Several of the many stewards who went through this cycle were Albert Rozar, who made one war patrol on *Gudgeon* before going to *Pargo*; Magnus Wade, who made five patrols on *Gunnel* and then put *Dentuda* in commission; and Anderson Royal, who made four patrols on *Silversides* before going to *Dragonet* in new construction.

The path from one submarine to another was not always easy, and sometimes the navy bureaucracy worked in mysterious, and often senseless, ways. After making four war patrols on *Plunger*, Steward Carl Kimmons was transferred back to the United States and assigned to the destroyer *Scott*. This was no place for a submarine sailor, and every day Kimmons put in for a transfer back to submarines but was continually turned down. While in the states, Kimmons saw the nearly all–Black crew of the destroyer *Mason* readying their ship for commissioning, the first major U.S. warship to be so manned, and thought "how wonderful it would be to be on that ship" (Kimmons). Still, he *was* a submariner and continued to put in for a transfer back to the boats. After three months, his request was finally granted, and his orders came for a return to submarine duty. There was just one problem: when Kimmons received his orders, *Scott* was in the middle of New York harbor getting ready for duty as a convoy escort in the Atlantic. He quickly packed his seabag and went to the quarterdeck for transfer by motor launch to shore. After his belongings were minutely inspected and items that were not issued by *Scott* confiscated, Kimmons was transported by motor launch across the harbor and put ashore in New York, left on his own to travel the long distance to the receiving station at Pier 90. As Kimmons later recalled, the *Scott*'s executive officer did not appreciate his constant transfer requests and "he got his revenge by inspecting my seabag, confiscating articles, and making me take the motor launch to get to shore.... However, I was so glad to be returning to submarine duty that I would have walked" (Kimmons). Carl Kimmons subsequently joined the commissioning crew of *Parche* in November 1943 and made her first three war patrols.

As the experiences of Carl Kimmons demonstrate, stewards were not always anxious to leave their boat, even if they were going to another submarine. Hosey Mays, a steward's mate on *Crevalle*'s first two war patrols, found the boat and her skipper, Hank Munson, a good one and didn't want to leave. However, when it came time for him to be rotated off the boat, he had no choice but to go. He would later serve in a submarine relief crew at Fremantle before going to *Bowfin*.

In addition to the normal rotating of crews, stewards and men of other rates were also sent off the boats for various other reasons. As previously discussed at length, sometimes this was due to disciplinary action. However, such action did not mean a man was off the boats for good. Officer's Cook 3rd Class Joseph Anderson made the first three war patrols of *Bowfin* but was sent off the boat for unstated disciplinary action. Two months later he went to *Flasher* for one patrol before going to shore duty. Sometimes men were sent off the boats because of accidents or medical reasons beyond their control. Steward's Mate Isaac Johnson, a 1944 enlistee from Texarkana, Arkansas, put *Sennet* into commission at Portsmouth, New Hampshire, in August 1944. While enroute to the war zone and transiting the Panama Canal, Johnson was on the pier helping to load supplies when he was hit by a torpedo truck. *Sennet* continued on to the Pacific, but Johnson was left at Panama and hospitalized for two months. He would later ride *Roncador* to Pearl Harbor but, with the conflict at an end, made no war patrols.

In an unusual situation, *Bluefish* had not one, but two men, Steward's Mates 2nd Class Isaac Mack and Bill Buffington, disqualified in January 1945 due to "chronic seasickness" (National Archives, reel 756). Mack lasted for 36 days, while Buffington only lasted 11 after coming aboard the boat at Mare Island, California, in December 1944. While the problem of seasickness was not itself an unusual one, the fact that two stewards on the same boat at the same time suffered prolonged bouts of this most uncomfortable malady harsh enough to force them out of the Submarine Force was uncommon. Another man who was forced out of submarines due to illness was Mess Attendant 2nd Class William Allison from Charlotte, North Carolina. After making one war patrol on *Grampus*, he was slated to go out on her next patrol in July 1942 when he fell ill with a throat infection. His replacement was another North Carolinian, Mess Attendant 3rd Class Donald Fenner from Halifax, who was serving on the submarine tender *Otus*. Little did William Allison know then that that throat infection would save his life. Donald Fenner and seventy shipmates were lost when *Grampus* was sunk eight months later while patrolling Blackett Strait in the Solomon Islands.

Probably one of the most unusual reasons for a steward being sent off a boat can be found in the case of Chief Steward Walter Wilson on *Trigger*. A native of Junction City, Kansas, Wilson served for eleven war patrols on that boat, along with her executive officer Edward Beach. However, in early 1944 Beach received orders sending him to new construction in Portsmouth, New Hampshire. As he reflects in his memoirs, he called Walter Wilson "to the wardroom and summarily dismissed him from the ship. No one was going to be able to say he had served in her longer than I, I said, handing him a just-made-up set of orders sending him to our squadron relief crew. He had richly earned a rest, I told him, and I wanted him to get it. Wilson, always the good sailor ... took the paper. We shook hands and bade each other goodbye" (Beach, *Salt and Steel*, p. 54). However, Beach had not got the best of Walter Wilson, for Beach's replacement on *Trigger* tore up his orders and Wilson made two more war patrols. He made 13 runs in all on *Trigger*, more than any other crewman on that boat.

Steward's Mate L.C. Fisher, who made the fourth war patrol of *Parche* in December 1944–January 1945 under Captain Woodrow McCrory. (Photograph courtesy of C. Kimmons.)

In the case of stewards voluntarily leaving their boat, the process was usually quite simple. After coming into port from patrol, the matter of their replacement was often made on their own if they wanted off the boat. After his third war patrol on *Parche*, Carl Kimmons "decided it was time to get off" when the submarine docked at Midway Island. He found his own replacement and swapped duty with L.C. Fisher. While Fisher went aboard *Parche* and served several war patrols, Kimmons stayed on Midway. As Kimmons later stated "I talked Fisher into taking my place. All the ship wanted was a warm body. They didn't care about not having attended submarine school" (Kimmons). Likewise, Sam Wallace, after serving four patrols on *Mingo*, needed a break and went ashore to find his replacement. This would turn out to be Mason B. Smith, who would stay on *Mingo* when Wallace returned to the boat for her sixth war patrol. As he recalls, Wallace came on board the submarine tender *Griffin* and went below deck where her stewards were involved in a card game. He asked Smith, "Man, you want to go to sea?" (Smith, Mason B.), and he agreed. They have remained friends to this day.

In reality, it was fairly easy for Black submariners to get off a boat if they so desired. Since submarine duty was voluntary, any man could ask off the boat at any time, and permission to do so was usually given. In the case of stewards and officer's cooks, it was probably even easier, as few submarine commanders were personally attached to the men that served them in this capacity. Often it happened that, upon returning from a war patrol, a steward seeking a replacement would go ashore to where the base stewards were quartered or go on board the submarine tender and seek out the steward's compartment below decks. Here, just as Sam Wallace did, he would ask if anyone would want to take his place on the boat for its next patrol. Often there was another steward, perhaps bored with relief duty and in need of a change of scenery, who was willing to take on this new challenge.

What were the reasons for men of the steward's branch wanting off the boat? Many times it was simply because they needed a rest from the rigors of being at sea, and shore duty was much more relaxing. However, there were also two other reasons that often factored in their decision to leave. The most powerful of these was the thought, some may call it a premonition, that their luck might be running out and that they might be on the next boat to be lost with all hands. As Sam Wallace on *Mingo* remembers, "I made five runs on *Mingo* and got off before the sixth because a lot of buddies were coming up missing. In other words, I was scared. The worst thing to hear was some meat head on the tender yelling down to you 'I bet you $100 that you won't make it back'" (Wallace).

Wallace, indeed, had reason to be worried. During the time between *Mingo*'s fifth and sixth war patrols in October and November 1944, the Submarine Force suffered more losses in a two-month period than at any other time during the war. Between October 3 and November 9, seven boats, *Seawolf*, *Shark* (2), *Tang*, *Escolar*, *Albacore*, *Growler*, and *Scamp* were lost with all hands. Another boat, *Darter*, was lost to enemy action, but her entire crew was saved by *Dace*. While nine men would survive from *Tang* as prisoners of war, the loss of so many boats in such a short time was a chilling reminder to the crews of other boats what fate might lay in store for them. Wallace was not the only man with such premonitions. Another was Walter Wilson on *Trigger*. Viola Wilson remembers that her husband, then a bachelor, just had to get off the boat after thirteen runs, fearing that if he stayed on too long he might never get the chance to marry (Wilson, Viola). Walter Wilson was right, for *Trigger*'s luck ran out on her next patrol, when she was sunk with all hands in March 1944 west of the Nanshei Shoto in the East China Sea.

Other stewards during the war may have left their boats because of such premonitions, though it may also be true that they just needed a respite. Like Sam Wallace, Steward's Mate Elijah Dawson on *Drum* took a break, serving on that boat's second through fifth war patrols, skipping the sixth, and was back aboard for two subsequent patrols. Another such man to serve in this way was Steward 3rd Class William Brandon on *Bang*. After making that boat's first four war patrols under Commander Anton

Chief Officer's Cook Walter Wilson and his wife Viola on their wedding day, August 11, 1945. Wilson made 13 war patrols on *Trigger* from 1942 to 1945, getting off just before her final, fateful patrol in which the entire crew was lost. The frame for this photograph is made of leather and was crafted by Wilson while doing duty on *Sirago* shortly after his marriage. (Photograph courtesy of V. Wilson.)

Gallaher, Brandon left the boat prior to her fifth patrol in December 1944 only to rejoin her for her sixth and final war patrol in March 1945. One man that left his boat not once, but twice, was Officer's Cook 3rd Class J.P. Buttrill. He made *Spearfish*'s first war patrol in February 1942, then was off for two patrols before joining again for that boat's fourth through ninth war patrols, from June 1942 to January 1944. He then left the boat for one war patrol only to return for *Spearfish*'s final two patrols of the war. Buttrill made a total of nine war patrols in all, and likely counted himself a lucky man. On his last war patrol in December 1944, *Spearfish*, now commanded by Cy Cole, was mistakenly attacked by an army B-24 Liberator bomber and was nearly sunk.

Another man who had luck on his side was new submariner Isaac Johnson. Top man in his class at Bainbridge, he quickly volunteered for submarine duty and was sent to New London. He was slated to go aboard the first new boat there that was heading off to war. However, his friend and fellow classmate, Steward's Mate 1st Class Benjamin Evans, had already scoped out the boat and was accepted as a steward by the captain of *Escolar*. Evans was from Pittsburgh, Pennsylvania, the father of two children, and could use the extra submarine pay. Despite the fact that, as Johnson states, "I wanted to go, that boat was supposed to be mine," there was nothing he could do, and he would have to wait for another boat to ship out on. Once again, the gods of fate were kind to one man, and at the same time harsh to another. Evans, Steward's Mate 2nd Class James Raley, and the rest of her crew were lost on *Escolar*'s first and only war patrol just months later, in October 1944, the likely victim of a mine in the Yellow Sea. However, not all stewards were as lucky as Isaac Johnson. Steward's Mate 1st Class William Rodney, who enlisted from Minnesota, served in the relief crew for *Snook* for three months in mid–1944. He must have liked what he saw, as he later joined the crew of *Snook* in August 1944 in time to make her seventh war patrol. It was a fatal move, as *Snook* would be lost with all hands, Rodney and Steward 3rd Class William Shelton included, two patrols later in April 1945.

Well-known steward William Knight may have been one of the luckiest men in the Submarine Force. He first served on surface craft, all of which were sunk after he left. Knight then went to submarines, serving on *Tunny*, and later transferred to *Whale*. Legend has it that Knight also served on *Pickerel*, making several patrols before that boat was lost in April 1943 with all hands. However, muster rolls for *Pickerel* show that Knight never served on her. Nevertheless, the perceived luck of William Knight would have future consequences for him and his career. After three war patrols on *Whale*, Knight wanted off the boat. That boat's captain, Albert "Ace" Burrows, had already looked over Knight's record "and decided he was never going to leave my boat…. No Sir!" (Reynolds, p. 43). When Knight wanted off for one patrol for "a pretty good reason," Burrows refused his request stating that "No, Willie boy. When we leave tomorrow you are going to be with us" (*ibid.*). William Knight would stay on *Whale* as long as Commander Burrows was in charge, who later stated, "Don't get me wrong. I'm not superstitious. Willie was just a fine boy, and I wanted him along" (*ibid.*). As a general rule, sailors were, and still are, a superstitious lot, and the story of William Knight just proves that the men of the steward's branch were not the only men to act on their premonitions.

While much of William Knight's story is more legend than fact, there were at least two stewards in the Submarine Force that survived the war despite what can only be termed close brushes with death. Perhaps the most incredible story is that of Eugene

Mosley, Jr. He made nine war patrols in all during World War II, all on boats which were sunk almost exactly a year after he left. He made one patrol on *Triton* in early 1942. A year later she was lost with all hands. From 1942 to 1943, Mosley made another five war patrols on *Gudgeon*. She too was lost a year after Mosley's departure. The same held true on his final boat, *Bonefish*. He made three war patrols on her from 1943 before leaving for other duty on June 12, 1944. The venerable *Bonefish* was subsequently lost with all hands on June 18, 1945, one year and one week after Mosley's departure. Was it mere coincidence, sheer luck, or divine intervention that saved Mosley from being lost not once, but three times? While we do not know Mosley's thoughts on the subject, we can be sure that there were times when he probably pondered this very same question.

Our final example of extraordinary survivor's luck, though others have been found, is that of Steward's Mate 2nd Class Paul Westley Sprigs on *Gudgeon*. He joined the crew of this famed boat on April 3, 1944, the day before she departed on her twelfth war patrol from Pearl Harbor. The boat then went to Johnston Island to fill her fuel tanks, and here Sprigs left *Gudgeon* for unknown reasons. Having made no prior war patrols, perhaps Sprigs left the boat due to illness or for some other reason. In any case, when *Gudgeon* left the island on April 7, 1944, she was short her normal compliment of two or three stewards, having only one, Steward's Mate Ambrosio Fernandez, aboard. The boat was never seen or heard from again, being lost with all hands due to unknown causes in late April or May 1944.

Another reason that caused many stewards to leave their boat for a stint of shore duty or duty in a relief crew was a change in command. Remember that stewards had firsthand knowledge of the experience and character of the officers in the Submarine Force and that the good and not-so-good captains were well known amongst them, as were the executive officers who would soon take command. Once a particular commander left his boat, either for another boat or for duty ashore, a steward had to decide whether to continue on that same boat with her new commander. If the incoming captain or newly promoted exec had a good reputation, it was likely a steward would stay. However, if the opposite were true, he might arrange a transfer off the boat as soon as possible. Sometimes this could be arranged immediately, other times it might not be arranged until after another war patrol had been completed. One example of a steward leaving his boat due to a change in command is that of Carl Kimmons on *Parche*. After putting that boat in commission and making three war patrols, one of which netted him the Congressional Medal of Honor, Commander Lawson Ramage left the boat and command of *Parche* fell to his executive officer, Woodrow McCrory. As Kimmons well recalls,

> I was glad to leave. I got off the *Parche* when Ramage got off because I thought his relief, Woodrow W. McCrory, would be more adventurous and dangerous. Battle surface was a dangerous exercise. Some of those targets were setups to lure a submarine to surface. Then the camouflage sideboards would come down and guns would be exposed. Some of our subs got trapped like that — and I believed McCrory would try it [Kimmons].

Another man who might have left the boat he was serving on because of her commander was Mess Attendant 1st Class Willie James on *Wahoo*. James made the first two war patrols of the famed *Wahoo* from August of 1942 to January 1943. The first of these was made under Commander Marvin Kennedy, the officer that commissioned *Wahoo*, while on his second run the boat was commanded by Kennedy but with a PCO, Dudley Morton. After this run under Kennedy and Morton, Willie James left *Wahoo* for good. Why James left this boat is unknown, and his reasons for doing so can only be guessed. Was it because James did not get along with either Kennedy or Morton? This is unlikely, as James was known to have gotten along quite well with both of them (Veder). Instead, it may be that James left *Wahoo* because it was soon clear that Dudley Morton would be taking over the boat, and James may have been apprehensive of Morton's daring and dangerous attack methods. Morton hated the enemy with a passion and was willing to do whatever was reasonably possible to sink Japanese ships, stating upon taking command that "*Wahoo* is expendable" (Blair, p. 381). Whether or not it was Dudley Morton's daring attack methods that made James leave *Wahoo* will never be known. However, it is a fact that after he left her, no Black steward ever served on *Wahoo* again. Her other Black steward, Mess Attendant 2nd Class C.J. Smith, had put the boat in commission at Mare Island and departed before she even made her first war patrol. For her final four war patrols, *Wahoo* only had Filipino stewards. Maybe this was because Morton only desired Filipino stewards on his boat. However, it is more likely, given Morton's daring tactics, that Black men of the steward's branch avoided serving on *Wahoo* because they surmised that there was less of a possibility of survival. If so, they were proved correct in October 1943, when *Wahoo* was sunk with all hands in the dangerous waters of La Perouse Strait off the Japanese island of Hokkaido in the Sea of Japan. This was an area that Morton had specifically requested for his field of operations on this patrol, as his last patrol in the Sea of Japan had been unsuccessful (United States Navy, *United States Submarine Losses World War II*, p. 65). With the devastating loss of *Wahoo*, the use of La Perouse Strait and further submarine operations in the dangerous area of the Sea of Japan were halted until June of 1945, a period of twenty months.

Whatever their reason for leaving the boat, whether on a temporary basis or for good, the fact that many good men could do so quite easily is curious. On examination of the character of such men as Carl Kimmons, Willie James, and a whole host of others, one is hard-pressed to understand why any ship captain would let such reliable and experienced men leave their command without some attempt at persuading them to stay. Possibly some did, like Commander Slade Cutter did with Steward's Mate J.C. Crawford in *Seahorse*. This was probably a rare exception. In today's navy such a thing might happen, but not in the navy of the 1940s, when Blacks were only grudgingly accepted in the United States Navy and certainly not on an equal basis. Having stated this, it must be said that there were exceptions to the rule, and there are some notable examples of stewards and officer's cooks who were perceived as valuable crew members and, as such, stayed with one submarine and her commanders for a longer term than was the norm. Such men, whose stories are told in these pages, include the likes of Walter Wilson (*Trigger*), George Lytle (*Drum*), Jim Stallings (*Haddock*), and Arthur Brown (*Narwhal*).

At War's End

By May of 1945, the submarine war in the Pacific was winding down. The men and boats of the Submarine Force had done such a thorough job that few targets remained. The Japanese merchant fleet was nearly annihilated, while the remaining units of the Japanese Navy struggled just to survive. With fewer targets to be found, American submarines did mop-up duty, sinking stray merchantmen and knocking off small coastal escorts and gunboats. While few major vessels of the Japanese Navy were even encountered in the last months of the war, whenever they were spotted, they were usually sunk. Just as it was in the beginning, so, too, were the men of the steward's branch present when the war came to its victorious conclusion. While few Black submarine stewards were to be found at the beginning of the war, now the Submarine Force had a large amount of seasoned veteran stewards to help train and instill the proper fighting spirit in those men who were new to submarines. When *Pargo* was on one of her final patrols in February 1945, she sank the Japanese destroyer *Nokaze*. On board *Pargo* was a mixture of new and old submariners, including Steward's Mate 1st Class George Bracey, who entered the navy in 1942 and went into submarines in 1943. His junior steward was Steward's Mate Christopher Sample, a relative newcomer.

Despite this example, many of the most experienced stewards were back in the states, helping to put new submarines into commission, and the last sinkings of the war were achieved by boats that had youngsters for stewards. In March of 1945, when *Threadfin* sank the frigate *Mikura*, newcomer Steward's Mate 1st Class Isaac Hargreaves was aboard, as was fellow 1944 enlistee Steward's Mate 2nd Class Leon Rochester. Another boat that went out on patrol in March 1945 was *Devilfish*, making her second war patrol. Aboard was 1943 enlistee, Steward 3rd Class Jesse Allen and a steward's mate by the name of Parish.

In one of the most unusual submarine incidents of the war, *Devilfish* was cruising west of Iwo Jima on March 20 at just about sunset when a Japanese plane rapidly approached. The boat quickly dove, and as she was heading down she was hit hard in the conning tower. Heavy flooding inside the boat resulted, but was soon brought under control. When *Devilfish* surfaced in the early evening hours, her persicopes and radar antennae badly damaged, she found a large amount of twisted bits of metal with Japanese markings that clearly resembled a plane's landing gear. It was now clear that *Devilfish* had been hit by a kamikaze, the only submarine so attacked and hit during the war. The boat was subsequently credited with destroying one enemy aircraft, thereby earning her crew the right to wear the submarine combat insignia.

In further late war action, when *Bluefish* sank the Japanese submarine *I-351* on July 14, 1945, she had two relative newcomers, Steward's Mates 2nd Class Barnard Crocket and Percy Boothe, aboard. When *Spikefish* sank the submarine *I-373* just one day before the war ended, on August 13, 1945, she had just one steward, 1944 enlistee Herbert Zanes from Columbus, Ohio. He must have been an able man, or perhaps Zanes had reenlisted, as he was promoted to steward 3rd class just before the boat departed on her final patrol.

Still, it must not be thought that the danger was over for submariners. Though the Japanese merchant and naval fleets were mortally wounded, they could still deliver a killing blow on occasion. Seven submarines, *Swordfish*, *Barbel*, *Kete*, *Trigger*, *Snook*, *Lagarto*, *Bonefish*, and *Bullhead*, were lost with all hands in 1945, proving that though victory was just around the corner, it would come at a high price. While all submarine losses were hard to bear for the men of the Submarine Force, the loss of *Lagarto*, *Bonefish*, and *Bullhead* in the waning months of the war was particularly painful. *Lagarto*,

The crew of *Devilfish* in 1945. They had the unique experience of being hit by a Japanese kamikaze pilot, the only submarine during the war to be so attacked. The steward in the photograph has not been positively identified. (Photograph courtesy of Jack Wood.)

commanded by the able and popular skipper Commander Frank Latta, was lost while on patrol in the Gulf of Siam in May 1945. Probably sunk by a radar-equipped minelayer, Steward's Mate 1st Class Albert Kirtley of Ohio and Steward's Mate 2nd Class Robert Green from Pennsylvania were among those that went down on *Largarto*. In mid–June 1945 *Bonefish,* one of Admiral Ralph Christie's favorite boats, was on her eighth war patrol, operating in the Sea of Japan under Commander Lawrence Edge. She was lost in a depth-charge attack by Japanese forces in the shallow area of Toyama Wan. Going down with her were two 1944 enlistees, Steward's Mates 2nd Class Quintus Cooley of Mississippi and William Epps, Jr., of Virginia. This was Cooley's first war patrol. The last U.S. submarine to be sunk in World War II was *Bullhead*. Commanded by E.R. Holt, she was probably sunk by Japanese army planes in the Java Sea off the island of Bali. Among her crew was Steward's Mate 2nd Class Hubert Hackett from New York and Steward's Mate 1st Class Percy Johnson, Jr. Lost on August 6, 1945, just over a week before war's end, the men of *Bullhead* were the last of 3,505 submariners killed in action during the war, 74 of whom were Black stewards. Throughout the war years, the loss of any submarine and her crew was, as one man stated, "simply devastating" (Hussey) to the rest of the men in the Submarine Force. Most submariners knew at least one or two, and sometimes more, men on any given

The side launch of *Menhaden* at Manitowoc, Wisconsin, on December 20, 1944. Among the stewards that served on her was Florida native Frank Emory Holloman. However, by the time *Menhaden* was ready to join the war, the war was over. (Photograph courtesy of J. Holloman.)

submarine, having known them from boot camp or maybe later on at one of the rest camps for submariners.

Despite these losses, more submarines and men were being readied back in the states to continue the submarine war if the need arose. While most of these boats, as it turned out, would not be needed, their building and the training of their men continued. Up in Portsmouth, New Hampshire, *Sea Leopard* and *Sirago* were being readied for war and almost made it to the Pacific. Aboard *Sea Leopard* was newcomer Steward's Mate Bruce Anderson and former *Sailfish* Steward Killraine Newton, a veteran patroller. Commissioned in June 1945, the boat had orders to proceed to the Pacific war zone but had yet to depart before the end of hostilities was announced. The same was true of *Sirago*, which was put into commission the day before the war ended. Her steward was Chief Walter Wilson, the seasoned veteran from *Trigger*. Meanwhile, building further south in Groton, Connecticut, and Philadelphia, Pennsylvania, were *Cobbler* and *Sabalo*. The first of these boats was commissioned at Groton six days before the war ended and had yet to receive orders for the war zone when the war ended. Had she

Steward's Mate 1st Class Jimmie Howard Jones (middle level, far left) and the crew of *Gurnard* arriving home at Hunters Point, California, after war's end in 1945. (Photograph courtesy of Glenn Milhorn.)

gone to the Pacific, she would have had a wealth of experience in her stewards alone, the veteran submariners Steward 1st Class Carl Kimmons and Steward's Mate 1st Class Willie James. *Sabalo*, on the other hand, nearly made it into the war. Built at the Cramp Shipyard in Philadelphia and commissioned in June 1945, she went off to war with new enlistee Steward's Mate Robert Jordan from New London, Connecticut. However, the boat was plagued with too many leaks and other mechanical problems and was forced to go back to Groton for repairs. Here she was when the war ended. Had she made it out on patrol, Jordan would have manned her 50-caliber machine gun during battle-station surface operations. And, finally, from the submarine yards at Manitowoc, Wisconsin, there was *Menhaden*. Commissioned in June 1945, her crew largely consisted of the men from *Darter*. That boat was lost on October 24, 1944, when she was grounded on Bombay Shoal in the Palawan Passage and could not be gotten off. However, all of her crew were rescued and most went to *Menhaden* in new construction, including her skipper, David McClintock. Among the newcomers to this experienced group was Steward's Mate Frank Holloman from St. Augustine, Florida. The boat almost made it to the war to avenge *Darter*'s loss but fell just short. When the war ended, she was undergoing training exercises in the Panama Canal Zone.

Steward 3rd Class Roscoe Munford Brown on the deck of *Tirante* in December 1945. This photograph, taken at Staten Island, New York, depicts Brown next to the boat's deck gun. Brown made both of his boat's action-filled war patrols under Captain George Street in 1945.

The last hours of the submarine war in the Pacific are rather symbolic of what this varied mixture of youngsters and veteran stewards, and indeed all submariners, went through to bring the war to its end. The last official sinking by a submarine in World War II was achieved by *Torsk* on August 14, 1945, just hours before hostilities ceased. Aboard her when she sank two 800-ton frigates was relative newcomer Steward's Mate 1st Class Percy Chavis and veteran Officer's Cook 1st Class George Thompson. Meanwhile, *Cavalla* had been on surface patrol off Tokyo Bay when hostilities ceased at one hour before midnight on August 14, 1945. Hours later, as her crew prepared to celebrate the end of the war with a dose for each man of "medicinal brandy" (Blair, p. 871), a Japanese plane swooped in and dropped a bomb that landed a short distance from the boat. As the plane maneuvered for another attack on *Cavalla*, the boat dived to safety, and the intended celebration was put on hold. Among *Cavalla*'s crew were veteran submariners Steward's Mate 1st Class Horace Farr and Steward's Mate 2nd Class Woodrow Wilson. You can bet that these men, and the entire crew of *Cavalla*, breathed a sigh of relief when they made it safely back to port.

Steward's Mate Rufus Jack Weaver, at top (far left), on the bridge of the German submarine *U-505* in 1945. The identity of the steward's mate next to him is not known. Weaver was part of the crew that rode the captured submarine all the way down the East coast on a war bond tour. (Photograph courtesy of R. Weaver.)

When the war officially ended on September 2, 1945 with the formal Japanese surrender ceremony in Tokyo Bay aboard the battleship *Missouri*, twelve submarines were there to represent that branch of the service that contributed mightily to the defeat of Japan. Among the many submarine stewards present to witness this historic event were Steward's Mate 1st Class Ivory Harper and Steward's Mate 2nd Class James Malone on *Archerfish*, Steward's Mate 1st Class Willie Waddell on *Haddo*, and Steward's Mate 2nd Class David Collier on *Hake*. What a sight it was when Collier was allowed a brief glimpse of the surrender scene through the periscope of *Hake*. It was one he would never forget.

With the end of the war now at hand, the United States Navy now had more submarines than she knew what to do with. Soon, many of these boats were decommissioned and put into mothballs for use at a later date. Others, boats that were older and had seen much wear and tear, were stricken from the rolls of the navy, stripped of whatever usable gear they had, and then were sold for scrap. Yet others were used in the atomic bomb experiments in 1946 in Bikini Atoll or were later sold to other nations.

What about the submarine stewards that manned them? What lay in store for them? One of the most unusual assignments that fell to some stewards at the end of

---

Opposite: This unusual photograph was probably taken just after the war ended in October 1945, perhaps at Pearl Harbor or back in the states. At left is *Pilotfish* with Chief Steward Tyree

Cornish at center (see arrow), while another steward is handling the lines to secure the boat. Note that *Pilotfish* has her hull number in white (386) painted on the bow, while *Loggerhead*, at right, is in the process of having her hull number painted back on by the crewman hanging over the side (on the right). These identifying numbers were removed on American submarines during the war so the Japanese could not track submarine movements; numbers were only restored when the war ended. (Photograph courtesy of the Cornish family.)

the war was their service on captured German U-boats. With the surrender of Germany in May 1945, a number of German submarines were surrendered intact to American naval forces and sent to several ports on the east coast for examination. Several were even sent on war bond tours, visiting many east and Gulf coast ports all the way from Maine to Texas. Former *Narwhal* steward Arthur Brown was sent aboard *U-530* at Portsmouth, New Hampshire, and rode her on a war bond tour all the way to Texas. Accompanied by a destroyer escort, the German submarine traveled on the surface only and never submerged. Another such man who performed steward duties on one of Hitler's captured submarines was Steward's Mate Rufus Weaver. A native of Louisville, Kentucky, Weaver enlisted in the navy in March 1945 and first served on the old school boat *R-1* before being sent aboard the famous *U-505*. This German submarine was captured intact with her entire crew by a hunter-killer group led by Captain Daniel Gallery in the escort carrier *Guadalcanal* on June 4, 1944, off the coast of Africa. The capture of *U-505* on the high seas was one of the outstanding actions of the submarine war on any front and was crucial in revealing many German secrets. The submarine was later sent on war bond tours and is now on display at the Museum of Science and Industry in Chicago. One can only smile at the irony of a Black man serving on a German submarine, something that Hitler himself could never have imagined possible. Unfortunately, even some American's were astounded to see a Black man aboard. Rufus Weaver, speaking of his time on *U-505*, said, "It was a wonderful tour until we hit the south," and remembered one spectator in one of the southern ports visited exclaim, "'Hey Ma, look! They got a nigger down here. I didn't know they had niggers on submarines'" (Weaver).

For those men with enough points to get out of the navy in 1945, a return to civilian life was theirs for the taking. Those men that needed more points would have to serve into 1946 or longer before their term of service was up. Once this happened, some stewards left the navy for good. Other men chose to stay in the navy and made it their career even when they had no such intention in the beginning. Yet others left the navy only to return, either by choice because of difficulty in finding civilian employment or by force via the draft system during the Korean War. No matter what path they chose, many of the men of the steward's branch continued to serve their family, community, and country in ways both big and small. However, not all of those submarine stewards that survived the war would live to reap the benefits of old age. Stewart DeHosnery, a steward on *Trout* for her first nine war patrols, would survive the war, but not for long. A resident of Oakland, California, he died at the young age of 27 on November 7, 1948, while being transported from his home to the Permanente Foundation Hospital. Publicly available records are strangely silent as to the possible cause for DeHosnery's death at such a young age. Perhaps it was due to a sudden accident or illness, but there are some indications that his death may have been a suicide.

While it was only natural that some World War II veterans would survive the war only to die from such rigors of everyday living as illness or accident, a few well-known and highly regarded Black submariners died during the course of their service after the war was over. The first to be lost in this manner were George Bracey and Roscoe Pennington. They were shipmates on the new nuclear submarine *Thresher* when she was lost with all hands during a test dive off the New Hampshire coast on April 10, 1963. George Bracey had made a number of war patrols on *Pargo* during the war and was a steward 3rd class at the time of his death. Roscoe Pennington, a native of Texas, had made six war patrols on *Sea Dragon* and *Spikefish* during the war and was considered an outstanding submariner. He would later change his rate to that of electrician and was one of the first men selected to attend nuclear power school for submarines. At the time of his death on *Thresher*, Pennington was a chief electrician's mate with twenty years in the service.

Tragedy would strike the United States Navy again in May of 1968 when the nuclear submarine *Scorpion* was overdue at Norfolk, Virginia, with her 99-man crew. Heading home from the Mediterranean, the boat never made her home port and was presumed lost on June 5, 1968. Eventually the sunken submarine was found 400 miles southwest of the Azore Islands. The cause of her loss has never been fully explained but was probably due to a weapons failure. On board *Scorpion* at the time of her loss was Steward 1st Class Joseph Cross. Not only was Cross the oldest man on board but he was also one of only two World War II submariners serving on the boat at the time. Cross had made eight war patrols during the war, including six on *Halibut*, and was one of the navy's best-known and popular stewards.

Finally, there is the sad case of Charles Richardson. A seasoned veteran, he made nine war patrols in all, including four on *Kingfish*, three on *Bluefish*, and two on *Nautilus*. He returned to the states with an Aussie war bride soon after the war ended and continued his navy career. He retired from active duty in 1963 after nearly twenty-five years of service. Sometime in 1967 he attempted to join the Groton, Connecticut, volunteer fire department, but was "blackballed due to his race" (Richardson). A short time later, Richardson also tried to gain membership in the United States Submarine Veterans, World War II organization.

Chief Commissary Steward Charles McKinley Richardson. A native of West Virginia, Richardson saw substantial action during the war, making nine war patrols in all on *Kingfish*, *Bluefish*, and *Nautilus*. After the war he changed his rate and later made the transition to nuclear powered boats. He is shown here with three of his children, (from left) Perditha, Kurt, and Londi, in the late 1950s. (Photograph courtesy of M. Richardson.)

Though eminently qualified to join this organization, he was declared "ineligible" (Richardson), yet again likely due to his race, and was denied the chance to become a member. All of these events were likely a crushing blow to this quiet and introspective man. Charles Richardson, veteran submariner, husband, and the father of five children, took his own life in October 1968 at the age of 48. The survivor of many battles under the sea during his military service, Richardson was yet another casualty, perhaps, in the war against racial prejudice that ravaged America in the 1960s.

Many submarine stewards chose to leave the navy for good and returned to civilian life once they had earned enough points for their discharge. Some returned to their hometown and home state to find work, while others established themselves in communities new to them. Not a few were surprised to find what changes were in store for them when they returned home. Steward Robert Goens from *Icefish* experienced both a bit of luck and surprise on his discharge. He missed the train that he was supposed to take that would carry him home only to find out that it had wrecked and many people were killed. Thinking his son was on that train, Robert Goen's father was getting ready to leave their home in Richmond, Indiana, for the scene of the accident when he received the happy call from his son, telling him that he had taken another train and was safe. Upon his arrival back home, Goens "saw my mother had a small baby with her, and I asked her who she might be babysitting for, and found out that I had a younger brother" (Goens). Goens would continue to live in his native state and, after working at various jobs, settled down as a health inspector for Wayne County for a number of years.

Other Black submariners turned civilian also led successful and productive lives. When North Carolinian Harold Hale from *Tunny* returned to civilian life, he chose the state of Massachusetts as his new home. Trained in the HVAC field, Hale worked for the Commonwealth of Massachusetts and the city of Boston for twenty years before his retirement. Another former submariner that worked in government was William Allison from *Grampus*. After leaving the service in 1947, he attended and graduated from Johnson C. Smith University in Charlotte, North Carolina. After a stint as a teacher, he worked for the Federal Railway Mail Service for 37 years, rising to the position of supervisor. Now retired, Allison is a writer and historian specializing in African American history. Other men that left the navy soon after the war ended were Jesse Debro from *Queenfish*, who worked as a cobbler and barber; L.C. Fisher from *Parche*, who worked as a chauffeur for actress and film star Katharine Hepburn at her Connecticut home; Albert Soles from *Cod*, who worked as a factory engineer; and Richard Lucas from *Raton*, who attended Fayetteville Teacher's College (North Carolina) and was a teacher for 37 years.

Three men who had outstanding civilian careers after serving as submarine stewards during the war are worthy of special notice. Hadwick Thompson from *Pollack* left the navy in 1945 and returned to his home in Oakland, California. First employed as an officer with the California State Police, he soon joined the Oakland Police Department in 1947. Along with friend, Clarence Williams, the two men were the first Black police officers ever in the city of Oakland. Thompson also earned a degree at San Francisco State University and later taught at the Institute of Police Science at Merritt College.

Another outstanding submariner turned community leader was Russell Donan. A native of Bowling Green, Kentucky, Donan made three war patrols on *Cobia* and rose to Officer's Cook 1st Class before leaving the service in 1946. He soon moved to Nashville, Tennessee, where he earned a bachelor's degree in health and physical education at Tennessee A and I University. He then moved to Richmond, Virginia, where he taught physical education and was the assistant football coach at Virginia Union University. He later earned a master's degree from NYU and served as a high school teacher and supervisor for the City of Richmond Department of Recreation and Parks for 22 years. A friend of the famous tennis player Arthur Ashe, Donan was instrumental in getting a gym built for Black youths in Richmond.

Finally, there is the career of former *Bluegill* steward Walter Patrick. Upon leaving the navy in 1946, Patrick returned to New Jersey, where he worked for the New Jersey Transit Bus Company for 27 years. However, preaching was his real calling. He became licensed to preach in 1966 and became an ordained minister in 1968 at Mount Olive Baptist Church in East Orange, New Jersey. After a period of study at several bible colleges, this "country boy at heart" (Patrick) returned to his native Virginia and was minister at Buelah Baptist Church in Chesterfield, Virginia, for 16 years. He later ministered at Bethiah Baptist Church in Amelia Court House, Virginia before retiring in 2001. In 1995 Walter Patrick was named one of "25 Who Have Made a Difference in Today's Amelia County" by newspaper writer Mike Salster. His counseling to area African American youths on the issues of premarital sex and helping them to "better themselves through education and get off the welfare treadmill" (Salster) has had a real impact on his community.

Many submarine stewards who left the service just after the war ended returned to civilian life for a brief time before reentering the navy. While the Korean War was a major reason for their return, some men came back because of economic necessity. With so many former servicemen returning to civilian life, jobs were often hard to come by in the years after World War II ended. While even white ex-servicemen had a hard time finding a job, it was even more difficult for former Black servicemen, due to prejudicial hiring practices and a climate of racism that had changed but little in most parts of the country. Hosey Mays of Denver, Colorado, former steward on *Crevalle* and *Bowfin*, left the navy in 1946 but returned in 1950 during the Korean War. He would soon change his rate from steward to electrician and later was an instructor at the navy's IC "A" school. He retired from the navy in 1967 as a chief electrician and later entered the private sector, working for Solar Turbines in San Diego. Likewise, Casper, Wyoming, native Bert Minor, formerly on *Crevalle*, left the service in 1946. He served in the navy again for a brief time during the Korean War and then returned to civilian life. Minor was a long-term employee at the post office in Casper before his retirement in 1983.

Other men who pursued different career paths before returning to navy duty were Willie James, Everett Davis, and Edward Neely. New Orleans native Willie James, formerly officer's cook on *Whale* and several other boats, put his culinary talents to work and opened his own restaurant. However, financial difficulties forced James out of the restaurant business and back in the navy by 1947 (Nalle). He would go on to have a long navy career.

Oklahoma native Everett Davis, formerly of *Lizardfish*, also had an unusual post–World War II career. He left the navy in 1946 and attended mortuary school in

Chicago but was recalled for Korean War duty. Davis subsequently changed his rate to that of hospital corpsman and retired from military life in 1968 as a chief. In civilian life he continued to serve the government as medical director for the Military Sealift Command in California.

Houston, Texas, native Edward Neely, formerly steward on *Billfish, Bowfin,* and *Hammerhead,* left the navy in 1945 to pursue a course of music study at Texas Southern University. However, hard economic times forced him to return to the navy in 1947. After a long and successful career, Neely retired from the navy in 1967 and returned to the private sector.

However, not all former submarine stewards that returned to the military to serve during the Korean War reentered the navy. Valdosta, Georgia, native Arthur Brown, the long-time steward on *Narwhal,* was drafted for service in the army during the Korean War. Serving in the 2nd Infantry Division until his discharge in 1951, this dyed-in-the-wool submariner found army life unpleasant and was quite happy when his time was up and he could return to civilian life.

While many submarine stewards left the navy for good once World War II had ended, there were a surprising amount of men who chose to stay in the service and continue their military career. Many men enjoyed the military life, while some men saw that there was a light at the end of the tunnel, so to speak, and that attitudes toward Black servicemen were slowly changing and might result in expanded future opportunities. The state of Blacks in the United States Navy was, indeed, changing, but ever so slowly. By August 1945, 95 percent of all Blacks in the navy were still employed in the steward's branch (Davis, p. 634). However, the situation for Blacks looked brighter starting in 1944 with the death of Secretary of the Navy Frank Knox. His replacement, James Forrestal, was sympathetic to the plight of Blacks in the navy and was very much in favor of integration. By 1945, training facilities were starting to be desegregated and ratings were being expanded for Blacks in auxiliary vessels. More change, hopefully, would come in the navy in the near future, and many seasoned submarine stewards would be there when it happened.

For those submarine stewards that chose the navy as their career, most served twenty years and then "retired" at an early age with a good government pension. Once retired, most of these men then entered the private sector and started a new career where they could earn a salary that would well augment the pension they received for their years of military service. Men such as Sam Wallace (*Mingo*), Anderson Royal (*Silversides* and *Dragonet*), Clark Cooper (*Tuna*), William Perry (*Sunfish*), Melvin Heisser (*Hoe* and *Rasher*), Dave Collier (*Hake*), Alfred Hall (*Pomfret*), Elvin Mayo (*Jack*), Woodrow Jones (*Pike* and *Redfish*), Leroy Toombs (*Guardfish*), and Earnest Danford (*Baya*) all served in the navy for twenty years before their retirement. Afterward, they worked at a variety of occupations, and, if stationed at New London, often remained in the area of Groton, Connecticut, close to the submarine base they had served for so many years. Other east coast ports that served as both submarine bases and the home for retired submariners include Norfolk, Virginia, and Charleston, South Carolina. For those men that were stationed on the west coast, mainly California, during the greater part of their career, San Diego, Oakland, and San Francisco were areas in which many retired submariners took up residence. Honolulu, Hawaii, was also another west coast retirement spot. Leroy Toombs was one unusual exception to this rule. Upon his retirement, he had a concession business in Alaska and is thought to have done quite well during the building of the Alaskan oil pipeline before returning to his native state of Kansas. Other men who had navy careers that lasted at least twenty years, and longer, include John Gray (*Tautog*), Leslie Hamilton (*Thresher, Billfish,* and *Brill*), Lacey Stevenson (*Barb*), Paul Ragland (*Barb*), Elijah Dawson, Jr. (*Drum, Finback,* and *Saury*), Mack Butler (*Dace*), Eugene Mosely (*Bonefish*), Herbert Odom (*Silversides*), Lonnie Jackson (*Trout*),Ulysses Reed (*Haddo* and *Hake*), Luther Bryant (*Haddo*), Houston Kennedy, Jr. (*Growler* and *Hardhead*), Bernard Heard (*Snook* and *Crevalle*), Willie Waddell (*Haddo*), Otha Toler (*Spikefish*), Julius Caesar Bowe (*Cero*), William Murray (*Plunger*), and George Lytle (*Drum*).

A number of men served in the navy even longer than the standard twenty years. Killraine Newton (*Sailfish*) served for 28 years, while Shirley Day (*Grayling* and *Thresher*) served for 26 years, as did the previously mentioned Joseph Cross (*Halibut*) before his loss on *Scorpion*. Had he not been lost, it is likely that Cross would have continued his career to the 30-year mark. Walter Wilson (*Trigger*) served for nearly 25 years and retired as a chief steward before going to work for the Portsmouth Naval Shipyard, while Wallace Coleman (*Pollack*) served for 25 years before going to work as a Connecticut State Auxiliary Trooper. Another man that served in the navy for nearly 25 years was the famed Dave Ball (*Rasher*). Following his retirement, he worked at Madison Square Garden in New York operating a concessions business. Given Ball's outstanding career as a navy boxer and softball player, this comes as no surprise. Then, there were those men that served in the navy for 30 years or more. This honor roll includes such men as brothers Albert Rozar (*Gudgeon* and *Pargo*) and Leonard Rozar (*Tuna* and *Saury*), Jim Stallings (*Haddock*), Carl Kimmons (*Plunger* and *Parche*), Sammy Major (*Picuda*), and Robert Coley (*Tambor* and *Bugara*).

Of all the submarine stewards listed that served in the navy for twenty years or more, there are three men that achieved a high level of distinction that is worthy of notice: Anderson Royal, Killraine Newton, and Carl Kimmons. Two of them, Kimmons and Newton, would rise from the enlisted ranks to retire as "mustang" officers.

Oklahoma native Anderson Peter Royal joined the navy in 1940 and first served in surface craft before transferring to submarine duty. He made five war patrols on *Silversides* and three on *Dragonet* by the end of the war. By 1949, Royal was a chief steward but had his mind set on changing his rate to that of an electronics technician (ET). Despite navy rules that were against him, all who knew Royal, including his commanding officers and friends, were aware of how smart this young man was and wanted him to succeed. While serving as an instructor at the steward school at the naval training center in San Diego in 1952, Royal was allowed to take classes at the fire control technician school. While he completed the coursework for this class, it was all done under the table and is something that is not part of his official record. Within two years, with the encouragement and help of the officers he served, Royal was officially enrolled in the electronics technician conversion school in 1954 and graduated third in his class in 1955. He was the only Black man in his class, and one of the first Black men ever in the navy to convert to the ET rating. As far as is known, the only man to convert earlier was Isaac Johnson, whose story will be told later on.

After serving on board the repair ship *Hooper Island* for a little over a year as chief electronics officer, Royal came back to the naval base at Treasure Island in 1956 and

Fire control technician school graduates at the Naval Training Center, San Diego, in 1952. At far left is Chief Steward Anderson Royal, an unofficial graduate of the school. Royal had an aptitude for electronics and, after being allowed to sit in on the sessions, finished third in the entire class. Several years later, Royal would officially change his rate to that of an electronics technician. Note that not only is Royal the highest rated man in his class, but also the longest serving. The three hash marks on his sleeve are indicative of his twelve years plus of naval service. (Photograph courtesy of A.P. Royal.)

worked as an instructor at the conversion school from which he had recently graduated with honors. Not only was Royal an expert on shipboard communications and radar systems, he also took a fatherly interest in those he was teaching and is well remembered to this day by many men who rose to command positions. Royal retired from active duty in 1960 but continued to have an impact on the navy. After graduating with a degree in industrial and vocational education at San Francisco State University, he served as a civilian instructor at the navy training school at Treasure Island and was one of the prime movers responsible for the development of today's electronics warfare technician (EWT) rating in the modern navy. Working closely with his friend and navy boss, Lieutenant Commander Killraine Newton, Royal taught the first EWT classes ever. Though Anderson Royal finally retired in 1979, it may be truly said that his influence on the navy is still being felt to this day.

Pennsylvania native Killraine Newton was drafted in the navy in early 1943 and after boot camp served on *Sailfish* for her final two war patrols before she was retired from war service. After riding *Sailfish* back to the states, Newton was transferred to new construction as part of the commissioning crew of *Sea Leopard* at Portsmouth, New Hampshire, just as the war was ending. Newton stayed in the service, and by 1950 he had reached the rate of chief steward. In 1955 he was accepted for the electronics technician conversion (ETC) program and after a year had cross rated to chief electronics technician. In 1959, Newton applied for warrant officer status and was accepted after achieving outstanding results in a fleet-wide competitive test. Because submarines at this time did not carry warrant officers, this was the end of Killraine Newton's submarine career. However, the change to surface ships was just another challenge to "Newt," and it was one in which he would rise to even higher levels. In 1962, Newton again tested high in fleet-wide competition and advanced from chief warrant officer to lieutenant junior grade. As an officer, Newton served on the auxiliary vessel *Lookout* as electronics officer and later became the director of the ETC school at Treasure Island and subsequently the director of the Electronic Warfare Development Department. Along with Anderson Royal, he is known as one of the founders of the navy's EWT rating. By the time of his retirement in 1971, Killraine Newton had achieved the rank of lieutenant commander, the highest rank ever achieved by any World War II steward.

Finally, there is the outstanding career of Ohio native Carl Kimmons. He enlisted in the navy in 1940 and was the honor man for class 13 at boot camp in Norfolk. After service aboard the destroyer *McFarland*, Kimmons soon volunteered for the Submarine Force. He made four war patrols on *Plunger* and three on *Parche* by war's end. In October 1947, following President Truman's order that opened all rates to Black serviceman, he was one of the first stewards to change their rate, going from steward 1st class to yeoman 2nd class. He subsequently served on *Medregal* and *Sea Robin* before being assigned to duty in Submarine Squadron 10 in 1951. By the following year, Kimmons rose to the rate of chief yeoman. He subsequently did shore duty for several years at the naval station, San Juan, Puerto Rico, as chief yeoman. While in Puerto Rico, Kimmons has the added distinction of having served as the mayor of San Patricio, a community of 1,300 military and civilian residents from November 1954 until his transfer to another duty station in 1956. Working in conjunction with a vice-mayor and a town council, Kimmons was the town's first mayor. Though this was an unpaid position, the popular and talented yeoman worked as both a trouble-shooter and liason between residents and the San Juan Naval Station that held jurisdiction over the community. In mid–1956, Kimmons was transferred to Submarine Division 101, serving aboard the tender *Fulton*. Here he advanced in rating to senior chief and master chief yeoman. Several years later, in 1961, Carl Kimmons was selected for the "Chief to JG" program, due to a shortage of junior officers in the navy. He subsequently attended Officer Candidate School in Newport, Rhode Island, and after graduation in May 1961 was assigned to the U.S. Navy Hydrographic Office in Washington, D.C. Here he worked as administrative, security, and top secret control officer, advancing in rank from lieutenant jg to lieutenant. In 1963, Kimmons was transferred to the submarine school at New London, handling administrative, security, and top secret control duties. Kimmons' final assignment was to the navy's underwater sound laboratory in New London, serving as security officer from 1968 to his retirement in 1970. He is the only former mess attendant ever to serve in every enlisted pay grade from E1 to E9, to become a commissioned officer.

The fact that so many World War II submarine stewards would later go on to achieve high levels of distinction in both civilian and military careers is indicative of the character, determination, and drive of these fine young men. Given just the slightest chance to succeed, they usually did so. In another, more enlightened era, such men as Killraine Newton, Carl Kimmons, and many other Black men like them, might have had the chance to become Annapolis graduates and, perhaps, rise to command their own submarine. Instead, they were the trail-blazers for the Black men of today's navy.

VI

The Submarine Navy During the Postwar Years

Following the end of World War II, the Submarine Force of the United States Navy underwent many changes and exciting new developments. In every decade, from the mid–1940s to the 1970s, these changes had an effect on all submariners, both Black and white. Sometimes the changes were internal, specifically affecting Black submariners, while at the same time the Submarine Force and, indeed, the entire United States military establishment was undergoing other rapid and profound changes as a result of the Cold War era. These changes affected not just Black submariners, but all U.S. military personnel and, by extension, the entire nation. Not only was it a new era in relations between the world's superpowers, it was also one cloaked in secrecy and fraught with peril. It is only just recently that the role of the Submarine Force in these world events has come to the attention of modern day historians. As such, some of the events herein described are being told for the first time ever in print by men who were there. However, there is much that has yet to be revealed. Though some of the Cold War activities of our nation's Submarine Force took place over fifty years ago, much of the information regarding them is still classified. This is especially true for those men on boats that performed missions in the 1960s and 1970s, but while specific details are lacking, we can at least get a sense of what these men experienced.

For each decade from 1945 to 1975, the following sections will cover the experiences of Black submariners who enlisted in the navy in the 1940s and 1950s in the areas of enlistment policies and advancement opportunities as well as operational duties and experiences. As in the previous chapters about submariners during the war years, this section covering the years up to 1975 is not a scientific or statistical study about the number of Blacks who served in the Submarine Force but rather an informal history told by the men that were in the service during this time period. There is one important difference: due to changes in navy policy (described fully in the next chapter) these men served in a variety of ratings and would no longer be solely restricted to the steward's branch of the navy.

One "tradition" that has changed but little through the years is the number of Black servicemen in the United States Navy. This branch of the service has always lagged in popularity in comparison to the army and marines when it comes to the number of Black enlistees, and this has continued to the present day. Following the end of the Vietnam War in 1972, navy enlistment of Blacks, as a percentage, has consistently matched that of the entire Black population in the United States, standing at about 12 percent in total (Edgerton, p. 186). Given the wide disparity among the number of the navy's surface craft versus submarines, it is no surprise that, even in the 1960s and beyond, few Black crewman, at most three or four men, were to be found in any given submarine crew. This same is true even today for a submarine's leadership group, consisting of officers and chief petty officers. In the year 2000, the Trident submarine *Nebraska* had only two Blacks among its complement of 33 officers and chiefs, a figure that is probably no higher on average than that of submarines, diesel or nuclear, in the 1945–1975 time frame. Indeed, it was not until 1982 that a Black officer would gain command of a submarine, this being Captain Chancellor "Pete" Tzomes of the nuclear powered fast attack submarine *Houston*.

While this postwar look at Black men and their role in the Submarine Force makes no attempt to explain why more Black men did not choose to enter its ranks, it does make one point abundantly clear. These men, some newcomers and some who were already navy veterans that switched to submarine duty, took every advantage of the opportunities that slowly became available to them and carried well the torch that was passed to them by their predecessors serving in World War II submarines.

THE END OF THE 1940S AND PRESIDENT TRUMAN'S DESEGREGATION ORDER

In the immediate years following the end of World War II, the navy operated under a system of double standards. By the end of 1945, the practice of segregated training for Black recruits was finally ended. This process began the previous year, when James Forrestal became secretary of the navy after the death of Frank Knox on April 28, 1944. By July 1944, segregated advanced training for Blacks was discontinued, though that for new recruits still continued. This affected Black men that entered the navy beginning in mid–1942 and attained rates other than that of steward. However, these men were almost never allowed to man ships that went to sea in combat areas. New recruit integrated training subsequently began in July 1945 and went into full effect within the year (Foner, pp. 171–72). Seemingly, the navy had achieved what it believed, at least under Knox, was impossible—full integration. Real integration, however, was yet to be achieved. Those men serving in both surface craft and submarines during the war as stewards remained as stewards and were not allowed to change their rate. As a result, the steward's branch, composed mostly of Blacks, as well as Filipinos and Guamanians, remained a separate and distinct branch in the navy hierarchy, and one based on the color line division.

Despite the fact that many submarine stewards and officer's cooks were ready and wanted to change their rating, they were not allowed to do so. Still, this did not deter such men as Carl Kimmons, Roscoe Pennington, and likely many others. Serving aboard

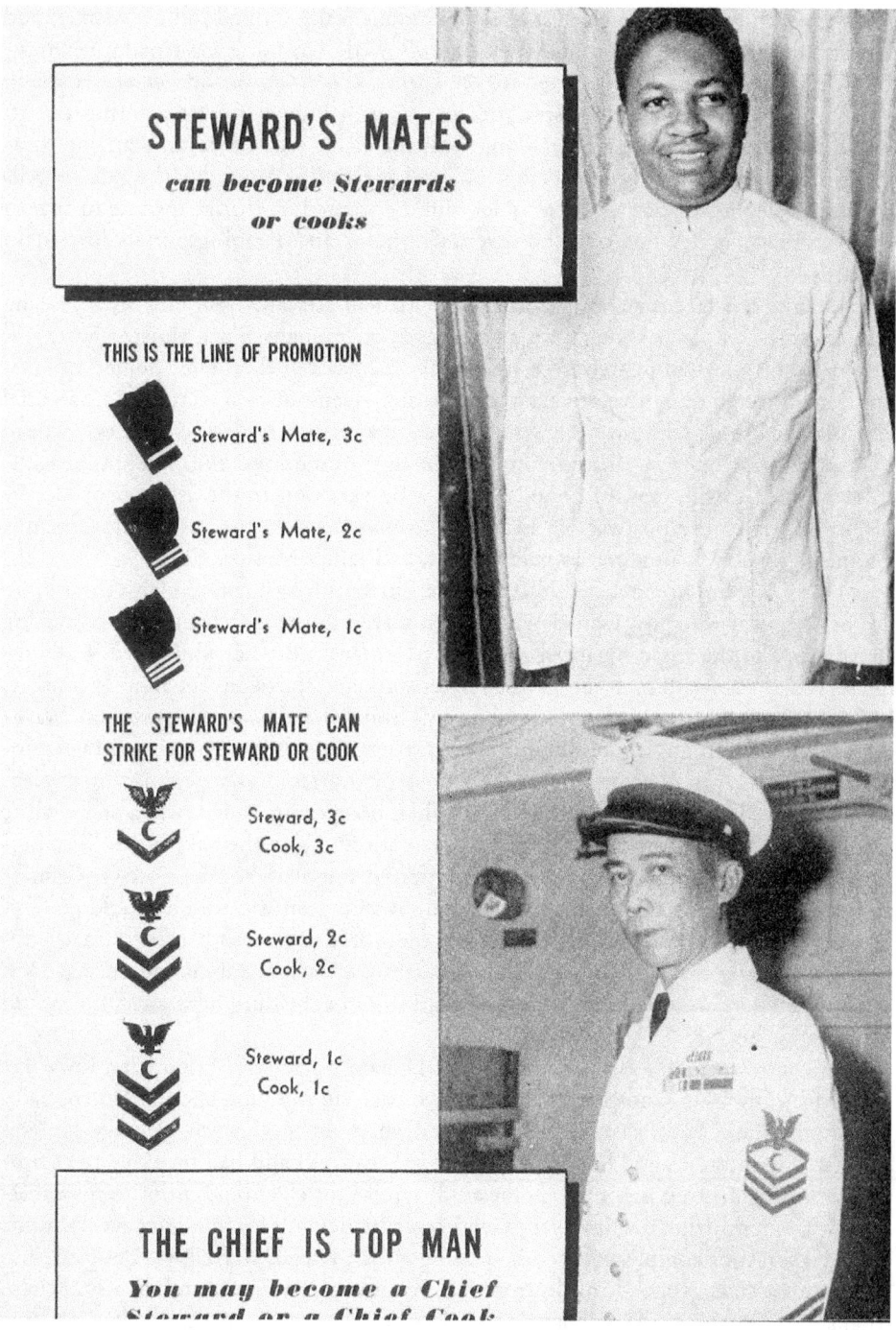

Illustration from the first steward's mate training guide produced by the navy in 1946, showing the line of promotion and rating badges for the steward's branch. (Official U.S. Navy photograph.)

Cobbler after the war as steward 1st class, Kimmons really wanted to be a yeoman and performed such duties as he could when time allowed. The same was true for Pennington, who after the war served as steward on *Tilefish, Cusk, Chivo,* and *Ronquil.* Though his official duties were that of steward, he was well known for frequenting the aft end of the boat in his free time, talking with the electricians, and familiarizing himself with the electrical components there, as well as crawling around in the battery wells (James Mosley). One day, if the navy let him, he wanted to change his rate to that of an electrician's mate. For now, however, Kimmons and Pennington would remain stewards.

Despite the fact that ratings other than that of steward were now slowly being opened to new recruits, though not all ratings at once, many Black enlistees were still automatically assigned to steward duty on the sole basis of their race. Sometimes this was done through deceptive or vague information given out by a recruiter to potential new Black recruits, while at other times those new recruits with no specialty in mind were automatically, as in earlier times when being a steward was the only option available, assigned to the steward's branch. The wide variation in the assignment of new Black recruits in the postwar era is amply demonstrated in the cases of future submariners Hosea Washington, Donald Burrell, and James Mosley.

Hosea Washington enlisted in 1946 from Pittsburgh, influenced by his three older brothers, all war veterans. Daniel Washington served in the merchant marine, making convoy runs to the frigid northern waters of Murmansk, Russia, while Fred Washington served as a steward on a submarine tender stationed stateside. Yet another brother, Melvin Washington, served stateside as a machinist mate on a minesweeper. Washington, though a high-school dropout, was a talented musician who played the trumpet. At boot camp Washington "spent most of my time as a regimental bugler" (Washington, Hosea), and did little else. When boot camp ended, when some white recruits were sent to musician's school in preparation to join the navy band, Washington wanted to go too. It was then that he found out that he was a steward's mate and could not go. As a sort of compensation, Washington was told he could go anywhere he wanted. It was then, remembering the words of his brother, Fred, that "submarine duty was easy" (*ibid.*), that Hosea Washington chose submarine duty at New London. He soon learned that being a steward was not the duty he wanted and would later change his rate.

In contrast, there was the experience of Donald Burrell of Mason City, Iowa. He enlisted in July 1946, and there seems to have been no question about what specialty he would pursue. A self-avowed electronics devotee during his school years, he "was fascinated with radios and ham radio operators" (Burrell) and had reviewed the Capitol Radio Engineering Institute's home study course for electronics prior to his enlistment without realizing that it was the navy's basic curriculum for training new electronic technicians. After completing recruit training at San Diego, Burrell was designated as a seaman 1st class assigned to Electronics A School at Treasure Island, San Francisco. After a 42-week course, he graduated as an electronics technician mate 3rd class in October 1947, one of the first Black men ever to do so. Unusual for that time period, Burrell "never discussed the steward rating with any recruiter" (*ibid.*).

Finally, there is the case of James Mosley, a native of Homestead, Pennsylvania. He enlisted in the navy in May 1948 "with the aspiration of being a naval aviator. At that time there was one African American aviator" (James Mosley). However, Mosley's aspirations would not be realized. As he recalls,

> I was denied the right to attend the school at the naval air station in Pensacola, Florida. During my medical and dental examination, I was informed that my "teeth didn't occlude properly" which was justification for failing my application for flight school. As a young man, I just accepted the decision and moved on. I found out later from a dentist that there was nothing wrong with my teeth. I was later assigned the rating of HR [Hospitalman Recruit] in boot camp at the Great Lakes Naval Training Center [*ibid.*].

While all three men joined the service at nearly the same time, their assignment expectations were not always met. Burrell's talents and knowledge were early recognized, and he was able to get the rating he wanted. Washington, on the other hand, despite his talent as a musician, was, unbeknownst to him, assigned to be a steward instead of a musician. It may be that his lack of a high school diploma affected him adversely. However, Washington would soon overcome the obstacles in his path and went on to have a fine navy career. The denial of James Mosley's initial career choice was, without doubt, affected by the fact that Blacks were still not regarded as acceptable for aviation training. Though he was subsequently assigned the hospitalman rating, he would excel at every service class he attended and has the distinction of being the first African American hospital corpsman to attend and graduate from the navy nuclear power school.

While some men wanted to change their rate and prepared for the day when that might happen, many submarine stewards were happy to remain in the steward's branch of the service. Veteran stewards that stayed in the service after the war were usually held in high regard for their years of valuable submarine service and wartime experience. Postwar enlistees into the submarine service, whether Black or white, looked up to all these "old-timers" and relied on them for help when it came to the qualification process. In particular, young Black men that entered the Submarine Force found in the stewards a friend and sometimes even a mentor in all things submarine related. One such enlistee was Kenneth Joyner from New York City. In talking about the stewards, he states that

> They were our fathers and big brothers.... I found a camaraderie and support system ... that developed into a mutual respect. They looked out for us.... I respected them for the tough jobs they were caste into strictly because of racism [Joyner].

There were times, however, when prejudiced submarine skippers worked to get Black stewards off their boat in the immediate postwar era. While the service of Black men may have been tolerable to some prejudiced naval officers due to the expediencies of war, service in the peacetime navy may have been more than they could bear. This seems incredible, given the fact of the fine performance of the men of the steward's branch during the war that had just ended. One example of this occurred on *Catfish* in 1947 while she was stationed in the Far East with the Seventh Fleet. A steward's mate from Alabama, name not disclosed, was summarily court martialed on the charge that he failed to properly rig the forward battery compartment for dive. While it is unknown

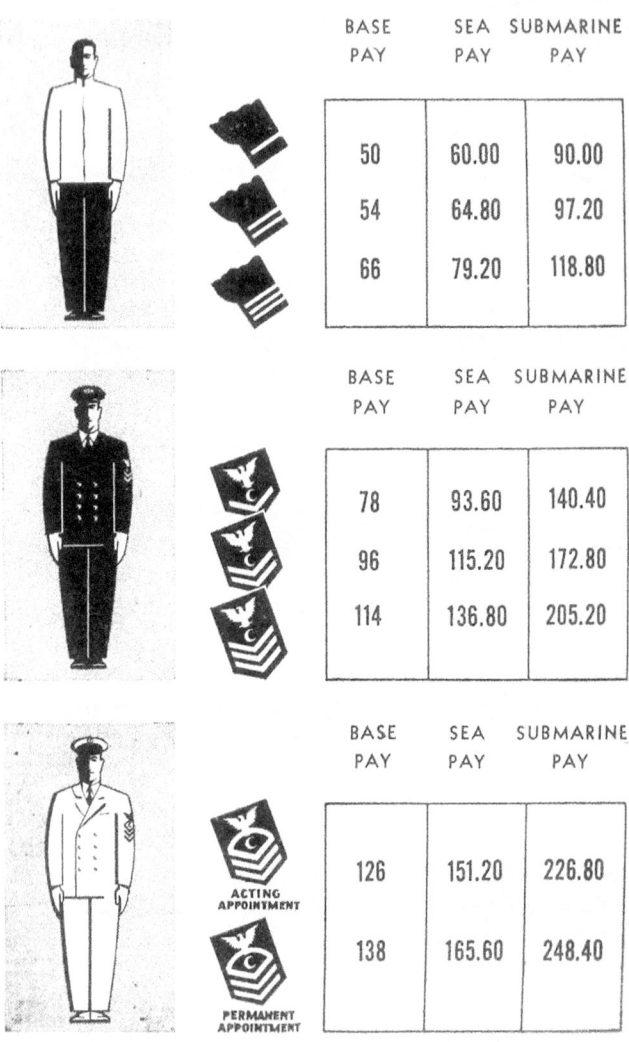

Illustration from the first steward's mate training guide produced by the navy in 1946. Depicted are the pay rates for each rating from steward's mate 3rd class to chief steward. (Official U.S. Navy photograph.)

if such a charge was warranted, it soon became apparent to the boat's junior officer, Hugh Latham, that the captain was intent on getting rid of the steward. When Latham overheard the captain and his executive officer discussing the case, the captain was heard to say "Get rid of this Black kid" (Latham). Fortunately, Latham intervened on the steward's behalf. When the court martial was later convened in the wardroom, Latham appeared to defend the man, much to the surprise of the executive officer, and asked that the case be dismissed. When asked on what grounds this should be done, Latham stated that the court martial was not a fair one and that he had overheard the captain already state what its outcome would be. Somewhat flustered, the court martial proceedings were temporarily adjourned while the executive officer, no doubt, went to consult with the captain. Upon his return a short time later, the court martial proceedings were quickly ended, without explanation and, more importantly for the steward involved, with no guilty finding.

The navy, despite the actions of some prejudiced officers, did begin to take more of a professional approach to the men of the steward's branch. In 1946, for the first time ever, a training manual for steward's mates was published by the Standards and Curriculum Division of the Bureau of Naval Personnel. This manual was not only a "self-study guide" for new steward's mates but also "a guide for officers working with Steward's Mates" (United States Navy, *Steward's Mates*, p. ii). What is most striking is the fact that this training manual, if only briefly, places its first emphasis on the fighting duties of a steward's mate, stating that "The Steward's Mate has a fighting job" (*ibid.*, p. 3) and citing three steward's mates that were decorated during the war for their military actions, including submariner Joseph Cross. While stewards were restricted by official policy prior to World War II from manning gun crews, practicality and the high level of performance by stewards in gun crews during the war changed navy policy. Now, steward's mates were not only told that they would be manning such gun crews but also that "Steward's Mates may be the entire gun crew from clip room to gunner" (*ibid.*, p. 4).

However, while this training manual was an attempt by the navy to place more of a professional emphasis on the men of the steward's branch, it also reinforced some of the old ways of thinking. As part of their duties, steward's mates were still expected to make an officer's bed and even shine his shoes, though it does not tell how this should be done, whether on, or off of an officer's feet. The business of shining shoes by stewards was always a source of friction between them and their officers and would remain so for quite some time. More bothersome was the fact that the men of the steward's branch, and they were that, indeed, were still referred to in official publications as "boy." The steward's mate that manned the galley is referred to in this manual as the "Galley Boy," while the steward's mate on watch is referred to as the "Watch Boy" (*ibid.*, p. 23), and so on. navy tradition, combined with racially biased attitudes, died hard, and it would take many years and an influx of a new generation of officers before the term "boy," as applied to the men of the steward's branch, went out of usage.

What the navy and other branches of the armed forces could not, and would not, do on their own — implement a desegregation program — was finally achieved through

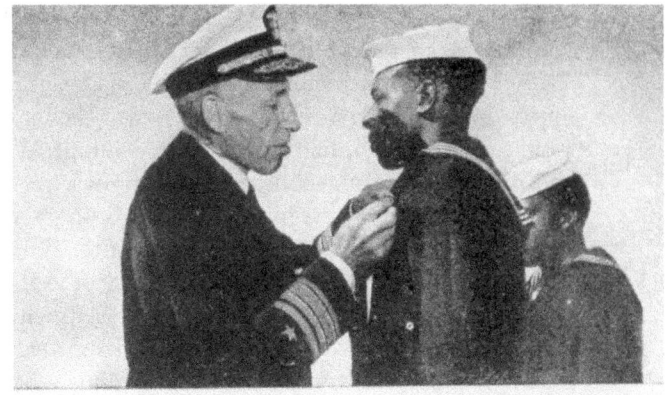

THE STEWARD'S MATE HAS A FIGHTING JOB

At Pearl Harbor on 7 December 1941, Dorie Miller, StM 1c, operated a machine gun firing at enemy attacking aircraft. Miller was awarded the Navy Cross.

In enemy-controlled waters, Joseph Cross, StM 1c, served on four submarine patrols which sank or damaged many Japanese ships. Cross got the Navy and Marine Corps Medal.

On 7 April 1944, off the Marshall Islands, Ed King, StM 2c, nearly lost his life in attempting to save a drowning shipmate. King received the Navy and Marine Corps Medal.

This page from a 1946 steward's mate training manual shows how the navy's attitude toward stewards was changed by their war-time performance under battle conditions. (Official U.S. Navy photograph.)

political expediency. President Truman's Presidential Advisory Commission on Universal Training was appointed in December 1946 and submitted its findings the following May. This advisory commission "strongly endorsed Universal Military Training and vigorously opposed all segregation in a citizen's army" (Foner, p. 179). Despite this, by the time a bill for universal military training was submitted to Congress, it was watered down and did not contain a nonsegregation provision. Undeterred, Black leaders pushed strongly for the end of segregation in the military and, in the end, it was the pressure they brought to bear that forced the situation. The issues of civil rights was one that "appealed strongly to Black voters" (Foner, p. 183), and Truman needed all the votes he could get during the 1948 election year. As such, President Truman took unilateral action on July 26, 1948, when he issued Executive Order 9981, declaring "that there shall be equality of treatment and opportunity for all persons in the armed services without regard to race, color, religion or national origin. This policy shall be put into effect as rapidly as possible" (History.Navy, p. 2). While Truman was criticized for the ambiguity of this executive order, subsequent questioning by the national press made it abundantly clear that his order was meant to end segregation in the military.

The enforcement of Truman's order was to be trusted to a commission established by Executive Order 9981, its seven members to be appointed by the president and to start their work January 1949 upon the commencement of Truman's new term. Chosen to lead this body was Charles Fahy, a native of Georgia. Two members of the subsequently named Fahy Committee were Black civil rights leaders. Hearings were begun by the committee in 1949, consisting of representatives from the leadership of each branch of the military. In regard to the navy, the fact that a high percentage of its Black personnel were in the steward's branch was a point of major concern. When the secretary of defense, Louis Johnson, asked for plans from all service branches on how equality of treatment was to be achieved, the navy responded that they were already following the guidelines established in Executive Order 9981. Johnson rejected the navy's response, and asked that they submit another plan. Acting on the recommendations of the Fahy Committee, the navy finally agreed, among other things, to allow men from the steward's branch to transfer to all other ratings and agreed to increase the number of Black enlisted men outside the steward's branch. On June 7, 1949 Johnson formally approved the navy's proposals, now making it possible for men in the steward's branch to change their rating (Foner, pp. 185–87).

It was also about this time that the navy changed its ratings designations for the men of the steward's branch. The E-1 to E-3 pay grades, formerly called steward's mates, designated as "StM," were now called stewardsmen, with their designation now being "TN." This was likely done for no other reason than to lessen the confusion that may have existed between the many navy rating designations that began with the letter "S." In conjunction with this, the petty officer pay grades were also changed for stewards. The official distinction in ratings between officer's cook and steward was now eliminated, and all such men were now referred to officially as stewards, their sole designation being "SD." Those stewards that became a chief petty officer were subsequently designated as an "SDC."

While the navy dragged its proverbial feet before making the changes sought by the Fahy Committee and Secretary of Defense Johnson, it was the army that fought these changes the most before finally coming up with an acceptable plan. The work of the Fahy Committee was the engine which drove change for Blacks in the armed forces, but it would take a full five years before official segregation was ended. It was not until 1954 that the separate recruiting of stewards was abolished and "specialty groups" (Foner, p. 193) were opened to all seamen. However, it must not be thought that this was the end of segregation and racial discrimination in the navy. It would take years before actual actions matched official policy and law, and some might even argue that it has yet to be fully realized even to this day.

With the change in policy initiated by Executive Order 9981, the gates were open, at least partially, for those men in the steward's branch who wanted to cross-rate to a specialty to which they had previously been denied access.

Stewards Sam Wallace (left) and Killraine Newton (right) in Shanghai, China, in 1947. The little girl pictured here used to help the stewards procure food at the local markets for a fair price for their boat. In return, the men befriended the girl and her family and provided them with food and other necessities to make their lives a bit easier in poverty-stricken postwar China. (Photograph courtesy of S. Wallace.)

However, though the opportunity existed for Black stewards to cross-rate, there were still many obstacles in their path. The biggest may have been a lack of education and the high rate of illiteracy found among many men in the steward's branch. A high percentage of these men came from the south, where educational opportunities above seventh grade, and sometimes lower, were denied to them on the basis of color. Such men who entered the navy during the war were usually promoted to higher ratings on the basis of their actions in combat situations. But now things were different. With the navy on a peacetime footing, promotion was now more often based on taking a test to determine one's ability. This is one reason why many wartime stewards that made the navy their career afterward never progressed much higher than steward 3rd class.

Another reason that stewards could not always cross-rate was, in part, due to navy regulations and the attitude of one's immediate commanding officer. For those men who, by 1949, had been in the steward's branch for ten years or something close to that, the ability to cross-rate to another specialty, even if they were perfectly competent to do so, was virtually impossible. With possible retirement coming up for such men in just ten years (assuming the standard 20-year hitch), the navy did not believe it cost-effective to put such efforts into training and schooling when the time spent in their new rate might be less than ten years. In an ideal situation, this makes perfect economic

Radioman Bruce Anderson in the radio shack of a submarine. Anderson was a former steward on *Sea Leopard* who later changed his rate. (Photograph courtesy of B. Anderson.)

sense, but Blacks had already been restricted when they enlisted and were further restricted even after Truman's historic order because of the racially biased practices of the past that continued to haunt them. The one exception to this, in some cases, was a change in rate from steward to commissaryman. The duties of both rates involving the procurement and distribution of food supplies, especially aboard a submarine, went hand-in-hand except for the fact that stewards were there to serve and wait on the officer corps. With the ability to change their rate, some stewards, among them Otha Toler, Claude Palmer, Edward Neely, and Charles Richardson, made the jump from the steward to the commissary branch, heretofore all white, and left behind the business of serving officers.

Additional restrictions were also sometimes placed by their commanding officer on those stewards who wanted to change their rating. Such action was probably a combination of prejudice or a desire to keep the immediate status quo, depending on the situation. Because a steward needed his captain's recommendation to change his rating, the steward had to tread carefully to make it happen. Bruce Anderson's skipper on *Sea Leopard* was not willing to recommend his change in rate to that of radioman until Anderson proved to him that he knew Morse code. Whether this was a delaying tactic by the captain or a requirement that he truly felt necessary is unknown. However, little did the captain of *Sea Leopard* know that Anderson already knew Morse code, having learned it as a Boy Scout in his youth. To his credit, the captain kept his word, and Anderson's switch to radioman was soon begun when he was sent back to Bainbridge, Maryland, for radio school in 1951.

Other 1940s-era submariners that changed their rate from steward to other specialties throughout the 1950s include Joseph Green (motor machinist), Hosie Washington (engineman), Anderson Royal (electronics technician), Killraine Newton (electronics technician), Gilbert Lomax (radioman), Isaac Johnson (electronic technician), Hosea Ferguson (commissaryman), James Owen (storekeeper), Carl Kimmons (yeoman), Roscoe Pennington (electrician's mate), Charles Williams (electrician), Herbert Odoms (electronics technician), and many more. In addition, a number of men who had left the Submarine Force as stewards at war's end would come back into the navy during the Korean War and were also able to change their ratings. Former steward Hosey Mays became an interior communications electrician, while Everett Davis became a hospital corpsman. The details of this change in rate for Carl Kimmons is quite interesting. Kimmons was one of the first stewards in the Submarine Force to change his rating after the war, doing so in October 1947 while serving aboard *Cobbler* in Key West, Florida. However, in order to change his specialty, Kimmons had to accept a reduction in rating, going from steward 1st class to yeoman 2nd class. This meant a reduction in both base pay and submarine hazardous duty pay. This economic loss is likely one reason that many stewards, prior to Truman's order, did not change their rating even when it was possible for them to do so.

Chief Electrician Charles Williams circa 1958. A steward in World War II, Williams changed his rate after the war and had a long navy career. (Photograph courtesy of C. Williams.)

While the late 1940s were a time of social change for Blacks in the navy, it was also an exciting and eventful time at the operational level for those men in the Submarine Force. While many of the boats built during the war were decommissioned, those boats that stayed in service saw a wide range of activities that represented both an expanded strategic use of the submarine as a weapon and the technological advances that accompanied their new role. Ironically, it was the activities of the antiquated S-boats operating in Alaskan waters during the war that presaged the actions of the boats of the postwar fleet. One of the earliest of these activities was Operation Highjump, a naval expedition to the Antarctic led by Admiral Richard Byrd. While one of the stated objectives of this mission was to train and test how the navy, its men and ships, could operate in such a frigid environment, it was also a show of strength in an area that would soon be contested by the world's super powers. Among the many ships to participate in this mission were the carrier *Philippine Sea*, the Coast Guard cutter *Northwind,* and the submarine *Sennet.* Aboard this boat were two veteran stewards, Officer's Cook 1st Class Edward McNair and Steward 3rd Class Robert Blue, Jr. McNair, a prewar submariner, had been stationed in the Panama Canal Zone at Balboa during part of the war and joined *Sennet* in 1946. This was his first fleet submarine, his prior service having been in the old S-boats. Blue, on the other hand, had been aboard *Sennet* for a year and a half, coming aboard in May 1945 and making her last war patrol.

The service of *Sennet* in Operation Highjump was dangerous and brief. She departed the submarine base at Balboa on December 10, 1946, and headed for Antarctic waters, crossing the Antarctic Circle on December 28 and rendezvoused with the main group of ships near Scott Island. One day later, she entered the dangerous pack ice and creeped southward toward the Pole. However, it was soon proved that the frigid, ice-filled waters were no place for a conventional submarine and that *Sennet* was in extreme danger. Despite a valiant attempt, on January 3, 1947, it was decided to withdraw the submarine from the core expedition, and she was taken in tow by the cutter *Northwind* and taken back toward Scott Island. Here, *Sennet* was thoroughly inspected to make sure the ice had not done major damage and, being found in good condition, she continued to serve Operation Highjump as a weather and radio relay station and, later, served as a lifeguard for the flights made by carrier-based aircraft to Little America. Following the end of this duty, *Sennet* steamed for Wellington, New Zealand, on February 4, 1947, and thence back to the submarine base at Balboa, where she arrived on March 13, 1947.

Another exciting and historic submarine cruise in the early postwar years was the voyage of *Sea Robin*, the first submarine ever to round Cape Horn. Once again, the objective of this mission was to provide cold weather training for submarine crews and was also a chance for the Navy Hydrographic Office to update nautical charts in these dangerous waters. Aboard *Sea Robin* when she departed the submarine base at Balboa on May 15, 1947, was Steward's Mate 1st Class John Kennon. He was a veteran of the boat, having joined her in May 1945 for her final war patrol and continued on her after the war. *Sea Robin's* voyage lasted 55 days and covered 12, 500 miles, her final destination being Portsmouth, New Hampshire. Despite "persistent storms, dense fogs and heavy seas" (Winslow, p. 129), and even a collision with a whale, *Sea Robin* rounded the Horn on the morning of June 1, 1947, and, continuing northward, was the first American warship to visit Port Stanley, Falkland Islands, in fifty years. She glided into Portsmouth on July 8 to successfully complete the historic voyage, adding *Sea Robin's* name to the long list of American Cape Horners dating back to the days of the clipper ship era.

While the voyages of *Sennet* and *Sea Robin* are high profile and exciting examples of the Submarine Force at work in the immediate postwar years, there were other boats performing work of a more classified nature. Aboard *Chopper* in 1947 was Officer's Cook 1st Class Sam Wallace. As part of her crew, he served aboard her during a simulated war patrol exercise to China. This voyage covered over 18,000 nautical miles and included stops in Japan, China, and Okinawa. As Wallace recalls, "I rode her [*Chopper*] to China and spent time ashore in Shanghai, on the Yangtze River. While in the Far East we would go out on exercises for ten or twelve days at a time, come back in

The USS *Sennet* during the third Byrd Antarctic expedition in early January 1947. At top is the *Sennet* in the ice pack, nearly surrounded by icebergs. At bottom are members of the crew after she was guided to safety. At far right in the last row is Officer's Cook 1st Class Edward McNair. (Photograph courtesy of the McNair/Pollard family.)

and provision, then go out again. On one cruise we sank an old Chinese destroyer for training. There was nothing to it, really" (Wallace). However easy such duty may have been for Wallace, *Chopper*'s patrol exercise was deemed a huge success, and the boat was awarded the Battle Efficiency Pennant, being rated one of the outstanding submarines of the Pacific fleet.

The USS *Sennet* was part of the third Byrd Antarctic expedition in early 1947 but had to be withdrawn due to the danger of her being crushed in the pack ice. The crew is here throwing a tow line to the Coast Guard cutter *Northwind*. Thought to be among the men at the bow is Officer's Cook 1st Class Edward McNair, who by this time was a ten-year submarine veteran. (Photograph courtesty of the McNair/Pollard family.)

Steward's Mate Reginald Bigelow on the deck of *Sablefish* heading into the North Atlantic in 1946. (Photograph courtesy of R. Bigelow.)

Other wartime stewards that recall their service during this time include C.V. Cooper, who served on *Diodon* out of San Diego from 1947 to 1949. This fleet boat was modernized at Mare Island Naval Shipyard beginning in 1947 and afterward, according to Cooper, "*Diodon* was the first boat to voyage outside the states with the new snorkle set-up" (Cooper). During his time aboard the boat, she participated in training exercises on the west coast and in Alaskan and Hawaiian waters. Operating closer to home was Steward 1st Class, soon to be Yeoman 2nd Class, Carl Kimmons on *Cobbler* and later, *Medregal*. Both these boats operated out of Key West, Florida, and conducted training exercises in antisubmarine warfare (ASW) in support of the fleet sonar school based there. These exercises were conducted in Caribbean waters with cruises to Guantanamo Bay, Cuba, as well as in the Atlantic as far north as Virginia. Another boat that was stationed out of Key West that performed similar duties was *Sea Leopard*. Aboard her were veteran stewards Jim Stallings, Killraine Newton, and newcomer Bruce Anderson. Yet another boat that saw some interesting duty during the late 1940s was *Sablefish*. Built during the war at the troubled Cramp Shipyard in Philadelphia, she did not enter active service until after the war had ended. Home-ported out of New London, she participated in ASW exercises on the east coast as far south as Bermuda and even made a three-week cruise to Greenland waters. Aboard *Sablefish* during this time was Steward's Mate 1st Class Reginald Bigelow, a 1944 draftee from Harrisburg,

Pennsylvania. Some of the highlights of his time aboard include the testing of a new type of submarine escape buoy and taking part in the activities in Havana, Cuba, memorializing the fiftieth anniversary of the loss of the battleship *Maine*.

In addition to the fleet submarine duties, there were also those boats and their crews that participated in the development and testing of new weapons and defense systems. One of the earliest of these boats was *Carbonero*. In April 1947 she was ordered into the submarine guided missile program, developing what would be the forerunner to today's modern ballistic missile submarine. Among the crewmen on board *Carbonero* during her work in developing the Regulus I missile guidance equipment were veteran submariners Steward 1st Class Anderson Royal, Steward 1st Class Otha Toler, Steward 2nd Class Isaac Johnson, and Steward 3rd Class Paul Jordan. The former executive officer of *Carbonero*, Lieutenant Commander Charles Rush, terms his boat "the happiest and most effective peacetime submarine imaginable. The story of how the ship saved the budding submarine guided-missile program from oblivion is virtually unknown today" (Rush). Should anyone still believe that all stewards ever did was serve coffee to their commanding officers, they'd better not tell it to Rush. In describing the "situation between an executive officer and four Black stewards," Rush uses such terms as "favorite people" and "professional mutual regard" to describe his stewards on *Carbonero* and remains friends with them to this day. There is no doubt that Royal, Toler, Johnson, and Jordan were valued crewmembers on this pioneer submarine. While working on the Regulus system, *Carbonero* worked out of Port Hueneme, California, near Oxnard. Her days were spent at sea launching and guiding missiles that were the forerunner to today's modern cruise missile. Nicknamed "loons" by the crew, they were really versions of the German V-1 buzz bombs used during the war. Logistical support for these operations was provided by the naval air base at Point Mugu. After a hard day's work, *Carbonero* would dock at Port Hueneme, and her crew would spend the evenings socializing and playing intramural team sports (Rush). *Carbonero* was, indeed, a happy ship, and Anderson Royal was grateful for his time aboard. He made chief steward in 1949 and was helped by his fellow enlisted men and officers when he decided to change his rating from steward to electronics technician.

Another participant in the submarine guided missile program was Steward 1st Class Harry Senior on *Cusk*. Senior was an experienced steward, having volunteered for the navy in 1942. During the war he served in Australia on the tender *Griffin*, as part of a submarine relief crew, and later served on the tenders *Bushnell* and *Pelias*. When he joined the crew of *Cusk* in 1946, it was his first submarine assignment. During his six years aboard the boat, he made cruises to Alaskan and northern waters and, on January 20, 1948, was witness to a historic event when *Cusk* became the first submarine ever to launch a guided missile from her deck.

On the eve of the Korean War, United States submarines were engaged in a wide range of activities, but probably none were as important as the stealth and spy missions to the far northern waters of the western Pacific Ocean as well as the far northern reaches of the Atlantic Ocean in the North Sea and beyond. Those missions to the western Pacific would come to be known as WESTPAC deployments and involved close surveillance of activities in Russian and Chinese territorial waters. Their mission was to observe at close range the activities of the Soviet navy and merchant fleets and learn all they could about their capabilities and strength without being detected. Aboard the submarines on these WESTPAC runs were "spooks," navy spies with special monitoring equipment designed to detect and record all aspects of Soviet military communications. What high flying U-2 spy planes were doing in the skies over the Soviet Union was also being done in the waters around the Soviet Union by American submarines. It was dangerous work. Among the first submarines to perform such duty was *Carp*, making two runs to northern waters in 1948 and 1949.

Spy missions such as these were also sent to the waters of the northern Atlantic and the Bering Sea. One of the first of these missions was called Operation Kayo and involved the submarines *Cochino*, *Tusk*, *Corsair*, and *Toro*. While the latter two boats were of the standard fleet type, *Cochino* and *Tusk* had been modernized, being fitted with snorkel technology that allowed them to stay under water for weeks at a time, and had also undergone the GUPPY conversion process, which gave them greater battery power and a more streamlined hull and conning tower. So configured, the *Cochino* and *Tusk* now possessed greater speed and endurance capabilities, perfect for the spy mission they were about to embark on. Among the men on board *Cochino* for this mission was

Chief Steward Otha Toler on *Carbonero* in 1949. A veteran of war patrols on *Plunger* during the war, Toler would later change his rate to that of commissary steward in the 1950s. (Photograph courtesy of C. Rush.)

Steward 1st Class Leotis Shelton, better known as "Pops" Shelton. He was a seasoned submarine veteran, having made all five of *Sandlance*'s war patrols during World War II. However, nothing could have prepared him for what was to come on this mission. Formerly aboard *Cochino* was long-time steward Sammie Major. Also a veteran with five war patrols under his belt, he was transferred off the boat just prior to her departure for Europe. As for *Tusk*, her stewardsmen included Hosie Washington, Joseph Holmes, and Henry Riley. At the time of this mission, Washington was a seasoned crew member, having been aboard *Tusk* since 1946, and was pulling extra duty in the engine room "doing the work of a fireman even though I was a stewardsman" (Washington, Hosea). It was his goal to change his rate from that of steward to fireman, with the goal of becoming an engineman. There was no better circumstance, perhaps, in which Washington could have made this change. The *Tusk* had a close-knit crew, and many of her experienced men, including such veterans as Chief Torpedoman Dave Veder and Beecher Allen, John Hoppes, and Henry McFarland of the engineering department, "were determined to make this Black boy a success" (*ibid.*). The hard work of Hosie Washington and the men of *Tusk* would soon come to fruition in this regard, but now, in August 1949, they had a mission to perform.

Operation Kayo began in July 1949 when the force of four submarines left the states for Great Britain. After training exercises with the British in sonar systems at Londonderry, Northern Ireland, during which time a navy spy came aboard, the force subsequently sailed to Portsmouth, England, where sensitive spy and sonar gear was installed aboard *Cochino*. By August 13, 1949, the force of four submarines were underway, steaming submerged in the Atlantic, due west of Ireland and heading toward Arctic waters close to the Soviet Union. Soon, the force would split up, with *Corsair* and *Toro* heading toward northeast Greenland, while *Cochino* and *Tusk* steamed through the Norwegian Sea. Once in the Barents Sea, the two boats split up, with *Tusk* doing sonar work while *Cochino* headed to the northern tip of Norway to commence her intelligence-gathering mission.

After four days of work, with little to show for her hard work, *Cochino* headed back to rendezvous with *Tusk*, where the two boats would subsequently engage in sonar exercises. However, weather in these polar seas was not always cooperative, and during the day of August 24, 1949, high winds and seas developed. In the early morning hours of August 25 the storm intensified, and *Cochino* became increasingly unable to ventilate properly the buildup of hydrogen gas in the after-battery compartment. Disaster struck just after eight in the morning when there was an explosion and fire in the after battery on *Cochino*. Captain Benitez immediately prepared his wounded boat to surface and fired off a message to *Tusk*, stating that he had fire aboard and was about to surface. Once on the surface, *Cochino* had to combat not only the emergency in her after battery but also the deteriorating weather. With the inside of his boat filled with smoke and toxic gas, Benitez ordered all hands to the bridge. Forty-seven men made it to the bridge, some being injured and some barely dressed. Eighteen men were still below in the after battery, five badly wounded, while Electrician's Mate 1st Class Martinez worked gallantly to disconnect the shorted batteries. However, another explosion ripped through the after battery just forty minutes after the first, and *Cochino* was now doomed. With no power at all, the sub was adrift in the frigid waters of the North Atlantic during a storm. However, *Tusk* soon arrived on the scene to conduct rescue operations. High seas prevented her from maneuvering close aboard, despite four attempts, and instead a lifeline was secured between the two boats. A raft was soon passed from *Tusk* to her wounded sister ship, filled with badly needed medical supplies. When the raft made its return trip from *Cochino*, manned by one officer and the civilian sonar expert who had volunteered to help, the raft overturned, and the men were rescued by crewmen from *Tusk* stationed topside to act as line handlers. By the time the two men from *Cochino* were aboard, one badly wounded, the two submarines had drifted a mile apart. In attempting to return to *Cochino*, *Tusk* was hit by a huge wave that swept ten of her crew and the wounded civilian from *Cochino* overboard. During the subsequent rescue operations, Stewardsman Hosie Washington was called topside to act as a line handler. As he recalls,

> We knew the ship [*Cochino*] was in trouble, but not how critical. We were in rough seas, and a large wave washed our men over the side. The rubber boat from *Cochino* flipped over, and those men were in the water, too. The call came that more line handlers were needed topside. That was when I went topside to

help with the recovery effort. I was no hero, I was just trying to do a job [Washington, Hosea].

During the rescue operations that ensued, Washington would call down the hatch for even more line handlers, but Stewardsman Henry Riley, still below, called back "There's no one left" (*ibid.*). It is unknown if Stewardsman Joseph Holmes was below at work or whether he was already on deck as a line handler. In spite of the herculean efforts of *Tusk*'s crew, conducted in treacherous seas, only four of the crewmen washed overboard were recovered. Seven men, including the civilian from *Cochino*, perished. Meanwhile, Benitez and the men on *Cochino* were waging an incredible fight to save their boat. The men left below had managed to power up the engines and auxiliary power was restored, giving them hope that they might yet save their boat. Once the situation was restored aboard *Tusk*, she steamed back to *Cochino*, and began to escort her back to port. It was a race against time, but one that would be lost. Just over five hours later, the hydrogen gas that had continued to build up in *Cochino*'s after battery exploded yet again, starting a fire. With the stormy seas now decreased, *Tusk* maneuvered alongside *Cochino* for the last time, while her frozen, battered, and tired crew crossed a wooden plank to *Tusk* and safety. Moments later, just before 2:00 A.M. on August 26, 1949, *Cochino* slid beneath the waves stern first. She sank one hundred miles from safe harbor on the coast of Norway. It was not until the two crews talked about their ordeal that *Cochino*'s crew learned of the loss of life on *Tusk* during the rescue operations. While steaming back to Hammerfest, Norway, Stewardsman Hosie Washington was back below working in the engine room as acting fireman. However, he was soon called to the wardroom to perform steward duties, as the men there, Riley, Holmes, and probably Steward 1st Class Leotis Shelton from *Cochino*, were short-handed now that both crews were aboard.

While Operation Kayo was a failure in the technical sense due to the loss of life, the loss of *Cochino*, and the inability to gather any useful intelligence data, it was, in many ways, a shining moment for the men of the Submarine Force. From Captain Benitez of *Cochino* and Captain Robert Worthington of *Tusk* all the way down to the lowest enlisted men in the navy hierarchy, including stewardsmen such as Hosie Washington, the *Cochino-Tusk* incident showed that their high level of training and courage could prevail even in the most dire of circumstances.

Overall, the era of the late 1940s was a time of transition, both for Black submariners and the Submarine Force as a whole. Not only was there social change for Black sailors that would soon lead to greater career opportunities but also a time of great advances in weapons technology. All of these things would come together in the decade to follow with spectacular results.

THE 1950s: ENTER THE NUCLEAR AGE

With the advent of the 1950s, Black men serving in the Submarine Force were still largely employed as stewards. However, with the changes brought about as a result of the Fahy Committee's findings, this would soon change. In the early 1950s, when stewards were still being recruited separately, many young Black men still came into the navy as stewards, often unknowingly. Among those future submariners that enlisted in the navy early in the 1950s were Kenneth Joyner (1950), Louis Slaughter (1950), Melvin Williams (1951), Frank Holloman (1951), Archie Denson (1952), Arthur O'Meally (1952), Jim Higgins (1953), Abraham Mozeak (1954), John O'Meally (1954), and John Wouldridge (date unknown). While all these men came into the service just a few years apart, their experiences were, in many cases quite different from each other.

The earliest of these men to enter the service was Kenneth Joyner, a native of New York City. As he relates, "I was very, very patriotic from World War II and couldn't wait to get in. I didn't know what I was going to meet with and didn't think about the 'Black' aspect, I was just enthusiastic about me joining" (Joyner). Joyner subsequently signed up for service as a High School Sea Recruit (HHSR) and was guaranteed an "A" school posting upon the completion of navy boot camp. The tests he took determined that he had an aptitude for electronics, not surprising as his father was an electrician, and after boot camp he went to radio school in Norfolk, Virginia. After a 16-week course of study, Joyner graduated as the class honor man and became rated as a radioman.

Of the remainder of the men listed above, Slaughter, Williams, Holloman, Denson, and Higgins became stewards. The experiences of Melvin Williams were probably typical of how many young Black men were assigned, or better yet, "unknowingly recruited," to the steward's branch with little say in the matter. Williams, born in 1933, was a native of East St. Louis, Illinois. Upon graduating from high school in 1951, he worked as a "gandy dancer" for a short time, laying railroad tracks for the Wabash Railroad, working in Ohio, Indiana, and Michigan. After a summer's worth of work, Williams moved to California and, after receiving draft notices for the Korean War, decided to join the navy. As he recalls,

> I loved boot camp because it wasn't segregated. We went through boot camp, and we went through small arms training and the rifle range.... I did real good on all my scores. They would always post them, and I remember asking my company commander what the initials "TR" (next to my name) was. He said "You are going to be a steward," and I said, "Well, I thought I was going to be guaranteed a school." He said "You will be guaranteed a school" ... and I said "But I want to try something else," and he said "Well, you'll have to work on that after you get out of boot camp, because right now they have you designated for this [steward] school."
>
> So, I went through boot camp, and they posted all those who were going to school, and boom. I looked, and I was going to steward school.... Things completely reversed. I happened to be the only African American in my company when I was in boot camp, and suddenly, when we assembled for the stewards school, it was 100 percent African Americans! And all of us at that time ... were high school graduates, and we were all wondering how did we get this assignment.... No one volunteered for this, so how did we all end up here? As we talked to some of the instructors who were stewards, ... the fact that this was a segregated organization ... became more of a reality. As we went on liberty, it was seldom that we saw anybody who was an African American who was not a steward. So we ended up going through steward school. I graduated as honor man ... the entire experience was quite a shock" [Williams, "Naval Historical Center Interview"].

Little did anyone know that the experiences of Melvin Williams as a young navy steward would one day, nearly 25 years later, result in vast and important changes for the men of the steward's branch.

The enlistment, or, more properly, reenlistment, of Frank Holloman in 1951 is also indicative of the times. Holloman was a former war veteran and submariner who had enlisted in late 1944 and rose to the rate of steward's mate 1st class before leaving the navy in 1946, having served in the crew of *Menhaden*, the submarine base at Guam, and on the tender *Bushnell*. However, upon leaving the navy, employment opportunities were hard to come by, and Holloman "planned to finish college in the navy, and had high hopes of getting into electrician's school. Of course, when I reenlisted, I had dreams of getting another rate other than steward's mate.... I was told the only way I could join was to enter the Mess Rating as a Stewardsman" (Petway article). In effect, Holloman was lied to by his recruiter and, despite his ability and prior service, was slated for the steward's branch from the start due solely to his race. The navy still had a long way to go before equal opportunity for minorities became a reality.

Steward's Mate 2nd Class Melvin Williams, Sr., would be the one to force the navy to change the steward's branch. Here he is shown in his early navy days before he became a submariner. (Photograph courtesy of M. Williams.)

One steward who tried to change his rate early on in his career was Columbus, Georgia, native Archie Denson. He enlisted in 1951 and, like Williams, also attended navy boot camp in San Diego and was assigned to steward duty. During that time, Denson had a chance to see the submarine base at Mare Island, and, as he puts it, "I liked what I saw" (Denson). Denson volunteered for submarine duty and first served on *Sterlet* in April 1953. He would later serve on *Besugo* for a year and a half and then *Capitaine* for over three and a half years. While on board these boats, Denson worked

Steward's Mate Archie Denson standing sonar watch on *Besugo* in the early 1950s. Stewards did more than just serve meals on submarines and qualified throughout the boat to stand watches. (Photograph courtesy of A. Denson.)

as a yeoman and electrician striker in an attempt to change his rate but met with little encouragement and advancement in grade. When he was transferred to shore duty at the naval air station in Corpus Christi, Texas, in 1961 Denson abandoned his attempt to change his rating. However, he was far from being done with the Submarine Force and, after a year of shore duty, saw service in the ballistic missile submarine *Ethan Allen*. He would end his outstanding submarine career as a master chief more than twenty years later.

Of those men listed previously who did not become stewards, Arthur O'Meally and John Wouldridge became radiomen. Arthur O'Meally entered the navy from New York City in 1952 and, after taking some tests, was designated an electronic field seaman recruit (EFSR). While attending both boot camp and radio school, he was the only Black man present. During this time, O'Meally recalls,

> One incident of racism that almost changed my career in the navy. While in boot camp I had to see a classifier that tried to send me to steward school until I reminded him of my EFSR designation. He then gave me another test and I was sent to Radioman "A" School [O'Meally, Arthur].

Just like his older brother, John O'Meally ran into the same problems when meeting with navy classifiers at boot camp. Recalling this meeting, O'Meally remembers that

> The counselor wanted to send me to school to be a steward. I told him during the interview that I was an electrician. He corrected me by saying, "You mean you carried tools for the electrician and helped him." I said no, I was the electrician and on some jobs I had a helper who carried my tools. He still didn't believe me I guess because he pulls out a sheet that had ten or fifteen questions concerning electrical work.... I responded to all the questions on the sheet correctly. He made the comment that I was the only person he had ever seen that ever got all those questions right. I was granted my wish and was sent off to electricians mate school in Great Lakes.... I still shudder when I think of how close I came to being assigned to be a steward. It would have been a short stay in the navy and I would be a very bitter person [O'Meally, John].

Finally, there is the case of Abraham Mozeak, a future submariner who enlisted in 1954 from Wilmington, North Carolina. Unlike some of the men listed previously, he was never steered toward being a steward and, as he states, "I was lucky that people seemed to listen to me" (Mozeak). While he took the required tests, just like all new recruits, he came out of boot camp as a fireman and struck for engineman. While working at the torpedo station in Keyport, Washington, he also went to deep sea diving school and achieved an auxiliary rating as diver 2nd class, qualified to dive to depths of up to 120 feet. While Mozeak was an engineman striker, he did a fair amount of diving and saw enough to know that there were few opportunities available in that area. As he would later recall, "I never saw a Black deep sea diver" (Mozeak).

All in all, for those Black men that went into the navy early in the 1950s, it was highly likely that, even with a technical background or aptitude, they would be steered toward being a steward. It was rare for a Black recruit to encounter a councilor who looked beyond race as a factor when helping to decide on a rating, but, as the experiences

Submariner Abraham Mozeak in the early 1960s. Behind him are several submarine tenders, including the *Apollo* (*AS-25*). (Photograph courtesy of A. Mozeak.)

of Joyner and Mozeak show, it sometimes happened. However, as the decade progressed and the separate recruiting of stewards was discontinued, fewer and fewer Black men were becoming stewards, instead choosing rates that were more geared toward their interests and abilities. One interesting illustration of this change can be found in the crew make-up of the submarine *Stickleback* in 1958. Of her 84-man enlisted crew in May of that year, only two were Black, a number that had held pretty constant in the Submarine Force since about 1943. However, neither of these men were stewards. John Phelps, Jr., was a torpedoman 3rd class, while William Stallings was an interior communications electrician 2nd class. The boat did have three stewards, but all were either of Filipino or Guamanian descent. Slowly but surely as the 1950s progressed, Black men in the Submarine Force, and the navy as a whole, were expanding into a variety of technical ratings.

Despite the fact that the rating of steward was one that was seldom chosen by new Black recruits, this did not mean that those Black submariners who were stewards were viewed as anything less than regular crewmen. Indeed, as they had during World War II, stewards were fully qualified on the submarines on which they served, and performed a variety of watch duties. Even when operating under peacetime conditions, the decisions they made and the actions they took were often of vital importance to their boat's safety. This is vividly illustrated by the actions of two seasoned stewards, Donald Wilson on *Sea Cat*, and Rufus Weaver on *Sea Owl*. Both men made the right decisions in critical situations that could have turned deadly had they not acted.

Wilson, a native of Columbus, Ohio, enlisted in the navy in late 1945 and went into submarines in 1950. From 1951 to 1953, he served aboard *Sea Cat*, based out of Key West, Florida. As a steward 3rd class, Wilson was standing watch in the after battery of *Sea Cat* one day out at sea when he noticed that a navy reservist electrician 2nd class, about to descend into the boat's battery well to check the battery acid levels, was wearing his rings, a watch, and had his keys attached to his belt. This was very much against procedure, as the metal items the electrician was wearing could come into contact with the batteries below and might cause a short or even an explosion and resulting fire. As Wilson recalls, "I yelled at him to stop ... thinking about the *Cochino-Tusk* incident scared me, and I acted on instinct" (Wilson, Donald). Wilson was later congratulated by his fellow enlisted men for his quick actions, and it was then, as he believes, that he became a real crew member, not just a steward. While the electrician involved in this incident was somewhat indignant and probably embarrassed at being yelled at, especially by a steward, the chief electrician on *Sea Cat* backed Donald Wilson, pointing out that when a qualified submariner like him spoke, it was for a reason. Because of his handling of this incident, Wilson would later be chosen for duty aboard *Nautilus*, the navy's first nuclear submarine.

An even more serious incident involving Steward Rufus Weaver took place on *Sea Owl* in 1956. While performing submarine school duty, taking along about forty students for training exercises in Long Island Sound, the boat was practicing diving with her executive officer in charge. While the boat was beginning to submerge, someone accidentally opened the main induction valve, flooding the engine room. Further trouble was averted when Weaver quickly closed the large 36-inch induction valve, located in the crew's mess, and the boat was able to blow her tanks and resurface. Had Weaver not acted quickly, as he was trained to do, more serious flooding could have resulted that might have put *Sea Owl* on the bottom in dire straits. His captain later told Weaver that, for his actions, he was eligible for a commendation but also told him that by doing so, the future career of the executive officer, who was the acting diving officer during the incident, would probably be in jeopardy. While the executive officer never thanked his steward personally for his actions, Weaver did not put in for the award. Stating that he was only doing his job, he believed that "glory doesn't mean anything to me if I didn't earn it" (Weaver, Rufus).

While the men of the steward's branch received much better treatment when serving in the Submarine Force, as opposed to the navy's surface craft, problems with race and and the demeaning tasks stewards were made to perform still cropped up from time to time within the service. Probably the only consolation to those stewards who were on the receiving end of such problems was the fact that their fellow stewards on such ships as aircraft carriers, cruisers, and the like had it much worse.

While many stewards suffered silently at the hands of the racist officers they served, choosing, as one man put it, "to wait them out" (Mozeak) until one or the other parties were transferred to another boat, not all were willing to take the treatment that was meted out to them, and they fought back. Veteran stewards, in particular, seemed often to be a target of discrimination and sometimes fought back. Younger stewards that came into the service after the war, too, were not always willing to accept the demeaning jobs that were sometimes demanded of them. Whether a veteran steward, or one just starting his career, there was a wide range of consequences for those men who bucked the status quo. The cases of William Perry, Dave Ball, and Howard Burton are illustrative of some instances when submarine stewards ran afoul, sometimes unknowingly, of the officers they served and the consequences that befell them.

William Perry was a long-serving submarine steward who enlisted in the navy way back in 1939 and first saw service on *Narwhal* that same year. A veteran of World War II, he made five war patrols on *Sunfish* and ended the war as an officer's cook 1st class on the *R-7* stationed stateside. In 1950 he was stationed at the New London submarine base when, with no advance notice, he was transferred out of the Submarine Force for duty in Washington, D.C. As he found out later, his integrity was questioned because he owned a spacious house and a nice car. Surely, his new commanding officer must have thought, such things could not be afforded on the salary of a lowly steward. What this officer didn't know was that Perry and his wife June worked hard for everything they owned and had spent their money wisely. Not only was Perry a first-class steward, but his wife worked as a nurse in the local hospital in Groton. Race, it appears, was really at the heart of the issue, for this commanding officer was also heard to have declared that "no nigger will work for me" (Perry). William Perry had no choice but to accept the transfer and uproot his family to a new home. On arrival in Washington, Perry saw duty as a policeman in the newly formed Armed Services Police Detachment. This unit helped local police in patrolling within a ten-mile radius of the capital and usually worked in cases involving servicemen.

However, things were not as easy when it came to his family. On arrival in

Chief Steward turned policeman William S. Perry in Washington, D.C., in 1952. Forced out of submarine duty due to his race, Perry was transferred to the national capital and worked as a member of the Armed Services Police detachment before he made it back to the Submarine Force several years later. (Official U.S. Navy photograph.)

Washington, attempts to get navy housing met without success, a common problem for many minority servicemen, and the Perry's were placed number 124 on a waiting list for military housing. It took a call to a Connecticut senator who knew well the Perry family to get this situation fixed in a hurry.

Perry's odyssey was not yet over. In July 1952, now two years out of submarines, William Perry received orders for new duty. The old submarine sailor had had enough and fought the move, writing a letter to the chief of naval personnel requesting that he be returned to submarine duty. Pleading his case, Perry stated that "I have served in submarines almost my entire career and desire to continue in them.... I am qualified in submarines, having qualified on board the *Narwhal 1* March 1941 ... and it is further believed that utilization of such training and experience will be in the best interest of the naval service" (Perry letter). The letter worked, and Perry, finally, was returned to submarine duty. In Perry's case, he did nothing wrong and there was no one incident that precipitated events. It was simply because of his color that he was sent out of submarines.

Chief Officer's Cook Dave Ball, a native of Arkansas, made four war patrols on *Rasher* and earned a Bronze Star for his service. After the war, he was a noted softball player for the Submarine Force, worked on the staff of the White House, and later switched his service to the naval air arm. (Official U.S. Navy photograph.)

Another man who left the Submarine Force, but never to return, was none other than Dave Ball. Not only was Ball the veteran of several war patrols on *Rasher* during the war, but he had also worked as a steward at the White House and was said to be held in high regard by Eleanor Roosevelt. Ball was also legendary for his sporting skills, including boxing during the war, and was a renowned navy softball pitcher in the postwar era. Ball was a chief steward in April 1954 when he suddenly left the Submarine Force for good, transferring to Fleet Aircraft Service Squadron 77 in Naples, Italy, for duty. Such a drastic change for this long-time submarine steward seems unusual, especially in light of the fact that Ball had just completed submarine escape training at New London in late December 1953, just four months prior. Why the sudden switch to the navy's air arm? Friends of Ball state that the problem was with Dave Ball's squadron commodore in New London, who demanded that Ball, as part of his duties, wash the commodore's car. Ball refused such duty, stating that he would quit the sub service before doing this, and, as such, held true to his word

(Collier). Ironically, while Ball lost his hazardous submarine pay, he supplanted this lost income by receiving hazardous flight pay when he worked aboard the aircraft of the secretary of the navy, flying out of the U.S. Naval Air Station at Paxtuxent, Maryland, from 1955 to 1959.

Another steward who refused to put up with some of the demeaning duties assigned to him was Steward 2nd Class Howard Burton on *Tusk* about the year 1955. Burton joined the navy as a steward in 1948 and first served on *Cobbler* and *Flying Fish* before later joining *Tusk*. During the time in question, Burton, along with Steward 3rd Class Woodrow Galbreath, a former *Nautilus* man, and a stewardsman by the name of Hardin, were on board for a week-long training run. Also on board was the division commanding officer. Things went wrong almost from the start. With *Tusk* operating in heavy weather and rough seas, cooking was difficult, and much of the gear had to be safely stowed away. However, one of the officers, a stickler for toast, insisted that toast be made for him. Burton told him, "Man, its too rough to make toast" (Burton). However, the officer insisted that toast would be made, whereby Burton "dug out the toaster and told him to make it him damn self.... The other officers came by to see what was going on. I was so mad I could hardly talk" (Burton).

Several days later, more trouble arose when the division officer asked that Burton wash his socks and underwear, to which Burton replied, "No, I'm a second class [steward], and I won't order my men to do it" (Burton). While Burton now admits, regarding these incidents, that "My pot boiled over quicker than it should have," he was clearly correct in that personal laundry chores were not a steward's job. However, even Burton knew that he had probably pushed things too far. As he recalls, "I went about my business, though it was in the back of my mind. After lunch I went by the officer's stateroom and saw the washing hanging up. I asked Galbreath if he had washed.... No, he didn't. I figured, I brought enough clothes to last me, a division commander should have, too" (Burton). After these incidents on *Tusk*, Burton "knew my time was up.... Nobody [officers]

The enlightened state of race relations on submarines versus that on surface ships nearly saved the career of former war-time steward Edgar Frazelle. (Photograph courtesy of E. Frazelle.)

were speaking to me. As we were coming into port and securing the boat, the yeoman called me and said that "Gabby" [Galbreath] and I were being transferred. I said, 'Man, get the hell out of here,' but he showed me the orders" (Burton). Howard Burton was subsequently transferred to the naval air station at Whiting Field in Milton, Florida, and was out of submarines for 29 months.

Despite such troubles, racial conditions in the Submarine Force were almost always better than those found on surface ships. As such, a number of stewards left surface craft to go to submarine duty and had successful subsequent careers in that area. Among such men were James Owens, Jr., and Charles Groom. One man who tried to find a better navy life, so to speak, by going to submarine duty was Edgar Frazelle. While his submarine career was short and ultimately unsuccessful, his career was likely similar to that of many stewards who served on surface craft in less than ideal conditions. Frazelle, a native of New Bern, North Carolina, enlisted in the navy in 1939, first serving on the battleship *Idaho* before being sent to the aircraft carrier *Hornet*. Edgar Frazelle was aboard the *Hornet* when she was attacked by Japanese aircraft off Guadalcanal on October 26, 1942, and sunk the next day. His battle station had been deep in the bowels of the ship as an ammunition passer, but he made it topside when the carrier was mortally wounded and was eventually evacuated to safety with the rest of her surviving crew by a destroyer sent to their aid. In his subsequent duty aboard transport vessels, he was again assigned to a battle station below and refused to do such duty. For this he was court martialed and, as he states, "labeled a troublemaker" (Frazelle). While Frazelle would serve out his time, ending up as a steward 3rd class by the time of his discharge in 1945, he had strong misgivings about the navy as a career and "didn't feel that I should be in the war.... I wasn't fighting for anything. Our country had jim crow racism and the navy was the worst perpetrator of racism" (*ibid.*).

Despite these feelings, Frazelle would volunteer for the navy yet again in 1950. Given the choice to come back in as either a steward 3rd class or a seaman 1st class, he "opted for steward third class, which was stupid" (*ibid.*). Frazelle would subsequently serve in New London, working in the base (bachelor officer quarters) BOQ and was the master of arms over the base steward barracks. After scoring extremely high on an intelligence test he was made to take, Frazelle was told to set up an appointment for evaluation as an OCS (officer candidate school), but, as he recalls, "Once they saw I was Black, they said I was too old.... I'll always believe that had it not been for my race and color, I would have gone further" (*ibid.*). Tired of surface craft, Frazelle, about the year 1954, volunteered for submarine duty, with the thought that he would like it better. As it turns out, it was better, and, as Frazelle relates, "I got along pretty well," and he liked the fact that, on submarines, "you leave your rating topside" (*ibid.*). However, there was one insurmountable problem — Frazelle experienced terrible seasickness. As long as his boat, *Grampus*, was submerged, he was fine, but when she rode on the surface it was a different story. Because of this problem, Frazelle left the Submarine Force within six months and would be out of the navy in the following year. As he relates, "I was fed up with the way I was treated.... Things went from bad to worse" (*ibid.*), and he was eventually discharged from the navy in 1955 after being busted from steward 1st class to steward 2nd class. While Frazelle would later go on to have an excellent civilian career, one can't help but wonder if successful submarine duty might not have resulted in a different ending to his naval career.

Prejudice was still an everyday part of life for most Blacks in the navy, but those submarine stewards that had served during World War II under skippers that were later promoted to higher command positions often had an inside edge. Having served closely with their wartime commanders, many stewards remained quite friendly with their skippers after the war and sometimes found in them a man who served both as a protector and an advocate when it came to advancement within their own navy career. Of the numerous examples of this type of friendship to be found, two are worth mentioning here. The first involves Elvin Mayo, the former wartime steward on *Jack* under Captain Thomas Dykers. While serving on *Corsair* out of New London in the late 1940s, Mayo became sick and was sent to the base hospital. He did not regain his health as quickly as he thought he should and complained to the hospital staff about his treatment. As Mayo tells it, a hospital officer came to him and said he was going to "ship my ass to Timbucktoo and out of submarines" (Mayo) for making trouble. Word soon got back to Dykers, who was in command of a squadron at the time, and he confronted the guilty officer in Mayo's presence and "told him that he was going to ship *him* to Timbucktoo" (*ibid.*) if he treated Mayo that way again.

Another example of this type of relationship involved Chief Steward Anderson Royal on *Carbonero* in 1950. Royal and his boat were involved in the testing of new weapons systems, but when the Korean War broke out, all submarines stationed on the west coast were ordered to Pearl Harbor to determine which would be deployed for the war. Very shortly after arriving at Pearl, Royal encountered Captain Creed Burlingame, his old skipper on *Silversides* during the war, who was now on the submarine command staff at Pearl. The two talked and exchanged pleasantries, and Burlingame inquired about Royal's four children. It was then that Royal told him, "Captain, I've got six children now" (Royal). Burlingame was amazed at how large Royal's family had become, and when he met him the next day, he told his old steward, "You've got nothing to worry about, you're going back stateside" (*ibid.*). *Carbonero* was indeed sent back to the states to resume her duty and made no Korean patrols. Though he never told anyone at the time, Anderson Royal believes to this day that Burlingame made certain that his former steward, his old friend, and the boat he was on would not be sent in harm's way. Given the fact that Burlingame later facilitated Royal's rate change to chief electronics technician, he is probably correct.

While the men of the steward's branch were the lightning rod for racial change in the navy, it is important to note that there had always been a dichotomy of sorts within all areas of the steward's branch itself, the Submarine Force included. On one side, there were those stewards that served directly aboard the boats and were part of a regular crew. With them may also be included those qualified submarine stewards that were currently performing shore duty. This second group of men were often sent to such duty against their wishes, such as Howard Burton, while at other times, some normally sea-going stewards asked for a period of shore duty so that they might have time to spend with their families or for other personal reasons. At such times as this, these stewards usually served at such submarine base divisions as the mess hall or the BOQ.

On the other side were those stewards who served high-ranking division officers or officers of flag rank. Though often officially attached to a particular submarine, these stewards seldom were seen on board as they were simply part of the "flag allowance" that every high-ranking officer had as part of his privileges. Stewards were assigned to such boats only because of its designation as an officer's flagship. The distinction between sea-going stewards and stewards assigned to a boat as part of a flag allowance had always existed but was seldom a problem within the Submarine Force prior to the war, as there were relatively few Blacks serving in this small branch of the service. In the postwar era, however, with many more units in the fleet, many of them manned by stewards who had put their lives on the line by making war patrols, the differences became greater. Not only were those stewards on the boats doing military duty, day in and day out, but many were also desirous of expanded opportunities outside the steward's branch. Those stewards in the Submarine Force that served in a flag-allowance position as officer's servants, however, often performed duties, such as personal laundry chores, washing cars, and serving as waiters at social gatherings and were often referred to by sea-going stewards in such derisive terms as "ass-kissers," "brown-nosers," "Uncle Toms," and worse (Weaver, Rufus). In part, this was because these stewards were doing the demeaning jobs that sea-going stewards were constantly fighting against.

What made matters even worse is the fact that many stewards that were part of a flag allowance had little submarine experience but yet were paid the hazardous duty pay for submarine service. How did this occur? It was simple, really, though vastly unfair to the regular-duty submarine stewards. Because officers of high rank often went out for a brief cruise on one of their submarines every month, perhaps for a few hours, maybe for the afternoon, their personal stewards usually went with them. These essentially land-based stewards didn't mind this at all, as it allowed them to qualify for submarine pay and, in some cases, to even "earn" their dolphins by "qualifying" aboard the boat in a ridiculously short space of time. Of course, the real submarine stewards saw these events for what they really were, but the matter was outside their control. While the navy must receive a lion's share of the blame for allowing such situations to exist, those flag-allowance stewards that took advantage of the situation must also share in the blame. At a time when many of the Black men in the steward's branch were striving to be recognized as the professionals that they were, some flag stewards served to perpetuate the old way of doing things. Having stated this, it must be said that there were exceptions to the rule.

There were a number of good men who served high-ranking officers yet were able to maintain their professionalism. Flag stewards were, after all, a part of the privilege of rank, and their assignment in this area was inevitable. Many of these stewards in the postwar era were older submariners who had made war patrols during World War II and had done their time at sea. Once in flag-allowance positions, men such as William Knight, Dave Ball, and Paul Ragland, and others maintained their professionalism ashore. Because of their wartime experience, they sometimes had the power to dictate what jobs they would and wouldn't do and the guts to make a stand if pushed to the limit. The experiences of Dave Ball, discussed previously, well illustrate this point. When pushed to do what he deemed to be a demeaning or inappropriate job, he acted on principle and refused to do it, choosing instead to leave the Submarine Force.

The types of incidents involving Ball, Perry, and Burton, coupled with a desire to move to another job of greater interest, were some of the reasons that many submarine stewards changed their ratings in the 1950s. Now that they were able to do so with less restriction, many men chose to leave the steward's branch and pursue new and challenging careers within the navy. Among the most interesting and accomplished of those submarine stewards that changed their rates were Isaac Johnson, Anderson Royal, and James Owens, Jr. Johnson was a wartime veteran who first served on *Sennet* and, after the war, for a long period on *Carbonero*. Following this, Johnson went to *Tilefish* as steward 1st class and later put in for a change of rating. On August 2, 1954, he went to Treasure Island to go to electronics technician conversion (ETC) school. After a year of intense study, the change became official, and Isaac Johnson was now an electronics technician 1st class. He was the first steward ever at Treasure Island, and probably the entire navy, to change his rate to that of an ET, beating out Anderson Royal for this honor by a month. After his conversion, Isaac Johnson returned to *Tilefish* for duty. His former fellow steward, Velton Parker, was still aboard and was happy for Johnson. As for the rest of the crew, they welcomed the popular Johnson back but, as he recalls, "They still looked at you as a steward, and there was some resentment at my changing rates" (Johnson). However, no real problems were encountered in subsequent submarine assignments for Johnson. On board *Tilefish*, Johnson was known first as a steward and then as an ET — on future boats he was known only as an ET, so there was no mistaking his duty.

The story of Anderson Royal and his pioneering change from chief steward aboard *Carbonero* to chief ET in 1955 has already been told, in part in a previous chapter, but it is worth reiterating that his change in rating was made with the full support not only of his former World War II commander but also the officer corps at the naval training center in San Diego where he worked. The amount of support Royal received has made him grateful to this day for the men who looked at his abilities without any regard to his color. In speaking about the officers who helped him get into ET school, Royal recalls that "They had more interest in me getting to school than I did myself" (Royal, Anderson P.). When he graduated from ETC school in 1955, Royal, the only African American in the group, was third in his class. Upon graduation, Royal was posted out of submarines to the repair ship *Hooper Island* and flew to Japan to join his new ship. Royal recalls vividly that when he stepped aboard, the word was

> "Oh, we got another chief steward...." Then the word spread — "we got a colored chief of electronics.... We got a nigger for a chief." I put on my best uniform, with the best decorations and the best submarine things, and things went well after that.... Later they said, "We got a good chief" [Royal, Anderson P.].

Finally, there is the change in rate for James Owens, Jr. Owens was a veteran of World War II who entered the navy in 1943 and saw service in the South Pacific aboard the carrier *Yorktown*. After the war, he switched gears and joined the Submarine Force, first serving on *Sea Robin* before gaining a berth on the first nuclear submarine, *Nautilus*. He would subsequently serve in nuclear boats the rest of his career, and while on *Sargo*, he changed his rate from steward to storekeeper. He was the first Black storekeeper in the Submarine Force. As he recalls today, "It was hard to be a storekeeper on submarines, and being Black was a multiplier.... I learned the navy did not give you anything, but anything in the navy you wanted, you had to work like hell to get" (Owens).

If the decade of the 1950s was a time of great change for Black submariners and the advancement opportunities that became open to them, the changes within the decade were even greater when it came to the submarines themselves and the operations in which they were involved. First and foremost of these new developments was the swift development of the nuclear submarine. Her keel laid at the Electric Boatyard in Groton, Connecticut, in June of 1952, *Nautilus* was the world's first nuclear submarine. In length, she measured 320 feet, just 8 feet longer than the Tench-class diesel boats that saw service in World War II. Powered by a nuclear reactor, however, she weighed in at just over 4,000 tons — 1,600 tons heavier than a fleet diesel boat. The story of this, the world's first nuclear-powered ship, and her development under the intense personal supervision of Rear Admiral Hyman Rickover is well known and needs no retelling here. However, what is little known is that Black sailors, too, were a part of her crew. Just like their white shipmates, the Black crewmen of *Nautilus* had to undergo rigorous and specialized training and had to be qualified throughout the boat.

The first Black personnel assigned to *Nautilus* were Steward 3rd Class Donald Wilson, a veteran submariner with two hash marks on his sleeve, Steward Shelley Cole, a veteran of one war patrol on *Catfish* in 1945, and Eddie Davis, a fireman. After their posting to the historic boat, both men, and, indeed, all the crewmen and officers of *Nautilus*, had months of hard work ahead of them. Their first assignment was to attend the navy's nuclear submarine propulsion school at the Westinghouse Atomic Power Division in Pittsburgh, Pennsylvania.

Chief Storekeeper James Owens, Jr., first served during World War II as a steward on an aircraft carrier and other transport vessels. He later volunteered for submarine duty and would become the first African American chief storekeeper in the Submarine Force. (Photograph courtesy of the Owens family.)

During the month-long course of study, Wilson, Cole, Davis, and the other men in the class became acquainted with the principles of nuclear power and its peculiar application to submarines and graduated from the Fourth Naval Training Group. From here, Wilson, Cole, and Davis, along with other crew, were sent to Idaho Falls, Idaho, for hands-on work with a prototype nuclear reactor. While the six-week course of study here was professional in every way, social and racial conditions were not as pleasant. Told of the color line in Idaho prior to his arrival, Donald Wilson found it all true. As he recalls,

> There were a lot of racial problems, and a place to stay was hard to get. A Black attorney named Reginald Reaves finally got me a third-rate room at the Hotel Idaho, close to the police station. I could not eat at local restaurants, and barbers would only cut my hair after hours.... Sometimes when people drove by us they spit at us and called us names [Wilson, Donald].

After their work was done at Idaho Falls, the *Nautilus* men were finally sent to the New London submarine base in Connecticut and finally went aboard their new boat. Much time was spent in class work ashore, while the rest of the time was spent aboard the boat after her launching in January 1954 while she was alongside the pier at the Electric Boat shipyard, waiting for the time when she would take to the waves. Finally, on January 17, 1955, *Nautilus* made history when she cast off her lines and became the first ship ever to sail under nuclear power. By this time, the Black personnel on the boat had changed. Wilson was still aboard as was Davis, but gone was Shelly Cole. He was replaced after the commissioning of *Nautilus* in 1954 by Steward 1st Class Thomas Emanuel. Veteran Steward 1st Class James Owens, Jr., also came aboard, replacing the lead steward, Limson, who was from the Phillipines.

Steward Donald Wilson of *Nautilus*. Wilson first qualified in diesel boats but was later chosen to serve on the world's first nuclear-powered submarine. On *Nautilus* he served several different tours of duty and was aboard when she made her first attempt to gain the North Pole. (Official U.S. Navy photograph.)

During her first months of sea trials prior to her formal commissioning in September 1955, Wilson well recalls the many surface tests and the constant supervision of Atomic Energy Commission (AEC) people and technicians from Westinghouse Atomic. Ever present was the strong-willed head of the navy's nuclear program, Rear Admiral Hyman Rickover. He was known not only for his hard-line approach but also for his strict attention to details, and he was involved in every aspect of the new boat's operations. While aboard *Nautilus*, Donald Wilson acted as the ship's barber, cutting hair for the officers, enlisted crew, and even

Rickover. He can rightfully lay claim to be the first man ever to cut someone's hair using nuclear power, an interesting, if somewhat obscure, distinction. One thing that is clear, however, is that Wilson and James Owens knew how to run an excellent wardroom. With Rickover constantly aboard, anything less than this would have been unacceptable. As in all newly built submarines, there were always construction details throughout the boat, both large and small, that needed attention and fixing. The wardroom and galley areas where Wilson worked were no exception, and he "pointed out problems with the wardroom and pantry area to Electric Boat people, and they were fixed because of my recommendations" (Wilson, Donald).

During his time on *Nautilus* leading up to her historic runs to the North Pole, Wilson spent his time getting fully qualified, as did the other men, as well as performing the duties expected of a steward. His battle-station duties were as phone-talker, manning the phones in the wardroom, a position given to him both out of tradition and for the fact that his voice was loud and easy to understand. While Wilson was interested in becoming a gunner's mate, it was a change he never actively pursued. In his off-hours, Donald Wilson spent time gambling with the crew and also studied to be a Mason. Because *Nautilus* was the navy's newest and most advanced submarine, her activities were kept secret, and even her crew had little knowledge of what duties she might see. As Wilson recalls, "We never found out about anything beforehand" (*ibid.*).

While the first years were filled with test runs to determine submerged endurance and speed capabilities for *Nautilus*, the navy and Rickover had a special mission in mind — the first ship ever to go to the top of the world and cross the North Pole, under the ice, from the Pacific to the Atlantic Ocean. Throughout maritime history, attempts to find a Northwest Passage by surface ships had resulted in many heroic, but ill-fated missions. It was the *Nautilus* that would finally achieve what many had tried before, and she did it the only way possible — under the ice. However, even on her first attempt to cross the North Pole, *Nautilus*, with Wilson and Owens aboard, was unsuccessful.

The secret mission began on August 19, 1957, when the nuclear boat left New London and headed toward the northern waters between Greenland and Norway, on the edge of the Arctic ice. Just eight years prior, the *Cochino* was lost in these very waters, and that fact must have lain heavily on the minds of *Nautilus*'s crew. The mission first became known to the crew, in all likelihood, when cold weather gear was stowed aboard the boat, but it was not officially announced until the *Nautilus* was under way. Once known, it was the subject of much discussion. Steward James Owens was heard to remark "that he had a fair amount of faith in the skipper to do the right thing" (Anderson, *Nautilus*, p. 75), but Donald Wilson was not as assured. While he, too, had faith in Commander William Anderson, he also remarked that "I'd still rather be in New London" (*ibid.*). What was most on Wilson's mind were the ill-fated expeditions of the past by men in wooden ships, such as that of the English explorer Sir John Franklin in 1847. As Wilson recalls, "The captain was in his stateroom and heard when I told Owens that I was afraid after hearing about all of those old ships that had been caught in the ice" (Wilson, Donald). Nonetheless, there was no turning back at this point, and Wilson, Owens, and the men of *Nautilus* were on their way.

Arriving at the edge of the pack ice, the boat made its first dive under the ice on September 1, 1957. Things proceeded well and the boat made steady progress toward the North Pole. While the goal was to proceed as far north as possible, the decision on whether or not to go for the North Pole itself was left to Commander Anderson. Despite having her periscope damaged and subsequently repaired in the harshest of conditions, *Nautilus* would have made it on her first try had it not been for a faulty gyrocompass. While the compass might have been regained its equilibrium, the effects in this extreme latitude on how accurately the compass might adjust itself were unknown, and the boat had to be navigated by a standard magnetic compass. After making it to 87 degrees north, about 180 miles from the North Pole, Anderson turned *Nautilus* around and headed her southward and out of the ice, unwilling to risk a navigational error that might put his boat and crew in danger.

Despite just missing her mark, the first attempt by *Nautilus* and her crew to cross the North Pole was a great achievement and proved just what a nuclear submarine could do. The days of the diesel submarine were numbered.

Upon her return to the states, *Nautilus* stopped at several ports, among them Miami, Florida. For Donald Wilson and James Owens, and probably Eddie Davis, this is where the voyage turned sour. All were excluded, because of their color, from participating in the ship's party that was held ashore. When the boat returned to her home port at New London, Wilson protested the treatment of the stewards by refusing to participate in any of the homecoming activities for *Nautilus*'s crew and, several months later, by January 1958, was off the boat at his own request. Owens and Davis, too, would soon be off the boat.

Steward Thomas Emanuel of *Nautilus*. Emanuel came aboard in time for *Nautilus*'s second, and successful, attempt to reach the North Pole, and it was the high point of his submarine career. Though Emanuel died at a young age in 1972, he has been honored by his hometown of Corona, New York, in Queens, by having a public school named after him. (Official U.S. Navy photograph.)

When *Nautilus* made her second, and successful, attempt to cross the North Pole in 1958, two Black stewards were aboard, Stewards Walter Harvey and Queens, New York, native Thomas Emanuel. After making the North Pole at 90 degrees north on August 3, 1958, and returning home, Harvey would later have the honor of presenting to Rear Admiral Rickover a piece of ice gathered from the top of the world. While Thomas Emanuel died in 1972, his accomplishments as part of *Nautilus*'s crew are not forgotten. In October of 2003, it was decided to give his name to a 400-seat prekindergarten to second grade early childhood school located on 47th Avenue in the Corona section of Queens, New York, to honor the Corona native for his navy achievements. It is an honor few submarine stewards have ever received.

On the heels of the historic submarine *Nautilus* there soon came a number of other nuclear boats, most of which had Black crewmen. Steward Earnest Danford served on *Seawolf*, the navy's second nuclear boat, and was part of her commissioning crew in

Chief Steward Walter Harvey (left) of the *Nautilus* is here shown presenting a chunk of ice from the North Pole to Admiral Rickover (far right) in celebration of the boat's successful voyage to the North Pole in August 1958. (Photograph by John Krawczyk; official U.S. Navy photograph.)

March 1957. Danford continued aboard *Seawolf* throughout 1957–1958, serving aboard her during her shakedown cruise off Bermuda, her training exercises in Key West, and her cruise across the Atlantic to take part in NATO exercises. Among the countries that *Seawolf* touched on during her early cruising days that is most remembered by Danford was that of South Africa. Another steward that served aboard *Seawolf* was Raymond Hopkins.

The third nuclear submarine to be launched by the Electric Boat Yard at Groton, Connecticut, was *Skate*. Like *Nautilus*, she was destined to see service in the Arctic ice. Among those that came aboard *Skate* just after she was launched in May 1957 was Chief Steward Woodrow Wilson Jones. A veteran of World War II, Jones was a seasoned submariner who had made war patrols on *Pike* and *Redfish*. However, the duty he was about to embark on would be different than that of any he had experienced before. Once the new boat was commissioned in December of 1957, just two days before Christmas, she conducted training exercises off New London and farther afield in the warm waters of Bermuda. In February 1958, *Skate* steamed across the ocean, visiting ports in England, France, and the Netherlands.

However, it was in Arctic waters that *Skate* would gain her fame. With Chief Jones aboard, she went to the Arctic first in August 1958, operating under the ice for ten days and traveling nearly 2,500 miles to become the second ship ever to reach the North Pole. Jones and *Skate* again went to the Arctic in March 1959, this time sailing 3,900 miles under the ice and surfacing at the North Pole, the first submarine ever to do so. When Woodrow Wilson Jones joined his fellow crew members to leave the warm confines of *Skate* and step foot in the ice and snow of the North Pole, he became just the second Black man in history to stand at the North Pole. Jones followed in the footsteps, albeit by a much easier route, of the first man ever to reach the North Pole, the Black explorer Matthew Henson, who had done so with the Peary Arctic Expedition fifty years earlier on April 6, 1909. For this pioneering voyage, *Skate* and her crew were awarded a Bronze Star in lieu of a second Navy Unit Commendation for her cold weather operations.

Yet another early nuclear boat that had several Black crewmen was *Sargo*, commissioned in October 1958. One of her stewards was the former steward on *Nautilus*, James Owens, Jr. However, Owens would soon change his rate from steward to storekeeper, the first Black ever to do so in the Submarine Force, and a replacement steward was needed. This man would be war veteran Mason Smith. A submariner since his days on *Mingo* in 1944, Smith had been on a destroyer escort vessel doing radar picket work as part of the DEW (Distant Early Warning) line and had had a stint of shore duty for the two years prior to his assignment to *Sargo*. When first commissioned, the boat, with Smith and Owens aboard, would make a 19,000 mile shakedown cruise in the Pacific and, in late 1959 was undergoing heavy training for a future run northward, to be discussed in the next section.

One of the last nuclear attack boats to be commissioned in the 1950s was *Skipjack*. When she was accepted for service on April 15, 1959, she had as her crew members at least two Black submariners, Chief Electronics Technician Isaac Johnson, and Hospital Corpsman 1st Class James Mosley. During her subsequent shakedown cruise in August 1959, *Skipjack* would be the first nuclear ship to pass through the Straits of Gibraltar and operate in the Mediterranean Sea. Just how far Black submariners had progressed by this time is demonstrated by the work of Hospital Corpsman Mosley. In addition to his trained duties, such as sewing back on the finger of the ship's cook that had accidentally been severed, Mosley also stood watch at a variety of stations. As he recalls, "I did everything. My battle-station position was that of helmsman, but I also stood watch as a radar/sonar operator and assisted the navigators" (James Mosley).

The final nuclear attack boat commissioned in the 1950s was *Seadragon*. Among her crew was Steward 1st Class Charles Groom. Groom was a veteran of World War II and served aboard the transport *Zeilen (APA-3)* from the end of 1943 to early 1946. As he recalls,

> We carried marines from San Francisco to such places as Tarawa and would take wounded men off the islands to hospital ships off shore. During the invasion of Luzon [January 1945], we were hit by a kamikaze attack in Lingayen Gulf, during which I was a gunner on a twin 20mm. When the kamikaze plane hit us, it killed about 17 men, including three stewards. I only got a scratch on my arm. We later took part in the operations off Iwo Jima before going back to the states" [Groom].

After the war Groom worked as a steward on the carriers *Midway* and *Antietam* before doing a stint of shore duty. His transfer to *Seadragon*, his first submarine, was due to the fact that the navy was then short on stewards. As Groom recalls, he took a ride on one newly built submarine that was out on sea trials and "kind of liked it.... When the admiral I was working for was transferred, I volunteered for submarines and went to sub school for eight weeks" (*ibid.*). One of the reasons Groom liked sub duty was the fact that "your rate didn't matter" when on a submarine, as all were qualified crewmembers (*ibid.*). After completing sub school, Groom was sent to *Seadragon* and was aboard for her commissioning on December 5, 1959. He would later, in the early 1960s, see some quite interesting duty aboard this, his first submarine.

Other historic nuclear submarines, such as the giant radar picket boat *Triton* and the first ballistic missile submarine *George Washington*, would also be commissioned by late 1959, but since their naval service did not fully commence until the following year, their activities will be covered in the next section. However, before leaving the 1950s, we must look at the activities of the tried-and-true diesel boats and the Black submariners that served aboard some of them. Though they were slowly being supplanted by the more modern nuclear boats, the diesel sailors and their boats still provided valuable and vital services to the navy.

Senior Chief Steward Charles Groom. Groom first did steward duty during World War II on a transport vessel and saw heavy combat action before voluteering for the Submarine Force in the late 1950s. (Photograph courtesy of C. Groom.)

Some Black submariners saw duty on a number of experimental submarines built or modified by the navy in the 1950s. The smallest of these boats was the 347-ton *T-1*, a vessel built primarily for training purposes and commissioned in October 1953. Among her small, 14-man crew was former wartime submariner, Steward 2nd Class Alfred Hall. Service on this boat out of Key West, Florida, primarily in antisubmarine warfare (ASW) exercises, was quite a change from the regular fleet diesel boats Hall was used to serving on. However, Hall would later serve on a much bigger boat when he received a posting to *Nautilus*, a submarine over ten times the tonnage of *T-1*.

Another, and more important, experimental submarine that had at least one Black crewmen was the radically designed *Albacore*. Aboard her from 1955 to 1962 was Chief Steward James Washington, yet another seasoned steward who had enlisted in 1938 and had been a submariner since 1941. The *Albacore* was of a vastly different design than the fleet boats that preceded her and, with her whale-shaped hull, was built solely for speed and great maneuverability underwater. As Washington recalls, most of her work was "top secret stuff" (Washington, James) and involved many different changes in the physical configuration of the boat. Among her operations during the late 1950s were cruises in both New London and Key West waters as well as operations off Guantanamo Bay, Cuba. In April of 1956, *Albacore*, with Washington and the rest of her crew aboard, was featured in the television show *Wide, Wide World*. For the first time ever, live film footage of a submarine diving was broadcast when *Albacore* took to the deep in the waters off New York City.

Another type of submarine activity that was developed in the late 1940s and in use throughout the 1950s was that of radar picket duty. Simply put, this involved converting a typical fleet submarine so that she carried a whole array of communications and electronics detection gear. So configured, such boats, spread out across the Atlantic Ocean, from the Arctic waters of the north to the warm waters of the Caribbean, served as part of the DEW (Distant Early Warning) line established in the sea and the sky to monitor Soviet activities and, if necessary, give warning of an impending nuclear strike against the United States. One of the boats that was assigned to and modified for this duty was *Tigrone*. Among the crewmen of this boat during the mid–1950s was legendary World War II submariner Steward 1st Class Joseph Cross. During his time aboard *Tigrone*, the boat made a number of cruises to the Mediterranean and to the Atlantic waters off England, Italy, and Spain. Her activities were air defense training exercises with U.S. and NATO forces. One former crewman of *Tigrone* fondly recalls Cross not only for being a good submariner but also for how well he treated his shipmates. During one Christmas, while the boat was home-ported in Norfolk, Virginia, Cross stayed aboard to voluntarily cook a holiday meal for the entire crew. He didn't have to do it — he wanted to do it, and it was a meal his shipmates wouldn't soon forget (Drewry).

Another World War II fleet boat that underwent a similar conversion process was *Cavalla*. Decommissioned after the war, she was recommissioned in 1951 with Steward 1st Class Paul Ragland, a veteran patroller during the war years on *Barb*, aboard for duty. A short time later, *Cavalla* was converted to a hunter-killer submarine (SSK designation) and was fitted with a wide array of new sonar gear specifically designed to aid in the hunt for enemy submarines. So equipped, she participated in many new weapons tests and participated in a variety of fleet and NATO exercises. Ragland would remain aboard *Cavalla*, his last submarine, for four years before going to shore duty in 1955.

Other boats operated in Mediterranean waters during the 1950s, including those boats that were sent there during the Mideast crisis in Beirut, Lebanon, in 1958. Among the fleet diesel boats sent to this area during this tense time was *Trutta*. Aboard her was Electrician's Mate 2nd Class John O'Meally, a 1954 enlistee who had been in submarines for about a year. *Trutta* was O'Meally's first boat, and he was just one of two Black crewmembers aboard. His experiences during this time, both aboard the boat and in the southern ports of Charleston, South Carolina, and Key West, are quite interesting. Despite the fact that there were few Black submariners aboard, O'Meally recalls that

> My acceptance by the crew was no problem as far as I could tell — the officers also did not treat me any different than the rest of the crew.... On the ship, I was doing the work of an electrician and got the respect my rank of second class petty officer called for" [O'Meally, John].

Ashore, however, it was quite a different story—this was, after all, the south in the 1950s. O'Meally remembers that, in Charleston, "there was no place I could go where the rest of the crew hung out.... The shipyard workers would give me the once over and mutter something under their breath but did not interfere with me" (*ibid.*). Key West, Florida, was no different for O'Meally. In describing the situation, he states that "I was a young 21-year-old from New York City, I had never been anywhere where there was an option as to how I would be treated. I had a lot to learn" (*ibid.*). And learn he did. Continuing his story, O'Meally says of Key West, "On the base there was no problem. Once outside the gate, however, you made a right turn and went to the dark side of town. That was the normal way of doing things in 1957 and that was that" (*ibid.*).

While making *Trutta's* Mediterranean cruise in 1958 off the coast of Beirut, O'Meally recalls that "It was uneventful for the most part," but things would change while she made her way home. O'Meally remembers that

> We were directed to intercept five Russian subs coming down the coast of Portugul heading for Gibralter. They were travelling on the surface with a Russian surface ship. We approached them and were getting some data when they detected us. They submerged, and for the next twelve hours or so we played the game of who has the most air. Nobody [on *Trutta*] made a sound, and the air was getting awfully thin. CO-2 absorbent was spread around the boat to get rid of exhaled gases. The Russians finally gave up and surfaced, and we continued to stay quiet for another two or three hours before coming up to snorkel depth [*ibid.*].

This type of cat-and-mouse game was common during the Cold War era and quite dangerous. While tracking Russian submarines, the Americans never knew if their opponent might turn hostile and try to torpedo them. While such an event never happened, as far as is known, all it took was one over-itchy finger on the trigger for either side to possibly precipitate another world war.

Not to be forgotten were those Black submariners serving in Pacific waters during the 1950s. One of these boats was *Tilefish*, with Steward 1st Class Arnold Duncan aboard and, from 1950 to 1953, Electronics Technician Donald Burrell. As Burrell recalls,

> *Tilefish* was the lead boat with the special signals intercept system, the latest technology.... We were assigned to classified intel missions but not on an exclusive basis. During that three years we made at least two WESTPAC deployments. There were tense moments caused by finding ourselves in an unswept World War II minefield or a violent typhoon, but such moments were common to all boats at that time [Burrell].

Another Black submariner who saw service in Korean waters was Kenneth Joyner. His submarine career as a radioman began on *Bashaw* in 1951 but was temporarily halted when he was transferred off the boat, against his wishes, after a confrontation with the chief of the boat (COB) over his assignment to mess cooking duties. Joyner subsequently served aboard the tender *Sperry* and was on the auxiliary-submarine rescue vessel *Chanticleer* when he finally made a return to submarine duty after volunteering for service on *Blenny* in early 1952. By now Joyner was a radioman 3rd class and was joining his new boat just as she was ready to make another WESTPAC run in Korean waters. As Joyner relates,

> For these runs, everything was blacked out on the sub, her hull number and everything. They were surreptitious operations and hard duty on a diesel submarine. You went a long time without a shower, and it was arduous duty in cold water — a miserable life as a sewer rat. But, it was also exciting.... We were submariners, the cream of the crop [Joyner].

During these operations, which ran from May to November of 1952, the boat made reconnaissance patrols in support of Korean War operations. Joyner particularly recalls the time when,

> Off the coast of Russia, *Blenny* was pinned down for several hours as an enemy trawler dropped depth charges around us. We could hear the explosions above and feel the vibrations straight to your soul. The skipper gave the order to dive ... so that we could sneak out of the area. Everyone on board was silent and apprehensive.... *Blenny* was a diesel boat, so we had to go slow and very quiet — on a submarine any sound that can be picked up on sonar is a dead giveaway. And the only sound that day was the beating of my heart. It was a real cat-and-mouse game played out at the bottom of the sea (*ibid.*).

While Joyner served aboard *Blenny*, he got along quite well with his other Black shipmates. He refers to Commissaryman 1st Class Claude Palmer as a "big brother" and fondly remembers visiting his home when they were ashore together. Palmer was a veteran of five war patrols on *Besugo*, and later changed his rate from steward to commissaryman. It is highly likely that these WESTPAC runs on *Blenny* were milk runs for Palmer as compared to his World War II days. Kenneth Joyner was also close to one of the boat's stewards, a man that could not read or write but nonetheless worked hard to put his sister through college. Joyner assisted him by reading his mail and writing letters home for him. Joyner always recognized what those Black submariners who came before him had accomplished and valued the advice they had to offer. As he puts it, "I couldn't have taken the crap that stewards did.... I always wanted to be in their 'family'" (Joyner). He also recognized that, "being on the cutting edge of the 'new navy,' I could not afford to slip. I was aware of setting precedent for future Black enlisted (men) and officers" (*ibid.*).

Following his service on *Blenny*, the boat on which he qualified and earned his dolphins, Joyner made yet another WESTPAC run, this time on *Sterlet*. As he recalls, after *Blenny* returned stateside to San Diego, he was "so enamored about the excitement of it all that I wanted to go back, so I asked for a transfer to the next boat going" (*ibid.*). The run he made on *Sterlet* was uneventful, but it was aboard this boat that Joyner experienced a bit of overt prejudice that was rare in submarines by this time. While in port, a group of men were down below playing pinochle, and Joyner and his partner were doing rather well. As he relates, one of the losers in this game, "a big guy, a midwest 1st class ET said 'Hey Ken, you going down to nigger town?' Well, I hit him in the mouth, and he fell back, startled. I went up to see the XO but he was in conference, so I went topside to cool off.... No one bothered me after that" (*ibid.*). This incident is, as far as Joyner can recall, the only one of its type during his entire naval career.

Donald Burrell, too, saw continued action in the Pacific after the end of the Korean War. Soon to be a chief electronics technician, Burrell went from *Tilefish* to *Carp* in late 1953. He would serve aboard *Carp* for nearly four full years, during which time he made three WESTPAC runs. When pressed for details of his service aboard this boat, Burrell states that "we completed three deployments during which we continued collecting intelligence and other assigned duties.... We completed some exciting missions which, I believe, are classified.... We collided with an iceberg, while submerged, and tore up the sail area. I managed a favorable citation during that adventure" (Burrell). Burrell's commendation from the commander of Submarine Squadron One of the United States Pacific Fleet, Captain C.C. Cole, reads, in part, as follows:

A part of the crew of *Blenny* during the Korean War in 1952. Radioman 3rd Class Kenneth Joyner is at top left, while next to him is World War II veteran patroller Claude Palmer. (Photograph courtesy of K. Joyner.)

> For meritorious achievement in the performance of his duties while serving on the USS *Carp* ... from 18 August 1955 to 8 October 1955. During a special mission of the *Carp* Chief Burrell exhibited outstanding qualities beyond that required or expected of his experience. During operations requiring peak performance of the electronic equipment, Chief Burrell led a repair party topside in the shears and in extremely cold weather he repaired a piece of defective electronic equipment in a minimum amount of time. This permitted *Carp* to continue her special mission in full operating condition. He thus contributed to a marked degree to the successful completion of a special mission of great importance [Burrell, "Citation"].

Not long after this incident, Chief Donald Burrell would soon begin to qualify for the position of Chief of the Boat (COB) on *Carp* and acted as COB when the man assigned to that duty was away. To the civilian uneducated in navy tradition, this might seem of small import, but in terms of submarine shipboard operations it was a position of huge responsibility, and one that, in the not too distant past, was rarely if ever assigned to a Black crewman no matter what his qualifications. The COB on any given submarine was usually the most-senior enlisted man aboard the boat and was one who had the respect of both his fellow enlisted men as well as the officers above him. It goes without saying that the COB would be regarded by all aboard as an outstanding submariner, and often (though not always) he was the man who had been on board that particular submarine the longest. While the COB position has evolved over the years, it has always been one in which the boat's commanding officer worked with, and through, the COB to ensure that his orders regarding shipboard operations were carried out to their fullest. In many cases, the captain used the COB position as in a "good cop–bad cop" scenario. Unpopular directives would come down from the captain to the crew through the COB, and it was the COB's job to make sure that the orders were followed, while decisions that were sure to be popular with the enlisted men were always communicated directly by the captain. In addition to this general scenario, the COB and the captain and other officers also held meetings to discuss such things as morale issues, disciplinary problems aboard the boat, and like issues. The fact that experienced Black submariners like Burrell were beginning to assume this important role in the 1950s was indicative of just how far the navy, in general, had come and how progressive the Submarine Force continued to be when it came to shipboard race relations. In hindsight, the achievement of gaining such a position by Burrell was significant, despite the fact that, at the time, his work in gaining qualification as Chief of the Boat was only done so as a means to further his career. It was not his intent to make history of sorts or to set precedents for future Black submariners, but he helped to do both just the same. During World War II there were many Black stewards that were more than qualified to act as COB, but their race and the navy's strict separation of the steward's branch from the rest of its enlisted rates made them an impossible choice. Men such as Jim Stallings (*Haddock*), George Lytle (*Drum*), Magnus Wade (*Gunnel*), and Walter Wilson (*Trigger*) all would have been excellent COBs and undoubtedly would have held this position had race not been an issue.

Returning to some of the submarine operations of the 1950s and the experiences of Radioman Kenneth Joyner, he also saw service aboard *Carp* when she made cruises to the Far East from 1956 to 1959. He had left the service for a brief time in 1953 but found civilian life less exciting. When he "thought about the good things in the navy" (Joyner) that he had left behind, Joyner went back to the navy. After working at shore position in South Boston for two years and attaining the rate of radioman 1st class, Joyner went back to submarines and joined the crew of *Carp*, making several WESTPAC runs. His position as a radioman with top secret clearance on these classified missions meant that Joyner "knew what was going on before the captain. I had to encrypt messages and copy them from Morse code and translate them" (*ibid.*). Like most men who served on such missions, Joyner is limited in the details he can divulge, even more than forty years later. One dangerous incident recalled by Joyner was one that he calls "the goddamn scariest time of my life" (*ibid.*). As he vividly recalls,

> While making a run in the cold, unfriendly waters of the northern Pacific Ocean, *Carp* had recharged the batteries…. At daybreak we surfaced going into a shallow harbor [location not divulged] with approximately sixty-five feet of water. Then out of nowhere we felt the bang and crunch of metal. We could hear the foreign language on the tape and knew we were in trouble. A sub-

marine [had] crossed over us and tore off and chewed up part of the sail; the sound head forward was detached, and the scopes were bent. This was every submariner's nightmare. We were 1.2 meters away from a watery grave — or worse. If we had been captured, there is no telling what would have happened to us. And we all knew it. A quiet panic set in all over the boat as we checked for internal damage. The watertight integrity was o.k., but the skipper, "Easy Ed" McCauley, was not. He chewed out the sonar tech. "How could you not hear another submarine overhead?" We stayed submerged for the rest of the day, cruising out of the harbor into international waters. Finally, at night, we were able to surface and assess the damage.... Thank God it was just the superstructure — so we were able to stay underway on our own power. But it had knocked out our sonar capacity, which heightened the stress level of the skipper and the crew. We couldn't ascertain the amount of damage to the other submarine. He surfaced immediately; his screw [propeller] had to have been severely damaged. That evening contact was made with our HQ in Japan. After informing them of the incident and the damage, we were instructed to proceed home at the best possible speed. Upon arrival home, a four-star admiral met us with the cover story — mum was the word. After all it was the Cold War.... When I look back after all of these years, I'm amazed at how young we were, how well trained and what a cohesive force we became [*ibid.*].

While *Carp* made various cruises to Alaskan and Russian waters, she also made a goodwill trip to Australia and participated in various exercises with some of our Asian allies. One thing that Kenneth Joyner remembers most is coming back to port after the grueling WESTPAC runs. As he recalls, "Comparatively speaking, we were rich when we came in, with six paydays waiting for us.... We were honchos over there with money to spend" (*ibid.*). Joyner did well on *Carp* and found out, as he initially believed, that being a submariner was his true calling. In 1959 he made chief radioman but would soon leave the boat for advanced training and further duty. However, we will hear more from Joyner when his submarine career in the 1960s is detailed. It would prove every bit as eventful as his experiences in the 1950s.

In our final look at the operational experiences of Black submariners in the 1950s, we have yet to relate the experiences of James Mosley on *Volador* in 1956–1958 as well as the decade's one operational submarine loss. First, Mosley's experiences: Having enlisted in 1948, Mosley served at several navy hospitals in Portsmouth, Virginia, and Bainbridge, Maryland, before going to hospital corpsman school. While serving at Bainbridge, one of Mosley's fellow hospitalmen there was the future comedian and television star Bill Cosby, whose father had been a submarine steward during the war. Mosley became a submariner in 1955, and by 1958 he was a hospital corpsman 1st class and had made several northern runs on *Volador*. The first of these commenced in August 1957, when she departed from Pearl Harbor for a 30-day patrol off the Kamchatka Peninsula near the Russian city of Petropavlovsk. During this time of intelligence gathering, *Volador* experienced engine problems while among the nearby Kurile Islands and, as Mosley recalls, "it was a close call, but we got back" (Mosley, James). During this time in the seas off the Russian coast, Mosley's boat encountered over twenty vessels, many of which were warships. By the end of the month, *Volador* was back at safe harbor in Yokosuka, Japan, the port from which many a northern run emanated. Another interesting run for Mosley on this boat came in late December 1957 when she

Hospital Corpsman 1st Class James Mosley. This photograph was taken in 1957 in Yokusuka, Japan, when he was stationed on *Volador* and made several western Pacific runs. (Photograph courtesy of J. Mosley.)

conducted a photographic reconnaissance mission in the frigid waters of the Sea of Okhotsk and went undetected. *Volador* subsequently returned to Japan in January of 1958, and from thence went stateside to San Diego via Hawaii. Soon after, Mosley was sent to the nuclear boat *Skipjack*.

Finally, though the 1950s peacetime exercises of the Submarine Force may have seemed routine and even mundane to the general public, they were often anything but that. Some of these exercises pitted ASW (antisubmarine warfare) groups of surface craft, such as carriers, cruisers, and always lots of destroyers, against submarines. The task of the submarine, the aggressor, was to try and penetrate the defenses of the surface craft and score a "hit." These exercises not only tested and honed the navy's ASW techniques in a live situation but also provided the Submarine Force with a chance to practice and refine their own tracking and attack procedures. Because this was a test of a submarine captain's ability as well as that of her crew, the pressure to perform well in these exercises was quite high.

Sometimes, however, things went wrong. Steward 1st Class William Green served on *Bergall* from April 1953 to September 1955, and during his time in submarines took part in many such exercises. However, none were probably as eventful as those that took place on October 30–31, 1954. While participating in an ASW exercise that covered thousands of square miles of ocean from the North Atlantic to the Caribbean, *Bergall* successfully penetrated the screen set against her and made a successful "attack." On the next day, October 31, 1954, the destroyers that had been bested the day before were not only increased in number but were also very aggressive, no doubt anxious to avenge the previous day's loss. In all the confusion, *Bergall* was hit while she was submerged by one of the destroyers. However, the well-trained crew, Green included, reacted quickly, and the boat was brought to the surface quickly without any flooding.

The sail of *Bergall* had a huge V-shaped gash where the destroyer *Norris* had sliced through her, disabling her periscopes, radar mast, and snorkel masts. Luckily, the boat's watertight integrity was fine, and she was escorted to the navy yard in Philadelphia by *Angler*, another diesel boat. William Green would not see action of such an exciting nature again until he served on *Triton* six years later.

Another incident of this type, only one that was more serious and involved the loss of a boat, was that of *Stickleback*. Aboard this boat when she left Pearl Harbor for antisubmarine warfare (ASW) exercises on May 29, 1958, were two Black crewmen, Torpedoman 3rd Class John Phelps, Jr., and Inter-Communications Electrician 2nd Class William Stallings. The routine exercises, performed in conjunction with the destroyer escort *Silverstein*, turned out to be anything but routine. At just about noon, the submarine was submerged and suddenly lost power, and *Stickleback* began going down in a hurry. However, the crew reacted quickly, and the main ballast tanks were blown. The boat began to head for the surface. The captain called for all hands forward, and the eight men in the after-battery compartment, including Phelps, raced forward. Just a minute later the order was given to the torpedoman aft to "load and shoot one red flare" (Barron and Meagher, p. 1). However, the chance to fire this distress signal failed because the torpedoman on watch at the time in the after battery, John Phelps, had already gone forward as previously ordered. Less than a minute after hitting the surface, more serious trouble occurred when *Stickleback* was rammed on the port side close to the control room by the *Silverstein*. With the water rising fast in the control room and the boat mortally wounded, the order was quickly given to abandon ship. Many men did so through the conning tower, some made it out through the aft end of the boat, while those trapped in the forward battery and the forward torpedo room made it out through the escape trunk hatch. Meanwhile, *Stickleback* was held afloat because the *Silverstein* was holding her bow in the submarine's mangled side. Had she backed clear of the wounded submarine, it was very likely that the boat would have quickly filled and sank, probably with loss of life. Instead, the entire crew escaped, and most waited topside to be rescued by the submarine rescue vessel *Greenlet*. Not long after the crew of *Stickleback* was rescued, the *Silverstein* backed clear, and the boat finally sank bow first in the deep waters off Honolulu, Hawaii.

Once again, American submariners proved their mettle and made the best of a bad situation. The loss of one diesel submarine, while unfortunate, was a small price to pay in return for the rescue of a well-trained submarine crew. What role William Stallings played during the loss of *Stickleback* is unknown. He was likely among that group of men that escaped through the conning tower. The role of John Phelps has already been discussed, but it is important to note that he was not held responsible for the ship's failure to launch a flare through the after torpedo tubes, where he was the torpedoman on watch. Instead, as one crewman noted, "He was just following orders" (Barron) when the captain ordered all men forward. Had the captain first ordered a flare to be fired, Phelps undoubtedly would have been on station to ensure the task was completed. The loss of *Stickleback* was hard on her crew and made worse when it was soon realized that her men would not be kept together for assignment on another boat. As was recalled by a crewman,

> We were like brothers; I mean the crew was really tight.... After all the work in the yards, the shakedown to Tahiti and the work up for WESTPAC, she was our

> home and we were proud of her and what we had done. I don't think anyone but another submariner can understand how close the crew gets and how much the boat means to you [Barron and Meagher, p. 4].

In summing up the decade of the 1950s for submariners, it is clear to see that it was a great leap forward in all areas. On the technology side, the decade started with a force that consisted entirely of diesel fleet boats. By the end of the decade, the diesel boat era was in its sunset, while the era of the nuclear attack boat was well in stride. With the launching of the first ballistic missile nuclear submarine in 1959, a new age of nuclear strike capability and deterrence through strength was begun that continues to this day.

Despite these great changes, the 1950s were an era of even greater change for Black submariners. With the start of the decade, most Black submariners occupied the position of steward and were recruited specifically for this rating. As the decade progressed, however, overtly biased recruiting practices were discarded, and fewer and fewer men were entering the steward's branch. Instead, they were able to choose the rate they had an aptitude for and, by 1960, Blacks were serving in all areas of operations. The initial phase of future submariner Steve Shelby's navy career is a shining example of this change. A native of Harlem, in New York City, Shelby enlisted in the navy in November 1958. He was designated as Seaman Recruit Nuclear Field and was likely one of the few Black men at the time signed up in this manner. As Shelby recalls, his "recruiter stated that he had never signed up a Black to be assigned to the nuclear program" (Shelby). Shelby, the youngest of the Black submariners interviewed for this book, subsequently went to interior communications electrician "A" school at Great Lakes and later attended submarine school. During this time he experienced no problems with discrimination. In August 1959 he was assigned to the diesel boat *Sabalo* at Pearl Harbor and was the only Black sailor aboard. He quickly proved his abilities when he qualified throughout the boat by November 1959, in the short space of just three months. He was well on his way to an outstanding submarine career.

Indeed, throughout the Submarine Force fleet, there were now Black submariners rated as radiomen, electricians, electronics technicians, sonarmen, interior-communication electricians, motor-machinists, enginemen, torpedomen, yeomen, commissarymen, storekeepers, stewards, and others. The days of Black sailors being thought of as just stewards was numbered. One small, but telling example of this was a rather comical situation witnessed by John O'Meally aboard *Guavina* in early 1959. O'Meally was aboard this vessel as an electrician's mate while she was being decommissioned at Charleston, South Carolina, and recalls a night when the crew was watching a movie in the mess hall:

> A Lieutenant Knapp called over to a Black sailor named John Sparks. He said "Hey Sparks, how about a cup of coffee." Now Sparks was close to the coffeemaker but he wasn't the one closest to it. Sparks answered, "No thanks, Mr. Knapp, I just had one." The lieutenant got up and got his coffee, and I think he learned something. This would not have happened on any ship but a submarine at that time because submarine sailors could get away with saying that [O'Meally, John].

Steve Shelby, a Harlem, New York, enlistee joined the navy in 1958, and first served on *Sabalo*. Twenty-one years later he would make Lieutenant Commander (LCDR) while serving on the nuclear missile boat *Thomas Jefferson*. (Photograph courtesy of S. Shelby.)

Many Black submariners were earning advancement to higher rates on a steady basis because of their intellect, skill, and leadership abilities, something that few would have thought possible just the decade before. Among such men were Kenneth Joyner (radioman), Hosea Washington (engineman), and Donald Burrell (electronics technician), all of whom became chiefs within the decade, while Burrell has the added distinction of having served as chief of the boat, acting. Let's not forget, too, those chief stewards that changed their rating to chief electronics technicians: Isaac Johnson, Anderson Royal, and Killraine Newton. However, in the case of Royal and Newton, the Submarine Force would suffer a loss when they were posted to duty on surface craft and, subsequently, as instructors. Notably, Newton went to surface craft when he became a warrant officer in 1959. Finally, there is also the continued advancement of Chief Yeoman Carl Kimmons. By 1959 he was advanced to senior chief, a newly established pay grade, and soon would become a master chief. The next step for him would be officer's candidate school. What is all the more interesting is that all these naval achievements by Black submariners came about during a tumultuous time when the civil rights era was gaining momentum in the United States. As Kenneth Joyner so aptly states, "During that time, racism was all around, every day, and you just couldn't forget the color of your skin" (Joyner). More changes were yet to come.

THE 1960S: BOOMERS AND FAST ATTACKS

If the 1960s were a time of drastic change for the country in terms of race relations and civil rights, for the Black men in the navy's Submarine Force it was a period in which goals and priorities were shifted to a higher level. Recruiting practices and opportunities had changed drastically, and now the focus was more on how Black men who had chosen the navy as a career path could gain greater representation in positions of command. The environment for doing so, however, in the Submarine Force was a paradox. While the Submarine Force itself was, as we have seen, an enlightened branch of the navy that provided opportunities for advancement based on ability and leadership capabilities, its small size, when compared to the sheer number of units in the surface fleet, made it difficult for steady advancement to occur without having to leave the force and go to surface ships. Thus, in some cases, the Submarine Force's best and most promising Black submariners would rise to officer positions only after being sent to surface ships (often against their own personal desires), leaving behind a leadership vacuum that had to be filled by those who would come after them. Because such men

Chief Steward Jim Eckford Stallings in the torpedo room of *Grenadier* in the late 1950s or early 1960s. Stallings was among a small group of stewards who made more than ten war patrols during World War II. He made thirteen patrols in all on *Haddock* from 1942 to 1945 and earned the Bronze Star. (Photograph courtesy of C. Groomes-Davis.)

as Killraine Newton and Donald Burrell, to name just a few, came from the ranks of the enlisted to become "mustang" officers, there was no guarantee that younger Black submariners would take their place.

Part of the problem here was with the Naval Academy at Annapolis, Maryland. Few Black midshipmen were accepted into the Naval Academy during the 1950s, and by 1962 the navy only had a total of 174 Black officers in their ranks. By 1964, this number had risen but slightly, to 188 Black officers (Davis, p. 656). There was definitely a "glass ceiling" in the navy when it came to the development and integration of Blacks into the navy's command structure, and change would continue to be slow in this area. It was not until 1968 that the navy's first Black ROTC unit was established at Prairie View A & M College in Prairie View, Texas, and it was not until 1971 that Annapolis enrolled 50 African American midshipmen, its highest number ever at the time (Foner, p. 217). When it is considered that, despite the size of the navy, the second largest branch of the nation's armed forces after the army, the smaller air force had over six times as many Black officers, it was clearly evident that the navy still had a long way to go. One of this small number of Black officers that chose the Submarine Force as his career was Chancellor "Pete" Tzomes. A native of Williamsport, Pennsylvania, he received an appointment to the U.S. Naval Academy after attending the State University of New York at Oneonta. Upon graduation from the Naval Academy in June 1967, Tzomes was commissioned an ensign and went to nuclear power school at Mare Island, California, for a year before going to submarine school at New London. He first served in the Blue crew of the *Will Rogers* and there became a qualified submariner. His later career will be discussed in the final section of this chapter.

In looking at advancement opportunities for Black submariners in the 1960s, we may look at it from two different perspectives — that of the men of the steward's branch and that of men who were rated in other specialties. First, the stewards. By the 1960s, veteran stewards were being recognized for their leadership abilities and were recognized for their achievements, both aboard the boats as well as ashore in base operations. A few examples of the commendations and recognition they received will suffice to show what true professionals they were. In April 1961, veteran Chief Steward Wallace Coleman was awarded a Meritorious Mast for his work at the Boston Naval Shipyard. While in charge of the BOQ from 1959 to 1961, Coleman's performance was cited as "outstanding," and his "knowledge of Naval Leadership, coupled with your initiative makes you a credit to the Naval Service" (Coleman, "Meritorious Mast"). Similarly honored was Chief Steward Jim Stallings, during the course of his naval service in Key West, Florida. Stallings, a distinguished World War II submariner, received at least two commendations for his work in the 1960s. The first of these occurred in July 1962 while aboard the diesel boat *Grenadier*. His commendation reads, in part,

> By your efforts and leadership you have enabled *Grenadier* to set the standards for Commander Submarine Division 121.... Your efforts, leadership, and knowledge welded an inexperienced submarine crew into an effective *fighting* [italics added] organization. For this you deserve full credit and are so commended [Stallings, "Letter of Commendation"].

High words of praise, indeed! Jim Stallings was recognized for his professionalism yet again in 1966, while ashore and serving at the naval air station heliport as part of

Helicopter Anti-Submarine Squadron One. While running that unit's BOQ, Stallings was chief over a large group of "steward's mates" and rendered "superior performance" while running a unit that was termed as "the best ever seen in the navy" (Stallings, "Letter of Recognition"). Clearly, whether afloat or ashore, Jim Stallings was a valued chief petty officer in the navy.

Another man who was cited for his outstanding performance was Chief Steward Rufus Weaver. While serving aboard *Cavalla* from February 1962 to September 1963, he was commended by commanding officer Edwin Williams for

> your ability as an outstanding lead steward ... in addition to duty in rate, you have served as Chief of the Watch, standing a topnotch watch, both in operating the hydraulic manifold and in supervising the watch.... [Y]ou have been a principal source in upholding the high morale of the personnel aboard *Cavalla* by your sense of humor and guidance of the younger sailors [Weaver, "Citation"].

It is interesting to note that the citations for Weaver and Stallings aboard *Grenadier*, recognize their abilities outside their normal duty as steward and show that these men were substantial contributors when it came to the task of forging a crew into an effective fighting force.

In other areas, too, stewards were recognized for their performance and abilities. Harry Senior, a submarine relief crewman during World War II, became Chief of the Boat, acting (COBa) while serving aboard the diesel submarine *Sarda* in the early 1960s. He would later see service on the fleet ballistic missile submarine *John Marshall*. Another steward that rose to even higher levels was World War II veteran Frank Holloman. He first joined the crew of *Menhaden* in 1945 but was too late to see any war action. After leaving the navy for a brief time in 1946, he resumed his submarine career in 1951 and met with great success. He served in the fleet ballistic submarine *Sam Houston* in the early 1960s and was commended for his work. As lead steward aboard the *Sam Houston*'s Blue crew for eight Polaris patrols, Holloman was recognized for his

> superior qualities of leadership above that required.... By your own efforts you have become highly qualified on the ship and given unstintingly of your time to improve the qualification of the rest of the crew. Further, you have served as Protestant Lay Leader and, by personal example and superior performance of duty, inspired a religious and moral character in the crew. You have organized and directed the efforts of the ship's Career Appraisal Team and raised the ship's already high reenlistment rate. Overall, your superior performance has materially contributed to the success ... of the Nation's vital deterrent force. Your conduct, leadership, and devotion to duty were in keeping with the highest traditions of the United States Naval Service [Holloman, "Commendation"].

This was not the first time Frank Holloman was commended for his work on *Sam Houston*. Having joined the boat as part of her precommissioning crew in late 1960, he was commended by her commanding officer, Daniel Brooks, in April 1965 for outstanding performance on *Sam Houston*'s first six Polaris patrols. Interestingly enough, fellow Black submariner and Blue crew member Chief Sonar Technician Robert Foster was also a notable contributor to the performance of *Sam Houston*. Like his friend Frank

Holloman, he put the boat into commission and was COB for six of the Blue crew's first eight Polaris patrols. He, too, was commended for his performance in April 1966 by Captain Brooks.

Despite his already high level of performance on *Sam Houston*, Chief Steward Frank Holloman would achieve even greater heights. In 1967–1968, while aboard the fleet ballistic submarine *Will Rogers*, he served as COB for that boat's Blue crew. His fellow shipmate, once again, was his friend Robert Foster. As a former COB himself, he undoubtedly was able to give Frank Holloman some good advice regarding his new appointment.

With men of such high caliber as we have detailed, might they, and many other stewards like them, have been candidates for further promotion as officer candidates? Sadly, the answer to this question is a resounding "No." The reasons for this were threefold: One of these was the perceived lack of education among veteran stewards by navy standards. Many men were the victims of southern education policies directed toward Blacks in the prewar years (and after, for that matter)

Chief Steward Harry Senior, circa 1959. Senior served in submarine relief crews during the war, but soon after joined the Submarine Force and made war patrols during the Korean War. The hash marks on his sleeve indicate his 16 plus years of service, one stripe earned for every four years of service. (Photograph courtesy of H. Senior.)

and were often denied a full grade-school or high-school education. Many of these men were self-taught in the areas of reading and writing and certainly were intelligent individuals. Through their skills and service they became chief petty officers, many rising to that position quickly during the war years. Afterward, in the peacetime navy, their possibilities for advancement were slowed considerably when they were judged on their background and schooling first and their accomplishments were but little regarded. Simply put, no further advancement was likely to occur for any steward with a low level of education.

A perfect example of this inequity is Jim Stallings. While making twelve war patrols on *Haddock* from 1942 to 1945, he rose to the rate of chief steward probably faster than anyone before him by the time the war ended. Interestingly enough, this is as far as Jim Stallings would go in rate. When he retired after a career of 30 years in the early 1970s, he was still a chief steward — his rate had not changed for 25 years. We have already seen the citations for Stallings' excellent performance, and his yearly evaluations, always highly favorable, show no reason why he might not have risen to master chief. The only reason that can possibly explain his lack of further advancement is the idea that, perhaps, the quick rise in rate at the beginning of his career left Stallings with nowhere else to go by the Bureau of Naval Personnel (BUPERS) standards. Whether or not this was the case is unknown, but the fact that Stallings had only received a seventh grade education while growing up in Mississippi was likely a mitigating factor.

Yet another reason for the lack of advancement for the men of the steward's branch was the "new racism" that prevailed in the navy during the Vietnam War era (Foner, p. 201). While the historic Civil Rights Act of 1964 ensured that, in theory, opportunity in the nation's armed forces for all servicemen would not be based on one's ethnic background, actual practices inevitably fell far short of this ideal. As one historian states, "when discrimination in its more blatant forms ended, it was replaced, just as in society as a whole" by one that was "more subtle, although no less immoral, than the more overt examples of bigotry, which have become less common in recent years" (*ibid.*).

Tied with the second reason is the third and defining reason why stewards could not, and would not, be promoted as potential officer candidates without a change in rate: The steward's branch, despite all the changes it had undergone from 1945 to the 1960s, was still an anachronistic branch of the navy based on racism. No matter what official pronouncements the navy might make, no matter what role individual stewards might perform on an individual basis on one boat or another, the men of the steward's branch were still viewed as a class of servants, of sorts, to be used by navy top brass as indicative of their rank and privilege. While Black men in other rates, especially technical ones, were eligible for promotion to positions of leadership, it was different for a steward. How could the navy promote a steward to officer? Such a man would then be ranked among those same men that he had formerly served, often on an intimate basis. At best, the idea would have been awkward — in the eyes of the navy it was unthinkable. Despite the leadership abilities of such men as Jim Stallings, Frank Holloman, and others, it would take an entire overhaul of the steward's branch and more enlightened thinking on the part of the navy before such change would occur.

In regard to the advancement opportunities for Black submariners who were in other ratings than that of steward, the story is a different one. A number of the men interviewed for this book who served in the postwar Submarine Force did quite well, some even advancing to officer status.

First, let us look at the career of submariner Donald Burrell. When we last saw Burrell, he was a chief electronics technician on *Carp*, and was veteran of many a WESTPAC run. He left that boat in 1957 to go to nuclear power school in Idaho and after completing the course there was assigned as an instructor. As he recalls, "I was also encouraged to apply for the LDO [Limited Duty Officer] program and for the NESEP [Naval Enlisted Science Education Program]. After I'd taken the tests, I received a call from an officer who I'd served with on the *Tilefish*. He strongly urged me to go

NESEP, to get the college education (probably the best advice I ever followed)" (Burrell). Burrell did indeed go to college beginning in 1959, graduated with a BS in electrical engineering from the University of Kansas at Lawrence in 1963, and was commissioned as a line officer upon the completion of his studies. Later that same year, he was sent to Officers Candidate School in Newport, Rhode Island. A winner of his class's leadership award, Donald Burrell was commissioned as a lieutenant junior grade (LTJG) on October 8, 1963, and reported to the nuclear power training school at Mare Island, California, for subsequent duty as an instructor. Unfortunately, Burrell was never again to serve on submarines. In 1967 he was sent to the guided missile cruiser *Oklahoma City* as electronics warfare officer and saw action during the Vietnam War in the Gulf of Tonkin and on more WESTPAC operations. In 1969, Burrell received a posting to guided missile destroyer *Gridley*, serving as combat information center (CIC) officer, with a promotion to full lieutenant. In 1971, Burrell was promoted to lieutenant commander and was posted to the NROTC unit at Prairie View A & M College in Texas. Burrell was later promoted to commander and retired in 1978. Though his performance and success as an officer occurred outside the Submarine Force, it was his performance within the Submarine Force during his early career that gave him his start.

Another submariner that had an excellent career was Hospital Corpsman 1st Class James Mosley. After serving on the diesel boat *Volador* in the mid–1950s, and on the nuclear boat *Skate* from 1958 to 1962, Mosley served aboard the fleet ballistic submarine *Thomas Edison* for three years until 1966. During this time, Mosley applied for the warrant officer program, Limited Duty Officer program, and the Medical Service Corps program. Despite the fact that Mosley had graduated "either first or within the top four … of numerous service schools" (Mosley, James), Mosley was never selected for any of the programs to which he applied. In 1964 he was on a list of 39 men to be considered for the medical service corps, but the list was subsequently reduced, and Mosley was not selected. Whether or not race was a determining factor in the decisions against him is unknown but is a possibility that must be considered. James Mosley would later retire as a senior chief hospital corpsman in 1968 after a twenty-year career, most of which was spent in submarines.

John O'Meally was another Black submariner who had a great amount of career success during the 1960s. In 1959 he was assigned to the guided missile submarine *Halibut*, operating out of Pearl Harbor and saw much exciting and clandestine action aboard this famed spy sub. While some of O'Meally's adventures on this boat will be described at a later point, his fine performance led to increased opportunities as time went on. Among O'Meally's shipmates on *Halibut* were three other Black submariners: Radioman 1st Class Bruce Anderson, formerly a steward; Steward 1st Class Fate Carter; and Machinist Mate (nuclear trained) Eddie Merriweather. As O'Meally recalls,

> There were no problems with being Black on the ship or the base. There was always the assumption that you were a steward when talking with someone that did not know your rate. I remember when I picked up my car that had been shipped over from the mainland, the chief in charge of the dock called me "Stew" in a friendly manner. He just assumed I was a steward. I said in an equally friendly manner that I was an electrician, and he should call me "Sparks" [O'Meally, John].

O'Meally enjoyed his service on *Halibut* and, as he says, "My life ... kept getting better.... It seemed like everything I touched on *Halibut* turned to gold" (*ibid.*). He made chief in 1962 and the following year successfully tested to serve as an engineering officer of the watch. This was normally an officer's job, and one in which few other enlisted men were qualified to perform in the entire Pacific fleet. Part of O'Meally's job on this watch was to bring the boat's nuclear reactor on line and start up the steam plant, a huge responsibility. O'Meally followed up this achievement by becoming COB on *Halibut* in 1965, a rarity at that time in the navy as a whole, and probably the only one at Pearl Harbor. In November 1966, O'Meally, like so many outstanding Black submariners before him, was transferred to shore duty as a recruiter in New York City. Soon after, he was selected to the warrant officer program and was promoted as such to warrant officer, level one. By the time he retired in 1975, John O'Meally was a commissioned warrant officer, level three (CWO-3). In reflecting on his submarine service during the 1960s, O'Meally remembers that "This was the time when the navy was changing, and there were some white stewards in the fleet. One of these stewards reported on board [*Halibut*] before I left the ship. So we had a submarine with a Black chief of the boat and a white steward. Who would have thunk it" (*ibid.*). As a sidelight, O'Meally was not the only Black aboard *Halibut* to rise to officer status. Eddie Merriweather, who declined to be interviewed for this book, later went on to become a lieutenant junior grade and left the navy after a 16-year career.

Equally impressive was the rapid advancement of relative newcomer Steve Shelby. From 1960 to 1965 he served on the nuclear attack boat *Skate* as an interior communications electrician. During his time aboard this boat, he had a number of Black shipmates, including Chief Steward Arnold Duncan, Chief Machinist Mate William McDaniels, Yeoman 1st Class Robert Williamson, and Machinist Mate 1st Class Abraham Mozeak. As Shelby recalls, "My success on *Skate* was mostly resulting from my professionalism and partly due to the mentoring I received from the other Blacks" (Shelby). Prior to leaving the boat in June 1965, Shelby had been a reactor operator and was qualifying as an engine room supervisor. While aboard, Shelby had applied for the NESEP program and, during his candidate interview with *Skate*'s officers, "was asked how I felt about being a Black officer and how I thought my wife would interact as a Black officer's wife. I explained that we were not concerned with any discrimination and would handle whatever was presented to either of us" (*ibid.*). Upon acceptance into the NESEP program, Shelby attended the University of Utah and earned a BS degree in computer science. As a new ensign in 1969, Shelby briefly left the submarine service to serve aboard the guided missile cruiser *Chicago*. One of only two Black officers on the ship, Shelby served as the Talos missile fire control officer and received excellent fitness reports from his white commanding officer, "a good old boy from Georgia" (*ibid.*). However, unlike others before him whose careers have been detailed in these pages, Shelby was destined to return to submarine duty. We will catch up with his subsequent submarine career in another section.

Another Black submariner who achieved notable success during the decade was 1950 enlistee Kenneth Joyner. After serving on *Blenny*, *Sterlet*, and *Carp*, he reenlisted in 1960 and went to advanced class "B" radio school in Bainbridge, Maryland. As he recalls, "It was really intense, like three years of college in one year.... I was the only Black in the class.... My main thing was not flunking out" (Joyner). Upon graduation,

Chief Radioman John O'Meally in the radio shack of *Halibut* in the early 1960s. O'Meally received several citations for his service on this famous boat. (Photograph courtesy of J. O'Meally.)

he served aboard *Halfbeak* for a time out of New London and, in 1962, was sent to the navy's instruction and leadership school in Norfolk, Virginia. Upon passing the required tests with flying colors, Joyner received a posting as an instructor at Officer's Candidate School in Newport, Rhode Island. His job was to teach junior officers, from ensigns through lieutenant commanders, in the area of communications. Not only was he the only Black instructor, but he was also the only enlisted one as well. As Joyner relates,

> I had to be on my toes; I had to be sharp, but I had the knowledge and the capability to do it. My relationship with the other instructors was great. I was the professional, with shipboard, not administrative, experience, and I got along with the students well. I even tutored Samuel Gravely, our country's first Black admiral, in communications when he was attending Naval Officer's War College across the street. He later became my boss. The whole instructor experience was a unique and different situation.... I missed the camaraderie of submarine duty, but it was still enjoyable [Joyner].

Joyner excelled in his instructor's role and in 1965 was assigned to FOCCPAC (Fleet Operation Control Center Pacific), a vital and top-secret joint command communications center in Hawaii. That same year he also became a senior chief radioman. A year later he would return to submarine duty aboard the fast attack boat *Plunger*, on which he served as COB. We will hear more from Kenneth Joyner and *Plunger* later in this chapter.

Finally, in regard to higher level advancement opportunities for Black submariners in the 1960s, there is the career of Abraham Mozeak. He served aboard *Skate* from 1962 to 1966 and would leave that boat as chief machinist mate. Following this, he served on the commissioning crew of the fleet ballistic submarine *Henry L. Stimson* and served aboard her in the Blue crew from July 1966 to May 1968. Following this, from 1968 to July 1971, Mozeak served in the Blue crew aboard the *James K. Polk*. While on this boat, Mozeak became the COB, an esteemed shipboard position that more and more was becoming open to Black submariners. In reflecting upon his time as COB, Mozeak remembers that "Mostly it was rather routine.... At first I expected some problems with whites, so I made sure Blacks were doing their jobs ... but I had no problems" (Mozeak).

One of the more unusual aspects of the job as COB was that, while the men were at sea, the COB's wife at home usually acted as a liaison for the other enlisted men's wives and helped them with the difficulties that might arise during the course of everyday life while their husbands were at sea. Abraham Mozeak was unmarried, so had no wife at home to act in this capacity. However, he was held in such high regard that a friend's wife (who was white) "volunteered to be my stand-in wife and did things for me" (*ibid.*) while the *James K. Polk* was out to sea. This progressive and family-type attitude, one where color did not matter, was typical of the Submarine Force and was yet another factor that fostered the successful career of many a Black submariner.

While Black submariners were able in this decade to further their career opportunities, we must also take a look at one veteran Black submariner who not only furthered his own career but also had a real interest in bringing more minorities into the navy's nuclear power program. This man was former wartime steward Isaac Johnson. After the war, he changed his rate to become an electronics technician. After serving on the nuclear attack boat *Skipjack* and the fleet ballistic submarine *Robert E. Lee*, he went to shore duty in California as a recruiter in 1961. Though assigned to the Los Angeles recruiting station, he attempted to persuade the navy to open a recruiting center in the predominantly Black area of Logan Heights in San Diego. The navy agreed to let Johnson do this on one condition: it could not mean any extra expense to the navy. An enthusiastic Johnson got to work and made it happen. The navy recruiting station in Logan Heights, manned solely by Johnson, opened in July 1962. For the next three years, until his time in the navy was up, Johnson spent two days a week doing recruiting duty in Los Angeles. At first it was difficult, and Johnson had to establish a measure of trust, not in himself, but in the navy. The navy was still, despite many changes, not held in high regard by Black men, but eventually Johnson would prevail. Many of the young Black men he recruited, in a place where no white recruiter would ever have been trusted, went on to serve in nuclear submarines. The remainder of Johnson's time was spent recruiting in San Diego.

Chief Electronics Technician Isaac Johnson. A native of Arkansas, Johnson joined the navy in 1944 as a steward and would be the first steward to change his rate to that of electronics technician in 1955. The dashing Johnson would later serve as an electronics technician on *Tilefish*, the nuclear attack boat *Skipjack*, and the FBM boat *Robert E. Lee* before encouraging the navy to let him open a recruiting office in San Diego's Logan Heights section in 1962. (Photograph courtesy of I. Johnson.)

This is just one example of how the navy was slowly changing. All it needed was outstanding men like Johnson to translate theory into actual practice when it came to expanding minority representation within its branch of the service.

Another man who performed similar duty to Isaac Johnson in the area of influencing those who might choose the navy as their career was Chief Steward Edward McNair. A veteran of three war patrols on the old *S-43* that joined the navy in 1936, he remained a steward after the war and would later graduate from the Navy Career Appraisal School at Pensacola, Florida, in the early 1960s. Before returning to submarine duty aboard the *Sam Houston* at the end of his career, McNair worked in Pensacola as a career appraiser, helping to advise new recruits of all races on what career options were open to them in the navy.

Senior Chief Steward Edward McNair is shown offering career advice to a young enlisted man. This photograph, taken after McNair had graduated from the Navy Career Appraisal School in Pensacola, is a unique reminder of just how far the navy had come in race relations by the early 1960s. (Photograph courtesy of the McNair/Pollard Family.)

In turning to the operational aspects of submarines during the 1960s, the era of the nuclear submarine was now in full force. Close on the heels of the world's first nuclear attack submarine, the *Nautilus*, was the first nuclear submarine, the *George Washington*, designed as a platform for launching ballistic missiles. This fleet ballistic missile (FBM) boat, the first of a new class, was commissioned in December 1959 and successfully test launched the first Polaris missile while submerged on July 20, 1960. She was originally planned as the nuclear attack boat *Scorpion*, but her name and designation were changed when she was lengthened with the addition of a 130-foot missile section, consisting of 16 missile tubes from which she could launch her newly designed Polaris missiles. With the start of the FBM submarine program, all named after prominent Americans, the defense triad of the United States was now complete. Whether by land, sea, or sky, America was now fully prepared to defend herself and retaliate, if need be, against any hostile nation. While the nuclear attack submarine was designed to operate against enemy shipping and warships in a more traditional, albeit

Chief Steward Rufus Jack Weaver made the transition from diesel-boat submariner to nuclear power in 1963, when he joined the crew of the FBM boat *George Washington*, depicted here. (Photograph courtesy of R. Weaver.)

much more stealthy, manner, the FBM submarine, nicknamed "boomers" by submariners for the power they packed, was deployed as a deterrent. Armed with potent, long-range missiles designed to hit prominent land targets, their patrols were designed as a show of force, of sorts, to let America's enemies know that we were out there, underneath the sea, watching and waiting, ready to respond in kind to any threat that might be unleashed against us. While opposing nations couldn't know where our FBM submarines were at any given time — there was strict secrecy involved about where they would operate — they certainly knew that they were out there, and that was all they needed to know.

Just as they were in the first nuclear boats, so, too, were Black submariners involved on the first FBM boats as valued crewmembers. Steward 1st Class Rufus Weaver was a crewmember on *George Washington* in the early 1960s and, as he recalls, "I don't know how I ended up on *George Washington*.... I had no [nuclear] schooling but qualified on board the boat as a member of the Blue crew and ... was fascinated with the missile system they had on board" (Weaver). Another Black submariner who did duty on an FBM boat was Melvin Williams. He first went to submarine duty in 1960 on board the diesel boat *Carp*. However, in 1961 he was part of the commissioning crew for the *Thomas Jefferson* as a steward 1st class. While aboard his first submarine, Williams recalls the "cramped conditions" and "sleeping with a Mark 25 torpedo ... that thing was cold!" (Williams, Melvin, Sr.). However, service on an FBM boat was vastly different. As Williams comments further regarding the accommodations on the *Thomas Jefferson*, "Now you're talking high class. All that room, unlimited water for showers, your own bunk ... no hot bunking" (*ibid.*).

The FBM boats, and all nuclear boats, were indeed a huge change from the diesel boats of World War II: They were larger and more crew-friendly, with roomier bunks, unlimited hot water for showering, and large mess areas where the crew could congregate in their off-hours. They even had a small library stocked full of books, and many FBMs would later be equipped with a full range of exercise equipment so that her crew could remain in shape during extended patrols. The old days of being a submariner were indeed becoming a thing of the past, as least where crew comfort was concerned. Stated even more succinctly, Chief Electronics Technician Isaac Johnson on the *Robert E. Lee* called such duty "plush all the way ... plenty of fresh food" and compared the differences of diesel boats versus the FBMs equivalent to that between "a Model-T and a brand new Cadillac" (Johnson).

Duty aboard the FBMs was a new way of doing things for the Submarine Force. There are few stories to gather from their crewmembers regarding service aboard these boats because such things as areas of operations and potential threats were, and still are, shrouded in secrecy. Operations were called by one man as "super secret," and were detailed only on a "need-to-know" basis (Mozeak). What secrets there are, or were, were likely not privy information for many of the men aboard, stewards included. However, even those submariners who have such knowledge of classified operations cannot relate the details due to security regulations that are in force at this date. If there ever was a case where an FBM submarine was close to launching her missiles at some target in Russia, China, or elsewhere, either by design or accident, it is a closely guarded secret.

The other reason that there are few stories to tell for those who made FBM patrols, also called Polaris deterrent patrols, is the fact that they were routine by design and not meant to cause excitement or stir up trouble. While a nuclear attack boat making a successful WESTPAC run was supposed to penetrate enemy waters and track Russian submarines to gather vital intelligence data, the FBM submarine did nothing of this kind. Instead, it cruised in a predetermined sector of either the Pacific Ocean, the Atlantic Ocean, or the Mediterranean Sea and usually deliberately avoided any surface craft that wandered into their area to avoid detection. The job of an FBM submarine and her crew was to stay on station and always be on alert should the order come to fire her missiles.

During this time, countless hours were spent in training and safety drills designed to prepare the men for any situation that might arise while on patrol. An FBM patrol usually lasted about ninety days, including several weeks for training and preparation prior to departure from home base, sixty days submerged on patrol nonstop, and about a week or so for the boat to return to port, from which her crew would be flown home. While the boat was submerged on patrol, its crew was isolated from the rest of the outside world and only received official navy communications regarding her operations. However, it was soon discovered that being so isolated for so long was demoralizing at times, especially to those men with families back home. It then became the practice of the navy, and it remains so today, to allow "familygrams" to be sent to the men on board at set intervals during the patrol. These messages from loved ones back home were short, about forty words long at most, and were strictly censored by the navy for content. Happy messages regarding the birth of a child, or an "I love you" from the wife were allowed. Bad news of any kind, such as a death in the family, were prohibited and would have to wait until a sailor arrived home.

Since it was vital to the nation's defense for an FBM boat to be always on patrol, each boat had two full crews, called the Blue and Gold crews. Each crew had her own captain, and while one crew was out on patrol, the other was at home on rest and relaxation leave and subsequent training prior to going back out on patrol. Barring any technical difficulties, this allowed an FBM boat to be always on patrol except when being refueled and reprovisioned. To keep the boats closer to their patrol areas, naval bases outside the continental United States were utilized. For those boats making patrols in the Mediterranean and Atlantic, the naval bases at Rota, Spain, and Holy Loch, Scotland, were used as points at which the crews could be switched, one crew flying home, the other crew due to come aboard being flown in from the states. For those boats making FBM patrols in the Pacific, the submarine bases at Pearl Harbor, Hawaii, and Apra Harbor, Guam, were used.

For the Black submariners that served aboard the FBM boats, it was, as war veteran Mason Smith remarked, "A different style of navy now. You had to requalify; you had to adapt and be able to keep pace" (Smith). They did indeed do that. After serving on the nuclear attack boat *Sargo*, Smith served aboard the *Ethan Allen* as part of her commissioning crew in 1961 and made four Polaris patrols as part of her Gold crew in both the Atlantic Ocean and the Mediterranean Sea prior to his retirement in 1963. Another man that served on the same FBM boat as Mason Smith was veteran submariner Robert Coley. As chief steward on the *Ethan Allen*, Coley served on her Blue crew and made seven Polaris patrols followed by two more in the Gold crew of the *Benjamin Franklin*. Among those men interviewed for this book who made the most Polaris patrols was Jesse Allen. A World War II veteran of five war patrols on *Devilfish*, he went to the FBM boat *George Washington* about 1960 and made 13 Polaris patrols in all, leaving the boat in 1970 as a chief steward. Asked to compare the Polaris patrols with those of World War II, he simply laughed and said, "It was different as night and day.... Those on the *George Washington* weren't as frightening" (Allen, Jesse).

One man who made Polaris patrols on *Kamehameha* about whom little is known is Chief Steward John Stone. Serving on the boat's blue crew from 1967 to 1969, he was nicknamed "Sheriff" and "was a big man, for submarines, and allegedly had been a Golden Gloves boxing champ. He occasionally enforced discipline in the steward's pantry by pinning the culprit to the bulkhead with his forearm" (Harrison). "Sheriff" John Stone is thought to have been an old-time steward who enlisted during World War II or before, though he is not known to have made war patrols and had previously served in submarines stationed at the Panama Canal Zone.

Other Black submariners not previously mentioned that made Polaris patrols throughout the 1960s include Sammie Major (*Patrick Henry*), James Owens, Jr. (five patrols total on the *Thomas Jefferson*, *Sam Houston*, and *George Bancroft*), Archie Denson (patrols on *Ethan Allen*, *Ben Franklin*, and *Will Rogers*), Alfred Hall (patrols on *George Washington* and *Daniel Webster*), and Charles Richardson (*Theodore Roosevelt*). Of these, all but Denson and Owens were wartime submariners. Another wartime submariner who served on an FBM boat was William Murray. Serving as chief steward on the *Robert E. Lee*, he can't help but laugh when he remembers how one of the stewards on that boat "would religiously slap Lee's face (a likeness of which was in the wardroom on display) each morning before serving breakfast" (Murray). Certainly, the irony of a Black man serving on a boat named after the greatest of all Confederate generals was not lost on this steward!

Many of the Black submariners who served on the FBM boats were well recognized for their service. In addition to Frank Holloman, whose citation on the *Sam Houston* has already been mentioned, we might mention a few others. One was former wartime steward Wallace Coleman. He was part of the commissioning crew of *Nathan Hale* in 1963 and made two Polaris patrols as part of her Blue crew. In December of 1964 he received a commendation from his commanding officer, Joseph Russel,

Steward 1st Class Sammie Major in the late 1950s. Major made several war patrols on *Picuda* during the war and later made the transition to nuclear power, serving on the FBM boat *Patrick Henry* during the 1960s. (Photograph courtesy of D. Major.)

> for outstanding performance of duty.... Your professional performance, behavior, adaptability, leadership, and military appearance have consistently been outstanding and in keeping with the highest tradition of the Naval Service.... [Y]ou have continually served the ship and your shipmates with great devotion as Protestant Lay Leader and as the Chairman of the Ship's Recreation Committee" [Coleman, "Commendation"].

Another man who made a name for himself in FBM boats was Melvin Williams, Sr. After first serving on the *Thomas Jefferson*, he put the *James K. Polk* in commission in 1966 and served in her for two years. Williams made nine Polaris patrols in all on the two boats and became chief steward while on *James K. Polk*. His reputation was such that he was transferred off the boat in 1968 and was sent for duty on the presidential

The commissary division of the FBM boat *Robert E. Lee* circa 1961. Chief Steward William "Bill" Murray is in the first row (second from right), while the names of the other stewards are unknown. Note that all the Black stewards in this photograph are qualified submariners, as demonstrated by the dolphins they wear, and that only Murray and the unidentified steward in the back row (center) are wearing the submarine combat insignia indicative of their war patrol service during World War II. (Official U.S. Navy photograph.)

yacht *Sequoia*, a heady appointment even for a steward of Williams' experience. As Williams later recalled, "I had a good reputation, but I didn't want it [duty on *Sequoia*].... When I asked why I was being sent there, they told me that they only took the best" (Williams, Melvin, Sr.). Melvin Williams' two-year stint on the prestigious presidential yacht from 1968 to 1970 would take him away from the submarine duty he had come to love but would lead to even bigger changes that would affect all of the navy's stewards in a very short time.

Submarine achievements for the decade were started off in grand style in February 1960 when the *Triton* commenced her historic voyage. The story of this unusual boat, commissioned in November 1959, and of the Black submariners that served aboard her is one well worth recounting. The *Triton* herself was of an unusual and groundbreaking design. Built for speed, her power plant consisted of not one but two nuclear reactors, one to supply steam to the forward engine room and drive the starboard propeller and another to supply steam to the after engine room and drive the port propeller. Because of this unique setup, *Triton* was a big submarine, weighing in at nearly 6,700 tons and measuring 447 feet in length but achieving great speeds underwater because of her streamlined hull. No nuclear attack boat came close to her in size, and only the "boomers," equipped to carry 16 Polaris missiles, exceeded her in tonnage. *Triton* was originally built and designed as a radar picket boat, the only nuclear boat ever built to receive this official designation (SSRN). However, her career as a radar picket boat was short, and she was later redesignated as an attack boat when the navy's radar picket submarine program was ended.

Among the Black submariners that put the historic *Triton* into commission was Steward 3rd Class Donald Wilson. He reported aboard *Triton* several months after her launching, in January 1959, and was likely chosen for duty on her because of his prior nuclear boat experience. Wilson, as has previously been told, served aboard *Nautilus* when she was first built and during her first Arctic run. After leaving the boat, he did a short stint of duty in Submarine Squadron 10 at New London, serving aboard the diesel boat *Entemedor*. Wilson well recalled how difficult it was going from a nuclear boat back to the old diesels: "They used to tease me when things went wrong, and I'd tell them no, it wasn't like this on *Nautilus*, where things had to run smooth" (Wilson, Donald).

Another Black submariner that put *Triton* into commission was Chief Engineman Hosea Washington. After changing his rate from steward to engineman in the early 1950s, Washington served on *Atule* and made first class engineman on *Ray*. Following this, Washington went to, of all places, Cleveland, Ohio, for shore duty. While there, he furthered his education to further his career. He had applied for service on nuclear-powered ships in 1955 but was told he needed to enhance his education to better his General Classification Test rating in order to be considered. Washington, a former high-school dropout, did just that in stunning fashion. First, he took a correspondence course in American History from John Hay High School that enabled him to receive his long-delayed high school diploma. Immediately after, Washington enrolled in classes at the United States Armed Forces Institute (USAFI) and later Fenn College (now Cleveland State University), completing coursework in algebra, geometry, trigonometry, and electricity. Soon after, he received his hard-earned reward when he was sent to nuclear power school in New London and afterward received a posting to *Triton* as part of her commissioning crew in 1959. As Washington recalls, "To learn about *Triton*'s two reactors we were sent for training to a land-based reactor at West Milton, New York, for about a year" (Washington, Hosea).

Three months after her commissioning, on February 15, 1960, *Triton*, with Wilson, Washington, as well as Black submariners Radioman 1st Class John Wouldridge, Chief Steward William "Joe" Green, and Steward 3rd Class James Ward aboard, began her shakedown cruise by heading toward the South Atlantic. Commanded by Captain Edward Beach, a renowned submariner from World War II who was one of the navy's most respected and liked submarine skippers, *Triton* commenced what would be a most historic voyage, the first submerged circumnavigation of the world. Beach was certainly happy with his new command and the men who served aboard *Triton*. At the start of the voyage, the mission still a secret, he visited every compartment in the boat to see how things were operating. In the number two reactor compartment located aft, the largest compartment in the boat, chief engineman, and also *Triton*'s chief chemist,

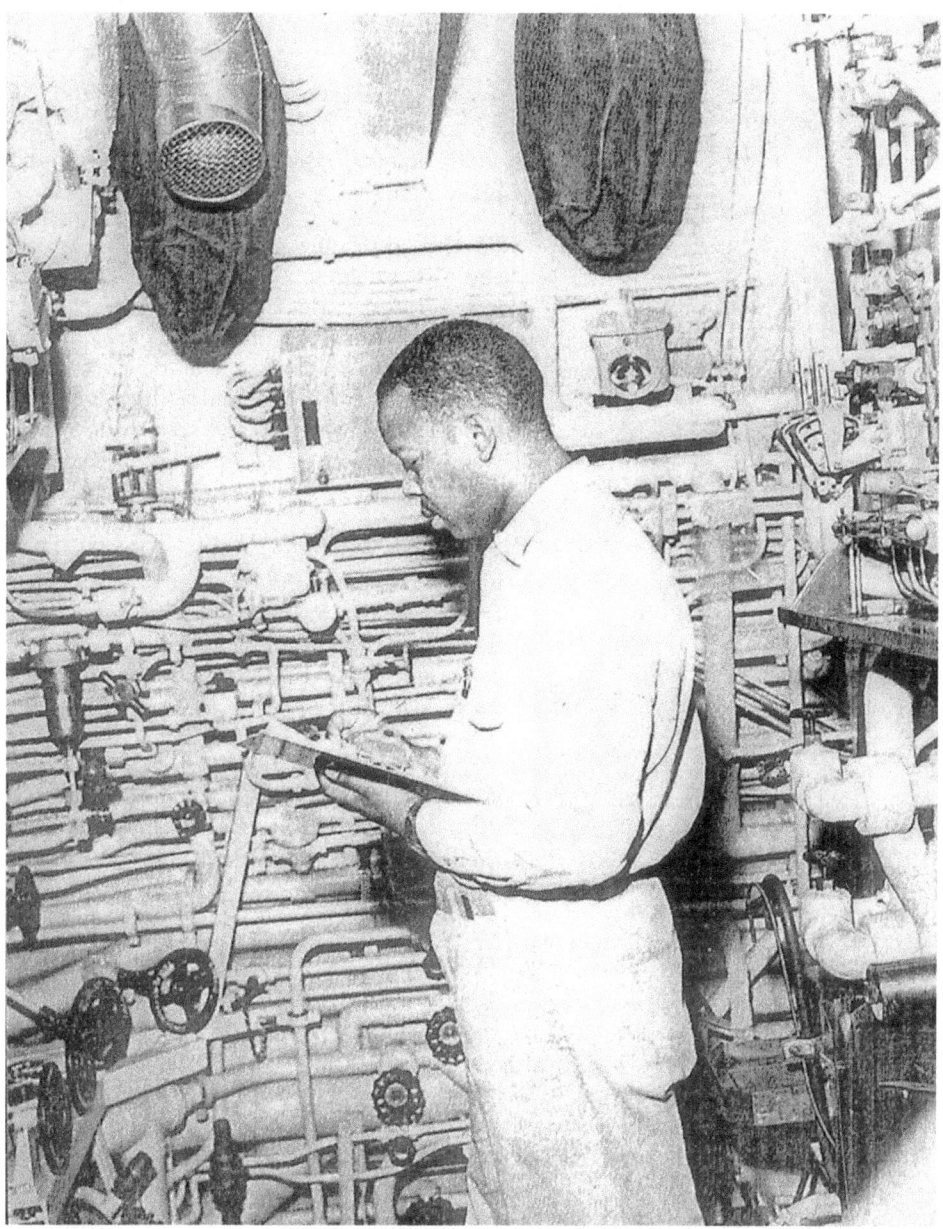

Chief Engineman Hosie Washington doing duty in the nuclear reactor compartment of *Triton* during her historic voyage around the world submerged in 1960. Washington served as the boat's chief chemist on the epic run. (Photograph courtesy of H. Washington.)

Hosea Washington was hard at work. As Beach relates, "A high-pitched roar of machinery reached my ears.... It sounded wonderful.... Washington ... our Chief Chemist, grinned happily at me. 'She sure sounds nice, Captain!' he shouted, his eyes dancing in his handsome Negro face. I nodded my agreement" (Beach, *Around the World Submerged*, p. 72). When Captain Beach returned to his stateroom later that day, Chief William Green, "known to most of the crew as 'Joe'" (*ibid.*, p. 81) was there to help him with his clothes. Like any attentive steward, Green easily deduced which way *Triton* was headed. Beach's record of his conversation with Green is a classic example of the give-and-take relationship between a steward and his captain:

> I peeled off the uncomfortable heavy garments and passed them to him. "Dry them out well, Green, and then put them away," I said. "I won't be needing them for a while." ... "It might be cold on the bridge up there in the North Sea, Captain," he said. "Maybe I'd better just fold these up and keep them where you can get at them." ... "Get out of here, Green," I said with feigned severity, "and take that gear with you." "Aren't we going up north, sir?" Green's carefully contrived expression — his big round eyes and innocently questioning face — were too much to hold, and he broke into a broad, white-toothed grin. "Are we going to keep heading down into the warm water, Captain?" [*ibid.*].

Chief Engineman Hosie Washington first saw service as a steward on *Tusk* before later changing his rate and serving in the twin-reactor powered *Triton*. (Photograph courtesy of H. Washington.)

Chief Steward William "Joe" Green probably knew where *Triton* was going before any other enlisted man on the boat. Following in the footsteps of the first man to circumnavigate the globe on its surface waters, the explorer Magellan, Beach guided *Triton* around Cape Horn and went west across the vast Pacific, passing through the Phillipine Islands and those of Indonesia and across the Indian Ocean. After rounding the Cape of Good Hope off the tip of Africa, *Triton* arrived back in the South Atlantic off St. Peter and Paul Rocks on April 10, 1960. Her voyage lasted just under 61 days and was completed totally underwater, except for one instance when she had to surface to transfer a seriously ill sailor to a waiting cruiser off the coast of Uruguay.

As Washington recalls, the voyage became routine.

> The hardest part was not becoming bored while off-duty. I brought along ten or twelve books to read and swapped them with others, and we also watched movies. For companionship after watch I usually hung out with the steward on duty. The only time we saw the outside world was when we had periscope liberty.... I can remember seeing the Straits of Magellan, Easter Island and Borneo [Washington, Hosea].

The term "periscope liberty" used by Washington refers to the times when Captain Beach brought *Triton* up to periscope depth and let those men who were interested take turns looking at some of the exotic locales they passed during the course of their circumnavigation.

While the voyage of *Triton* was an outstanding and exciting achievement for the navy, it may also stand as a milestone, of sorts, for Blacks in the navy as a whole and the Submarine Force in particular. While Washington, like most submariners in his position, is disinclined to place any special merit on the part he may have played in his boat's successful voyage, the fact remains that few Black chiefs in the Submarine Force had such important responsibilities on a boat as important as *Triton* as Washington had. His achievements here would lead Hosea Washington to even more responsibility.

Following her historic voyage, Steward 3rd Class Donald Wilson left *Triton* for a brief period of shore duty in Washington, followed by orders to report aboard a destroyer. An experienced submariner with nuclear training, Wilson wanted nothing to do with surface craft. All it took was a call to BUPERS and the mere mention of Admiral Rickover's name to get his orders changed. Soon, by 1963, Donald Wilson was back aboard *Nautilus*. He would subsequently retire from active duty in 1966.

Chief Steward William "Joe" Green of *Triton*. He was the lead steward for the boat's historic submerged circumnavgation of the world in 1960 and probably knew where *Triton* was headed well before any other crewmember onboard. (Photograph courtesy of the Green family.)

As for Hosea Washington, he stayed aboard *Triton* after her historic voyage when she assumed her duties as a radar picket boat for a brief time. This included a deployment to Europe as part of the Second Fleet to participate in NATO exercises and later patrols and exercises with the Atlantic Fleet. In 1962, when *Triton* was sent to Portsmouth, New Hampshire, for conversion to an attack submarine, Washington left her for duty at the submarine school in New London. Here he organized and taught a class in nuclear propulsion shaft components for three years. In 1965 he was one of 22 men up for officer's commissions but was the only man to be turned down. Whether this was due to his race is unknown, but, as Washington reflects, "It just wasn't the right time for me.... I have no complaints" (Liburd). Washington, forever to be remembered as a *Triton* crewman, would retire from the navy as a senior chief engineman in 1967, his career a long and valuable one. Ironically, that very same year, *Triton* became a victim of defense cutbacks and was put on the inactive list. She would never again sail the high seas.

Another historic nuclear boat that was a one of a kind like *Triton* was the guided missile submarine *Halibut*. Launched in January 1959 and commissioned in January 1960, this unique nuclear boat was the first and only boat designed to carry the Regulus I missile system. A radical departure from other submarines, her main deck was higher above the waterline than most submarines and had a large turret forward with a hatch that opened into her missile compartment. Halibut launched her first guided missile enroute to Australia on March 25, 1960. Among her crewmembers was Electrician 1st Class John O'Meally. His recollections of duty aboard *Halibut* are quite interesting and indicative of the high tension that accompanied missions to Soviet waters:

> I reported aboard as a 1st class electrician and remained on board for the next seven years. During this time we made seven North Pacific patrols. These patrols consisted of going within range of our targets and maintaining our missiles in a firing position for ninety days at least, and one patrol we were gone for a hundred and five days. We would then transit back to Pearl.
>
> This was our primary job, keeping our target covered. What we did while we were up there was collect data on the Soviet navy's operations in any way we could. If this was done by sneaking around their operations or going close to their coast, we did it. We were able to film their launch of a missile from one of their submarines which showed that the missile had a range much longer than we believed. On our seventh patrol we were detected and were held down for about thirty hours before we were able to escape. Every time we would lose a ship we would run into another. The weather favored them, and there were seven destroyers. Each time we would turn toward the open sea, they would drop a [depth] charge to prevent our going in that direction. They [the Soviets] knew they had a nuke by the speed we would make and the time we were remaining submerged. They called out the helicopters just like we do. They weren't that good, and as soon as the weather changed so that we could find a thermal layer we were able to lose them. Before that happened we went to battle stations and had flooded two torpedo tubes. All that was needed was to open the outer doors and shoot. We finally got away and went out about fifty miles to get the boat back in shape. We still had over sixty days left on this patrol, so after a few days we were back into the area and back to collecting visual and audio intelligence.
>
> While we were in Pearl we would operate on a weekly training basis. Our patrol cycle was not as rigid as the Ballistic subs years later. We were the only nuke boat making those runs. The other boats having missile capability were diesel driven and were older. The rotation schedule was always dependant on which of these units were able to make a patrol, which were broke down.... As a result, we were always at sea [O'Meally, John].

The vital duty that O'Meally performed aboard *Halibut* is reflected in the citation he received from Rear Admiral Eugene Fluckey for his performance during the course of that boat's seventh patrol in the spring of 1964. Detected by the Soviet navy, O'Meally remained on duty as the Engineering Officer of the Watch "for over fifteen hours as we attempted to elude the Russian ships that were trying to surface us" (*ibid.*). His citation reads, in part,

> For meritorious achievement in the performance of duty.... Chief O'Meally's outstanding performance ... enabled the Commanding Officer to successfully complete an operation of great value to the Government of the United States. His leadership, application of professional skill, and devotion to duty were in keeping with the highest traditions of the United States Naval Service [O'Meally, "Citation"].

For his last year on *Halibut*, the highly regarded O'Meally was the COB and received yet another citation for work from March 1965 to August 1966. During this time, *Halibut* was overhauled and converted to a fast-attack submarine after the demise of the Regulus program, and O'Meally was responsible for the overhaul on all the boat's electrical equipment. Once the boat was readied for her many spy missions to follow, John O'Meally was transferred off the boat to shore duty. Though he never again would serve on submarines, his career was always closely linked to the Submarine Force. After a short term of duty as a recruiter in New York City, O'Meally was promoted to warrant officer and transferred to Syosset, New York, to work as a special project technical representative at the Sperry Corporation. His job was to monitor the company that had the contract for navigation systems used by the Submarine Force. He would later serve as engineering officer aboard the submarine rescue vessel *Sunbird* and well remembers one particular incident that occurred:

> At dinner one night the CO was commenting on the racial problem in the country. He looked at me and said that I did good and what did "my people" want. I replied that yes, I felt I did fairly well in the navy, but if everything was equal, as it should be, I would be sitting in his chair by now. It was a quiet dinner after that [O'Meally, John].

We have already discussed the service of Black submariners aboard the "boomers"— now it is time to turn our attention to those that served aboard the nuclear fast-attack submarines. Twenty-three of this type of boat were built and launched during the decade, beginning with the ill-fated *Scorpion* in 1960 and ending with *Grayling* in 1969, and a large number of Black submariners served in their crews. One of these men was former Arctic veteran, Chief Steward Woodrow Wilson Jones. Upon returning from the North Pole on *Skate* in 1959, he was transferred to the commissioning crew of *Scorpion* in October 1959. During Jones's time aboard, until early 1961, *Scorpion* participated in NATO exercises and made operational visits to England and Scotland.

Another man who served in fast-attack boats was Chief Steward Charles Groom. He went aboard *Seadragon* in 1959 as part of her commissioning crew and participated in yet another historic Arctic submarine event, the first submarine transit of the Northwest Passage. *Seadragon* departed from Portsmouth, New Hampshire, on August 1, 1960, and headed north. Her destination was the Pacific. Moving through the frozen wastes of Davis Strait, Baffin Bay, and Lancaster Sound, she then transited Barrow Strait, Viscount Melville Sound, and McClure Strait to reach the Beaufort Sea on August 21, 1960. Soon thereafter, she reached the North Pole and subsequently headed south, reaching Nome, Alaska, on September 5, and Pearl Harbor on September 14, 1960. For this spectacular voyage, *Seadragon* and her men received the Navy Unit Commendation. Charles Groom later went aboard the newly commissioned fast-attack boat

Sculpin and made at least one WESTPAC run on her between May and August of 1962. Other men that served in fast attack boats include Steward Jim Higgins, who served on the commissioning crew of *Pollack* from 1961 to 1964 and on *Haddo* from 1966 to 1968. During his time on the later boat, Higgins and the crew helped earn the boat a Navy Unit Commendation (1966), and Meritorious Unit Commendation (1967). Other men that served on fast-attack commissioning crews include Steward Howard Burton (*Sculpin*, 1961) and Louis Slaughter (*Haddo*, 1962–1964). Chief Machinist Mate Hollis Sims, a native of Newnan, Georgia, served on the fast-attack *Dace* from 1966 to 1971, during which time she earned a Naval Unit Commendation in 1967. He would later become an officer.

One fast-attack boat that was well crewed with a contingent of Black submariners was *Skate*. As was previously mentioned, she had not only a Black chief steward but also a Black 1st class yeoman, a Black chief machinist mate, as well as Machinist Mate 1st Class Abraham Mozeak and Interior Communications Electrician 1st Class Steve Shelby. Mozeak and Shelby, among the others, were participants in what may be termed the last of the great Arctic submarine voyages when, on July 7, 1962, *Skate* headed from New London toward the North Pole for yet another mission. This time, her mission was to rendezvous under the ice at the North Pole with *Seadragon*, which departed Pearl Harbor for the same destination five days later. The mission was a success, with the rendezvous begun on July 31, 1962, and completed on August 2 when both boats surfaced at the Pole and exchanged greetings. With this accomplishment, the men and boats of the Submarine Force could truly claim to be the hailing conqueror of the Arctic. Following the mission, both Steve Shelby and Abraham Mozeak stayed aboard *Skate* for several years, conducting local operations out of New London. When the boat went to Norfolk, Virginia, for nuclear refueling and overhaul in mid–1965, Shelby would leave the boat and continue his career in other areas. Mozeak did likewise, though he did not leave *Skate* until 1966 and was present for part of her overhaul routine. After a brief period working in the overhaul crew of the diesel boat *Dogfish*, Mozeak would see subsequent duty in FBM boats.

As with most other classes of submarines, the duties of the fast-attack boats were sometimes routine and sometimes daring. Of the former, there is little in the way of exciting or historic events to speak of. For the latter, there is much that is hinted at but little that can be told due to the classified information involved. However, for any boat that earned a Meritorious, Navy, or Presidential Unit Citation during our time-frame in question, we can be sure that they were involved in dangerous missions vital to our country's defense.

One such boat to be so honored was *Plunger*, which received the Navy Unit Commendation (NUC) for her operations in the winter of 1966 and received another NUC for combined operations in summer 1968, spring 1969, and winter 1970. She also received the Arleigh Burke Fleet Trophy for 1969. One of her key crewmen during the time in which the above awards were earned was experienced submariner Senior Chief Radioman Kenneth Joyner. He had previously been working at the FOCCPAC communications center in Hawaii but was growing tired of it. As he relates,

> FOCCPAC ... was a top secret control center during the Cold War and Vietnam War in the sixties. Every commander had an emergency control center located there in the event of an impending nuclear attack. Control of any situation

could be maintained from this location. In spite of FOCCPAC being the focal point of the war, highly classified, and a hot spot of activity, being inside a tunnel from sunup to sundown was too much isolation and not my idea of the navy.... When I was asked if I would care to go on the *Plunger* ... I was ecstatic [Joyner].

Just like other men that served on these "spy" boats, Joyner can give but the barest of details regarding his experiences. Brief though they may be, they are still enlightening:

> I requalified for nuclear power submarines while on *Plunger* ... during the course of my regular duties. She served as the Submarine Force flagship. So it came as a surprise to me that now the *Plunger* was a very disruptive command. The crew hated the skipper, morale was very low, and there was a lot of outward bitching. Yearly, every boat has to go through board inspection for the license to operate a nuclear plant. The *Plunger* ... passed, but morale was so low the skipper was relieved of command. The new skipper, six-foot five-inch Nils Ron Thunman ... was smart, intense. After he came aboard and I re-qualified ... in late 1966, I was made Chief of the Boat — the first Black chief to be assigned to the prestigious and arduous position on the *Plunger*.... We sailed into Chichi Jima and Iwo Jima [off Japan] routinely. Many submarines conducted "back-to-back" patrols from Adak [Alaska] to maintain their rigorous schedule, rather than return to Pearl Harbor.
>
> On one of our runs, we were on patrol near Vladivostok. As part of my job, the XO and I saw the skipper everyday to get the daily plan. But on this day he was uptight ... things on this patrol seemed to be at a standstill. Not an enemy vessel anywhere. He called me in and said "Chief, how much booze do we have aboard?" I said that I would check with Doc [the pharmacist's mate] for the booze. The skipper said "I want to have a Monte Carlo night; set it up." And that's what I did. We had gambling games just like Las Vegas, with one section of the crew on duty and the rest getting drunk. My mistake was that I had no one who could relieve the watch. After that, the crew would have run through hell with a gasoline suit on for the captain. Later, we encountered the Whiskey class sub [Russian] we were looking for and got all sorts of data [*ibid.*].

The events that Kenneth Joyner allude to during his time on *Plunger* well reflect the tension that accompanied such submarine missions to the Soviet coast during the Cold War. In learning all that they could about the various types of Soviet submarines, such as the Whiskey, Echo, Gulf, Zulu, and Yankee-class boats to name a few, it was hoped that American boats could catch a Soviet submarine heading out on patrol and sneak up behind her and commence a dangerous operation known as "trailing." By skillfully following in the wake of a Russian submarine, undetected for days, weeks, or even a month, much could be learned about how Soviet submarines operated, their individual tendencies, and their underwater sound signatures. The Soviets, too, tried to trail American submarines and might have had a few minor successes, but they usually failed because their submarines were inferior in technology in many aspects and often noisier. In other cases, when it was thought that a Russian submarine might be trailing one of our FBM boats, a fast-attack boat was deployed to the area to try and confuse the Russians by masking the sound signature of the FBM boat. Too, sometimes the Russians knew when they were being trailed and tried to elude their pursuers, resulting in some minor collisions and many near collisions.

For the unlucky American submarine that was detected in Soviet or foreign waters, then the game became one of trying to avoid being "surfaced." Once one of our boats was detected, the Soviets would send a whole array of antisubmarine warfare vessels, from trawlers to destroyers, and even deployed helicopters to try and box in the American submarine. If they were lucky, and they usually weren't with our nuclear boats, they might force one to the surface. This would, of course, be embarrassing to the American government and might be somewhat of a public relations coup for the Soviets. Even if an American submarine was not surfaced, by pursuing them the Soviets could certainly shake her crew up and, probably a secret hope of the Soviets, might even sink or severely damage one. As Joyner chillingly states, "We understood ... our fate. Should we disappear *nothing* would be said" (*ibid.*). Those who served on the nuclear attack boats saw dangerous service, indeed, but men like Joyner did the jobs asked of them, and did them well. In regard to *Plunger* and her winning of the "highly coveted" Arleigh Burke Fleet Trophy, Kenneth Joyner received a letter of commendation from Commander Thunman, stating, in part, that "Your exceptional performance as Chief of the Boat significantly contributed.... I wish to commend you for your leadership, professionalism and devotion to duty. WELL DONE" (*ibid.*).

Despite the huge contribution of the nuclear powered submarine fleet, we must not forget the old diesel boats. They still gave tried-and-true service in many roles, both dangerous and routine, and many Black submariners served aboard them. *Bang*, with war veteran Chief Steward Sam Wallace aboard, operated in the Mediterranean Sea in 1961 and was stuck at Toulon, France, for 22 days with a disabled engine. In addition to overseas duty, many of the diesels worked out of various home ports in the United States serving as training boats in all aspects of fleet activities.

While the nuclear boats were in the ascendancy, the old diesels were still used to make dangerous WESTPAC runs. One man who served on two such boats was 1952 enlistee Arthur O'Meally, the older brother of submariner John O'Meally. He had previously served on a destroyer, in several shore positions and, most recently, on an auxiliary oiler vessel. In May 1964 he requested submarine duty and "after several tests, physical and medical, I reported aboard my first 'boat,' USS *Cusk*.... No sub school. Direct input" (O'Meally, Arthur). In talking about the limited amount of discrimination he experienced during his navy career, Chief Radioman Arthur O'Meally has this humorous story to relate when he first reported for service aboard the destroyer *Rowe* and his subsequent experiences:

> I discovered that my unusual name created an image that was shattered when I showed up. In fact, my Chief ... told me they that they were expecting a red-headed Irishman. I was the only Black in my division.... I was a 1st class radioman [RM 1] when I reported aboard USS *Cusk*, one of two Blacks aboard. The other Black was a 1st class engineman, who was affectionately called "Pappy." ... Two days after I reported aboard [at Pearl Harbor] we left for a four-month deployment to WESTPAC.... The trip was very exciting to me, being my first duty aboard a submarine.... I stood lookout watches, helm and planes watches, took orders from lower-ranked personnel when learning or performing tasks I was unfamiliar with. Three-and-a-half months later in the

harbor at Naha Okinawa, I earned my dolphins, was thrown over the side, and began my life as a full fledged *submariner* [*ibid.*].

In his two years on *Cusk*, O'Meally participated in "several special operations (SpecOps) cruises, training cruises, and another WESTPAC deployment" (*ibid.*). In describing his experiences during this time, from 1964 to 1966, he gives us these interesting observations:

> My tour of duty on submarines was like every other type of job — a combination of boredom and excitement. It can best be described as long periods of tedium interrupted by short periods of stark *terror*. A lot of those "terror" moments cannot be discussed, but some of them had to do with weather. While on the USS *Cusk*, we were on a "SpecOp" in the South China Sea area when we ran into a typhoon. The *Cusk* had to surface because we could not stay submerged indefinitely like a "nuke." Being on the surface in a submarine in a typhoon is *not* one of your favorite places to be. We were on the surface, and the sea was mountainous, forcing us to raise our "snorkel" mast in order to run our diesels. The head valve on the raised snorkel kept cycling, open and shut, because of water hitting the sensors. Fortunately, we were headed north, while the storm was headed in a southerly direction. It took about two days to reach calmer seas. Two days of sandwiches, soup, and coffee. We were being tossed around too much to cook any type of meal. After another day or so of squaring the boat away, cleaning, restoring gear, and checking equipment, we went back into normal patrol routine ... *tedium*. Heavy weather was always a problem on the diesel boats [*ibid.*].

Following his duty on *Cusk*, Arthur O'Meally did 13 months duty on the diesel boat *Tiru*. Once again, O'Meally observes that:

> The 13 months I spent on *Tiru* were exciting, hectic, and very diverse. Again, I was the only Black aboard but we had four Filipino cooks and stewards aboard. When I reported aboard, *Tiru* was in the last stages of a shipyard period. In fact, she was just coming out of dry dock. By the middle of June [1966], having completed sea trials, we were ready for whatever we were assigned to do. In September we were to participate in a joint exercise in the Coral Sea, off the coast of Australia.... After a successful operation and some outstanding liberty in Brisbane, we left for the Phillipines. Our first night out, which was a heavily overcast night, no moon, no stars, on a calm flat sea, we ran aground on Fredericks Reef. Fortunately we were running on the surface. Again, I was the senior communicator on board, and over the next 72 hours I processed and sent over 50 thousand coded groups of [radio] traffic. This being 1966, this was before computerized communications, I had to send all the traffic by hand using a speed key (which I still have sitting on my desk). After getting off the reef, we were in Brisbane for damage evaluation, and then went to the navy shipyard in Yokosuka, Japan, for repairs. At the completion of repairs we went on one SpecOp, and then returned to Pearl Harbor, more than six months after leaving. I was then transferred [*ibid.*].

Despite these adventures, Arthur O'Meally would see even more action in the early 1970s when he served on his first, and only, nuclear attack boat.

Before leaving the decade of the 1960s behind, we must first tell the sad stories of two operational losses. Both were totally shocking, completely unforeseen, and involved heavy loss of life, including well-known Black submariners that were part of their crew. The first of these two losses occurred on April 10, 1963, when the new nuclear attack boat *Thresher* sank off the coast of Portsmouth, New Hampshire, with the loss of all 129 men and civilian technicians aboard. *Thresher* was conducting sea trials after completing an overhaul at the Portsmouth Naval Shipyard and was lost due to a piping failure on her initial deep-dive test. Aboard were two Black crewmen, Steward 3rd Class George Bracey and Chief Electrician's Mate Roscoe Pennington. Both were veterans of World War II and had made a number of war patrols as stewards, Bracey on *Pargo* and Pennington on *Seadragon* and *Spikefish*. Both were fine men, and a loss to their friends, family, and community. Bracey was described as "an ardent church worker and was an ordained deacon at the People's Baptist Church of Portsmouth, N.H." (U.S. Navy, *United States Ship* Thresher, p. 22). He was also a Mason and left behind his mother, his wife Letha, and seven children. As part of *Thresher*'s commissioning crew, he had already received a letter of commendation from his first captain, Commander Dean Axene, for his fine performance.

Chief Electrician's Mate Roscoe C. Pennington of *Thresher*. Pennington was a veteran steward of World War II, making war patrols on *Seadragon* and *Spikefish*, before changing his rate in the 1950s. He would later go to nuclear power school and was part of the crew of the new attack boat *Thresher* when she was lost in April 1963. (Official U.S. Navy photograph.)

The other Black man serving on *Thresher*, Roscoe Cleveland Pennington, was well known in the Submarine Force and was highly regarded for his dedication and perseverance. He started out as a submarine steward in 1943 but always had an interest in all things electrical. On the postwar boats on which he served, he often spent his off-duty hours in the after battery compartment, learning from the electricians on duty there. While aboard *Ronquil* at San Diego in 1956, Pennington was a steward 1st class and within several years had cross-rated to electrician's mate 1st class. Soon after, he attended nuclear power school at New London but had to drop out for academic reasons. One man who attended nuclear power school at nearly the same time as Pennington, known as "Penny" to his friends, was John O'Meally. As he recalls,

> At the reactor facility I met a sailor named Roscoe Cleveland Pennington. He was in the class ahead of me. He invited me to share the apartment that he had rented.... Penny was an older sailor who had been in the navy during the war. He was an orphan in Texas and went into the navy at seventeen. He made a few war patrols on submarines and was a no-nonsense sailor.... Penny was one tenacious person when attempting to accomplish something. He failed his first attempt to complete nuke school. Now this would normally end your career in the nuclear navy. However, Penny tried so hard and displayed such a degree of comprehension of the subject matter that the powers that be decided to send him through the school for another try. Like a pit bull, he locked on to the math that beat him the first time around and would not let go until he whipped it. He was like that. I remember when he failed to make chief petty officer due to his getting a low score on the test. He told me he was going to make it the next time he took the test. One day about a week before the test, he had a day off. That morning, when I was going to work, I left him sitting at our kitchen table in his PJs with all of his books and papers studying for the exam. That was 0700 [7:00 A.M.] in the morning. At six o'clock that evening when I returned, he was still there in his PJs studying. There were cigarette butts all over the place. He had spent the entire day hitting the books. He made chief that following May like he said he would. When Penny completed nuke school, the school wanted him to stay as an instructor. He declined this offer and was assigned to the USS *Thresher* [O'Meally, John].

Prior to his loss on *Thresher*, Roscoe Pennington was that boat's leading chief reactor technician and, in September 1961, was part of a group sent to the David Taylor Model Basin in Washington to evaluate *Thresher*'s performance. He later was part of a motivational team formed by the navy to tour the country and visit high schools to inform students of the opportunities available in the nuclear navy. How many future Black submariners he might have inspired on this tour can never be known. The high regard in which Pennington was held remains evident, even to this day. Pennington Hall, a training facility dedicated on April 10, 1974, and named in his honor, stands today at the naval submarine school at the New London Submarine Base in Groton. The sentiments expressed by fellow Black submariner James Mosley are likely ones that were shared by many: "Roscoe was a dedicated person and a good friend. I still miss him" (Mosley, James).

One interesting, and rather strange, sidelight to the loss of *Thresher* is the fact that so many men felt an attachment to her in one way or another. Because of her large crew, and the close-knit atmosphere of the submarine community in general, many submariners had a friend or two or at least someone they knew on *Thresher* when she was lost. Also, just like the loss of any famous ship, its hard not to find a submarine sailor from that time stationed in the northeast who claims he was supposed to have been aboard *Thresher* on the day of her fateful voyage but, for some reason or another, somehow lucked out.

In the case of Chief Steward Rufus Weaver, however, truth is indeed stranger than fiction. Weaver was serving aboard the diesel boat *Cavalla* in March 1962 when a new steward was needed for *Thresher*. The personnel officer for Submarine Development Group Two wrote to Weaver's executive officer, stating that

> I have exhausted all efforts of trying to solve the problem of providing a steward for *Thresher*.... However, no luck. The only way for solving the problem is to transfer Weaver to *Thresher* thereby giving them two of the three stewards they rate (Garcia, SD1 leaves the first part of April). Therefore you should expect to have orders for Weaver to *Thresher* awaiting you upon your return to NLON [New London]. Weaver should plan on going to *Thresher* reporting NLT [no later than] 10 April [Weaver, "Memorandum"].

Rufus Weaver was subsequently informed of this transfer and awaited his official orders. However, in typical navy fashion, and luckily for Weaver, the orders for him to report to *Thresher* were not cut until April 12, 1963, two days after her loss, and did not arrive on *Cavalla* until April 16. By then, of course, the orders were useless, and the papers instead remained as a souvenir of the quirky nature of fate. If all had gone according to the navy's wishes, Weaver should have been on *Thresher* for her last dive. Most of his friends thought that Weaver *was* on *Thresher*. When the news of her loss came through over the base radio station at New London, fellow Black submariner and friend John Wouldridge, the former radioman on *Triton*, was on duty as radioman and was among the first to hear of the event. He soon called Weaver's residence and was stunned to have his friend answer the phone. Like many others, he thought Weaver was gone with *Thresher*. Sadly, Chief Steward Napoleon Garcia, a native of the Phillipines and a prisoner of war at the hands of the Japanese at age 15, was never transferred off the boat and was among those lost on April 10, 1963.

Finally, just as the navy was getting over the loss of *Thresher*, another nuclear boat, *Scorpion*, was lost in May 1968. It was a tragic way to end an otherwise spectacular decade in the annals of the Submarine Force. In retrospect, it may be that *Scorpion* was doomed from the start, at least in the eyes of any superstitious sailor. The name *Scorpion* was originally assigned to a nuclear submarine that was begun at the Electric Boatyard in Groton, Connecticut, in November 1957. However, when the hull was changed to accommodate a missile compartment, her name was changed to *George Washington*, and she became the world's first FBM boat. Name changes for any vessel were often considered bad luck, so consider that strike one. The new nuclear boat *Scorpion* was subsequently launched in late 1959. Though she was the sixth navy ship to bear this name throughout its history, her immediate predecessor was another submarine (*SS-278*) that was lost with all hands on her fourth war patrol in January 1943. How much confidence this inspired in her commissioning crew is unknown, but maybe this was strike two. Despite this, *Scorpion* had an active and accomplished record at the beginning of her career. She received the Navy Unit Commendation in 1962 for her work in developing nuclear submarine hunter-killer tactics and was active in Atlantic Fleet activities through 1966.

However, the defense budget was tightened late in the 1960s, and *Scorpion* was one of the few boats that had yet to receive a safety overhaul designed to prevent accidents like the one that caused the loss of *Thresher*. Despite this, *Scorpion* went to Norfolk, Virginia, for nuclear refueling and overhaul in early 1967. While there, her crew was augmented with the addition of Steward 1st Class Joseph Cross in July 1967. Not only was he the only Black submariner aboard *Scorpion*, but he was also her oldest and most seasoned submariner. A native of Louisiana, Cross had joined the navy in 1942 and made eight war patrols on *Halibut*, earning a Bronze Star. He had previously served on the nuclear boats *Triton* and *Shark*, both of which were stationed out of New London. However, Cross was anxious to get a posting to a boat home-ported at Norfolk, as his family, wife Anna Mae and son Joseph Fabian, were living there. He accepted a posting to *Scorpion*, even when his navy friends begged him not to. By then, *Scorpion*'s reputation had fallen, and she was widely referred to as the USS "Scrap Iron" by those who knew that the boat was not in top condition (Washington, Hosea).

By early 1968 *Scorpion* had completed her overhaul and refresher training and, with Cross as her lone Black sailor, headed for the Mediterranean in February 1968. She served with the Sixth U.S. Fleet there and made port calls at Rota, Spain, and Taranto, Italy, before heading for home. She was reported off the Azore Islands on May 21, 1968, and was due home at Norfolk six days later. Anna Mae Cross waited for her husband on the dock at Norfolk along with the rest of the crew's families, but *Scorpion* never arrived that day. Sadly, she would never make home port, and her 99-man crew was presumed lost on June 5, 1968. The navy diligently searched for the lost submarine and finally found her on October 30, 1968, sunk in over 10,000 feet of water southwest of the Azores. While the cause for her loss is still inconclusive, many signs point to the fact that she was probably lost due to a weapons failure when one of her torpedoes was accidentally activated while still aboard, called a "hot run," and subsequently exploded, killing all on board. The loss of Steward 1st Class Joseph Cross is illustrative yet again of the many ironies to be found in life in the Submarine Force. He started his submarine life by surviving many a close call against the Japanese during World War II only to die at the hands, perhaps, of an American torpedo 25 years later. As one man who served with Cross, and knew him well, stated, "Cross went down on *Scorpion* and is still serving, still on patrol to this day" (Drewry).

1970–1975: An End and a Beginning

In these final years under consideration, we will first take a look at some of the Black submariners whose careers we have been detailing and follow them to their conclusion. We will then address the racial atmosphere that prevailed in the navy during this critical and often troubling time in our nation's history and see how an ex–submarine steward, working with a progressive Chief of Naval Operations, showed the navy how to reform its much-abused steward's branch.

The changing of the guard among submariners in general, well underway by the early 1950s, was completed in the early years of the 1970s. As the postwar years passed, the World War II submariners began to retire and were replaced with younger men who manned even mightier submarines. Just as the diesel boats gave way, slowly at first, to those that were nuclear powered, so, too, did the old war veterans, both Black and white. Many Black submariners from this time retired in the years 1961–1964, having put in their twenty-year tour of duty. Many, however, went longer, serving their country into the 1970s. Among them were the highly esteemed Carl Kimmons, who retired

A native of Philadelphia, Chief Steward Fate Carter served on the famed spy-boat *Halibut* in the early 1960s. He would later retire as a Master Chief Steward. (Photograph courtesy of L. Slaughter.)

as a full lieutenant in 1970, one of only two former wartime submarine stewards who later became "mustang" officers. Following him was another man of distinction, the only other wartime steward to join the ranks of the "mustangs," Killraine Newton. He retired in 1971 as a lieutenant-commander. Some of the other remaining wartime submarine stewards who had made war patrols also retired early in the decade. Jesse Allen retired as a chief steward in 1971, while Sammie Major retired as a steward 1st class in 1973.

Other Black World War II veteran stewards that later became submariners and served into the 1970s include Harry Senior; James Owens, Jr.; and Fate Carter, Jr. Harry Senior, who "loved submarines" (Senior) last served on the FBM boat *John Marshall* before going to shore duty about 1965. He subsequently became an instructor for more than four years, teaching at the steward's school in San Diego before retiring in 1970 as a chief steward. He might have risen to be senior chief (E-8 pay grade) but decided not to test for the higher rate as he thought that this would get him posted out of submarines, something he could not bear.

Chief Storekeeper James Owens, Jr., formerly a steward, saw his last submarine service on the FBM boats *Sam Houston* and *George Bancroft* before going to shore duty and retiring in 1973. His final two duty stations were in Washington, D.C., and New York as a navy recruiter. Now retired and living in Wayne, New Jersey, he had this to say when asked about his generation's contribution to the next generation of Black submariners: "I feel it was pride in our work, faith in our future, and faith in our country. So we pushed ahead with what we had to do to make a good solid foundation. In the service today, the foundation is solid; the opportunities are plentiful" (Owens).

Another long-serving submarine steward that retired in the 1970s was Master Chief Steward Fate Carter, Jr. Having enlisted in the navy from his hometown of Philadelphia in 1944 at the age of 17, he retired in 1974 after a 31-year career that included service on many submarines, both diesel and nuclear. He is well remembered for his intelligence and the kindness he exhibited to younger submarine recruits that served under his guidance. Fate Carter, Jr., passed away in the late evening hours of December 7, 2000, just as "Taps" was being played after the late evening news. By his side, demonstrative of the close-knit relationship between submariners, was friend and fellow submarine steward Louis Slaughter. Among Carter's final written words were those stating that "I was blessed to have a wonderful life.... I tried to treat everyone the way I wanted to be treated" (Carter).

Among those postwar Black submariners that retired in the 1970s who were not rated as stewards were Kenneth Joyner, Abraham Mozeak, and the brothers Arthur and John O'Meally. As was common with many submariners from this time who went on to attain a higher rating, all spent the remaining four or five years of their navy career in shore duty billets of some importance. Following his years on the attack boat *Plunger* from 1966 to 1970, Kenneth Joyner put in for shore duty. When he left *Plunger*, he had the distinction of being her longest serving crewman, having been on the boat even longer than her captain. He subsequently served for four years at the Naval Communications (NAVCOM) Station at Barber's Point in Honolulu, Hawaii, and was assistant to the officer in charge of communications. As he recalls, "It was a plum assignment. I had it made and I had a good staff" (Joyner). Faced with the unappealing prospect of going back to sea duty in 1974, Kenneth Joyner retired as a senior chief radioman that same year, having served in the navy for 25 years. Reflecting on his career, he states, "I am very proud of my naval career. It was a unique period in American history; I lived through integration [in the navy] and came through honorably" (*ibid.*).

Abraham Mozeak was yet another Black submariner who would end his career on a high note. After serving in the Blue crew of the FBM boat *James K. Polk* from 1968 to 1971 as both chief of the boat and chief auxiliary equipment technician, Mozeak went to shore duty at the Navy Training and Publication Department (NTPD), working as a technical adviser and writer from July 1971 to July 1974. While in this billet, Mozeak performed to a high level and was advanced to master chief petty officer (E-9) in July 1972. While no longer serving in submarines, his task was an important one for future submariners. As a master chief machinist mate, his job was to plan, develop, and write the "Blue Book," a rate-training manual for machinist mates 3rd and 2nd class. This Abraham Mozeak did with exceptional skill, as demonstrated by both his yearly evaluation report and the letter of appreciation he received from the officer in charge of navy training support at the Washington Navy Yard, in Washington, D.C. In his evaluation, it was said of Mozeak that "He can be relied upon [to] perform the most difficult task.... He possesses a superior knowledge of all phases of his rate" (Mozeak, "BUPERS Report"). The letter of appreciation also lauds his "untiring personal efforts, conscientiously applied" and called his contributions "a true asset in this accomplishment" (Mozeak, "Letter of Appreciation"). The bespectacled Mozeak, who was at first denied submarine duty in 1960 because he wore glasses, retired from the navy in 1974, having served in submarines for eleven years of his 20-year tour of duty.

The brothers John and Arthur O'Meally also ended their careers in the 1970s. As has previously been related, John O'Meally left submarines for good in 1966 and had an exceptional conclusion to his career, retiring in 1975 as a commissioned warrant officer, level three (CWO-3). In summing up his naval career, he had this to say:

> Looking back on my career in the navy, I feel that I was never denied anything because of my race. Sure, I saw people grind their teeth when they had to salute me as we passed, but some Blacks did it also.... Submarine people were special; we were all young, and I never looked for any discrimination. I was too busy getting ahead and enjoying myself.... I saw the navy change for the better in

race relations.... When I became an officer, I detected a feeling of pride from the stewards — like they were happy to have a minority to serve. I treated them much better than the other officers.... [T]hat's when I got a look at how petty some whites, and I suspect some Blacks, can be toward those they think are below them. I had an officer tell me how much he hated Filipinos. I don't think this idiot realized he was talking to a minority. Since I was an officer, he expected me to agree with him. I didn't [O'Meally, John].

While his younger brother had served in submarines at sea from 1957 to 1966, Arthur O'Meally, got a later start, joining the Submarine Force in 1964 after spending the first twelve years of his naval career in surface craft and other shore assignments. After serving on his first boats, the diesel submarines *Cusk* and *Tiru* from 1964 to 1968, Arthur O'Meally served out the rest of the decade of the 1960s at the NAVCOM Station in Honolulu, Hawaii, working as watch supervisor of the VLF (very low frequency) transmitter that sent out submarine broadcasts in the Pacific. After serving in this important billet for two-and-a-half years, O'Meally attended a specialized communications school and then was sent "to my first and only 'nuke' boat, USS *Guardfish*" (O'Meally, Arthur). He reported aboard *Guardfish* in April 1970 while she was undergoing an extensive overhaul at the Ingalls Shipbuilding yard in Pascagoula, Mississippi, and was one of three Black submariners assigned to the boat. The others were Sonarman 1st Class Harold Wilson and a commissaryman 1st class named Jones.

In June 1970, Arthur O'Meally was slated for promotion to chief petty officer and went through the traditional ceremonies that attended his "putting on the hat" (i.e., now able to wear the visored cap of a chief petty officer). Among the humorous traditions of the United States Navy when this event occurred was that of answering a list of mock "charges" by the man about to become a chief. While O'Meally's superiors undoubtedly had "charges" of their own against him, so did someone else. Now outranking his fellow submariner and older brother, and perhaps sensing an opportunity for a little brotherly payback, CWO-2 John O'Meally offered a few "charges" of his own to the chief of the boat on *Guardfish*. Among them were "I have known the defendant for most of my life and have found him to be the type who rapidly becomes drunk with power," and "check his collar devices, as I am missing all my old ones, and I heard him say something about not wanting to look like a boot chief" (O'Meally, John). Taking it all in stride, Arthur O'Meally answered all the "charges" against him and soon, indeed, was wearing the hat of a chief petty officer.

In the following year, *Guardfish*, with O'Meally aboard, went to sea, arriving at Pearl Harbor in September 1971. During a period of tests and evaluations, Arthur O'Meally, the lead radioman aboard, qualified as chief of the watch and diving officer of the watch. *Guardfish* and her crew were subsequently deployed on a variety of special operations ("SpecOps") in Soviet waters, including an arduous period of back-to-back SpecOps missions from February to June of 1972. During this five-month period, *Guardfish* and her crew spent only three days in port, while the remainder was spent at sea submerged. While it may have been the beginning of an era of détente between the Soviet Union and the United States, with SALT (Strategic Arms Limitation Treaty) agreements soon to come, underneath the sea it was still business as usual for the men of the Submarine Force. Russian submarines were out there, and still had to be closely monitored. Once again, while the activities of our Cold War–era submariners are still largely classified, Arthur O'Meally has this event to relate, one that earned the boat and her crew the Navy Unit Commendation, that occurred while he was aboard *Guardfish* in May–June 1972:

> USS *Guardfish* ... tracked a Soviet ECHO II nuclear powered submarine for 26 days. Trail was established on 12 May 1972, sixty miles north of Tsushima Straits [Japan]. The ECHO II, designated "Papa 07," continued southward transiting eastward. At a point due west of Okinawa and 15 miles west of Kumeshima, Papa 07 turned southeast into the Phillipine Sea. Once in safe navigable waters, he set a course direct for the Bashi Channel [between the Phillipine Islands and Taiwan] into the South China Sea. *Guardfish* trailed him for 26 days, gathered a wealth of information on his operating procedures, and then broke it off. We had stayed within a mile of this ECHO II and had remained *undetected* the entire time [O'Meally, Arthur].

In addition to this type of danger, there was always the cold and harsh weather to deal with when making such runs in the Northern Pacific Ocean, and the runs of *Guardfish* were no exception. Again, Arthur O'Meally:

> On one occasion, while on patrol we received a casualty to our #1 periscope. We were unable to lower it. That cut our submerged speed to three knots. We were ordered into Adak, Alaska, to get our "scope" changed. Between our position at that time and Adak was reported some extremely heavy weather, state-5 seas. We made it to Adak in about a week. Because of the speed limitation and the weather, it was quite a trip. At one point ... we were taking 20-degree rolls to port and starboard. An exciting transit. We arrived, changed the scope, checked it out, and resumed patrol [*ibid.*].

The "biggest thrill" of Arthur O'Meally's naval career, and one of the biggest in his entire life, was

Chief Radioman Arthur O'Meally in his dress white uniform. The thrill of his life was conning the nuclear attack boat *Guardfish* out of Hong Kong harbor while acting as officer of the deck in the early 1970s, a time when there were no Black submarine commanders. (Photograph courtesy of A. O'Meally.)

when he made his last trip on *Guardfish* late in 1973. The excitement of this event is still reflected in O'Meally's voice even today and is one he is rightfully proud of. As he vividly recalls:

> I had been studying, with the concurrence of my skipper, Commander D.C. Minton III, to qualify as OOD surface [Officer of the Deck–on the surface]. When we left Hong Kong on our way to Yokosuka, Japan, I was allowed to take her out. It was quite a rush, being "in command" of an 80-million-dollar piece of government hardware. I went from "driving" on the surface, to "diving" the boat submerged [*ibid.*].

The importance of O'Meally serving as OOD and conning *Guardfish* out of Hong Kong is difficult to gauge, but it is at least indicative of just how far Black submariners had progressed over the years. While it is unknown how many other enlisted men like O'Meally were trusted with such high tech pieces of "government hardware," if even for only a short time, the number was likely small, and the number of Black submariners so entrusted probably even smaller. When it is remembered that, at this time, there had not yet even been a Black officer promoted to command of a submarine, this career achievement of Arthur O'Meally is truly remarkable.

Following his duty on *Guardfish*, O'Meally was sent to shore duty at the Naval Submarine Training Center Pacific (NSTCP) in Pearl Harbor after attending instructors school in San Diego. At NSTCP, O'Meally was the area supervisor and lead instructor for a computerized communication system designated "VERDIN," his job being to develop and teach lesson plans for both its operation and maintenance. For several years thereafter, he spent nine weeks teaching the course followed by two weeks of revising and improving the curriculum, subsequently repeating the process during the course of his tenure. As he relates, "This tour as an instructor was the most satisfying. I really enjoyed it" (*ibid.*). Arthur O'Meally retired as a chief radioman in January 1978, having served the Submarine Force for 14 years and his country overall for 26 years. Whether or not Chief Petty Officer Arthur O'Meally ever deigned to salute his younger brother John, who had advanced to warrant officer status during his navy career, is unknown, but both deserve to be saluted for their outstanding submarine careers. The unique bond they share as both brothers and fellow submariners is one that remains strong to this day.

In concluding the personal accounts of Black submariners we have previously mentioned, we must also look at the careers of three men who joined the Submarine Force in the 1960s and served into the 1980s. These men were Steve Shelby, Hollis Sims, and Chancellor Tzomes. Steve Shelby, it will be recalled, enlisted in 1958 and joined the Submarine Force in 1959; he first served on *Sabalo* and *Skate*. In 1969, after earning a degree in computer science at the University of Utah as part of the NESEP program, he was commissioned as an ensign aboard the guided missile cruiser *Chicago*. As Shelby recalls, "I had a yearning to go back to subs and got my orders [in 1971] just before we left for Vietnam" (Shelby). He was subsequently assigned to the FBM boat *John Marshall*, serving in her Blue crew as assistant navigator, communicator, and sonar officer. While Shelby recalls no problems with discrimination aboard this, or any other boat he served on, his account shows that a sense of humor was always helpful;

Just after being interviewed by the CO [commanding officer] for my Officer of the Deck [OOD] qualifications, the ship was at periscope depth at night. The control room was rigged for black [lights in the control room were darkened] so the OOD would be able to see out of the periscope. I was standing near the periscope stand when the CO asked if it was I. He had me come to look out of the periscope at the snorkel head valve. This was to show me that without a moon, it was hard to see the head valve indicator. When I was finished, I jokingly said to the OOD ... that he better not rig control for black when I was there again. The CO asked what I had said. He was floored, because I was the first Black officer that he had under him. However, his predisposition did not affect our relationship, and he was not racist.... When the CO invited me to his home, to have the required naval tradition first meeting with the wife, he asked me, "How did you get out of Harlem." My wife and I had a good laugh.... It should be noted that even in the '70s, I was considered an oddity to some people which is evidenced by not being saluted, "Oh I thought you were a Chief," or having a Black sailor exclaim, "*All* right, there is a Black Lieutenant" [*ibid.*].

Following his service on *John Marshall* from March 1972 to June 1974, Steve Shelby served for two years as the officer in charge of the Polaris Training and Evaluation Program (PTEP) at New London. In the performance of this duty, Shelby had the important task of supervising six enlisted men and one civilian to conduct testing and evaluation of weapons and navigation personnel that served on the FBM boats. He was routinely required to prepare and give briefings to both commanding officers and officers of flag rank. In August 1976, now a lieutenant, Shelby went back to sea once more, this time on the Blue crew of the FBM boat *Thomas Jefferson* operating out of Pearl Harbor. Here, as he recalls, "I was navigator and senior watch officer. By this time I had nothing to prove. I did my job and had an excellent working relationship with my men, CO and XO. I made LCDR [lieutenant commander] during my next to last patrol in 1979" (*ibid.*)

In November 1979, Steve Shelby went to shore duty, serving as the director of communications at the NSTCP. Shelby retired from there in June 1981, having served 24 years in the navy with almost his entire career, except for his 18 months on the cruiser *Chicago*, spent in the Submarine Force and related commands. Upon his retirement he received a Navy Commendation Award for his outstanding performance.

Another Black submariner who went from enlisted man to officer rank and served into the 1980s was Hollis Sims. After serving on the nuclear attack boats *Dace* (1966–1971), *Batfish* (1971–1974), and *Philadelphia* (1974–1975) as a chief machinist mate, in June 1975 Sims was selected for the warrant officer program and was commissioned as a chief warrant officer. Because submarines have no billets for warrant officers, Sims was assigned to the submarine tender *Holland* as assistant Radcon (Radio Control) officer. He later served on the staff of Submarine Squadron Fourteen at Holy Loch, Scotland, and later as a ship coordinator, supervisor of shipbuilding and conversion, at Groton, Connecticut. He also served, up to 1983, as a planning officer at submarine base Pearl Harbor and on the staff of the Commander, Submarine Force, Atlantic Fleet, rising to the rank of lieutenant commander.

Finally, there is the account of the Black submariner who made history, Chancellor Tzomes. After first serving as an officer on the Blue crew of *Will Rogers* in 1969,

Tzomes reported to the attack boat *Pintado* in late 1970 as part of her precommissioning crew. While aboard, he completed his engineer officer qualifications and, in April 1973, was assigned as engineering officer on the attack boat *Drum*. Tzomes served on this boat until August 1976, subsequently doing shore duty on the nuclear propulsion examining board on the staff of the commander in chief, Pacific Fleet. Chancellor Tzomes went back to sea in November 1979, serving as executive officer aboard the attack boat *Cavalla* for three years. In April 1983, Tzomes made history when he was ordered to Norfolk, Virginia, to take command of the nuclear attack boat *Houston*. By rising to this position of command, Chancellor "Pete" Tzomes became the first ever Black submariner to rise to his own command. From stewards in another era to commanding officers in a new age, the cycle for Black submariners was now nearly complete.

In turning our attention to the area of racial equality and opportunity in the navy in the 1970s, the story is one of ultimate success. However, the navy, like the rest of the country, had to be shown the way to success, and change would not be easy. To set the stage, the early 1970s were a tumultuous time in American history. On the home front, the disturbances of the 1960s were still fresh on the minds of most Americans, Black and white. These included such events as the race riots in the Watts section of Los Angeles (1965–1966) and more recently in Newark, New Jersey, and Detroit (1967), and the assassinations of Robert Kennedy and Martin Luther King (1968). The 1970s didn't start out much better — the Vietnam War was spiraling out of control, and casualties were growing. So, too, was discontent at home against the war heightening, culminating in the tragic incident that took place at Kent State University (Ohio) on May 4, 1970, when four students were killed after a contingent of the Ohio National Guard fired into a crowd of students protesting the war. Other events, too, were happening that would shape our nation's history, including the election and reelection of Richard Nixon and his subsequent fall from power in 1974, just a year after the Vietnam War had ended. Amidst all of these events, the navy, too, had its good moments and bad, many of which reflected the state of the nation as a whole. Perhaps the most interesting and, for our story, the most significant event of the early 1970s was the promotion of Admiral Elmo Zumwalt, Jr., to the post of chief of naval operations in July of 1970.

At the age of 49 in 1970, Zumwalt was the youngest ever chief of naval operations and was a forward-thinking man. From the start he had a vision of how the modern navy should operate and communicated his directives via the now famous "Z-grams," a series of more than 100 orders issued during the course of his tenure that implemented sweeping changes in many aspects of navy operations. While many officers of flag rank supported the changes implemented by Zumwalt, there were many naval officers who preferred the old way of doing things. One admiral said of Zumwalt that he was "the first chief of the navy to recognize changes in society which have necessitated changes in the navy," while another officer, commenting on his changes, stated that "while a much-needed breath of fresh air is sweeping through the navy, many of my colleagues prefer the musty odor of ancient times" (Foner, p. 249).

One of the areas in which Zumwalt made the most drastic changes was that of race relations in the navy. His directives in this area affected not only Black submariners but Blacks in the entire navy. They began with Z-gram 57, which was issued in November 1970. In seeking "to eliminate many of the most abrasive policies" of the navy, Zumwalt now stated that "in the case of haircuts, sideburns, and contemporary clothing styles, my view is that we must learn to adapt to changing fashions" (Zumwalt, "Z-gram 57"). He decreed that those enlisted men who chose hair or clothing styles "at variance with the taste of their seniors" (*ibid.*) would not be penalized. This was a big issue for many young Blacks who had entered the navy and were previously forced to conform in their style of dress and hairstyles to what their white officers deemed appropriate. Now, Black sailors who were so inclined could sport Afro-style haircuts, sideburns, and contemporary clothing styles that reflected the rising sentiment of "Black Power" and "Black Pride" without being penalized for doing so.

The navy under Zumwalt even changed its recruiting practices and, with the new recruiting slogan of "You can be Black and Navy Too," made a concerted effort to gain new Black recruits, especially amongst its officer ranks (Foner, p. 240). Too, the navy began to step up its various community outreach programs to specifically encourage Black youths in inner-city areas. Despite its less than attractive reputation, it was hoped that the "new" navy could be seen as a viable career choice for minorities and whites alike.

Here again, one may argue that the Submarine Force was in the forefront when it came to such programs. They started in the early 1960s when Chief Roscoe Pennington was part of an outreach program to various high schools designed to attract enlistees for the navy's nuclear power program. As previously related, former steward, and now Chief Electronics Technician Isaac Johnson also started a minority recruiting program for the navy's nuclear power program in San Diego in 1962. A later example of this type of program, just preceding the Zumwalt era, was one in May 1969 in which Black submariner Kenneth Joyner, chief of the boat on the nuclear attack boat *Plunger*, was a proud participant. Steve Jackstadt, a former teacher in Los Angeles at the Watts 66th Street School, now teaching economics at Punahou School in Honolulu, suggested to the navy the idea that they help sponsor a visit to Hawaii by children from the school in Watts. The commander of the Submarine Force Pacific Fleet agreed with the idea and subsequently sponsored five children who visited Hawaii for ten days. In addition to attending classes at Punahou School, the youngsters also toured the submarine base, had lunch aboard *Plunger*, and were presented cards making them honorary submariners. Calling this event "One of the highlights and privileges of my tenure as COB of *Plunger*," Joyner further recalls that "It was a pleasure to see these children's faces while they toured the submarine and ate lunch with us.... By the time they left, the students were using terms like 'shipover,' 'ship out,' 'off duty' and 'head' like veteran navy men" (Joyner).

Recognizing that "ours must be a navy family that recognizes no artificial barriers of race, color, or religion. There is no Black navy, no white navy — just one navy — the United States Navy" (Zumwalt, "Z-gram 66"), Admiral Elmo Zumwalt issued his famous Z-gram 66 in December 1970 to address the issue of equal opportunity and race relations in the navy. This directive was the result of a series of study groups consisting of Black officers, enlisted men, and their wives who met to discuss race problems within the navy and presented their findings to Zumwalt, the secretary of the navy, and others. Zumwalt was stunned at what he learned. In the opening paragraph of Z-gram 66, Zumwalt candidly admits that

Stewardsman Louis Slaughter served on the nuclear attack boat *Haddo* from 1962 to 1964. The time had certainly changed when he took one of his officers to captain's mast for inappropriate orders in 1970. (Photograph courtesy of L. Slaughter.)

Prior to these meetings, I was convinced that, compared with the civilian community, we had relatively few racial problems in the navy. However, after exploring the matter in some depth.... I have discovered that I was wrong—we do have problems, and it is my intention ... to take prompt steps toward their solution.... What struck me more than anything else was the depth of feeling of our Black personnel that there is significant discrimination in the navy [*ibid.*].

As a result of what Admiral Zumwalt learned, his Z-gram on this subject targeted many issues that were of significance for Black personnel at all levels. After addressing the issue of communication and an increased dialogue, Zumwalt goes on to discuss the matters of discrimination in regard to navy housing; the appointment of minority affairs officers and minority wives in navy-wives ombudsman groups; the stocking of suitable goods for Black personnel at navy exchanges and commissaries in regard to ethnic cosmetics, toiletries, grooming aids, foods and produce; the employment at every base or station of at least one qualified Black barber or beautician; entertainment programs that include events of interest to minority personnel; and the stocking of navy libraries, wardrooms, and clubs with a selection of books, magazines, and records by and for Black Americans. The implementation of these changes on a timely basis would be followed up with visits to major navy installations by LCDR William Norman, a Black officer who was Zumwalt's minority affairs assistant. Those individuals who felt that they were the victims of discrimination could even request a captain's mast hearing to get the issue resolved.

While the Submarine Force was probably the least of the navy's problems when it came to race relations, even here problems cropped up from time to time. One individual who did take advantage of the navy's more sensitized approach to minorities was

Steward 1st Class Louis Slaughter. While serving aboard the FBM boat *James K. Polk* in 1970, Slaughter "took the executive officer, a southerner, to captain's mast for ordering me to wash his clothes — something that was not in my job description.... I won the case" (Slaughter). However, when his enlistment was up later that year, Slaughter decided not to reenlist, even though he was due to make chief, because "I thought I would have been black balled" (*ibid.*) for taking an officer to captain's mast.

Despite all of Admiral Zumwalt's progressive actions, it would take some time and much problem solving before his vision of a cohesive navy without racial barriers was realized. By 1972, problems within the service still abounded, especially in the area of navy housing and the number of minority officers, which was growing at only a small rate. However, things would get worse before they got better. In October and November of that same year there occurred racial flare ups on three navy ships, the oiler *Hassayampa* and the aircraft carriers *Kitty Hawk* and *Constellation*, that would once again bring the issue of racial discrimination to the forefront on the national stage.

One area of race relations that became a focal point in the navy was its steward's branch. By now, this minority branch of the service was comprised of predominantly Filipinos, but also had other races, including large numbers of Blacks and hispanics, and even a small number of caucasians. It was clear, especially to outsiders, that this branch of the navy was an anachronistic one that not only treated minorities as inferior beings but one that also wasted tax payer's money. While the men within the steward's branch continued, as they always had, to do good work, the various ways in which they were misused by the officers they served was rapidly becoming unacceptable. National newspaper columnists like Jack Anderson began to question the need for high ranking officers to have someone else shine their shoes, make their beds, and walk their dog. So, too, did such high ranking politicians as Senator William Proxmire of Wisconsin begin to question the expense of having stewards serve as personal valets for officers. When he began handing out his dubious Golden Fleece awards in the early 1970s to organizations within the government that wasted tax payer's dollars in a big way, Proxmire not only targeted expensive and questionable military projects but many relatively smaller expenditures as well. These included not only the legendary toilet seat for the air force that cost $400 but also the navy's questionable use of the men of the steward's branch.

As a result of this kind of publicity, guidelines were established that limited the personal use of stewards during the early 1970s. Starting in December 1970, based on Zumwalt's orders, flag officers could only use stewards for official navy functions. If they were used on a personal level, such service had to be optional and performed on a paid basis. In September 1973 the Senate passed a further amendment limiting the use of stewards as servants for officers, but still it was not enough.

Pressure was even brought to bear on the navy from an unusual source — the Phillipine government. Since it was men from these islands that by now predominated the steward's branch, their concern was that their citizens, who had a long-standing tradition of serving as stewards in the navy, were not being treated on an equal basis with other naval personnel who were either white or served in other rates. It seems yet another small piece of bitter irony for Black servicemen that it would take protests from a foreign government, trying to protect their own citizens, to prod the United States Navy to do the same for their own minority servicemen.

While there can be no doubt that Admiral Zumwalt wanted to achieve racial equality in the navy, when it came to the steward's branch and how it should be reformed, he needed guidance and leadership from someone who was a well respected steward, knew the ins and outs of the rate, and had a plan for implementing change in a manner that was satisfactory to all. Not surprisingly, it would take a submarine steward to get the job done and get it done right. While the forward-thinking actions of Admiral Elmo Zumwalt have been well documented and written about, few know that it was Master Chief Steward Melvin Williams who ended the era of the steward in the United States Navy almost single handedly. So, let us now follow the career of Melvin Williams, and end our account where it began in the first place, with the men of the steward's branch.

When we last left Melvin Williams, he went from the FBM boat *James K. Polk* to the presidential yacht *Sequoia* in 1968. Here he would serve for two years in a most distinguished, and very political, environment different from any he had ever been in before. In reflecting on his time aboard *Sequoia*, Williams relates that;

> The combat ships were navy. The presidential yacht was political.... It was a Washington idea, and it was used for political reasons ... international politics. We took out people to wine and dine during the time I was on there, such as the Russian ambassador Dobrynin. We'd take out the Secretary of State Dean Rusk and many foreign dignitaries. We seldom took the President out. The Nixon girls would get the boat; Lyndon Johnson would come out every now and then; Hubert Humphrey would come out every now and then. But, normally it was a lot of staffers and congressional people who used the vessel. Basically, what we did was take the yacht out — we never left the Potomoc and Anacostia rivers. So we'd just go out, and we'd cruise the river, and we'd have parties.... Sequoia gave the opportunity for international agreements to be made [Williams, National Historic Center interview].
>
> Sequoia was a showboat.... No one treated us [the stewards] bad; we were like celebrities and talked to such people as the secretary of the navy, and Senators John Chafee and John Warner [Williams, Melvin, Sr.].

From this high profile appointment, Melvin Williams went to another important billet, the Secretary of the Navy — Chief of Naval Operations Flag Mess at the Pentagon in 1970. As the lead steward on duty here, Williams ran the dining room and related facilities where the secretary of the navy, the chief of naval operations, and many assistant secretaries and three-star admirals dined on a regular basis. Such an appointment might have been a daunting one for most stewards, but not for Williams. While his previous experience on the presidential yacht made the transition easier, and he already knew many of the Pentagon personnel from the time they had spent on *Sequoia*, Williams had an even better reason for feeling at ease in the Pentagon, "I had done twenty years in the navy by this time, and I felt like an equal" (*ibid.*). More importantly, Williams was interacting on a regular basis with such men as Admiral Zumwalt and Secretary of the Navy John Chafee. These were men who wanted to change the navy's record when it came to race relations, and Williams knew he had an eager audience. Seizing the moment, Melvin Williams hashed out a plan to merge the commissary branch of the navy with the steward's branch to create an entirely new rate, drafting it at his kitchen table at home during times when he was off duty. While Melvin Williams will one day write the complete story of his outstanding life and naval career and bring to light the full details of his work in helping the navy to abolish the steward's branch, his brief account here is extremely enlightening:

> The timing was right. I also wanted to help Admiral Zumwalt, who was a most honorable man, and I wanted to help the navy.... I also knew that I had the ear of Admiral Zumwalt. There had been rumors that there was a pending merger of the mostly white commissaryman rating and the mostly minority stewards rating. The problem was, that the navy did not know how to do it. How to bring to an end 93 years of discrimination and institutional racism with a single stroke.... I began to do some research and found out that they were indeed about to merge the two groups; however, as expected, it was not going to be fair to the Stewards, and they had not eliminated the steward stigma. I interceded — I wrote a proposal and position paper for Admiral Zumwalt which addressed the steward's problems.
>
> One of the problems was promotions. Because we were about to merge, I looked at the pending promotion picture. I found out that the commissarymen were scheduled for a 78 percent promotion rate while the stewards were scheduled for a 5 percent promotion rate. We had to stop the pending promotions — we failed on that one.... While researching I discovered why so many [stewards] ... could not be promoted while ... on active duty.... I found that 58 percent of all the jobs in the steward's branch were for grades E-1 through E-3. No wonder so many of us were lucky to retire at E-6 [steward 1st class]. On the other hand, the commissaryman rating only called for 11 percent E-1 through E-3. This was Institutional Racism and I was mad.... All of these years [stewards] had taken exams ... retiring with less than deserved. The proposal that I wrote for a merger plan allowed for fair play and equity and the elimination of perceived menial work as a profession. Admiral Zumwalt liked it and had me chair a board of stewards from the fleet to develop the plan so the navy could study it. Myself and 12 other stewards met at the Bureau of Naval Personnel August 5–9, 1974. I had already written the proposal and other members agreed that it was good. We then spent the rest of the time designing our new rating badge and giving our new rating a name. We came up with mess management specialist (MS).
>
> After our work, we met with a room full of admirals, including the chief of naval personnel and the assistant secretary of the navy to give a briefing. I gave the presentation. I told them that I was speaking for generations of former stewards who had served the navy well. For them, you owe us a better life. I let them know I was knowledgeable of the press, the position the navy was in, and the politics of it.
>
> Our proposal called for a new name and for those who served in it to be professional and experts.... To be eliminated from our rating were bed making, shoe shining, dog walking, shopping, and all manner of things that should not be a permanent job.... We wanted to upgrade our image so that we could be hired in the expanding hospitality field when we left the navy.... Our new shore duty would be in "managing" all the BEQs, BOQs, and BQs in the navy. We would also manage the shore duty messes.... I also recommended that they convene a board of commissarymen to see how they felt. When they met, they didn't have anything to add. They liked it.

However, their senior chiefs refused to touch it and left the navy in droves. On January 1, 1975, the stewards were no longer a navy rating. When I received my copy of the guidelines for the new rating [mess management specialist], I was surprised to see that the navy had adopted just about every recommendation that I sat in my kitchen and wrote.... When the promotions were awarded in 1975, the [former] stewards were promoted at a rate of 70 percent. Within a year, there was no former steward that anyone knew that had not been promoted [Williams, "Keynote Presentation"].

Master Chief Steward Melvin Williams had, indeed, grabbed the bull by the horns and done what others before him could not or would not do. He reformed the steward's branch from the inside and, by doing so, gave it a new identity and the respectability that stewards had for so long deserved but had been denied to them by the navy. For his efforts, Williams was awarded the Meritorious Service medal and remains appreciative to this day for having had the honor to work with Admiral Elmo Zumwalt. Without Zumwalt's wisdom, Williams' plans for reforming the steward's branch may have fallen on deaf ears. It seems very fitting, then, that the abolishment of the steward's branch coincided with the end of Zumwalt's tenure as the chief of naval operations.

However, Melvin Williams was not yet through. After the new rating was put into effect, he wanted to be sure that his plan worked as well aboard a navy ship as it did in theory. To this end, he went back to sea for two years, this time on the destroyer tender *Piedmont*. While he dearly would have enjoyed going back to submarine duty, Williams knew that this wasn't where problems would crop up. Unofficially, the men of the Submarine Force had solved most racial problems years ago — it was on the larger surface ships where the new rating needed testing. As Williams recalls,

> I was assigned to the USS *Piedmont* ... in Norfolk. Upon my arrival I was assigned as the division chief; I was also put in charge of the general mess, officer's mess, chief's mess, and the 1st class mess. I was asked to chair the Striker Board, Sailor of the Quarter Committee, Ombudsman Committee, Human Relations Committee, serve as EEO counselor and then was appointed as command master chief. I thought, how am I doing all this? Maybe its because I was no longer "only" a steward, but now a mess management specialist. I have often wondered if I had come on board with our old quarter moon insignia on my sleeve, would I have been asked to do these things? I think I know the answer [Williams, interview].

Williams' plan had indeed worked, and former stewards, including many Black submariners, would now reap the benefits as mess management specialists and would gain the promotions they so richly deserved. Two such men were former stewards Frank Holloman and Archie Denson. When we last left Holloman, he had served aboard the *Will Rogers* as chief of the boat of the Blue crew in 1967–1968. He well knew what Melvin Williams was talking about in regard to promotions for stewards. As Holloman would later recall, after he had reenlisted in 1951,

> I began taking all the exams for advancement, and the following two years I made the two rates. For all the guys ... who complain about being in a rate for a long time, I can sympathize, because I remained SD2 [steward 2nd class] for nine years. The reason was simple, I didn't have enough time in grade; I always

Master Chief Mess Management Specialist Frank Emory Holloman, circa 1976. He served on many diesel and nuclear boats during his extensive navy career beginning in 1944, culminating with his tenure as chief of the boat on the *Will Rogers* before going to shore duty. Once ashore, the work of this Tuskeegee Institute–educated man was equally impressive. (Photograph courtesy of J. Holloman.)

passed every exam. I can recall with a great deal of pride one navy captain looking at my uniform and saying, "Where are your hash marks? ... There are no second class stewards in the navy without hash marks!" The problem was, I had only been in the navy three years, and I had not earned any hash marks [Petway, p. 13].

As a former cadet at the Tuskeegee Institute in Alabama, Holloman was a highly intelligent and well-educated man. In many ways, it is not surprising he would never again serve on submarines, as his talents would be put to use for a wider audience. He subsequently became a steward advancement examination writer at the naval examining center at the Great Lakes naval training center and, subsequently, the naval education and training center at Ellyson Field, Florida, from September 1969 to August 1975. During this time, which included the transition period from steward to mess management specialist, Frank Holloman advanced to the rate of master chief in 1970 and was awarded the Navy Achievement Medal. His citation states, in part,

[H]e wrote 72 examinations annually — a number unequalled in the history of the navy advancement system.... [H]e undertook the simultaneous training of four newly assigned training ... and examination writers.... The dedication, perseverance, long hours and hard work devoted to these tasks are clear evidence of his sincere interest in, and regard for, not only the training and advancement of the men in his rating, but also those who benefit from the services they render. His total dedication ... and his distinctive achievements reflect credit upon himself and the United States Naval Service [Holloman, "Navy Achievement Medal Citation"].

Shortly after receiving this award, Holloman would state that

Opportunities for Blacks in the navy are better today [1976] than ever before, we just have to take advantage of these opportunities and go out and get it ... it's there waiting. Not only have the educational advantages changed a great deal, the racial problems are nothing at all like they used to be.... I can remember when a white man would get upset if a Black man used the same wash basin as he; things like that are not even given a second thought anymore [Petway, p. 13].

Holloman would later do shore duty at the naval air station in Pensacola, Florida, where he was in charge of the officer's BOQ and supervised 86 men. He later went to Naval Supply Systems Command in Washington, D.C. After serving on eleven submarines and achieving a navy career of 30 years, Master Chief Frank Holloman retired in May 1979.

Archie Denson was serving as chief steward on the FBM boat *Will Rogers* from 1966 to 1968. From late 1968 to late 1975, Denson did shore duty, first serving at the Navy Medical Center in Bethesda, Maryland, followed by duty at the Naval Academy in Annapolis. He went back to sea in October 1975 on the nuclear carrier *Nimitz* and was now rated as a master chief mess management specialist (E-9 pay grade), a rate he might never had achieved if the old steward's branch were still around. Denson did two years of carrier duty, stating that "No one [stewards] liked carrier duty" (Denson) and participated in one nine-month Mediterranean cruise. However, always a submarine man,

Denson went back to submarine duty in 1977 after nearly a ten-year absence. He served on the FBM boat *Ulysses S. Grant* for seven months and was the chief of the boat for the Gold crew before going back to shore duty in late 1978. He retired as a master chief in 1982 after attending human resources management school in Memphis, Tennessee, and doing a final stretch of shore duty at Annapolis. In an effort to extend his enlistment, the navy offered him a transfer to fast-attack submarine duty, but Denson declined. After 30 years of serving his country, sixteen of which were spent in submarine duty, he knew his time had come.

Finally, what about that architect of change for the men of the steward's branch, Melvin Williams? After two years on Piedmont, and discovering that, indeed, his plan had worked, Master Chief Mess Management Specialist Melvin Williams decided the time had come to move on and retired from the navy in 1978, having served his country honorably for 25 years. However, Williams's impact on the navy was not yet ended. The plan this proud submariner implemented remains in effect today. Though the name for

Steward Archie Denson made the transition from diesel to nuclear boats and retired as a master chief after a long and successful navy career. (Photograph courtesy of A. Denson.)

this rate has changed yet again, to that of culinary specialist (CS) in 2003, the professional functions that its men perform today have remained the same as was envisioned by Master Chief Williams over twenty-five years previously. Ironically, in the same year he retired, 1978, Williams' son, Melvin Williams, Jr., graduated from the United States Naval Academy and followed in his father's pioneering footsteps. He would choose the Submarine Force as his career path beginning in 1980 and never look back. He was executive officer of the nuclear attack boat *Louisville* during Operation Desert Shield, serving on that boat from 1989 to 1992. In 1993 he gained command of the Trident submarine *Nebraska*, serving as captain of her Gold crew from 1994 to 1997.

Having gained command of his own submarine, Williams, Jr., joined the ranks of what is now called The Centennial Seven. These men were the first Black submariners to command a submarine during the first 100 years of the Submarine Force's existence. The other men of The Centennial Seven, and their first commands, were the previously mentioned Chancellor Tzomes (*Houston*), Tony Watson (*Jacksonville*), William Bundy (*Barbel*), Joe Peterson (*Dolphin*), Cecil Haney (*Honolulu*), and Bruce Grooms (*Asheville*). Demonstrating just how far the Navy had progressed, all but two of these men were Naval Academy graduates. Bundy and Peterson were enlisted men who became "mustang" commanders. Some of these men, benefiting from the trail blazed by Black submariners of an earlier time, advanced even further in rank, including Melvin Williams, Jr. He is now a rear admiral in command of Submarine Group Nine in Bangor, Washington. As his father, Master Chief Melvin Williams, recalls after spending a day on *Nebraska*,

> I had lunch in the wardroom and reflected on many thoughts as I was served my meal.... I looked up at the mess management specialist who was serving my food and saw that he was a white American. I looked up to the head of the table and in the commanding officer's seat, I looked into the face of my son.... I get choked up thinking about it now [Williams, "Keynote Presentation"].

The times had indeed changed a great deal. America's Black submariners had finally achieved what they had deserved all along. Taking advantage of the smallest of opportunities that was granted them in World War II, America's submarine stewards proved their worth as fighting men many times over. When opportunities were gradually expanded after the war, Black submariners of all rates seized the moment and quickly soared to heights that were unexpected by all but them. Today, the color of a man's skin in the Submarine Force is seldom an issue, but we must always keep in mind that it wasn't always this way. Should the navy occasionally stray into the bad habits of the past, it might be well for them to keep in mind these solemn words from W.E.B. Dubois's *The Souls of Black Folk* (p. 163):

> Would America have been America without her Negro people?

Great submariners, great men like Carl Kimmons, Anderson Royal, Sam Wallace, Arthur Brown, and the others whose stories have been told in these pages, already know the answer to that question. Now, so might we all.

VII

Histories of Black Submariners

In this chapter are the firsthand accounts of 37 living Black submariners that served during World War II, and 44 biographies of Black submarine stewards who served during the war but who are now deceased or too ill to give their own story or cannot now be located. Much of the information in these biographies, such as submarines served on and service dates, come from crew muster rolls from individual submarines, while additional information and anecdotes have been supplied by family members, friends, and former shipmates. Because access to the personnel records for World War II veterans by law is primarily limited to direct family members and their descendants, this information could only be used to the fullest when supplied to the author by a family member. This was done so in many instances.

The number of war patrols made by most of the men who gave firsthand accounts range from a low of one or two war patrols to a high of twelve, the number of runs made by Arthur Brown on *Narwhal*. A few men made no war patrols due to varying circumstances. All of the firsthand histories in this section come directly from the men themselves, in their own words, as told directly to the author. Some were communicated in written form, while others were given during oral interviews, often conducted in more than one session. Introductory or explanatory comments were added by the author to help clarify or give additional information where it seemed needed to help place the experiences of an individual submariner within the context of the submarine war overall. The sources quoted within this portion can be found in the bibliography at the end of this work.

A few additional notes about these accounts are also in order. Every attempt has been made by the author to verify information given by a veteran submariner. To the best of my knowledge, the accounts found herein are true and accurate. However, it must be said that not all activities on a submarine were recorded in the official histories (see the account of Robert Goens, for example), nor do fellow shipmates always agree on the details of a particular event. In rare cases such as this, I have sorted out the details as best as possible and presented my findings in the explanatory paragraph following a given narrative.

Another source of confusion and debate are the sinkings attributed to a given submarine. Submariners are proud of their boat's accomplishments, and rightly so, and fondly remember the number of ships and tonnage sunk on a given patrol. These are usually wartime accounting figures that were claimed by a submarine commander and often accepted by his superiors. However, the Joint Army-Navy Assessment Committee (JANAC) was formed at war's end to examine the sinkings claimed by American submarines during the entire war. Based on imperfect and incomplete Japanese records obtained at war's end, many of these claimed sinkings were denied by JANAC for lack of evidence. Thus it was that a submarine's overall official score for a given war patrol was often reduced, sometimes drastically, resulting in discrepancies between what a submarine crewman believed was sunk versus what was, in the end, officially credited. The discrepancies in JANAC's flawed findings are many, but I have decided to follow the lead of other naval historians in this matter and accept their findings as published in Roscoe's work. These figures, when used, will also be found in the author's explanatory comments following a given history.

Finally, there is the matter of the use of hull numbers. All United States Navy vessels, including submarines, are given both a name and a hull number with a letter prefix that identifies the particular class to which that ship belongs. For submarines, that prefix is "SS." In addition, all United States Naval vessels have the designation "USS," for "United States Ship," attached to their name. Thus, the submarine *SS-167* is also known as the USS *Narwhal*. For clarity's sake and in an effort to keep the text as clear as possible and avoid needless repetition, I have chosen not to use either hull numbers or the designation "USS" when referring to a given submarine but instead just the name of the submarine. The only exception to this will be when there were two submarines with the same name that served during the war. Examples of this might include the submarines *Sealion*, *Perch*, *Shark*, and *Runner*. Each of these are boats lost during the war whose name was later given to another submarine that also saw war service. In this case, I will identify which submarine is being referred to by using her hull number. A list of all the hull numbers for submarines referred to in the text will be found in Appendix D or the index. All vessels referred to by name in the narratives are submarines unless otherwise identified.

CARROLL LOUDEN ALLEN

Carroll Louden Allen was born on October 9, 1914, in Brunson, South Carolina, the son of Norman and Adell Allen. He was educated in the local public schools and left his father's farm at the age of sixteen to go out on his own. He took up the trade of a bricklayer, learning its intricacies from his uncle, Richard Riley, and his first wife's stepfather, Abe Hicks. That same year, about 1934, he was married to his first wife, Arthree Hicks. Together they had three children, sons Carroll Junior and Harold Hurley and daughter Clara Elizabeth.

Nearly ten years later, Carroll Louden Allen enlisted for military service, joining the navy at Columbia, South Carolina, on December 20, 1943. He was not the first Allen to fight for his country, nor would he be the last. His uncle Sherdon Warner had served in France during World War I. Military service was a tradition in his family. At the age of 29, he was one of the older steward's mates to serve in submarines. His son, Harold Hurley Allen, can still recall when he went off to war:

> It was before dawn when he woke all of us up to say goodbye. I didn't see him again until I saw a bearded man get off the Greyhound bus as I walked to the store to buy groceries for my mother, Arthree. At first I didn't recognize him as he got off the bus, because of the beard. I had never seen him with a beard before. I ran to him and hugged him about his legs. We embraced and walked home together [Allen, Harold Hurley].

From the time he went into the navy, until the time he came home, Carroll Louden Allen had seen quite a bit of action.

Allen went aboard *Puffer* on April 19, 1944, just four months after joining the navy. He must have done good duty prior to going to submarine duty, as he came aboard the boat already rated as a steward's mate 1st class. He made five war patrols in all, patrols five through nine for *Puffer*, until he left the boat at war's end. During this time, he made patrols under captains Frank Selby and Carl Dwyer, and the boat sank an officially credited five ships for nearly 14,000 tons. One incident that Allen used to tell his children about from his submarine days was the time, probably on *Puffer*'s seventh war patrol in February to March 1945, when the boat encountered a few mines, and he was "directed by the ship's captain to shoot mines floating on the surface from the deck of the sub" (Allen, Harold Hurley). At war's end, Allen had attained the rate of officer's cook 2nd class.

After the war was over, Allen returned home, done with military service for good. However, the joy of his return home was soon dampened with the death of his wife, Arthree, due to tuberculosis in 1945.

Allen remarried in 1946, wedding Louise Young of Fairfax, South Carolina. With her he had two sons, Herman and Donald O'Carroll. Donald is now a corrections officer for the city of New York. Carroll Louden Allen and his family stayed in Brunson, where he built up his brick-laying business. By the time he moved his family north to Brooklyn, New York, in 1962, he had built many buildings in the area and trained many local masons. In New York, he ran his own company, Allen and Sons Construction, and worked on many projects, including the Sheffield's Farm Development on Fulton Street in Brooklyn. After the death of his wife, Louise, in New York, Carroll Allen moved back to South Carolina, where he was married to the former Mabel Johnson. He resided there until his death on March 12, 2001.

Although he is gone, the tradition of military service has continued with his sons and his granddaughter. His son, Carroll Louden Allen, Jr., served in the army from 1959 to 1962 and was a Nike guided missile fire control crewman with the Third Missile Battalion. He was also the first in his family to attend college. Another son, Herman Allen, joined the air force in 1966 and had a 26-year career. Having done photographic maintenance work in direct support of processing intelligence information collected by the SR-71 and U-2 spy planes, Herman is a veteran of the Gulf War and retired as a senior master sergeant. Inspired by both her father, Herman, and her grandfather Carroll Allen, Adrienne Allen enlisted in the navy in 1992. Not unlike her grandfather, her service as a woman in the navy came at a time when opportunities were beginning to expand. When she went to sea with VFA-147 Squadron on the carrier

Nimitz in 1995, working as an aviation electrician striker on FA-18 fighters, she was one of the first females in that squadron. While on the *Nimitz* she made two WESTPAC runs, later transferring to shore duty. As of this writing, Adrienne Allen is an aviation electrician 2nd class on the carrier *George Washington* with VFA-131 Squadron, serving in support of Operation Enduring Freedom in Iraq.

JESSE ALLEN

Jesse Allen was born in Spartanburg, South Carolina, in August 1926 and entered the navy on August 16, 1943. Right away he knew he wanted submarine duty.

> I picked the navy because I'd seen a submarine movie picture and was a bit of a daredevil. I went to boot at Bainbridge and then to New London. I was on the *R-5* and rode her to Bermuda. I was on her until December, when I was sent to Portsmouth on the *Devilfish* detail. I put her into commission. While at Portsmouth, we had six weeks of submarine schooling. We had components class, and in the morning would tour the boats that were being built to learn about them. I qualified throughout the boat. We had an outstanding crew, Mann was a good captain. For battle stations, I worked on the torpedo reload while submerged. Surface, I was an ammo passer. The man that worked with me was a steward striker named Parish from Atlantic City, New Jersey. I never saw him after the war [Allen, Jesse].

Allen served on *Devilfish* throughout the war under Captain Stephen Mann, making all four of her war patrols. Coming to the war late in the game, *Devilfish* and her crew, through no fault of their own, found few targets to attack and achieved no credited sinkings. However, when the boat was hit by a Japanese kamikaze attack on March 20, 1945, her crew had at least earned the right to wear the submarine combat insignia for engaging the enemy. Of his time aboard, Allen has this to say;

> We were never really depth-charged that badly. One of the most scary things was passing through the mine fields. You could hear the boat rubbing against the mines and never knew if one might go off. The kamikaze attack was scary, too. I was in the torpedo room forward, and it hit the conning tower just as the sun was setting.
>
> I had no problems with my color on *Devilfish*. We all had to work together and had no time for shit like that. Besides, I made sure to know how the captain liked things and always got that situation straightened out first on any boat I was on [*ibid.*].

At the end of the war, Jesse Allen put *Devilfish* out of commission at Mare Island and then served on *Sea Cat* in China until 1949. From 1949 to 1951 he worked at the Great Lakes training school, and from 1951 to 1952 did duty on the escort carrier *Corregidor*, traveling to both Europe and Korea. Allen went back to submarine duty in 1952, putting *Lionfish* out of commission at New London in 1952–1953, and then went to Norfolk, Virginia, to serve in Submarine Squadron Six on *Tench* from 1953 to 1957. Allen then worked at the navy supply school in Athens, Georgia, for two years before joining the crew of the FBM boat *George Washington*. He subsequently made 13 Polaris patrols on this pioneer missile boat before leaving her for shore duty in 1970. Allen worked at the BOQ in New London until his retirement from the navy as a chief petty officer in July 1971. Now aged 75, he lives in Ledyard, Connecticut.

WILLIAM ALLISON

William Allison was born in Providence Township, North Carolina, on July 5, 1921. He was raised on a farm there, near Charlotte by his great-grandmother Roxie Harrison-Jones. Born in 1854, she had once been a slave in Virginia before the Harrisons moved further south. Life in the south in the 1920s and 1930s was not an easy one. The farm of Allison's grandparents was constantly vandalized; his barn was burned down several times and his livestock killed. The last of these fires occurred in 1928, and soon after the family lost their farm, unable to financially survive the fires. Allison and his family later became sharecrop farmers. Though William Allison was too young to plow, he recalls that one year they harvested one bale of cotton that fetched exactly $13.26. In recollecting his younger days, he recalls:

Steward 2nd Class William Allison in 1945. Allison made one war patrol on *Grampus* in 1942 before going to tender duty due to a throat infection. He would survive the war, but *Grampus* would not. (Photograph courtesy of W. Allison.)

> I was too young to be seriously concerned about racism and segregation. I kept busy learning where the best fishing holes were, the locations of strawberry patches, the wild plum thickets, and the black walnut trees.... When I had money, I would order books from Sears Roebuck and Company. In the winter I built rabbit boxes and caught rabbits.... My only encounter with politics, that I remember, was seeing a poster with Franklin D. Roosevelt's picture on it when he was running for President in 1931 [Allison].

In commenting on his naval service, Allison recalls:

My career in the United States Navy began on December 18, 1941. I was sworn in at Charlotte, North Carolina, and sent to Norfolk, Virginia, for training. I was there for approximately one month. Near the middle of January 1942, about 135 of us were placed on a train in Portsmouth, Virginia. Days later, we arrived at Treasure Island, California. I was able to go to San Francisco a few times before leaving for Pearl Harbor.

A group of us were loaded on the USS *Anderson* to be sent to Pearl Harbor. I was assigned to the submarine base.... We arrived on about February 27, 1942. I was appalled at the devastation caused by the Japanese attack on December 7, 1941.

While at Pearl Harbor, I went to Honolulu a few times. We had to go during daylight hours and we had to carry gas masks. What I saw in Honolulu was hard to believe. Servicemen with gas masks on their shoulders were standing in long lines, waiting their turns to enter houses of prostitution. I had never seen anything like that before in my young life.

On April 27, 1942, I was assigned to the submarine, USS *Grampus*.... The next morning we left Pearl Harbor on the ship's second war patrol.... Our destination was the Caroline Islands. We were assigned one of the entrances to Truk Atoll. We practiced a diving run after we were underway. At 2000 hours, our escort left us; we were on our own. Once we reached enemy waters, we had to dive at about 0400 hours and stay submerged until dark. We then had to charge our batteries.

On May 17, 1942 we were attacked by a Japanese destroyer. They shot a large hole through a part of the superstructure as we were diving. The Japanese dropped many depth charges. I don't have the words to tell how frightened I was. I stood near the hatch to the forward torpedo room and prayed. I thought it was the end for us, but thanks be to God, we survived. A few hours later, we were trying to sink ships again.

After our patrol duty was over, we headed for Fremantle, Western Australia. We went through the Molucca Strait, then into the Banda Sea and the Timor Sea, and finally into the Indian Ocean. We arrived at Fremantle, Australia, on June 17, 1942. We had been at sea for approximately 50 days. Curtheal Black from James, Texas, was the other steward's mate on the *Grampus*. Curtheal suggested that I go on liberty first. I took the bus into Perth. As I was strolling along the street, I noticed that everyone was watching me. Many of the folks there had never seen a Black man. It was a day when I received two haircuts. I was told that they had never cut my type of hair before. So between two barber shops, I received a decent haircut. As was the procedure then, the crew was given two weeks rest and recreation at a hotel at Cottesloe, a few miles from Fremantle.

As we were about to leave ... on the *Grampus*' third war patrol, I became ill with a throat infection. I could not leave with the ship. Donald Fenner from Halifax, North Carolina, took my place.... The *Grampus* had a sad ending. On February 11, 1943 ... the *Grampus* left Brisbane, Australia, on her sixth war patrol from which she failed to return. The manner of her loss remains a mystery.... Once [after the war] when we were in Charlotte, North Carolina, I suggested to my wife that we should stop in Halifax to see if we could locate members of Donald Fenner's family. We were able to find his mother. This was 29 years later [*ibid.*].

After making his one and only war patrol, William Allison recovered from his illness and did duty aboard the submarine tender *Otus*. After spending six months back in the United States while his ship was being overhauled at Mare Island, William Allison went back to Australia on the *Otus*. He was later at Milne Bay, New Guinea, and there was transferred to a patrol craft, the *PC 479*. This vessel did escort duty around New Guinea, and Allison was aboard her during the invasion of Cape Gloucester, New Britain, on December 26, 1943. During the many air attacks while escorting ships to Rabaul, Allison and the crew of *PC 479* shot down two Japanese planes. One incident that Allison recalls while aboard *PC 479* is too humorous to ignore:

> Once I took over a British merchant ship. At Finschafen, New Guinea, a fellow shipmate and I were visiting the merchant ship. I observed *PC 479* leaving without us. I ran up to the bridge of the merchant ship and turned on the signal light and called *PC 479*. It turned back to retrieve us [*ibid.*].

William Allison would return stateside in December 1944 and subsequently served at the naval air station, San Diego. He then did duty in Salton Sea, California; Litchfield Park, Arizona; and on the converted escort carrier *Siboney* in the Aleutian Islands. He received an honorable discharge from the navy at Seattle, Washington, on October 27, 1947. After his military service, Allison attended Johnson C. Smith University in Charlotte, North Carolina, and was a school teacher for one year. He then worked for the Railway Mail Service, a branch of the U.S. Postal Service. After 37 years of service there, he retired in 1989 as a general supervisor. A father to three children, two daughters and one son, William Allison now devotes most of his spare time to historical research and writing and lives in Temple Hills, Maryland. He has completed one work, entitled *Race, Religion, and Slavery in Providence Township*, a history of his hometown area, and is currently at work on a history of slavery in the United States.

BRUCE ANDERSON

Bruce Anderson, known as "B.O." to his friends, was born and raised in Williamsport, Pennsylvania. He enlisted in the navy in 1944 at the age of 17.

> I had not yet graduated from high school but later got my GED. I had to get my parents' permission to enlist, and my father signed for me. I went to boot at Bainbridge, Maryland. That was a big change. I'd never run into out-and-out segregation like that before, and it hit me full blast. I volunteered for sub duty and went to sub school at New London. Because there was a shortage of submariners, both my boot camp and sub school time were shortened. I served on the *O-2* school boat for indoctrination and also on the *Sturgeon*, where I qualified. Frank Holloman was on there, too. After six months, I was sent to Portsmouth [New Hampshire] to commission *Sea Leopard*. I was on there with [Killraine] Newton. We were just heading out when the war ended, so we went to Key West. On the *Sea Leopard* there were six Andersons, so they just called us by our initials. I was on *Sea Leopard* for about six years until I changed my rate. Once my captain recommended me for the switch, I went back to Bainbridge for radio school and then to Norfolk, Virginia. I served on the early

warning picket boats and later decommissioned *Pompon*. I was later sent to Mare Island for the new boat, *Halibut*, and took her to Pearl Harbor [Anderson, Bruce].

For a number of years, Bruce Anderson served as a radioman on the nuclear spy boat *Halibut*, whose activities he is not at liberty to discuss. He has this to say about the qualifying process during his years of service;

> I served on eight boats, four of which were different classes. I had to qualify on each class. The time to do this (six months) was the same, the paperwork, drawings, and documents were the same. I did not attend full submarine school, however, [I] was required to go through the escape tower and tank and on board stood helm, bow, and stern plane watches as well as lookout watches when on the surface. During battle station gun action I was also part of various gun crews. I liked sub service. It was a close band [*ibid.*].

Bruce O. Anderson spent the final four years of his time in the navy doing shore duty and was offered the warrant officer program but declined as it would have meant another ten-year commitment to the navy. Married, with two children, Anderson worked in civilian life as a commercial boiler inspector for the state of Rhode Island. He is proud of his service as a submariner and had this reaction when he visited the *Nautilus* memorial and Submarine Force Library in Groton, Connecticut, in 1988:

> When we walked through the entrance, I felt a great sense of pride in having been an integral part of the Submarine Force, but after viewing all of the displays and photographs, I became depressed and very angry at what I perceived to be a glaring discrepancy. Here I had spent 17 years serving aboard submarines and had known at least a hundred more Black sailors who had done the same thing, and yet in all of the photographs, with the exception of one crew photo, Blacks were invisible; there was no evidence that they had ever existed or made any meaningful contribution within the Submarine Force [*ibid.*].

Anderson and other retired Black submariners would later speak out in protest about this lack of acknowledgement of the contribution of Black men in the Submarine Force, which later resulted in having the photo and Bronze Star citation for wartime steward George Washington Lytle become a permanent display at the Submarine Force Museum. Bruce Anderson is now retired and lives in Providence, Rhode Island.

DAVE BALL

Ball was born on November 21, 1919, at Texarkana, Texas. He joined the navy on February 3, 1936, at Little Rock, Arkansas, and retired from active duty on August 28, 1959. His records show that he received not only the Presidential Unit Citation during his career but also the Silver Star and the Bronze Star. After completing boot camp at Norfolk on June 9, 1936, Ball first served on surface ships, including the auxiliary transport *Herbert*, the destroyer *Leary*, the cruisers *Indianapolis* (1936–1940) and *Portland*, and then went to submarine duty on February 17, 1940. He first served on the *S-22* for six months in 1940 and subsequently on the patrol craft *Falcon* (1940–1941), the submarine *Marlin* (1941), the auxiliary net-layer *Locust* (1941–1942), the submarines *O-4* and *O-6* (1942–1943), and then to the submarine *Rasher* (1943–1944) as a chief officer's cook. It was on this last boat that Ball made four war patrols between June 1943 and July 1944 and earned some of the decorations mentioned previously. Ball is also famous for having worked at the White House for presidents Roosevelt and Truman, and his staff duty there is noted on his honorable discharge certificate under the heading "Qualifications." However, the date of this service is unknown.

For the rest of the war, Dave Ball did shore duty as part of *Puffer*'s flag allowance and subsequently in SubDiv 121, ComSup Seventh Fleet, Submarine Repair Unit 137, and ComSubRon 18 and ended the war at the submarine base in New London. His subsequent assignments included *Corsair* (1945–1947), the tender *Howard W. Gilmore* (1947), and the submarines *Odax, Bluegill, Cutlass,* and *Sarda,* but his service times are uncertain. In 1954, as previously related, Ball left the Submarine Force and went to the naval air arm for duty. While based at the naval air station at Patuxent River, Maryland, Ball was cited for outstanding service a number of times, including one from Vice-President Richard Nixon in 1959 while traveling with him to Russia and in two instances by Admiral Arleigh Burke (1956 and 1957). Dave Ball was also up for an award for "extraordinary heroism" (Ball document fragment, dated 30 July 1959), but for what action is unknown. This may have resulted in the Silver Star he is known to have received. Ball retired from the navy on August 28, 1959, after a 23-year career.

Upon his retirement, Ball is known to have worked at Madison Square Garden in New York, but little else is known of his post-navy career. Unfortunately, it did not last long, as records indicate he died in Argentia, Newfoundland, on June 26, 1965. The circumstances surrounding his death are unknown.

Dave Ball is best remembered by his contemporaries for his almost-legendary status. Stories abound about how it was President Roosevelt that pulled strings to get him to sub duty (very doubtful, as he was in the Submarine Force early on, and they needed volunteers), and about his special connections with Eleanor Roosevelt (undocumented, but very likely). While he was stationed in Key West, Florida, it has been recounted by many of Ball's friends that should they end up in the custody of the military police, all it took was one call by Ball to obtain their release. This may very well be true, given that Ball did work for President Roosevelt, whose Little White House was right there in Key West. In addition, it has also been discovered that Dave Ball carried on a correspondence with Reverend Martin Luther King in 1959, the nature of which is unknown.

Finally, no account of the legendary Dave Ball would be complete without some overview of the sports skills that made him a legend. His boxing career has already been noted. Ball was also a renowned softball pitcher for teams formed from the various commands, both submarine and naval air, under which he served. He was probably the most dominant softball pitcher in the navy on the East Coast from 1945 to 1956. Referred to variably as a "portly" or "chunky" right-hander, he won countless games. While aboard *Corsair* in 1947, his team won the Atlantic Fleet softball tournament with a 1–0 victory over Guantanamo Bay, Cuba, in 15 innings. Ball went the distance and was the winning pitcher. In 1949, he sported a record of 16–2, and fanned 20 men in one game. In 1953, while pitching for the Submarine Force All-Stars, he tossed a one-hitter and beat the Marines 8–1. In 1956, while pitching for the air arm, his team won the ComAirLant softball tournament with a 1–0 victory. Called a "fireballer," he won two no-hit, no-run games in a row to lead his team to the title. Alex Drury, a former shipmate on *Rasher* during the war with Ball recalls that his baseball shoes were bronzed and on display at the Norfolk naval base at one time but have since been lost.

George Bracey

George Bracey was born on December 18, 1919, the son of Lela and Milton Bracey of Jackson, Mississippi. He attended local schools and was in the Civilian Conservation Corps before the war. He enlisted in the navy on October 9, 1942, and went to boot camp at Norfolk, Virginia. He first saw sea duty on the carrier *Ranger* until volunteering for submarine service on June 18, 1943. He was one of the few stewards to go to submarine school at New London, and afterward he was assigned to the newly commissioned *Pargo*. He served on that boat from August 1, 1943, to June 1, 1945, and made seven war patrols in all under captains Ian Eddy and David Bell.

Steward 3rd Class George Bracey. A World War II veteran who made war patrols on *Pargo*, the Mississippi native was lost on the nuclear attack boat *Thresher* on April 10, 1963. (Official U.S. Navy photograph.)

After the war, Bracey served on the tender *Griffin*, the destroyer *Vogelgesang*, and the diesel submarines *Bluefish*, *Clamagore*, *Thornback*, *Razorback*, *Sea Poacher*, and *Amberjack*. In July 1960 he was assigned to the nuclear attack boat *Thresher* and was lost when she went down on April 10, 1963. Bracey received commendations for his service and outstanding performance while on board both *Razorback* and *Thresher*. He widow, Letha Bracey, now resides in Mississippi.

Arthur Brown

Arthur Lee Brown, a native of Valdosta, Georgia, was born on March 30, 1927, and joined the navy in January 1943 at the young age of 15.

> I lied about my age when I went in, told them I was born in 1927. My parents let me do it because they wanted to make me happy. I did it because I wanted

Officer's Cook 3rd Class Arthur Brown of *Narwhal* in 1945. The Valdosta, Georgia, native made twelve war patrols on the old V-boat from 1942 to 1944 and dealt with more refugees, passengers, and rescued aviators than any other submarine steward on any boat during the war. For him, his submarine career was a unique education, and one that he thoroughly enjoyed. (Photograph courtesy of A. Brown.)

to help win the war! From Georgia in January 1943 I went to Norfolk and from there to Treasure Island in March 1943. No sub school, no sir! I went to a destroyer base at San Diego. When word came in that two men were needed, I volunteered right quick, and ten minutes later went down to the pier. I wanted a battleship but didn't see any. The only ship I saw looked like a submarine. I told the driver I didn't want to go on a sub, but he told me, "It's too damn late now, the orders have been cut." I went aboard the *Narwhal* on April 17, 1943. We loaded 100 troops on board for the Attu-Kiska invasion and went north to Alaska. I nearly froze to death; it was so cold. The other steward aboard was [Andrew] Linthicum. I later served with [Johnny] Green and another Brown [James]. We had a lot of colors on the boat! [Frank] Latta was in command. I liked the man; he was a good man, the best. I made twelve runs on *Narwhal* and learned things about life, surviving, and getting along with people. Yes, I've been lucky, I got along good and never had a trouble. My shipmates still treat me good today. I think the 37 months on submarine duty helped me more than four years at Dartmouth or Yale!

I bunked in the forward battery and during battle station below manned the phones in the wardroom. On battle surface I worked in the magazine with 105-pound shells, hoisting them topside. I was a weak young man. I also did a lot of surface lookout duty. I never received any training until we came into Pearl from Alaska. I qualified there, then we went to Midway. We would operate out of Australia.

Yeah, I remember being depth-charged alright. Some were so close, they broke the light bulbs overhead, and one time we developed a leak in the engine room, and salt water mixed with the batteries to make chlorine gas. I helped bucket the water out with other guys. I was very hot and scared, but we were lucky. The scaredest I've ever been was when the Japs caught us on the surface at night in the Phillipines. We had to travel a ways out before we could dive, and they worked us over pretty good with depth-charges. I made twelve runs on *Narwhal*, and she was a good boat.

Off duty while on patrol I hung out in the radio shack with Sylvester [the radioman]. We listened to Glen Miller, and also music by Strauss and Beethoven. It was the first time I ever heard that kind of music, and I loved it. Just a few years ago, my daughter took me to Vienna, and it all started on the *Narwhal*. I enjoyed our time in Australia and the liberty there. I stayed out of trouble, but was late one time coming back to the boat due to the train. I had a written certificate explaining why I was late, and the XO talked to me, so everything was fine. I was off *Narwhal* in December 1944 as a petty officer, a steward 3rd class and went back to the states and had 30 days' leave [Brown, Arthur].

Arthur Brown's twelve runs on *Narwhal* are among the most war patrols made by any submarine steward. During his time aboard the boat throughout 1943–1944, three ships were sunk. More importantly, this large V- boat was used on numerous occasions to conduct special missions, which included landing commando parties, transporting badly needed supplies, and rescuing large numbers of refugees. In effect, she did it all. Brown's first seven patrols were conducted under Captain Frank Latta, a well-respected and talented submariner. Once Latta left the boat, Brown served under her former executive officer, Captain Jack Titus, for four patrols and made one last patrol in

October 1944 under Captain William Holman. Afterward, old *Narwhal* was withdrawn from combat duty.

> After I returned from leave, I went back to New London and just hung around the barracks. I had a lot of free time and went to New York and Boston. When I went back to sea, I rode the *R-18* down to Guantanamo for training duty till the end of the war. That was no tough duty, and we took her up to Portsmouth to decommission her. I then got on the *U-530* and we went all the way to Texas to sell War Bonds. This was all on the surface, no submerging. Then we took her back to New London. I got out of the navy in February 1946 at Jacksonville, Florida. I served three years and one month. I went back to finish high school in 1948 but was drafted in the army for Korea. I was in the Second Division and got out in 1951. No more military for me. If I could do it all again [submarine service], I would. Where do you want me to sign! I'll always be a submariner! [*ibid.*].

Now retired and living in Valdosta, Georgia, Arthur Brown has three children, including one son who has served in the Marine Corps. A true southern gentleman in every sense of the word, he has remained friends with many of his former shipmates on *Narwhal* from sixty years ago and enjoys attending submarine veteran reunions whenever he can.

Mack Butler

Mack B. Butler was the son of Easley Butler, and his hometown was Tallulah, Louisiana. He enlisted in the navy on July 7, 1943, at Shreveport, Louisiana, and volunteered almost immediately for submarine duty while at boot camp. He was soon sent to Pearl Harbor and did flag duty, attached to *Silversides*, before joining the crew of a new boat, *Dace*, on October 27, 1943. The skipper at this time was Captain Joseph Enright. Butler would subsequently make all seven of *Dace*'s war patrols from October 1943 to June 1945. The first patrol was conducted by Captain Enright, the next four by Captain Bladen Claggett, and the final two by Captain Otis Cole. During this time, six ships were sunk worth over 28,000 tons, including the Japanese heavy cruiser *Maya*.

However, *Dace* is probably best remembered for rescuing the crew of *Darter*, which ran aground off the island of Palawan on October 25, 1944. It was probably the most harrowing time of all in Mack Butler's submarine career. With *Darter* in danger of being captured, *Dace* and her crew came to the rescue. They transferred the 85-man crew of the stranded boat to their own by using rubber rafts and, once they were safely aboard, worked to destroy *Darter* so she wouldn't fall into Japanese hands. They first tried four torpedoes, but this didn't work. Next, they tried using their deck gun, but this also failed. With Japanese aircraft and destroyers focusing their attention on the stranded submarine, *Dace* wisely headed back to Brisbane, Australia, with 165 men on board. With all the extra men aboard, food supplies soon ran low, and it is certain that the stewards aboard, Butler and James Gaylor, were taxed to their limit, even though they had the help of the stewards from *Darter*.

Mack Butler (center) and shipmates from *Queenfish* on the beach on Guam in late 1945. Butler was a veteran patroller on *Dace* during the war and was fully qualified throughout the boat. (Photograph courtesy of John Nash.)

Mack Butler continued on *Dace* through the end of the war and in late 1945 was transferred to the crew of *Queenfish*. He stayed aboard this boat until 1949 to 1950 and was a popular and respected crewmember. Former shipmate John Nash remembers him as "the guy who taught me how to "spit shine" my shoes" (Nash, John) and bunked near him in the forward torpedo room. Another man who recalls Butler is former shipmate Ken Jacobs:

> He was a hell of a nice guy who got along with most of the crew. I really didn't have too much contact with Mack except on those occasions that I was in the forward battery taking readings on the batteries under the deck of the wardroom. Mack and I would talk, mostly in generalities. He always had this broad grin on his face. People just liked him. He was involved with saving my eyesight. I had gotten battery acid in my eyes while taking a reading on the forward battery. Our skipper pulled me out of the battery well and called to Mack to fill the officers' galley sink with water. Mack did that…. Indirectly, he along with the skipper saved my eyesight [Jacobs].

Following his service on this boat, nothing else of Butler's submarine career is known. Upon retiring from the navy, after making it his career, Butler lived in New London and worked at the submarine base commissary. He is thought to have died around the year 1999.

WALLACE COLEMAN

Wallace Coleman was born on June 27, 1920, in New Orleans, Louisiana, the son of Sanders and Evelyn Coleman. He enlisted in the navy on July 2, 1940, at New Orleans. After boot camp, he first worked at the United States Naval Academy at Annapolis, Maryland, before being sent overseas in the early years of the war to Australia. Here he served in Naval Repair Unit 89 at Brisbane, a unit primarily devoted to working on submarines. Coleman later did flag duty and was an officer's cook 2nd class by the time he joined the Submarine Force on September 30, 1944. On this date, he joined the crew of *Pollack*, an older boat that had just been withdrawn from combat duty following her eleventh war patrol. Though old, the boat still performed valuable duty, serving as a training boat for antisubmarine warfare units. Wallace Coleman, though he made no war patrols, served on *Pollack* until August 1, 1945, and by the time the war was over he was an officer's cook 1st class. A love of submarines was not the only thing that caught Wallace Coleman's eye while he was in Australia. He also found his future wife, Emma Beryl Martin, a seventeen-year-old "spinster" from Brisbane. The two were wed on October 3, 1944 and soon went to the United States.

Once home, Wallace Coleman continued his naval career, while Emma Coleman had to get used to life as an American. When it came to race, things were much easier,

Officer's Cook 2nd Class Wallace Coleman. A native of New Orleans, Coleman served for much of the war in Australia wth Naval Repair Unit 89 before going to submarine duty aboard *Pollack* in 1944. (Photograph courtesy of the Coleman family.)

she soon found out, in Australia than in her adopted homeland. While visiting the Coleman family in New Orleans in the late 1940s, she was asked, as a Black woman, to sit in the back of the bus. She defiantly refused to do so, foreshadowing the actions of Rosa Parks in Montgomery, Alabama, nearly ten years later. Meanwhile, Wallace Coleman would stay in submarines, serving on the diesel boats *Amberjack*, *Corsair*, *Trutta*, *Tusk*, and *Sarda* during his career. He also did squadron and shore duty at New London; Key West; Charleston, South Carolina; and the Boston Naval Shipyard. He received a number of commendations for his leadership during his career, which have already been discussed in detail. His last submarine was the FBM boat *Nathan Hale*, on which he qualified as part of her Blue crew on December 1, 1964. Chief Steward Wallace Coleman retired from the navy on January 18, 1965, having served 25 years.

As a civilian, Coleman served as a sergeant in auxiliary Connecticut State Troop E and as a security guard at both Electric Boat Company and the Foxwoods Resort Casino. He and his wife Emma had five children, sons Wallace Jr., Lawrence, and Mark, and daughters Cheryl and Yvonne. Wallace Jr., now deceased, joined the marines and later worked as a supervisor at the Electric Boat Company. Son Lawrence joined the navy like his father and served as a medic 3rd class in Vietnam. While his father was not crazy about him joining the navy and going off to war, once he decided to do so, Wallace Coleman helped his son anyway that he could. Coleman died in November 1996, and his wife Emma passed away a month later. To honor his memory, his Connecticut State Trooper unit had an honor guard at his funeral and lined their patrol cars along the road leading to the cemetery with lights flashing and sirens blaring.

ROBERT COLEY

Alabama native Robert Coley was age 18 when he enlisted in the navy in early 1941 from Montgomery. Though he had not finished high school, he would later complete his education. First, however, he had a war to fight.

> I went to navy boot camp at Norfolk, then to San Diego and on to Pearl. No sub school. On December 7, 1941, I was on the sub tender *Pelias* when we were attacked. I later joined *Tambor* at Pearl, the *SS-198*. I rode her for six war patrols as a steward's mate 2nd class. I had to qualify on everything in the boat. On battle station submerged my position was in the forward torpedo room. On surface I was a reloader on the 5-inch gun. Ninety-nine percent of the crew was good, I never had a problem [Coley].

Coley made six war patrols on *Tambor* from March 13, 1942, when he went aboard, to July 19, 1943, when he was transferred off to Submarine Division 161. On his first patrol under Captain John Murphy, the boat was deployed for the Battle of Midway in May 1942. On four subsequent patrols, from July 1942 to February 1943, Robert Coley served under Captain Stephen Armbruster. During this time, *Tambor* sank three ships and also performed mine-laying duty. Coley's final patrol on the boat was made under Captain Russell Kefauver in May 1943, resulting in one enemy cargo vessel destroyed. Coley was not yet done making war patrols.

After shore duty in division, I was sent back to New London for new construction on *Bugara*. While waiting for her, I served on *Mackerel* and *Barracuda*. I made one patrol on *Bugara* after she was commissioned, and I got off her at Fremantle. I was then in a relief crew. I then did shore duty for three years, which was much harder. I'll always be a submariner! [*ibid.*].

After the war, Robert Coley stayed in the navy and had a successful 30-year career. He was married to Julie Primus in December of 1947 and has two sons and two daughters. Both his sons and one daughter would later become navy veterans. Coley was out of submarines for a time, assigned to the battleship *Mississippi* and later the destroyer escorts *Jenkins* and *Philip*. On the last named ship, Coley was aboard during the first H bomb test. He then returned to submarine duty, serving on the conventional boats *Remora* and *Grayback* before going to the missile boats. He would subsequently make seven FBM patrols as part of *Ethan Allen*'s Blue crew and made two more on the Gold crew of *Benjamin Franklin*. Coley ended his submarine duty by serving on the nuclear attack boat *Gurnard* and retired as a senior chief steward in 1971 while stationed at Naval Air Station Saufly Field, in Pensacola, Florida. He currently resides with his wife in Montgomery, Alabama.

David Collier

David Collier is a native of Steubenville, Ohio. He was both working and going to school when he was drafted in late 1944 at the age of 18.

I was working in a steel mill and going to school when I was drafted. I already had two older brothers in the army. I went to boot camp at Bainbridge. I got along fine there, as the barracks chief's name was also Collier. I volunteered for sub duty and was sent to New London. There I stayed in the stewards' barracks and worked for the officers. I went to sub school for a short time, then served on the O-boats they used for training. Eventually I was shipped to Mare Island [California] by cattle train. I was assigned to *Hake*, replacing a steward named Moore. The other steward that served with me was Tyree Cornish. We had a good group on the boat, and the only prejudice I saw came from an electrician's mate while I was qualifying. My battle station positions were the regular ones: submerged I was in the forward battery or pantry, and surface I was an ammo passer. I did one patrol and then was aboard when we were at the Japanese surrender ceremony in Tokyo Bay. The skipper, Haylor, let me look through the periscope at what was going on. After going back to Pearl, I rode *Hake* to New London, and from there went to New York, Staten Island [Collier].

Following his war service, David Collier stayed in the navy for more than twenty years. He later changed his rate to that of commissaryman and served on the diesel boats *Argonaut*, *Requin*, *Sea Devil*, *Besugo*, and *Ronquil*. He then served on the tender *Sperry* before going to the nuclear boat *Skate*, where he had to requalify for nuclear power. He retired from the navy in 1967 as a commissaryman 1st class. Dave Collier then worked for Electric Boat in Groton before his final retirement. He has one daughter, Stephanie, and still resides in the Groton area.

CLARK COOPER

Clark Verlin Cooper, better known as CV Cooper or just plain "Coop," joined the submarine service in 1944 and made four war patrols on the submarine *Tuna*. The *Tuna* saw only marginal success during the war, sinking a total of only four ships during her thirteen war patrols. During Cooper's time aboard, the submarine was commanded by James Hardin for two patrols followed by Edward Steffanides for the boat's final two war patrols. For the final months of the war, the *Tuna* operated out of Australia, having previously been stationed at Pearl Harbor.

> I was drafted into the navy at the age of 23 in 1944. I was living in Fort Worth, Texas, at the time, working at a packing plant, and was a high school graduate. I was sent to Bainbridge, Maryland, for boot camp training and there volunteered for submarine duty. After boot camp, I was sent to New London for training. Afterward, I was sent to Mare Island, California, and from there took an LST to Midway and the war zone. I was assigned to the *Tuna* and made four war patrols on her, three of which were deemed successful. Things were always dangerous aboard submarines, especially the closer to Japan you got. One place that was really dangerous was the Makassar Strait. ... That was a tough area to get in and out of [Cooper].

It was not far from this area that the boats *Barbel* and *Tuna* were on patrol in February 1945 along with other submarines. *Barbel* was subsequently lost with all hands on February 4, sunk by Japanese aircraft. *Tuna* was the last boat to make contact with her before she was lost.

> Hardin and Steffanides were my kind of people. ... They respected you; they were religious, and they wanted to come home! Before we fired a torpedo, there was silence in the boat, and we would bow our heads and say a prayer for everyone, even the enemy. Then it would be "Fire one," and so on. During battle-stations submerged, my position was to man the phones in the forward battery, and for battle-stations surface I helped man the 50-caliber machine gun on deck. My fellow stewards on *Tuna* were men named Buchanon and Whitfield. I ended the war by getting appendicitis while at the Phillipines and was sent back to the States on the tender *Gilmore*.
>
> Back home, I was sent back to submarine duty and joined the *Lapon* at Staten Island, New York. This was in late 1945. I still remember what a severe winter it was then. I served on *Lapon* until 1947, then got transferred back to the west coast. I was then assigned to the *Diodon*. This was the first submarine to go outside the United States with the new snorkle setup. I was on her two years. I remember one time that one of our crew stole the ship's bell and sold it. ... It ended up in a bar where us sailors used to go and was returned. By the time I was on *Diodon*, I had made Steward 2nd class.
>
> I left her after two years and did some years of shore duty, working for the captain at the line school in Monterey, California. I later was sent to Kingsville, Texas. By this time I was steward 1st class and went back to sea in the submarine *Catfish*. I was on her for a year-and-a-half before going to the tender *Neurius*, where I served for nearly another two years. Then I was sent back to San Diego to work at the squadron BOQ. From there, I later went back to Pearl

Clark Cooper retired from the navy in 1965. He rose to the rank of chief steward in a career that began in 1944 aboard the *Tuna*. (Photograph courtesy of C.V. Cooper.)

Harbor in 1965. By this time I was an E-7 mess specialist and had held that rank for five years.

One thing that happened to me after I retired was this. ... I was driving through town in my car, which has a decal that reads "Submarine Veteran of World War II." When I got out, a fellow asked me if that was my car I was driving.... I said, "Of course it is, why would you ask that." He said he had noticed the decal and didn't think that Blacks served on submarines during the war. I told him I would bet him 500 dollars on that.... I still carry my submarine card in my wallet to this day that shows I made war patrols. He never did bet me. Most people today don't know about us stewards and the job we did. I'm old and sick now, but I can't complain and thank God for every day I'm alive [*ibid.*].

Clark Cooper now resides in San Jose, California, and, though his health is not what he would like it to be, he has the support of such friends as fellow submariner Anderson Royal to keep his spirits high.

TYREE CORNISH

Steward 1st Class Tyree Cornish circa 1950. Note the silver dolphins on his chest and the three hash marks on his sleeve, an indicator of his twelve-plus years in the navy. (Photograph courtesy of the Cornish family.)

Tyree Cornish was born in Stamps, Arkansas, on February 22, 1920. He enlisted in the navy at Garland City, Arkansas, in July 1937 at the age of 17. Because he was then underaged, his mother had to sign for him, which she did. Cornish went to boot camp at Norfolk, Virginia, afterwhich he first served on surface craft. His first assignment was the aircraft carrier *Lexington*, where he was part of a large contingent of mess attendants. Later, in 1939, Cornish was serving on the cruiser *Tuscaloosa* when he crossed the equator for the first time and received the proper initiation from King Neptune and his gang on April 17. From this time until mid–1942, Cornish's service is uncertain, although he may have served on the destroyer *Blakeley* prior to her torpedoing by a German U-boat in the Caribbean in early 1942. While back stateside in 1942, Cornish met his future wife, Ruby Hamilton, and they were married on December 24, 1942. Their only child, daughter Gloria, was born the following year on November 14, 1943, at Oak Knoll Hospital in Oakland, California. She has the unique distinction of being the first African American baby to be born there.

Tyree Cornish served during part of the war at the Panama Canal Zone, where he reenlisted in the navy on February 14, 1942. It is unknown why Cornish volunteered for the Submarine Force, but he joined his first submarine, *Hake*, at Pearl Harbor in time for her final war patrol off Formosa that lasted 49 days. He still recalls to this day his first depth-charging and the prayers that he made to help him get through the terrifying ordeal. Like fellow steward Dave Collier, Officer's Cook 2nd Class Tyree

Cornish was aboard *Hake* at the Japanese surrender in Tokyo Bay on September 2, 1945. After his service on *Hake*, Cornish joined the crew of *Pilotfish* and served on her into 1946.

Following the war, Tyree Cornish continued his service in the Submarine Force. He served during the Korean War and retired after a thirty-year career of active duty on August 1, 1968. He then served in the Fleet Reserve for another ten years, giving him forty years of navy service. Cornish, now retired, lives in Oakland, California, with Ruby, his wife of more than 60 years. Though his memory has grown hazy due to age and the effects of Alzheimer's disease, he is lovingly cared for by his wife and daughter Gloria and still loves to talk of his exciting years in the navy and his time on submarines.

JOSEPH CROSS

Joseph Cross is probably the best-known submarine steward of World War II among all submariners from that time period. He was born on October 4, 1920, at Maringoiun, Louisiana, and joined the navy when he enlisted at New Orleans on May 12, 1942. Cross went almost straight to submarine duty from boot camp at Norfolk, Virginia, coming from the tender *Beaver*. He joined the crew of the newly commissioned *Halibut* on June 22, 1942, under Captain Phillip Ross. Cross and his crew very soon went out to the war zone, heading first to Pearl Harbor. From there she made her first two war patrols in Alaskan waters in August and October 1942. Cross would make the first eight war patrols of *Halibut*, serving under Captain Ross for the first five and Captain Pete Galantin for the final three.

During his time aboard, the boat was very successful, sinking an officially credited eight ships for nearly 35,000 tons. Cross's contribution during this time was vital. Known as an exceptional lookout, his actions saved the boat on one patrol from almost certain destruction by enemy aircraft. For this deed, he was awarded the navy and Marine Corps Medal. A decorated submariner, he also received the Bronze Star and the Navy Unit Commendation ribbon for his war action. Cross's second skipper, Captain Galantin, would later say of Cross, "He was a small wiry man with a ready grin and the best night vision in the boat. When we attack on the surface at night, I keep him

Steward 1st Class Joseph Cross. He was a veteran of eight war patrols on *Halibut* but lost his life when the nuclear attack boat *Scorpion* went down off the Azore Islands in late May 1968. (Official U.S. Navy photograph.)

The submarine combat insignia card of Earnest Danford on *Baya* in 1945. Only those patrols that were deemed "successful," meaning contact with the enemy was made, earned a submariner the combat insignia and successive stars. (Photograph courtesy of E. Danford.)

on the bridge" (Galantin, p. 74). Several sources have stated that Cross made war patrols on *Tigrone*, but this is incorrect, as he did not serve on that boat until the 1950s time period.

Other submarines that Cross served on after *Halibut* after the war include *Tambor*, *Sirago*, *Sea Lion*, and *Tigrone* and the nuclear boats *Triton* and *Shark*. With the desire to be home ported in Norfolk, Virginia, where his wife, Anna Mae, and son Joseph Fabian lived, he transferred to the nuclear attack boat *Scorpion* in July 1967. He was lost with that boat and her entire crew in May 1968 when she sank off the Azore Islands while heading back to Norfolk from duty in the Mediterranean Sea.

Though Cross was now gone, he was not forgotten. Ten years after his death, in 1978, a new enlisted men's dining facility at the New London Submarine Base was named in his honor. That same year, his 18-year-old son, Fabian, was a freshman at Georgia Tech University.

Earnest Danford

Earnest Danford, an 18 year old from Waycross, Georgia, was drafted into the war in mid–1944. He had previously graduated from high school and had taken some classes

Steward 3rd Class Ernest Danford. He was a veteran patroller on *Baya* during World War II. (Courtesy of E. Danford.)

at Georgia Normal Agricultural College. Because he wasn't taking classes at the time he was drafted, he was unable to gain a student deferment and went off to war.

I was sent to Bainbridge and volunteered for sub duty. I was later sent to California and took a Dutch freighter to Australia. From there, I took a train all the way across Australia to Perth-Fremantle. I was on the USS *Baya* for three patrols. I liked her crew, and they treated me well. I had a bunk in the fore torpedo room, and during some attacks I was in the conning tower as the control room scopeman. The most dangerous thing I recall is when we ran up some river in the South China Sea and blew something up. When leaving the area, we were caught and scraped the bottom in only eighty feet of water. I later got off the boat after the war at Honolulu [Danford].

Danford made three patrols on *Baya* from February 1945 through July 1945, all under Captain Ben Jarvis. During this time, *Baya* sank four ships, which was a pretty good score at this point in the war. Danford's most dangerous time aboard, though he did not know it then, was on May 2, 1945, when *Baya* attacked a small convoy in the Gulf of Siam with another boat, Captain Frank Latta's *Lagarto*. Twice Danford's boat was driven off by radar equipped escorts, and achieved no success. *Lagarto* was not so lucky. She and her entire crew were lost during their attacks on the convoy, sunk by an escort vessel.

After the war, Ernest Danford, known to his friends as "Danny" or "Scooby-Doo," served on a number of boats for 20 years, including the diesel boats *Brill*, *Tench*, and *Balao*. He later put the nuclear boat *Seawolf* into commission in 1957, riding her to South Africa and places beyond. He retired in 1963 as a steward 1st class and then worked for the post office and the United Nuclear Company.

Alonza Davis

Alonza Davis is a native of Altheimer, Arkansas, a small town just north of Pine Bluff. Born in 1924, he joined the navy in early 1943 at the age of eighteen and went to submarines soon after. Though his memories from this time period have faded a bit, he still recalls his service on *Pargo* with both pride and humor.

Yeah, *Pargo* was a good boat ... good crew, and I liked Captain Eddy. I made a couple of patrols on her before I was off the boat doing relief duty. My best friend on there was Little [Albert] Rozar. We used to run together all the time, but I haven't seen him since the war. "Mose" [R.D. Mosley] was on there, too. I used to tease him about his sea sickness. I'd kinda forgotten, but I guess I did miss the boat several times. Once it was back in the states, and once it was while we were at Johnson Island. I was just jiving with my friends and plain missed the boat. After that, they used to kid me, said they had one man on the maneuvering watch just to look for Alonza [Davis, Alonza].

Davis made *Pargo*'s first four war patrols under Captain Ian Eddy, during which time she sank four ships. He went aboard on August 17, 1943, and left the boat prior to her fifth patrol on August 15, 1944. Alonza Davis's wife, Christine, passed away in 2000, and he currently resides in Philadelphia, Pennsylvania. As a result of this interview, he was put in touch with his old friend and shipmate, Albert Rozar.

EVERETT DAVIS

Everett Davis was born on December 9, 1925, in Grant, Oklahoma. His mother's name was Olivett Smith. Prior to joining the navy, from 1942 to 1944, he lived in Lawton, Oklahoma, and worked at the Fletcher Funeral Home in Chickasha, Grady County, Oklahoma, as an assistant embalmer. He attended school through at least a part of high school but did not finish high school.

Everett Davis was drafted into the navy on June 23, 1944, and went to boot camp at Bainbridge, Maryland. While there, he volunteered for submarine duty and went to New London for three weeks of training. One of his training vessels was the *S-15*.

Davis was subsequently assigned to a relief squadron for overseas duty and was sent to Norfolk, Virginia, for subsequent transport to the Panama Canal

Above: Chief Hospitalman Everett Davis. A submarine steward during the war, Davis later changed his rate and became a hospital corpsman. With his mortuary experience both before the war and after, he would later have the important task of helping to identify the remains of soldiers killed in the Vietnam War. (Photograph courtesy of M. Davis.) *Opposite:* The military service record of Everett Davis, as recorded by his mother. Davis, a native of Oklahoma, made several war patrols on *Lizardfish*, but, as this record notes, almost didn't made it to the Pacific. (Photograph courtesy of M. Davis.)

Military Service Recor[d]

NAME Everett E. Davis

BRANCH OF SERVICE U.S. Navy

PLACE OF ENTRANCE Bainbridge, Maryland

DATE June 23   **RANK** S.T.M. 1/c

FIRST ASSIGNMENT New London, Connecticut

RECORD OF PROMOTION U.S. Submarine

RECORD OF TRAINING AND DOMESTIC SERVICE

After 3 weeks training in New London Conn. was sent to Norfolk Va. On the 10th of Nov his first submarine mission on his way to Panama his boat was torpedoed and the whole crew was picked up by a liberator and sent back to Pan. He spent some time in hospital as he had a cold.

RECORD OF FOREIGN SERVICE AND COMBAT

On Nov 23 at 1/2 o'clock Eastern war time left for Pan... made the trip alright the Sable Church stood in prayer and gave thanks to God for his goodness.

RECORD OF CITATIONS AND AWARDS

Rejoined Navy AWOL 3 Jan

RELEASED FROM SERVICE Norman   **DATE** 1946 February 21   **RANK** O'Dean S.T.M. 1/c

Zone. He departed November 10, 1944, for Panama, but the boat he was on was torpedoed. He and others on the ship were rescued by Liberator aircraft and taken back to Norfolk, where he was hospitalized briefly for a cold.

Davis subsequently departed for Panama again late in November, and this time made it safely. He continued on to Pearl Harbor, where he did relief duty before joining the crew of *Lizardfish,* a newly commissioned boat from Manitowoc, on March 31, 1945. He was a steward's mate 2nd class at this time. Davis made two war patrols on his boat, both under Captain Ovid Butler. The first, departing from Pearl Harbor, commenced in April 1945 and ended at Fremantle, Australia, 52 days later. His second war patrol departed from Fremantle in June 1945 and lasted 39 days. On both patrols, no official sinkings were achieved. Davis would later tell his wife, Mildred, that Captain Butler was "a very good man" (Davis, Mildred), and that he would never forget his first depth-charging. One of Davis's battle station positions was to man the deck gun crew. By the time the war ended, Everett Davis was a steward's mate 1st class. He was discharged from the navy on February 21, 1946, having served one year and eight months.

Upon leaving the navy, Davis married his wife Mildred in 1947 and they had three children, Gwendolyn, Everett Jr., and Donald. Both sons were army veterans, with Donald doing two tours of duty in Vietnam. Once a civilian, Davis completed his high school education and went to mortuary school in Chicago. However, he would soon reenter the military when he was drafted for service in the Korean War.

Serving once again in the navy, Davis changed his rate from steward to hospital corpsman. His duty stations included the naval hospital at Kodiak, Alaska, from 1951 to 1956, the naval hospital at Sasebo, Japan, from 1959 to 1963, and the San Francisco naval hospital. One of his most prominent duties during this time was his work identifying the remains of soldiers killed in the Vietnam War. Davis also earned a PhD in sexually transmitted diseases from the Columbia University Extension Program. When he retired from the navy, Davis was a chief hospital corpsman. He would subsequently serve as medical director for the Military Sealift Command and the naval supply center in Oakland, California, before finally retiring in 1997.

As of this writing, Everett and Mildred Davis reside in Richmond, California. Everett Davis now has Alzheimer's disease and could not be interviewed for this book. However, he remains in good physical health and is lovingly cared for by his wife of 56 years.

Lewis Davis

Lewis Davis was a native of Huge Springs, Texas. He enlisted in the navy at Tyler, Texas, on September 23, 1942, and went aboard *Plaice* as part of her commissioning crew at Portsmouth, New Hampshire, on February 12, 1944, as a steward's mate 2nd class. His prior service is unknown. Davis made all six of *Plaice*'s war patrols, the first being in June to July 1944. At this same time, Davis was promoted to steward's mate 1st class. The first four patrols Davis made were conducted by Captain Clyde Stevens and the last two under Captain Richard Andrews. On the very first patrol, *Plaice* and her crew attacked a Japanese battleship. The boat was credited with four official sinkings

Steward's Mate Lewis Davis (back row, far right) and the crew of *Plaice* ashore for rest and relaxation. Davis, nicknamed "Tex" by his shipmates, made all six of his boat's war patrols and was well known for his sense of humor. (Photograph courtesy of B. Butcher.)

during the war. Known as "Tex" to the crew, the likeable Davis was called by one shipmate, ship's cook Bill Butcher, "the most relaxed person on the boat ... never uptight, always loose. ... After a depth-charging, he would always comment, 'They didn't get us yet!'" (Butcher). Butcher further comments that "Tex enjoyed the *Plaice* parties. Here everybody was a submariner. Beer, fishing, sports, games, cookouts, tug-of-war with other submarine crews. Our commissary officer always led us in singing sub songs" (*ibid.*). Lewis Davis stayed on the boat through the end of the war. His life details after submarines are unknown, but he is still, 60 years later, fondly remembered by his old crew.

SHIRLEY DAY

Shirley Day was born on October 26, 1918, in Oakwood, Texas, to Charlie and Lula Day. He had one brother, Wilson, and six sisters, Zethel, Sammie, Lucille, Ruth, Carnie, and Charlene. He attended Palestine, Texas, public schools and would later join the CCC. As he would later write:

> I left Palestine on April 14, 1937, to join the Civilian Conservation Corps Camp, and it was while enrolled in the CCC program that I had an opportunity to join the United States Navy. I did so on April 14, 1939. When I was recruited, I was informed that I would receive board and $21 per month. I replied that I did not care about the $21. If the navy fed me I would be satisfied. The officer said they had to pay me in order to keep the bookkeeping straight. My initial training was received at the Naval Academy in Annapolis, Md. My duties were those of a mess attendant, but I was later promoted to the position of steward. At that time Black sailors were assigned only to menial tasks. In 1940 I was sent to New London, Conn., where I was assigned to my first submarine, the USS *Tambor*. Throughout my Naval career, I served on the USS *Grayling*, from which I made four war patrols ... the USS *Thresher* ... the *Medregal*, the *Charr*, the *Carbonero*, and the *Salmon*, from which I retired on June 9, 1959. My travels took me to many parts of the world, including Europe, the Philipines, the Caribbean, the Panama area, and Australia. I hold the Combat Insignia with three stars, two of which are silver. Often now when I look back at some of the close calls I had, sweat breaks out on my forehead. At the time I was experiencing some of those happenings, I was not aware of the danger. I guess sometimes, it does pay to be ignorant [Day, p. C-6].

In addition to the submarines listed, Shirley Day also served briefly on the *Triton* at Portsmouth, New Hampshire, from June 2 to June 26, 1941, holding the rate of mess attendant 1st class. Just months later, he would go to a newly commissioned boat, *Grayling*, under Captain Eliot Olsen. He boarded her on August 4, 1941, from Submarine Squadron 6 and, just nine days before the Pearl Harbor attack, was court-martialed on November 28, 1941, for missing his ship's sailing. He pled guilty. He departed with *Grayling* on her first war patrol in January 1942 and made two subsequent patrols that year, all under Captain Olsen, in March and July. In addition, the boat was deployed for fifteen days in support of the Battle of Midway operations, thus supporting Day's claim of four patrols while on *Grayling*. While aboard, the boat sank one cargo ship of nearly 7,000 tons.

Day left the boat on September 29, 1942, going to flag allowance duty. He surely counted himself a lucky man, for both boats he served on in 1941 and 1942, *Triton* and *Grayling*, were sunk later in the war with all hands. Fellow shipmate on *Grayling*, Richard Baker, calls Day "a very popular guy, pretty savvy" (Baker), and he states that Day was one man who helped him greatly when he had to qualify for submarine duty. He also states that Day's battle station position on the boat was in the forward battery as a phone talker.

Following his time on *Grayling*, Day did flag allowance or relief duty until returning to combat in December 1943, when he joined the crew of *Thresher* for her eleventh patrol of the war. Now an officer's cook 3rd class, Day came aboard the boat at Midway Island and served under Captain Duncan McMillan. During the months of December 1943 and January 1944, *Thresher* saw substantial action when she sank four cargo ships worth over 14,000 tons and sank a trawler with her deck guns. She also attempted to attack an aircraft carrier group but was driven off. Once this patrol ended, Day left the boat for shore duty once again.

While he claimed to have made seven patrols on *Thresher*, Day was mistaken, and an examination of the crew records does not bear this out. He was aboard for one patrol only. It has also been stated that Day made patrols on another boat that was lost, *Harder*, but this, too, is incorrect and not borne out by official crew records.

Following his retirement from the navy, Shirley Day lived in Vallejo, California, with his wife, Laura, before returning to Palestine, Texas. He worked for the Disabled American Veterans Group No. 26 for twelve years, and performed more than 10,000 hours of volunteer work. Shirley and Laura Day had two sons, stepson Charles Holmes and adopted son Gregory Day. Day died on April 20, 1997, in Palestine, Texas and is buried in the Reed Cemetery.

Jesse Debro

Jesse Debro, Jr., was born on August 31, 1918, and was living in the area of Knoxville, Tennessee, when he went to war in 1944 and served on *Queenfish*.

> I was drafted into the war and kinda talked into sub duty. My wife, Bessie-May, and I had six children when I went into the navy and seven when I got out in late 1945. The captain on *Queenfish* [Charles Loughlin] was a swell guy. I was a steward and served cups of coffee to the officers. Some of those guys seemed to drink thirty or forty cups a day. I also helped to reload torpedoes sometimes. I was treated great on the boat, never had a problem. One of the funniest things I remember is while we were ashore in between patrols, and I acted as a baseball umpire at one of our games. There was a big fight after I called a ball a strike, but I stayed out of it. After the war, I lived in West Virginia for a time, worked at repairing shoes and at a barber shop [Debro].

Jesse Debro, Jr., put *Queenfish* into commission at Portsmouth, New Hampshire, in early 1944 and made all five of that boat's war patrols. For her first two war patrols, the men of *Queenfish* were awarded the Presidential Unit Citation. One former, unidentified crewman has this to say about Debro:

> Debro was a deacon in a small Black Baptist Church in Knoxville. When we picked up some survivors ... he gave up his bunk in the forward room and he and I "hot bunked" for the rest of the patrol.... We were friends and "bunk brothers." There was one crew member who professed to be an atheist, and he was always giving "Deacon," as he was known, a hard time about why God didn't stop the war. Deacon just sluffed [*sic*] it off and went on about his business. We were tied up at Pearl ... and I had the deck watch from 1200 to 0400, so I was biding my time to go on watch. I noticed that this man had Deacon cornered in the outboard seat next to the wall and was really giving him a going over about how useless his religion was.... Deacon, being the gentleman he was, kept laughing and grinning. Finally, the man hit a nerve about how did he know that there was a God, and Deacon laughed like he always did and asked the question, "Who made the grass green?" That really shook the man, and he went into a long dissertation on photosynthesis, but Deacon just grinned at him and asked again, "Who made the grass green?" This went on until I went on watch at 1200. I came off watch at 0400, and they were still at it. Finally, the man had enough, and he made some uncomplimentary remark about ignorance,

and as he went through the watertight door into the control room, Deacon Debro yelled after him, "Who made the grass green?," and he and I held each other up laughing [Hall, Harry].

As of this writing, 85-year-old Jesse Debro lives in Knoxville, near his son Jesse Debro III.

NATHAN DOGAN

Nathan J. Dogan, thought to be from Chicago, was a prewar submarine steward. He first went into the navy in 1938, possibly earlier. He was at New London when he reenlisted in the navy on July 8, 1942, and on September 18, 1942, he joined the commissioning crew of *Gurnard* at Groton. He would subsequently make five war patrols on this successful boat, all under Captain Charles Andrews. The first patrol began in November 1942 and was conducted in European waters. No sinkings were achieved. It was not until Dogan and the crew of *Gurnard* made it to the Pacific that she really saw action. The first war patrol for this boat from Pearl Harbor began in June 1943, while Dogan made his last patrol in April to May 1944. During this time, *Gurnard* and her crew sank nine ships for 51,000 tons.

Dogan, who was promoted to officer's cook 1st class on June 30, 1943, was a very popular crew member. Fellow shipmate Frank Foulke says of Dogan, "He was a great

Officer's Cook 1st Class Nathan Dogan with crew members of *Gurnard*. Dogan would make five war patrols on this very successful boat, and always kept his shipmates relaxed even during the toughest of moments with his colorful commentary. (Photograph courtesy of F. Foulke.)

guy ... very intelligent, and a person you would like to have for a friend" (Foulke). Dogan was also cool under pressure during the many depth-charge attacks that the crew of *Gurnard* was forced to endure and is well remembered for his colorful statements about submarine warfare. Two of the best, remembered by shipmate Glenn Milhorn, were: "It's a hard fight with a short stick," and "When you shoot at a destroyer and miss, it's like hitting a wildcat in the ass with a banjo" (Milhorn). It was comments like these that kept the crew and wardroom of *Gurnard* in high spirits. Nathan Dogan was transferred off *Gurnard* on June 24, 1944, after she ended her fifth war patrol at Fremantle, Australia, and sent to Submarine Division 121 for relief duty. Nothing further is known of Dogan.

RUSSELL DONAN

Russell Donan was born in Edmonton, Kentucky, on March 14, 1922. He went to school through the tenth grade before he left to join the navy on August 6, 1940, at the age of eighteen. He was inducted at Bowling Green, Kentucky, and went to boot camp at Norfolk, Virginia. He volunteered for submarines right away and was assigned to the *R-3* for his first submarine duty. He later served out of New London on the *R-5* and

Officer's Cook 1st Class Russell Donan in 1946. A native of Kentucky, Donan made a number of war patrols on *Cobia* and was well-regarded by his shipmates. This dashing photograph shows him in dress uniform, with his submarine combat insignia and campaign bars. As was regulation at the time, note that his chief's hat has the simple "USN" logo only, and not the anchor insignia that was worn by white chief petty officers. (Photograph courtesy of M. Donan.)

R-7 before being assigned to the commissioning crew of *Cobia* at Manitowoc, Wisconsin, on March 29, 1944. Serving under Captain Albert Becker, Donan made three patrols aboard the boat, the first commencing from Pearl Harbor in June 1944. Success was immediate, as three ships, worth over 11,000 tons, were confirmed sunk. After the second patrol in September to October 1944, the boat was sent to Fremantle. On Donan's last patrol, December 1944 to January 1945, *Cobia* and her crew sank one enemy ship. Former shipmate Jim Marion says of Russell Donan that he was "an awfully fine young man," and recalls that he did lookout duty in addition to his steward duties (Marion, Jim). Officer's Cook 2nd Class Russell Donan left the boat on February 10, 1945, transferred to Submarine Division 182 for duty. He later did flag duty on *Bashaw* and *Kraken*, and immediately at war's end was a member of the prize crews assigned to bring captured Japanese submarines from Japan to Guam. His final duty, until his discharge on August 1, 1946, was on the tender *Sperry* and *Carp*.

While on leave, Russell Donan married his school sweetheart Mary Rebecca Mayfield (Mae) on March 19, 1946. They would have one daughter, Rosalind Marie. Once a civilian, Donan returned to school to get his diploma and then moved to Nashville, Tennessee, where he attended Tennessee A&I University from 1947 to 1950, earning a BA in health and physical education. The Donans subsequently moved to Richmond, Virginia, where Russell taught physical education and was the assistant football coach at Virginia Union University from 1950 to 1956. He would later return to school and earn a master's degree and teach at Essex City High School in Tappahannock, Virginia. From 1962 to 1984 he also worked for the City of Richmond Department of Recreation and Parks, where he was instrumental in getting a gym built for Black students. Donan retired in 1984 at the age of 62 and was an avid hunter and loved to fish and golf. He died on July 5, 1992, and is survived by his wife Mary Donan.

Donald Fenner

Donald Fenner was born on July 15, 1922, in Smithfield, Virginia, the son of Frank and Cosy Fenner. He was the fourth of eight children, the others being Ernestine, Frankie, James, Lethia, Rudolph, Erie, and Florence. The family lived in Halifax, North Carolina, and Frank Fenner was a farmer who, from time to time, helped with his brother's logging business in Virginia. Frank Fenner also worked in a barber shop on weekends to support his large family. Donald attended public schools into his high school years, but his education was interrupted when he volunteered for the navy and was inducted on August 15, 1940, at Richmond, Virginia. He had just turned eighteen. He subsequently went to boot camp at Norfolk and from there went to the California.

Fenner was assigned there to the battleship *Tennessee* and sailed on her from California to Bremerton, Washington, on December 2, 1940, arriving four days later. At this time, Fenner was doing fine in the navy, but things would soon change. The battleship soon made its way to Pearl Harbor, Hawaii, and it was probably on this long passage that Donald Fenner found out what it was really like to be Black and in the navy. In an undated letter home to his mother, Cosy, probably written in early 1941, he states that

> I am having some trouble with some officers.... I am coming out of the Navy. Its no place for Coloreds ... when I first came in I thought I would like it but things have changed. All the Colored boys are getting out [Fenner letter].

Fenner, however, would not leave the navy but instead join the Submarine Force. The exact date he did so is unknown. His first boat was probably *Sailfish*, from which he was transferred to *Snapper* on October 31, 1941. Fenner would subsequently serve on *Snapper* under Captain Hamilton Stone until May 28, 1942, making two war patrols during this time. Though the boat achieved no sinkings during this early phase of the war, Fenner and his boat were quite busy. In December 1941 during her first patrol, *Snapper* evacuated members of the command staff at Java, soon to be in Japanese hands, to Australia. Most of these men were code breakers who had already been evacuated when Corregidor fell, and their safe delivery was of prime importance.

The second patrol of *Snapper* with Donald Fenner aboard commenced in March 1942, and though no successful attacks were mounted, it also ended in dramatic fashion.

A nearby boat, *Searaven*, had evacuated a large number of Royal Australia Air Force personnel on Timor and, while heading toward Australia, experienced a fire in her after battery. Trying to battle the fire, and dead in the water, she needed help. *Snapper* came to the rescue by throwing the wounded boat a line and towing her part of the way to Australia. This would be Fenner's last patrol on *Snapper*.

The boat returned to Fremantle, Australia, on April 25, 1942, and the men were given a period of rest. Here, Fenner, now a mess attendant 2nd class, was transferred to the tender *Otus*, where he did duty in a relief crew until July 8, 1942, when he was sent aboard *Grampus*, getting ready to head out on her third war patrol. Fenner was needed because another mess attendant on the boat, William Allison, had come down ill. At this early stage in the war, the captain of *Grampus* was probably glad to have an experienced steward with war patrols under his belt as a replacement, while it is also equally likely that Fenner was more than happy to get off the large tender and back to the more friendly submarine crews. It would be a fateful move.

Donald Fenner would subsequently make four war patrols on *Grampus*, the first under Captain Edward Hutchinson in July to August 1942 and the final three under Captain John Craig. While no official sinkings were achieved on these patrols, they were conducted aggressively, resulting in much action for her "battle-wise" (Blair, p. 375) crew. When *Grampus* departed on her sixth patrol of the war in February 1942, Donald Fenner and her crew under Captain Craig were never seen

Mess Attendant Donald Fenner, in a photograph taken circa 1941. This photo was probably taken at San Francisco or Pearl Harbor while Fenner was still a battleship sailor. He later volunteered for submarine duty and was lost on *Grampus*. (Photograph courtesy of F. Young.)

again. It is believed that they were sunk in the Solomons on the night of March 5–6, 1943 by a Japanese destroyer, though this is far from certain.

At the time of his death in 1943, Donald Fenner was 20 years old. His family still resides in Halifax, North Carolina. While no monument has been erected to his memory, the author is now working with the family to see that he finally gets one. When he does, Donald Fenner will finally have come home.

LC FISHER

LC Fisher was born on September 4, 1922 in Sampson City, Florida, the son of Charles and Lillie Turner Fisher. He was orphaned while young and at age eight moved to New York state, where he was raised by a Jewish family. During his entire adult life he went by the name "LC". His date of enlistment in the navy is uncertain, but by late 1944 he was on Midway Island in the Pacific as part of the submarine relief crews stationed there. He made his first and only war patrol on *Parche*, making that boat's fourth war patrol under Captain Woodrow McCrory from December 1944 to February 1945. As has already been related, he served as a replacement for Carl Kimmons. From that time until his death forty-nine years later, Fisher and Kimmons remained close friends. The remainder of Fisher's naval career is unknown, though he likely returned to relief duty on Midway after his one war patrol before the war ended. It was here that Fisher often spoke of his upbringing and the Jewish family that raised him.

After the war, LC Fisher married the former Ethel D. Green in Reno, Nevada and would continue serving in the navy for twenty years. In 1954 he moved to New London. After his retirement, he was an avid photographer. However, his main focus after the navy was his devotion to religion. Fisher attended theological seminary in New York, graduating in 1969. In addition to working as a chauffeur for movie stars Katharine Hepburn and Robert Goulet in Connecticut, Fisher was the senior pastor of the Pentecostal Rescue Mission of the Church of God in Christ in New London. Reverend Fisher founded the Pentecostal Rescue Mission in 1969 and would serve for twenty-four years as its driving force until his death on December 5, 1993. At his death he was survived by his son Leonard, and daughter Diana.

ROBERT GOENS

Robert Goens was age 17 when he enlisted in the navy from his hometown of Richmond, Indiana. Prior to his military service, he was a typical all–American kid, a four sport captain in track, basketball, baseball, and football at his local high school. In 1944, after going to boot camp at Bainbridge, Maryland, he went to submarine duty and put the *Icefish* into commission at Manitowoc, Wisconsin. He would subsequently make all five of that boat's war patrols and decommissioned the boat before his naval service ended in 1948.

> When I was to report for submarine duty, I got down to the pier late. I had overslept and was late and had missed that boat, which was later sunk. And that's when I got assigned to the *Icefish* [Goens].

The commissary division of *Icefish* in January 1946. The man at far left is Steward 2nd Class John Oscar Ellis, an Alabama native who joined the navy in 1941 and served in submarine relief crews during the war. At the far right is Steward's Mate Robert Goens. A native of Richmond, Indiana, Goens made all five of *Icefish*'s war patrols and later helped to decommission the boat at Mare Island. (Photograph courtesy of K. Jamcson.)

It is unknown for sure which boat Goens is referring to, but it may have been *Golet*, which had been recently commissioned at Manitowoc and was heading our for the war zone about the time that *Icefish* was launched. *Golet* was lost with all hands on her second war patrol in June 1944.

> We had a great crew on *Icefish*, and I had no problems because of my color. It was a close-knit crew, and Captain Peterson was a beautiful skipper — I'd have died for that bastard! On battle stations submerged I served as a striking torpedoman; on the surface I was the kickman on the 40mm gun. I also served as a lookout and became chief of the lookout crew. I made all five war patrols on *Icefish*, including two to Tokyo Bay. On one run, I was generally to be in the forward room but had gone to the control room when water began flooding in the forward room. We were ordered to close all watertight doors. By the time I got to the forward torpedo room, the door had closed, and I was trapped in the officer's quarters between the control room and the torpedo room. I was ordered to hold the door because I was quite strong at the time and there were six men in the area that was flooded. Naturally, they were trying to get out the door, but it had to be held so as not to jeopardize the entire ship. I could see their faces

> looking through the glass, begging us to open the door. They were able to get to air pockets and breathe until they could be rescued [*ibid.*].

This incident Goens refers to occurred on the first war patrol of *Icefish* on October 26, 1944, when the boat was severely depth-charged after an attack and suffered much damage in the forward compartments. Despite this, the boat recovered and was well christened on this first patrol, sinking two enemy vessels during 61 days of operations. Goens goes on to state:

> There was another incident in which we had a run in with a Japanese troop transport, resulting in 10,000 Imperial Marines being in the ocean. ... A man on deck began shooting at men destined to drown and kept this up until his gun was red hot. Knowing they were going to drown, I prevented him from doing any more shooting.... I was put on report, and the skipper asked to see me. As a result of this ... the chief gunner was transferred [*ibid.*].

This incident described by Goens is not to be found in official records, causing some uncertainty as to its validity. *Icefish* herself did not sink any Japanese troop transports during the war, and her patrol reports indicate no such action. Two possibilities present themselves. The first, and most unlikely scenario, is that *Icefish* during one of her patrols came across Japanese troops in the water from a transport sunk by another submarine and, subsequently, machine-gunned them. While such action, which was neither condemned nor condoned by the submarine high command, could have taken place and not have been recorded in the official log, it seems unlikely, as no former crewmen can recall such an incident and, more importantly, *Icefish* was not operating in an area where a large troop transport was sunk by any other submarine. It is more likely that Goens, instead, is mistakenly recalling an incident that did occur on *Icefish*, one that is not officially recorded but is attested to by former crewmembers. During one of her patrols, *Icefish* had a small surface action and captured a small boat, perhaps a trawler or a sampan. On board were two Japanese military officials and five or six Malaysians. All were taken prisoner except one of the Japanese, whom the war patrol report describes as having escaped by jumping into the water and swimming away rather than be taken prisoner. Despite this official version, crew members recall a different ending, stating that the man did indeed escape but was shot and killed in the water with a sidearm by one of the crew, probably for the reason that it would be unwise to risk the possibility of the man being rescued and pinpointing the location of an American submarine. Why Captain Richard Peterson did not report this is unknown, but it probably was to protect his crew, and himself, from any scrutiny regarding the incident that might have resulted (Jameson). In continuing his wartime accounts, Goens goes on to say:

> Another time was in San Francisco. I went to a bar and was dancing with the ladies. This went on until 2 A.M., and I had been enjoying dancing with one particular lady, quite attractive, and was thinking of going a little further ... when I discovered that this lady was a man. This was a gay bar, and we were not aware of such things, I being from Indiana.... As a result, a huge fight erupted, and the entire place was smashed to smithereens. We were able to get out before the shore patrol arrived.... I got out of the navy in 1948 and for brief

periods of time I was a machine operator in a factory, a bartender, and a blind installer. My main occupation was as a health inspector with the Wayne County [Indiana] Health Department, dealing with air and water pollution, hazardous spills, and food inspections [Goens].

Robert Goens is now retired and lives in Marion, Indiana, with his wife, Gloria. He has three children, Dr. Bruce Goens, Michael Goens, and Jo-Ellen Goens, by a previous marriage.

John Gray

John Andrew Gray was a long-serving submarine steward about whom little is known other than his World War II service. This record alone is well worth mentioning. Gray enlisted in the navy on November 18, 1941, at Norfolk, Virginia, and was soon in the Submarine Force. He was assigned to the crew of *Tautog* on April 9, 1942, under Captain Joseph Willingham, just prior to her departure for her second war patrol. Gray joined the boat as a mess attendant 3rd class. He would subsequently make eight war patrols on this top-scoring submarine under two different captains. His first three war patrols, from April 1942 to November 1942 were made under Captain Willingham, while the last five patrols, from December 1942 to January 1944, were conducted by Captain William Sieglaff.

While *Tautog*'s record is too extensive to cover in detail, she sank 14 officially credited enemy ships worth over 40,000 tons while John Gray was aboard. Included in these totals are two Japanese submarines, the *RO-30* and *I-28*, that were sunk on Gray's first-ever war patrol. John Gray left *Tautog* on January 31, 1944, as an officer's cook 2nd class and was transferred to Submarine Division 141 for flag duty. However, he would soon return stateside and perform recruiting duty at Bainbridge, Maryland. Draftee Isaac Johnson well recalls Gray and all the medals on his uniform that inspired him to volunteer for submarine duty while at Bainbridge in April 1944.

After the war, John Gray is known to have had an extensive navy career, though his duty assignments and stations are not fully known. One of these was overseas in Japan.

William Green

William Lee Green was born on December 17, 1926, at Asheville, North Carolina. He would later move to Knoxville, Tennessee, where he graduated from Austin High School in 1944. Weighing in at 177 pounds and playing the guard position, Green, who wore number 32, was a starter for the Austin High School Panthers in the fall of 1944. His team was undefeated through their first seven games. William Green would later put his football skills to work while in the Submarine Force. Green enlisted into the navy on February 2, 1945. He did graduate from high school, but was in the navy when the time for the graduation ceremony came around. His grandfather, who "was so proud of him enlisting to serve our country, sat and received his high school diploma for him on the scheduled June graduation" (Green).

William Green went to boot camp at Bainbridge and volunteered quickly for submarine duty. He was first sent to New London and from there went to Pearl Harbor. Later in the year, he would go aboard his first submarine, *Chivo*, on which he would serve from 1945 to 1951. During his time on this boat after the war, he served with another wartime steward named Joe Green. *Chivo* returned to the states late 1945 or early 1946 and was based at San Diego. While there, William Green played football for various submarine division intramural teams from at least 1946 to 1948. While playing for the "I" team in 1946, he played his old high school position of right guard and wore his lucky number 32. He was the only Black athlete on the squad. In contrast, when he played for the submarine team in 1948, he was one of four Black men on the squad. The times were slowly changing. It was also in 1948 that William Green married Claree Jefferson of Vicksburg, Mississippi, while in Arizona. The two had first met in San Diego.

Following his duty on *Chivo*, Green transferred to *Cavalla*, on which he served from March 1951 to February 1952. He was then sent to the New London naval submarine base, where he served on the submarine rescue vessel *Tringa* from April 1952 to April 1953. Green then went aboard *Bergall*, on which he served from April 1953 to September 1955. During this time, Green's boat was involved in a number of antisubmarine warfare exercises in the Atlantic, one of which was quite eventful and has previously been described. He may have even been aboard when the boat was deployed to the Mediterranean on several occasions.

Following this service, William Green was transferred for squadron duty, serving on the staff at Submarine Division 181 in New London from September 1955 to about 1959. In the course of this duty, Green was nominally attached to the flagship *Irex*. Green's next submarine duty was probably the most exciting of his career. In November of 1959 he went to the crew of the radical new nuclear boat, *Triton*. During his time on this boat, which lasted at least through mid-1961, Green made the famous first submerged circumnavigation of the world under Captain Edward Beach, which has previously been detailed.

Following his time on *Triton*, Green did shore duty at Davisville, Rhode Island, for a time before returning to sea duty on the FBM boat *Ethan Allen*. He would serve in her Gold crew before retiring from the navy as a chief steward on August 5, 1964. William Green, who died on January 7, 2000, in New London, and his wife Claree had eight children. They are daughters Artelia, Barbara, Charlene, Delva, Penny, and April, and sons William Jr. and John. Both sons served in the army, while Green's eldest daughter, Artelia, followed in her father's footsteps. She joined the navy after finishing college and went from boot camp to Officer's Candidate School. She would serve in the navy for 14 years, rising to the rank of lieutenant commander. Her dad was "most proud of his number-one child" (Green). Another daughter, Charlene, has also continued the navy tradition, working as a civilian for the navy for the last 25 years.

Harold Hale

Harold Herbert Hale, a native of Algoma, West Virginia, was born on February 8, 1919. His father was a coal miner, his mother a traveling cook. He enlisted in the navy on October 17, 1939, at the age of 20.

> I went to the navy because I didn't want to be a coal miner. I went to boot camp at Norfolk, Virginia, then was sent to San Diego. I caught the battleship USS *Mississippi* at Long Beach. We went from there to Bremerton [Washington] and then to Pearl. Later, we went to the east coast and did convoy duty for Lend Lease. I can remember when the *Hood* and *Bismarck* chase was going on and was in Iceland on Pearl Harbor day (December 7, 1941). It was at Reykjavik that I saw the midnight sun while I was in Iceland [Hale].

Once the war had begun, the *Mississippi* went back stateside, first to Norfolk and then to San Francisco. It was here that Harold Hale, after spending two years on a battleship, went to submarine duty.

> While in California, I put in for sub duty and took a physical. I was accepted and given a two-week furlough. I went from Treasure Island to Pearl Harbor, and was only there for two or three weeks before I was sent back to Mare Island to put *Tunny* into commission. By then I was a mess attendant 1st class. I made the first three war patrols on *Tunny* then was off for the fourth after we were overhauled in the states. I worked in the BOQ and then went back for the fifth war patrol. On that last patrol we were awarded the Presidential Unit Citation for sinking a sub, and we had also hit an aircraft carrier [*ibid.*].

Hale is indeed correct: *Tunny* was awarded the PUC after this patrol. Led by Captain John Scott, she found the Japanese submarine *I-42* off Palau and sank her with four torpedoes. The resulting explosions from this attack rattled both the commander and crew, causing Scott to dole out a ration of whiskey for the crew. The aircraft carrier Hale is referring to was actually attacked on *Tunny*'s second war patrol in April 1943. In one of the most daring attacks of the war, Captain Scott encountered a force of three Japanese carriers and was able to maneuver into position and attack two of them. It was initially thought that one, and possibly both, of the carriers had been sunk, but it was not to be. The carrier *Taiyo* was damaged, and the other carrier escaped after the torpedoes *Tunny* fired exploded prematurely. In speaking of his time on *Tunny*, Hale recalls that:

> I liked submarine duty. Captain Scott and the other officers, [Gordon] Underwood, [Jack] Titus, and Greenfield were men that made you feel good. Being depth-charged was no fun, and anybody that says they're not afraid, they're a liar. But, we had to grin and bear it. On *Tunny* I qualified in the forward battery, on the telephones, and the forward escape hatch. On the surface, I was on the 20mm gun crew and remember one time when it jammed up on us. I left the boat after her fifth war patrol in about April 1944 at Brisbane, Australia, and worked at the BOQ there. I was sent back to the states as part of the commissioning crew of *Manta* with skipper Madley out of Portsmouth [New Hampshire]. Furlough there was good. I went with another steward named Neal from Kentucky, and we let the good times roll. I took *Manta* back to Midway, where I spent the last eight months of the war. When the war was over, I was done with the navy. I left as a steward 1st in 1945 [*ibid.*].

After the war ended, Harold Hale settled in Boston and attended Peterson Technical School, gaining a degree in the HVAC field. He worked for the state of Massachusetts and the city of Boston for twenty years before going into the private sector.

He married his wife, Doris, in 1947 and has a daughter named Cheryl. Hale retired in 1989 and recently moved from the Boston area to Raleigh, North Carolina, where he resides as of this writing.

ALFRED HALL

Alfred Leander Hall was a resident of New London, Connecticut, when he was drafted into the navy on December 3, 1943. Born on August 12, 1925, Hall, whose father was from Petersburg, Virginia, was working on submarines at the Electric Boatyard in Groton as part of a riveting gang. There seemed to be no doubt what type of service he might choose.

> I was drafted in 1943 and sent to Bainbridge, Maryland. We were there six weeks and were just a Black company. There was no mingling with whites. I was then sent to New London and went aboard *Pomfret* after she came down from Portsmouth. At the sub base I did go through Spritz's navy. He was a great chief, but stewards got less training than the other guys. I qualified on *Pomfret* and made all six runs on her. I started out as a mess attendant and ended the war as a steward 2nd class. My battle stations were to man the XJA phones forward, and I was a sighter on the 5-inch gun. Our crew was close, like a family, and Captain Hess was a great skipper. During our patrols, we got depth-charged often, and at the end of the war we were on lifeguard duty and picked up five flyers. Then we learned the bomb was dropped. I got off *Pomfret* at Pearl and rode *Razorback* to the states. I was then at Mare Island and later San Diego. I later went back to Pearl on a freighter. I knew a lot of the stewards in the war, Joe Cross, Dave Ball, I knew 'em all [Hall, Alfred].

The first patrols Hall made on *Pomfret* were fraught with danger and adventure of a rather unusual nature. While Hall recalls Captain Hess quite well, the boat's first captain was Frank Acker. On the boat's first patrol in June 1944, Acker was aggressive and almost chased a few ships through an enemy minefield before being prevailed on to change his mind. He also attacked a Japanese battleship, went close to the Japanese coast and fired on a village with his deck gun, and when leaving the area ran aground on a mud bank for several hours before an escape was made. On his second patrol, Acker became severely ill, and his executive officer had to take over temporary command. Though paralyzed from the waist down, Acker resumed command for a brief time, directing an attack on two ships and sinking one of them. With an ill skipper badly in need of medical attention, *Pomfret*'s patrol was cut short, and the boat made it back to Saipan through a typhoon after being out a month. With Captain Acker gone for medical reasons, his replacement on the boat's last four patrols was John Hess. Hall's adventures on *Pomfret* would continue when, on her fourth patrol, in February 1945, the boat did lifeguard duty off Tokyo Bay and performed a feat of daring by rescuing two downed U.S. aviators and one Japanese pilot. All in all, *Pomfret* was indeed a valuable addition to the fleet.

Following his war service, Alfred Hall, known as "Sunny" to his friends, stayed in the navy 22 years before retiring in 1965 as a steward 3rd class. Of his later submarine service, he has this to say:

Some of the boats I served on include *Chopper* and *Nautilus*. I was on the *Nautilus* after her historic run. It was a prestigious boat, and I was very proud to have her name on my uniform. I also commissioned the Polaris sub [FBM] *George Washington* at New London and rode the *Daniel Webster* [an FBM boat] out of Scotland. When I retired, I was only a steward 3rd because I got busted at captain's mast. Us stewards were usually treated better in foreign countries than [in] our own, especially Charleston and Key West. We usually made our own parties in these places, separate from whites. Still, the navy was good, gave me travel to different places, and opportunity [*ibid.*].

Once his military service was over, Alfred Hall worked for the Electric Boat Company, and later as a cook for the Hilton Hotel in Hartford, Connecticut, and later was a cook supervisor at the Hartford City Jail. Prior to his death in 2004, he resided in Dunedin, Florida.

Leslie Hamilton

Leslie Hamilton is notable for his total of ten war patrols on three different boats during the war. He first enlisted in the navy on September 27, 1939, and was inducted at Birmingham, Alabama. Nothing about his personal life is known. It is also unknown when Hamilton first went to submarine duty.

Hamilton's first known boat was the battle-hardened *Thresher*, which had seen heavy action since the first days of the war in 1941. Leslie Hamilton went aboard this boat as a mess attendant 1st class in time for her fourth war patrol in June 1942 and made a total of five patrols before leaving *Thresher*. If this was his first war patrol, it was quite an indoctrination to submarine warfare and one that was experienced under the roughest of conditions. Departing for the Marshall Islands under Captain William Millican, the boat sank one officially credited ship and would have had more if her torpedoes worked properly. The boat was nearly lost when, after attacking one convoy, she was driven deep and depth-charged. When the noise had stopped, something unusual then happened. The boat was hooked by a grapnel thrown overboard by a Japanese patrol vessel. Her intent was to pull *Thresher* by force to the surface and then finish her off or capture her. Hooked by the stern like a fish, the boat slowly rose. Initial attempts to lose the grapnel were unsuccessful, and the worst-case scenario was prepared for. All confidential materials and the radio decoding equipment were destroyed, and demolition charges were placed in the boat to prevent her from falling into enemy hands intact. Luckily, the continued efforts of Captain Millican and the crew paid off, and they eventually got free before being surfaced. However, they were subsequently depth-charged, and in twelve hours took 41 depth-charges and two bombs. Leslie Hamilton and the crew were lucky to survive.

Hamilton's successive patrols on *Thresher* were not nearly as exciting but action-filled nonetheless. On the boat's sixth war patrol in December 1942 to January 1943, the crew attempted to sink a cargo ship by deck gun action, and the boat was nearly rammed. On the next patrol, in March 1943, the boat attacked a destroyer but was driven off and received a good pounding. Hamilton's final patrol on *Thresher* came in April to May 1943 under Captain Harry Hull, and no sinkings were achieved. By the time Hamilton left the boat in May or June 1943, he was an officer's cook 1st class.

Hamilton likely did squadron or relief duty but was back in action on November 1, 1943, when he joined the crew of *Billfish* under Captain Frederic Lucas in time for her second war patrol. Just like his first patrol on *Thresher*, this one was also nearly his last. While operating in the Makassar Strait, the boat was severely depth-charged on November 11, 1943, and was nearly lost. With the captain incapacitated and the pressure hull of the boat ruptured, Chief Engineer and Diving Officer Charles Rush assumed command and worked twelve long hours to save the boat and lead her out of danger. Hamilton, unlike many of the men who were sure they were going to die, remained calm throughout the ordeal. He would make a second patrol on the boat, this time under Captain Vernon Turner, before leaving the boat for squadron duty on April 7, 1944.

Soon after, Hamilton was sent stateside to New London and assigned to the commissioning crew of *Brill* on October 26, 1944. Described by shipmate William Whelen as "a bit aloof, but a great guy," "Ham," as he was nicknamed, was a respected and well-liked crew member. He made all three of this boat's war patrols when she made the war zone in early 1945, all under Captain Harry Dodge. The first commenced from Pearl Harbor in January 1945 and ended in Fremantle, Australia. The last two patrols emanated from Fremantle in May and July of 1945. Because she entered the war at a time when targets were very scarce, *Brill* achieved no official sinkings during the war.

Hamilton was certainly respected for the many war patrols he had made, and he used to tell the story of the time when *Thresher* was nearly reeled to the surface by the Japanese. Leslie Hamilton left *Brill* close to the war's end, on August 10, 1945, while at Perth, Australia. He would later have a career in the postwar navy and served on the east coast at New London. The submarines he served on after World War II are unknown, as are the details of the rest of his life.

L.T. Hammond

Lewis T. Hammond, who goes by the initials L.T., was born in Sheffield, Alabama, on February 15, 1924. He was 19 and working for the Tennessee Coal and Iron Mine Company when he was drafted into the navy in June 1943.

Officer's Cook 2nd Class L.T. Hammonds of *Batfish*. He made all seven of his boat's war patrols during World War II. (Photograph courtesy of L.T. Hammonds.

I served in the navy two years, ten months, and a day and got out in 1946. I went to boot camp at Norfolk. I was young and didn't care about the segregation there. I was used to it, being from Alabama. It was there I volunteered for subs ... not for the extra money, but because I was young, thought I'd try it out. I was sent to New London. I took swimming tests but didn't go to [sub] school. I put the *Batfish* into commission at Portsmouth and made five successful patrols. We had a good crew. I was the only Black man. The other steward was a Filipino. My battle stations were in the officer's quarters [submerged] and the 50-caliber machine gun on surface. Lots of time we caught the devil. The most dangerous thing I remember was when we were going from the Atlantic to the Pacific and a German sub fired on us. We had a good crew on *Batfish*, and I was treated very well. It all depended on the crew you were with. When we were running out of Australia, I liked that. That was a good time. I didn't see the navy as a career and hadn't thought about it when I got out in '46 [Hammond].

L.T. Hammond served aboard *Batfish* for at least her first six war patrols and possibly her final one as well. While heading to the war zone in the fall of 1943, *Batfish*'s future career, perhaps, was foreshadowed when she was fired upon by a German submarine while heading toward the Panama Canal Zone. While this attack was unsuccessful, *Batfish* would be ready when the tables were turned. Under captains Wayne Merrill and John Fyfe, the boat sank three confirmed ships on her first five war patrols. On her sixth war patrol, while off Formosa in February 1945, *Batfish* and her crew earned the title of "Champion Submarine Killer," when they sank three Japanese submarines, the *I-41, RO-112,* and *RO-113* in the space of three days.

At the war's end, Lewis T. Hammond went back to Alabama and worked at a steel mill until his retirement in 1987. He has a wife, Janie, and two daughters, Beverly (Jones) and Cynthia (McCray), and currently resides in Bessemer, Alabama.

JOHN HARRIS

John Calvin Harris's fame, if you will, lies in the fact that he was an early Black submariner, if only for a brief time, and also for the length of his service. He was born in Nansemond County, Virginia, just south of Norfolk, on November 3, 1892. When he joined the navy at Norfolk on January 2, 1914, he was a resident of Portsmouth, Virginia. A small man, he was only 5 feet, 3 inches in height, and weighed 124 pounds. His first duty station was on the submarine tender *Fulton* at New London, Connecticut. His enlistment expired in October 1917, but he immediately rejoined the service and was now a mess attendant 1st class. His discharge for this date notes that he now had tattoos of an eagle, shield, and two flags on his body. He was a true sailor by this time, no doubt! Harris made the equivalent of officer's cook 3rd class in 1919 while still on the *Fulton* and apparently stayed on board until 1923.

Though the records are unclear, it appears as if Harris went aboard the *S-1* under Captain Ralph Christie in September 1923. His activities aboard this boat have already been noted. When he left the boat in December 1924, he was an officer's cook 2nd class. Whether he transferred off the boat on his own is unknown. He subsequently served on the light cruiser *Savannah* and the destroyer *Maury* in 1925 before going to the auxiliary submarine rescue ship *Chewink*. He served on this craft from December

1925 to September 1927 and then went to the *Camden* (type of ship unknown, possibly a light cruiser or an auxiliary vessel), on which he served until May 9, 1930. He became an officer's cook 1st class on February 12, 1928. In 1930, Harris left active service for the Naval Reserve, from which he was retired in April 1939 due to a physical disability. However, his service was not over. Harris returned to active duty during World War II, serving at the New London Submarine Base in its defense force from June 30, 1942, to August 21, 1945.

Arthur Haynes

Arthur Haynes is a native of Kansas City, Kansas, and joined the navy in late 1943. Prior to this, as a civilian, he held a job in a meat packing plant as a shipper.

> I went to boot camp at Bainbridge, Maryland, and while I was there I volunteered for submarine duty. One of the reasons I did was because one of the stewards came to talk to us about submarine duty, a man from Kansas City named Leroy Toombs who had been on subs for five years or something. I don't know ... I guess I liked his uniform and all the medals he had on it [Haynes].

Experienced submarine stewards were sometimes sent back to the states to do some recruiting duty at the Bainbridge Naval Training Center. With all the new boats coming into the fleet, more stewards would be needed to man them. One man who did such duty was the above-mentioned Leroy Toombs. He had joined the navy in 1940 from Kansas City and made four war patrols on *Guardfish* from May 1942 to May 1943, rising to officer's cook 3rd class. Sometime late in 1943 he was sent back to the states for recruiting purposes just as Haynes was going through Bainbridge.

> I made three war patrols on *Chub*, all successful. My battle station topside was to man the 5-inch gun, and I also did lookout duty. I was treated very well on *Chub*, just like any other crewmember. On one patrol in 1945 we rescued two airmen. One of them was Morris Perkins, a frightened 18-year-old kid. I just got him a cup of coffee and talked to him. We still see each other to this day. I ended the war as a steward, not a steward's mate, and left the navy in December of 1945 [*ibid.*].

Chub made three war patrols between February and August of 1945 under the command of Cassius Rhymes, Jr. She was credited with sinking one vessel, a Japanese minesweeper, and rescued three downed aviators before the war ended.

Arthur Haynes currently lives in Kansas City, Kansas, with his wife Elsie. They have two sons, Brian, who became a lieutenant-colonel in the army, and Mark, who played professional football with the New York Giants and Denver Broncos before his retirement from the NFL in 1990.

Curtis Hill

Curtis Hill is another prewar submariner about whose career little is known. He was born in 1918 to Virgil and Judy Hill and lived in Warren, Arkansas, a rural town about 100 miles from Little Rock. His mother worked in a saw mill to support the family, but education was important and she saw to it that her three boys, Curt, Jerry, and Sanfuel, all attended school. Curt is described by his brother as a "good student" and a young man with "an extremely outgoing personality. He never ever walked anywhere, he was bubbly, always on the run. Everyone in town knew Curt" (Jones, Jerry). Curt Hill graduated from the Bradley County Training School in Warren in 1935 and joined the navy soon after. The family was excited for Curt, but also sad to see him go. Judy Hill "wanted nothing but the best for Curt and reluctantly agreed to the navy" (*ibid.*).

Hill attended boot camp at Norfolk, Virginia, and upon being granted boot leave, returned home for a brief visit. His brother Jerry Jones would later state that "Curt was the talk of the town. ... They took pride in him, and he visited every one he knew" (*ibid.*). His early service is unknown, but it is thought that he was stationed at Norfolk. Early on, Hill was "discouraged because he could only become a steward," but afterward, making the best of the situation, "decided he might go into cooking and become a pastry chef" and accepted what the navy would give him (Jones, Sanfuel).

Officer's Steward 3rd Class Curtis Hill circa 1938. Hill was a pre-war submariner who did squadron duty with the Atlantic Fleet Submarine Force during World War II. This photograph shows him in dress uniform before he joined the Submarine Force and served on *Bonita*. (Photograph courtesy of J. Jones.)

In 1938 Hill was aboard the battleship *Texas* and made a European cruise on her. The ship left Virginia in June 1938 and subsequently visited France, docking at Le Havre; Copenhagen, Denmark; and Portsmouth, England, in late July before returning home on August 9, 1938. While overseas, Curt Hill took the opportunity on his 48-hour leave to visit Paris with four other mess attendants. Upon his return to the states, Hill subsequently served in surface craft, including the cruiser *Vincennes* and the *Geer* (type of ship unknown).

Hill went to submarine duty about the year 1939, although this date is not certain. He was stationed about this time at Pearl Harbor and served aboard the boats *Bonita* and *Barracuda*. He rode the latter boat to the Panama Canal Zone and from there to New London, just prior to the attack on Pearl Harbor, and served at the submarine base in New London doing flag duty during the war. He did not make any war patrols. By 1944, Curtis Hill became a chief steward and was serving flag duty for the commander of submarines, Atlantic Fleet. For much of his postwar career, Curt Hill was stationed in New London. What boats he may have served on is unknown, although he is thought later on to have done a stint as a navy recruiter in Brooklyn, New York. He retired from the navy in 1961 as a chief steward.

Hill was popular with his fellow stewards and was well liked for his great personality. Fellow submariner Sam Wallace recalls that "Curt had a smile that would light up a room — I can still see that smile today.... He was a good church man, too" (Wallace). Curt Hill, deceased since February 1988, and his wife, Sonia, had eight children, including son Curtis Jr. who now resides in Cheshire, Connecticut.

LONNIE JACKSON

Born on April 1, 1918, in Savannah, Georgia, Lonnie David Jackson enlisted in the navy on June 2, 1936, at Raleigh, North Carolina. Nothing about his early years is known, nor is it known when he first went into submarines. However, he was a submariner well before the war. He was part of the commissioning crew of *Trout* at Portsmouth, New Hampshire on November 15, 1940, and would stay aboard that boat for more than two years. From December 1941 to January 1943, Lonnie Jackson made seven war patrols on *Trout*, the first four from December 1941 to June 1942 under Captain Frank Fenno. His final three war patrols were conducted by Captain Lawson Ramage from August 1942 to January 1943, the last two of which originated from Australia.

During Jackson's entire time on board *Trout*, she sank a confirmed four enemy ships for nearly 11,000 tons. However, she is probably best remembered for her evacuation of bank gold from Corregidor in the Phillipines in early 1942. For this achievement, a daring and dangerous one previously described, all members of the crew, Jackson included, were awarded the Army Silver Star on order of General Douglas MacArthur. At about the same time, Lonnie Jackson was also promoted to officer's cook 3rd class for meritorious service, and, on this same date, March 22, 1942, Jackson was both discharged from duty and immediately reenlisted in the navy. Jackson was hospitalized for a brief time at the Naval Hospital, Pearl Harbor, starting on July 10, 1942. While the cause for this is unknown, he was back in time to join the boat for its next patrol. While aboard *Trout*, Jackson was esteemed by all, and remembered by fellow shipmate Radioman Dean Brown as "gentle, a polite guy, a top-notch submariner" (Brown, Dean).

Jackson left the boat on March 13, 1943, going to squadron duty. He would soon be sent stateside, where he was stationed at the submarine base, New London. For a brief time, from September 4 to 11, 1943, he was assigned to *Corvina* and reenlisted yet again while aboard her. Whether he had a chance to be part of her crew and opted not to, or was just doing relief duty, it was fortunate he did not stay aboard, as *Corvina* was lost with all hands on her first war patrol in November 1943. Jackson's old boat, *Trout*, suffered a like fate in February 1944 when she was also lost with her entire crew. In this respect, Lonnie Jackson lived a charmed life.

At war's end, Lonnie Jackson stayed in the navy and made it his career. While his specific submarine assignments are unknown, he was stationed at both New London and Norfolk during his career and at many other places. He retired from the navy in early 1968, having served over 31 years, and attained the rank of master chief (E-9). To most stewards, he was known as "Big Jack," respected by his contemporaries, and looked upon as a father figure by the younger stewards.

After retiring from the navy, Jackson worked for the government as an electrical data processor until his final retirement about 1981. Following this, Jackson loved to spend his time fishing, working his garden, and being with his family. He and his wife, Anne E. Jackson, had three sons, William, Lonnie Jr., and Robert, and two daughters, Avis Annette and Avis Yvette. Lonnie Jackson died in Norfolk, Virginia, after an extended illness on January 1, 2004, and is survived by his children, eight grandchildren, and three great-grandchildren. Among those that helped look after Lonnie Jackson during his final illness was friend and fellow submariner Killraine Newton.

ZEDELL JACKSON

Zedell Jackson was a native of Topeka, Kansas, and was born in 1925. He joined the navy on October 11, 1943, at the age of 17 and attended boot camp at Bainbridge, Maryland. While there, he volunteered for submarine duty and was first assigned to the old *S-15*. Soon after, on June 10, 1944, he joined the commissioning crew of *Icefish* under Captain Richard Peterson at Manotowoc, Wisconsin. Jackson made at least one war patrol on the boat and possibly several others. On the first war patrol for *Icefish*, with Jackson aboard, two cargo ships were sunk between October 24 and 26, 1944, the only sinkings achieved by the boat during the war.

When Zedell Jackson left the boat is unknown, but he subsequently did duty on the tender *Howard W. Gilmore* in Australia and returned stateside where he received his discharge at Bremerton, Washington, on March 28, 1946. His final rate was that of officer's cook 2nd class. Zedell Jackson joined the navy reserve on June 16, 1947, and was discharged from there on August 22, 1950, having seen no active service during that time.

Upon leaving the navy, Zedell Jackson married and lived in Washington state. He has several children, including a daughter and son Zedell Jr., who resides in Walla Walla, Washington.

WILLIE JAMES

Willie James is another wartime steward who served on a number of famous boats and made a high number of war patrols. He is said to have been a native of New Orleans, Louisiana, and enlisted from there into the navy on December 17, 1941. No doubt he was inspired by the Japanese attack on Pearl Harbor less than two weeks before. James went to boot camp at Norfolk, Virginia, and likely volunteered for submarine duty while there. His first submarine assignment was on *Drum*, where he went aboard as mess attendant 3rd class prior to her first war patrol in April to May 1942. This patrol was conducted by Captain Robert Rice and was highly successful, resulting in the destruction of four ships worth over 20,000 tons in 56 days. One of these was a large sea-plane tender.

James left the boat after this first run and likely did squadron duty before joining the crew of what would be one of the most famous submarines of the war, *Wahoo*. James went aboard this newly commissioned boat, commanded by Captain Marvin Kennedy, on August 21, 1942. Coming from Submarine Division 101, he was a mess attendant 1st class by now. His prior promotion to mess attendant 2nd class probably came as a result of *Drum*'s successful patrol months earlier. James made the first two patrols of *Wahoo*, both conducted by Captain Kennedy. The first was in August to September 1942 and the second in November to December 1942. The second patrol was most interesting, as a prospective commanding officer (PCO), Dudley Morton, was aboard. He would soon take over *Wahoo* from Kennedy and conduct some of the most aggressive and productive patrols ever made. The boat sank just one ship under Kennedy's command but would sink another nineteen under Morton in just a year before her loss. Fellow shipmate Dave Veder recalls Willie James as "a great guy," and remembers that he was very friendly with Morton and that they joked around with each other during their one patrol together (Veder). However, James left the boat on January 11, 1943, before Morton took command of *Wahoo*. His reasons for doing so are unknown and have previously been speculated upon.

For several months after, James did squadron or relief crew duty before joining the crew of *Whale* on May 5, 1943. Coming from the tender *Sperry*, he was a steward's mate 1st class, and by May 31 was promoted to officer's cook 3rd class. While the crew records for *Whale* regarding Willie James's service are incomplete, it is almost certain that he made seven war patrols on the boat between May 1943 and January 1945. The first three of these patrols were conducted by Captain Albert Burrows and the final four under Captain James Grady. During these patrols, the boat sank five ships worth nearly 32,000 tons, including a large aircraft ferry. Floyd "Doc" Erickson, the pharmacist's mate on *Whale*, well remembers James as a "gourmet cook" who also made cookies for the crew. He also recalls that James' battle station position was manning the phones in the forward battery. Another former crewman, Ensign Peter Nalle, also recalls James fondly. He states that

> Willie never drank when he went ashore.... Instead, he gambled. Shooting craps was his game, and being sober he always brought home a lot of cash. I once asked him what he did if the game was crooked. "Oh, Mister Pete, I just quietly fold and move on. I don't want to get in no fights." I am sure Willie could take care of himself very well if he had to [Nalle, Peter].

Nalle also recalls with relish James' cooking skills:

> Willie was an excellent cook. As with most subs, the officers ate the crew's mess but we always laid in a store of condiments, spices, curries, and assorted goodies to liven things up. Willie, for instance, if the main dish were stew would convert it to a curry with six or seven boys [side dishes]. He would make enough for some of the old Phillipine or China hands on board. We still had a few, but in general the crew did not go for spicy dishes.... The only disaster Willie made, as I remember, was a flaming plum pudding. Not having brandy or rum, he used cigarette lighter fluid [*ibid.*].

After James' seventh war patrol on *Whale*, the boat was sent stateside, arriving at San Francisco Bay on January 25, 1945, and docking at Mare Island the next day. Willie James, having made ten war patrols, was finally home. He subsequently left that boat and was sent to new construction at Groton, Connecticut. He was part of the commissioning crew of *Cobbler*, along with another veteran patroller, Carl Kimmons, when the war came to an end in August 1945. James served on this boat into 1946 but apparently accepted a discharge, at least for a brief time, from the navy.

During his brief return to civilian life, James returned to New Orleans and opened a restaurant with his wife Etta. Unfortunately, this venture did not succeed, and James returned to the navy in time to gain his old rate back. In June 1948 he was stationed at Key West, Florida, doing high-level flag duty. Now a chief officer's cook, James was in charge of the stewards taking care of President Truman's party that was then visiting. When his old shipmate, Peter Nalle ran into him there, he was surprised to see James, and asked about President Truman and what his party did while visiting. James replied,

> Well, Mister Pete, I can't tell you no confidences, but I can say they are the poker-playingest group I ever did see. We serve them dinner at 1930 [7:30 P.M.], and they start playing as soon as the boys get the table cleared. Then all we have to do is bring ice and whiskey and empty the ash trays 'til 4:30 in the morning, They grab a bite to eat, go to sleep and get up at noon. The president reads a little mail in the afternoon, and then they start all over again (Nalle, Peter).

Nothing further is known about the career of Willie James, and he is now deceased. However, he will always be remembered as one of the best of the submarine stewards, and a most likeable individual. James should not be confused with another man by the same name that enlisted from Alabama and served on *Picuda* during the war.

ISAAC JOHNSON

Isaac Johnson, "Dr. J" to his friends, was born on June 12, 1926, at Texarkana, Arkansas. He enlisted in the navy on April 13, 1944.

> My brother, Joe Peterson, Jr. (Pete), entered the navy in 1934. He was in one of the first groups to enlist as mess attendants during the Roosevelt administration. Pete would come to Texarkana, Arkansas, with his navy uniform on and was greatly respected by the Blacks as well as whites in the community. I vowed when I became of age I would enlist and serve under him. Joe and his wife were living in Pearl Harbor when the Japanese attacked. We didn't hear from the Red Cross until two weeks later, notifying us that they were safe. These two acts increased my determination to join the navy. My parents moved from Texarkana to Chicago in 1943 in search for jobs and a better life. I then volunteered for the navy in 1944 and was sent to recruit training at Bainbridge, Maryland, where Blacks were tolerated, but we weren't received with welcome arms. I was surprised to find the same segregation as in Texarkana, and it was obvious that training was different for white trainees versus Blacks. Near the end of recruit training, Chief [John] Gray came to Bainbridge Center and told about the

> increased pay, the good food on submarines, and [that] it was too small to segregate the crew. That *sold* me, and I volunteered. I was sent to New London, and I still remember going on that first sub and smelling the diesel oil. I wondered if I made the right choice [Johnson].

The full story of how and why Isaac Johnson volunteered for submarine duty and how he came "that close" to going on the doomed *Escolar* has already been told. So, too, has his time aboard his first boat, *Sennet*, with Captain George Porter already been detailed.

> Now in Panama, the *Sennet* was tied up along the dock there loading supplies. I remember going on the pier along side of the submarine when a torpedo truck hit me. I was hospitalized at Balboa Navy Hospital for two months. After recovery, I was assigned to *Roncador*, enroute to Pearl Harbor. When we arrived, the war had ended. We then headed for the USA to be decommissioned in time for VJ Day [*ibid.*].

After the war, Johnson stayed on *Roncador* for a short time and was soon posted to *Carbonero*, where he served for eight years.

> While on *Carbonero* we were assigned to the WESTPAC area every eighteen months. We'd go to the far north waters near Russia and keep an eye on their ships coming down and take pictures of them. Real top secret stuff. And the weather — Boy, was it cold! I was glad when we went back to California to take part in the early testing of submarine-borne missile weapons systems and do the Loon testing [*ibid.*].

Nicknamed "Loons" by the crew, the details of this testing on *Carbonero* has been previously discussed. Following his duty on this boat, Isaac Johnson subsequently served on *Tilefish*. While on this boat the navy needed electronics technicians and established the ET conversion school at Treasure Island, California. Isaac Johnson holds the distinction of being the first steward ever at Treasure Island to make this change, going from steward 1st class to electronics technician 1st class. Isaac Johnson's subsequent career as an ET on *Tilefish*, his conversion to nuclear power, and his service on board the nuclear boats *Skipjack* and *Robert E. Lee* have already been discussed at length, as has been his work as a navy recruiter in San Diego. He retired from the navy on April 12, 1965, as a chief electronics technician.

Upon leaving the navy, Isaac Johnson attended college at Cal-Western University and earned a BA degree in mathematics in 1967. He would later earn a master's degree in 1968 and earn a doctorate of philosophy in leadership and human behavior in 1975 from U.S. International University in San Diego. Dr. Johnson's teaching assignments, all in San Diego, include Dana Junior High School and O'Farrell Junior High School; he was later an administrator at Hoover High School and Gompers Junior High School. In addition to his teaching career, in 1976 Johnson went into business for himself as owner and operator of Dr. J's Liquor Store in San Diego, which was formerly owned by ex–San Diego Chargers running back Paul Lowe.

Dr. J, now retired, has lived in Houston, Texas, for the past three years. He is the proud father of twin daughters, Kara and Kirsten, and his youngest daughter, Kindra. All of his daughters have followed in their father's footsteps and have earned their master's degrees, while Kindra was at one time a cheerleader for the Houston Texans in the National Football League.

WOODROW WILSON JONES

Woodrow Jones was born on December 25, 1918, in Bolivar, Tennessee, the son of Eddie and Evie Jones. His was a large family, Woodrow being just one of 27 siblings and one whose descendants went back to slave times in Tennessee. Jones was working at a hotel in Louisville, Kentucky, when the war broke out, and very soon after, on December 29, 1941, enlisted into the navy at the age of 23. He went to boot camp at Norfolk, Virginia, completing his training there on January 31, 1942. He first served for eleven days (March 20–31, 1942) on the *Rigel*, an auxiliary repair ship, before being assigned to the battleship *West Virginia* on March 31, 1942. He would serve aboard her for almost exactly a year before switching to submarine duty.

Jones joined the crew of *Pike* under Captain Louis McGregor on March 5, 1943, and served on her until February 12, 1944. During this time, he made two war patrols on *Pike*, one in March to April 1943, and another in July to August 1943. During both patrols, Jones and the crew saw substantial action, though only one enemy ship was sunk. Jones' second patrol on *Pike* would be the last for both him and his boat. After Captain McGregor attacked and badly damaged the Japanese aircraft carrier *Taiyo* off the island of Saipan, his boat was severely depth-charged by destroyer escorts and was so badly damaged that she was withdrawn from combat duty and sent stateside for use as a training boat.

So, back to the United States went both McGregor and Woodrow Wilson Jones, and both were assigned to new construction at Portsmouth, New Hampshire. Their new boat would be *Redfish*. While back in the states at nearby New London, Jones chanced to meet a young lady from nearby Norwich in the fall of 1943 while he was shopping. Ms. Florence Jubrey was in a hurry, trying to get on her way to a prayer meeting, but Woodrow Jones was immediately smitten and had to know who she was. Soon after, the two began a whirlwind courtship. Knowing he was about to ship overseas for another tour of duty, Jones asked for Ms. Jubrey's hand in marriage in December 1943. Upon the advice of her godmother, Florence Jubrey agreed, and she soon found out that Jones had already bought her a ring. The two were wed on February 26, 1944.

Returning to duty, Woodrow Jones put *Redfish* into commission on April 12, 1944, with Captain McGregor and soon headed off to the war zone again. However, perhaps mindful of his new wife at home, Jones made no further war patrols. He was transferred off *Redfish* prior to her first war patrol on July 23, 1944, and went to squadron duty. From July 1944 to April 1945 he worked in Submarine Divisions 44, 202, and 101 before doing relief duty on *Flying Fish* in April to May 1945. He subsequently returned to squadron duty, serving in Submarine Divisions 101 and 361 from May to August 1945. He returned to his old boat *Redfish* in August to September 1945, serving on her for a month after her belated return to the war zone. The boat had taken a severe beating on just her second patrol after McGregor sank the Japanese carrier *Unryu* in December 1944 and barely survived the ordeal. She would not make another war patrol.

At war's end, Jones rode another boat, *Redfin*, back to New London and his anxious wife. In the postwar era he served on the diesel boats *Whale, Grouper, Piper,* and *Spikefish*, before going back to squadron duty for ten years, from June 1947 to May 1957, at New London. When Woodrow Wilson Jones went to sea again in 1957, it was aboard a whole new type of boat. This time, he was on the nuclear attack boat *Skate*, which he rode to the North Pole in a historic voyage that has already been detailed. He served on *Skate* from May 1957 to October 1959, subsequently going to another nuclear attack boat, *Scorpion*. He served on her from October 1959 to August 1961, from which he went back to squadron duty. Woodrow Wilson Jones retired as a chief steward on August 17, 1962, after a twenty-year navy career.

Upon leaving the navy, Jones worked for General Dynamics (Electric Boat Division) in Groton, Connecticut, for 24 years. He was an active Mason, and a dedicated member of the Evans Memorial A.M.E. Zion Church in Norwich for 56 years. The Woodrow Wilson Jones Educational Center at Zion Church is named in his honor. At his death on July 14, 2000, Jones left his wife of 56 years, Florence, and a daughter, Beverly Louise Jones.

Chief Steward Woodrow Wilson Jones in 1944. A native of Tennessee, Jones entered the navy before World War II and made several war patrols on *Pike* before going to new construction duty at New London in 1944. (Photograph courtesy of F. Jones.)

CARL KIMMONS

Carl Eugene Kimmons is among the most distinguished and respected Black submariners of his time, pure and simple. He was born and raised in Hamilton, Ohio, and joined the United States Navy in 1940. By the time he retired thirty years later in 1970, he was the first man ever to have enlisted as a mess attendant and serve in every enlisted pay grade to become a commissioned officer.

> I enlisted at twenty years of age in the U.S. Navy in Cincinnati, Ohio, on June 4, 1940. After seeing one of those recruiting movies about how great

being a sailor was, I was very eager to get in. After enlisting, I was put on a train for the naval training center at Norfolk, Virginia. At Wheeling, West Virginia, the conductor moved all the African Americans into a segregated car for the journey into Virginia. At the naval base, Norfolk, I was assigned to Unit B East. In addition to the officer in charge, there was a Filipino steward named Abad who was in charge of my Class 13. There were also some African American stewards, an African American first class machinists mate, and an African American first class storekeeper. The storekeeper was very light and could have been "passing" for white. But African Americans can recognize African Americans.

When my class departed after training, I was held over until September 1940 because I was assigned to the Glass House for duties as a yeoman. LTJG E.B. Billingsley commanded the unit. As the typist in the Glass House, I typed his name so many times that it is printed indelibly on my mind. My typing class in high school did me good, but after my class had departed, I was eager to get to the fleet. Before World War II broke out, the common feeling among American sailors was "give us a rowboat and a machine gun and I'll take care of those Japs." We used to laugh at the Japanese who were buying tin cans from the USA. We didn't realize that Japan would have the last laugh.

I was sent by train across the United States to Mare Island, California, where I was assigned in September 1940 to the recommissioning crew of the USS *McFarland*. It was an old four-stack destroyer being converted to a seaplane tender, with extra space for an enlarged wardroom for the officers and space for carrying aviation gasoline. After commissioning, the *McFarland* was sent to Pearl Harbor for a homeport. We always tied up at the submarine base piers. We left port on December 6, 1941, to be included in a safety net for some army B-17's that were flying to Hawaii. In those days, the powers that be had navy ships stationed every 500 miles from the mainland to Hawaii just in case one of the planes developed trouble and had to abort the mission. The *McFarland* had the station closest to Hawaii, so we left the submarine base the day before the attack. So we missed the action on December 7. Thank goodness. We were diverted to another Hawaiian Island to remain until Pearl Harbor was cleared.

While on *McFarland* I used to hang out around the yeoman's shack in my off time because I could type and wanted to be a yeoman instead of a mess attendant. On one of my ships the yeoman let me handle the ship's logs. On the back of the ship's logs in those days was the requirement to put in all the navigational data — a lot of figures. Most typists didn't like to use figures, but I was eager to do yeoman's work, so I became very good at it. In the later years this was done away with. All they had to do was type "Same as SOPA" (Senior Officer Present Afloat — which meant the same navigational data as the big boss on a large ship).

After requesting submarine duty, I was transferred in April 1942 to the *Plunger*. The skipper was Lieutenant Commander D.C. White. I don't remember anything particular about him. On the *Plunger* I was advanced to officer's cook, 3rd class.

You asked about the routine for stewards. I can only remember some. The steward's bunks were in the forward torpedo room — which was next to the forward battery where the officers ate and slept. When we got up in the morning, we cleaned off the table in the wardroom and prepared for breakfast. We prepared breakfast in the pantry. Lunch and dinner were prepared by the ship's cook in the galley, and we just transported them to the pantry. But not breakfast. We prepared that. After breakfast, we cleaned the wardroom, the pantry, the officer's rooms (including making the beds), and the forward battery. We always kept a coffee pot going. The duty steward would take coffee to the control room and to the bridge when called upon to do so. It was always a pleasure going to the bridge because it would give the steward a chance to breathe some fresh air — and maybe spend a few moments there gazing at the scenery. When necessary, one of the stewards would blow the officer's head — depending where we were, of course.

About stewards qualifying on submarines in the early days, we only had to qualify in the forward torpedo room because that is where our bunks were and in the forward battery because that is where the wardroom was. After I learned how to blow the officer's head, I was in. I had drawings of all the ship, but no one was interested after I relieved one of the torpedo men from having to take care of the officer's head in the forward torpedo room.

I made the second, third, fourth, and fifth war patrols on *Plunger*. The fifth war patrol brought a new skipper, LCDR Raymond H. Bass. He was later to be my squadron commander, Submarine Squadron Ten aboard the USS *Fulton* in New London when I was a yeoman in Submarine Division 101 after the war. On the *Plunger* my assigned battle station submerged was in the forward torpedo room helping reload the fish. Battle station surface, I was on the 50-caliber machine gun. Of course, we never had a battle station surface during my runs [Kimmons].

During Kimmons' time on *Plunger* from April 1942 to July 1943, the submarine made four war patrols. The first of these, in June 1942, was to the area of the East China Sea. Not only was it a productive patrol, resulting in the sinking of two Japanese merchant vessels, it was also historic in terms of the tactics used. The boat's skipper, David White, sank one the ships with an unusual shot from astern. Known as an "up the kilt" shot, it was the first of its kind during the war that resulted in a sinking and one of only five or six succesful attacks of its kind during the entire war (Roscoe, *Submarine War*, pp. 148–9). On the next patrol, *Plunger* achieved no sinkings but had plenty of action. Newly equipped with SJ radar, she attacked a *Natori*-class Japanese cruiser off Truk. After firing four torpedoes, all of which missed, the submarine dove deep. She crashed into the bottom, damaging her hull and new sonar gear, forcing her back to Brisbane, Australia, for repairs (Blair, p. 330). On Kimmons' third patrol, *Plunger* achieved no sinkings and sailed back to Pearl Harbor. On his final patrol aboard *Plunger*, Kimmons again saw much action when it came to torpedo work. Now commanded by Bass, *Plunger* sank two large merchant ships north of Truk (Roscoe, p. 232).

> In July 1943 I was transferred to the mainland and wound up on the destroyer USS *Scott*. That was heartbreaking for a submarine sailor. We submariners think that we have such important duties aboard ship that we are indispensable. When we are transferred and standing on the pier and throw off that number-one line and the ship leaves without such a vital part, we all wonder, "How did they do that?"
>
> In July 1943, in Philadelphia, I married, and am still married to, my high school classmate Thelma Jean Lewis. Every day I would put in a chit to return

to submarine duty. The executive officer, LCDR H.H. Holt — who used to initial all papers with "H3" — would tear my chit up in front of me. Somehow, one chit got through, and I was transferred in November 1943 to the USS *Parche* at Portsmouth, New Hampshire. The skipper was Commander Lawson P. Ramage. The ship went through the Panama Canal. In Panama I had my first encounter with segregated water fountains labeled "gold" and "silver." I took a drink from both of them. The water tasted the same!

I made the first, second, and third war patrols on the *Parche*. My battle station assignment was as a phone talker in the forward battery. During the second war patrol, the *Parche* made a surface attack on a Japanese convoy. During forty-six minutes of action on the surface, the *Parche* fired nineteen torpedos scoring with fifteen. During that historic battle, those of us below only knew that the skipper sent the lookouts he didn't need below. We only had a vague idea what was going on. One of the ships was so close to our submarine that it could not depress its deck gun enough to get off a shot. Commander Ramage was awarded the Congressional Medal of Honor, the first living submariner to receive this award [*ibid.*].

Kimmons' time aboard *Parche* was, indeed, filled with action. On her first patrol, "Red" Ramage and his men sank two freighters in the Luzon Strait. *Parche*'s second war patrol is one of the most famous in the annals of submarine history. The patrol, made in company with the boats *Hammerhead* and *Steelhead*, started out slowly, with the sinking by deck gun of a small patrol craft, but the battle in the early morning hours of July 31, 1944, has been called "the wildest of the submarine war" (Blair, p. 681). Ramage and his men, while surfaced, attacked a large Japanese convoy in the early morning hours. While the Japanese tried to ram *Parche*, and fired at her with deck guns, "Ramage dodged and twisted, returning torpedo fire for gunfire" (*ibid.*). When all was done, *Parche* was officially credited with sinking two ships and shared in the destruction of another with *Steelhead*, for a total of 19,200 tons of enemy shipping sent to the bottom. The third patrol of *Parche* resulted in no sinkings and ended with *Parche* safely escorting the submarine *Sailfish*, with her radio transmitter out of commission, back to the island of Saipan.

When Commander Ramage, who was a great skipper and a great guy, was transferred after the third patrol, I decided it was time to get off too. His executive officer, W.W. McCrory, had been elevated to command. I thought that McCrory would be an over-anxious fighter since he was on the patrol on which Ramage had been so aggressive. So, during our two week stay at Midway, I looked for someone to take my place on *Parche*. I talked L.C. Fisher into taking my place and was transferred at Midway Island to Submarine Division 241 in December 1944. I stayed on Midway Island in Submarine Division 241, 242, and 321 until June 1945.

In August 1945, I was transferred as steward 1st class to the *Cobbler*. I served on her with Steward Willie James. World War II officially ended on September 2, 1945. I did a lot of yeoman work on the *Cobbler*. The yeoman in charge trained me so he could take a 30-day leave.

In October 1947, I changed my rate to yeoman, 2nd class. I accepted a reduction in rating in order to change from steward to yeoman. That was the only way to get it approved from the squadron. Officers' cooks and officers' stewards wore the chief petty officer's uniform minus the "crow" (American Eagle) on the sleeve and the anchor on the cap. Changing from steward to yeoman meant a complete change of uniform. It also meant a reduction in base pay and submarine hazardous duty pay. On changing my rate, I was transferred across the pier in Key West, Florida, to the *Medregal*. I made yeoman 1st class and was transferred in January 1949 to shore duty to SubGruOne, New London Group, Atlantic Reserve Fleet in Portsmouth, New Hampshire.

In April 1950 I was transferred to *Sea Robin*, serving until July 1951, when I was assigned to the Flag Allowance of Submarine Squadron Ten. I served in Submarine Division 101 and made chief yeoman, acting appointment. In July 1953, I was transferred to shore duty at the naval station, San Juan, Puerto Rico, as chief yeoman. I served there until June 1956 when I was transferred back to Submarine Division 101 aboard the tender *Fulton*. I was advanced in rating to senior chief yeoman and then to master chief yeoman.

I was selected in a new program that we called "chief to JG" program. The navy was short on junior officers, and to fill the gap certain chief petty officers were selected to be commissioned as limited duty officers. I was assigned to the officer candidate school in Newport, Rhode Island, in May 1961. Upon graduation, I was assigned to the U.S. Navy Hydrographic Office, Washington, D.C. There, I was the administrative officer, the security officer, and the top secret control officer. I was advanced from lieutenant junior grade to lieutenant. I was very excited about the opportunity of becoming an officer. After being a yeoman you know about all the red tape you have to go through. As an officer I could cut this red tape, make decisions, and stand by them.

I was transferred in October 1963 to the U.S. Naval Submarine School as administration officer, where I served until April 1966. Then I became group secretary for Submarine Development Group Two, handling administration, security, and top secret control. My final assignment in the navy was the U.S. Navy Underwater Sound Laboratory, New London, Connecticut. I reported in July 1968, served as security officer, and retired from the U.S. Navy on July 31, 1970, after thirty years of service.

All the while I was in the navy, I really did not have any instances where segregation became a problem. When I was attached to the *Plunger*, one of the officers wanted me to shine his shoes while they were on his feet. I convinced him a better job could be done if they were off his feet. He complied. All the crews accepted me for what I was, steward or yeoman, and I was treated with respect. When I became a commissioned officer and was stationed in New London, Connecticut, some white sailors would see me coming and rather than have to salute a Black officer, they would cross the street. This became very noticeable.

There were three Black barber shops; the most popular one belonged to a former steward named Strong, in the New London area that cut the hair of Black sailors. I went to the barbershop aboard *Fulton*, when I was assigned to Submarine Division 101, and sat in the chair. The Filipino barber said he did not know how to cut the hair of Blacks. I told him to do the best he could because in two weeks it wouldn't make any difference because of the hair growth. He cut it. Then, when I was attached to a unit on the submarine base, I went to the base barbershop. They gave me the same response, and I gave them my response. They cut it. I only say this because last Saturday when I was getting my hair cut at the sub base barbershop, there were four African

Lieutenant Carl Eugene Kimmons. A native of Hamilton, Ohio, he made seven war patrols during World War II and is the only steward ever to hold every enlisted man rating and rise to officer rank. (Photograph courtesy of C. Kimmons.)

Americans getting their hair cut. Little did they know that I was the one that got things started there. Now, all barbers have to have a course in cutting the hair of African Americans. In the old days the navy exchange did not carry any products used mainly by African Americans. Now they are all over the place. We have come a long way!

After retirement from the navy, I attended Connecticut College and received a bachelor's degree, magna cum laude, then a master's degree from the University of Connecticut, and a Sixth-Year Certificate from Southern Connecticut State University. Starting in 1973, I taught social studies at Clark Lane Junior High School, Waterford, Connecticut, for ten years. Then I was assigned to Waterford High School, where I taught for twelve years. I had a great advantage in being a teacher after serving in the navy. That navy background enabled me to perform in a much more efficient manner. I could "hack it" because I had been to "hack it" school!

In February 1965 I became a private airplane pilot. I owned my own airplane, a Cessna 140 tail dragger, for twenty-six years. We tail dragger pilots think we are the best because it takes more skill to land and takeoff with the wheel in the back!

I dislike retirement immensely. I am a volunteer at the Retired Activities Office at the submarine base New London. I am a volunteer at Lawrence and Memorial Hospital. I am a volunteer in AARP's 55 Alive Mature Driving Course. I have been appointed for a three-year term as a commissioner in the senior Citizens Department, Waterford, Connecticut, and I am a volunteer leader in an exercise program [*ibid.*].

As of this writing, Carl Eugene Kimmons lives in Waterford, Connecticut, with his wife of more than sixty years, Thelma Jean. They have three grown children, Karen, Larry, and Kimberly. Recently, in November 2002, Kimmons was inducted into the Holland Club, an organization for submariners who have been qualified in submarines for fifty years or more. Carl is also active with the local chapter of World War II Submarine Veterans and even designed the logo used on the caps they wear and the Submarines Lost at Sea banner used to remember those submariners lost during the war. Though he has been retired from the navy for well over thirty years now, he is still remembered by his peers, both Black and white, as the consummate submariner.

William Knight

William Knight is yet another man about whom little is known, but an aura of legend surrounds him. He enlisted in the navy on November 16, 1939, at Norfolk, Virginia, and first served on surface craft. When the war began, he may have been on the carrier *Lexington* and is said to have been transferred off at Pearl Harbor just a week before she was sunk at the Battle of the Coral Sea on May 8, 1942. He was subsequently assigned to the cruisers *Astoria* and then *Vincennes*, both of which were sunk off Guadalcanal in the Battle of Savo Island in August 1942. However, before their loss, Knight had apparently volunteered for submarine duty.

By February 1943, William Knight was an officer's cook 3rd class and was doing flag duty. His officially assigned flagship was *Pickerel*, however he was only nominally attached to this submarine and made no war patrols on her. Knight left flag duty and went to *Whale* as part of her regular crew on February 26, 1943. His legendary status, akin to a cat with nine lives, grew when, in April 1943, his old flagship *Pickerel* was sunk with all hands off the island of Honshu. That made four ships that Knight had served on and were sunk after he had left. Captain Albert Burrows on *Whale* was not about to let this happen to him, deciding about Knight that "he was never going to leave my boat" (Reynolds, p. 43). He followed through on his promise, and Willie Knight made three war patrols under Burrows from May 1943 to January 1944. Burrows relinquished his command in February 1944 to Captain James Grady, and at the same time Knight left the boat, going to flag duty on *Tambor* with Burrows on February 16, 1944.

By late 1944, Burrows was back in the states at New London, and Willie Knight was with him. Knight later did flag duty on *Mackerel*, went to the old *Permit* on July 28, 1945, and subsequently to *Snapper* on September 5, 1945. The last two boats were based out of New London and were older boats withdrawn from combat service and used for training duty.

Willie Knight's postwar career is unknown, except for the fact that he remained on flag duty with Captain Burrows, with whom he had undoubtedly formed a unique friendship that was first based on superstition. After the war was over, former *Whale* crewman Floyd Erickson visited his old captain while at New London and was surprised when the man that brought him a cup of coffee was none other than Willie Knight. Pleasantries were exchanged, and when Erickson asked Captain Burrows about the arrangement, he just smiled and said "I'll have Willie with me until I retire" (Erikson).

Richard Lucas

Richard Ralph Lucas was born in 1927 in North Carolina. He was drafted in 1944 for military service at the age of 17, but stated his age as 18. He had just graduated from high school, where he was a basketball and baseball athlete, when his draft notice came.

> My main reason for going into the service at 17, which I did with my parents' permission, was economic. I was one of twelve children, and already had three brothers in the army. I was sent to boot camp at Bainbridge, where I volunteered for sub duty, then was sent to sub school at New London. I was screened very closely, asked a lot of questions, and took many tests for sub duty. From New London I went to San Francisco and was on a sub relief crew. I was supposed to go on the *Bluefish* but was hospitalized. I later took a troop ship to Honolulu, where I was assigned to the new sub tender *Orion*. In early 1945, *Raton* came in and aboard her was my friend and high school classmate Richard Smith. I asked for a posting to the boat and got it. I made one war patrol, *Raton*'s last before the war ended.
>
> I liked Captain Gus Gugliotta, and found submariners liberal minded. But, when we went ashore, we [stewards] went our way, they [white crew members] went theirs. I served in the forward torpedo room and took turns standing watch with the others. I remember being depth-charged, but also felt that it was the one you didn't hear that you worried about.

After the war was over, we went to Staten Island [New York] and then to the sub base at the Panama Canal Zone. I didn't have enough points to get a discharge, so I was in until 1947. I sometimes wish I had stayed in the navy [Lucas].

At the end of his service, Richard Lucas married in 1950 and has five children. He attended Fayetteville Teachers School in North Carolina and taught in various grades as well as drivers' education class for 37 years before his retirement in 1987. He currently resides in Rocky Mount, North Carolina, and owns and operates his own dry cleaning business.

GEORGE WASHINGTON LYTLE

While little is known about big George Lytle, he has an impressive war record. When he joined the navy is uncertain, but it was probably sometime between 1938 and 1939. He joined the commissioning crew of *Drum* in November 1941 as a mess attendant 1st class and made her first ten war patrols. The first three patrols were conducted by Captain Robert Rice, from April to October 1942, and the next four were under Captain Bernard McMahon from November 1942 to September 1943. Lytle was virtually one and the same with *Drum*, for he would continue on with her, making two more runs under Captain Delbert Williamson, from November 1943 to May 1944, and a final run under Captain Maurice Rindskopf in June to July 1944. Only Rindskopf, who had served as executive officer on the boat, made more patrols on the boat than Lytle. During Lytle's time on *Drum,* she sank twelve ships worth over 60,000 tons, including a large seaplane tender on their first patrol. Lytle was one of the few stewards during the war to win a Bronze Star. Rindskopf believes this was not only for his overall service on the boat but may also have been related to his final patrol on *Drum* when Lytle and the deck gun crew saw action in sinking a sampan and taking several prisoners, and later when they shot up an island-based radio station. By the time George Lytle left *Drum*, he was an officer's cook 1st class.

After the war, George Lytle stayed in the navy and worked out of New London. The boats he served on are unknown. Upon retiring from the navy, Lytle was active in veteran's organizations and attended reunions with his old crew from *Drum*. Even in his old age, he was a giant of a man and cut an impressive figure. When he became ill in 1986, Captain O.B. Adams, a former ensign on *Drum* during the war, wrote to his old shipmate these encouraging words:

> You were such a robust and vital person that it is difficult for me to believe that illness could ever strike at you. You were the number-one morale booster in the boat, handling those shells as number-one loader of the deck gun and stomping up and down the passageway in your depth-charge shoes. I just wanted to tell you to hang in there and fight with your stamina of old [Adams, "Letter"].

However, Lytle eventually lost his battle and passed away in 1987. His photograph and Bronze Star citation are now on display at the Submarine Force Library and Museum; George Washington Lytle is the only African American submariner to be so honored. This came about because of pressure placed on the museum by Lytle's friends and fellow stewards to see that not only would Lytle honored but also that the contribution of men of the steward's branch as a whole would be recognized. They picked a good man to represent them.

SAMMIE MAJOR

Sammie Major was a native of Florida, born in Cocoa Beach on October 30, 1926, and living in Fort Pierce when the war broke out. Previously working as a truck driver, he enlisted at the age of 17 into the navy and was inducted at Jacksonville, Florida, on January 28, 1944. He lied about his age to get in the navy, a fact that was not discovered by his family until after his death decades later. He went to boot camp at Bainbridge, Maryland, where he volunteered for submarine duty. He joined the crew of *Picuda* on December 17, 1944, from squadron duty at Pearl Harbor and

Steward 1st Class Sammie Major, a veteran patroller on *Picuda* during World War II. The Florida native was part of a crew that earned the Presidential Unit Citation for their outstanding war patrols. (Photograph courtesy of D. Major.)

made that boat's last two war patrols under Captain Evan Shepard. For taking part in his boat's fifth war patrol in December 1944 to January 1945, during which she sank several ships in wolf pack operations, Sammie Major and her crew received the Navy Unit Commendation. Major made his, and the boat's, final war patrol under Shepard in March to April 1945 and subsequently went stateside.

After the war, Major served on *Cochino* from December 1945 to August 1947, *Odax* from August 1947 to August 1949, shore duty from 1949 to 1958, *Barracuda* from September 1958 to January 1960, *Archerfish* and *Halfbeak* from January 1960 to February

1963, and the FBM boat *Patrick Henry* from January 1963 to January 1965. He subsequently did shore duty and retired as a steward 1st class on October 1, 1973, having served in the navy 30 years.

Major married his wife, Doris, in Fort Pierce, Florida, on May 17, 1951, and they had three children: Tammie, Harney, and Anthony. Once he was a civilian, Major worked at Pfizer Chemical Company in Groton, Connecticut, and was living in Waterford at the time of his death.

Elvin Mayo

Elvin Adair Mayo was born on August 25, 1925, in the small town of Avinger, Texas.

> It was a small town.... You blink your eyes and you'd go right through. Well, it might've been 5,000 people or so.... My parents were Alvin and Bennie. We were real poor. My father was more or less a sharecropper. We grew cotton and corn, and my grandmother had peach trees.... She had huge peaches. I don't know of anyone poorer, and I always wondered about my father, whether he wasn't sick all the time. My father had been gassed as a soldier in World War I. I had three sisters and a brother. His name is Garland, and we still talk every week.... I never went to high school, except for maybe a month or so. I went out to Dallas to work, then came back home and was picking cotton. That's why I wanted to get out and join the navy. I had a cousin from Texas, he was called "Rooster," and he went down on one of the boats. I don't know which one. That's why I picked the navy. I was in the navy reserve when I was called up.
>
> At boot camp [Bainbridge] when I went in the navy, I wasn't around Black people, but I was used to that. Mostly where I grew up it was white people, and I ate and slept at their houses with my friends. Many of them [stewards] brought trouble on themselves. When I was sent to New London, I was there for maybe a month. I had adaptability. Now here I am, no high school, no sub school, no nothing, and I'm going to submarines. I was then sent to California, Mare Island. I tried to get on a boat [*Pargo*] with "Little" [Albert] Rozar, but the captain said he already had enough stewards. So I took a tender overseas, the *Griffin*, I believe. I didn't like that. The ship was too big.... I couldn't take it. I said to myself, "I got to get me a submarine. I got to get out of this place."
>
> I was on the rail, watching all the subs coming in from patrol. I had my eye on the *Jack*. The next time they came in, I went to see the captain, this tall slim guy. I said, "Captain, can I have a word with you, please?" He said, "What do you have in mind?" I said, "I want to come on your boat." I told him, "I'm trying to pick a boat that's going through the war," and I told him I liked the look of his boat.... "You're meticulous and neat." He laughed and said OK, and told me to go to the squadron to get the orders cut.
>
> I found a home on *Jack*. I told the captain [Thomas Dykers], "I'm from Texas." He said, "I'm from Louisiana," and I said, "We're next door neighbors." When I went on the boat, the captain told the crew "Mayo is just like one of

us ... there will be no racist slurs, no name calling." He told me not to handle problems myself, "Just come down to my stateroom, that's what I'm here for." The crew treated me just like their brother.

Once while in Australia, at Perth, I was in a place and guys from one boat were calling me nigger. One of my crew, maybe the chief of the boat, I don't remember, went in there and told them "Mayo is part of my crew. There will be no more racist slurs made. If you're calling him a name, you're calling me one," and that was that.

The thing was, even when he [Captain Dykers] got to be a big wheel, he never forgot me. Even when he made admiral, same thing. Captain [Albert] Fuhrman [Dyker's successor on *Jack*] told the crew the same thing as Dykers. I could ask him anything. I was the only Black man on the *Jack*, and captains Dykers and Fuhrman, they molded me, told the crew I was the same as them, could go where they did. When Fuhrman took over, he said "I'm not going to sea without Mayo." I was the good luck charm.

I qualified throughout the whole boat on *Jack*. In battle station submerged, I worked in the forward battery, manning the phones, watching for leaks. Once or twice I did lookout duty and helped reload torpedoes. One time I was lying in my bunk, when I heard this drip, drip, drip. Something didn't sound right, so I called up that we had a leak in the forward torpedo room. They checked and found that the water in the bilges was at a high level. I never liked being depth-charged, never got used to that, but going through Makassar or Lombok Straits, going through at night, was dangerous. I ended up riding *Jack* through the end of the war, and a bit after [Mayo].

Mayo enlisted in the navy on November 23, 1943, and went aboard *Jack* from Submarine Division 122 on May 22, 1944. He subsequently made her last five war patrols, during which time she sank seven ships under captains Arthur Krapf and Albert Fuhrman and rescued one downed aviator. Elvin Mayo was the only Black steward ever to make a war patrol on *Jack*, all the rest being from the Phillipines.

After the war, Elvin Mayo served aboard *Ling*, *Corsair*, and *Trout*. throughout the 1940s and 1950s. In 1961 he commissioned the FBM boat *Abraham Lincoln* but didn't like this duty. He then went to the old diesel boat *Jallao*, where once again he was a "good luck charm." When the boat was sent to the troubled Mediterranean area to serve with the U.S. Sixth Fleet from January to May 1962, he was in charge, once more, of "bringing the boat back," especially through the minefields off the coast of Albania. Following this cruise, Mayo ended his career with a stint of shore duty at Freehold, New Jersey, before his subsequent retirement as a steward 2nd class in 1964. He then worked at the Portsmouth Naval Shipyard. Elvin Mayo passed away in Rochester, New Hampshire, in October 2003.

Hosey Mays

Hosey Mays was a resident of Denver, Colorado, when he was drafted into the navy in March of 1943. He had previously worked for the Union Pacific Railroad as an attendant in a dining car. He attended boot camp at the Unit K West facility in Norfolk, Virginia, where his life changed drastically.

> I was in one of the last classes at Norfolk before they opened Bainbridge. All the stewards were trained at Unit K West, and there were guys from all over the U.S. there. Culturally, it was a deep shock going from Denver to Norfolk when it came to how Blacks were treated. I needed money, so I volunteered for the boats. I spent one day in sub school, then was sent to Building 16, the officer's mess, where a Filipino steward was in charge. At the time, I didn't know how good I had it. I had lots of liberty! The *Crevalle* came down from Portsmouth, so I was sent aboard her. I worked on the reload crew in the fore torpedo room and as first loader on the 4-inch deck gun. I made the first two war patrols on *Crevalle* with another steward's mate, Tim Pennyman [Mays].

Mays' initiation to submarine warfare was an eventful one. On her first patrol in November 1943, under skipper Hank Munson, *Crevalle* attacked four ships, including an 18,000-ton Japanese escort carrier. She paid for this attack when she was subjected to heavy return fire from both the carrier and her destroyer escort. *Crevalle*'s deck gun crew, too, got in on the action on this patrol when she battle-surfaced and sank a small freighter. While Munson and the crew were credited with sinking four ships, including the carrier, postwar accounting reduced the official score to just one ship. Still, it was an outstanding first patrol, and was one that netted Munson a Navy Cross. During *Crevalle*'s second war patrol in January 1944, again under Hank Munsun, Mays and the rest of the crew again saw much action and would have sank a Japanese submarine had their torpedoes not exploded prematurely. In addition to laying a minefield near Camranh Bay, off the Vietnamese coast, *Crevalle* was officially credited with one sinking, and Munson was awarded a second Navy Cross.

> Hank Munson was an outstanding captain and a fair man. I was promoted a grade every time he received a Navy Cross. Not all captains did this for their men. *Crevalle* was a good boat, and I didn't want to leave her, but both of us stewards left the boat when Munson did. Pennyman went to *Rasher* with Munson, and I went to a relief crew at Perth-Fremantle. Australia was a great place, though we were warned there would be a $2000 fine for fraternizing with aborigines. While on leave, we [stewards] had our own housing and weren't bothered as long as we kept clean. We had our own girls, played cards, listened to music, and were able to get excess chow from the boats that were coming in off patrol. After a few months, I went aboard *Bowfin* [*ibid.*].

Hosey Mays is indeed correct, his promotions did come quickly while aboard *Crevalle*. When he left that boat in February 1944, he had been in the navy less than a year and was already a steward 3rd class. After working on a relief crew for several months, Mays went to *Bowfin* on April 25, 1944. On this boat he made two war patrols under John Corbus, whom Mays calls "outstanding." The first of these began in April 1944 and resulted in one shared sinking. After a refit at Majuro Atoll, *Bowfin*'s sixth patrol of the war and Hosey Mays' fourth was a wild one that began in July 1944. It was one in which nine Japanese ships were attacked and believed sunk, and even a bus, parked on a wharf, was destroyed. Like so many other sinkings, however, postwar analysis only credited *Bowfin* with just one ship sunk. Following this patrol, Hosey Mays was now a steward 2nd class and was still on the boat while she went through an extended overhaul. However, Mays missed the boat when she sailed on her next patrol in December 1944 and was subsequently transferred to Squadron 30 at Pearl Harbor. From there he went back to Australia, serving at Perth until the war's end.

> On the boats I was treated outstanding, though you didn't always hear about things or events ashore — ship's parties — and wasn't invited. I was irked when some officers banged on my bunk to bring coffee to the bridge at all hours. The regular crew was fine, but ensigns would use the buzzer instead of getting their own coffee, even if I was off duty. Australia was a good place. We were called "Black Yanks," and the kids wanted to feel our hair and skin. We were taken into people's homes — there was no prejudice. I left Australia in October 1945 and went back to New London. I was discharged in 1946 and was in the navy reserve and was called back in 1950 for Korea. I stayed in the navy for 17 years. In January 1953 I changed my rate to IC electrician and retired as a chief in 1968 [*ibid.*].

After Hosey Mays came back in the navy, he first served at Mare Island and recommissioned the boats *Bluegill* and *Besugo*. He was on *Sterlet* when he changed his rate and was no longer a steward. He then served on *Atule* and *Grenadier* out of Key West, Florida. He was on the latter boat for five years and calls it "the best boat of my whole navy career." In talking about the camaraderie aboard *Grenadier*, he states:

> A white chief electrician, "Low Voltage" Miller, took me under his wing. He taught me everything and was my mentor. When I relieved him as chief, he went to his bunk and presented me with a bottle of Canadian Club whiskey [*ibid.*].

After leaving *Grenadier*, Hosey Mays became an IC instructor at the naval school in San Diego for three years. He retired in 1968 and stayed in the San Diego area, where he still resides today.

EDWARD MCNAIR

Edward McNair was born in Savannah, Georgia, on October 25, 1917, the only son of Jesse and Hattie McNair. He obtained an eighth-grade education before leaving school. He later enlisted in the navy on February 5, 1936, and went to boot camp in Norfolk, Virginia. After graduating from either Mess Attendant Class Three or Four, which were called two of the very finest group of mess attendants taken through at Norfolk and were referred to as "the cream of the crop," McNair soon volunteered for submarine duty. His first-known submarine service occurred on June 5, 1937, when he was aboard the *Narwhal* during her deep-submergence dive off Pigeon Point, California, to a depth of 346 feet. Prior to World War II, McNair would later serve in Submarine Group One at New London, Connecticut, and on the *S-47* and *S-45* before joining the crew of *S-43* on June 27, 1939. He would stay on this boat throughout the war. The old *S-43*, built in 1923, made three war patrols from Brisbane, Australia, from April to October of 1942 before being sent back to the states. In two patrols under Captain Edward Hannon, and one under Captain Francis Brown, the boat operated in the Solomon Islands but sank no enemy ships in patrols that lasted an average of 30 days each.

Senior Chief Steward Edward McNair. A native of Georgia, "Mac" was a real sailor's sailor. (Photograph courtesy of the McNair/Pollard family.)

Later in the war, Edward McNair was stationed at Submarine Base Balboa in the Panama Canal Zone, where he reenlisted on February 5, 1942, for two years. After the war, he served on *Sennet*, making an Arctic cruise on her, whose details have already been discussed. McNair later served on the diesel boats *Sea Cat*, *Sea Poacher*, and *Bergall*. From about 1957 to 1959 he left submarine duty for a brief time to serve on the aircraft carrier *Forrestal* (CVA-59) as chief steward. On this huge floating island, McNair was in charge of a large compliment of stewards and was also a member of the ship's boxing team. He often used his connections with the Submarine Force to try to get well-regarded stewards to come on the *Forrestal* with him.

Edward McNair was well known throughout the Submarine Force in New London and is described by fellow steward Sam Wallace as "a natural comedian, very talkative, a good sailor's sailor" (Wallace). He was also known for his outspokenness, especially in the area of race relations and the navy, and he even angered at times his fellow stewards. Though he could be tough, he was fair-minded and was driven to help others to choose the right career path in the navy. McNair was also known for being a very smart man. He was a graduate of the navy's Career Appraisal School in Pensacola, Florida, details of which have already been discussed, and ended his career with a tour of duty on the FBM boat *Sam Houston*. Edward McNair retired from active duty on January 31, 1966, as a senior chief steward (E-8), having served 30 years.

Upon retirement, he worked for Electric Boat Company for a short time before attending the University of Connecticut. He first graduated with a bachelor degree in history, and later earned a masters degree in education. He subsequently worked as a substitute teacher.

Edward McNair was interested in local politics and sought, unsuccessfully, the Democratic nominations for state representative and mayor in Ledyard, Connecticut. Convinced that Blacks could not win local elections without better organization, McNair joined the Connecticut Federation of Black Democratic Clubs and later founded the New London County Black Democrats group as well as similar organizations in Ledyard. In 1977 he was honored by the State Federation of Black Democratic Clubs with their Man of the Year Award. McNair was also active in the town of Ledyard, serving on the Democratic Town Committee and the zoning board. His many civic activities, too numerous to list here in full, included the Ledyard Historical Society, the Kiwanis Club of Groton, and the West Side Community Action Committee. He was a Third Vice President in the Connecticut NAACP.

Edward McNair married Helen (Bryan) McNair on June 18, 1955. He has four children, son Cornell McNair (Jewett City, Connecticut), daughters Elena Pollard (Ledyard, Connecticut), Thomasina Smith (deceased), and Perditha Catheau (Australia). Edward McNair, who is survived by seven grandchildren, three great-grandchildren, and one great-great-grandson, died on July 3, 1981.

BERT MINOR

Bert Minor was born in 1926 in Casper, Wyoming, and was raised and went to school there into early adulthood. Despite growing up in the west, racial prejudice was still a factor in everyday life for the Black families that lived in Casper, and regular schools for Minor were, as he puts it, "off limits." He was a high school senior, aged 18, and spent his spare time working until he was drafted in 1944.

> After being drafted, I was sent to Bainbridge, a separate training facility for Blacks. While I was there I also did some boxing. I volunteered to go to New London for sub duty. I was there for two months and was trained at steward school. I learned the basics of stewardship, not seamanship, for two months. I felt bad about being a steward and didn't like serving food. I was then sent to Mare Island by train and worked at the officer's quarters for a short time. I missed the first boat I was supposed to go on and was soon transferred to a sub group and went to Honolulu by liner. I then went to Saipan on the sub tender *Orion* and, after a couple of months, was transferred to the tender *Proteus*.
>
> In April 1945 I was sent aboard *Crevalle* and made one war patrol under Captain Steinmetz. I was not treated so good at first, and [I] had a chief electrician that kept bothering me and calling me "Jaycox," the steward who was on with me. I eventually set them straight. I qualified aboard the boat in about a month and a half.
>
> On my one patrol, we went with the Hellcats wolf pack into the Sea of Japan. During this time, our motors gave us some trouble, and a mine cable was caught in our screws. When we went through the LaPerouse Strait, we fired on a little ship. My battle station position was to man the headphones in the forward compartment and to relay orders [Minor].

During this last war patrol of *Crevalle*, the boat was commanded by Everett Steinmetz and ventured into the Sea of Japan as part of a nine-boat wolf pack called the Hellcats. The submarines were subdivided into three groups, with *Crevalle* serving under Commander Earl Hydeman's Hepcats. During this patrol, Minor's boat sank three Japanese cargo ships in three days. However, one boat, *Bonefish*, was not so fortunate. She was lost with all hands during this operation.

> At the end of the war, I was at Midway, and we were ready to head out for another patrol. We were one hour from heading out when the war was over. The base was then all lit up, and guns were fired in celebration. We then went back stateside to New York, and I got out in 1946. In my case, I felt like I went through it [submarine experience] alone and did not feel like a part of the crew. I know some of the white guys felt bad about that [*ibid.*].

After leaving the navy, Bert Minor returned to Casper, Wyoming. He went to junior college there, and began working for the post office in 1948. He was called back into the navy during the Korean War but spent his time at a reserve base in Florida. After this service, Minor returned once more to Casper and resumed his work with the post office. He retired from there in 1983 and then went to work for the Conoco Oil Company, where he has worked for the past 15 years. Bert Minor has one daughter from a prior marriage.

EUGENE MOSLEY, JR.

Eugene Mosley, Jr., enlisted in the navy on April 4, 1940, at Nashville, Tennessee, and attended boot camp at Norfolk, Virginia. Though he entered with Class 10 there, an illness forced him to miss a large part of his training, so he graduated with Class 11 instead. Upon graduation, he went straight to submarine duty, serving on the old school boats *S-29* and *R-11* at New London. He was at Pearl Harbor on December 7, 1941, when the Japanese attacked, probably doing relief duty on the tender *Pelias*. On the evening of December 6, he had been picked up by the shore patrol for some infraction and was held overnight. Mosley was in the brig at the submarine base on the morning of the attack, but once the attack began the brig was emptied, and Mosley went back to his ship.

On January 1, 1942, Mosley, now a mess attendant 2nd class, was transferred to the crew of *Triton*. He made her second war patrol under Captain Willis Lent in January to February 1942, and two ships were sunk in the East China Sea. After being depth-charged for the first time, he had second thoughts about submarine duty and, as he later told his friend Carl Kimmons, "I had no hair on my chest until after that first depth charge during which I was frightened to tears" (Kimmons, Carl).

On February 18, 1942, Mosley was transferred to *Gudgeon*. He probably made one war patrol on this boat under Captain Elton Grenfell, and possibly more, riding her to Australia before going to squadron duty. Because crew records for this boat were not available to the author, Mosley's exact dates of service on *Gudgeon* are unknown. He was serving in Submarine Division 162 at Fremantle when he went to *Bonefish*, the pride of Admiral Christie's fleet, as an officer's cook 3rd class on November 21, 1943. Serving under Captain Thomas Hogan, Mosley made three patrols from November 1943 to May 1944, during which four ships worth 10,000 tons were sunk. On his final patrol, Captain Hogan and the crew sank a Japanese destroyer in exciting fashion with a "down the throat" shot. As far as is known, this was Eugene Mosley's last combat action of the war. Like William Knight, Mosley, nicknamed "Boot" to distinguish him from an older steward by the same name, led a rather charmed life. All the submarines on which he made war patrols, *Triton*, *Gudgeon*, and *Bonefish*, were later lost with all hands during the war.

After the war, Mosley was based mostly on the east coast and served on the following ships: the diesel submarines *Corporal*, *Torsk*, *Dace*, *Cuttlefish*, and *Entemedor*; the FBM boat *Thomas Edison*; the submarine tenders *Orion* and *Fulton*; and the auxiliary ships *Chewink* and *Kittiwake*. Mosley passed away in 1981. (When looking at Appendix D, Eugene Mosley should not be confused with Steve Mosley, who made war patrols on *Bowfin* and *Cabrilla*.)

R.D. MOSLEY

Texas native Robert Daniel Mosley, known to his friends as "R.D.," enlisted in the navy at age 18 on January 26, 1943, from Tyler, Texas. He would give nearly three years of military service for his country, making two war patrols on two different submarines.

> I went to boot camp at Norfolk, Virginia, and then went to sub school at New London. I was part of the commissioning crew of *Pargo* in April 1943. I recall one dive we made during a training run where something went wrong and things got real hairy. My ears rang after that. I was treated well by the crew,

and Bell [the executive officer] was a lifesaver. He helped me out a bit. One bad thing I remember is the officers' sons calling me names while we were at New London, but the officers themselves I had no problem with. A Filipino chief steward on *Pargo* taught me how to qualify, and I did fine as a steward, as I had taken homemaking in school. I served as a loader on the 4-inch gun and in the fore torpedo room while I was aboard [Mosley, R.D.].

Mosley served on *Pargo* from her commissioning to October 28, 1943, during which time one war patrol was conducted, with no sinkings credited, under Commander Ian Eddy.

After serving on *Pargo*, I served on *Sailfish* and made one patrol on her. We sank a Japanese carrier and were awarded the Bronze Star for this patrol in November 1943. I then rode her back to the states, where we stayed for awhile, and I was transferred off at Mare Island in 1944. Once I got off the boat, I served in the officers' mess ashore and also did relief duty. I got out of the navy in late 1945 due to poor health and went back to school. But, jobs were hard to find, so I worked at the naval hospital in Long Beach, California, and later at Camp Pendleton [*ibid.*].

R. D. Mosley's second, and final war patrol for him, was *Sailfish*'s tenth of the war. Commanded by Captain Robert Ward, the boat and her crew achieved distinction when they sank the Japanese escort carrier *Chuyo*, 20,000 tons in size, on December 4, 1943, off the island of Truk. Whether or not Mosley received a Bronze Star for this action is unknown, but the boat and her crew were awarded a Presidential Unit Citation for the achievement. This was the first enemy carrier sunk by American submarines, but it came at a price. Aboard *Chuyo* were 21 POWs from the lost submarine *Sculpin*, and all but one were killed when the Japanese carrier went down after three torpedo hits. *Sailfish* also sank a large cargo ship on this patrol and was then sent back to the states for a long period of overhaul and modernization. During this time at Mare Island, Mosley was still aboard but was reduced in rate to a steward's mate 2nd class by court-martial in March 1944 for reasons he cannot now recall. Mosley was transferred off *Sailfish* at Mare Island on June 17, 1944.

R.D. Mosley currently resides in Whitehouse, Texas, with his wife. He has three children, including one son who served in the army.

WILLIAM MURRAY

William Herriot Murray, known to his friends as "Bill," was born on May 11, 1924, on Sandy Island, Georgetown County, South Carolina. When he was drafted into the navy on May 14, 1943, he was living in the Parkersville section of Pawleys Island, South Carolina. This community has remained his home to this day.

I attended boot camp in Norfolk, Virginia, and after boot camp I went to sub school in New London, Connecticut. As I recall, my stay in training was less than six weeks. Among the few things I most vividly recall about my training period in New London includes my going through the so-called battery of tests to determine psychological suitability to serve in submarines and qualifying in

Steward's Mate William "Bill" Murray in early 1943. He first served on *Plunger* in the fall of 1943 and made five war patrols in all. While being depth-charged was no fun, the most terrifying moment of his young navy career came at captain's mast in 1944, simply for following his captain's orders. (Photograph courtesy of W. Murray.)

the procedures of escaping from a sunken submarine. ... In the chamber of the escape training tank during the pressurization process ... at about the 11- or 13-pound pressure level, I started lightly bleeding through the nose. The operator of the chamber stopped the pressurization process and asked me if I wanted to continue. I told him I wanted to continue ... after all, there were about seven people in the chamber, and as the only Black person I was not going to be the one to abort that escape process. So, it continued, and just before the proscribed pressure level was reached, the bleeding ceased, the pain subsided.... In less than two weeks after ... I was out of sub school and on my way by rail to California. I boarded a troop ship, I believe at Vallejo, which took me to the submarine base at Pearl Harbor. By the end of July 1943, I had been assigned to my first submarine, the USS *Plunger SS-179* [Murray].

Records indicate that Murray went aboard *Plunger* on September 21, 1943. The lead steward on the boat at this time was Officer's Cook 3rd Class Otha Toler. Bill Murray's first two war patrols on *Plunger* were under Captain Raymond Bass, a man whom Murray holds in high esteem to this day. On his first patrol, *Plunger*'s ninth of the war, in November 1943, Murray and the crew did duty on one of the ten submarines deployed in support of Operation Galvanic, the effort to capture the Gilbert Islands. Murray's second patrol on *Plunger* was most eventful. In February 1944, Bass sank three ships, including one large Japanese cargo ship with a shot that has been termed "one of the best shots of the war (Blair, p. 587). Following this successful attack, *Plunger* was held down for hours and received a prolonged depth-charging. In May 1944, Murray's happiness aboard his boat ceased when Captain Edward Fahy took command.

> Lieutenant Commander Edward Fahy's assignment was not what I would call now a period of nostalgia.... It did not take long for the entire crew to realize

that we were not fortunate enough to have inherited another commanding officer of Commander Bass's caliber. In any case, while out on this patrol, we lost total use of one engine. A second engine was malfunctioning to the extent of rendering it most unreliable. The situation was sufficiently crucial to force us to seek emergency repairs at the nearest friendly port. So we limped into the port of Brisbane, Australia. While we were in the shipyard at Brisbane, an officer placed me on report for refusing to carry out his direct order.... I was subsequently court-martialed and found guilty as charged [*ibid.*].

Steward 1st Class William "Bill" Murray in the late 1940s. He made five war parols on *Plunger* during the war and, after the war, served on many boats, including *Sea Robin*. (Photograph courtesy of W. Murray.)

Bill Murray's account of his court-martial in September 1944 is detailed in full within these pages. During his two patrols under Captain Fahy, the last being in July 1944, *Plunger* had little success and sank no enemy ships. In speaking about his final two war patrols on *Plunger*, Murray recalls several incidents of interest.

> I found humor in watching ... a bigoted officer who was shot in the buttocks when our sub was caught on the surface during a pilot-down risqué and was strafed by a Japanese plane. This bigot had the nerve to ask me, "What do you think of me now?" My response was, "The evidence is clear." He asked, "What the hell do you mean by that?" I said, "You were running!" ... I also derived satisfaction out of seeing Lt. Commander [Fahy] canned for ramming the pier upon our return to Pearl Harbor after having court-martialed me at sea [*ibid.*].

By the end of 1944, the old *Plunger* was withdrawn from service, and Bill Murray rode her back home to the states and served on her through the early part of 1945. Though court-martialed and busted to a steward's mate 2nd class in September 1944, Murray was promoted back to steward's mate 1st class on January 1, 1945, by his new commanding officer.

In 1945 ... we brought the *Plunger* back to the states and decommissioned her in Portsmouth, New Hampshire.... When the war ended, I was serving aboard a boat in New London. We had completed a shakedown and were preparing to return to sea.... Later, I had the choice of mustering out of the navy or remaining in. I think I opted to leave the navy as soon as it was possible. In December of 1945, I was mustered out of the navy and returned home and went back to high school and started building a house on the $4,000 I had saved during the war. I ran out of money before the house was completed. The GI Bill school payment was not forthcoming, even though I had been in school for four months. The job market was not at all appealing at 45 cents per hour. So, in early May of 1946, I opted to return to the navy. Despite two court-martials for reasons of bigotry, I later rose to become the lead steward on an FBM boat [*ibid.*].

Bill Murray stayed in the Submarine Force and served on a variety of boats after the war, including *Sea Robin*, in the late 1940s and the missile boat *Robert E. Lee* in the early 1960s. After retiring from the navy on August 16, 1966, Bill Murray returned to Pawleys Island, South Carolina, where he now works as a real estate broker.

Edward Neely

Edward Neely was born on September 15, 1924, in Houston, Texas, and graduated from Phyllis Wheatley High School in 1941. He worked for a year and a half before he enlisted in the navy on January 15, 1943.

I went to boot training in Norfolk, Virginia, and then received orders to go to Portsmouth to put *Billfish* into commission in April 1943. I made one patrol on her, then went to *Bowfin* and made three patrols on her. Captain [Walter] Griffith was a good man. *Bowfin* was the best boat I served on because the officers knew what they were doing. One of my battle stations was to help reload torpedoes [Neely].

On Neely's one patrol on *Billfish*, conducted in August 1943, several ships were damaged, but no confirmed sinkings were made. This patrol was conducted in tandem with another boat making her first war patrol, *Bowfin*. Neely was transferred off *Billfish* in mid–October 1943 and went to a relief crew in Perth-Fremantle. It's a good thing he did, for *Billfish* took a severe pounding her next patrol and was very nearly lost. On February 28, 1944, Edward Neely went back to submarine duty, this time on *Bowfin*. He would make three patrols on that boat from his arrival, until he left her in December 1944. The first was under Captain Walter Griffith and the last two under Captain John Corbus. On his first war patrol on *Bowfin*, conducted by Griffith, excellent success was achieved when three ships were sunk. But, success did not come easy, and the boat was attacked during her patrol at almost every single turn. Neely and *Bowfin*, during the course of this patrol, were depth-charged, attacked by aircraft, and shot at by shore guns. No wonder that Neely has high praise for Griffith, the man who got them home safely after all that adventure.

> I made one last war patrol on *Hammerhead* late in the war, and when the war was over in 1945, I got out. I went to college at Texas Southern for two years, studying music. But, times were tight, and I reenlisted in 1947. I did twenty years and served on the submarines *Sealion* (II), *Redfin*, *Grenadier*, and *Becuna*. I retired as a commissaryman 1st class and then worked for Electric Boat [*ibid.*].

Neely came aboard *Hammerhead* in July 1945 and made her seventh and final war patrol, during which two ships were sunk under Captain Frank Smith. On August 1, 1945, just before the war ended, Neely was promoted to officer's cook 3rd class.

Edward Neely was married in Houston, Texas, in 1954 to Dorothy Ewing, a school teacher and guidance counselor. Currently residing in Silver Spring, Maryland, they have three children, including two daughters, Judith and Gwendolyn, and one son, Captain Edward Neely, who is in the army medical service and chief resident of neurology at Walter Reed Army Hospital in Washington, D.C.

KILLRAINE NEWTON

Killraine Newton was born in Bryn Mawr, Pennsylvania, but came from Virginia roots. His ancestors go back to the slave days in old Virginia. He graduated from A.T. Johnson High School in Westmoreland County, Virginia.

> I was the product of a broken home. My father told me I would have to be twice as good to succeed, but I already knew I was! The key influence on my life was my grandmother. She raised me, and she said I would go to school, or she'd kill me! I was 20 years old when I went into the navy. I was drafted kicking and screaming. I had been working at a CCC camp and also had a defense job as a supply clerk in the Yorktown Naval Mine Depot, Yorktown, Virginia. I went to boot at Bainbridge, Maryland, and went into subs at Vallejo, California, on *Sailfish* [Newton].

Newton, known as "Newt" to his friends, was drafted into the navy at Richmond, Virginia, on August 28, 1943, and after boot camp was sent to Mare Island, California. Here he was highly thought of, as he was a steward 3rd class by the time he went aboard *Sailfish*, coming off a modernization refit at Mare Island, on June 17, 1944. He soon made his first war patrol under Captain Robert Ward in July 1944.

> On *Sailfish* I relieved a steward named Mosley, and served with [Allen] Batts. My shipmates were a fine group of men, and Bob Ward was a fine commander. We became dear friends, and he later rose to be an admiral. Never had any problems with racism. I was very strong, and people didn't mess with me, and I was educated. I qualified throughout the boat, just like everyone else. My battle station position was to man the phones in the forward battery. After the torpedoes were fired, I counted off the seconds before they hit. Topside, I was a machine gunner. My on-board service was most dangerous [*ibid.*].

Killraine Newton made two war patrols on *Sailfish*, the last she would make before being withdrawn from combat and sent stateside as a training boat in early 1945. Newton is right about the danger. On his first war patrol, *Sailfish* was part of three-boat

Steward's Mate Allen Batts (row 2, third from left) and Steward 2nd Class Killraine Newton (next to Batts) on the conning tower of *Sailfish* in early 1945. (Photograph courtesy of Ray Bunt.)

wolf pack sent to the Luzon Strait. The boat attacked a convoy, sinking one cargo ship, and tried to attack a Japanese battleship group but was prevented from doing so by her escorts. On Newton's second war patrol, *Sailfish* performed lifeguard duty off Luzon. Newton was kept busy below decks when Ward and the crew rescued 12 downed aviators, going into a minefield to do so. *Sailfish* also saw surface action when she sank a Japanese patrol boat with her deck gun. The patrol ended when the boat's radio transmitter went dead and *Parche* had to escort her back to Saipan for repairs.

> After being sent stateside, I later went to the commissioning crew of *Sea Leopard*. While a steward after the war, I played on the sub force softball team as a catcher. I started out Dave Ball on his pitching career. He was only an umpire at first! He did throw hard, and my hand would hurt after we were done.
>
> Some of the boats I served on after the war were *Sea Leopard*, *Chopper*, *Spinax*, and *Pomodon*. I was on *Chopper* when she was in Shanghai a few years after the war.
>
> I became a chief steward in 1950 and was a leader in the steward's branch when I cross-rated in 1955. Admiral Ward was an assistant to the secretary of the navy, and I had the mutual respect of Admiral Grenfell. I applied for and was accepted for the electronics technician conversion program. After one

year of intense training, I cross-rated from chief steward to chief electronics Technician.

In 1959 I applied for and got warrant officer status and was out of submarines; they did not have Warrant Officers. I wasn't saddened by leaving sub duty but welcomed it as a way to improve my career. In 1962 I participated in a fleet-wide competition and was advanced from chief warrant officer to lieutenant junior grade. As director of the ECT school at Treasure Island, I hired brilliant men and former stewards as instructors. Among them were Ike Johnson and A.P. Royal, the smartest man I know. When I became director of the Electronic Warfare Development Department, it was Royal and I that developed the EWT rating and designed the navy's training program for the new rating [*ibid.*].

Once out of submarines, Newton served on the USS *Lookout* as her electronics officer and on the USS *Wright*. He retired in 1971 as a lieutenant commander, the highest rank ever achieved by a former steward, and later served as the director of the Housing Management Department for the city of Norfolk, Virginia. He was the first Black person to ever hold this position. Newton remained close friends with his first commander, Robert Ward, and the two became lifelong friends. When Ward passed away, Newton was with him, and afterward helped to arrange for his burial at Arlington National Cemetery. Killraine Newton's old shipmates on *Sailfish* hold him in high esteem to this day and wonder how much further he would have gone if he had had the same opportunities as they had. Newton is married to the former Georgia Hope of San Francisco, California, and they reside in Virginia Beach, Virginia. They have twin sons that joined the Naval Reserve and later became firefighters.

CLAUDE PALMER, JR.

Claude Palmer, Jr., was born on October 6, 1925, in Phenix City, Alabama. He joined the navy on December 8, 1943, and was inspired to volunteer for the Submarine Force after watching the movie "Destination Tokyo." Upon completion of boot camp, he was sent to New London, where he first served on the school boat *O-6* and later went to *Mackerel*, where he first qualified. On June 19, 1944, he went aboard *Besugo* at New London as part of her commissioning crew. Palmer made all five of the boat's war patrols from September 1944 to July 1945 and saw quite a bit of action. The first three patrols were conducted by Captain Thomas Wogan and resulted in the sinking of four enemy ships worth nearly 16,000 tons. The first patrol in September to October 1944 was most harrowing for Palmer. Several men were injured during battle surface action, and the boat also had to drive at flank speed to go the rescue of another boat, *Salmon*, which had been severely depth-charged and was badly damaged. Palmer's final two patrols were conducted by Captain Herman Miller and were equally exciting. On the final patrol of the war for Palmer and *Besugo* in June to July 1945, they sank two ships, one of which was the German submarine *U-183*. She had been flying a Japanese flag and was quickly sunk, with one officer surviving to tell the tale. Palmer and fellow steward Lewis Jackson were probably the only submarine stewards ever during the war to tend to a captured U-boat officer.

After the end of the war, Palmer headed back to the states and when he made it to San Diego, he met his future wife Viola Nicholas on his first day home. Palmer would continue in the Submarine Force and was based on the west coast. He would later change his rate to that of commissaryman and serve on *Blenny* during the Korean War. Palmer retired from the navy on February 23, 1965, and subsequently worked for the post office until his final retirement in 1983. Claude Palmer, now deceased, and his wife, Viola, had four children: Shana, Donna, Denise, and Kesha.

WALTER PATRICK

The exciting story of Walter Patrick's submarine career has been detailed in parts throughout this book already. His pre-navy life is in many ways typical of that of many future stewards that came from the south and is worth recounting here in some detail.

> I was born in the year 1924, sixth child in a family of eleven siblings. My mother and father were Joseph and Pinkie Jane Booker Patrick. I was born at Truxillo, in Amelia County, Virginia. I grew up on a real small two-acre farm, with garden spot and a small corn patch and a little wheat which was cut and threshed by hand.... We rented some land for farming, but after giving a fourth to the landowner, we had so little left. The children worked the little farm, while our father worked a neighboring white farmer's farm by the day for $1.00 a day, of which he had to take half of his pay in food, salt meat, dried beans, peas, and potatoes. He had $2.50 left out of his weekly pay.
>
> In the winter time I was kept home from school many days at the age of nine and helped my father cut logs, after walking over two miles to the woods. I was kept out of elementary school by my father until age seven, when school authorities threatened my father with court action.
>
> At the age of twelve I had read the first five books of the Bible. I learned to read early by my mother's teaching. My father became a wayward father after the death of my mother at my age of thirteen. He would desert us at times.... Once in school, I skipped second grade and kept a grade A grade throughout elementary school. I spent two years in the sixth grade with straight A's, all because of too many days absent. I finally graduated from the seventh grade a few days from my sixteenth birthday. I took entrance tests for high school, and passed with a high score. ... Because I did not have the funds for bus fare, no decent clothes to wear, I went to work in the timber business cutting logs and doing sawmill work and farm work. I went into the C.C.C., Civilian Conservation Corps, where I stayed for six months. My pay was $30 per month, of which I was given $5 and $25 was sent home for me, but my father wasted it all. After mother died, only three of us boys, Samuel, James, and I, remained with my father, while my sisters Florence and Gussie, and my baby brother John, were taken to New Jersey by my aunt. So, we had a hard way to go. So, I stayed in the C.C.C. six months and was discharged at my request. At seventeen-and-a-half years old I went to New Jersey until my induction in the navy.
>
> I was inducted in the navy on August 9, 1943, and went to boot camp at U.S.N.T.C., Bainbridge, Maryland. After four weeks of rigorous training, we broke boot and were given a nine-day leave. Most of our training period consisted of drilling, obstacle course, swimming, and boat rowing. When I left boot camp, I knew very little about the navy [Patrick].

The story of how Walter Patrick went to submarine duty, though he originally wanted to serve on surface ships, has already been told, as has his account of his submarine school training. He was subsequently assigned to the commissioning crew of *Bluegill*, which joined the fleet in November 1943 under the command of Captain Eric Barr, Jr.

> So, off to war I went. We left New London, Connecticut, on December 24, 1943. The first day out we hit a storm and stayed in high seas for days, of the which I was seasick for nine days. Finally we arrived in Key West, Florida, about the first week of January 1944. On my first liberty in Key West someone picked my pocket and stole my wallet. So, when I came back to the base gate, I was held at the base gate until someone came to identify me. Some time the last of January 1944 we left Key West on our way to the Pacific. After some liberty in Panama City and exercises in Panama Bay, we came to the Galapagos Islands on February 25, 1944, where we were initiated into Davy Jones's Locker.... From February 25, 1944, at the equator, we headed deep into the Pacific [*ibid.*].

Patrick's initiation rights while crossing the equator have also been previously told. *Bluegill* and her crew then proceeded to her home base at Brisbane, Australia. She departed for her first war patrol in April 1944, headed for Davao Gulf in the Phillipine Islands after a three-day stay in Milne Bay, New Guinea. Her first cruise would be memorable in more than one way for Walter Patrick.

> We were near the island of Sonsoral [the Palau group] when we sank our first ship, a Japanese light cruiser, *Yubari*. The first time I had heard real exploding depth-charges. The cruiser was refueling, so I was told. A Jap plane circling the area dropped light bombs or some other explosives to ward us off. Captain Barr ordered our sub into firing position, with commands to the forward torpedoman to ready the forward tubes, then ordered firing a spread of the six forward torpedo room tubes. The torpedoman replied "Torpedoes away and running." Numbers one and two missed the target and four made hits.
>
> The captain reversed the sub direction as a destroyer was bearing down on us very fast. The captain ordered firing from the stern tubes, and all four torpedoes missed the destroyer. ... We got a terrific pounding. Depth-charges were so close the vibrations would shake the boat, blew out [light] bulbs, cork was popping off the bulkhead. It was around 1000 [10:00 A.M.] when we started this attack and about 1300 [1 P.M.] when the battle ended. The destroyer would go somewhere, reload, and make continued runs on us.
>
> We surfaced that night [April 27, 1944] and went on the hunt again. The next ship we sank was a big cargo ship which was being escorted by two DE's [destroyer escorts]. We took quite a beating that time. The target did not sink but burned through that night. The captain let the men take a look through the periscope to see the burning ship. The next morning [May 1, 1944] we surfaced and finished sinking the target with the 5-inch deck gun. After firing 100 rounds the ship went down. Then we sank an oil tanker. By this time, we had almost exhausted our supplies, so we were sent to the Admiralty Islands to pick up supplies.... I had begun to wonder if I would ever walk on the soil again [*ibid.*].

Patrick did, indeed, reach solid ground again, when *Bluegill* returned to port at Brisbane. In addition to his baptism under fire, he had also undergone a traumatic series of events with the lead steward on the boat, a man named David Huntley, which has previously been recounted in detail. Despite his misgivings, Walter Patrick, called "Pat" by his shipmates, was aboard *Bluegill* when she departed on her second war patrol in July 1944. It would be Patrick's last patrol of the war.

> On this patrol we were sent to a new area in the vicinity of Halmahera Island [south of Davao Gulf]. Near our patrol area we spotted a Jap convoy which we chased all night. We sneaked in on them, and the tin cans [destroyers] picked us up and made repeated runs on us but did not drop any ash cans [depth-charges]. Finally, the convoy got ahead of us but left two small escorts trailing it. As we started to go past them, they turned and made a run on us and dropped three depth-charges directly over us. Light bulbs fell out of the overhead lamps; some water valves blew off. All were soon repaired. I was very nervous by now and tiptoed through the officer's compartment, which was my battle station while on battle station submerged. When I passed the chief's compartment, I looked in and saw the chief yeoman sitting on the floor, rocking from side to side vigorously, his arms wrapped around his knees. He was in a bad way, he had already bitten his fingernails till some of them bled. I heard that he was never mentally sound again.
>
> So, after that depth charge attack we stayed down about an hour, then we came up to periscope depth. The captain looked around and decided to surface. The Japs had some big ships in this convoy that the captain wanted to get. So, we surfaced and gave chase. We were going at flank speed when the diving alarm blasted twice. I heard the shouts over the sound system, "Clear the deck! Clear the deck! Dive! Dive!" By the time the lookouts managed to lock the watertight door, we were already into the dive.... I was in my bunk, which was in the forward torpedo room, when I leaped out and hit the deck, grabbed my sandals, had one sandal on and reaching for the other when there were two ear-splitting blasts astern, and the diving angle became even greater. All loose items were sliding toward the forward of the boat. I was holding to the side of shipmate Blackmyer's bunk where he also held on and reached for my hand, and I reached for his. We grasped hands and he said, "Goodbye Pat." I said goodbye to him and dry swallowed trying to rid myself of the lump in my throat. All the while we were sliding faster and faster, deeper and deeper. We could hear Lieutenant Beckman spitting out orders such as, "Blow bow ballast tanks," "Flood after tanks," "Elevate bow planes." When we were about 200 feet or more deep, the sub began to shake as though it would come apart. After this, the bow started to rise higher than the stern ... until finally it came on an even keel. My, my! What a time! If you could have heard the shouts, the crew sounded like spectators when their favorite home run hitter had hit a grand slam. I heard later that our Lieutenant Beckman had received the Bronze Lifesaving Medal for saving our lives.
>
> When we had leveled off, we began to survey our ship's damage. Most of the damage was in the rear of the sub, some water was shooting into the stern torpedo room, the propeller shaft was bent. The bombs did not make a direct hit on our sub, but hit the water 42 feet astern.... After this, we were ordered to go into Brisbane, Australia, for repairs. While repairs were being made, all hands were given fourteen days leave at the submarine rest camp at Coolangatta [*ibid.*].

Walter Patrick never made another war patrol on *Bluegill* due to incidents previously described. After being busted a grade for his actions to get off *Bluegill*, Patrick worked for a time at the Darwin Sub House, then went to the submarine base at Fremantle for several months before serving on the sub tender *Eurayle*. He then went to Pearl Harbor, Guam by way of Okinawa, and on to Sasebo, Japan, after the war was over. While in Japan, he worked on the refit of two captured Japanese submarines and ended the war as a steward 3rd class. While on *Eurayle*, he worked under Executive Officer John De Tar, a former submarine skipper, and was the acting chief steward in charge of 35 enlisted men. He now had to decide whether or not to make the navy his career.

> According to my commissary officers, the executive officer, Commander J.L. De Tar, I had handled my job well. When I got enough points to be discharged, they made me a great offer. If I shipped over to the regular navy for four years, I would be made full chief steward in six months and would be recommended for commissary officers school. But I had second thoughts. I had held the chief's position for seven months without any major problems.... Meals on time, big Thanksgiving and Christmas dinner with all the trimmings, all operating on the budget given me. I did it all on the steward 3rd class pay rate without a raise in salary. I could not trust them. Then again, I had my childhood sweetheart back in Virginia waiting for me, a sweet young lady by the name of Lillian Barley. So, I accepted my navy discharge and came home and changed that young lady's name to Mrs. Lillian Barley Patrick; so it is to this day [*ibid.*].

After returning to civilian life in 1946, Patrick and his wife married in 1947 and lived in New Jersey, where he worked for New Jersey Transit Bus Company for more than 27 years. However, religion was his true calling. Calling himself a "country boy at heart," he became licensed to preach in 1968 and was ordained in 1968. He first preached at St. Peters Church in Newark, New Jersey, for more than five years and subsequently was the pastor at Mt. Olive Baptist Church in East Orange, New Jersey. Walter Patrick furthered his education by getting his GED first and then attended college at the Northeastern Collegiate Bible Institute of Essex Fells, New Jersey, and later the Bowls Institute of Bible Studies in Elizabeth, New Jersey. Turning down a call from a large church in Morristown, New Jersey, he moved back to his native Virginia, pastoring for 16 years at the Beulah Baptist Church in Chesterfield, Virginia. After pastoring at the Bethiah Baptist Church in Amelia County for eleven years, he is now retired. However, he still preaches when called upon to do so.

He has three children: Walter Wayne, who followed in his father's footsteps, serving in the navy for two years and is now a minister; Sandra, a graduate of Howard University; and Linda-Marie. The pastoring that Walter Patrick began while aboard *Bluegill* in 1944 continues to this day. He is the chaplain of the local Tidewater Chapter of the World War II Submarine Veterans group and has been recognized by the local press as being one of 25 local men "Who Have Made a Difference in Today's Amelia County" (Salster).

In November 2003 Walter Patrick was able to relive his more memorable experiences from his time on *Bluegill*, perhaps also bringing to pass a long-desired bit of closure to his abruptly ended submarine career. With his wife Lillian and daughters

Linda-Marie and Sandra, Patrick made the 1,066 mile trip to Branson, Missouri, for a ship reunion. As Patrick relates,

> I had the opportunity to meet with 32 men with whom I had the privilege of sharing duty. During that meeting we were all just like brothers, with hearty hand shakes and many hugs. To see Captain E.L. Barr was the epitome of our three-day meeting. When we first met after more than 58 years, Captain Barr made this statement to me: "Walter, I've waited for this day to see you again." We then shared a big hug [*ibid.*].

ROSCOE PENNINGTON

While much of his career has already been discussed, following are more details on one of the best known of all Black submariners. Roscoe Cleveland Pennington was born on October 3, 1924, in Fort Worth, Texas, the son of Willie Pennington. He attended local schools in Fort Worth and subsequently joined the navy on January 15, 1943. After attending boot camp, he volunteered for submarine duty and was sent to Pearl Harbor as part of a relief crew. He soon went to his first submarine, *Seadragon*, being assigned to that boat from Submarine Division 21 on September 16, 1943. He made three patrols on this boat from September 1943 to May 1944, the first two under Captain Royal Rutter and the final patrol under Captain James Ashley. Following his service on *Seadragon*, Pennington left the boat on September 10, 1944, for relief duty with Submarine Division 44. This duty lasted for just over a month before he joined the crew of the newly commissioned Portsmouth-built boat *Spikefish*. He went aboard the boat on October 21, 1944, and made two war patrols under Captain Nicholas Nicholas. He made one final war patrol under Captain Robert Managhan in April to May 1945 before leaving the boat on June 30, 1945, for relief duty. On none of Pennington's six war patrols were any official sinkings achieved. At war's end, Pennington was doing flag duty in Submarine Division 282 before serving aboard *Sea Dog* from August 25 to September 19, 1945. By the end of World War II, Pennington was a steward's mate 1st class.

After the war, Pennington served on the diesel boats *Tilefish*, *Cusk*, *Chivo*, and *Ronquil* and made chief steward. His rate change to that of chief electrician's mate has already been detailed. While on *Chivo* in 1960, his boat entered San Francisco naval shipyard for an extended overhaul. His friend, former steward and now chief electronics technician, Anderson Royal recalls that

> It was during this time that he informed me of his fervent desire to change his rate to electrician. Consequently, I invited him over to stay with me, and we could study during this overhaul period. I could see lines of determination in his face! I regard this individual as one of the most unrelenting and dedicated individuals that I have ever known! He passed his electronics training course with flying colors! [Royal, Anderson].

As has also been discussed in detail, Pennington later went to nuclear power school and was subsequently lost on the nuclear attack boat *Thresher* on April 10, 1963. He left behind his wife, Doris, his son, Gregory, by a previous marriage, and countless friends. On April 10, 1974, 21 years after his death, Pennington was honored with the dedication of Pennington Hall, a training facility at the naval submarine school intended for advanced simulated training in ship-control casualties. The memory of Roscoe Pennington is still important to many Black submariners even today. While interviewing veterans for this book, the author encountered many men who were concerned that the career of Roscoe Pennington be recorded.

WILLIAM PERRY

William Sidney Perry was born on June 8, 1920, in Prospect, Virginia. He was living in south Philadelphia when he enlisted into the navy on July 19, 1939. His father, Don, had told him this might be a good way to see the world, so Perry gave it a try. He went to boot camp at Norfolk, Virginia, and soon volunteered for submarine duty. He joined the crew of *Narwhal*, one of the big V-boats, on December 13, 1939, and in mid–1940 rode her to Pearl Harbor. He crossed the line on July 10, 1940, thereby qualifying as a "shellback," and on March 1, 1941, was fully qualified as a submariner.

Perry left *Narwhal* on September 2, 1941, and went to ashore to do relief and flag duty. In December 1941 he was a steward for Admiral Husband Kimmel, the Commander in Chief of the Pacific Fleet, and it was Perry who awoke Kimmel on the fateful morning of December 7, 1941. Perry quickly woke the admiral and told him there was trouble, and later recalled that "When I woke up, Pearl Harbor was on fire, and I was handed a machine gun" (Perry).

After that historic day, William Perry continued doing relief crew and flag duty, serving in Submarine Division 62 until May 2, 1942. After a short stint of relief and further flag duty on *Gudgeon* and *Narwhal*, he was assigned to the newly commissioned Mare Island boat *Sunfish* on August 11, 1942. Perry would make five war patrols on this boat, all under Captain Richard Peterson. The first patrol commenced in November 1942, and his last patrol was in October to November 1943. During Perry's time on board, the boat sank three ships worth over 8,000 tons. The patrols of this boat were not always successful, but her fourth patrol was the most harrowing. One ship that was torpedoed blew up with such force that it jarred the boat violently. After another attack, *Sunfish* received such a violent depth-charge attack that her skipper thought that it would "rip off the conning tower" (Blair, p. 456). During his time on submarines during the war, Perry found Peterson to be a "nice" skipper, and was always treated well by his crew (Perry). However, while his time as a submariner was memorable, he will always remember with clarity that morning of December 7, 1941, when he had to wake up Admiral Kimmel.

Following his time on *Sunfish*, Perry left on December 23, 1943, to resume his flag duties. By the time he was off the boat, he was an officer's cook 3rd class. On August 3, 1944, Perry went back to the states and was stationed out of New London. From September 28, 1944, to the end of the war, he served on the training boat *R-7* and ended the war as an officer's cook 1st class.

On February 24, 1945, Perry would marry Ethel June Brown of Groton. Not a bad catch for William Perry, as his wife had been an honors nursing student at

Lincoln Hospital in New York City from 1942 to 1945 and was now a registered nurse. When she later worked at Lawrence Hospital in New London, Connecticut, she was the first Black nurse there in over thirty years and later became head nurse. Of course, Perry himself was a pretty good catch and, as his wife now states, "He's quite the ace in my book" (Perry).

Later that year, 1945, William Perry was sent to the Cramp Shipbuilding Yard in Philadelphia and went aboard the mechanically troubled boat *Sablefish*. He would remain on her through all of 1946 and most of 1947. Following a period of flag duty, Perry was suddenly transferred out of the Submarine Force to Washington, D.C., in 1950. This move, a racially motivated one, has already been discussed at length. Perry subsequently worked as a policeman for the Armed Services Police Detachment at the naval gun factory there until he wrote a letter asking that he be reassigned to submarine duty. He eventually got what he wanted. Perry subsequently served in Squadron 12 at Key West in 1953 and also served as a steward instructor for a time. He retired from the navy on November 16, 1959, as a chief steward. He would later work at General Dynamics in Groton, Connecticut, as a security guard, and also worked as a carpenter and a cook.

William Perry and his wife June have two daughters, Jacquelyne and Rhonda, and currently reside in Groton, Connecticut. Due to a stroke that William Perry suffered in 1996, he was unable to be directly interviewed. However, June Perry was most helpful in gathering information relative to her husband's career and helping him to answer a questionnaire supplied by the author. William Perry subsequently passed away in 2004.

Chief Steward William Sydney Perry. The Virginia native first qualified for submarine duty on *Narwhal* in 1939 and made war patrols on *Sunfish* during World War II. (Photography courtesy of J. Perry.)

JOHN PHILLIPS

Little is known about John Joseph Phillips except what is found in crew records and, more importantly, what his wartime skipper, Captain Pete Galantin, has written about him. Phillips went into the navy at Brooklyn, New York, on August 25, 1943. After completing boot camp, probably at Bainbridge, nothing is known of his first year in service until he joined the crew of *Halibut* on August 31, 1944. He would come aboard as a steward's mate 1st class, serving under Captain Galantin for one war patrol. However, this patrol was probably the most harrowing event ever in the young Phillip's life. The skipper of *Halibut* describes Phillips as a "tall, good looking, young steward's mate from New York's Harlem" (Galantin, p. 252) and recounts how he was puzzled by the loss of a day when the boat and her crew crossed the International Date Line on October 12, 1944. He further describes Phillips as being "a neophyte sailor ... slight ... and articulate" (*ibid.*, p. 233). Having been aboard for just one patrol, John Phillips certainly must have impressed his wartime skipper to have been remembered by him more than forty years later.

During *Halibut*'s tenth war patrol in late 1944, the boat attacked a convoy near Formosa on November 14 and paid severely for it. *Halibut* was attacked by enemy aircraft and wracked by explosions that nearly wrecked her conning tower. During this time, Phillips was stationed in the forward battery, where chlorine gas formed from incoming water coming in contact with the boat's batteries. Despite absorbing what one historian calls "one of the most devastating depth-charge attacks of the war" (Blair, p. 771), *Halibut*'s crew saved their boat and limped safely back to port. *Halibut* was so badly damaged that she was withdrawn from combat duty. John Phillips rode her back to the states at Mare Island, leaving the boat on February 16, 1945.

PAUL RAGLAND

Paul Francis Ragland was born on April 10, 1922, at Baltimore, Maryland, the son of Hezekiah and Viola Ragland. He had two sisters, Janice and Gloria, and two brothers, Herbert and Morris. Morris and Gloria Ragland were twins. He met his future wife, Letha, in Baltimore in 1939. Ragland volunteered for the navy on December 15, 1942. His brother Herbert was in the army, so Paul knew from him that the navy might be a better place to serve. Ragland went to boot camp at Norfolk, Virginia, and there volunteered for submarine duty. By April 1943 he was at the submarine base in Pearl Harbor, and on September 29, 1943, he went aboard *Barb* under Captain John Waterman as a steward's mate 1st class. Ragland would subsequently make seven war patrols on *Barb* through July 1945 and was a witness to some of the most outstanding submarine action of the entire war.

Ragland's first two patrols were conducted under Captain Waterman through April 1944 and resulted in the sinking of one enemy ship. Not much to brag about. However, the next five patrols were conducted under Captain Eugene Fluckey, and they made history. In patrols from May 1944 to July 1945, Fluckey, Ragland, and the crew of *Barb* sank 16 ships worth over 94,000 tons. This score made *Barb* the third highest scoring submarine when it came to tonnage sunk in the war. No captain sank more tonnage than Fluckey did on his patrols, and only three captains sank more ships overall. Ragland was there to witness it all and, more importantly, always made it back to base safely. While the exploits of *Barb* cannot be described here in detail, Fluckey was one of the few captains who had the combination of luck and skill to sink a Japanese aircraft carrier. *Barb* and her crew sank the escort carrier *Unyo*, 20,000 tons, in August 1944. Though Fluckey was daring, he was not foolhardy, and his crew was fond of him. Paul Ragland was no exception, "He loved Fluckey" (Ragland).

Following these wildly successful patrols, Ragland left *Barb* in July 1945 and went to *Moray*. He stayed on this boat until January 1946, when he served subsequently on *Tigrone*, and then went to shore duty at Mare Island from January to July 1946. Ragland subsequently did duty on the tenders *Sperry* and *Nereus* and then on *Tusk* before going aboard *Guavina* in September 1946. He would serve on her for four years, one fellow steward being Donald Wilson, before going to *Cavalla* in September 1951. This would be his last boat, as in September 1955 he went to shore duty, first in COMSUBRON 14, and then to COMSUBLANT. He retired from the navy on December 15, 1964, as a steward 1st class.

Steward's Mate Paul Francis Ragland (right) and his brother, army veteran Herbert Ragland. Paul Ragland, a native of Baltimore, served in the Submarine Force during the war, making patrols on the hard-hitting *Barb* under Captain Eugene Fluckey. (Photograph courtesy of L. Ragland.)

Paul Ragland and his wife had seven children: Paulette, Brenda, Paul, Jr., Cheryl, Francine, Janet, and Tonya. Paul Ragland died on March 14, 1973, at the young age of 50. His wife, Letha, now resides in New London, Connecticut.

CHARLES RICHARDSON

Charles McKinley Richardson was born on September 16, 1920, in Huntington, West Virginia. He enlisted in the navy at Richmond, Virginia, on March 15, 1940, and went to boot camp at Norfolk, Virginia. He soon volunteered for submarine duty and on July 8, 1940, was sent to New London, where he served aboard the school boat *R-14* and became a qualified submariner. From 1941 to early 1942 Richardson's service is unknown, but on May 2, 1942, he joined the commissioning crew of *Kingfish* at Portsmouth, New Hampshire. He subsequently rode her to the war zone and would make four patrols under Captain Vernon Lowrance. The first of these commenced in September 1942 and the last ended in August 1943 at Fremantle, Australia. All these patrols began at Pearl Harbor, and all but the last ended there. During his time on *Kingfish*, Richardson rose to officer's cook 3rd class and participated in the sinking of five enemy ships worth nearly 24,000 tons. Richardson and Captain Lowrance apparently got along quite well.

After departing *Kingfish* in September 1943, Richardson did relief duty on the tender *Pelias* and flag duty from *Puffer* before going back to sea on *Bluefish*. He was assigned to this boat under Captain George Porter on December 10, 1943, in time for her third war patrol. By this time, he was an officer's cook 2nd class. From this time until he left the boat on July 12, 1944, Richardson made three war patrols on *Bluefish*, the first under Porter and the final two under Captain Charles Henderson. During this time, five ships, mostly oil tankers, were sunk for over 26,000 tons. Promoted to officer's cook 1st class on January 1, 1944, Richardson left the boat in July for duty at Submarine Division 162. He would subsequently serve in a relief crew on the tender *Orion* until going aboard *Nautilus* on October 17, 1944.

Now, Richardson was in for a whole new experience. Instead of making the standard war patrols, he would be involved in a multitude of special missions that were the norm for the big V-boats like *Nautilus* and *Narwhal*. On his first patrol in October 1944, the boat was commanded by Captain George Sharp and had two missions. The first was to land men and 20 tons of cargo on the island of Luzon, in the Phillipines. This was done with success on October 23–27. Four days later, Richardson and the crew were sent on an even more dangerous mission. Their job was to destroy the American submarine *Darter*. She had stranded on Bombay Shoals, and her crew was rescued, but the boat was still stranded and intact. *Nautilus* and the crew fired 88 rounds from their 6-inch deck gun on the wreck, scoring 55 hits, but it was all for naught. Though a wreck, *Darter* would remain where she was for some years even after the war was over. On his second mission, this time under Captain Willard Michael, the mission was to land 90 tons of supplies on the island of Mindanao. This was done over three days, January 20–23, 1945. When Charles Richardson left *Nautilus* on February 2, 1945, he had nine war patrols to his credit.

Richardson stayed in Australia for a time, where he met his future wife, Moyna, and would later bring her home as a war bride. Before leaving Australia, Richardson, as part of Task Force 71-6, helped to close the submarine bases at Perth and Brisbane.

With the war over, Richardson stayed in the navy, changing his rate to that of commissaryman. He subsequently served on the diesel boats *Tile fish* (out of Pearl Harbor 1945–1950), *Bumper*, *Tusk*, *Clamagore* (at Key West), and *Harder*; performed shore duty at the naval communications station in San Juan, Puerto Rico, from April 1956 to April 1958; and served on the destroyers *Power* and *Hawkins* (1958–1959) before returning to New London for duty. After two years of shore duty from 1959 to 1961, Richardson went to the FBM boat *Theodore Roosevelt* in July 1961 as part of her Blue crew. A year later, in November 1962, Richardson went back to diesels, joining the crew of *Entemedor* for three months until his retirement from the navy on February 20, 1963.

Charles and Moyna Richardson had five children, sons Kurt and Londe, and daughters Perditha, Dorothy, and Kara. Charles Richardson worked for a time as a security guard at the Electric Boat Division of General Dynamics. He attempted to join the Groton, Connecticut, Volunteer Fire Department but was denied probably because of his race. He also attempted to join the local United States Submarine Veterans chapter along with several other friends and was similarly denied membership due to his race. Likely distraught over these incidents, Charles Richardson took his own life on October 1, 1968, at the age of forty-eight.

ANDERSON ROYAL

Anderson Peter Royal was born in Slick, Oklahoma, near Tulsa, on June 8, 1922. He would join the navy, on the advice of his father, in 1940, thus beginning a military career that would last, in various forms, for nearly forty years. His is an incredible story.

> My father, Will Royal, was a runaway slave from West Virginia at the age of 12. He was told to run away by his father, a slave who worked on a plantation and didn't want his son to be "nothing but another cotton picker." His mother cried hard, but Will, with five buffalo nickels given to him, was told to hop a train to Chicago and follow the sign of the Indian Chief to Oklahoma Territory. In Chicago, Will was offered a job as a dishwasher by a white man and was given some food. Remembering what his father had told him about trusting white folk, when the man turned his back, Will ran off and found the train with the sign of the Indian head, the same as on the nickels given to him, and took it south to Arkansas. All alone, he was befriended and taken in by a family and later moved to Oklahoma Territory.
>
> In World War I he went overseas, worked in the stables caring for army horses. Once he was back home, he got jobs working in the Oklahoma oil fields and construction. Will—boy, could he climb—was often sent to the top to cap the wells of the wooden derricks in the swirling Oklahoma winds. My mother, Curmilla, was part Native American. She loved sports and could outrun anyone on the block. She was tough and could box, too. I myself played baseball, football, and boxed. But my mother also believed in education. While she herself had only a fourth grade education, she was smart. On day she said to me "Son, you may have three times the education I have, but I have something you don't ... I can make a living!"

> Our family lived in Tulsa during the 1921 race riots. My father never talked about it, but my mother always blamed the Blacks for bringing slavery to Oklahoma. My father would come back by teasing her about how the Indians foolishly made war on the white soldiers, using a bow and arrow against guns. Oh boy, this made my mother mad! I saw how hard my parents had to work, but education was important in our family. I didn't go to school until age six, but my mother and sisters pushed me. I could write my name and say the ABCs before I was four. I went to a Catholic school through ninth grade, then finished high school in the public schools.
>
> As a kid, we were forced to save money, it being the Depression. Both me and my younger brother, John, had paper routes, and I even bought a bicycle on credit. In Tulsa, I was a shoe shine boy on Saturdays and worked for a professor at Langston University. I didn't attend college there, and Negroes couldn't go to Tulsa. When I was out of school, there were no jobs to be had. My dad, a World War vet, advised me to go in the navy, not the army [Royal].

On July 2, 1940, having just turned 18, Anderson Royal enlisted in the navy from Dallas, Texas. He went to boot camp, Class 15, at Norfolk, Virginia, and in early 1941 was sent to the destroyer base at San Diego, California. Here, he joined the crew of *McFarland*, an old four-stack destroyer originally built in 1920 that was now being recommissioned. He rode her to Pearl Harbor for duty, battling sea sickness along the way. Serving with him was his new friend, Carl Kimmons, another future submariner.

> I was on *McFarland* from 1941 to 1942. We were in the Marshall and Gilbert Islands, at Coral Sea, and the Battle of Midway. The educational officer on board allowed me to read all their books on board, but I had to do it clandestinely. I loved those books. I really wanted to be a signalman and spent a lot of time on the bridge, just watching. Signal flags are an art to master. One time, I confirmed the dates of a golf tournament for the captain by signal with another destroyer. I thought he'd be angry, but he was happy! He said, "You got it down, man!" I also did lookout duty, and took my turn at the helm. I was a sailor!
>
> When Pearl Harbor was attacked, we were out to sea, ten miles off LaHaina Roads doing lifeguard duty for bombers coming to Hawaii. After the attack, we couldn't come back to Pearl until the top line ships were back. Kimmons spent most of his time in the ship's office. He loved to help with typing and read all the BUPERS manuals. He was the one that found out about enlisted Negro personnel being needed for submarines. But, our ship was undermanned, and they didn't want us to go. The BUPERS notice should have been posted on the bulletin board but was not. They probably just said, "Tell 'em no candidates for *McFarland*." Both Kimmons and I were interested in sub duty, but only one of us could go, and he went first. Later, I went to the *Silversides* [*ibid.*].

It was while on destroyer duty that Anderson Royal, known as either "Andy" or "AP" to his friends, also gained the nickname "De Lick." In his wartime book entitled *Silversides*, author Robert Trumbull tells the story of how Royal got his moniker:

> He got the name in the Marshalls. During that raid he was on deck watching the bombardment of a Japanese installation on an atoll. Royal counted eleven Japanese on the beach, but after the destroyer fired, he could only see two, and

they were running. Royal was jumping up and down … "Dat's de lick!" he yelled. "Dat's de lick!" Somehow this story reached the *Silversides*, and Royal became "De Lick" [Trumbull, p. 96].

Anderson Royal finally went to submarine duty in mid–1942, joining the crew of the new boat *Silversides* for her second war patrol in July under Captain Creed Burlingame and Executive Officer Roy Davenport.

> I liked the extra pay for submarine duty and kept thinking about my mom and dad, how they could use it. My parents couldn't believe it and were afraid to cash the check!
>
> Captain Burlingame was from Kentucky. He was a good man, and a good sailor. He knew what he was doing, and we got along very well. Davenport was good, but he was more a tactical guy, and very religious. He would give me chocolate bars for cleaning his room. I made all four of my patrols with Captain Burlingame, and all but one with Mr. Davenport. I qualified throughout the boat, the whole boat. I had to know what all those valves and instruments were for because you never knew what might happen. I was also strong and did duty as a helmsman for short stretches. I did a lot of signaling, too, especially when going out, and we had to request permission to leave port [Royal].

Steward 2nd Class Anderson Peter Royal on *Carbonero* in 1949 at San Diego. Serving with fellow wartime stewards Isaac Johnson and Otha Toler, Royal and the crew of *Carbonero* were involved with the navy's early submarine missile program. (Photograph courtesy of C. Rush.)

Wartime author Robert Trumbull recorded that Royal, being a destroyer sailor, didn't want to qualify for his dolphins at first, which angered some crewmen. This seems out of character for Royal and is something he doesn't recall. However, Royal soon would qualify aboard *Silversides* to the fullest. As Trumbull relates, "Royal wanted to know what would happen if such-and-such valves *didn't* work.... There came a proud day eventually when "De Lick" qualified on the *Silversides* from bow to stern, and Davenport commended him over the ship's announcer system" (Trumbull, pp. 96–7).

> I recall being depth-charged many times. That's not something you easily forget. On a destroyer, we used to drop them; now I was on the other end. One patrol we had lots going on. We had a man who had to have an appendectomy and had to be operated on by the pharmacist's mate. Me and the other mess attendant had to clean the room before they operated. That same patrol we fired a bunch of torpedoes at a ship, but one was stuck in the tubes, hanging half in and half out. Now that was a tricky situation. Here we were in enemy waters, with depth-charges going off ... not too close to hurt us, but close enough for us to hear, and we got this problem torpedo. Well, the captain formed a bucket brigade, and we trimmed the boat by taking water from the bilges forward aft. Then the forward torpedo room was secured with just the men needed to do the job; I wasn't one of them, and we fired the torpedo again. We didn't know what would happen, but we got rid of it without it blowing us up! [Royal].

Royal made four patrols on *Silversides* from July 1942 to June 1943. During this time, the boat and her crew sank an officially credited seven ships for over 43,000 tons. The most memorable of these runs was Royal's third, which began in December 1942. Not only did a man have to have an emergency appendectomy (he survived), but there was also the torpedo problem that Royal mentions. In addition, the boat and her crew were nearly lost, not once, but twice. The first time occurred when they attacked what was thought to be a Japanese submarine (it turned out to be a destroyer), and one of their torpedoes prematurely exploded close on, blowing the stern of the boat out of the water. The boat was then held down by the destroyer and given a working over. When the boat tried to surface, on Christmas Eve day 1942, aircraft patrolling overhead pounced on her and dropped three bombs. Her bow planes jammed, *Silversides* headed for the bottom, but her crew was able to recover quickly, and the situation was eventually brought under control. It had been a close call.

Anderson Royal was transferred off *Silversides* after four patrols in late June or early July 1943 and was eventually sent stateside to new construction. He joined the commissioning crew of *Dragonet* at the Cramp Shipyard in Philadelphia under Captain Jack Lewis. Like most Cramp-built submarines, *Dragonet* was plagued with numerous mechanical problems and took so long to get to sea that her skipper dubbed her "the Reluctant *Dragonet*" (Blair, p. 806). It probably gave little inspiration to the crew that the first Cramp boat to put to sea, *Escolar*, was sunk on her first patrol with all hands lost. *Dragonet* would be the second Cramp-built boat to make a patrol, beginning in December 1944 and lasting 49 days. Her luck would be quite a bit better than that of *Escolar*, but it would still be a close call.

> Captain Jack Lewis was a fine officer. My fellow steward was [Frank] Patrick. He was a good guy, a good dancer, from Kentucky. That first patrol was something. We got along the Japanese coast, surfaced at night, and dove the next morning. We hit an uncharted coral reef and put a hole in the fore torpedo

room. The chief closed off the bulkheads. It was a high-pressure situation. We surfaced early at night and assessed the damage, but it was too bad, and we couldn't dive. We headed back to Pearl on the surface through 5,186 miles of water. We ran at flank speed during the night and, lucky for us, made no contact with the enemy, or any friendly ships. We were very lucky. We made it back to Midway; they put a plate on the damaged area, and we returned to Mare Island. I lost all my things in the fore torpedo room, which was totally flooded, during that patrol, and spent a lot of anxious moments on lookout duty. On our next patrol, I was on the lookout crew and told by Captain Lewis that I was the best lookout man. We did some screening and lifeguarding duties on my last two patrols. When the war ended, I was a steward 1st class and went back to Mare Island to decommission *Dragonet*.

Overall, I never had any problems, and was always treated well. I had a lot of people that helped me during my career. Too, I was realistic minded about the race question that confronted the navy during the war. I knew winning the war was the number one objective ... the other question would be dealt with later [Royal].

Royal made three war patrols on *Dragonet*, the first two under Captain Lewis, from December 1944 to May 1945, and a third under Captain Gerald Hinman in July to August 1945. Though the boat achieved no sinkings during her patrols, she will always be remembered for the outstanding seamanship displayed by her captain and crew to save the damaged boat and bring her home safely.

With the war at an end, Anderson Royal went home and married his sweetheart, Merion. Together, they would have eight children. Royal did shore duty from 1945 to 1948 at Mare Island. In 1948 he went back to submarine duty, joining the crew of *Carbonero*, a fleet boat now being used to test an experimental missile launching system. Aboard were three other stewards: wartime veterans Otha Toler and Isaac Johnson and newcomer Paul Jordan. However, the boat had too many stewards, so Royal, not wanting to displace others who were aboard before him, put in for a transfer to shore duty. The story of how this wartime steward, a veteran of seven war patrols, changed his rate is an interesting one.

> *Carbonero* had four stewards but was only supposed to have two. I put in for a school but was later order to recommission another sub. These were orders that I was told cannot be changed. A few days later, I was ordered to NTC [Naval Training Center] San Diego, so I called Captain Burlingame, who had a friend in BUPERS, to settle the dispute. I was sweating things out, but the captain resolved it, and I was transferred back to *Carbonero*. They must have been thinking "Where do we put this colored boy?" Well, I qualified in every compartment on one patrol, and I made chief on that boat. You didn't have to be a hotshot to succeed, just study. On *Carbonero*, I had an electronics technician who helped me out, and I also took a correspondence course in 1949 on electronics repair. With a wife and four kids I had to be able to fix radios and TVs to earn extra money.
>
> In 1951 I went to the NTC San Diego to become an instructor at the steward school there. While I was an instructor, I continued to do TV repairs on the side and even took home LCDR Jennings' TV to fix. He was the commander of the steward school and a man at the end of his rope with his TV. I fixed it for

> him. In 1952, while I was an instructor, I was allowed to sit in on FTC [Fire Control Technician] "A" school classes. Now, I was going to school every day for 16 weeks and teaching. I graduated, unofficially, as it was all under the table, with an 83.6 grade in the middle of the class. However, I was happy with my career.
>
> In 1953 I was asked if I would apply for the ET conversion school. My Captain and XO said, "I bet he can do it," so I applied, but the personnel office said no. BUPERS stated emphatically that "applicants with more than ten years of naval service will not be admitted." At the time of my submission, I had 13 years of naval service. In all honesty, I can understand the justification of the personnel officer's adamant position. And moreover, upon entering the program in the fall of 1954, I had more than 14 years of naval service. The CO and XO of NTC, and Captain Burlingame of COMSUBPAC staff faced a seemingly impossible task! He was elated to hear about my schooling and had his friend in BUPERS help get things done. In late 1953 he called me at home to tell me I got the ET school. I tell you, I was mystified. I couldn't believe it. I was told to keep it under my hat until the orders officially came down, which was six months later. I couldn't tell anyone, but I wanted to shake those orders right in the face of the personnel officer. I tell you this though, those men, my commander, the XO, Captain Burlingame, they took more interest in me going to school than I did myself. I left NTC in July 1954 to go to ET conversion school. I was the only African American in the class, but had no color problems [*ibid.*].

Anderson Royal, after much hard work in balancing family life and a grueling course schedule, graduated from ET conversion school on September 2, 1955. He was just the second steward ever to convert to the ET rating at Treasure Island (the first was friend and former shipmate Ike Johnson), and the first ever chief steward to go through the conversion process there. With the help not only of his wife but of fellow classmates who were white, Royal graduated third in his class. Upon graduation, Royal took a course in radar at Long Beach, California, and was subsequently assigned to the repair ship *Hooper Island*, and, in late 1955, flew to Japan to join his ship. He would not serve in submarines again. His last shipboard stay was a short one.

> We had a good group on that ship, and I got along well. They said, "We finally got someone who has pride in our quarterdeck." The ET techs developed a habit of being cleancut and well-dressed and were very proud. I was the repair officer in charge of the IC, ET, and FT sections and oversaw all their chiefs. We did repair work on LSTs and destroyer escorts. However, in March or April 1956, I received an urgent letter from BUPERS asking for volunteers for instructors for the school at Treasure Island, so I put in for that duty. The CO wouldn't let me go. He said, "Wait a minute, you just got here, you haven't finished your sea duty yet." He didn't look at me as a Negro anymore. Well, I stayed on that ship until we came back to the states at Long Beach. Then I went to naval command school at San Diego for instructor training for four weeks. At this time, I was offered the warrant officer program but declined.
>
> I then reported to Treasure Island in September 1956 as an instructor at the ET School. When I got there, I was questioned upon my arrival, and they

all said "You just left here." Well, now we had a little social crisis. Now we got this one Black here, and many of the white instructors car-pooled to work together everyday. But, it all worked out fine. I taught shipboard communication and radar systems and also SS [submarine] radar. I loved radar! I did this duty, teaching chiefs and first class men, until the end of my career with the navy. I never did think about going aboard the nuclear submarines. It wasn't that I thought I couldn't make it in nuclear power school, no, but I just loved to teach. That was what I wanted to do. I retired on July 16, 1960. The navy wanted me to stay and offered guaranteed shore duty, but I refused. It was time for me to help my wife Merion raise our eight children [*ibid.*].

Following his retirement, Anderson Royal led a very active second life. He worked for the defense contractor Raytheon for a time doing shipboard work. Now 38 years old, he was known affectionately by his coworkers as either "Daddy" Royal or "Chief" Royal. However, education was always on his mind, in one form or another, and he always wanted not only to better himself but also help others. From 1960 to 1962 he earned an associate's degree in science from San Francisco City College while still working off and on for Raytheon. He subsequently attended San Francisco State's Teacher College and graduated in 1964 with a degree in industrial and vocational education. He was an honors student, and his children teased him by saying that "Daddy is older than the teachers!" He then returned to working for the navy, but this time in a civilian capacity.

In the summer of 1964 I was doing work for Raytheon at the San Francisco naval shipyard on radar systems when a supervisor there noticed that I liked teaching people and encouraged me to put in for their apprentice training program. I became an instructor at the apprentice training school there, and several months later became the chief of instructors for that program. I had the last say on students in the program. My policy was to turn around — not turn down — students that needed help.

In 1967 I went to work for Commander [Killraine] Newton, who was in charge of the navy's Electronics Warfare Development Department at Treasure Island. He wanted me as an education specialist to develop instructor training guides and coursework for a new rating. Now, there were no minorities in the civilian area at this time working for the navy, but Newton, he stuck up for me, saying that "Royal is ably qualified." Now, the way the navy operated, there was the rating of radarman, who operated the system, and electronics technician [ET], who maintained the radar equipment and many other electronics on board a ship.

Our job was to start a class to teach radar men to maintain their own equipment, and BUPERS was asked to establish a new rating, called Electronic Warfare Technician [EWT]. Now radar operators were invaluable, and there weren't enough of them in the navy then, so this opened the door for the new rating. They could then maintain their own equipment, since the regular ET, already overwhelmed with repairs, did not know how to operate the radar he was repairing. Newton wrote up the justification for the new rating and got the necessary funds for the project. We wrote up the curriculum for BUPERS. We worked 7:00 A.M. to 10:00 P.M. every day just trying to get a pilot class and

> justification for the new rating. When we went to Washington, D.C., to make our presentation, we knew we were walking into a minefield, but we got it. I chose the rating badge myself. The pilot class ran in 1971–1972 for 48 weeks. I taught it and made the test items and validated the program as we went along. I was nailed to that teaching platform like Jesus to the cross, day in and day out. But, we had very positive feedback. Newton made it happen. He wanted EWTs to be as sharp as any ET in the navy, wanted them [the navy] to know we had arrived [*ibid.*].

Royal's friend and fellow submariner Killraine Newton retired from the navy in 1971, and in 1974 the Electronics Warfare Department moved from Treasure Island to Pensacola, Florida. Royal went there too, now serving a dual role in a civilian capacity as command education advisor and as command equal employment opportunity advisor at the naval technical training center, Corry Station. Once again, Anderson Royal was in a position to do the two things he loved most — teach and help people. Of all his military service, both as a sailor and as a civilian, this duty was the most satisfying of his career.

> Working for the navy, my job was to make sure that fair employment practices were in place for *all* civilians working on the base, not just Blacks, but women as well. We started an upward mobility program and a summer hire program. Previously these were all for white individuals, but I visited Negro churches and other areas to get people for the program. Some of the places I saw in Pensacola, the poverty, I didn't know we had places like that! It all boiled down to this: When you see someone trying to do their best, you don't look at color anymore. You don't do that [*ibid.*].

Royal stayed for one year in Pensacola before moving back home to California. During his time in Florida, he accomplished much and was held in high regard by both his colleagues at Corry Station and those in the educational field at large. In June 1975, "As a noted specialist in occupational education" (Southern Association of Colleges and Schools, "Letter"), he was invited by the Southern Association of Colleges and Schools to join a team that was slated to visit the army infantry school at Fort Benning, Georgia, for evaluation purposes. When Royal left for California in October 1975, it was said of him that "NTTC Corry Station will be losing a valuable asset today.... Mr. Royal has accomplished a great deal during his year stay" (Corry Log, 10/31/1975, p. 8).

Anderson Peter Royal returned to California in late 1975 and went back to Treasure Island as the director of the academic department and also continued his service as an EEO advisor. He finally retired in 1979. Now retired and living in Hattiesburg, Mississippi, Royal spends his time visiting family and his many submarine friends. He is an enthusiastic attendee of the yearly mess attendant reunions and enjoys catching up with his old submarine friends whenever he can. His former boss and longtime friend, Lieutenant Commander Killraine Newton calls Royal "The most brilliant person I know" (Newton), and when his friends speak of him, the term "great guy" comes up frequently. Though his earlier career leaves no doubt that he was as fine a submariner as there ever was, he will always be known for his kindness and compassion and for his extraordinary ability to pass his knowledge on to others.

ALBERT ROZAR

Albert Rozar was born in 1919 and raised in Dublin, Georgia. A high school athlete who excelled in basketball, football, and baseball, he volunteered for the navy on August 14, 1941. He was inspired to do so by an older man he knew that had served in the navy during World War I.

> I went to boot at Norfolk. From there I went to Mare Island, where I went to machine gun school. I then went to Honolulu. I rode one patrol on *Gudgeon* as a mess attendant 1st class, leaving Pearl Harbor on December 11, 1941. It was the first patrol of the war into Japanese waters. I then went to *Pargo* for some patrols. I was the senior steward aboard, and my job was to man the XJA telephone in the forward battery. On battle surface I was on the 40mm gun. All the patrols were frightening. We had a good crew on *Pargo* and I liked captains Eddy and Bell. Alonza Davis, a steward's mate from Texas, was my friend. I was a loner, not a drinker, and mostly roomed with Davis ashore. I was not happy about being a steward, but did it without fuss [Rozar, Albert].

Albert Rozar, referred to by other stewards as "Little Rozar" (a name he does not care for) to distinguish him from his older brother, Leonard "Big" Rozar, made five

Officer's Cook 1st Class Albert Rozar coming topside. Rozar, a Georgia native, made patrols on *Grudgeon* and *Pargo* during the war. (Photograph courtesy of A. Rozar.)

war patrols in all on *Pargo*. Rozar went aboard *Pargo* on October 27, 1943, and was transferred off a year later, on October 25, 1944. His first patrol, *Pargo*'s second of the war, was conducted under Captain Ian Eddy in October and November 1943. Testing a new concept, *Pargo* was part of just the second wolf pack ever organized, operating with *Harder* and *Snook*. However, communications were poor, and while attacking the same convoy, *Snook* came close to sinking *Pargo*. After this patrol, Rozar and his boat went back to Mare Island for new engines.

They returned to the war in early 1944, heading out on patrol in March. This, too, was an active patrol. *Pargo* encountered two Japanese cruisers off Davao Gulf but was prevented from scoring a kill by depth charges from both aircraft and escort vessels. Albert Rozar made the next two patrols on the boat, one under Captain Eddy in June 1944 and a final one under Captain David Bell in September 1944. During Rozar's time aboard *Pargo*, Captains Eddy and Bell sank a combined total of six ships.

> After serving on *Pargo*, I was on the staff of Commodore Wilkins at Midway and was back to Pearl by war's end. I then went back to Mare Island and from there to New London. I put *Greenfish* into commission in 1946 and was aboard until 1948. On April 10, 1948, I married my wife, Hermine Evelyn Gary, in New London, Connecticut. I was then on the staff at New London. In August 1953 I went to Norfolk and was on *Cobbler* until 1955. From there I went to *Shark* [*SSN-591*] but never went to sea. I then went back to staff duty on *Orion* at Norfolk, and retired as a senior chief in 1971 [*ibid.*].

Albert Rozar and his wife still reside in Norfolk, Virginia, today. They have two children. Their only son, Vaughn Rozar, now deceased, served in the air force and later earned a master's degree in teaching. Their daughter, Catrina, also earned a college degree and now works as a nurse.

LEONARD ROZAR

Leonard Cicero Rozar was born in 1917 and raised in Dublin, Georgia, along with his younger brother and fellow submariner Albert Rozar. He volunteered for the navy on November 28, 1939, embarking on a subsequent thirty-year career as a submariner.

> I volunteered in 1939 for the navy. No army for me.... I'd heard devious things about them. I went to Norfolk for training at Unit K West. There was no steward training. We did general military stuff, some weapons and marching. The training was segregated, all Blacks together. I was there for twelve weeks. While waiting for my assignment, I worked at Unit B East. When I came out, I was a mess attendant 3rd class. I had boot leave, then went straight to Pearl Harbor. I left the Monday after Easter Sunday 1940 to go to Pearl. Right away I went to the boats. Before the war, I served on *Pompano, Pollack,* and *Plunger*.
>
> Late in 1940, with shadows of war on the horizon, I was sent to Mare Island as part of *Tuna*'s commissioning crew. We had a heck of a crew, the other steward was a guy named [Eddie] Gordon. Commander DeTar was a badass, with no sub talent. He worked on a rescue boat before submarines. I was a qualified

soundman aboard, and my battle station was in the forward battery. Sometimes I was on the standby sound gear, and also in the control room, ready to pull the demolition plug if needed. I made three runs on *Tuna* [Rozar, Leonard].

Rozar, known as "Big Rozar" to other stewards, served on *Tuna* from September 30, 1941, to November 3, 1942. His first two patrols were made under Captain John DeTar, a rather strange character who was somewhat mistrustful of his own crew. In two patrols made between January and May 1942, DeTar sank two ships. On his third patrol, Rozar served under Captain Arnold Holtz and departed Pearl Harbor in July 1942 for the frigid waters of Alaska. No sinkings were recorded by *Tuna* this run, though she did land an army party on a small island.

> After I left *Tuna*, I worked in the Submarine Division 42 at Pearl Harbor and almost immediately went to *Saury* under Captain Tony Dropp. I made six patrols on her and saw a lot of action. Dropp was a good captain — the best — and he got us through some rough times. On two of these runs I served with William Cosby, Bill Cosby's dad [*ibid.*].

Rozar's time aboard *Saury* was filled with excitement and danger. Things started out on Rozar's first patrol on *Saury* quite well. Newly skippered by Captain Anthony Dropp, the boat and her crew headed out in May 1943 on patrol and proceeded to sink four enemy ships, thereby erasing 20,000 tons of Japanese shipping. It was one of the best war patrols by any submarine so far. Little did Dropp, Rozar, and the rest of *Saury*'s crew know it would be the last ships they would sink.

Departing for their next patrol in July 1943, the boat was nearly lost. On the night of July 30, while attacking a convoy, things went wrong, and a Japanese destroyer unknowingly collided with *Saury*, taking out her periscopes. The boat returned to Pearl Harbor after being out only thirty days and was lucky to have survived. Two patrols later, in February 1944, Captain Dropp took a shot at sinking the Japanese carrier *Unyo* but was driven off by her destroyer escort. While *Saury* was heading back off patrol to Midway, she was hit by mountainous waves and took a large amount of water down the conning tower. Though no men were lost, the boat was a sitting duck on the surface for nearly a day while her damage was repaired. Luck was once again on Dropp's side, as well as the rest of the crew, and *Saury* made it back safely.

Leonard Rozar's final patrol on the boat came in September and October 1944 when, as part of Operation King Two, she provided lifeguard support for the air strikes on Okinawa. Now under Captain Richard Waugh, she rescued one aviator. After six grueling patrols, Rozar's time on *Saury*, which was herself being withdrawn from combat duty, was over.

> I went back to New London in early 1945 and went to *Sailfish*. I later went back to squadron duty, New London. Other boats I was on after the war were *Flying Fish*, in 1951–1952, *Chopper* out of Key West for three years, and *Spikefish* for two years. I was in the squadron at New London in 1962, then went to Athens, Georgia, for four years as the chief in charge. I then went to Norfolk for twenty months and was on the cruiser *Little Rock*. I didn't like that duty at all. After being on the sub fleet staff at San Diego, I retired in 1969 as a senior chief [*ibid.*].

After his retirement, Leonard Rozar worked for the border patrol and for the postal service. Married since 1954, he has five children and resides in San Diego, California.

HARRY SENIOR

Harry B. Senior, a native of South Carolina, joined the navy in 1942 at the age of 17.

> I wanted to go in the navy. During high school I worked at the naval air station in Jacksonville, Florida, for two years and liked it. I went to Norfolk for boot camp and from there was sent to Treasure Island. I then went to the submarine tender *Griffin* at Pearl Harbor. I later went to Brisbane [Australia] and ended up in Perth. One of the men with me on the *Griffin* at Perth was Dave Ball. Well, I volunteered for submarine duty, but I had no choice, and they put me in a relief crew. Learning was by on-the-job experience. I did go in the decompression chamber that was on the *Griffin*. In the relief crew, we were on a sub for two weeks after they came in. Electricians and all rates went on. I worked on cleaning up the forward battery area and after went on the tender to serve. Later in 1945 I was on the [tender] *Bushnell* and was a steward 2nd class, then went to *Pelias* [Senior].

Once the war was over, Harry senior finally got his wish and got posted to submarine duty. He would later change his rate to that of commissaryman.

> I went on the USS *Cusk* in 1946 and was on her for six years and made 1st class. We were working on the early missile system. After I got off her, I went to one boat that I can't recall and then to *Tivo* for three years. I was then sent to the squadron in New London in 1957 working for ComSubLant [Commander Submarine Atlantic Fleet] and made chief in 1958. I didn't like shore duty one bit and wanted to get back on a boat. I went to *Sarda* and was assistant chief of the boat and then back to Squadron 12. I then served on the USS *John Marshall* and then for four or five years was an instructor at the commissary steward school in San Diego before retiring in 1970. I could have made senior chief, and my captain wanted me to go up for E-8, but I didn't want to. Once you made E-8 [senior chief] you were out of subs. I loved subs and didn't want that [*ibid.*].

During his time on *Cusk* during the 1940s, Senior operated primarily out of San Diego, but the boat did make one cruise to Alaskan waters. Now living in Orange Park, Florida, Harry Senior worked as a mechanic in a nuclear plant in Waterford, Connecticut, after his naval service was over before his retirement in 1990.

SPAULDING SETTLE

Spaulding Bedford Settle enlisted into the navy at Newark, New Jersey, on July 10, 1943. He attended boot camp at Bainbridge, Maryland, where he volunteered for submarine duty. He subsequently went to Treasure Island, California, and from there boarded a troop ship, the *Sea Pike*, and went to Australia. His destination was Brisbane.

There he did flag duty attached to *Bluefish* before being transferred to the crew of *Tinosa* on January 3, 1944, as a steward's mate 1st class. He would make seven war patrols on this lucky boat, the first three under Captain Donald Weiss and the last four under Captain Richard Latham.

Settle's submarine career started out auspiciously, as the boat and her crew sank four ships worth 16,000 tons on a patrol that commenced in January 1944. It was on this patrol that Spaulding Settle first qualified in submarines. On two further patrols, conducted from March to July 1944, four more ships were sunk to the tune of 24,000 tons. Following this patrol, *Tinosa* went stateside to Mare Island for overhaul. When Settle and the crew returned to action, their new leader was Captain Latham. His luck was not as good as that of Weiss, and only three ships were sunk on four patrols during the time period from December 1944 to June 1945. On some of these patrols, lifeguard duty was performed, and the boat picked up a total of ten aviators during this time.

Spaulding Settle stayed on *Tinosa* through the end of the war and into late 1945, ending the war as an officer's cook 3rd class.

MASON SMITH

Mason B. Smith was born in Georgia on December 9, 1925, and raised just outside of Atlanta. When he was drafted for military service in April 1944, little did he know that he would make it his career.

> I was one of seven children. My mother was a school teacher, a college grad from Clark University in Atlanta. My dad was a laborer on our own farm. I went to school through ninth grade and worked at a variety of jobs. I worked at a department store, bicycle delivery for a grocery store, and later on in cafeterias. I was drafted in April 1944, and after I was inducted and took the physical exam, I went to the man in the white shirt. There was not much of a choice, so I went into the navy.
>
> Things were pretty typical at Bainbridge; nothing we didn't see in the south before. There were a whole bunch of recruiting stewards there. Everybody was gung-ho in those days, with the patriotic movies and all. When I finished boot, I talked to a psychiatrist and was sent to New London. I received steward training there, but not much sub duty. I was only there two or three weeks and remember when they were piping in news about the D-Day invasion over the radio. I was shipped west to Mare Island, and from there to San Francisco to a troop transport heading for New Guinea. From there I was part of a replacement group and was sent on a destroyer to Fremantle, Australia.
>
> I was assigned to a relief crew on the sub tender *Griffin* in about August 1944 but wasn't there very long. I was on the tender below deck when this steward named Sam Wallace, whom I didn't know, came to me and said, "Man, you want to go to sea?" I said yes. My first war patrol was on *Mingo* in November 1944 without Wallace. On my second and last patrol, Sam was back on the boat. We had a pretty good crew, but I was green. I qualified in the fore part of the boat by the end of the second war patrol.
>
> As for being a steward, you just did it. What the heck? I went along with the

flow and was calm outside, even if I was churning inside at times. I did have some good experiences with some fine officers, and Captain Madison was a fine guy.

My first depth-charging happened in the South China Sea. You never forget that. I recall we were running on the surface one night, and we lost some guys during a storm. We were on our way back out to war patrol, two days out of Pearl, when the war ended. By then I was a steward's mate 1st class [Smith].

Smith made two war patrols on *Mingo*. The first was in November to December 1944 under Captain Joseph Staley and lasted 52 days. One large cargo-passenger ship was sunk during this patrol. On the second outing, conducted in February to April 1945 under Captain John Madison, the patrol lasted 87 days when the boat was caught in a typhoon and lost three men overboard. *Mingo* was forced to rely on her auxiliary motor to get her back to base.

Steward's Mate Mason B. Smith of Mingo in 1945. Smith originally did tender duty before going to submarines in 1944 as a replacement steward. He would remain a submariner for most of his navy career. (Photograph courtesy of M. Smith.)

I stayed on *Mingo* and was part of her decommissioning crew. I then worked at headquarters in San Francisco for an admiral, then went back to subs in Hawaii. I think it was *Brill* I was on from 1947 to 1949, and then I went back to the states. I was thinking of getting out but reenlisted. In the early '50s I was on a destroyer escort, a radar picket ship that was part of the DEW line. I did shore duty at Mare Island from 1954 to 1957. About 1958 I went to nukes and went on *Sargo* to replace James Owens. I made the ice run in 1960 to the North Pole and got off soon after, say December 1960. I then went to *Ethan Allen* and put her in commission [August 1961]. I was on her gold crew and made four [Polaris] patrols in the Atlantic and the Mediterranean.

It was a different style of navy now. You had to requalify; you had to adapt and be able to keep pace. We had a good CO on the *Ethan Allen*. The patrols lasted three months, and we were submerged for two months. We flew back and forth from Holy Loch [Scotland] to join the boat. I made chief, E-7, and retired in 1963 after twenty years. I've had a heck of a good life! [*ibid.*].

Mason B. Smith now lives in Stockbridge, Georgia, with his wife, Celia. Together, they have two children, daughters Amy and Nicole. To this day, Smith is friends with

Sam Wallace, the man who persuaded him to go aboard a submarine on patrol for the first time way back in 1944.

Albert Soles

Albert Soles was born on March 26, 1924, and is a native of Dallas, Texas. His father, Pete, owned a cleaning and pressing shop and was considered a fine tailor, while his mother, Flossie, was a housewife. His brother, George, would serve during the war too, in the army. Albert Soles volunteered for the navy on January 26, 1942.

> I was young and ready to go. I lied about my age — told them I was 18 when I was really 17. My parents didn't mind, and they let me do it. I went to boot at Norfolk. I was in the squadron in 1943 when I went on *Cod*. I made two patrols on her under Captain [James] Dempsey. He was a quiet little guy, and he did right by me. I qualified throughout the whole boat and was helped out by the XO. The first time we were depth-charged, I just prayed we'd come out of it. After that boat, I did more squadron duty and then went on *Ray* for three or four patrols. Captain [William] Kinsella was a big, good guy. He liked me pretty good. In all the boats I was on, my battle station was in the fore torpedo room pretty much, nothing topside. We made some rugged runs on those boats, and on *Ray* scored us some good tonnage. The *Ray* was pounded with depth charges a couple of times while I was on her. We had good crews on the boats I was on [Soles].

Albert Soles went aboard *Cod* in the fall of 1943 and made her first two war patrols under Captain James Dempsey. On the first patrol in October–November 1943, no sinkings were achieved. On the second patrol in January–February 1944, the boat sank two ships worth 9,800 tons while patrolling off the island of Halmahera. However, things went downhill when most of the crew became ill, and the patrol was cut short. Soles was one of the few who remained healthy. Following this, Soles went to squadron and relief-crew duty. He had previously been on the relief crew for *Bluefish* when he was transferred to *Ray* on June 28, 1944. He would subsequently make three eventful patrols on this boat under Captain William Kinsella and was a participant in the destruction of over 38,000 tons of Japanese shipping.

On Soles's first patrol on *Ray* in July–August 1944, the boat sank three ships in one convoy alone and a total of five ships overall for 26,000 tons. One tanker that was destroyed was hit with 22 torpedoes before she finally sank.

His second patrol was even more eventful and fraught with danger. Conducted during September–October 1944, the boat patrolled in tandem with *Cod* off Manilla and claimed five ships sunk, not all of which were credited. Perhaps the most dangerous time was on October 14, 1944, when *Ray* was attacked by a Japanese plane and was forced to dive. However, the upper conning tower hatch became jammed, and the boat started to fill with water. Forced with the decision to continue the dive and drown the men in the conning tower or risk further air attack by surfacing to save his men, Kinsella surfaced the boat. Luckily, though the conning tower was two-thirds flooded, his men were saved. Soles was in the fore torpedo room when this incident occurred and recalls vaguely the "hectic times" before the situation was brought under control.

Officer's Cook Albert Soles on *Ray* in 1944. A native of Texas, Soles made war patrols on *Cod* during the war and saw even heavier action during several patrols on *Ray* under Captain Kinsella. (Photograph courtesy of A. Soles.)

Later, *Ray* refueled at the island of Mios Woendi before heading back out to sea. Such a patrol as this, when a boat comes in for a brief refueling or reloading and goes back out, is referred to as a "double-barreled patrol." Though it officially counts as one war patrol, they are often lengthy and this is probably the reason why Soles recalls four war patrols on *Ray*. The boat's adventures were far from over on this double-barreled patrol. She would land men and supplies on the island of Mindoro and picked up two downed aviators, three refugees, two American POWs originally captured at Corregidor, and one high-ranking guerilla leader. When back out hunting for ships, Kinsella and his crew attacked the Japanese heavy cruiser *Kumano* with three other boats, but were driven off by bombs and depth charges. After this patrol, *Ray* and her crew proceeded to Pearl Harbor for a well-deserved period of rest.

Prior to his next patrol, Albert Soles reenlisted for another two years of duty on March 25, 1945. In April–May 1945 Soles made his third and last war patrol on *Ray*, and his last of the war. On this patrol, things were considerably quieter, and no sinkings were achieved. By the time he left *Ray* on June 17, 1945, Albert Soles was an officer's cook 3rd class.

After the war, I served on some boats, including *Besugo*. I thought about making the navy a career, but there was one officer that made it hard on me, so I decided to get out. This was on *Besugo*, when I was told I had to requalify in the entire boat, I think because we got refitted with the snorkel. I didn't think that was right, and even the squadron commander, who was my old XO on *Cod*, said, "I qualified this man personally," and said there was no need. But I had to, anyway. I left the navy on April 11, 1947, That year I married my wife Landonia. I got called back in for the Korean War and served aboard the tenders *Beaver* and *Bushnell* and the sub *Spinax*. I went in January 3, 1951, and got out April 5, 1952. Afterward, I worked for a paper company and an engineering company, each for 20 years [*ibid.*].

Now retired, Albert Soles and his wife live in Carrollton, Texas. They have five children, including two sets of twins: daughters Faith and Joy, and son Jean and daughter Celene. They also have another son, Greg. The navy tradition in the Soles family is now at three generations. One son did duty on an aircraft carrier, while one grandson has done duty as a navy recruiter in the Dallas area.

Jake Spurlock

Jake Spurlock was born in Texas about the year 1911. In 1930 he lived in Plainview, Texas, and worked as a hotel porter prior to joining the military. His first entry into the navy is uncertain. The crew muster rolls for *S-28* state that he enlisted on April 24, 1942, at Houston, Texas, but it is possible that he was reenlisting at this time for another term, given his age. On March 2, 1943, Spurlock was sent to the submarine base at Dutch Harbor, Alaska, to join the crew of *S-28*. Rated as a mess attendant 1st class, he was 32 years old, older than most submarine stewards at that time. He subsequently made two war patrols on the old S-boat under Captain Vincent Sisler. The first was conducted in July 1943 and the next in September. On this final patrol for *S-28*, she sank a Japanese gunboat in the Kuriles, being one of the few S-boats to achieve success in these Alaskan-based war patrols.

Being stationed at Dutch Harbor was no picnic. The weather was, at best, foggy and rainy, and at its worst it was the coldest Arctic conditions imaginable. When the men were off duty, there was no fancy hotel for them! Instead, they stayed in Quonset huts just trying to stay warm. Spurlock's fellow shipmate and friend on *S-28* was Jim Lewis. He well recalls the old steward:

> Spurlock was a good guy.... I still remember the time we were ashore in our huts drinking, with foxholes right outside, when a wave of Japanese bombers hit. Everyone in the hut, including ole Jake, ran outside, heading for the foxholes or the boat. I followed Jake, who was carrying several bottles of beer. He weaved back and forth, headed first for the foxholes, then toward the boat. Well, he had big feet and got all tripped up. He skinned his elbows bad but never lost a drop of beer [Lewis].

By the end of 1943, Spurlock was promoted to officer's cook 2nd class on December 31, 1943, and was headed toward warmer duty. *S-28* was withdrawn from Alaskan service and sent to Pearl Harbor in early 1944 to serve as a training ship for the destroyer fleet based there. While Jim Lewis left the old S-boat, Spurlock continued on her. Sadly, he and the rest of her 50-man crew were lost during a sonar training exercise on July 4, 1944. Commanded by Captain J.G. Campbell, the boat sank in deep water off Pearl Harbor for reasons unknown.

JIM STALLINGS

Jim Eckford Stallings was born on July 27, 1921, in Starkville, Mississippi, to Sam Ella and Jimmie Lee Stallings. He had one sister, Virginia, with whom he attended Oktibbeha County public schools. As was common at the time, he was forced to leave school after the seventh grade. The biggest influence in his life was his grandmother, Minerva Stallings, who helped to raise and care for him. As he grew older and with tight economic times, Stallings became frustrated about the lack of work and decided to join the navy. While he was curious about the world, many of his friends thought he was crazy to join because he could not swim. This did not deter Stallings, and he joined the navy on November 27, 1939. He went to boot camp at Norfolk, Virginia, and from there was assigned to aviation squadron VP-12 in San Diego. Here he served from February 1940 until November 1940, when he joined a submarine relief crew at Pearl Harbor, serving on *Narwhal* and the old boat *Dolphin*. Jim Stallings was at Pearl Harbor until February 1942, when he was sent stateside. His family believes that he may have been wounded at the attack on Pearl Harbor, since he possessed a Purple Heart decoration, but this claim is unsubstantiated. There is no record of him having been awarded this medal. However, the possibility does exist, as some of Jim Stallings's service records show inaccurate dates, and there seems to be no doubt that he was on the scene at the time.

In any case, Stallings was sent to Portsmouth, New Hampshire, in February 1942 (not 1941 as the records indicate), where he received submarine training before joining the commissioning crew of *Haddock* on March 14, 1942. Stallings was aboard for her patrol under Captain Arthur Taylor in July to August 1942 and would stay for eleven more patrols, making his final war patrol in April to May 1945 under Captain Albert Strow. Serving under captains Taylor, Roy Davenport, John Roach, William Brockman, and Strow, no one served as long on *Haddock* as Stallings did. While aboard, Stallings saw much action, especially under Captain Davenport, who won a number of Navy Crosses for his outstanding patrols. Jim Stallings's battle submerged position was in the wardroom as a phone talker, and on the surface he helped to man the 20mm gun. For his outstanding and lengthy service, he was also awarded the Bronze Star, an award seldom given to submarine stewards. On February 16, 1945, he was promoted to chief officer's cook, probably the youngest man ever to earn this rate, and the quickest.

At war's end, Stallings went back to the states and served the rest of his career in Key West, Florida. The submarines he served on, all diesel boats, were *Aspro* (1945 — no patrols), *Piper* (late 1945), *Runner II* (1945–1946), *Sea Leopard* (1946–1948), *Corporal* (1948), the tender *Howard W. Gilmore* (1948–1951), *Sea Cat* (1956–1957), and *Grenadier* (1960–1964). On some of these boats only flag duty was performed and no voyages were actually made. Chief Stallings was highly regarded, and received many commendations for his service, which have previously been discussed. Late in his career, still at Key West, he was in charge of the BOQ at the naval air station.

After 33 years in the navy, Stallings finally retired in 1972. He was married to his wife, Leoncia, on July 27, 1958, and they were together until her death in 1996. Stallings, nicknamed "Big Jim," is described by his niece Carrie Grooms-Davis as having been "a towering figure, but a gentle-giant, a very giving person"(Grooms-Davis, Carrie). He died on April 24, 2002, at his home in Key West, Florida.

LACEY STEVENSON

Stevenson is another early submariner whose career is mostly unknown. Born on July 12, 1913, he was a native of Boley, Oklahoma, and his friends used to hear him tell how his family, which was part Native American, came to Oklahoma on the Trail of Tears (Weaver). It is unknown when Lacey Stevenson first joined the navy. However, since the records show that he reenlisted in the navy in New London on April 23, 1942, it seems reasonable to assume that he originally joined in 1938. Given his birth date, he may have even joined the navy earlier, perhaps as early as 1934. When he re-upped in 1942, he was an officer's steward 2nd class (OS-2).

Steward 1st Class Lacey Stevenson. A pre-war submariner from Oklahoma, Stevenson made three European war patrols on *Barb* under Captain John Waterman. (Photograph courtesy of R Weaver.)

While Stevenson mostly did duty at New London and the Panama Canal Zone during the war, he did make three patrols on *Barb*. He joined that boat under Captain John Waterman at her commissioning in Groton on July 8, 1942, and made one war patrol in support of the North Africa operations and two other patrols in European waters. All these patrols were made under Captain Waterman from October 1942 to February 1943. Like every other war patrol made in European waters by American submarines, no sinkings were achieved.

Lacey Stevenson was promoted to officer's steward 1st class

on October 1, 1942, and subsequently left *Barb* on March 11, 1943, going aboard the tender *Beaver* for medical treatment and duty. His further military activities are unknown, and he is thought to have retired from the navy in 1958. Lacey Stevenson soon returned to his native Oklahoma and was a resident of Oklahoma City when he died on July 1, 1997.

Ezell "Tommy" Strong

Little is known about submarine steward Tommy Strong and his career in the navy. He entered the service on December 19, 1939, at Dallas, Texas, and saw service on the coastal defense submarine *Mackerel* from March 1941 to April 1942. He also served briefly on *Growler* before she departed for the war zone. According to fellow shipmate Michael Geletka, Strong was well educated with a degree of some type. Strong is best known for the barbershop he operated in the New London–Groton, Connecticut, area after his retirement from the navy. His establishment was a well-known gathering place for retired submarine stewards for many years until he passed away.

Patrolman Hadwick Thompson of the City of Oakland (California) Police Department. Done with patrolling the seas in a submarine during the war, Thompson took on an even greater challenge, perhaps, when he patrolled the streets of Oakland as one of its first African American police officers. (Photograph courtesy of L. Thompson.)

O'Neal Thaxton

Thaxton is yet another steward of which too little is known. He was born on October 6, 1921, and joined the navy before the war. He was a crewman on the small, coastal defense submarine *Marlin* from 1941 to 1943. He probably made the two Atlantic war patrols conducted by this boat under Captains George Sharp and Paul Grouleff in 1942. While no sinkings, as was the norm, were achieved, the patrols were still filled with danger. The biggest problem was being attacked by friendly aircraft that might mistake them for a German U-boat. One former shipmate on *Marlin* describes Thaxton as "a wonderful person and nobody did any better at his job" (Lester). It was also recalled how many of the crew members used to joke with the Irish lads on the boat about Thaxton's name, which gave new meaning to the term "Black Irish." Following this duty, Thaxton was part of the commissioning crew of *Pampanito* at Portsmouth, New Hampshire, on November 6, 1943. He was now a steward 1st class but did not go off to war on this boat. He was later sent to Mare Island for duty, and from there he joined the crew of *Cero* at Pearl Harbor for her seventh war patrol under Captain Raymond Berthrong. Thaxton went aboard the boat on February 6, 1945. During his one patrol, the boat sank several cargo ships. O'Neal Thaxton left *Cero* on June 19, 1945, being transferred to Submarine Division 282 for flag duty from *Tilefish*. No futher details of Thaxton's career are known, except for the fact that he continued to be stationed on the east coast and lived in the New London area. Sometime after his retirement, he moved to Monroe, Louisiana, where he died in July 1985.

HADWICK THOMPSON

Hadwick Alvin Thompson was born on November 17, 1919, in Willows, California, the son of Hadwick and Edna Thompson. He had two sisters, Adell and Betty. Thompson grew up in Willows and worked on the family farm and later in their catering business. The Thompson family was from a pioneering family in California, descended from the Black pioneer Alvin Coffey. Hadwick Thompson, Sr., was the only Black man to farm rice in northern California and attended the University of California's College of Agriculture at Davis after fighting in World War I. When he came home, "he was invited to join the Willows chapter of the American Legion and they named it after him. Some white people never let him know he was Black" (Fleming, p. 1).

Following in his father's footsteps, Hadwick Thompson graduated from Willows High school in 1938 and joined the navy to serve his country on January 11, 1939. He was inducted at San Francisco and subsequently went to the naval training center at San Diego for basic boot training. Following this, he went to Norfolk, Virginia, for steward training. It was a totally different world than the one he was used to. As he would later say, "I'm a fourth-generation Californian and I didn't know how things were down there" (Snapp). After completing this class, Thompson was assigned first to the auxiliary cargo ship *Capella* and then went on the destroyer *Ramsey*. He was aboard this ship at Pearl Harbor when the Japanese attacked on December 7, 1941. As he vividly recalls,

> I saw this lone plane coming in, and it couldn't have been more than 200 feet above our bow.... I said to the guy standing next to me, "Damn! They're low!" And he said, "Well, you know how those flyboys are; they're horsing around again." Then I looked again and I said, "Horsing, hell!! Look at the rising sun on that wing!" And a second later he dropped the first bomb. Then they started

coming in from all sides.... When they started to dive to drop those torpedoes, I could look them right in the eye [*ibid.*].

Hadwick Thompson soon ran to the bridge of the destroyer and grabbed a machine gun, helped by his gunnery officer.

Thompson continued to serve on *Ramsey* into 1942, with the ship doing mostly antisubmarine warfare work. Thompson would later say that he went to submarines because "they took men off the small ships, who were used to being in close quarters, and put them in submarines" (*ibid.*). Hadwick Thompson went aboard *Pollack* on July 31, 1942, as a mess attendant 2nd class. Twelve days later he was promoted to mess attendant 1st class. He would make five war patrols on the boat from October 1942 through August 1943. The first three were conducted by Captain Robie Palmer and produced no sinkings. Also aboard was George Grider as executive officer. He was a popular officer, as was Palmer, and one highly respected by Thompson. Thompson's last two patrols on the boat were under the guidance of Captain Bafford Lewellen and were highly successful, resulting in the sinking of four ships worth 11,000 tons from May to August 1943.

Thompson well remembers one time when *Pollack* was pinned down by enemy destroyers for eighteen hours, stating that "half the crew had already passed out from lack of oxygen ... and we were taking depth-charges every minute" (*ibid.*). This incident referred to probably occurred on Thompson's final war patrol in August 1943, after Lewellen and his crew had sunk a large transport that was carrying supplies and 1,200 Japanese troops to Tarawa. While the troops were rescued, they never made it to Tarawa, possibly saving "the lives of untold numbers of U.S. Marines" (Blair, p. 455).

During his time on the boat, Thompson served in the forward torpedo room as a phone talker during battle station activities. He was promoted to steward 3rd class on July 14, 1943, and rode the boat back to the states when she went for an overhaul to Mare Island in fall of 1943. While back home, he married his sweetheart, Lily Aubert, whom he had met earlier at a YMCA dance, on October 8, 1943. Thompson, however, stayed with *Pollack* and returned to Pearl Harbor but left prior to her next patrol on February 28, 1944. Hadwick Thompson subsequently served at the naval hospital at Pearl Harbor and Oakland, California, before he was discharged from the navy on September 20, 1945. During the war, he had married his girl — now he was coming home.

While Hadwick Thompson's postwar career has been discussed previously in detail, it is well worth mentioning again that he went on to become the first Black police officer for the city of Oakland in May 1947 and was very active in community affairs. Hadwick and Lily Thompson had three children, sons Hadwick Jr. and Emile, and a daughter, Michele. The Thompsons were married for 59 years before Hadwick's death in Kaiser, California, on July 30, 2002, at the age of 82.

OTHA TOLER

Otha Toler was a native of Little Rock, Arkansas, being born to Bertrand and Frances Toler on March 16, 1923. He went to school in Little Rock and gained an eighth grade education. Among his friends and classmates was another boy that would also join the navy when he grew to manhood, Sam Wallace. Otha Toler joined the navy on October 2, 1941, and was inducted in his hometown. He went to boot camp in Norfolk and would serve for over a year on auxiliary ships before volunteering for submarine duty. His first submarine duty, and his most extensive during the war, was on *Plunger*. He joined her at Pearl Harbor on April 12, 1943, as a steward's mate 1st class and would make four war patrols under Captain Raymond Bass. The first of these was conducted in April to May 1943, resulting in two ships worth 15,000 tons being sunk. Another three patrols, from June 1943 to December 1943, would follow, resulting in another four ships sunk worth 13,000 tons.

After four patrols on *Plunger*, Toler transferred off the boat on February 2, 1944, to Submarine Division 41 for duty. He would perform squadron and relief duty for over nine months, including a stint aboard *Spikefish* for

Otha Toler "behind bars" in Honolulu in early 1941. The young steward's mate, a native of Arkansas, is actually depicted here at one of Honolulu's tourist attractions. He first served on surface craft before going to submarine duty in 1942. (Photograph courtesy of C. Kimmons.)

two months from August 16 to October 31, 1944. During his time on *Spikefish*, no war patrols were made. Toler next went to sea on *Croaker* for her third war patrol, coming aboard from Submarine Division 282 on November 25, 1944. Toler made at least two, and possibly three, war patrols on this boat. The first was made under Captain William Thomas in December 1944, while the second was under Captain Francis Boyle in March 1945. During these two patrols, the boat only was credited with the shared sinking of one enemy ship. Toler may also have been aboard for *Croaker's* short fifth war patrol, which lasted only 22 days in April to May 1945 and was conducted by Captain Thomas. Otha Toler left the crew of *Croaker* on May 6, 1945, going back to squadron duty.

After the war ended, Otha Toler returned stateside and served in submarines on the west coast. Upon his return, he went to night school to gain his high school diploma and married Willa Mae Ventress in California on August 4, 1951. Together they had two sons, James and Pyron Stewart, and six daughters, Faye, Arcora, Gwendolyn, Barbara, Karen, and Reba.

As far as his navy career is concerned, Otha Toler served on a number of diesel boats, including *Carbonero*, with friends and fellow stewards Isaac Johnson and Anderson Royal, from 1947 to 1951, the experimental hunter-killer submarine *Barracuda* in 1951 to 1952, and *Queenfish* in the mid–1950s. Otha Toler would later, about 1954, change his rate to that of commissaryman while at San Diego, going from steward to commissaryman 1st class. Following the end of his sea duty, Toler worked at the San Francisco Navy Yard at the mess facility there from 1963. He retired from the navy in 1963 as a chief commissary steward with 23 years of service. Otha Toler died on October 8, 1998, at San Francisco.

MAGNUS WADE

Magnus Augustus Wade was born on August 15, 1918, in Columbia, South Carolina. While his father died while he was young, his mother worked as a cook to support Magnus and his sister Hattie. His mother was his biggest influence in his early life, and she made sure that he got an education. Wade did just that, earning his high school diploma in the Columbia school system. Both he and his sister would join the military, with Hattie being the first and joining the army. She later became an army nurse during World War II. Magnus Wade went the military route, too, joining the navy on November 22, 1939, at Raleigh, North Carolina. Wade subsequently went to boot camp at Norfolk, Virginia, and was part of Class 11 at Unit K-West. Upon completing boot camp, Wade first went to the old destroyer *Fairfax* as a mess attendant 3rd class and subsequently served on the old submarine tender *Beaver* and the yacht *Vixen*, which was used by the command staff at the New London submarine base as a flagship. Wade was aboard this ship in late July 1941 when President Franklin Roosevelt came to New London aboard the Presidential yacht *Potomoc* enroute to a subsequent meeting with Winston Churchill on the heavy cruiser *Tuscaloosa* in the North Atlantic on August 3, 1941.

It was not long after this that Wade, perhaps influenced by his fellow stewards in New London, volunteered for submarine duty. He first served on the school boats *O-4* and *R-5* before going aboard the *S-48*. From this old boat, called by one historian "the worst of the S-boats" (Blair, p. 882n), Magnus Wade transferred to the new boat *Gunnel* on April 4, 1943. Now serving under Captain John McCain, Jr., Wade was an officer's cook 2nd class. The boat had just returned from European waters where she conducted her first war patrol and was now headed for the Pacific. Left behind to worry about Wade was a young lady named Dorothy Edith Robinson, whom he had met at a USO club in New London in 1942. When Wade returned to the states for new construction in 1945, he married her.

After arriving at Pearl Harbor, and going through the normal training exercises, *Gunnel*, with Wade aboard, departed on her first war patrol in Pacific waters in June 1943. This patrol was a good one, with *Gunnel* and her crew sinking two cargo ships worth over 13,000 tons. Following this patrol, the boat was sent back to Mare Island for new engines. The engines she and a number of other boats were originally commissioned with, those of the H.O.R. type (called "whores" by the motor macs), were extremely unreliable and constantly broke down. *Gunnel* was the first to get new motors and returned to Peal Harbor by late October. Magnus Wade would subsequently make three more patrols with Captain McCain from November 1943 to July 1944, the last of these being conducted from Fremantle, Australia, from May to July 1943. Most of the time on this long patrol was spent in support of the air strikes on Surabaya. During his time on the boat, Wade was a valued crewmember on *Gunnel*. He was promoted to officer's cook 1st class on April 1, 1944, and liked Captain McCain. The boat's gunnery officer, and later executive officer, Joe Vasey, well recalls Magnus Wade. Of him, he has this to say:

Officer's Cook 1st Class Magnus Augustus Wade circa 1945. Wade, a native of South Carolina, made five war patrols on *Gunnel* under Captains John McCain and Guy O'Neil before going to new construction and *Dentuda*. (Photograph courtesy of D. Wade.)

> He was a superb steward's mate, 1st class, I believe, and later promoted to chief. More than that, he had a sparkling personality and a keen sense of humor. His quips had all of us laughing even in the most perilous situations. About six-foot-two-inches, he bumped his head going through the hatches more than the rest of us but never lost his ability to joke about it. He was the skipper's favorite and helped relieve the stress on the "old man" with his quips, often in the middle of depth-charge attacks. During battle stations–gun action, he manned a 50-caliber machine gun and took great pride in this. He was an expert gunner. For battle stations submerged he was responsible for rigging and security of the forward battery [Vasey].

On July 4, 1944, Magnus Wade left *Gunnel* prior to her sixth war patrol and went to relief crew duty in Submarine Division 121. He went back to the boat on October 6, 1944, and would make one last patrol, this time under Captain Guy O'Neil. This patrol, which commenced in October 1944 and resulted in the sinking of three ships, ended at Fremantle, Australia. Magnus Wade left *Gunnel* for good in early 1945 and went stateside. On February 14, 1945, before going back to the war zone, he married Dorothy Robinson. On March 12, 1945, he joined the crew of *Dentuda*, commanded by his old skipper, John McCain, and would make her one and only war patrol in May to June 1945 as the war was winding down. Wade served on this boat through the end of the war and after September 1945. He would subsequently go to shore duty in Submarine Divisions 342 and 52 before receiving his discharge from the navy on December 20, 1945. Magnus Wade continued as a submariner in the naval reserve, and changes his rate to that of commissaryman 1st class. He served on a variety of submarines until his discharge from the Naval Reserve as a chief commissaryman on July 11, 1969.

As a civilian, Wade worked as a carpenter and for the state of Connecticut as a construction supervisor for highway maintenance facilities. He soon transferred to the state health department as health facilities construction inspector and later retired as a plan reviewer. After his retirement, Magnus Wade and his wife, Dorothy, who together would have three foster children, owned and operated WADOT Farm in Oakdale, Connecticut, specializing in decorative and exotic plants. Magnus Augustus Wade, veteran of seven war patrols, died in 1998.

Sam Wallace

Sam Wesley Wallace is a native of Little Rock, Arkansas. Born on December 16, 1922, he joined the United States Navy on September 9, 1940, being signed in by his father at the age of seventeen. Soon after boot camp was over, he requested a transfer to the Submarine Force and never looked back. During World War II, he made six war patrols on the submarine *Mingo*, serving as officer's cook 2nd and 1st class from her commissioning in January 1943 to the end of hostilities and her return back to the states in September 1945.

> It took me nine months to join the navy. I was just a skinny kid back then and had to gain weight so the navy would accept me. I went in at age seventeen and didn't finish high school. I've always regretted that. I went to boot camp at Norfolk and afterward was assigned to the naval air station at Norfolk, Virginia. I served for a few months in air squadron VP-54 and worked aboard the USS *Curtis*, a seaplane tender. After spending my time going up in planes at Norfolk and making sandwiches, I was asked to go to submarine duty. I still remember the ride on an Eastern Steamship boat up the coast. Its something how people changed and acted different as we traveled north.
>
> In March 1941 I got orders for the submarine base in New London. First I served on the USS *Vixen*, a yacht that served as the fleet flagship. My boss was Commander R.H. Smith. It was easy duty, and I had an open gangway. … When Smith wasn't there, I didn't have to be there either. While I was

Steward 1st Class Sam Wallace. He made six patrols on *Mingo* during the war. (Photograph courtesy of S. Wallace.)

there we aided in trying to rescue the *O-9,* with no success. This happened off Portsmouth, New Hampshire. [Wallace].

The *O-9* belonged to an older class of submarines that were brought out of mothballs as World War II approached. These O-class boats, all built from 1917 to 1918, measured approximately 520 tons in size and carried a crew of about 35 men. They were used during the war years at New London as training boats for new Submarine Force recruits. Though badly outdated, they were useful in freeing up more-modern submarines for active war service and for getting new submariners acclimated to underwater operations. The *O-9* was lost with her thirty-four man crew during training exercises when she failed to surface in June 1941.

> After Smith was killed in a plane crash, I went to submarines. There was no sub school for stewards and most commissary personnel and little training. It was a deal where they gave you a pencil and paper, and you took notes. The first boat I served on was the *O-6*, when I relieved Dave Ball. We had operational training in the waters off Maine, and I qualified for submarines in the *O-6*. Many did not like our captain, but I got along fine. You soon find out in the navy that if a commander doesn't like someone, they can put salt on their tail right quick, if you know what I mean! After the attack on Pearl Harbor, we had to do double watches to protect the boat, which was funny. Hell, *O-6* was just a rust bucket! I served on that boat until January 1943. By this time I had gone from mess attendant 3rd class to officer's cook 3rd class.
>
> Then they came to me and asked if I wanted to go to war. I said I wasn't angry at anyone, but off I went anyway. I stayed in New London until we put the *Mingo* in commission. We headed for the Pacific Fleet in Pearl Harbor. Our tender was the USS *Griffin*. The first skipper of *Mingo* was a handsome fellow and well liked. We made the first two war patrols out of Pearl, then left for Mare Island for new engines in the last of 1943 [*ibid.*].

The Mingo was commanded on her first two patrols by Commander R.C. "Red" Lynch. In June 1943 he took Mingo to the waters off Palau for her first patrol, and on her second, in September, to the waters off Truk. During this patrol the boat was credited with damage to a 17,500 ton aircraft carrier. However, during these first two patrols the Mingo was constantly plagued by engine problems. Equipped by the navy with new HOR engines, they proved to be a dismal failure. Lynch would later state that *Mingo* "had the worst engines of the lot ... an extreme danger to the ship and crew" (Blair, p. 512). The boat was subsequently sent back to California to be re-engined and was out of the war for nearly four months.

> After overhaul with new engines, we left for patrol. Our new skipper was J.J. Staley — the best! After the third patrol we stopped in Brisbane, Australia, and went into dry dock for sonar work and rest and relaxation. After leaving Brisbane we proceeded on our fourth patrol. After the patrol we pulled into Perth, Australia [Wallace].

For *Mingo*'s third and fourth war patrols, the boat was commanded by Lieutenant Commander Joseph J. Staley. On her third patrol, which commenced in February 1944, *Mingo* had yet more engine problems, forcing her to put into Milne Bay, New Guinea, and thence to Brisbane for further repairs. In June 1944, during her fourth war patrol, *Mingo* finally had some luck, sinking a large Japanese destroyer on July 7 in the South China Sea.

> On our fifth run we were on lifeguard duty to pick up flyers. We picked up sixteen of them. We had to go in close to an island, and the draft was low so that

we couldn't dive. We put the bow of the boat right on shore and with life rafts picked up four aviators. As we were leaving, one of our own planes had their bomb bay doors open, ready to drop bombs on us. We finally got Ole Glory topsides in time. The skipper, Madison, was one of the best ship handlers I ever saw, but he was so nervous the night before our mission that he drank a fifth of scotch [*ibid.*].

On this fifth war patrol, *Mingo* was now commanded by John Madison. Departing base in August 1944, she was assigned lifeguard duty in the Makassar Strait to cover a strike made by B-24 Liberators of the Thirteenth Air Force on Balikpapan, Borneo. Her job was to rescue any aviators that were shot down into the surrounding waters. *Mingo* arrived at her station early and got into a surface battle with several Japanese trawlers. The next day she rescued six downed airmen adrift in their life rafts. In the following days the men of the *Mingo* rescued ten more men ashore. During this time, the *Mingo* was mistaken for a Japanese submarine and was bombed by U.S. aircraft. Luckily, the bomb landed 300 feet away, and friendly contact was established (Roscoe, p. 470). This mission by *Mingo* was one of the most outstanding ones of its kind during the war. Lifeguard duty was no easy task, but it was yet another invaluable service provided by the men of the Submarine Force.

> I made five runs on *Mingo* and got off before the sixth because a lot of buddies were coming up missing. In other words, I was scared. The worst thing you needed to hear was some meat head on the submarine tender yelling down to you, "I bet you $100 that you won't make it back." I just went on board the tender and found someone to take my place on *Mingo*'s sixth run. His name was Mason Smith. I didn't know him then, but he is a friend of mine to this day. I returned to *Mingo* for her seventh and last run in February 1945. A typhoon came up while we were on this patrol and hit us from astern, driving the boat down seventy-plus feet. We lost a lieutenant JG and a 3rd class quartermaster. We nearly sank before getting the conning tower hatch closed. After the storm, we never found a trace of our shipmates. Our ship had rolled at least fifty degrees from one side to the other, and all our electrical systems were out in the control room. So we had to go back to Perth for new supplies. After leaving for patrol, we got through Lombok Strait — a hell hole. We took after a large convoy and ran flank speed to get ahead of them. Then all four main engines went out, we only had the dinky engine to use. We could only make seven to nine knots and could not dive. We were at sea 87 days. I had shipmates I had not seen in two months. The submarine *Jack* was trying their best to sink us. It took a lot before they found out we were friendly. There was another boat that had us in their scope. The good Lord was with us [Wallace].

The incident that Wallace describes was not an uncommon one during the war. Because submarines often operated in groups, known as wolf packs, and passed other boats that were on their way to or from their patrol stations, sometimes a friendly boat was mistaken for an enemy submarine, and an attack was begun. Luckily, friendly contact would be made and disaster averted. No U.S. submarine sank another during the war, though several were lost by attacks from "friendly" surface ships or aircraft.

> Most stewards were pretty good people. I got along with everyone, and never had any problems with any of my skippers. One of my captains was a real

sailor's sailor. We even bet ten dollars on who had the best looking girlfriend in port. Of course, I knew I would win, as I had seen the captain's girl. When he saw my girl, he said that she was the "most beautiful woman I've ever met," and later paid up. During the time I was ashore for one patrol during the war I served the secretary of war's son, Stimson, and other officers.

After the war I rode *Mingo* back to the states and ended as an officer's cook 1st class. After the war, I served on *Chopper*, for a couple of years. I rode her to China and spent time ashore in Shanghai, on the Yangtze River. The many people living there in such poor conditions was a sad sight to see. While in the Far East we would go out on exercises for ten or twelve days at a time, come back in and provision, then go out again. On one cruise we sank an old Chinese destroyer for training. There was nothing to it, really. We didn't even dive to do it.

In 1950 I went to the sub tender *Proteus* in New London. I later helped to recommission the *Bowfin* and remember how the crew stole a hatchcover in the dead of night from another laid-up boat. I also recommissioned the submarine *Rock*. I later served shore duty, making chief in 1959. Then I went to *Hardhead*. It had a deep-south crew, but I liked them. The last boat I served on was the worst ever, the *Bang*. The crew was good, but the wardroom was terrible. The captain didn't know what was going on, and I remember running around the Mediterranean at flank speed with no regard for the rules of the road. We ended up, because of this, spending 22 days in Toulon, France, with a broken engine that no one knew how to fix.

I retired in June 1962 as a chief steward, E-7. I could have gone higher, but my lack of education hurt me. The only time I ever experienced any real prejudice was while I was stationed at Key West, Florida. I had my car, a Buick, impounded by the shore police down there all for a twelve dollar ticket. However, my commanding officer soon put things to right.

Once I retired from the navy, I lived and worked in Fort Dodge, Iowa, for three-and-a-half years. Then I moved back to Connecticut, where I worked for General Dynamics, Pratt and Whitney, and for a long time at Pfizer Chemical as a chemical operator. When I finally retired in 1983, I moved to back to Fort Dodge, Iowa, with my wife, Dorothy. Now I spend my time golfing when I can and have even had three holes in one after the age of seventy. Some time ago, a friend of mine in Norfolk ran into a man I had served with while on *Chopper*. He was a white man, a mess cook, and we worked side by side. Color means nothing to me.... It's what's inside a man that counts. Well, that mess cook reached the rank of captain. Can you believe it? One thing he said was, "Sam led me down the right path." When a person says that, it makes you feel good. I sure have had a good life [*ibid.*].

Sam and Dorothy Wallace had three children, all boys who are now grown. Today, you can still find Sam Wallace in Fort Dodge, Iowa. Though his wife has since passed on, and he has survived a bout with cancer, he remains what he has always been — a friendly, outgoing, and caring man. He may live in the cornfields of Iowa today, far from the sea, but he remains a submariner at heart. Soon after making his acquaitance, its not hard for one to understand why all who know him consider him one of the best shipmates and friends a man could ever have.

STRAUTHER WALLACE

Strauther Wallace entered the navy on November 25, 1942, at Memphis, Tennessee, and probably attended boot camp at Norfolk, Virginia. Little is known about him except for what his wartime captain has written. Wallace probably volunteered for submarine duty at boot camp, or shortly thereafter; nine months later, in September 1943, and probably earlier, he was doing flag duty at Pearl Harbor, nominally attached to *Silversides*. On August 15, 1943, Strauther Wallace was transferred to *Halibut* as a steward's mate 1st class. His commander was Captain Pete Galantin, who was also new to the boat. Wallace would make five war patrols with Captain Galantin from August 1943 to November 1944, *Halibut*'s last patrols of the war. On Christmas Day 1943, Captain Galantin details Strauther Wallace's service by stating that "Wallace balanced carefully as he came forward from the galley bearing the huge platter on which was the turkey for the wardroom. His shining face had a great grin as he placed the platter carefully before me" (Galantin, p. 140). Wallace was certainly well liked by his captain, who describes him as "an experienced submariner, a big, burly, likeable man" (Galantin, p. 233). Wallace was promoted to steward 3rd class on May 1, 1944, and, like his junior steward, John Phillips, Strauther Wallace was stationed in the boat's forward battery when she was bombed and nearly sunk while on patrol in November 1944. Wallace was transferred off the boat for new construction duty at Mare Island on January 31, 1945. His assignment, though not known for certain, was probably the new boat *Stickleback*.

JAMES WASHINGTON

South Carolina native James Washington entered the navy in 1938. His 26-year career in the navy led him from service on one of the oldest boats in the Submarine Force to one of its most advanced and top secret submarines.

> I enlisted in 1938 and went to boot camp at Norfolk. I was in class 17. I then went to the [light cruiser] *Boise* at Guantanamo, Cuba, and then to the [light cruiser] *Raleigh*, which was a flagship. I was on her from 1939 to 1941, then to subs, which I volunteered for. My first boat was *Cuttlefish*. I qualified throughout the boat, and my battle station was in the forward battery. I made three runs under captains [Martin] Hottell and [Elliott] Marshall. I liked Hottell, but have no comment about Marshall. I have nothing to say. I liked sub duty, and the liberty was better than in the surface ships. I remember our third patrol off the Japanese Island of Honshu when I was the lookout. I spotted a plane coming in from shore, and it was so close I could see the face of the pilot. By this time I was the only one topside and was the last man down before the bombs were dropped. I later went to *Pompon* and put her in commission. I did six war patrols on her. Captains [Earl] Hawk and [Stephen] Gimber were both great guys. We were out of Australia. In 1945 I went back to the states for new construction [Washington, James].

Washington's first three war patrols, conducted early in the war, were on one of the fleet's oldest boats, the old V-boat *Cuttlefish*, which was built in 1932. The first two runs, made under Captain Hottell in January and April 1942 produced no sinkings. On the first patrol, most of the crew got sick from cleaning fluid fumes from chemicals used in the engine room.

Washington's third patrol on the old V-boat in July 1942 was the last for the boat, considered an antique, before she was retired from service. It was also a most dangerous one. Patrolling in Japanese waters, not only was the boat harassed by aircraft, as described by Washington, but it also collided with a destroyer one night at midnight. When *Cuttlefish* tried to dive to safety, her conning tower hatch jammed. Luckily, it was quickly closed by the heroic action of several crewmembers.

In early 1943, Washington was stateside at Manitowoc, Wisconsin, as part of the commissioning crew of *Pompon*. After the boat was commissioned on March 17, 1943, Washington made her first six patrols from July 1943 to July 1944. The first three patrols, all in 1943, were conducted under Captain Earl Hawk, the last three in 1944 under Captain Stephen Gimber. During all his patrols on the boat, she and her crew were responsible for sinking three enemy ships. James Washington left *Pompon* prior to her seventh patrol while she was at Majuro Atoll on December 23, 1944. Like many stewards, Washington had his own specialty dish that was a favorite with the wardroom on *Pompon*. In his case, it was French toast. Former shipmate Nathan Henderson well recalls that one officer, Frank Wall, "tried repeatedly to get James's recipe for French toast ... unsuccessfully" (Henderson).

> I ended the war as a cook 1st class. Back home I put *Sailfish* out of commission, then did squadron flag duty at New London from 1945 to 1947. Then I was on *Trumpetfish* to 1950. In 1950 I put the *Grampus* in commission in Boston, then went to *Diablo* in Norfolk. I was on *Albacore* from 1955 to 1962. That was top secret stuff, and I was chief on that boat [*ibid.*].

Following his duty on *Albacore*, an experimental submarine, Washington did shore duty in Boston for 18 months before retiring from the navy in 1964. He lived and worked in Boston until he moved back to South Carolina, his native state, in 1979. He currently resides in Charleston, South Carolina.

RUFUS WEAVER

Rufus Jack Weaver was born on August 8, 1927, in Louisville, Kentucky, and, like many Black youths of his time, had a rather tumultuous upbringing.

> I was strictly a ghetto city boy. My mother died when I was two, and my father was a typical Black man in the south, with no skills and no trade. He did work as a bricklayer for a time for the WPA. When I was seven, he was jailed for a long time, so my brother and I were put in a detention home for several months until my grandparents came and got us. My grandmother was an invalid, but they took us in. We lived in a four-room house with an outdoor privy, outdoor water, and no electricity. We lived like this for two years. It was a disciplined and structured life. We were treated rough and took a hell of a beating. My grandfather, a minister, was very brutal, who believed in the old idea of spare the rod and spoil the kid. The only good thing was we got to go to school, where they treated us very well.

Steward Rufus Jack Weaver in the galley of *Sea Owl*. Weaver became a fixture on the boat, serving on *Sea Owl* for twelve years in the post-war era. (Photograph courtesy of R. Weaver.)

When we finally went back with Dad, I was very happy for a while. But, he soon returned to his old ways, and I left home when I was 14. I had to, I couldn't put up with my father anymore. I lived with a friend who got me a job at a restaurant. I was a pretty smart kid and later joined a government program that taught kids a trade. I was a welder and got real good at it. I could weld aluminum well and was going to ship out to Connecticut to work there, but they discovered I lied about my age. I later worked in a railroad yard and a paint factory but got fired from both for rebelling against white authority. I tried to join the navy, but they wouldn't take me at first because of my age.

I went to work at a restaurant owned by a German couple, the Axeman's. Minnie Axeman and her husband treated me like a son. I learned to cook, and Mrs. Axeman took me shopping. I learned German and went to the Catholic Church. They also clothed me, using colors that Black people didn't normally wear, such as yellow and white sweaters! The Axeman's played a major role in my life for bettering myself. Whenever I felt down, Mrs. Axeman always said "You can do it," and told me to keep trying. She always encouraged me to do more. I joined the navy at Mrs. Axeman's insistence on March 8, 1945, though my father had to sign for me. I knew I would be a food handler, but I didn't know about being a servant.

I went to boot camp at Bainbridge for three months. I really enjoyed it. It was a military life. I met a lot of strange people — 97 percent of my company was illiterate, so I was the company clerk. I charged guys to write letters home for them. I volunteered for submarine duty because I was attracted by the pay, $72 a month, plus it meant coming north. I didn't want to go to Mare Island [California] for surface ships.

In June 1945 I went to New London for training on how to serve on a sub. It was all white instructors. From there, I got sent to Bangor, Maine, and picked up the sub *R-1* at the navy base in Casco Bay. We were treated very well there. New London was very prejudiced, but it was well hidden. I went in a restaurant in New London one time, and no one would wait on me. There was the all Black kitchen staff looking out at me, and the manager tried to ask me to leave, but I wouldn't.

I did get into a little trouble in Maine when I first got there. I insulted a navy admiral, Admiral Brown of the 1st Naval District. I was off duty, reading a comic book and eating a triple-decker ice cream when he walked by, and I didn't salute him. I was hauled in by the MPs, but I explained that I didn't see him. I was cheered when I returned to the ship.

I qualified on *R-1*, and it was wonderful duty. We went down to Key West. There, we were depth-charged by a "friendly" bomber. My battle station position was in the forward battery submerged, and on surface I was a hot shellman, dealing with the spent shell cartridges.

From the *R-1* I was sent to the *U-505*, possibly at Fall River, Massachusetts. I rode her for a War Bond tour. It was a wonderful tour until we hit the south. In one city, I heard one kid say, "Hey ma, look! They got a nigger down here. I didn't know they had niggers on submarines." When we were in Miami, the crew got the key to the city, but this didn't apply to me. The tour ended in Texas.

I then traveled with a DE [destroyer-escort] that had five or six stewards aboard to a boatyard in Hingham, Massachusetts. Here we worked on putting boats out of commission. It was choice duty. We lived in barracks and ate on the boat. Though we stayed tied up to the pier, I still drew sub pay.

I worked on *Spikefish* and *Seadragon* in early 1946. Here, I was injured when I fell through a hatch and was sent to the Chelsea Naval Hospital near Boston. When I got out, I went back to *Seadragon* and was then sent back to New London to the overhaul shop. This was lousy duty. There wasn't nothing in New London, no subs to get on.

Late in the year, this is 1946, I was sent to the sub base in Panama. The transport I was on was like little Georgia on the high seas. The captain was from Mississippi and the exec a Georgian. The stewards were restricted on the boat and couldn't do anything [Weaver].

Once at Panama, Rufus Weaver did a month's worth of duty on the submarine tender *Orion* before going aboard *Sea Owl* in December 1946. For the next twelve years, Weaver became a fixture on the boat and was a popular crewmember. Not only was he a good steward but he was also a fine submariner. The time that he helped avert disaster during a diving exercise while aboard *Sea Owl* has already been told. Here are some other highlights of his duty as a "real *Sea Owl* Hooter" during the time from 1946 to 1958.

When I first went aboard, there were a couple of stewards. One was Alexander Love, an old sailor, a steward 3rd class, and the other was Gene Ramsey. He came in the navy when I did. He was my best friend. He taught me a lot and was educated. Later on, we had another chief steward, Bill Talton. During this time, we were stationed on the Pacific side at Balboa. One of the things we did was track Russian ships. We also did firing exercises. While on the 5-inch gun crew we were shooting at the top of a mountain or something, and I was hit with a hot shell and injured.

I well remember one time we had swim call in the Pacific. We'd have guys with a rifle or a .45 [pistol] on deck while we got to go swimming. You'd dive off the deck and come up on the bow plane. I was one of the last to come out this time when someone cried, "Shark! Get Weaver out!" Well, they made a human chain and got me out with a shark ten feet behind me. I never went on another swim call!

Duty on *Sea Owl* was mostly all good. We were allowed to go to all the ship's parties and treated well. We had one real religious skipper we called "John the Baptist." He always insisted on an early Sunday breakfast and was so religious it was sickening. One time I was up for court-martial for not doing something to his satisfaction. Well, we had a community cake that we baked each month for the guys' birthdays. This time it was the captain's birthday, so I got a book and studied how to make an angel food cake. I baked him an open Bible cake. It had five pages, was five layers high, and all decorated with some Bible passages on the top in frosting. I put it in the wardroom. I saw the Captain look at the cake, and he was crying. My court-martial was in the trash can. He was so proud of that cake. No one had ever been that nice to him before, and we became the best of friends.

We later took the *Sea Owl* to Portsmouth and changed her to a snorkel. On one run late in December I was told to order Christmas candy and have turkeys brought aboard. We couldn't say anything to anyone; we were going on a special assignment. The other steward was a guy named Brewster, a big guy, six-foot four. We made a run to Murmansk [Russia] and would stay down all day and surface at night. The weather was so bad we broached at one point. We returned to the states in January. When it came time for me to leave the boat in 1958, it was hard.

I then served on the *Irex* at New London. She was a river boat there; we never went anywhere. I was there for nine months. Then I worked shore duty at the base BOQ in New London. I ran the mess and linen locker. The captain of the base was strict, but I got along with him. While I was doing this, I also helped guys get their GED and taught them math and English, even white guys. During this time, I was also the secretary of an all–Black social club called Club Cosmo. Its members were mostly stewards. We had about 20 members, paid dues, and even bought our own place. We met and talked but also did things for the community, like send kids to camp. Some of the members were Gene Ramsey, Joe Green, Lacey Stevenson, and Jimmy Jones, a coast guard steward.

After two years on shore, I went to *Cavalla*. I made chief in the year-and-a-half I was on her. This was in 1962. They wanted to throw me overboard into the water like they usually did when you made chief, but I said, "No way," not after what happened the last time I went in the water on *Sea Owl* [*ibid.*]!

From *Cavalla*, Rufus Weaver received orders to report to the new nuclear attack boat *Thresher* at Portsmouth, New Hampshire, in April 1963. The story of how he missed the final, fateful voyage of this submarine has previously been detailed. In September 1963, Weaver was transferred to the Blue crew of the FBM boat *George Washington*.

> I don't know how I ended up on the *George Washington*. I had no nuclear schooling, and I qualified on board the boat during the first patrol. The patrols lasted sixty days, and we were in isolation at its height. I was fascinated with the missile system, but was scared of the boat itself. With its cooling system and all those huge pipes, all I could think about was the *Thresher* and how she was lost because one of her pipes had failed. I rode the *George Washington* for about a year and got off when she went into overhaul at EB [Electric Boatyard]. I did squadron duty for the last six or seven years of my career, then I retired from the navy [*ibid.*].

Rufus Weaver retired from the navy on March 1, 1965, as a chief steward. Introduced to his future wife, Marguerite, by fellow steward Lacey Stevenson, Weaver married in 1954 and had five children: Jimmy, Henry, Charlie, Catherine, and Eric. In civilian life, Weaver worked for the Pfizer Chemical Company for 25 years but also had many outside pursuits to keep him busy. A self-described "jack of all trades," he has dabbled as a writer, a portrait artist, and, most notably, worked as an inventor. His most notable achievement, for which he received a patent, was his development of a stair-climbing wheelchair. Rufus Weaver has this to say about his overall career as a steward in the navy:

> Our contributions toward operations of shore stations and ships were really necessary for smooth operations ... no matter how demeaning they were to the performer. I really have no regrets or bitterness toward the people who perpetuated this condition. It saved a lot of young Black guys who had nothing to look forward to ... and I have some long-lasting friends [*ibid.*].

Rufus Weaver, who is now retired, continues to work as an inventor. A resident of New London, Connecticut, he was inducted into the Holland Club in October 2002 for being a qualified submariner for over fifty years.

CARL WHITE

Carl Lee White joined the navy from Macon, Georgia, when he enlisted on June 23, 1941. He had previously worked at a CCC camp in Florida before returning to his native state.

> I joined the navy when I was nineteen. I was tired of working in the cotton fields. I went to boot camp at Norfolk, Virginia, for six weeks, where I was declared honor man in my class. I then went to Annapolis, serving as a mess attendant on an old Spanish wooden ship they used. I then became interested in subs and volunteered for them. I was sent to New London and went to sub school. I was on an O-boat they used as a school boat. During the war I was on

Paddle, *Mingo*, and some other boats. We'd go out training and then go back to port to head out for patrol. We was in Pearl Harbor, Hawaii, and also Marshall Islands, New Guinea, and the Phillipines. I earned three stars on my sub pin [White].

During the war, White made three war patrols: the two maiden patrols of *Paddle* under Captain Robert Rice, and one on *Mingo* in November 1944 under Captain Joseph Staley. On his first war patrol on *Paddle* in July to August 1943, White's boat sank one cargo ship. After his second patrol during October to November 1943, *Paddle* was sent back to Mare Island to be refitted with new engines. Carl White left the boat on February 25, 1944, going to the naval hospital at Mare Island for duty. He later went back to the war zone and was in a relief crew before going aboard *Mingo* for her sixth war patrol in November 1944 under Captain John Madison. During this patrol, the boat and her crew sank a large passenger-cargo ship. Carl White was off *Mingo* after this patrol, replaced by veteran steward Sam Wallace.

> My nerves were bad and praise the Lord that I made it. Other subs I served on [after the war] were *Chub*, *Mackerel*, *Hawkbill*, and *Catfish*. I don't remember the dates. I was then done with submarine duty and was transferred to the light cruiser *Oklahoma City*. I made a world cruise on her. During the bloody Korean War, I was on the *Randolph* [a carrier]. Being African American, my years of service were not easy. I earned an honorable discharge and retired in June 1962 with 22 years [*ibid.*].

Now retired, Carl White lives in Compton, California, and is a member of the Unit K West, Unit B East veterans organization for former stewards and cooks.

JOHN WESLEY WHITEHEAD

John Wesley Whitehead, born on June 8, 1922, and a native of Alabama, moved to Waukegan, Illinois, in his early teens. In an effort to avoid being drafted, he moved to California and worked at the Mare Island Naval Shipyard. He was drafted anyway and went into the navy at San Francisco on March 5, 1943. His interview, in which he makes it clear he did not like his service in the navy as a steward, is brief and candid.

> After I was drafted, I was sent to Norfolk. There were signs all over the place that said "Sailors and dogs not allowed." The segregation there — I didn't expect that. It left a bad taste in my mouth. After boot camp I got sent to Pearl Harbor. I was on a carrier for a week then volunteered for sub duty. I did so because I didn't want to get shot or wounded. I wanted to die quickly or come back home in one piece. So, I went on *Flying Fish* for three patrols.
>   Oh, the officers were mostly good. [Glynn] Donaho was alright, [Robert] Risser was much better. Kilgore, the gunnery officer was a nice guy. I also remember Small and LCDR Chase, who was related to the coffee company with that name. The crew didn't want no kind of friendship at all, and they let you know. It was like I wasn't worth anything. When we passed each other in the boat, it was like they were meeting a dog in the tight spaces. They'd get way to side, like they didn't want to touch me.

After those patrols, I wanted off the boat, and the feeling was probably mutual. I got off at Mare Island as a steward's mate 1st class and went back to work at the shipyard and did a little welding, which was my old job before I was drafted. When I got out in December 1945, I was a 3rd class metalsmith. Today, I sometimes get invitations for the boat's reunions. I don't go. There was no friendship back then, what do they want with me now? [Whitehead].

John Whitehead's three war patrols on *Flying Fish* began on October 3, 1943, when he went aboard, and ended on April 26, 1944, when he left the boat at San Francisco. His first patrol in October 1943 was made under Captain Donaho. It was a harrowing one. The boat sank one ship and attacked and damaged a Japanese aircraft carrier. During the attack, one of the boat's torpedoes detonated close on, rocking the boat violently. Whitehead's second war patrol, *Flying Fish*'s eighth of the war, was conducted November to December 1943 under a new skipper, Robert Risser. During this patrol, which lasted 59 days, the boat had great success, sinking two large ships for nearly 19,000 tons of shipping destroyed. On Whitehead's final patrol February to March 1944, again under Risser, three ships worth 10,000 tons were sunk in 49 days. In an attempt to conduct a follow-up interview with John Whitehead, the author's request was denied. He clearly had no desire to talk about his navy career. His wife, Ruby, had this to say: "I think John is bitter when he thinks about the things he had to endure while serving. The navy really didn't want the truth told what he did on those patrols. I tell him he is blessed to be alive and healthy" (Whitehead, Ruby).

John Whitehead married his wife, Ruby, in 1947. They would later move back to the North Chicago, Illinois, area. After the war, John Whitehead became a minister and still preaches today. He and his wife currently reside in Oakland, California, and are very proud of their granddaughter who graduated in the class of 2000 from Yale University.

WALTER WILSON

Walter Pye Wilson was born on December 23, 1912, at Junction City, Kansas, the son of Louis and Ophelia Pye. He was orphaned at a young age and had one brother, James P. Owens. Walter Wilson enlisted in the navy on December 18, 1934, at Little Rock, Arkansas. After completing boot camp training at Norfolk, Virginia, he was first assigned to the aircraft carrier *Ranger*, going aboard her on March 5, 1935. He would stay on this ship for his first four years in the navy. He reenlisted in the service at Pittsburg, Pennsylvania, on December 28, 1938. Tired of carrier duty, Wilson soon volunteered for submarine duty. He became a submariner in February 1939 when he was assigned to the commissioning crew of *Sargo* at Groton, Connecticut. During the prewar years he would subsequently serve on *Seal* and was later sent to the navy yard at Mare Island, California, where he was stationed when the war began. On January 31, 1942, Walter Wilson returned to sea when he commissioned *Trigger* at Mare Island and soon headed off to war in the Pacific. Thus began an incredible period of wartime service that was equaled by few men.

Walter Pye Wilson would stay on *Trigger* from January 1942 to February 22, 1945, making thirteen war patrols in all. The first of these war patrols was conducted under Captain Jack Lewis and was in support of fleet operations during the Battle of Midway in May 1942. A second war patrol, also under Captain Lewis, was conducted in Alaskan waters in June 1942. Following this frigid outing, during which no ships were sunk, Walter Wilson would make another eleven war patrols under Captains Roy Benson (four patrols), Robert Dornin (three patrols), and Frederick Harlfinger (four patrols), from September 1942 to January 1945. On almost every one of these patrols, at least one ship was confirmed sunk, and on two patrols under Captain Dornin, four ships were sunk each outing. By war's end, *Trigger* and her crew were among the leaders in both the number of ships sunk and the amount of tonnage destroyed. Steward Walter Wilson was an able contributor to this success, and some of his activities on the boat have already been detailed. Only one man, junior officer, and later executive officer, Edward Beach, would come close to serving on *Trigger* as long as Wilson. During their time together, they forged a friendship that would last for over thirty years. But, in the end, Wilson served on *Trigger* longer even than Beach. It should be here noted that other naval historians generally credit *Trigger* as having made only eleven war patrols during the time Walter Wilson was aboard. Not included in their reckoning is the short patrol made under Captain Lewis at the Battle of Midway in 1942 and a similarly short war patrol in November 1944 when the boat was part of an unsuccessful wolf pack. In all, during his time aboard the boat, Walter Wilson and the crew of *Trigger* sank 16 ships, thus sending nearly 84,000 tons of Japanese shipping to the bottom of the Pacific. For this achievement they earned two Presidential Unit Citations and one Navy Unit Commendation. By October 1, 1943, Walter Wilson was promoted to officer's cook 1st class, and just over a year later, on November 16, 1944, was promoted to chief officer's cook for meritorious service.

Despite this success, there was one thing missing for Wilson. He wanted to get married and have a family. Though Wilson was a very popular and highly respected crewmember, he was a quiet man and one who "had his Bible with him during the war" (Wilson, Viola). When *Trigger* came into port and it was time for liberty, Wilson, who was older than most of the sailors aboard, "was disturbed by the young women that used to meet the returning sailors and sometimes just stayed on the boat" (*ibid.*). By early 1945, Walter Wilson just "had a feeling" (*ibid.*) that now was the time to act. He went to his skipper and asked off the boat for her upcoming patrol, stating that "Captain, If I stay on this boat I may never get married" (*ibid.*). He was subsequently transferred to Submarine Division 281 for flag duty and was soon sent back to the states for new construction duty. The old salt was eerily correct, for less than two months later, old *Trigger* was sunk with all hands. Stunned when he learned the news, Wilson said a prayer for his departed shipmates but also thanked God for his safe return.

Walter Wilson would soon find the wife he longed for. He met Miss Viola Bailey, a young lady from Baltimore who was in Portsmouth, New Hampshire, visiting her sister, and the two soon formed an attachment. As she would later recall, "He had a very quiet manner and a beautiful smile" (*ibid.*). They were married on August 11, 1945, just two days before his new boat, *Sirago*, was commissioned at Portsmouth under his old skipper, Captain Fritz Harlfinger. It was tough for Wilson to go to sea and leave his new bride behind, but go he did. To pass away the hours in his spare time on his first long cruise after being married, he painstakingly crafted a frame out of hand-tooled leather in which he intended to display his wedding picture. That frame, and the picture within, is still a cherished memento to this day, nearly 60 years later, for Viola Wilson.

In the postwar years, Walter Wilson continued to serve in submarines, serving on *Sirago*, *Sablefish*, *Tusk*, and *Spinax*. About 1949 he was sent to the Boston Naval Shipyard, where he soon joined the commissioning crew of *Grampus*. He would later serve on *Sarda* and *Argonaut* before, fittingly enough, joining the commissioning crew of another new boat, *Trigger*. Once again, Wilson was serving with his old friend, Captain Edward Beach, who was the skipper of this new boat named in honor of its worthy predecessor. It somehow seemed right to have these two old hands from the old *Trigger* aboard to give the new boat a proper start when she was commissioned on March 31, 1952.

Wilson would serve aboard *Trigger* for nearly two years, but it was getting harder for him to go off to sea and leave his wife alone for such extended periods. He always saw to it that his wife was properly set up before he went to sea, getting her the things *she* needed to pass the long hours she spent waiting for him to return home. When she expressed an interest in sewing and artwork, he surprised her with a new sewing machine and a plentiful supply of art crayons and pencils before he went off to sea. Wilson's attentiveness to his wife was equally reciprocated by Viola early in their marriage. When Wilson was at sea, Viola sewed him a fine bathrobe, lovingly crafted out of a gray corduroy fabric that she carefully chose. When Walter Wilson returned home from a long cruise, he soon spotted the bathrobe and put it on at once. From then on, until he had to return to duty, the bathrobe seldom left his body. Without a doubt, it was a tangible symbol of the peaceful homelife Walter Wilson had always wished for and found forever when he met and married Viola Bailey.

Eventually the time came when it was time for the old submariner to return from the sea for good. In January 1954, after 19 years of continuous sea duty, Walter Pye Wilson requested and was granted permission to transfer to shore duty. He was subsequently stationed at the Portsmouth Naval Shipyard and retired from active duty on July 15, 1956. He then worked at the shipyard as a civilian warehouseman, though he was still in the naval reserve. Wilson retired from the navy altogether on December 1, 1964, having served for thirty years. He continued working at the Portsmouth Naval Shipyard until finally retiring on December 30, 1977. Perhaps longing for the wide-open space that had eluded him for so long while serving in cramped submarines, Walter Wilson and his wife bought an old farm in the Maine countryside where they lived for many happy years with their daughter Winnifred. Both Walter and Viola Wilson were devoted church members, while Walter enjoyed woodworking and refinishing old furniture. Sadly, Walter Pye Wilson did not get to enjoy his retirement for long. The old submariner passed away on October 22, 1978, at the age of 65. Despite his physical absence from her life for over 25 years now, Viola Wilson still talks about her husband with a wide smile and a sparkle in her eye, stating that "He never left me; he will always be with me" (*ibid.*).

Appendix A.
The Steward Rating System, 1939–1974

The following rates are listed from the lowest rating held when a man first joined the navy to the highest rating obtainable during each time period. The rating of officer's cook or officer's steward was equal in terms of pay grade and the duties they performed on submarines and were usually based on an individual's preference.

1939–1943

1. Mess attendant 3rd class (E-1)
2. Mess attendant 2nd class (E-2)
3. Mess attendant 1st class (E-3)
4. Officer's cook or steward 3rd class (E-4)
5. Officer's cook or steward 2nd class (E-5)
6. Officer's cook or steward 1st class (E-6)
7. Chief Officer's cook or steward (E-7)

1943–1948

During this time period the rating system remained the same as that of 1939–1943, except that the term "mess attendant" was replaced by that of "steward's mate" for grades E-1 to E-3. Grades E-4 to E-7 remained the same.

1948–1958

During this time period the rating system remained the same as in 1943–1948, but terminology changed. Pay grades E-1 to E-3 were now referred to as "stewardsman" (TN), while pay grades E-4 to E-7 were now only known as "steward" (SD), with the formerly optional designation of "officer's cook" dropped altogether.

1958–1974

Two additional pay grades were added in 1958. All other rates remained the same until the designation of "steward" was dropped altogether starting in 1975 and replaced with that of mess management specialist (MMS).

1. Stewardsman 3rd class (E-1)
2. Stewardsman 2nd class (E-2)
3. Stewardsman 1st class (E-3)
4. Steward 3rd class (E-4)
5. Steward 2nd class (E-5)
6. Steward 1st class (E-6)
7. Chief steward (E-7)
8. Senior chief steward (E-8)
9. Master chief steward (E-9)

Appendix B.
Black Submarine Stewards Killed or Lost During World War II

Key to Abbreviations Used:

- MA- Mess Attendant
- OS- Officer's Steward (Petty Officer)
- OC- Officer's Cook (Petty Officer)
- Stm- Steward's Mate
- St- Steward (Petty Officer)
- Ck- Officer's Cook (Petty Officer)

Numbers refer to the class within each grade.

	Date	*Name*	*Rate*	*Submarine*
1.	1/24/42	Nathaniel Johnson	MA-1	*S-26*
2.	8/42	Herbert J. Arvan	MA-2	*Grunion*
3.	8/42	Cornelius Paul, Jr.	MA-2	*Grunion*
4.	1/10/43	Percy J. Olds	OS-2	*Argonaut*
5.	1/10/43	Willie D. Thomas	OC-2	*Argonaut*
6.	2/43	Arthur R. Massey	MA-2	*Amberjack*
7.	2/43	Wallace Montague	MA-1	*Amberjack*
8.	3/43	Curtheal Black	OS-3	*Grampus*
9.	3/43	Donald M. Fenner	MA-1	*Grampus*
10.	3/43	John D. Dabney	OC-3	*Triton*
11.	3/43	Herman T. McCalop	MA-1	*Triton*
12.	6/43	Charles Laws	MA-2	*Runner*

Appendix B: Black Submarine Stewards Killed or Lost During World War II

	Date	Name	Rate	Submarine
13.	6/12/43	Willie D. Young	Stm-2	*R-12*
14.	9/43	Wesley L. Leonard	Stm-1	*Pompano*
15.	9/43	Sherman Ganious	Stm-1	*Pompano*
16.	9/43	Samuel Nelson	Stm-2	*Cisco*
17.	9/43	Albert W. Williams	Stm-1	*Cisco*
18.	10/7/43	Curtis Glenn	Ck-2	*S-44*
19.	10/7/43	Herman M. Mitchell	Stm-2	*S-44*
20.	10/12/43	Isaac Cabase	St-1	*Dorado*
21.	10/12/43	DeWitt Harris	Stm-2	*Dorado*
22.	11/16/43	Russell A. Brooks	Stm-2	*Corvina*
23.	11/16/43	Eddie Jackson	Ck-2	*Corvina*
24.	12/43	Earl Cheatham	Stm-1	*Capelin*
25.	12/43	Finon Perry	Stm-2	*Capelin*
26.	1/22/44*	Louis Jones	Stm-1	*Herring*
27.	2/44	Raymond P. Dews	Stm-1	*Scorpion*
28.	2/44	Nearest Fergerson	St-3	*Scorpion*
29.	3/44	John E. Ewell	Stm-2	*Trout*
30.	3/44	Albert S. Lewis	Stm-2	*Trout*
31.	3/44	Calvin C. Millner	Stm-1	*Trout*
32.	3/26/44	Leroy Ellis	St-1	*Tullibee*
33.	3/26/44	Ripley Washington, Jr.	Stm-1	*Tullibee*
34.	6/1/44	Timothy Burkett	Ck-1	*Herring*
35.	6/1/44	Nathaniel Campbell	Stm-2	*Herring*
36.	6/14/44	William E. McCulough	Stm-1	*Golet*
37.	6/14/44	George Sterling, Jr.	Stm-3	*Golet*
38.	7/4/44**	Levi Bolton	Stm-1	*S-28*
39.	7/4/44	Jake Spurlock	Ck-2	*S-28*
40.	7/26/44	Elliot Gleaton, Jr.	Ck-2	*Robalo*
41.	7/26/44	Davie L. Williams	Stm-1	*Robalo*
42.	8/13/44	Clyde Banks	Ck-3	*Flier*
43.	8/13/44	John C. Turner	Stm-1	*Flier*
44.	8/24/44	James E. Cromwell	Stm-2	*Harder*
45.	8/24/44	Robert Moore	Ck-2	*Harder*
46.	10/24/44	Richard E. Hooker	Stm-1	*Shark 2*
47.	10/24/44	George W. Pittman	Ck-2	*Shark 2*

*Lost overboard enroute to seventh war patrol.

**Loss is questionable, as Bolton's name later appears on the crew muster rolls for *Rasher* in late 1945.

Appendix B: Black Submarine Stewards Killed or Lost During World War II 387

	Date	*Name*	*Rate*	*Submarine*
48.	10/24/44	Ralph F. Adams	Stm-2	*Tang*
49.	10/24/44	Rubin M. Raiford	Ck-3	*Tang*
50.	10/24/44	Howard M. Walker	Stm-1	*Tang*
51.	10/44	Benjamin Evans	Stm-1	*Escolar*
52.	10/44	James A. Raley	Stm-2	*Escolar*
53.	11/7/44	James L. Carpenter	Stm-2	*Albacore*
54.	11/7/44	Willie A. McNeill	Stm-2	*Albacore*
55.	11/7/44	Sylvester M. Wright	Stm-2	*Albacore*
56.	11/8/44	Bennie Cleveland	St-3	*Growler*
57.	11/8/44	Willie Flippens	Stm-2	*Growler*
58.	11/16/44	Odio Bass	Stm-2	*Scamp*
59.	1/45	William P. Grandy	Stm-1	*Swordfish*
60.	1/45	Vernon Kirk	St-3	*Swordfish*
61.	2/4/45	Nathaniel Thornton	Stm-1	*Barbel*
62.	2/4/45	Arthur J. Wharton	Stm-1	*Barbel*
63.	3/45	William H. Dawson	Ck-3	*Kete*
64.	3/45	Calvin F. Dortche	Stm-1	*Kete*
65.	3/28/45	Andrew J. Carter	Stm-1	*Trigger*
66.	3/28/45	Nathaniel E. Thompson	Ck-2	*Trigger*
67.	4/45	William J. Rodney	Stm-1	*Snook*
68.	4/45	William E. Shelton	St-3	*Snook*
69.	5/3/45	Robert Green	Stm-2	*Lagarto*
70.	5/3/45	Albert Kirtley	Stm-1	*Lagarto*
71.	6/18/45	Quintus L. Cooley	Stm-2	*Bonefish*
72.	6/18/45	William H. Epps, Jr.	Stm-2	*Bonefish*
73.	8/6/45	Hubert B. Hackett	Stm-2	*Bullhead*
74.	8/6/45	Percy Johnson, Jr.	Stm-1	*Bullhead*

Appendix C.
Top Stewards During World War II by Number of War Patrols

The service of Black stewards during the war in the Submarine Force can be measured to the greatest extent by the number of war patrols they made. A total of 785 Black stewards have been identified (see Appendix D) as having made war patrols from 1941 to 1945. Just over 84 percent of these men made anywhere from 1 to 5 war patrols. However, a small group of Black stewards, 126 in number, made from 6 to 13 war patrols, and thus must be considered among the best of the best both for their abilities as submariners and their devotion to duty. A war patrol could last as short as seven days, as occurred in some instances, or last up to seventy-eight days, the longest patrol of the war conducted by *Sculpin* in May 1942. The average war patrol lasted about fifty days. Thus, for a man that made 13 war patrols, his time spent in combat situations at sea measured a total of nearly 21 months. For a man that made 6 war patrols, his time in combat measured about 10 months.

Following is a list of the Black stewards known to have made more than 5 war patrols, and the boat(s) they served on. An asterisk (*) indicates a man who was killed in action during the course of his service. See appendixes B and D for further details.

10–13 War Patrols Made

1. Jim Eckford Stallings (*Haddock*)—13
2. Walter Pye Wilson (*Trigger*)—13
3. Arthur Brown (*Narwhal*)—12
4. Nathaniel Elton Thompson (*Trigger, Tullibee, Trigger*)—12*
5. Earl Williams, Jr. (*Nautilus, Tuna, Piranha*)—12
6. Comer Howze (*Dolphin, Sunfish, Apogon*)—11
7. Ward Morris Majors (*Tautog, Tench*)—11

8. William Wright Roston (*Grayling, Finback*)—11
9. Louis Lee Epps (*Nautilus, Finback*)—10
10. Jeffie Frye (*Kingfish, Lamprey*)—10
11. Leslie Hamilton (*Thresher, Billfish, Brill*)—10
12. George Washington Lytle (*Drum*)—10
13. Claude J. McKay (*Drum*)—10
14. Leonard Cicero Rozar (*Tuna, Saury*)—10
15. Willie Jay Thompson (*Sawfish, Pogy*)—10

8–9 War Patrols Made

16. William Joseph Boulet (*Halibut, Queenfish*)—9
17. J.P. Buttrill (*Spearfish*)—9
18. Elijah Dawson, Jr. (*Drum, Finback, Drum*)—9
19. Stewart Alexander DeHosnery (*Trout*)—9
20. Eddie Gordon (*Tuna*)—9
21. Lee Montgomery Jackson (*S-30*)—9
22. Albert Leon Morris (*Gato, Greenling*, Peto)—9
23. Eugene Mosley, Jr. (*Triton, Gudgeon, Bonefish*)
24. James Woodley Patton (*Puffer*)—9
25. John Henry Prophet (*Growler*)—9
26. Charles McKinley Richardson (*Kingfish, Bluefish, Nautilus*)—9
27. James Washington (*Cuttlefish, Pompon*)—9
28. Ripley Washington, Jr. (*Sawfish, Tullibee*)—9*
29. Levi Bolton (*S-30-S-28-Rasher*)—8
30. Bennie Lawrence Brown (*S-28, Hardhead*)—8
31. Timothy Burkett (*Herring*)—8*
32. Robert Coley (*Tambor, Bugara*)—8
33. Joseph Cross (*Halibut*)—8
34. Joe Caesar Evans (*S-32*)—8
35. James Lewis Gaylor (*Snapper, Dace*)—8
36. Elliot Gleaton, Jr. (*Shad, Robalo*)—8*
37. Edward Ross Napier (*S-18*)—8
38. Willie James (*Drum, Wahoo, Whale*)—8
39. James Edward Johnson (*Grouper, Peto*)
40. David Frank Leeks (*Tambor, Triton*)—8
41. Steve Emry Mosley (*Bowfin, Cabrilla*)—8
42. Lunie Joseph Neal (*Narwhal*)—8
43. James Dorsey Oliver (*Bluefish, Rasher, Bluegill*)—8
44. William Fairfield Rapier (*Silversides, Tunny*)—8
45. Ulysses Grant Reed (*Haddo, Hake*)—8
46. William Dee Robinson (*Gato, Growler*)—8
47. Willie Edward Vaughn (*Trigger, Kingfish*)—8
48. Hall Jackson Wall (*Gato*)—8
49. James E. Wade (*S-35*)—8

7 War Patrols Made

50. Kenneth Barfield (*Tarpon, Baya, Bergall*)
51. George Bracy (*Pargo*)
52. Orange Bradley (*Hoe, Hawkbill*)
53. Luther Bryant (*Haddo*)
54. Mack B. Butler (*Dace*)
55. James Carpenter (*Pogy, Plaice, Whale*)
56. Leroy Cox (*Flying Fish, Seal*)
57. Joseph Milsted Deville (*Tinosa, Steelhead, Argonaut* 2)
58. Joseph George (*Guardfish*)
59. John Andrew Gray (*Tautog*)
60. Warren Hammond (*Haddock, Flying Fish*)
61. Lewis T. Hammonds (*Batfish*)
62. Edmund Richard Hannah, Jr. (*Pollack*)
63. Bernard Madison Heard (*Snook, Tilefish*)
64. Lonnie David Jackson (*Trout*)
65. Walter Jonkins (*Pompon*)
66. Carl Eugene Kimmons (*Plunger, Parche*)
67. Daniel McCormick (*Gar, Bonefish*)
68. Otis Morgan (*Redfin*)
69. John Willie Moore, Jr. (*Hake*)
70. James William Phifer (*Paddle*)
71. Paul Francis Ragland (*Barb*)
72. Anderson Peter Royal (*Silversides, Dragonet*)
73. Isiah Thomas (*Herring, Whale*)
74. Otha Lavada Toler (*Plunger, Croaker*)
75. John Clyde Turner (*Cod, Tinosa, Flier*)*
76. Carlos A. Tuttle (*Peto, Quillback*)

6 War Patrols Made

77. Columbus Adams (*Sunfish*)
78. Carrol Louden Allen (*Puffer*)
79. Milton Arder (*Paddle*)
80. Willie Bailey, Jr. (*Hake, Blackfin*)
81. James Lee Baker (*S-35, Nautilus*)
82. Isaac Bell (*Sealion II*)
83. Charles Henry Bivens (*Grampus, Triton, Salmon, Jallao*)
84. Curtheal Black (*Grampus*)*
85. Primas Alexander Blacknall (*Cabrilla, Cod*)
86. William Thomas Bynum (*Burrfish, Spadefish*)
87. Bennie Cleveland (*Growler*)*
88. John D. Dabney (*Triton*)*
89. Frank Lewis Davis (*Pilotfish*)
90. Lewis P. Davis (*Plaice*)

Appendix C: Top Stewards During World War II by Number of War Patrols

91. William Berkley Denson (*Bream*)
92. Melton Evans (*Gudgeon*)
93. Chester W. Epps (*Burrfish*)
94. Donald M. Fenner (*Snapper, Grampus*)*
95. Montierde Filemon (*Sealion II*)
96. Whaylon O'Neal Fisher (*Kingfish*)
97. Nellis Freeman (*Guardfish, Peto*)
98. Jim Mack Glover (*Gunnel*)
99. Charlie Gober (*Skate*)
100. Lonnie Hadden (*S-23*)
101. Alfred Leander Hall (*Pomfret*)
102. Arthur Harmon, Jr. (*Pilotfish*)
103. Robert Harris, Jr. (*Spearfish, Sawfish, Skipjack*)
104. Henry Hinton (*Gar, Cero*)
105. George Ingram (*Pampanito*)
106. Buck Jones, Jr. (*Guavina*)
107. Leonard Henshaw Keith (*S-44, Narwhal*)
108. Lyle Pleasant Lengue (*Bream*)
109. Wesley Lewis Leonard (*Pompano*)*
110. Charlie Morgan Lewis (*Lapon, Muskallunge*)
111. Andrew Linthicum, Jr. (*Narwhal*)
112. Fred Lee Moss (*Shad*)
113. Elijah Rowles, Jr. (*Bang, Bluefish*)
114. Spaulding Bedford Settle (*Tinosa*)
115. William Everett Shelton (*Snook*)*
116. William Sherman (*Raton*)
117. John Singleton (*Caiman, Pintado*)
118. Talmon Stallworth (*Ray, Tilefish*)
119. Thomas James Trigg (*Grenadier*)
120. Magnus Augustus Wade (*Gunnel, Dentuda*)
121. Wade Walker (*Gabilan*)
122. Willie Walton (*Pogy*)
123. Sam Wesly Wallace (*Mingo*)
124. Clyde Ware (*Bashaw*)
125. Curtis Clark Washington (*S-23*)
126. Robert James Williams (*Guavina*)
127. Charles Woodley (*Balao*)

Appendix D.
Black Stewards of World War II

The following is a boat-by-boat listing of most of the Black stewards that served during the war from 1941 to 1945. In most cases, this information was obtained from enlisted man muster rolls on microfilm held at National Archive II in College Park, Maryland. The reel numbers for these records can be found in the bibliography. The following listing represents nearly all of the Black stewards that made Pacific war patrols on both fleet and S-boats. In an attempt to view all such records at the National Archives, those for the fleet boat *Toro* were missing and could not be consulted. For two other boats, *Argonaut I* and *Sea Raven*, portions of their records were missing or damaged and may not be complete. In regard to S-boats, most of them were withdrawn from war service by the end of 1943, so men who served after this time have not been recorded here. While those fleet and S-boats that made both Atlantic and Pacific war patrols are recorded here, those S- and R-boats, and the antiquated *Bass, Bonita,* and *Barracuda* fleet boats that only made Atlantic war patrols in 1942 are not.

For those men who went aboard a submarine from late 1944 onward, it will be noted that their date and place of enlistment are often lacking. This is due to the fact that such information was no longer required by the navy to be filled in by a boat's yeoman when preparing his crew lists. Where such data for the same individual was found in another location, it has been added to those boats he served on late in the war. Finally, it should be noted that some boats never carried a Black steward in their crew throughout the entire war or the times during which they made war patrols, and thus they are not listed. These boats, numbering fourteen in all, were *Grayback, Perch I, Pickerel, Sargo, Seawolf, Sealion I, Shark I, S-27, S-36, S-37, S-38, S-39, S-40,* and *S-41.*

For this work, Black submarine stewards have been identified by their rate first (see Appendix A), by their place of enlistment (when known), and by their name. Since no white individuals served as stewards in the navy during this time, stewards were either Chinese (rare), natives of the Phillipine Islands or Guam, or they were Black Americans. Using these three factors, determining the ethnicity of a given boat's stewards was usually possible. In the few cases where the ethnicity of a steward is in question, it has been so noted.

The data for the submarines listed shows that 975 men served as stewards on board them. Of this total, 190 made no war patrols but served as relief crewmen. The remaining 785 men, representing 81 percent of the total, made at least one war patrol. Those men who served on boats that sortied for the battle of Midway in 1942 for about fifteen days have had this credited as one war patrol to their total, even if the navy or some historians have not recognized it as such.

A number of the men listed have entries for several different boats, indicating that they either made war patrols on more than one boat, served in a relief crew on more than one boat, or did a combination of relief duty and war patrol duty on different boats. As a reminder, relief crewmen only served aboard a given boat while she was in port, helping to clean it up and ready it for her next patrol. In the comments section for each man, I have included pertinent information where it was available. The term "flag" duty or allowance is found frequently, and simply means that a man was nominally attached to the boat listed because she was a flag ship, but he was not physically on the boat and made no war patrols while performing flag duty.

Key to Abbreviations Used

	AL	Alaska
	AOL	Absent over leave
	ATRC	Advanced training relief crew
	AWOL	Absent without leave
	BNS	Boston Naval Shipyard
	CM	Captain's mast/court martial proceedings
	CZ	Canal Zone, Panama
	DC	Deck court (similar to captain's mast)
	DH	Dutch Harbor, Alaska
	EOW	End of war 9/1945
	JA	Japan
	KIA	Killed in action while on patrol
	Lost	Death due to a noncombat situation
	MAN	Manitowoc, Wisconsin
	MI	Mare Island, California
	NC	New construction at one of the submarine shipyards stateside
	NL	New London Submarine Base
	NOK	Next of kin list, filed when a submarine went out on patrol
	NRU	Navy repair unit, a shore-based facility
	Ns	References a nonsubmarine or nontender vessel
	PH	Pearl Harbor submarine base
	PNSY	Portsmouth Naval Shipyard
	SD	San Diego, California
	SF	San Francisco, California
	SRU	Ship repair unit, a shore-based facility
	TF	Task force
	TI	Treasure Island, California
	USNH	United States Naval Hospital
	WP	War patrol

Note: Each submarine listed also includes that boat's official hull number.

Submarine	Last Name	First Name	Middle	D.O.E.	Place of Enlistment	Date on Board	Date Off	Rating On	Rating Off	War Patrols	Notes About Service
Albacore	Brown, Jr.	Albert		12/4/41	Raleigh, NC	3/24/43	3/29/43	MA-2	MA-2	0	Relief duty only
Albacore	Carpenter	James	Louis	11/29/42	Washington, DC	9/27/44	KIA	Stm-2	Stm-2	1	Lost with boat 11/7/44 in mined waters off Japan
Albacore	Gardner	Sylvester		7/6/39	Richmond, VA	6/1/42	after 9/42	MA-1	MA-2	1	Reduced in grade; Date off uncertain
Albacore	McNeill	William	A.	5/11/44	Raleigh, NC	10/28/44	KIA	Stm-2	Stm-2	1	Lost with boat 11/7/44 in mined waters off Japan
Albacore	Wright	Sylvester	M.	5/9/44	Raleigh, NC	10/1/44	KIA(?)	Stm-2	Stm-2	1	Crew records show transfer to SD 61 on 10/28/44; KIA status uncertain
Albacore-218	Berger	Otis	Lee	3/3/42	Richmond, VA	6/1/42	10/10/44	MA-3	Ck-2	10	Comm crew; Made all boat's WPs before her final loss
Amberjack	Nunn	Paul	Lloyd	11/13/40	Indianapolis, IN	6/30/42	11/16/42	MA-2	MA-2	3	Off to Guardfish
Amberjack-219	Montague	Wallace		3/15/40	Raleigh, NC	6/19/42	KIA	MA-2	MA-1	3	Lost with boat on 2/16/43 near Rabaul
Angler	Evans	John	Henry	ca. 1944		5/18/45	EOW	Stm-2	Stm-2	1	On from ATRC
Angler	Hearn	Marvin	R.	4/2/40	Cincinnati, OH	10/1/43 (1st)	6/19/44	Ck-2	Ck-1	3	On at NL, off to relief duty
Angler	Hearn	Marvin	R.	4/2/40	Cincinnati, OH	9/9/44 (2nd)	5/14/45	Ck-1	Ck-1	2	Off at SF
Angler	Marble	Johnie	unk.	6/5/45			EOW	Stm-2	Stm-2	1	
Angler	Patrick	Walter	ca. 1944		Newark, NJ	5/31/45	6/5/45	Stm-1	Stm-1	0	Relief duty only, prior on Bluegill
Angler	Strother	Elijah	B.	7/8/43	Albany, NY	10/1/43	9/6/44	Stm-2	Stm-1	4	On at NL
Angler-240	Davis	Edward		11/29/43	Gilmer, TX	6/12/44	EOW	Stm-2	Ck-3	4	On from Puffer flag
Apogon	Johns	Francis	Elijah	5/1/43	Columbia, SC	9/13/43	8/10/44	Stm-2	Stm-1	4	On from S-17
Apogon	McDonald	Eugene		5/4/43	Washington, DC	9/11/43	9/13/43	Stm-2	Stm-2	0	Relief duty only
Apogon	McNamee	Charles	Casey	12/22/42	Coco Solo, CZ	7/16/43	6/4/44	St-2	St-1	3	Comm Crew; Possibly enlisted first in 1938
Apogon	Myers	Theodore		12/17/41	New Orleans, LA	7/16/43	9/10/43	Stm-1	Stm-1	4	Comm Crew
Apogon	Palmer	Robert		4/10/43	Indianapolis, IN	8/12/44	EOW	Stm-2	St-3	4	
Apogon-308	Howze	Comer		9/3/41	Birmingham, AL	6/5/44	EOW	CK-2	unk.	5	Prior on Sunfish

Boat	Last Name	First Name	Middle	Hometown	Enlisted	Rate	Rank	WPs	Notes
Archerfish	Brown	William	Allen			10/26/44	EOW	Stm-2	Stm-3	3	CM 10/45, reduced from Stm-1; Present at Tokyo Bay surrender
Archerfish	Harper, Jr.	William	Ivory	Lubbock, TX		7/30/44	Stm-1	Stm-1	1	On from tender Proteus; Deceased 12/1986
Archerfish	Hughes	William	A.	Louisville, KY		9/8/43	Stm-2	Stm-2	0	On at NL, off to same; Relief duty only; Deceased 8/1/2000
Archerfish	Lewis	William	Vincent			6/4/45	EOW	Stm-1	Stm-1	1	Made boat's final WP; Present at Tokyo Bay surrender ceremony
Archerfish	Malone	James				6/13/45	EOW	Stm-2	Stm-2	1	Made boat's final WP; Present at Tokyo Bay surrender ceremony
Archerfish	Scott	Levi	Frank	Charleston, SC		5/15/44	5/21/45	Stm-2	Stm-1	4	Off to USNH SF; Deceased 7/1993
Archerfish	Stone	Herman	P.	New York, NY		9/4/43	11/13/43	Stm-1	Stm-1	0	A straggler; failed to return from liberty in CZ
Archerfish	Young	Donald	Augustus	Atlanta, GA	unk.	10/29/43	5/13/44	Stm-2	Stm-2	2	On from NL; declared a straggler 5/13/44
Archerfish-311	Bristow	Henry	unk.	Raleigh, NC	unk.	11/13/43	7/30/44	Stm-2	Stm-1	3	On from S-13; Deceased 10/6/1997
Argonaut 1	Thomas	Willie	D.	unk.	7/15/39		KIA	OC-2	OC-2	3	Date aboard and number of WPs uncertain
Argonaut 1-166	Olds	Percy	J.	Little Rock, AR	Pre-War(?)		KIA	OC-3	OC-2	3	Lost with boat 1/10/43 south of New Britain
Argonaut 2	Baptiste	Joseph	Clifton	New Orleans, LA	12/15/41	1/15/45	6/26/45	Ck-2	Ck-2	0	On at PSNY, off prior to WP
Argonaut 2	Barnes	Warren	G.			unk.	unk.	Stm-1	Stm-1	0	Relief duty only
Argonaut 2	Blevins	Charles	B.	Baltimore, MD	2/2/37	unk.	unk.	Stm-2	Stm-2	0	Relief duty only
Argonaut 2	Branton	Sterling	W.			unk.	6/7/45	Stm-1	Stm-1	0	Off to Carp
Argonaut 2	Deville	Joseph	Milsted	Houston, TX	10/21/42	6/3/45	EOW	St-3	St-3	1	Prior on Tinosa, Steelhead
Argonaut 2	Doxey	Henry	W.			unk.	unk.	Stm-1	Stm-1	0	Relief duty only
Argonaut 2	Fisher	Earl				3/24/45	EOW	St-2	St-2	1	On at NL

Submarine	Last Name	First Name	Middle	D.O.E.	Place of Enlistment	Date on Board	Date Off	Rating On	Rating Off	War Patrols	Notes About Service
Argonaut 2	Greene	Joe	William	12/8/43	Lexington, KY	1/17/45	3/28/45	St-3	St-3	0	On from Cachalot, off to Salmon
Argonaut 2	Jones, Jr.	Edward	Monroe	8/2/44		11/14/44	EOW	Stm-2	Stm-2	1	Comm crew, on at PNSY; Made boat's only WP
Argonaut 2-475	Madison	Lester		4/2/42	Houston, TX		6/9/45	St-3	St-3	0	Prior on Tang
Aspro	Johnson	Robert	Lee	1/19/43	Columbia, SC	11/24/43	11/28/43	Stm-1	Stm-1	0	Relief duty only
Aspro	Lyman, Jr.	William	Leonard	unk.		6/24/45	EOW	Stm-2	Stm-2	1	Comm crew, on at PNSY
Aspro	Micheaux	Henry	Auston	4/29/43	Detroit, MI	7/31/43	11/24/43	Stm-2	Stm-2	0	On at PNSY, off to ATRC
Aspro	Sherman	John		6/5/42	Nashville, TN	7/31/43	9/2/44	Stm-1	Ck-2	4	
Aspro	Smith	William	Thomas	7/9/43	Philadelphia, PA	11/28/43	6/30/44	Stm-2	Stm-1	3	Probably same man as William T. Smith on Hawkbill
Aspro	Walker	Samuel		11/29/43	Columbus, GA	6/30/44	EOW	Stm-2	Stm-1	4	NOK wife Purlie Walker, Omaha, GA
Aspro-309	Doss	Roy	Elmer	12/29/43	Chattanooga, TN	9/3/44	EOW	Stm-2	Stm-2	3	On from ATRC; NOK sister Nettie Johnson, Chattanooga, TN
Atule	Ellis, Jr.	Arthur		3/31/44	Little Rock, AR	6/21/44	3/27/45	Stm-2	Stm-1	2	
Atule	Griffith	Monroe	Wickliffe		Chicago, IL (?)	8/2/44	EOW	Stm-2	St-3	4	On at NL, made all this boat's WPs
Atule	Redcross	Floyd	Walter	unk.		3/27/45	EOW	Stm-1	unk.	2	
Atule-403	Brown	Quincy	Timothy	4/28/43	Oklahoma City, OK	6/21/44	8/4/44	Stm-2	Stm-2	0	
Balao	Carter	Andrew	Jordan	5/8/43	New York, NY	12/8/43	1/31/44	Stm-1	Stm-1	1	On from Peto, Off to TF 72 Relief, Lost on Trigger
Balao	Cobbs	Ervin	T.	4/1/41	San Francisco, CA	9/30/43	12/8/43	Stm-1	Stm-1	0	On from Guardfish, off to Peto
Balao	Cooper	Charlie		3/20/43	Columbus, GA	2/27/45	EOW	Stm-1	Stm-1	3	Made boat's final 3 WPs
Balao	Gardner	Sylvester		7/6/39	Richmond, VA	7/23/43	9/30/43	Ck-3	Ck-3	1	On from Guardfish, off to same
Balao	McLeroy	Inman		unk.		2/27/45	EOW	Stm-1	Stm-1	3	Made boat's final 3 WPs

Boat	Last	First	Middle	Enlist Date	City	Start	End	Rating 1	Rating 2	#	Notes
Balao	Sigue	Junius		11/18/42	New Orleans, LA	2/28/43	7/23/43	MA-2	Stm-2	0	Off to Guardfish
Balao	Woodley	Charles		8/17/42	St. Thomas, VI	2/4/43	1/3/45	MA-2	Ck-3	6	First enlisted in 1938 (?)
Balao-285	Biser	Anthony		4/8/43	New Orleans, LA	1/31/44	1/31/45	Stm-2	Stm-1	3	Transferred from SRU
Bang	Bass	Jesse	Phillip	unk.		10/25/44	EOW	Stm-2	Stm-2	3	Made boat's final 3 Wps
Bang	Brandon	William	Theodus	7/19/43	Detroit, MI	2/8/1944 (1st)	12/31/44	Stm-1	St-3	4	From O-3
Bang	Brandon	William	Theodus	7/19/43	Detroit, MI	3/11/45 (2nd)	EOW	St-3	St-3	1	Back on from relief duty
Bang	Holt	Carl	Chester	8/10/43						0	Off at New York
Bang	Rowles, Jr.	Elijah		12/1/42	Birmingham, AL	12/4/43	2/7/44	Stm-2	Stm-2	3	On from O-6
Bang-385	Barrett	Samuel	James	7/11/44	Yonkers, NY	12/31/43	9/30/44	Stm-2	Stm-2	1	
Barb	Clark	Dallas	Clinton	4/2/43	Richmond, VA	12/31/44	2/5/45	Stm-2	Stm-2	0	Relief duty only
Barb	Coley	David	Franklin	unk.		9/22/43	9/30/43	Stm-2	Stm-1	2	Made boat's final 2 Wps
Barb	Dodds	Roosevelt		5/13/42	Cleveland, OH	2/18/44	EOW	MA-3	MA-3	0	Comm crew, off at NL
Barb	Jackson, Jr.	Elmer		4/23/43	Cleveland, OH	7/8/42	8/5/42	Stm-2	Ck-3	4	On from O-6
Barb	Jones	William	Lee	1/19/43	Charlotte, NC	8/9/43	10/18/44	Stm-2	Stm-2	1	Prior on Cod
Barb	King	Eugene		12/4/39	Birmingham, AL	10/18/44	12/18/44	OC-3	Ck-2	1	On from flag duty, date off uncertain; Probably 1 Europe WP
Barb	Ragland	Paul	Francis	12/15/42	Baltimore, MD	5/19/43	ca. 9/1943	Stm-1	Ck-2	7	On for boat's final 7 WPs
Barb	St. Clair	Major		12/18/41	Raleigh, NC	9/29/43	EOW	MA-1	Stm-1	0	Off to tender Beaver, medical treatment and duty
Barb	Stevenson	Lacey		4/23/42	New London, CT	8/5/42	5/26/43	OS-2	OS-1	3	Comm crew, off to tender Beaver for medical; Prior enlist in 1938
Barb-220	Black	Solomon		12/4/41	Little Rock, AR	7/8/42	3/11/43	Ck-3	Ck-3	0	On from Plunger flag, off to USNH
Barbel	Dance	Samuel	Lee	11/28/38	Philadelphia, PA	9/22/43	9/23/43	Ck-1	Ck-1	0	From Sealion; Relief duty only
Barbel	Thornton	Nathaniel		11/30/43	Hattiesburg, MS	4/15/44	5/8/44	Stm-2	Stm-1	4	Lost with boat 2/45 off Palawan Passage
Barbel	Vaughn	Francis		6/6/42	Birmingham, AL	7/14/44	KIA	Stm-3	St-2	1	Comm crew
Barbel	Wharton, Jr.	Arthur	J.	3/4/41	Louisville, KY	4/3/44	8/25/44	Stm-1	Stm-1	3	Lost with boat 2/45 off Palawan Passage
						8/25/44	KIA				

Submarine	Last Name	First Name	Middle	D.O.E.	Place of Enlistment	Date on Board	Date Off	Rating On	Rating Off	War Patrols	Notes About Service
Barbel-316	Brown	Henry		1/18/44	Columbus, GA	4/3/44	7/15/44	Stm-2	Stm-3	0	CM 6/44; Reduced in rate
Barbero	Butler	Nathaniel	Lewis	unk.	Columbus, OH	8/28/45	EOW	Stm-2	Stm-2	0	
Barbero	Eliston, Jr.	James		1/18/44	Columbus, OH	4/29/44	EOW	Stm-2	Stm-1	2	Made all of this boat's WPs
Barbero	Smith	Henry	Lee	3/28/44	Little Rock, AR	6/3/44	8/29/44	St-3	St-3	0	Transferred from New London
Barbero	Suber	Willie	David	5/12/44	New York, NY	1/20/45	1/22/45	Stm-2	Stm-2	0	Relief duty only
Barbero-317	Buchanan	Paul		11/16/43	Buffalo, NY	6/5/44	7/21/44	Stm-1	Stm-1	0	On from O-4, off to USNH #10 for treatment
Bashaw	Lackey	Pless	Dupe	10/16/41	Raleigh, NC	10/25/43	1/1/45	St-3	St-2	4	On from NL
Bashaw	Pette, Jr.	Hosey		5/17/44	Houston, TX	1/24/45	3/20/45	Stm-1	Stm-1	1	
Bashaw	Ware	Clyde		7/24/43	Detroit, MI	10/25/43	EOW	Stm-2	St-2	6	On at NL
Bashaw-241	James	Frank		12/7/43	Hattiesburg, MS	3/20/45	EOW	Stm-1	St-3	1	Qualified 7/1/45; CM 7/30/45; prior on Bergall
Batfish-310	Hammonds	Lewis	T.	6/1/43	Sheffield, AL	8/21/43	EOW	Stm-2	Ck-2	7	This boat's only Black steward; Made all of this boat's WPs
Baya	Danford	Ernest		1944	Waycross, GA	1/27/45	EOW	Stm-2	Stm-1	3	
Baya	Jordan	Carey		8/6/42	Macon, GA	7/2/44	1/13/45	Stm-1	Stm-1	2	
Baya	Wallace	Willie	Sam	11/13/43	Richmond, VA	5/20/44	7/3/44	Stm-2	Stm-2	0	
Baya	West, Jr.	Thomas		unk.		11/6/44	EOW	Stm-2	St-3	4	
Baya-318	Barfield	Kenneth		10/23/41	Raleigh, NC	5/20/44	11/6/44	Stm-1	Stm-1	1	Prior service on Tarpon
Becuna	Robinson	Nathaniel		5/16/44	Portsmouth, VA	11/4/44	1/1/45	Stm-2	Stm-1	1	
Becuna	Suber	Willie	David	5/12/44	New York City, NY	1/23/45	8/14/45	Stm-2	Stm-1	3	
Becuna	Summerville	James	Tracy	11/30/42	Little Rock, AR	5/27/44	11/4/44	Stm-2	Stm-2	1	
Becuna	Thomas	Montell	Francis	2/23/44	Harrisburg, PA	5/27/44	8/3/44	Stm-2	Stm-2	0	Comm crew
Becuna-319	McClinton	John	T.	9/18/43	Chicago, IL	8/3/44	1/23/45	Stm-2	Stm-2	2	
Bergall	Barfield	Kenneth		10/23/41	Raleigh, NC	11/23/44 (1st)	11/29/44	Stm-1	Stm-1	0	On from ATRC, relief duty only, prior on Tarpon
Bergall	Edwards	Cecil	Earl	3/26/43	Akron, OH	2/19/45	EOW	Ck-3	Ck-3	3	
Bergall	James	Frank		12/7/43	Hattiesburg, MS	6/12/44	12/31/44	Stm-2	Stm-1	1	On at NL

Boat	Last	First	Middle	Date	Place	Date	Date	Rate	Rate	#	Notes
Bergall	Jones	Andrew	Vernon	4/4/44	Wilmington, NC	8/18/44	11/24/44	Stm-2	Stm-2	1	Off to ATRC
Bergall	O'Bryant, Jr.	Robert		6/7/42	Indianapolis, IN	11/30/44	12/2/44	Stm-2	Stm-2	0	Relief duty only
Bergall	Payne	Ralph	Lester	unk.		12/2/44	2/4/45	Stm-2	Stm-2	2	Off to Bluegill flag
Bergall	Pennyman	Timothy	Matthew	2/26/43	Cleveland, OH	6/20/45	EOW	St-3	St-3	0	Prior on Crevalle and Rasher
Bergall	Stricklin	Alfred	Franklin	2/24/42	New Orleans, LA	6/12/44	8/16/44	Stm-1	Stm-1	0	On at NL
Bergall-320	Barfield	Kenneth		10/23/41	Raleigh, NC	1/4/45 (2nd)	6/17/45	Stm-1	St-3	3	Off to ns Anthedon for treatment
Besugo	Jackson, Jr.	Lewis		unk.		3/18/45	EOW	Stm-1	Stm-1	2	
Besugo	Matthew	John	A.	unk.		12/18/44	2/16/45	Stm-2	Stm-2	0	Off for Relief duty and medical treatment
Besugo	Palmer, Jr.	Claude		12/8/43	Columbus, GA	6/19/44	EOW	Stm-2	Stm-1	5	Made all this boat's WPs
Besugo-321	Hodges, Jr.	Charles		7/10/40	Macon, GA	6/19/44	12/5/44	Ck-3	Ck-3	2	
Billfish	Cannada	Leroy	Carson	3/29/44	Cincinnati, OH	9/28/44	3/8/45	Stm-2	Stm-1	1	Off to ATRC
Billfish	Coley	Robert		8/21/41	Birmingham, AL	10/11/43	11/1/43	Ck-3	Ck-3	0	Relief duty only, on from Puffer flag, prior on Tambor
Billfish	Colvin	William		unk.		5/7/45	EOW	Stm-1	Stm-1	1	On from Bluefish flag
Billfish	Hamilton	Leslie		9/27/39	Birmingham, AL	11/1/43	4/7/44	Ck-1	Ck-1	2	Prior on Thresher, later on Brill
Billfish	Mitchell	John		4/5/43	Chicago, IL	4/18/44 (2nd)	4/13/45	Stm-1	Stm-1	3	On from tender Pelias flag
Billfish	Mitchell	John		4/5/43	Chicago, IL	10/15/43(1st)	1/9/44	Stm-2	Stm-1	1	On from Puffer flag, off to Bluefish flag
Billfish	Neely	Edward	Timothy	1/15/43	Houston, TX	4/20/43	10/14/43	Stm-2	Stm-2	1	Comm crew; On at PNSY, off to flag duty, later on Bowfin
Billfish	Robinson	Jerome	Clark	unk.		2/26/45	EOW	Stm-2	Stm-2	2	On from MI, prior on Moray
Billfish	Scott	Windfield		8/10/40	Nashville, TN	4/20/43	10/14/43	OC-3	Ck-3	1	Comm crew; On at PNSY, off to flag duty, relief duty 4/7–4/18/44
Billfish-286	Bolden	John	Francis	9/20/39	Charleston, SC	1/9/44	9/14/44	Ck-3	Ck-2	3	On from Bluefish flag
Blackfin	Jones	Robert	Lawrence	5/17/43	Birmingham, AL	9/17/44	9/30/44	Stm-1	Stm-1	0	Relief duty only

Submarine	Last Name	First Name	Middle	D.O.E.	Place of Enlistment	Date on Board	Date Off	Rating On	Rating Off	War Patrols	Notes About Service
Blackfin	Kinmon	Marvin	Barnell	4/4/44	Dallas, TX	7/4/44	EOW	Stm-2	Stm-2	4	On at NL
Blackfin	Stricklin	Alfred	Franklin	3/7/42	New Orleans, LA	9/30/44	12/26/44	Stm-1	Stm-1	1	
Blackfin	Turner	Frank		unk.		12/26/44	2/28/45	Stm-2	Stm-2	1	Off to tender Griffin
Blackfin	White	James		unk.		7/17/45	EOW	Stm-2	Stm-1	0	
Blackfin	Young	Lavester	Anderson	8/28/43	Atlanta, GA	7/4/44	EOW	Stm-1	St-3	4	On at NL
Blackfin-322	Bailey, Jr.	Willie		7/27/43	Columbus, GA	2/28/45	EOW	St-3	St-2	2	
Blackfish	Adams, Jr.	Culasket		3/27/43	Columbia, SC	8/13/43	2/29/44	Stm-1	OC-3	2	Off to relief duty; Later on Seahorse
Blackfish	Baptiste	Joseph	Clifton	12/15/41	New Orleans, LA	7/22/42	3/20/43	MA-3	MA-1	3	Comm crew; Made boat's first 3 WPs in European theatre
Blackfish	Carter	Andrew	Jordan	8/15/43	New York, NY	2/26/44	7/28/44	Stm-1	Stm-1	1	On from relief duty, later lost on Trigger
Blackfish	Clayborn, Jr.	Arthur		unk.		11/17/44	EOW	Stm-2	Stm-1	3	Fully qualified; On from Peto flag duty; Made boat's final WPs
Blackfish	Durham	John	E.	unk.		11/17/44	6/13/45	Stm-1	Stm-1	2	On from Guardfish flag
Blackfish	Johnson	Burnett		unk.		6/7/45	EOW	Stm-2	Stm-2	1	Made boat's 12th and final WP
Blackfish	Nealy	Junior		10/26/43	Raleigh, NC	6/2/44	11/17/44	Stm-2	Stm-2	1	On from, and off to Guardfish flag duty
Blackfish	Sappington	John	Edward	1/29/42	Macon, GA	3/31/43	ca. 6/1944	MA-2	MA-1	5	Made boat's last 2 Europe WPs, and first 3 in Pacific
Blackfish	Walker	Clarence		4/16/43	Jacksonville, FL	2/29/44	6/29/44	Stm-2	Stm-2	0	Relief duty only
Blackfish-221	Williams	Clifford		4/29/43	Detroit, MI	6/2/44	11/17/44	Stm-2	Stm-1	1	Made boat's 9th WP
Blenny	Crite	Emery	Wilson	2/4/45		2/4/45	4/4/45	Stm-2	Stm-2	1	Off to USNH
Blenny	Pritchett	John	Nimbus	7/20/43	Camden, NJ	7/27/44	EOW	Stm-1	Stm-1	4	On at NL
Blenny-324	Cranley	William	Andrew	10/13/43	Camden, NJ	7/27/44	1/14/45	St-3	St-3	1	On at NL
Blueback	Stevenson	John	Samuel	unk.		5/4/45	EOW	Stm-1	Stm-1	0	On after final WP
Blueback	Walker	Herman	Melwin	unk.		8/8/45	EOW	St-2	St-2	0	On after final WP

Boat	Last	First	Middle	DOB	Hometown	Enlist	End	Rate1	Rate2	WPs	Notes
Blueback	Woody	Frank		8/30/44			6/17/45	9/17/45	Stm-1	Stm-1	0	On after final WP; Off to tender Sperry
Blueback-326	Arnold	Carle	Newman	4/26/44	Philadelphia, PA		8/28/44	EOW	Stm-1	Stm-1	3	Comm Crew; Made all this boat's WPs
Bluefish	Buffington	Bill	B.	10/6/44	Columbus, OH		12/30/44	1/10/45	Stm-2	Stm-2	0	On at MI, off, disqualified due to seasickness
Bluefish	Crockett	Barnard	E.	7/7/44	Chicago, IL		1/11/45	1/29/45	Stm-2	Stm-2	0	Relief duty only
Bluefish	Fowler	James		5/3/43	Washington, DC		7/12/44	12/31/44	Stm-2	Stm-2	1	Off to MI, recommended for disqualification
Bluefish	Mack	Isaac		6/15/44	Philadelphia, PA		12/5/44	1/10/45	Stm-2	Stm-2	0	On at MI, off, disqualified due to chronic seasickness
Bluefish	Oliver	James	Dorsey	1/13/43	Omaha, NE		5/24/43	12/11/43	Stm-2	St-3	2	On at NL
Bluefish	Reid, Jr.	Cicero		1/6/43	Norfolk, VA		1/11/45	6/16/45	Stm-2	Stm-1	2	On from tender Orion
Bluefish	Richardson	Charles	McKinley	3/15/40	Richmond, VA		12/10/43	7/12/44	Ck-2	Ck-1	3	Prior on Kingfish, later on Nautilus
Bluefish	Rowles, Jr.	Elijah		12/1/42	Birmingham, AL		1/29/45	EOW	Stm-1	Stm-1	3	
Bluefish	Sublett	Robert	L.	10/28/41	New Haven, CT		5/24/43	7/23/43	Ck-2	Ck-2	0	On at NL, off at Coco Solo, CZ
Bluefish	Wallace	Harry		6/4/42	Jacksonville, FL		7/22/43	12/31/44	Stm-1	Ck-1	2	On at Coco Solo, CZ-CM 9/28/44, reduced from Ck-1
Bluefish-222	Boothe	Percy	Leon	unk.	Raleigh, NC		6/16/45	EOW	Stm-2	Stm-2	1	On for boat's final 2 WPs
Bluegill	Dowdell	Homer		unk.	Alabama		ca. 3/1945	EOW	Ck-3	Ck-3	2	
Bluegill	Huntley	David	Calvin	5/17/41	Birmingham, AL		11/11/43	ca. 6/1944	Stm-1	Stm-1	1	Prior on Cero; Comm crew at NL; Made boat's first WP
Bluegill	Oliver	James	Dorsey	1/13/43	Omaha, NE		ca. 9/1944	EOW	Stm-1	St-3	4	On at Fremantle, made boat's final 4 WPs
Bluegill	Patrick	Walter		ca. 1944	Newark, NJ		11/11/43	ca. 9/1944	Stm-2	Stm-1	2	Made boat's first 2 WPs; AWOL prior 3rd WP, later on tender Euryale
Bluegill-242	Bartie	Loundis		ca. 1943			ca. 6/1944	ca. 2/1945	Stm-2	Stm-1	3	Made WPs 2-4
Boarfish	Cox, Jr.	William	Henry	unk.			9/21/44	12/7/44	Stm-2	Stm-1	0	Comm crew

Submarine	Last Name	First Name	Middle	D.O.E.	Place of Enlistment	Date on Board	Date Off	Rating On	Rating Off	War Patrols	Notes About Service
Boarfish	Davis	Albert	Delbert	unk.		9/21/44	EOW	Stm-2	St-3	4	
Boarfish	Johnson, Jr.	Robert		1/4/43	Birmingham, AL	8/26/45	EOW	Stm-1	Stm-1	0	From tender Howard Gilmore
Boarfish	Nicholson	Samuel	Jeff	unk.		12/1/44	5/7/45	Stm-2	Stm-1	3	
Boarfish	Warren	Joe	Junior	unk.		5/7/45	EOW	Stm-2	Stm-1	1	
Boarfish-327	Brown	Eugene		10/30/43	Baltimore, MD	5/6/45	5/7/45	Ck-3	Ck-3	0	Relief duty only
Bonefish	Colbert	Sammie		1/10/44	Cincinnati, OH	6/30/44	2/4/45	Stm-2	Stm-1	2	Off at Hunter's Point, CA
Bonefish	Cooley	Quintus	Leon	unk.		3/31/45	KIA	Stm-2	Stm-2	2	From Tilefish flag; Lost with boat 6/1945 in Sea of Japan
Bonefish	Epps, Jr.	William	Henry	9/7/44	Chester, VA	3/31/45	KIA	Stm-2	Stm-2	2	Lost with boat 6/1945 in Sea of Japan
Bonefish	Johnson	Augustus		9/16/43	Macon, GA	8/31/44	2/2/45	Stm-2	Stm-2	1	From Puffer flag; CM 2/45; reduced from Stm-1
Bonefish	McCormick	Daniel		8/25/42	Mare Island, CA	6/30/43	8/31/44	Ck-3	Ck-1	5	Prior on Gar; Deck Court 7/43; Off for discipline
Bonefish	Mosley, Jr.	Eugene		4/4/40	Nashville, TN	11/21/43	6/12/44	Ck-3	Ck-3	3	
Bonefish	Turner	Otis	C.	7/14/42	St. Louis, MO	5/31/43	10/26/43	Stm-2	Stm-3	1	CM 10/43; Reduced in rate, off to tender Pelias
Bonefish-223	Bolton	Lincoln	David	7/12/44	Detroit, MI	1/31/45	3/3/45	Stm-2	Stm-2	0	On from MI
Bowfin	Mays	Hosey		3/6/43	Denver, CO	4/25/44	12/16/44	St-3	St-2	2	Prior on Crevalle; Off because missed sailing of the boat
Bowfin	McDonald	Eugene		5/4/42	Washington, DC	6/22/43	7/1/43	Stm-2	Stm-2	0	On from NL, off to same for disciplinary action
Bowfin	Mosley	Steve	Emry	9/6/41	Key West, FL	5/1/43	4/20/44	Ck-3	Ck-2	4	Comm crew; CM 2/29/44, reduced from Ck-1
Bowfin	Neely	Edward	Timothy	1/15/43	Houston, TX	2/28/44	ca. 12/1944	Stm-2	Ck-3	3	Prior on Billfish; On from Puffer flag, later on Hammerhead
Bowfin	Odoms	Edward	Arnold	5/19/44	Washington, DC	12/9/44	EOW	Stm-1	St-3	3	On from MI

Boat	Last name	First name	Middle	Birth date	Birthplace	Date 1	Date 2	Rate 1	Rate 2	#	Notes
Bowfin	Patterson	Jones		11/28/42	Nashville, TN	5/1/43	6/30/43	Stm-2	Stm-2	0	Comm crew; CM 6/30/43 AOL for 2 1/2 hrs, put in solitary 10 days
Bowfin	Turner	Charles		4/6/44	Columbus, OH	12/26/44	EOW	Stm-2	Stm-1	3	
Bowfin-287	Anderson	Joseph	Robert	12/16/41	Richmond, VA	7/1/43	2/25/44	Stm-1	Ck-3	2	Off to Puffer flag for disciplinary action. Later on Flasher
Bream	Harris	James	Leo	4/10/45	Mottite, AL	8/10/45	EOW	Stm-2	Stm-2	0	On at MI
Bream	Hilton	Earnest		8/23/43	Camden, NJ	4/10/45	EOW	St-3	St-3	1	On at MI
Bream	Lengue	Lyle	Pleasant	3/4/40	Nashville, TN	1/24/44	8/10/45	St-1	St-1	6	On at NL, off at MI
Bream	Sherman	John		6/5/42	Nashville, TN	6/17/45	9/1/45	Ck-2	Ck-2	0	Off at MI
Bream	Stricklin	Alfred	Franklin	3/7/42	New Orleans, LA	12/16/44	12/4/45	Stm-1	Stm-1	3	Prior on Bergall
Bream-243	Denson	William	Berkley	9/24/43	Cleveland, OH	1/24/44	8/10/45	Stm-2	St-3	6	On at NL, off at MI
Brill	Hamilton	Leslie		9/27/39	Birmingham, AL	10/26/44	8/10/45	Ck-1	Ck-1	3	Comm crew; Prior on Thresher and Billfish; Made all this boats WPs
Brill-330	Bryant	George	Albert	ca. 1944	New York	10/26/44	12/5/45	Stm-2	Stm-1	3	Comm crew at NL; Made all this boat's WPs
Bugara	Coley	Robert		8/21/41	Birmingham, AL	11/15/44	5/15/45	Ck-2	Ck-2	1	Made boat's first WP, prior on Tambor
Bugara	Gamble	Vernice		unk.		11/15/44	6/21/45	Stm-2	Ck-3	2	Comm crew; Off to tender Howard W. Gilmore
Bugara-331	Harris, Jr.	William	Thomas	7/30/42	Raleigh, NC	5/6/45	EOW	Stm-1	Stm-2	2	Made boat's final 2 WPs
Bullhead	Hackett	Hubert	Byron	unk.	New York	1/8/45	KIA	Stm-2	Stm-1	3	On at NL; Lost with boat
Bullhead	Johnson, Jr.	Percy		unk.		12/4/44	KIA	Stm-2	Stm-1	3	On at NL; Lost with boat
Bullhead-332	Brown	Solomon		unk.		12/4/44	7/29/45	Stm-1	Stm-1	2	On at NL; Off to tender Clytie for duty and medical treatment
Bumper	Bonman, Jr.	Wrispus		unk.		12/9/44	12/26/44	Stm-2	Stm-2	0	Comm crew. Off to ns Falcon at NL
Bumper	Bonneau	Marion		unk.		4/21/45	6/20/45	Stm-1	Stm-1	2	
Bumper	Brown	Richard	Edward	unk.		7/2/45	EOW	Stm-2	Stm-2	1	

Submarine	Last Name	First Name	Middle	D.O.E.	Place of Enlistment	Date on Board	Date Off	Rating On	Rating Off	War Patrols	Notes About Service
Bumper	Lyman, Jr.	William	Leonard	unk.		12/22/44	4/21/45	Stm-2	Stm-2	0	On from ns Falcon; Off to USNH #10 for treatment
Bumper	Rowles, Jr.	Elijah		12/1/42	Birmingham, AL	8/31/45	EOW	Stm-1	Stm-1	0	
Bumper-333	Armstrong	Ulysses	J.	unk.		12/9/44	EOW	Stm-1	St-3	2	
Burrfish	Epps	Chester	W.	7/8/43	Cincinnati, OH	9/14/43	EOW	Stm-2	Stm-1	6	On at PNSY
Burrfish	Rogers	Will	H.	6/30/42	Birmingham, AL	9/14/43	12/14/43	Stm-1	Stm-1	0	At USNH Key West 11/29 to 12/9/43
Burrfish	Roquemore	Leonard		unk.		12/20/44	EOW	Stm-2	St-3	2	
Burrfish	Sanders, Jr.	Leonard		unk.		12/29/44	EOW	Stm-2	Stm-1	2	
Burrfish-312	Bynum	William	Thomas	9/16/43	New Haven, CT	12/1/43	1/2/45	Stm-2	Stm-1	4	On from R-14
Cabezon	Guery	Ernest	Parker	unk.		1/17/45	EOW	Stm-2	Stm-2	1	On from ns Falcon
Cabezon	Tucker	Douglas	Conley	unk.		12/30/44	EOW	Stm-2	Stm-2	1	Transferred from Sub Base New London—Commissioning
Cabezon-334	Adams	Howard		unk.		12/30/44	2/5/45	ST-3	St-3	0	Comm crew
Cabrilla	Freightman	Maurice	Ameil	3/2/43	Jackson, MS	6/25/44	7/30/45	Stm-1	Stm-1	4	On from Puffer flag, off at MI
Cabrilla	Gregory	Willie	E.	9/10/43	Richmond, VA	2/6/44	2/17/44	Stm-2	Stm-2	0	Relief duty only
Cabrilla	Johnson	Augustus		9/16/43	Macon, GA	2/17/44	6/25/44	Stm-2	Stm-2	4	Off to tender Orion
Cabrilla	Mosley	Steve	Emry	9/6/41	Key West, FL	6/23/44	EOW	Ck-2	Ck-1	4	Prior service on Bowfin
Cabrilla	Smith	Herman		3/23/40	Dallas, TX	9/11/43	6/25/44	Ck-2	Ck-2	4	Off to Puffer flag
Cabrilla	Talton	William	Marion	unk.		1/27/45	EOW	Stm-2	St-3	2	On at MI
Cabrilla-288	Blacknall	Primas	Alexander	1/15/43	Memphis, TN	5/24/43	2/5/44	Stm-2	Stm-1	2	On at NL; later on Cod
Cachalot	Lamb	George	R.	10/14/41	Norfolk, VA	unk.	5/8/42	MA-2	MA-2	0	Relief duty only; Off to Plunger
Cachalot	Taylor	William	Franklin	11/13/39	Richmond, VA	2/26/40	after 12/42	MA-2	OC-3	4	Pre-war submariner; Made all this boat's WPs
Cachalot-170	Davis	Leroy		12/17/41	Birmingham, AL	5/12/42	after 12/42	MA-2	MA-2	3	Made boat's final WPs before relegation to training ship duty

Boat	Surname	Given	Middle	Date	Hometown	Date1	Date2	Rate1	Rate2	#	Notes
Caiman	Singer	Earl	Clifford	8/9/43	Columbus, OH	7/17/44 (1st)	2/17/45	Stm-1	St-3	1	On at NL; NOK mother Gladys Singer, Marietta, OH
Caiman	Singer	Earl	Clifford	8/9/43	Columbus, OH	7/1/45 (2nd)	EOW	St-2	St-2	1	On from tender Clytie
Caiman	Singleton	John		12/1/42	Charleston, SC	2/17/45	EOW	Stm-1	St-3	3	On at NL; Off to USNH
Caiman	Turner	Charles	Robert	4/6/43		7/17/44	10/2/44	Stm-2	Stm-2	0	
Caiman	White	James		unk.		10/4/44	2/7/45	Stm-2	Stm-2	1	NOK mother Anna White, Philadelphia, PA
Caiman-323	Johnson	Henry	Emanuel	unk.		2/5/45	EOW	Stm-2	Stm-2	3	Relief duty only
Capelin	Dyson	James	Carson	3/27/43	Columbus, GA	8/21/43	9/19/43	Stm-1	Stm-1	0	
Capelin	Perry	Finon		5/14/43	Cleveland, OH	10/14/43	KIA	Stm-2	Stm-2	2	On from Pompon; Lost w/ boat 12/43 Celebes Sea
Capelin	Spellman	Fronzell	Lincoln	5/28/42	Dallas, TX	6/22/43	8/30/43	Stm-1	Stm-1	0	Tried by Deck Court; Relief duty only
Capelin-289	Cheatham	Earl		3/30/43	Nashville, TN	6/4/43	KIA	Stm-2	Stm-1	2	On at PNSY; Lost with boat 12/43 Celebes Sea
Capitaine	Jackson	Charlie		unk.		8/26/45	EOW	Stm-2	Stm-2	0	Aboard after hostilities with Japan ended, prior to official surrender
Capitaine	Miller	Furman		unk.		1/26/45	4/30/45	Stm-2	Stm-2	0	Comm crew, on at NL; Off to tender Bushnell
Capitaine	Sled	William	Henry	unk.		4/25/45	8/25/45	St-3	St-3	2	On for both WPs
Capitaine-336	Thompson	Freddie	Lee	unk.		1/26/45	EOW	Stm-1	St-3	2	Comm crew; Made both WPs
Carbonero	Dison	James	Carson	unk.		2/7/45	EOW	Stm-1	Stm-1	2	Comm crew; Made all boat's WPs
Carbonero-337	Howell, Jr.	Benjamin		unk.		2/7/45	EOW	Stm-2	Stm-1	2	Comm crew; Made all boat's WPs
Carp	Horsey	Barnard	Thomas	unk.		2/28/45	3/17/45	Stm-1	Stm-1	0	Comm crew only
Carp	Polk	Ben		unk.		3/21/45	9/22/45	Ck-3	Ck-3	1	On from Tarpon; Made boat's only WP
Carp	Roundtree	Curtis	D.			3/16/45	EOW	Stm-2	Stm-2	1	Made boat's only WP
Carp-338	Smith, Jr.	Ernest	Matthew	unk.		2/28/45	3/17/45	Stm-1	Stm-1	0	Comm crew only

Submarine	Last Name	First Name	Middle	D.O.E.	Place of Enlistment	Date on Board	Date Off	Rating On	Rating Off	War Patrols	Notes About Service
Catfish	Cole	Shelley		12/4/43	Tennessee(?)	3/19/45	EOW	Stm-1	Stm-1	1	Fully qualified; After war served on first nuclear boat, Nautilus
Catfish-339	Dillingham	John	Charles	9/30/44	unk.	3/19/45	EOW	Stm-2	Stm-2	1	Made boat's only WP
Cavalla	Calhoun	James		10/14/43	Columbia, SC	2/29/44	3/14/44	Stm-2	Stm-2	0	On at NL, off at MI
Cavalla	Childress	Lincoln	Alexander	7/8/43	Washington, DC	2/29/44	4/16/45	Stm-1	Stm-1	4	On at NL, off to Cavalla flag
Cavalla	Farr	Horace		5/8/43	Indianapolis, IN	6/22/45	EOW	Stm-1	Stm-1	1	On from SRU 137; Present at Tokyo Bay surrender
Cavalla	Gambie	Walter		1/12/43	Jacksonville, FL	3/11/44	1/28/45	Stm-2	Stm-1	3	On from Cuttlefish; Off to Relief duty
Cavalla	Robinson	Leo	J.	1/6/44	Detroit, MI	3/18/44	3/31/44	Stm-2	Stm-2	0	On from O-4 at NL, off at NL
Cavalla	Roston	Edwin	Augustus	unk.		1/24/45	6/22/45	Stm-1	Stm-1	3	
Cavalla	Wilson	Woodrow		unk.		4/19/45	EOW	Stm-2	Stm-2	2	On from Cavalla flag; Present at Tokyo Bay surrender
Cavalla-244	Baker	Wilson		10/13/43	Des Moines, IA	3/31/44	5/23/44	Stm-2	Stm-2	0	On from Cuttlefish; Off to Relief duty
Cero	Ellis	Leroy		5/8/43	Coco Solo, CZ	7/4/43	11/20/43	St-1	St-1	1	Prior enlistment in 1939
Cero	Ethridge	Miller	D.	3/25/43	Columbus, GA	12/2/43	1/29/44	Stm-1	Stm-1	1	From Tinosa Flag; "On 2nd War Patrol," off to Fulton
Cero	Hinton	Henry		7/31/41		6/19/45	EOW	St-3	St-3	1	On from Tilefish flag
Cero	Huntley	David	Calvin	5/17/41	Birmingham, AL	9/5/44	2/3/45	St-3	Stm-1	1	Demoted by DC 1/31/45, off at MI
Cero	Jones	Paul	Jesse	5/8/41	Birmingham, AL	9/6/44	EOW	St-2	St-2	3	On from Nautilus
Cero	Porter, Jr.	James		7/5/43	Indianapolis, IN	3/23/44	7/4/44	Stm-2	Stm-1	2	On from NRU 144, off to Nautilus
Cero	Thaxton	O'Neal		unk.	Louisiana (?)	2/6/45	6/19/45	St-1	St-1	1	On at MI, prior on Marlin, Pampanito, off to Tilefish flag

Boat	Last	First	Middle	Date	City	Date2	Rate1	Rate2	#	Notes
Cero	Wheeler	Willie	Edward	2/6/42	Nashville, TN	1/29/44	Stm-2	Stm-2	0	On from Fulton, off to NRU 135
Cero-225	Bowe	Julius	Caesar	4/29/43	Detroit, MI	7/4/43	Stm-2	St-2	5	On at NL, Comm crew
Charr	Crawley	William	A.	10/13/43	Camden, NJ	9/4/44	St-3	St-3		Dates aboard and number of WPs unknown
Charr	Diggs	Roy	Alvro			ca. 1945	St-3			Dates aboard and number of WPs unknown
Charr	Shelton	unk.		unk.		ca. 1946	Stm-1	Stm-1		Dates aboard and number of WPs unknown
Charr	Wilson	Bennie		5/8/43	St. Louis, MO	ca. 1944	St-3	St-3		Dates aboard and number of WPs unknown
Charr	Collins	George		2/3/44	Birmingham, AL	ca. 1945	Stm-1	Stm-1		Dates aboard and number of WPs unknown
Charr-328	Walker	Herman	Melvin	unk.		ca. 1945	Stm-1	Stm-1		Dates aboard and number of WPs unknown
Chub	Williams	Wylie		unk.		10/21/44	St-2	St-2	2	On at NL, tried by DC 10/29/44
Chub	Haynes, Jr.	Arthur	Lee	1944	Kansas City, KS	7/6/45	Stm-2	Stm-1	1	Transferred from Sub Div 222
Chub-329	Porter	Eli	J.	9/28/42	Jacksonville, FL	EOW	Stm-2	St-3	3	Transferred from Sub Base New London
Cisco	Williams	Albert	W.	8/20/42	Pittsburgh, PA	EOW	Stm-2	Stm-2	0	On at NL, off at USNH, NL for treatment
Cisco	Nelson	Samuel		2/3/42	Philadelphia, PA	7/15/43	Stm-1	Stm-1	1	On from ns Chewink, Lost with boat 9/1943 in Sulu Sea
Cisco-290	Bryant	Edward	Lavern	6/27/42	Kansas City, MO	KIA	Stm-2	Stm-2	1	Comm Crew, Lost with boat 9/1943 in Sulu Sea
Cobia	Chavis	Simon		2/2/44	Columbia, SC	KIA	Ck-3	Ck-3	4	Relief duty only
Cobia	Donan	Russell		8/6/40	Louisville, KY	4/17/45	Stm-2	Stm-2	0	On at NL
Cobia	Garris	Henderson		9/29/43	Richmond, VA	6/21/44	Ck-2	Ck-2	3	On at NL
Cobia	Kirk	Harold	Roosevelt	unk.		2/10/45	Stm-2	Stm-2	0	Off to tender Gilmore
Cobia	Thomas	Eugene		unk.		6/9/44	Stm-1	Stm-1	2	
Cobia	Bland	Samuel	Lee	unk.		2/12/45	Stm-2	Stm-2	2	
Cobia-245						5/8/45	Stm-2	Stm-1	1	

Submarine	Last Name	First Name	Middle	D.O.E.	Place of Enlistment	Date on Board	Date Off	Rating On	Rating Off	War Patrols	Notes About Service
Cod	Cox, Jr.	Charles		8/11/42	St. Louis, MO	ca. 7/1944	ca. 10/1944	Stm-1	Stm-1	2	Made WPs 4 and 5
Cod	Jones	William	Lee	1/19/43	Charlotte, NC	6/21/43	ca. 8/1943	Stm-2	Stm-2	0	Comm crew at NL
Cod	McCall	Gus	Armstrong	1/31/42	Columbia, SC	ca. 4/1944	ca. 7/1944	Stm-2	Stm-2	1	Made boat's 3rd WP, prior on Nautilus
Cod	Nealy	Junior				ca. 6/1945	EOW	Stm-1	Stm-1	1	Made boat's final WP, prior on Blackfish
Cod	Soles	Albert		1/26/42	Dallas, TX	ca. 9/1943	ca. 3/1944	Stm-1	Stm-1	2	On WPs 1, 2, later on Ray
Cod	Turner	John	Clyde	10/23/42	Atlanta, GA	ca. 4/1944	ca. 7/44	Stm-1	Stm-1	1	Made boat's 3rd WP, later on Tinosa, lost on Flier 8/13/44
Cod-224	Blacknall	Primas	Alexander	1/15/43	Memphis, TN	ca. 7/1944	EOW	Stm-1	Stm-1	4	Made boat's final 4 WPs
Corvina	Jackson	Eddie		6/2/38	Nashville, TN	8/6/43	KIA	Ck-3	Ck-2	1	Comm Crew. Prior on Sturgeon. Lost with boat 11/43 by enemy sub
Corvina	Jackson	Lonnie	David	3/23/42	Pearl Harbor	9/4/43	9/11/43	Ck-2	Ck-2	0	Orig. enlist 1938, re-enlist on board, prior on Trout
Corvina-226	Brooks	Russel	Alexander	5/14/43	Cleveland, OH	8/6/43	KIA	Stm-2	Stm-1	1	Comm Crew, Lost with boat 11/43 by enemy sub
Crevalle	Duniver	Robert		unk.		ca. 2/1945	ca. 6/1945	Stm-2	Stm-2	1	On boat's 6th WP, off at Fremantle, Australia
Crevalle	Gregory	Willie	E.	9/10/43	Richmond, VA	ca. 4/1944	ca. 11/1944	Stm-1	St-3	3	Made WPs 3-5 for this boat
Crevalle	Heard	Bernard	Madison	11/2/40	New Orleans, LA			Stm-2	Stm-2	0	Relief duty only, date unknown
Crevalle	Jaycox	John	A.			ca. 2/1945	EOW	Stm-2	Stm-1	2	Made boat's final 2 WPs
Crevalle	Keith	Leonard	Henshaw	8/9/40	Pensacola, FL			Stm-1	Stm-1	0	Relief duty only, date unknown
Crevalle	Mays	Hosey		3/6/43	Denver, CO	ca. 7/1943	ca. 3/1944	Stm-2	Stm-1	2	On at NL-Made boat's first 2 WPs, later on Bowfin
Crevalle	Minor	Bert		ca. 1944	Casper, Wy	ca. 4/1945	EOW	Stm-2	Stm-1	1	Made boat's final WP
Crevalle	Pennyman	Timothy	Matthew	2/26/43	Cleveland, OH	6/24/43	ca. 3/1944	Stm-2	Stm-1	2	Comm crew; Made boat's first 2 WPs, Later on Rasher

Boat	Last	First	Middle	Birthplace	Birth date	Join date	Off date	Rate in	Rate out	WPs	Notes
Crevalle	Pittman	Louis						Stm-1	Stm-1	0	Relief duty only, date unknown
Crevalle	Wilson	John						Stm-2	Stm-2	0	Relief duty only, date unknown
Crevalle-291	Davis	Waymon		Shreveport, LA	1/26/43	ca. 4/1944	ca. 11/1944	Stm-1	Stm-1	3	Made WPs 3-5 for this boat; Later on Rasher
Croaker	Dance	Samuel	Lee	Philadelphia, PA	11/28/38	8/14/45	EOW	CCK	CCK	0	Relief duty only
Croaker	Lewis	Claude		Atlanta, GA	11/23/43	4/21/44	5/25/44	Stm-2	Stm-2	0	Off at MI
Croaker	McCants	Jimmie		Columbus, GA	10/13/43	10/13/44	11/25/44	Stm-1	Stm-1	0	On from Pike. Relief duty only
Croaker	Morgan	Henry	L.	Richmond, VA	3/24/43	4/21/44	9/15/44	Stm-1	Stm-2	1	Reduced in rate 8/31/44
Croaker	Toler	Otha	Lavada	Little Rock, AR	10/2/41	11/25/44	5/6/45	Ck-3	Ck-3	3	Prior on Plunger
Croaker-246	Armbrister	Leo	B.	Jacksonville, FL	4/25/44	9/15/44	EOW	StM2c	St-3	5	
Cutlass	Bell	Charlie			unk.	3/17/45	EOW	Stm-1	Stm-1	1	Made boat's only WP
Cutlass	Gamble	Harry	Rudolph		unk.	5/17/45	EOW	Stm-2	Stm-2	1	From Falcon flag for duty
Cutlass	Larrimore	Julius			8/2/44	11/14/44	5/16/45	Stm-1	Stm-1	1	Comm crew; Off at Pier 92, NY
Cutlass-478	Wylie	John	Lee		unk.	5/17/45	EOW	Stm-2	Stm-2	1	On from O-2
Cuttlefish	Bullocks	Joseph		Houston, TX	12/13/41	4/11/42	7/6/42	MA-3	MA-2	1	Off at PH
Cuttlefish	Lackey	Pless	Dupe	Raleigh, NC	10/16/41	7/7/42	after 12/42	MA-2	MA-1	1	Made boat's final WP before relegation to training ship duty
Cuttlefish	Washington	James	Henry	Raleigh, NC	11/10/33	5/13/41	after 12/42	MA-1	OS-3	3	Later on Pompon
Cuttlefish-171	Alston	Cicero		Pearl Harbor, HI	3/22/40	1/21/42	4/11/42	MA-1	MA-1	1	Pre-war submariner (original enlist ca. 1936); Made boat's first WP
Dace	Fulton	Edward		Philadelphia, PA	12/28/41	9/6/43	10/27/43	Stm-1	Stm-2	0	On at NL, off to Silversides
Dace	Gaylor	James	Lewis	Raleigh, NC	11/17/39	10/20/43	EOW	Stm-3	St-3	7	On from Cero; Demoted from St-2 on 4/30/45
Dace	Irving	Lorenzo		Memphis, TN	4/23/43	7/23/43	9/6/43	Stm-3	Stm-2	0	On at NL, off at NL for medical reasons
Dace	Johnson	Robert	Lee	Columbus, SC	1/19/43	9/6/43	10/20/43	Stm-1	Stm-1	0	On at NL; off to relief duty on Cero

Submarine	Last Name	First Name	Middle	D.O.E.	Place of Enlistment	Date on Board	Date Off	Rating On	Rating Off	War Patrols	Notes About Service
Dace	Welch	Namon		8/31/42	Birmingham, AL	7/23/43	9/6/43	Stm-1	Stm-1	0	On at NL; off at NL for medical treatment
Dace-247	Butler	Mack	B.	7/7/43	Shreveport, LA	10/27/43	EOW	Stm-2	Stm-1	7	On from Silversides; 3/44 Qualified "in excess"
Darter	Jones	Paul	Jesse	5/8/41	Birmingham, AL	10/31/43	3/22/44	St-3	St-2	0	On from Mackerel
Darter	Lewis	Alphonse		10/7/42	Chicago, IL	3/22/44	8/31/44	Stm-1	St-3	2	
Darter	McCullough	Chester	Vallees	6/12/43	Columbus, GA	9/30/43	10/24/44	Stm-2	St-3	4	On at NL; evacuated with entire crew when boat grounded
Darter	Sublett	Horace		8/10/40	Nashville, TN	9/30/43	10/31/43	Ck-1	Ck-1	0	On/off at NL
Darter-227	Griddle, Jr.	Frank		9/10/41	Dallas, TX	12/10/43	10/24/44	Stm-2	Stm-1	4	Evacuated with entire crew when boat grounded
Dentuda	Wade	Magnus	Augustus	11/22/39	Raleigh, NC	3/31/45	EOW	Ck-1	Ck-1	1	Prior on Gunnel, on at NL
Dentuda	Williamson	Edward	James	unk.		12/30/44	EOW	Stm-1	St-3	1	On at NL
Dentuda-335	Smith	Eugene		unk.	Charlotte, NC (?)	12/30/44	EOW	Stm-2	Stm-1	1	On at NL; NOK mother Elizabeth Smith, Charlotte, NC
Devilfish	Parish	unk.		ca. 1944	Atlantic City, NJ	9/1/44	EOW	Stm-2	Stm-1	4	
Devilfish-292	Allen	Jesse		8/16/43	Columbia, SC	9/1/44	EOW	St-3	St-2	4	On from R-5
Dolphin	Blue	Edward	L.	12/16/41	Birmingham, AL	8/31/42	after 12/42	MA-1	MA-1	1	Made boat's final WP in Alaskan waters
Dolphin	Flakes	Henry		10/10/41	Nashville, TN	3/9/42	7/18/42	MA-2	MA-2	2	Off to storeship Talamanca
Dolphin	Green	Edmund	B.	9/25/41	Los Angeles, CA	5/9/42	after 12/42	MA-2	MA-1	3	Made boat's final WPs, including one Alaskan
Dolphin	Howze	Comer		9/3/41	Birmingham, AL	12/4/41	8/14/42	MA-3	MA-3	3	Made all of boat's Pacific WPs; Later on Sunfish and Apogon
Dolphin-169	Black	Solomon		12/4/41	Little Rock, AR	8/16/42	after 12/42	MA-1	MA-1	1	Made boat's final WP in Alaskan waters
Dorado	Cabase	Isaac		unk.		ca. 8/1943	Lost	St-1	St-1	0	Boat lost with entire crew 10/43 enroute from NL to Panama, cause unk.

Boat	Last	First	Middle	Enlisted	Hometown	Onboard	Departed	Rating1	Rating2	WPs	Notes
Dorado-248	Harris	Dewitt		unk.			ca. 8/1943 Lost	Stm-2	Stm-2	0	Boat lost with entire crew 10/43 enroute from NL to Panama, cause unk.
Dragonet	Patrick	Frank	Leonard	7/23/43	Evansville, IN	3/6/44	6/25/45	Stm-2	Stm-2	2	
Dragonet	Royal	Anderson	Peter	7/2/40	Dallas, TX	3/6/44	EOW	St-2	St-1	3	Prior on Silversides
Dragonet-293	Hilliard, Sr.	James	S.	unk.		6/25/45	EOW	Stm-2	Stm-2	1	
Drum	Dawson, Jr.	Elijah		7/10/40	Norfolk, VA	ca. 7/1942 (1st)	ca.6/43	MA-2	MA-1	4	Back on for WPs 7-8; later on Finback and Saury
Drum	Dawson, Jr.	Elijah		7/10/40	Norfolk, VA	ca. 8/1943 (2nd)	ca.2/44	CK-3	Ck-3	2	
Drum	James	Willie		12/17/41	New Orleans, LA	11/1/41	ca. 6/1942	MA-3	MA-2	1	First WP only, later on Wahoo and Whale
Drum	Lytle	George	Washington			11/1/41	ca. 9/1944	MA-1	Ck-1	10	Comm crew-On at PNSY; Made boat's first 10 WPs; Bronze Star
Drum	McKay	Claude	J.	ca. 1942		ca. 11/1942	EOW	MA-2	Ck-1 (?)	10	On boat's final 10 WPs
Drum	Royal	Arthur	Morris	1/24/42	Kansas City, MO	ca. 6/1943	ca. 8/1943	Stm-1	Stm-1	1	Made boat's 6th WP; Later on Guardfish and Narwhal
Drum-228	Bloom	William		ca. 1944		ca. 12/44	EOW	Stm-2	Stm-1	2	Made boat's final 2 WPs
Entemedor-340	Watts, Jr.	Earl		unk.		4/6/45	EOW	Stm-1	St-3	1	Made boat's only WP
Escolar	Raley	James	A.	ca. 1944	North Carolina	6/2/44	KIA	Stm-2	Stm-2	1	Lost with boat on 1st WP ca. 10/17/44 in the Yellow Sea
Escolar-294	Evans	Benjamin		ca. 1943	Pittsburgh, PA	6/2/44	KIA	Stm-1	Stm-1	1	Lost with boat on 1st WP ca. 10/17/44 in the Yellow Sea
Finback	Dawson, Jr.	Elijah		7/10/40	Norfolk, VA	8/31/44	4/30/45	Ck-3	Ck-2	3	Prior on Drum
Finback	Epps	Louis	Lee	7/18/41	Nashville, TN	12/16/42	8/31/44	MA-2	St-3	7	Off to Drum flag duty
Finback	Johnson	Oscar		unk.		4/30/45	7/14/45	Stm-1	Stm-1	0	
Finback	Peeples, Jr.	Washington		11/10/41	Cincinnati, OH	2/28/42	3/19/42	MA-3	MA-3	0	On from Plunger flag; undesirable discharge 3/30/42
Finback	Rankins, Jr.	Thomas	John	12/23/41	Cleveland, OH	3/13/42	2/20/43	MA-3	OS-3	3	On from O-4, off at Midway

Submarine	Last Name	First Name	Middle	D.O.E.	Place of Enlistment	Date on Board	Date Off	Rating On	Rating Off	War Patrols	Notes About Service
Finback	Robinson, Jr.	John	Haywood	unk.		10/31/44	EOW	Stm-2	Ck-3	2	Made boat's final 2 WPs
Finback	Roston	William	Wright	6/3/40	New Haven, CT	2/27/43	ca. 10/1944	MA-1	MA-1	7	On at Midway-Prior on Grayling
Finback	Spriggins	Arreater	Johnie	10/22/41	Dallas, TX	9/23/42	12/5/42	MA-2	MA-2	1	
Finback-230	Chandler	Vernon	Wincey	8/6/41	St. Louis, MO	2/28/42	4/30/42	MA-3	MA-2	0	On from Flying Fish, off to Haddock flag duty
Flasher	Cox, Jr.	Charles		8/11/42	St. Louis, MO	9/30/43	3/31/44	Stm-1	Stm-2	1	On at NL
Flasher	Fowler	James	Louis	5/3/43	Washington, DC	3/31/44	6/30/44	Stm-2	Stm-2	1	On from tender Orion
Flasher	Freightman	Maurice	Ameil	3/26/43	Jackson, MS	11/7/43	4/4/44	Stm-1	Stm-1	1	On at NL, off for disciplinary action
Flasher	Page	Clarence	Henry	3/31/43	Huntington, WVA	6/30/44	EOW	Stm-1	Stm-2	4	5/31/45 reduced for theft of .45 auto & AOL
Flasher	Sartin	George	Melvin	12/31/41	New Orleans, LA	8/30/44	EOW	Ck-2	Ck-2	3	
Flasher	Singleton	Oscar		11/25/42	Charleston, SC	9/30/43	11/1/43	Stm-2	Stm-2	0	On from Cachalot, off as a straggler
Flasher-249	Anderson	Joseph		12/16/41	Newport News, VA	4/14/44	8/30/44	CK-3	CK-3	2	From Puffer flag, prior on Bowfin
Flier	Findley	Edgar		7/3/43	Nashville, TN	10/18/43	7/19/44	Stm-2	Stm-1	1	On at NL, off to Puffer flag
Flier	Turner	John	Clyde	10/23/42	Atlanta, GA	7/19/44	KIA	Stm-1	Stm-1	1	On from Puffer flag, lost with boat 8/13/44 in Balabac Strait
Flier-250	Banks	Clyde		12/15/41	Cincinnati, OH	10/18/43	KIA	Ck-3	Ck-3	2	Lost with boat 8/13/44 in Balabac Strait
Flounder	Garris	Henderson		9/29/43	Richmond, VA	12/18/43	1/5/44	Stm-2	Stm-2	0	Relief duty only from PNSY
Flounder	Haroney	Johnnie	Warren	3/17/43	Columbus, GA	7/27/44	10/5/44	Stm-1	Stm-1	1	On from Bashaw flag, off to SRU 134
Flounder	Jones	James	Lee	unk.		7/1/45	EOW	Stm-2	Stm-2	0	On at NL
Flounder	Meadows	Clifford		unk.		1/6/45	1/12/45	Stm-1	Stm-1	0	Relief for hospit'z'd steward
Flounder	Singletary	Emanuel	Lee	3/18/44	Raleigh, NC	10/20/44	EOW	Stm-2	St-3	2	On from Nautilus
Flounder	Taylor	Chester	Valentina	8/17/43	Pittsburgh, PA	11/24/43	12/13/44	Stm-2	St-3	4	On at NL, Comm crew

Boat	Last Name	First Name	Middle	Date	Place	Date2	Rate1	Rate2	Rate3	#	Notes
Flounder	Williams	Johnnie	B.	12/16/41	Dallas, TX	11/29/43	Stm-1	St-3	2	On at NL; Comm crew
Flounder-251	Bledsoe	Henry		unk.		1/12/45	Stm-2	Stm-1	2	Made boat's final 2 WPs
Flying Fish	Chandler	Vernon	Wincey	8/6/41	St. Louis, MO	1/31/42	MA-3	MA-3	0	On from ns Falcon, off to Finback
Flying Fish	Cox	Leroy		8/22/40	Macon, GA	8/13/42	MA-2	OC-3	4	On from Drum flag; CM; Direct disobedience of orders 9/30/42
Flying Fish	Crawford	J.	C.	1/22/43	Macon, GA	7/28/44	Stm-2	Stm-1	0	Relief duty only, prior on Seahorse
Flying Fish	Hammond	Warren		7/18/40	Philadelphia, PA	2/12/44	Ck-3	Ck-3	2	Prior on Haddock
Flying Fish	Hinton	Henry		7/31/41		4/29/45	St-3	St-3	0	On "for instruction"
Flying Fish	Laster	Robert		10/13/42	Dallas, TX	5/29/45	Stm-1	Stm-1	1	
Flying Fish	McDuffy	Newgene		12/3/43	Springfield, IL	EOW	Stm-2	Stm-2	3	On from tender Sperry
Flying Fish	Reid	Cecil	Hampton	2/26/44	New York City, NY	9/1/44	Stm-2	Stm-2	1	
Flying Fish	Robinson	Elrey		2/27/44	Columbia, SC	9/1/44	Stm-3	Stm-2	1	
Flying Fish	Thacker	Wiliam	Odell		unk.	5/7/45	Stm-1	Stm-1	1	
Flying Fish	Vall	Edward	George	11/25/42	New Orleans, LA	7/23/43	Stm-1	Stm-1	0	On from Drum flag
Flying Fish	Whitehead	John	Wesley	3/5/43	San Francisco, CA	10/3/43	Stm-1	Stm-1	3	Off at San Francisco
Flying Fish	Wisner	Frank		5/10/41	St. George, Bermuda	8/31/43	Ck-3	Ck-3	0	On from Snapper flag, off to tender Holland
Flying Fish	Yates, Jr.	Rosco	R.	12/16/42	New York City, NY	1/22/42	MA-3	MA-3	2	6/22/42; CM; direct disobedience
Flying Fish-229	Arnold	Edwin		10/21/41	Birmingham, AL	5/27/43	OS-3	St-3	1	Off to relief duty on tender Sperry
Gabilan	Cox, Jr.	Charles		8/11/42	St. Louis, MO	6/8/45	Stm-1	Stm-1	1	
Gabilan	Nixon	Tallie		8/27/43	Columbus, GA	12/28/43	Stm-2	Stm-2	1	
Gabilan	Walker	Wade		8/12/43	Camden, NJ	12/28/43	Stm-2	St-3	6	Made all this boat's WPs
Gabilan-252	Blevins	Charles	B.	11/2/43	Little Rock, AR	6/21/44	Stm-2	Stm-2	4	
Gar	Carpenter	Richard	Lee	6/5/40	Indianapolis, IN	9/30/43	Stm-2	Stm-2	0	Relief duty only
Gar	Cherry	Harry		4/9/43	Cincinnati, OH	5/31/44	Stm-1	St-3	3	On tender Orion from 11/13 to 12/31 1944
Gar	Goode	Claude		12/16/41	Houston, TX	6/25/42	MA-2	MA-2	3	On from Tambor flag, off to tender Pelias

Submarine	Last Name	First Name	Middle	D.O.E.	Place of Enlistment	Date on Board	Date Off	Rating On	Rating Off	War Patrols	Notes About Service
Gar	Hinton	Henry		7/31/41		9/9/41	1/31/43	MA-3	MA-1	5	Made boat's first 5 WPs
Gar	James	Jacob		1/14/44	Columbus, GA	11/13/44	12/29/44	Stm-1	Stm-1	0	Relief duty only
Gar	Lago	Anthony		12/16/41	New York, NY	9/30/43	10/8/43	Stm-2	Stm-2	0	Relief duty only
Gar	McCormick	Daniel		8/5/36	Little Rock, AR	4/14/41	6/22/42	OC-3	OC-3	2	Off to Tambor flag, later on Bonefish
Gar	Peery	George	Wesley	3/15/42	New Orleans, LA	5/31/44	EOW	Ck-3	Ck-3	3	CM 5/28/45, reduced in grade from Ck-2
Gar-206	Campbell	Nathaniel		7/26/43	Richmond, VA	10/3/43	11/9/43	Stm-2	Stm-2	0	On at NL, off to Tambor flag, later lost on Herring
Gato	Brown	Henry		unk.		1/4/45	1/10/45	Stm-3	Stm-3	0	Relief duty only
Gato	Dewitt	John	H.	4/7/36	San Diego, CA	12/31/41	9/28/42	OS-3	OS-3	2	Comm crew; Re-enlist 1942 for 4 years; Off to tender Fulton
Gato	Holt, Jr.	Herman	L.	unk.		1/13/45	EOW	Stm-1	St-3	3	On from Gilmore; Made final 3 WPs; Present at Tokyo Bay surrender
Gato	Jackson	Elmer	J.	unk.		1/10/45	5/24/45	Ck-3	Ck-3	2	Made boat's 11-12th WPs
Gato	James	Jacob		unk.		5/24/45	EOW	Stm-1	Stm-1	1	Made boat's final WP; Present at Tokyo Bay surrender ceremony
Gato	Lebeau	Clifton	J.	9/16/40	New Orleans, LA	4/16/44	ca. 11/1944	Stm-1	Stm-1	2	On from Guardfish flag
Gato	Lewis	Albert	Sylvester	5/17/43	Richmond, VA	ca. 7/1943	9/6/43	Stm-2	Stm-2	0	Off to Plunger, later lost on Trout
Gato	Linthicum, Jr.	Andrew		11/10/39	New York, NY	11/17/43	11/17/43	St-2	St-2	0	Off to Navy dispensary #89
Gato	Moore, Jr.	John	W.	8/3/39	Detroit, MI	12/31/41	2/14/42	MA-1	MA-1	0	Comm crew; On at NL, off at same — medical
Gato	Morris	Albert	Leon	12/21/41	Des Moines, IA	2/9/42	3/13/43	MA-3	MA-1	4	Made boat's first WPs; Off to Gato flag
Gato	Payne	Roosevelt		11/25/41	Birmingham, AL	1/22/42	3/17/42	MA-3	MA-3	0	On for flag duty only; Off to cruiser Helena
Gato	Postell	Andrew		unk.		12/11/44	1/15/45	Stm-2	Stm-2	0	Relief duty only; Off to tender Gilmore

Boat	Last	First	MI	Date1	Hometown	Date2	Rate1	Rate2	#	Notes
Gato	Robinson	William	D.	12/20/41	Salt Lake City, UT	3/13/43	OC-3	OC-2	4	On from flag duty; WP data estimated
Gato	Sanders	Charles	F.	8/14/40	Raleigh, NC	unk.	Stm-1	Stm-1	0	Relief duty only
Gato	Vaughn	Willis	E.	unk.		12/4/44	St-2	St-2	3	Made boat's final WPs; Present at Tokyo Bay surrender
Gato-212	Wall	Hall	Jackson	1/15/42	Mare Island, CA	12/4/44	MA-1	Ck-1	8	Prior enlistment ca. 1938; On from tender Fulton; Off to NC
Golet	Sterling, Jr.	George	E.	11/10/42	Los Angeles, CA	11/30/43	Stm-1	Stm-1	2	Comm Crew; Lost 6/14/44 off Honshu, JA
Golet-361	McCulough	William	E.	7/8/43	Raleigh, NC	11/30/43	Stm-2	Stm-2	2	Comm Crew; Lost 6/14/44 off Honshu, JA
Grampus	Bivens	Charles	Henry	2/2/37	Baltimore, MD	9/30/41	MA-1	MA-1	1	Later on Trinn, Salmon, Jallao
Grampus	Black	Curtheal		6/5/40	Dallas, TX	9/30/41	MA-3	OS-3	6	Native of James, TX; Lost with boat 3/1943 in Solomon Islands
Grampus	Fenner	Donald	M.	8/15/40	Richmond, VA	7/8/42	MA-2	MA-1	4	On from tender Otus, prior on Snapper; Lost with boat 3/1943 in Solomon Islands
Grampus-207	Allison	William	A.	12/18/41	Raleigh, NC	4/28/42	MA-2	MA-2	1	Off to tender Otus
Grayling	Day	Shirley		4/15/39	Houston, TX	8/4/41	MA-1	MA-1	4	CM 11/41 for missing ship, off to Plunger flag
Grayling	McAphee	Homer		2/26/42	Birmingham, AL	8/26/42	MA-3	MA-2	2	On from Trout
Grayling	Roston	William	Wright	6/3/40	New Haven, CT	10/13/41	MA-1	MA-1	4	Later on Finback
Grayling-209	Criss	Scott		12/10/41	New Orleans, LA	9/24/42	MA-1	MA-1	2	
Greenling	Giles	Edward	Dewitt	7/27/43	Pittsburgh, PA	6/30/44	Stm-2	Stm-2	0	Relief duty only
Greenling	Griffin	Ezra		9/4/43	New York, NY	2/21/44	Stm-2	St-3	4	On from Tambor
Greenling	Morris	Albert	Leon	12/21/41	Des Moines, IA	5/17/43	Ck-3	Ck-2	4	On from Peto flag, off to Tambor
Greenling	Porter	Parree		pre-4/1942	New Orleans, LA	2/21/43	MA-3	OC-3	4	Off to tender Fulton
Greenling	Williams	Thomas		1/24/43	Raleigh, NC	7/31/44	Stm-1	Stm-1	0	Relief duty only

Submarine	Last Name	First Name	Middle	D.O.E.	Place of Enlistment	Date on Board	Date Off	Rating On	Rating Off	War Patrols	Notes About Service
Greenling-213	Carter	Edward	Daniel	1/26/44	Newark, NJ	7/31/44	EOW	Stm-2	Stm-1	3	On from Tambor
Grenadier	Craig	Jacob	Delbert	8/23/39	Birmingham, AL	5/31/41	2/3/42	MA-3	MA-2	0	On from Mallard; 1/1942 CM, off to tender Pelias
Grenadier	Hamilton	Frank	Garret	11/6/40	Norfolk, VA	1/7/42	6/24/42	MA-1	MA-1	2	On from ns Antaeus
Grenadier	Trigg	Thomas	James	10/28/41	Houston, TX	2/3/42	POW	MA-3	MA-1	6	Boat lost 4/21/43, POW in Japan until liberated 9/13/45
Grenadier-210	Brooks	Reginald	Hamilton	9/15/39	Brooklyn, NY	5/1/41	1/7/42	MA-1	MA-1	0	Comm crew; off to ns Antaeus
Grouper	Allen	John	Harvey	2/26/41	Birmingham, AL	8/12/42	8/27/42	MA-2	MA-2	0	Relief duty only
Grouper	Brown, Jr.	Albert		12/4/41	Raleigh, NC	2/12/42	1/6/43	MA-3	MA-2	4	Comm crew; Made boat's first WPs; Off to tender Fulton
Grouper	Collier, Jr.	William	Clint	2/4/39	Nashville, TN	2/12/42	3/22/42	MA-2	MA-2	0	Comm crew; On at NL; Off to O-4
Grouper	Freeman	Nellis		1/24/42	Houston, TX	1/6/43	12/19/43	MA-2	MA-1	4	
Grouper	Hale	Harold	Herbert	10/17/39	Richmond, VA	7/26/42	ca. 8/1942	MA-1	MA-1	0	Assigned to Tunny detail
Grouper	Johnson	James	Edward	12/17/41	Raleigh, NC	ca.11/1942	ca. 8/1944	OC-3	Ck-2	7	On from Peto flag; Records illegible ? WP data
Grouper	Perkins	Robert	Leo	7/10/43	St. Louis, MO	12/26/43	EOW	Stm-2	St-3	5	NOK mother Lucinda Perkins, Troy, MO
Grouper	Sterling	Vance	D.	unk.		8/27/42	10/31/42	MA-2	MA-2	1	Made boat's 2nd WP; off to Gato flag
Grouper-214	Strickland	Frank	Bernie	9/16/43	Raleigh, NC	7/11/44	EOW	Stm-3	Stm-1	3	On from Peto flag; NOK father Bernie Strickland, High Point, NC
Growler	Flippens	Willie		unk.		10/14/44	KIA	Stm-2	Stm-2	1	Lost with boat 11/8/44 off Mindoro
Growler	Kennedy, Jr.	Houston		8/28/43	Nashville, TN	4/30/44	10/31/44	Stm-2	Stm-2	2	On from tender Sperry, later on Hardhead
Growler	Prophet	John	Henry	12/19/41	San Francisco, CA	4/30/42	5/31/44	MA-3	St-3	9	On from O-6, off to Silversides flag

Boat	Last Name	First Name	Middle	Enlisted	Hometown	Date	Date 2	Rate 1	Rate 2	#	Notes
Growler	Robinson	William	Dee	12/20/41	Salt Lake City, UT	3/20/42	12/31/42	MA-3	MA-1	4	On at NL, off to Gato flag
Growler	Strong	Ezell	Tommy	12/19/39	Dallas, TX	4/30/42	5/42	unk.	MA-1	0	Off at NL
Growler-215	Cleveland	Bennie		7/16/42	Macon, GA	7/21/43	KIA	Stm-3	St-3	6	On from Peto flag; Lost with boat 11/8/44 off Mindoro
Grunion	Newsome	Alfred		12/15/41	Detroit, MI	4/25/42	5/15/42	MA-2	MA-2	0	On from tender Beaver, deserted boat 5/15/1942
Grunion	Paul, Jr.	Cornelius		5/3/38	Birmingham, AL	4/11/42	KIA	MA-1	MA-2	1	CM 5/42 reduced in rate; Lost with boat 8/1942 off Alaska
Grunion	Starling	Vernon	C.	9/12/41	Pittsburgh, PA	4/11/42	5/2/42	MA-1	MA-1	0	Relief duty only
Grunion-216	Arvan	Herbert	J.	12/16/41	New Orleans, LA	5/23/42	KIA	MA-2	MA-2	1	On from S-48; Lost with boat 8/1942 off Alaska
Guardfish	Cobbs	Ervin	T.	3/1/43	San Francisco, CA	3/1/43	8/23/43	MA-1	MA-1	2	On from tender Fulton, off to flag duty
Guardfish	Cooper	Charlie		3/20/43	Columbus, GA	6/12/44	10/25/44	Stm-1	Stm-1	2	Made WPs 8-9
Guardfish	Estill	John	Jackson	3/19/43	Nashville, TN	11/24/43	6/12/44	Stm-1	Stm-1	2	On from Pompon
Guardfish	Freeman	Nellis		1/24/42	Houston, TX	5/8/42	8/10/42	MA-3	MA-3	0	On at NL, off to Gato flag
Guardfish	George	Joseph		10/30/41	Macon, GA	5/19/43 (2nd)	7/31/44	Stm-1	Stm-1	4	On from tender Fulton; CM 7/1944, reduced from Ck-3
Guardfish	George	Joseph		10/30/41	Macon, GA	8/10/42 (1st)	2/15/43	MA-2	MA-1	3	On from Gato; Off to flag duty
Guardfish	Hilton	Harry	Bobby	2/28/44	Los Angeles, CA	6/12/44	7/31/44	Stm-3	Stm-3	1	Made WP #8
Guardfish	Jackson	Leon	Clinton	8/10/43	Pittsburgh, PA	8/15/44	1/27/45	Stm-1	Stm-1	2	Made WPs 9-10
Guardfish	Kelly	William	A.	unk.		2/10/45	EOW	Stm-1	St-3	2	Made boat's final 2 WPs
Guardfish	Parker	George		unk.		11/26/44	EOW	Stm-2	Stm-1	3	Made boat's final 3 Wps
Guardfish	Royal	Arthur	Morris	1/24/42	Kansas City, MO	8/23/43	11/24/43	Stm-1	Stm-1	1	On from Peto flag, off to Pompon
Guardfish	Taylor, Jr.	Robert				11/11/44	11/26/44	Stm-1	Stm-1	0	Relief duty only
Guardfish	Tombs	Leroy		10/19/40	Kansas City, MO	5/8/42	5/1/43	MA-1	OC-3	4	Off to flag duty; Later was a recruiter for sub stewards at Bainbridge
Guardfish-217	Byrd	Robert		unk.		11/10/44	11/19/44	Stm-1	Stm-1	0	Relief duty only

Submarine	Last Name	First Name	Middle	D.O.E.	Place of Enlistment	Date on Board	Date Off	Rating On	Rating Off	War Patrols	Notes About Service
Guavina	Cooksey	Max	Baxter	unk.		1/22/45	3/15/45	Stm-1	Stm-1	1	On from ns Anthedon
Guavina	Gober	Charlie		8/16/43	Columbus, GA	8/19/45	8/28/45	St-2	St-2	0	Relief duty only
Guavina	Jones, Jr.	Buck		8/27/43	Columbia, SC	2/23/43	EOW	Stm-2	Stm-1	6	Comm crew; Made all this boat's WPs
Guavina	Prophet	John	Henry	12/19/41	San Francisco, CA	8/24/45	EOW	Stm-1	Stm-1	0	Prior on Growler
Guavina	Smith	John	Emmett	9/1/42	Cleveland, OH	1/10/44	1/28/44	Ck-3	Ck-3	0	On at MAN, off at Algiers, LA
Guavina	Williams	Robert	James	11/26/43	Little Rock, AR	1/26/44	7/24/45	Stm-2	Ck-3	6	Off at MI; Made all this boat's WPs
Guavina	Wilson	Bennie		5/8/43	St. Louis, MO	12/23/43	1/10/44	Stm-1	Stm-1	0	Comm crew
Guavina	Wilson	George	Willie	unk.		3/15/45	EOW	Stm-2	Stm-2	1	Made boat's final WP
Guavina-362	Arnold	Elmer	Ward	unk.		1/11/45	1/21/45	Stm-2	Stm-2	0	Relief duty only
Gudgeon	Butts, Jr.	Eugene	J.	8/7/41	Macon, GA	11/1/41	4/20/42	MA-3	MA-3	2	On at PH; Off to tender Pelias
Gudgeon	Evans	Melton		5/3/38	New Orleans, LA	5/29/41	ca. 1/1943	MA-1	OC-2	6	On from cruiser Richmond; 2/20/42 Meritorious advance to OC-2
Gudgeon	McAphee	Homer		2/26/42	Birmingham, AL	5/4/42	5/25/42	MA-3	MA-3	0	Relief duty only
Gudgeon	Mosley, Jr.	Eugene		4/4/40	Nashville, TN	2/18/42	3/7/43	MA-2	OC-3	5	On from Triton; Off to same; later on Bonefish
Gudgeon	Perry	William	Sidney	7/19/39	Philadelphia, PA	5/4/42	5/22/42	MA-1	MA-1	0	Relief duty only
Gudgeon	Sprigs	Paul	Westley	unk.		4/3/44	ca. 4/7/44	Stm-2	Stm-2	0	On at start of final WP, likely off at Johnston Island; Boat then lost.
Gudgeon-211	Rozar	Albert	H.	8/14/41	Macon, GA	Dec-41	2/1/42	MA-1	MA-1	1	Made boat's 1st WP; Late addition to roster and not listed as such
Guitarro	Collier, Jr.	William	Clint	2/4/39	Nashville, TN	1/30/45	EOW	Ck-1	Ck-1	1	Made boat's final WP
Guitarro	Farr	Horace		5/8/43	Indianapolis, IN	2/29/44	12/11/44	Stm-2	Stm-1	3	On at New Orleans, LA
Guitarro	Smith	Sylvester		4/23/43	Detroit, MI	9/2/44	1/30/45	Stm-2	Stm-1	2	Relief duty 11/30 to 12/10 1944

Boat	Last Name	First Name	Middle	Enlist Date	Hometown	Onboard	Off	Rate1	Rate2	WPs	Notes
Guitarro	Summerville	James	Tracy	11/30/42	Little Rock, AR	12/11/44	EOW	Stm-2	Stm-1	2	Made boat's final 2 WPs
Guitarro-363	Cameter, Jr.	Aleve		9/10/43	Philadelphia, PA	1/26/44	2/10/44	Stm-2	Stm-2	0	Comm crew
Gunnel	Glover	Jim	Mack	12/24/42	Macon, GA	10/11/43	EOW	Stm-1	St-3	6	On from ns PC 1260
Gunnel	Jacobs	Adolphus		12/14/39	Birmingham, AL	1/14/43	10/6/43	MA-1	Ck-3	1	On from tender Beaver, AWOL on 10/5/43
Gunnel	Lago	Anthony		12/16/41	New York City, NY	8/20/42	1/14/43	MA-2	MA-2	1	On at NL, off to tender Beaver; Made boat's first European WP
Gunnel	Larkie	Arthur		4/23/43	New Haven, CT	7/18/44	10/7/44	Stm-1	Stm-1	1	On at MI
Gunnel	Little	Jimme	Dave	unk.		3/12/45	5/27/45	Stm-2	Stm-2	0	
Gunnel	Pace	Andrew	Jack	7/6/37	Louisville, KY	8/20/42	10/9/42	MA-1	MA-1	0	On at NL; 9/30/42 AOL
Gunnel	Wade	Magnus	Augustus	11/22/39	Raleigh, NC	4/4/43 (1st)	7/4/44	Ck-2	Ck-1	4	On from S-48, off for one war patrol
Gunnel	Wade	Magnus	Augustus	11/22/39	Raleigh, NC	10/6/44 (2nd)	3/12/45	Ck-1	Ck-1	1	Back from Relief duty, off to NC Dentuda
Gunnel	Williams	Johnnie	B.	12/16/41	Dallas, TX	4/11/45	5/23/45	unk.	unk.	0	Relief duty only; Off to tender Fulton
Gunnel-253	Butler	Franklin	P.	6/26/42	Dallas, TX	9/24/42	4/9/43	MA-2	MA-2	1	On at NL, off to S-48; Made boat's first European WP
Gurnard	Dogan	Nathan	J.	7/8/42	New London(re-up)	9/18/42	6/24/44	OC-2	Ck-1	5	Prior enlistment in 1938, from Chicago(?)
Gurnard	Harris	James	Lee	unk.		7/7/45	7/28/45	Stm-2	Stm-2	0	Relief duty only
Gurnard	Hearn	Marvin	R.	4/2/40	Cincinnati, OH	6/25/44	9/5/44	Ck-1	Ck-1	1	Made boat's 6th WP
Gurnard	Jones	Jimmie	Howard	12/11/42	Jacksonville, FL	6/25/44	EOW	Stm-2	Stm-1	4	Made boat's final 4 WPs, off stateside
Gurnard	Penn	James	Paul	4/28/44	unk.	9/28/44	7/24/45	Stm-2	Stm-1	3	Off at MI
Gurnard	Sanders, Jr.	John	H.	11/29/43	St. Louis, MO	3/24/44	6/25/44	Stm-2	Stm-2	1	On at MI, off to tender Griffin for treatment
Gurnard	Smith	Henry	L.	3/28/42	Little Rock, AR	9/18/42	1/19/44	MA-2	St-3	4	Comm crew, off at MI; Made boat's first 4 WPs
Gurnard	Spoonhour	Alfred	Earl	10/9/43	Harrisburg, PA	9/19/44	9/28/44	Stm-1	Stm-1	0	Relief duty only, prior on Harder

Submarine	Last Name	First Name	Middle	D.O.E.	Place of Enlistment	Date on Board	Date Off	Rating On	Rating Off	War Patrols	Notes About Service
Gurnard-254	Blevins	Charles	B.	11/2/43	Little Rock, AR	2/12/44	3/24/44	Stm-2	Stm-2	0	On from Bainbridge, off at MI
Hackleback	Atkins	Charles	Lester	unk.	Columbus, OH	5/15/45	EOW	Stm-2	Stm-1	1	Made boat's final WP
Hackleback	Guilford	William	L.	9/8/43	Columbus, OH	8/4/44	EOW	Stm-1	St-3	2	Comm crew; on all WPs
Hackleback	Moore	Johnnie	Lee	1/30/43	Memphis, TN	3/10/45	5/13/45	Stm-1	Stm-1	0	Relief duty only
Hackleback-295	Richardson	Gilbert	A.	5/11/44	Philadelphia, PA	8/4/44	EOW	Stm-2	Stm-2	2	Comm crew; Made all WPs; Reduced in grade at CM 12/44 for AOL
Haddo	Reed	Ulysses	Grant	1/28/42	New Orleans, LA	10/9/42	7/31/44	MA-1	Ck-2	6	Comm crew
Haddo	Saxon	Bennie		11/16/43	Chicago, IL	7/31/44	EOW	Stm-2	Stm-1	4	Made boat's final WPs-Present at Tokyo Bay surrender
Haddo	Waddell	Willie	Mitchell	4/5/44		10/28/44	EOW	Stm-2	Stm-1	3	Qualified 7/2/45; Present at Tokyo Bay surrender
Haddo-255	Bryant	Luther		5/18/40	Raleigh, NC	10/9/42	10/25/44	OC-2	Ck-1	7	Comm crew
Haddock	Chandler	Vernon	Wincey	8/6/41	St. Louis, MO	4/20/42	5/9/42	MA-2	MA-2	0	Relief only, on from Finback flag, off to Herring flag
Haddock	Fulton	Edward		7/9/43	Philadelphia, PA	11/30/43	EOW	Stm-2	Ck-2	5	On from Silversides flag; Made boat's last 5 WP's
Haddock	Hammond	Warren		7/18/40	Philadelphia, PA	12/28/42	11/43	MA-2	Ck-3	5	On at PH; later on Flying Fish
Haddock	Stallings	Jim	Eckford	11/27/39	Jackson, MS	3/14/42	EOW	MA-2	CCK	13	Pre-war on Dolphin at PH; Made all this boat's WPs
Haddock-231	Bryant	William	L.	9/11/41		3/14/42	10/11/42	MA-3	MA-2	2	Comm crew, off to Wright
Hake	Boyd	Charles	L.	unk.		7/1/45	EOW	Stm-2	Stm-2	1	Made boat's final WP; Present at Tokyo Bay surrender ceremony
Hake	Collier	David	S.	ca. 1944	Steubensville, OH	6/1/45	EOW	Stm-2	Stm-2	1	Made boat's final WP; Present at Tokyo Bay surrender ceremony

Boat	Last Name	First Name	Middle	Enlist	Hometown	Report	EOW	Rate1	Rate2	WPs	Notes
Hake	Cornish	Tyree		7/14/42	Canal Zone	3/31/45	EOW	Ck-2	Ck-2	1	Pre-war enlist in 1937; Made boat's final WP; At Tokyo Bay
Hake	Edwards	Cecil	Earl	3/26/43	Akron, OH	7/31/44	10/31/44	Ck-3	Ck-3	1	Made boat's 6th WP
Hake	Johnson	James	Horace	8/20/42	Macon, GA	10/30/42	8/12/43	MA-3	MA-2	2	On at NL, off at NL; Made boat's first 2 European WPs
Hake	Moore	Robert		8/29/41	Birmingham, AL	11/2/42	12/1/42	MA-1	MA-1	0	Temporary relief duty only from Harder
Hake	Moore, Jr.	John	Willie	3/9/37	Detroit, MI	11/11/42 (1st)	7/26/44	OS-2	St-1	5	On from Falcon
Hake	Moore, Jr.	John	Willie	3/9/37	Detroit, MI	10/11/44 (2nd)	6/1/45	ST-1	St-1	2	Back on from relief duty
Hake	Pace	Andrew	Jack	7/5/37	Louisville, KY	10/30/42	11/2/42	MA-1	MA-1	0	Relief duty only; off at NL for medical treatment
Hake	Patterson	Jones		11/28/42	Nashville, TN	7/31/43	10/21/43	Stm-2	Stm-2	0	Off at MI
Hake	Petty	Thomas	G.	unk.		6/1/45	6/23/45	Stm-2	Stm-2	0	Relief duty only
Hake	Reed	Ulysses	Grant	1/28/42	New Orleans, LA	10/31/44	3/31/45	Ck-2	Ck-2	2	Prior on Haddo
Hake-256	Bailey, Jr.	Willie		7/27/43	Columbus, GA	10/31/43	10/31/44	Stm-2	St-3	4	On at MI; Off to Relief duty, back on before 7/45
Halibut	Cross	Joseph		5/12/42	New Orleans, LA	6/22/42	2/17/44	MA-3	OS-3	8	On from tender Beaver
Halibut	Gill	Marion	Bentley	9/21/44	Atlanta, GA	2/16/45	7/18/45	Stm-2	Stm-1	0	On from Jack, off at PNSY; Boat retired due to battle damage
Halibut	McCrobey, Jr.	John		7/29/43	Nashville, TN	2/21/44	8/21/44	Stm-2	Stm-2	1	On from Tambor flag
Halibut	Murphy	Willie		12/4/41	Macon, GA	6/22/42	6/26/42	MA-2	MA-2	0	Relief duty only from tender Beaver at NL
Halibut	Nelson	Samuel		2/3/42	Philadelphia, PA	5/1/42	6/9/42	MA-1	OS-3	0	On from S-1, off at USNH, NRI
Halibut	Phillips	John	Joseph	8/25/43	Brooklyn, NY	8/31/44	2/16/45	Stm-1	Stm-1	1	On at MI, off at MI
Halibut	Scott	Albert	Lee	unk.		2/13/45	2/16/45	Stm-3	Stm-3	0	On from Skate, relief duty only
Halibut	Smith	Herman		unk.		2/16/45	EOW	Ck-1	Ck-1	0	Possibly same man that served on Cabrilla

Submarine	Last Name	First Name	Middle	D.O.E.	Place of Enlistment	Date on Board	Date Off	Rating On	Rating Off	War Patrols	Notes About Service
Halibut	Wallace	Strauther		11/25/42	Memphis, TN	8/15/43	1/31/45	Stm-1	OS-3	5	On from Silversides Flag, off at MI for NC
Halibut-232	Boulet	William	Joseph	3/4/42	Houston, TX	5/1/42	8/12/43	MA-3	Stm-1	5	On at NL, later on Queenfish
Hammerhead	Neely	Edward	Timothy	1/15/43	Houston, TX	7/1/45	EOW	Stm-1	Ck-3	1	Prior on Bowfin
Hammerhead	Spencer	Curtis	Redmond	unk.		2/1/45	EOW	Stm-2	Stm-1	4	Transferred from SubDiv 261
Hammerhead	White	James		unk.		4/26/45	7/1/45	Stm-2	Stm-2	2	Made boat's final 2 WPs
Hammerhead 364	Brown	Eugene		10/30/43	Baltimore, MD	3/1/44	4/26/45	Stm-2	Ck-3	5	On at MAN
Harder	Moore	Robert		unk.	Alabama (?)	ca. 10/1942	KIA	unk.	Ck-3	6	On boat from commissioning to loss in 8/1944 with all hands; off Luzon, P.I.
Harder	Spoonhour	Alfred	Earl	unk.		ca. 3/1944	ca. 7/1944	Stm-2	Stm-2	2	Made boat's 4-5th WP; *not* lost with boat
Harder-257	Cromwell	James	Edward	unk.	Richmond, VA	ca. 8/1944	KIA	Stm-2	Stm-2	1	Lost with boat on 6th WP, 8/1944 off Luzon, P.I.
Hardhead	Hatcher	L.	C.	10/20/43	Cincinnati, OH	4/18/44	12/25/44	Stm-2	Stm-1	2	On at MAN
Hardhead	Jones	George	E.	unk.		8/31/45	EOW	Stm-2	Stm-2	0	
Hardhead	Kennedy, Jr.	Houston		8/28/43	Nashville, TN	3/20/45	10/1/45	Stm-1	Stm-1	3	Prior on Growler, discharged from Navy 10/45
Hardhead	Sherman	John		6/5/42	Nashville, TN	12/31/44	3/20/45	Ck-2	Ck-2	1	Made boat's 3rd WP
Hardhead	White	Harry	Edward	unk.		5/31/45	8/31/45	Stm-2	Stm-1	2	Made boat's final 2 WPs
Hardhead-365	Brown	Bennie	Lawrence	6/20/39	New Orleans, LA	4/18/44	5/31/45	Ck-2	Ck-1	4	On at MAN, Pre-war on Plunger
Hawkbill	Bradley	Orange		7/26/40	Raleigh, NC	1/21/45	3/31/45	Ck-1	Ck-2	1	Prior on Hoe; CM, reduced in grade 2/45
Hawkbill	Buchanan	Paul		7/2/45	Buffalo, NY	8/1/45	EOW	Stm-1	Stm-1	0	On from Boarfish, prior on Tuna
Hawkbill	Fanning	Lonzo		9/21/43	San Francisco, CA	5/17/44	5/31/44	Stm-2	Stm-2	0	Relief duty only

Boat	Last	First	Middle	Place	Date1	Date2	Rate1	Rate2	#	Notes
Hawkbill	Matthews	Edward		Camden, NJ	5/28/43	5/31/44	Stm-2	Stm-1	0	Off to USNH, Balboa, CZ for treatment
Hawkbill	Pogue	George	E.	Louisville, KY	10/7/43	11/15/44	Stm-1	Stm-1	1	Made boat's 2nd WP
Hawkbill	Robinson	Ernest		Jackson, MS	7/28/44	1/31/45	Stm-2	Stm-1	3	Made boat's final 3 WPs
Hawkbill	Smith	William	T.	unk.	3/4/45	8/1/45 EOW	Stm-1	Stm-1	2	Probably same man as William Thomas Smith on Aspro
Hawkbill	Strother	Elijah	B.	Albany, NY	7/8/43	1/24/45	Stm-1	Stm-1	0	Relief duty only
Hawkbill	Wilson	Bennie		St. Louis, MO	5/8/43	5/17/44	Stm-2	Stm-1	2	On at MAN
Hawkbill-366	Arnold	Claude		New Orleans, LA	9/3/42	7/31/44 1/27/45 1/31/45 6/30/45	Stm-1	St-3	4	Off to relief duty on tender Clytie; back on at EOW
Herring	Campbell	Nathaniel		Richmond, VA	7/26/43	1/29/44 KIA	Stm-2	Stm-2	2	Lost with boat 6/1/44 in the Kurile Islands
Herring	Chandler	Vernon	Wincey	St. Louis, MO	8/6/41	5/9/42	MA-2	MA-2	0	Relief duty only, on from Haddock, off to Shad
Herring	Jones	Louis	Hill	Louisville, KY	5/15/41	1/22/44	Stm-1	Stm-1	1	Deceased — Cause of death: drowning by Board of Invest.; line of duty; Next of kin not notified; Remains buried at sea.
Herring	Scott	Lewis		New Orleans, LA	4/1/42	5/8/42	MA-3	MA-3	0	On at Norfolk-a deserter since 8/22/42
Herring	Thomas	Isaiah		New Orleans, LA	4/1/42	5/8/42 1/23/44	MA-3	Stm-2	6	On at Norfolk,VA-CM 11/43, confined 10 days, reduced in grade
Herring-233	Burkett	Timothy		Birmingham, AL	9/15/39	9/1/42 KIA	OC-3	Ck-1	8	On from S-21, lost with boat 6/1/44 in the Kurile Islands
Hoe	Beasley	Oliver	O'Neal	Columbus, GA	1/20/44	6/29/44 9/15/44	Stm-2	St-3	1	Off for medical treatment; NOK wife Annie Beasley, Atlanta, GA
Hoe	Bradley	Orange		Raleigh, NC	7/26/40	12/16/42 10/22/44	MA-1	Ck-1	6	On at NI; NOK father John Thomas Bradley, Maysville, NC

Submarine	Last Name	First Name	Middle	D.O.E.	Place of Enlistment	Date on Board	Date Off	Rating On	Rating Off	War Patrols	Notes About Service
Hoe	Heisser	Melvin		5/24/41	New Orleans, LA	12/16/42	3/5/44	MA-2	Ck-3	3	On at NL, later on Rasher
Hoe	Marable	Earl	Richard	7/16/43	Boston, MA	3/26/44	6/29/44	Stm-2	Stm-1	1	Made boat's 4th WP
Hoe	Parker	James	Albert	5/1/44	Philadelphia, PA	9/15/44	EOW	Stm-2	Stm-1	3	NOK wife Margaret Parker, Philadelphia, Pa
Hoe	Robert	Oscar	Lee	1/5/43	Little Rock, AR	11/8/44	4/8/45	Stm-1	Stm-1	2	Made boat's last 2 WPs
Hoe-258	Baker	Wilson		10/13/43	Des Moines, IA	4/9/45	EOW	Stm-2	Stm-2	0	Prior on Piranha
Icefish	Ellis	John	Oscar	unk.		12/2/44	EOW	Stm-1	Ck-3	4	On from Shark flag duty
Icefish	Fanning	Lonza		9/21/43	San Francisco, CA	6/12/44	7/8/44	Stm-2	Stm-2	0	Comm crew; Off at NAS, Algiers, LA
Icefish	Goens	Robert	Milton	4/17/44	Indianapolis, IN	7/6/44	EOW	Stm-2	Stm-1	5	Comm crew at MAN; Made all of boat's WPs
Icefish	Hill, Jr.	Willie	L.	12/14/43	Memphis, TN	6/10/44	8/3/44	Stm-2	Stm-2	0	Comm crew; Off to USNH at Balboa, CZ
Icefish-367	Jackson	Zedell		4/17/44	Kansas City, MO	8/5/44	12/6/44	Stm-1	Stm-1	1	On from S-15; Off to tender Gilmore
Jack	Gill	Marion	Bentley	9/21/44	Atlanta, GA	1/31/45	2/13/45	Stm-2	Stm-2	0	Relief duty only, off to Halibut
Jack-259	Mayo	Elvin	Adair	11/23/43	Tyler, TX	5/30/44	EOW	Stm-2	Stm-1	5	
Jallao	Adams	Willie		11/19/43	Philadelphia, PA	7/8/44	6/14/45	Stm-2	Stm-1	3	Comm crew
Jallao	Bivens	Charles	Henry	2/2/37	Baltimore, MD	7/8/44	4/2/45	St-1	CST	2	Possible prior enlistment in 1940 or before
Jallao	Buie	John	E.	unk.		4/10/45	EOW	Stm-1	Stm-1	2	Made boat's final 2 WPs
Jallao-368	McCants	Jimmie		10/13/43	Columbus, GA	7/2/45	9/21/45	Stm-1	Stm-1	1	Made boat's final WP
Kete	Dawson	William	Howard	7/6/43	Evanston, IL	7/31/44	KIA	Ck-3	Ck-3	2	Comm crew; Lost with boat 3/45 off Nansei Shoto, JA
Kete-369	Dortche	Calvin	Frederick	1/7/44	New Haven, CT	7/31/44	KIA	Stm-1	Stm-1	2	Comm crew-Lost with boat 3/45 off Nansei Shoto, JA
Kingfish	Fisher	Whaylon	O'Neal	2/25/43	Baltimore, MD	9/30/43	5/11/45	Stm-2	St-2	6	On from Puffer flag

Boat	Last	First	Middle	Date	Hometown	Date	Date	Rate	Rate	Rate	#	Notes
Kingfish	Frye	Jeffie		5/13/42	Little Rock, AR	5/13/42	4/30/44	MA-3		OC-3	7	On at NL, off to Silversides flag, later on Lamprey
Kingfish	Justice	John	Enger	unk.		5/31/45	6/6/45	Stm-2		Stm-2	0	Relief duty only
Kingfish	Mobery, Jr.	Eddie		2/18/42	Birmingham, AL	7/29/44	9/30/44	Stm-2		Stm-2	0	On at MI
Kingfish	Neal	John	Albert	unk.		9/30/44	EOW	Stm-2		St-3	4	Transferred from Com-Sub 43
Kingfish	Richardson	Charles	McKinley	3/15/40	Richmond, WVA	5/20/42	9/30/43	MA-3		Ck-3	4	On at PNSY, later on Bluefish and Nautilus
Kingfish	Vaughn	Willie	Edward	11/25/42		4/23/44	EOW	St-3		St-3	5	
Kingfish-234	Wansley	Ellis	Leonard	unk.		6/17/45	EOW	Stm-2		Stm-2	1	Made boat's final WP
Kraken	Dawson	George	H.	ca. 1944		9/8/44	unk.	Stm-2		unk.		Comm crew at MAN; Boat made 4 WPs
Kraken-370	Thomas	Alfredo		8/17/42	St. Thomas, VI	9/8/44	unk.	Stm-1		unk.		Comm crew at MAN; Boat made 4 WPs
Lagarto	Green	Robert		unk.	Pittsburgh, PA	10/14/44	KIA	Stm-2		Stm-2	2	Lost with boat 5/3/45 in Gulf of Siam; NOK wife Dorothy Green, Pittsburgh, PA
Lagarto-371	Kirtley	Albert		1944(?)	Columbus, OH	10/14/44	KIA	Stm-2		Stm-1	2	Lost with boat 5/3/45 in Gulf of Siam; NOK wife Susan Kirtley, Springfield, OH
Lamprey	Frye	Jeffie		5/13/42	Little Rock, AR	11/17/44	EOW	St-3		St-2	3	Prior on Kingfish
Lamprey	Suber	Willie	David	5/12/44	New York, NY	8/30/45	EOW	Stm-1		Stm-1	0	
Lamprey	Templeton, Jr.	Clarence	Maxi	unk.		11/17/44	7/13/45	Stm-2		Stm-1	2	Off to Cavalla flag
Lamprey-372	Todd	Clarence	B.	unk.		7/13/45	EOW	Stm-2		Stm-1	1	
Lapon	Bunday, Jr.	James	Henry	unk.		6/22/45	8/25/45	Stm-1		Stm-1	0	
Lapon	Edwards	Cecil	Earl	3/26/43	Akron, OH	4/18/44	6/7/44	Ck-3		Ck-3	1	Made boat's 4th WP
Lapon	Holmes	William	A.	unk.		4/14/45	EOW	Stm-2		Stm-1	1	Made boat's final WP
Lapon	Huddleston	Paul	Emil	unk.		11/15/44	5/4/45	Ck-1		Ck-1	1	Made boat's 7th WP
Lapon	Jackson	Raymond	Freeman	unk.		5/4/45	6/22/45	Stm-2		Stm-2	0	Relief duty only
Lapon	Lewis	Charlie	Morgan	8/5/41	New York City, NY	5/15/43	5/15/43	Stm-1		St-3	4	On at Coco Solo, CZ
Lapon	Minor	George	William	6/10/55	Ports, VA	1/23/43	5/15/43	OC-2		OC-2	0	Comm crew, off at CZ

Submarine	Last Name	First Name	Middle	D.O.E.	Place of Enlistment	Date on Board	Date Off	Rating On	Rating Off	War Patrols	Notes About Service
Lapon	Orr	Charles	Wesley	11/16/42	Los Angeles, CA	2/20/43 (1st)	4/15/44	MA-2	Ck-3	3	On from O-4; Made boat's first 3 WPs
Lapon-260	Orr	Charles	Wesley	11/16/42	Los Angeles, CA	6/18/44 (2nd)	10/31/44	Ck-3	Ck-2	2	Back on for 5-6 WPs
Lionfish	Colston	Sam		unk.		11/1/44	EOW			2	Comm crew at BNS; Made both of boat's WPs
Lionfish-298	Jones	Lewis		unk.		11/1/44	EOW			2	Comm crew at BNS; Made both of boat's WPs
Lizardfish	Bolton	Levi		1/31/42	Kansas City, MO	12/30/44	4/1/45	Stm-1	Stm-1	0	Prior on S-28, off to USNH, later on Rasher
Lizardfish	Davis	Everett	Clifford	1944	Norman, OK	3/31/45	EOW	Stm-2	Stm-1	2	On from S-15
Lizardfish	Hines, Jr.	Andrew		unk.		12/30/44	3/4/45	Stm-1	Stm-1	0	
Lizardfish-373	Johnson	James	Horace	8/20/42	Macon, GA	8/21/45	EOW	Stm-1	Stm-1	0	
Loggerhead	Major	James	Alexander	unk.		2/9/45	EOW	Stm-2	Stm-1	1	Qualified 7/15/45
Loggerhead-374	Young	Daniel	VanDoren	unk.		2/9/45	EOW	Stm-2	Stm-1	1	Qualified 7/15/45
Macabi	Campbell	Thomas	Jerome	unk.		3/29/45	EOW	Stm-1	St-3	1	Comm crew at MAN; Made boat's only WP
Macabi	Jones	Melvin	Erman	unk.		3/29/45	7/19/45	Stm-2	Stm-1	0	Comm crew at MAN; Off to relief duty prior to WP
Macabi-375	Moore	Oscar	Henry	unk.		7/19/45	EOW	Stm-2	Stm-2	1	On from relief duty; Made boat's only WP
Mackerel	Blue, Jr.	Robert		5/11/42	Nashville, TN	6/20/42	unk.	MA-3	MA-3	1	Atlantic WP data uncertain; Later on Sennet
Mackerel	Carter	William		1/7/42	Indianapolis, IN	4/25/42	6/5/42	MA-3	MA-3	1	On from Norfolk; Court Martial 7/42; Off to Mackerel
Mackerel	LeBeau	Clifton	Joseph	9/16/40	New Orleans, LA	4/4/42	5/11/42	MA-3	MA-3	0	Relief only, off at Norfolk, VA
Mackerel-204	Strong	Ezell	Tommy	12/19/39	Dallas, TX	3/31/41	4/25/42	MA-2	MA-1	0	On from Growler; AWOL; straggler on 4/26/42

Boat	Last	First	Middle	Birth date	Birthplace	Enlist	Discharge	Rate1	Rate2	WPs	Notes
Manta	Hale	Herbert	Hale				9/14/44	10/4/44	St-2	St-2	0	Pre-commissioning detail; Off for medical treatment
Manta	Justice	John	Enger	unk.			10/18/44	5/7/45	Stm-2	Stm-2	0	Comm crew only
Manta	Murray	Clennon		unk.			10/18/44	EOW	Stm-1	Stm-1	1	Made boat's only WP
Manta-299	Singleton	Early	Lee	unk.			5/7/45	EOW	Stm-1	Stm-1	1	On from Snapper relief
Marlin	Carter	William		1/7/42	Indianapolis, IN		6/6/42	EOW(?)	MA-3	MA-3	1	Atlantic WP data uncertain; On from Mackerel
Marlin-205	Thomas	Isadore	D.	3/3/41	Greenwood, SC		9/18/41	8/22/42	MA-1	MA-1	2	Made both of this boat's Atlantic WPs; Off at NL
Mingo	Smith	Mason	B.	ca. 4/1944	Atlanta, GA		ca. 10/1944	EOW	Stm-2	Stm-1	2	On from tender Griffin
Mingo	Wallace	Sam	Wesly	9/9/40	Little Rock, AR		1/10/43 (1st)	ca. 10/1944	Ck-3	Ck-2	5	On at NL from O-6, off to tender Griffin
Mingo	Wallace	Sam	Wesly	9/9/40	Little Rock, AR		11/1/44 (2nd)	EOW	Ck-2	Ck-1	1	Back on from tender Griffin
Mingo-261	White	Carl	Lee	6/23/41	Macon, GA		ca. 10/1944	ca. 1/1945	Ck-3	Ck-3	1	Prior on Paddle and Muskallunge
Moray	Booth	Raymond		unk.			1/5/45	EOW (?)	Stm-2	Stm-2	1	Comm crew; On at Philadelphia; Boat made 1 WP
Moray	Ragland	Paul	Francis	12/15/42	Baltimore, MD		ca. 7/1945	EOW	Ck-2	Ck-2	0	Prior on Barb
Moray-300	Robinson	Jerome	Clark	unk.			1/5/45	ca. 2/1945	Stm-1	Stm-1	0	Comm crew; On at Philadelphia, later on Billfish
Muskallunge	Brown	Joseph		unk.			7/29/45	EOW	Stm-1	Stm-1	1	Made boat's final WP; Present at Tokyo Bay surrender ceremony
Muskallunge	Burt, Jr.	Eugene		6/6/40	Birmingham, AL		7/5/44	EOW	Ck-1	Ck-1	5	Present at Tokyo Bay surrender ceremony
Muskallunge	Collier, Jr.	William	Clint	2/4/39	Nashville, TN		3/15/43	9/23/44	OC-3	Ck-1	4	On at NL; Re-enlisted 3/1943 for 2 years
Muskallunge	Henderson	Marshall		unk.			7/17/45	EOW	Stm-1	Stm-1	1	Made boat's final WP; Present at Tokyo Bay surrender ceremony

Submarine	Last Name	First Name	Middle	D.O.E.	Place of Enlistment	Date on Board	Date Off	Rating On	Rating Off	War Patrols	Notes About Service
Muskallunge	Larkie	Arthur		4/23/43	New Haven, CT	1/20/45	7/17/45	Stm-1	Stm-1	1	On for boat's 6th WP
Muskallunge	Lewis	Charlie	Morgan	8/5/41	New York, NY	10/7/44	7/29/45	St-3	St-2	2	On for boat's 5-6 WPs
Muskallunge	Mallory	Clyde	Cicero	7/7/43	Pittsburgh, PA	12/16/44	2/27/45	St-3	St-3	0	Off at MI
Muskallunge	Nelson	William		12/1/42		3/15/43	4/19/43	Stm-2	Stm-2	0	On at NL, off to same
Muskallunge	Thomas	Alfredo		8/17/42	St. Thomas, VI	4/17/43	3/1/44	Stm-2	Stm-1	2	On at NL, later on Kraken
Muskallunge 262	White	Carl	Lee	6/25/41	Macon, GA	ca 3/1944	10/18/44	Ck-3	Ck-3	2	Prior on Paddle, later on Mingo
Narwhal	Arnold	Edwin		10/21/41	Birmingham, AL	4/22/42	4/29/42	MA-2	MA-2	0	Relief duty only
Narwhal	Brantley	John	Westley	12/16/43	Hattiesburg, MS	4/28/44	EOW	Stm-2	Stm-2	5	Made boat's final 5 WPs
Narwhal	Brooks	Joe	Lee	12/16/41	Birmingham, AL	4/30/42	7/1/42	MA-2	MA-2	1	On at PH
Narwhal	Brown	Arthur		1/15/43	Macon, GA	4/17/43	11/22/44	Stm-2	Ck-3	12	On at SD, later on U-530
Narwhal	Brown	James		7/15/43		4/3/44	11/22/44	Stm-1	Stm-1	5	
Narwhal	Brown	Ralph		1/14/43	Jacksonville, FL	4/17/43	8/29/43	Stm-2	Stm-2	3	On at SD
Narwhal	Clark	Lilton	Robert	12/20/38		9/30/41	8/20/43	Ck-2	Ck-1	5	12/10/42 re-enlisted on board
Narwhal	Everett	James	Anthony	9/18/41	Raleigh, NC	12/31/41	3/11/43	MA-3	MA-1	3	2/1943 CM, 3/1943 to SF for bad conduct discharge
Narwhal	Green	Johnny		12/20/43	Dover, DE	7/25/44	4/23/45	Stm-2	Stm-1	3	Off at NL
Narwhal	Hays	George	Allen	6/17/39		9/30/41	4/17/42	MA-2	MA-1	3	Off for flag duty
Narwhal	Heisser	Melvin		5/24/41	New Orleans, LA	4/23/44	4/24/44	Ck-3	Ck-3	0	Relief duty only, prior on Hoe and Rasher
Narwhal	Keith	Leonard	Henshaw	8/9/40	Pensacola, FL	8/29/43	4/14/44	Stm-2	Stm-1	5	CM 4/1944, reduced from St-3
Narwhal	Linthicum, Jr.	Andrew		11/19/39	New York City, NY	12/31/41	10/21/43	MA-2	St-2	6	Off to TF 22 relief
Narwhal	McCall	Gus	Armstrong	1/31/42	Columbia, SC	8/20/43	10/22/43	Stm-2	Stm-2	1	Off to TF 22 relief
Narwhal	Neal	Lunie	Joseph	9/25/41	Louisville, KY	7/2/42	ca. 4/1944	MA-2	St-2	8	On at PH
Narwhal-167	Royal	Arthur	Morris	1/24/42	Kansas City, MO	1/2/44	4/3/44	Stm-1	Stm-1	1	Prior on Drum, Guardfish
Nautilus	Baker	James	Lee	4/7/42	Louisville, KY	4/5/44	12/19/44	Stm-1	Stm-1	5	Boats 1st Black steward since 9/42; Off to ATRC

Boat	Surname	First	Middle	DOB	Birthplace	Date1	Date2	Rate1	Rate2	WPs	Notes
Nautilus	Carpenter	Savoy			Richmond, VA	2/3/42	3/17/42	MA-3	MA-3	0	Relief duty only
Nautilus	Davis	Alonza	Lee		Little Rock, AR	ca. 1942	3/28/42	Ck-3	Ck-3	0	Prior on Pargo, on from TG 71.6
Nautilus	Epps	Louis	Lee	7/18/41	Nashville, TN	4/15/42	8/7/42	MA-2	MA-2	3	On from Argonaut; WP number includes sortie at Battle of Midway
Nautilus	Fields	Alonzo	Emerson	9/6/38	Cincinnati, OH	6/20/41	3/31/42	MA-1	MA-1	0	Off at MI to Whale
Nautilus	Jones	John	Joseph	1/31/44	Philadelphia, PA	8/13/44	4/19/45	Stm-2	Stm-1	4	Made boat's final 4 WPs
Nautilus	Linthicum, Jr.	Andrew		11/10/39	New York, NY	10/29/40	ca. 12/15/41	MA-2	unk.	0	Pre-war submariner, on at SF, later on Narwhal
Nautilus	McCall	Gus	Armstrong	1/31/42	Columbia, SC	3/17/42	ca. 6/1942	MA-3	MA-2	0	On at SF; From 10/42 to 4/44 boat had no Black stewards
Nautilus	Olds	Percy	J.	7/15/39	Little Rock, AR	3/4/42	3/12/42	OS-3	OS-3	0	Temp. relief from Argonaut, lost on same 1/10/43 off New Britain
Nautilus	Rapadas	George		8/15/39		11/16/40	2/12/42	OS-2	OS-2	0	Off to USNH MI; Possible prior enlistment in 1935
Nautilus	Richardson	Charles	McKinley	3/15/40	Richmond, VA	10/7/44	2/2/45	Ck-1	Ck-1	2	Prior on Kingfish and Bluefish, off to TG 71.6
Nautilus	Stewart	James	David	2/3/42	Raleigh, NC	3/17/42	3/26/42	MA-3	MA-3	0	Relief duty only
Nautilus-168	Williams, Jr.	Earl		1/29/42	Dallas, TX	3/17/42	9/8/42	MA-3	MA-2	4	On at SF, off to Narwhal flag; WP total includes Midway sortie
Paddle	Anderson	Joseph		12/16/41	Newport News, VA	3/29/43	4/30/43	Stm-1	Stm-1	0	Later on Flasher
Paddle	Arder	Milton		4/24/43	Marion, AR	3/15/44	EOW	Stm-1	St-3	6	From Snapper flag
Paddle	Burt, Jr.	Eugene		6/6/40	Birmingham, AL	5/9/43	5/17/43	OC-2	OC-2	0	Relief duty only, on from O-2, off to tender Griffin
Paddle	Eldridge	Fred	W.	9/8/43	Newark, NJ	2/12/44	3/13/44	Stm-2	Stm-2	0	On at MI, off to Snapper flag
Paddle	Harris	Willie	C.	6/15/39	Philadelphia, PA	6/30/43	9/8/43	OC-2	OC-2	1	Made boat's 1st WP
Paddle	Phifer	James	William	12/18/41	Raleigh, NC	10/5/43	EOW	Stm-2	Ck-3	7	Made all but this boat's 1st WP

Submarine	Last Name	First Name	Middle	D.O.E.	Place of Enlistment	Date on Board	Date Off	Rating On	Rating Off	War Patrols	Notes About Service
Paddle	Smith	Justice		5/15/40	Raleigh, NC	3/29/43	5/6/43	OC-3	Stm-1	0	CM 4/30/43, reduced in rating
Paddle	Walker, Jr.	Luster		5/28/43	Akron, OH	9/30/43	10/5/43	Stm-2	Stm-2	0	Relief duty only
Paddle-263	White	Carl	Lee	6/23/41	Macon, GA	4/30/43	2/25/44	Stm-1	Ck-3	2	On at NL, off at USNH MI; Later on Mingo
Pampanito	Byrd	Robert		unk.		ca. 6/1944	ca. 10/44	Stm-1	Stm-1	2	
Pampanito	Ingram	George		ca. 1942		ca. 2/1944	EOW	Stm-1	St-3	6	On for all her WPs
Pampanito	Johnson	John	Lewis	1/2/43	Tyler, TX	ca. 10/44	EOW	Stm-1	Stm-2	3	CM ca. 1/1945, reduced in rate
Pampanito	Payton, Jr.	Albert				ca. 2/1944	ca. 6/1944	Stm-1	Stm-1	1	
Pampanito	Smith	John	Franklin	unk.		11/6/43	ca. 2/1944	Stm-2	Stm-2	0	Comm crew at PNSY; off before 1st WP
Pampanito-383	Thaxton	O'Neal				11/6/43	ca. 2/1944	St-1	St-1	0	Comm crew at PNSY; off before 1st WP, later on Cero
Parche	Braxton	Leroy		unk.		ca. 2/1945	EOW			2	Made boat's last 2 WPs
Parche	Fisher	L.	C.	unk.	New York (?)	ca. 12/1/44	ca. 2/1945			1	On at Midway for war patrol
Parche-384	Kimmons	Carl	Eugene	6/4/40	Cincinnati, OH	11/20/43	12/1/44	Ck-2	Ck-1	3	Prior on Plunger; On from ns Scott, off at Midway
Pargo	Bracy	George		10/9/42	Jackson, MS	8/1/43	6/1/45			7	On from carrier Ranger; Made all Pargo's WPs
Pargo	Davis	Alonza	Lee	ca. 1942	Little Rock, AR	8/17/43	8/15/44			4	Later on Nautilus
Pargo	Mosley	Robert	Daniel	1/26/43	Dallas, TX	4/26/43	10/28/43			1	Comm crew at NL; Later on Sailfish
Pargo	Rozar	Albert	H.	8/14/41	Macon, GA	10/27/43	10/25/44	St-3	St-1	4	Prior on Gudgeon
Pargo	Sample	Christopher				10/25/44	7/9/45			2	Made boat's last 2 WPs
Pargo	Shoemaker	Lee	E.			6/6/45	7/12/45	6/6/45		0	Relief duty only
Pargo-264	Williams	Charles	M.	ca. 1942	Louisiana	6/6/45	EOW			0	
Perch 2	Domio	Wilfred	Joseph	8/7/43	New Orleans, LA	1/7/44	3/5/45	Stm-2	Stm-1	4	Comm crew; Made boat's first 4 WPs

Boat	Last	First	Middle	Enlisted	Hometown	Start	End	Rate1	Rate2	WPs	Notes
Perch 2	Matthews	Joe		unk.	Houston, TX	3/10/45	EOW	Ck-2	Ck-2	3	Made boat's last 3 WPs
Perch 2-313	Rowlins	Edward	J.	12/14/42	Houston, TX	9/11/44	EOW	Stm-1	Stm-1	5	On from relief duty; Made boat's last 5 WPs
Permit	Bass	Thomas	Lee	unk.	Norfolk, VA	9/19/45	EOW	Stm-2	Stm-2	0	
Permit	Knight	William	Edward	11/16/39		7/28/45	9/5/45	Ck-1	Ck-1	0	On from Snapper, prior on to Whale
Permit	Lucas	Isiah		10/31/42	Little Rock, AR	6/14/43	6/18/43	Stm-2	Stm-2	0	Relief duty only, on from Plunger
Permit-178	McGuire	James	Thomas	12/6/38	Louisville, KY	12/1/42	1/24/43	MA-1	MA-1	0	12/8/42 re-enlisted for four years, on from ns Dewey, later on Plunger
Peto	Coleman	Henry		7/18/42	Birmingham, AL	6/4/43	9/28/44	Stm-1	St-3	5	On from flag duty, off to NC at MI
Peto	Ellis	Jones		1/24/42		9/28/44	10/15/44	Stm-1	Stm-1	0	Relief duty only
Peto	Freeman	Nellis		1/24/42	Houston, TX	9/1/44	4/24/45	St-3	St-2	2	On from MI; NOK niece Effie Collier, San Antonio, TX
Peto	Johnson	James	Edward	12/17/41	Raleigh, NC	11/21/42	6/8/43	MA-1	OC-3	1	On at MAN, off to flag duty
Peto	Johnson, Jr.	William	Lemard	unk.		12/20/44	EOW	Stm-1	Stm-1	3	On from Drum flag
Peto	Morris	Albert	Leon	12/21/41	Des Moines, IA	8/31/44	12/20/44	Ck-1	Ck-1	1	On from Shark flag; NOK wife Gladys Belle Morris, Des Moines, IA
Peto	Smith	Robert	Wayward	unk.		4/24/45	EOW	Stm-2	Stm-1	2	Made boat's final 2 WPs
Peto	Tuttle	Carlos	A.	5/9/39	Birmingham, AL	11/21/42	8/31/44	OC-3	Ck-2	6	On at MAN, off to NC; Later on Quillback
Peto-265	Walker	Clarence		4/16/43	Jacksonville, FL	7/31/44	9/4/44	Stm-2	Stm-2	0	On from ATRC, off to MI
Picuda	James	Willie		1/15/40	Birmingham, AL	7/31/44	10/15/44	St-3	Stm-1	0	CM 9/44, off to tender Bushnell
Picuda	Lieteau	Joseph	Phillip	9/21/40	New Orleans, LA	12/31/43	12/29/44	Stm-1	Ck-3	4	Made boat's first 4 WPs
Picuda	Major	Sammie		1944	Jacksonville, FL	12/17/44	EOW	Stm-1	Stm-1	2	Made boat's last 2 WPs
Picuda	McCoy	James	Davenport	7/15/43	Chicago, IL	10/16/43	4/30/44	Stm-2	Stm-2	1	Made boat's 1st WP
Picuda	Ward	John	Vincent	1/17/42	New York, NY	10/16/43	12/31/43	Stm-1	Stm-1	0	

Submarine	Last Name	First Name	Middle	D.O.E.	Place of Enlistment	Date on Board	Date Off	Rating On	Rating Off	War Patrols	Notes About Service
Picuda	Warren	Benjamin	Sanders	1/20/44	Houston, TX	4/30/44	12/29/44	Stm-3	Stm-2	4	Prior on Pipefish
Picuda-382	Whitfield	Orial		3/1/40	Jacksonville, FL	12/17/44	EOW	St-3	St-3	2	Training/Relief duty only
Pike	Baxter	Leonard	F.	unk.		12/13/44	EOW	Stm-2	Stm-1	0	On from Sturgeon
Pike	Bell	Howard	L.	unk.		6/11/45	EOW	Stm-2	Stm-2	0	On from Sturgeon
Pike	Bigbee	Robert	Lee	1/19/44	Cleveland, OH	7/14/44	6/16/45	Stm-2	Stm-1	0	Training duty only; Off at NL
Pike	Finley	Napoleon		12/1/43	Jacksonville, FL	2/11/44	4/28/44	Stm-2	Stm-2	0	Training/Relief duty only; Off to Sterlet
Pike	Forrest	Clifton	H.	unk.		6/11/45	EOW	Stm-2	Stm-2	0	On from Sturgeon
Pike	Gray	James		1/18/43	Columbia, SC	1/13/44	3/15/44	Stm-2	Stm-2	0	Training/Relief duty only; Off to PNSY
Pike	Hamilton	Frank	G.	11/8/40	Norfolk, VA	11/23/42	unk.	MA-1	MA-1	?	On from Nautilus; Date off and WP data uncertain
Pike	Johnson	R.	L.	9/16/40	New Orleans, LA	5/11/44	EOW	Ck-3	Ck-3	0	Training duty only; On from O-7
Pike	Jones	Woodrow	Wilson	12/29/41	Louisville, KY	3/5/43	2/12/44	MA-1	Ck-3	2	Made boat's final 2 WPs; Boat withdrawn from combat duty to battle-damage
Pike	McCants	Jimmie		10/13/43	Columbus, GA	4/7/44	5/24/44	Stm-2	Stm-2	0	Training/Relief duty; Off to Croaker
Pike	Prophet	John	Henry	12/19/41	San Francisco, CA	8/22/44	6/11/45	St-3	St-3	0	Prior on Growler, off at NL
Pike	Rozar	Leonard	Cicero	11/28/39	Macon, GA	11/23/42	12/22/42	MA-1	MA-1	0	Relief duty only; Off to Saury
Pike	Smith	McKenney		2/23/44	New York, NY	5/24/44	9/14/44	Stm-2	Stm-2	0	Training/Relief duty only; Off to Sub Squadron 1 for duty
Pike	Smith	Milton		9/24/43	Chicago, IL	1/28/44	4/1/44	Stm-2	Stm-2	0	Training/Relief duty only; Off to Piranha
Pike	Smith	Roy	E.	3/2/44	Huntington, WVA	5/1/44	5/10/44	Stm-2	Stm-2	0	Training duty only; Off to Sea Fox

Boat	Last Name	First Name	Middle Name	Enlistment Date	Birthplace	Date1	Date2	Rate1	Rate2	#	Notes
Pike-173	Wade	James	Earl	9/7/38	Nashville, TN	7/18/44	12/13/44	Ck-2	Ck-2	0	AWOL 3 days, reduced from Ck-1 12/44
Pilotfish	Davis	Frank	Louis	6/23/42	San Diego, CA	2/9/44	EOW	St-3	St-3	6	Made all of this boat's WPs; Present at Tokyo Bay surrender
Pilotfish	Harmon, Jr.	Arthur	A.	6/3/43	Springfield, IL	4/27/44	EOW	Stm-1	St-3	6	Made all this boat's WPs; Present at Tokyo Bay surrender
Pilotfish	Kemp	Leon		7/31/43	Atlanta, GA	12/16/43	4/27/44	Stm-2	Stm-2	0	Comm crew only
Pilotfish	Smith	David	Leon	3/10/42	Indianapolis, IN	12/16/43	ca. 2/1944	Ck-3	Ck-3	0	Comm crew only
Pilotfish-386	Wright	Joseph		unk.		5/21/45	EOW	Stm-2	Stm-2	2	Made boat's final WPs; Present at Tokyo Bay surrender
Pintado	Blue	Joseph		unk.		4/15/45	EOW	Stm-2	Stm-1	2	NOK father James Blue, New Orleans, LA
Pintado	Gallop	James	Butler	unk.		1/27/45	EOW	Stm-1	Stm-1	3	NOK wife Esther Gallop, Sharon Hill, PA
Pintado	Johnson	Isaac	Webson	8/11/43	Chicago, IL	1/1/44	2/29/44	Stm-2	Stm-2	1	On from S-48
Pintado	Knowlton	Frank		6/7/43	Detroit, MI	2/29/44	9/30/44	Stm-1	Stm-1	2	On from tender Sperry
Pintado	Scruggs	Willie	Hubert	unk.		10/9/44	1/27/45	Ck-1	Ck-1	1	
Pintado	Simpson	James	Leslie	unk.		1/27/45	EOW	Stm-2	Stm-1	3	On from SRU; NOK wife Vera Simpson, Greensboro, NC
Pintado	Singleton	Charles	Willie	unk.		unk.	1/1/45	Stm-1	Stm-1	3	May be same man as John Singleton
Pintado-387	Singleton	John		12/1/42	Charleston, SC	1/1/44	unk.	Stm-1	unk.	3	May be same man as C.W. Singleton
Pipefish	Clay	Frank		1/27/44	Chicago, IL	7/29/44	EOW	Stm-2	Stm-1	5	On from Silversides; CM 9/44 for failure to obey orders
Pipefish	McMillan	Hayward		unk.		10/26/44	EOW	Stm-2	Stm-1	4	
Pipefish	Smith	Nathaniel		unk.		10/28/44	EOW	Stm-2	Stm-1	4	Transferred from CSD-42
Pipefish	Theirse	Leroy	Bede	11/20/42	New York, NY	1/22/44	10/28/44	Stm-1	Ck-3	2	Made boat's 1st 2 WPs
Pipefish	White	Wilbert		unk.		10/14/44	11/1/44	Stm-2	Stm-2	0	CM 10/30/44 AOL and disobedience of orders

Submarine	Last Name	First Name	Middle	D.O.E.	Place of Enlistment	Date on Board	Date Off	Rating On	Rating Off	War Patrols	Notes About Service
Pipefish-388	Whitfield	Orial		3/1/40	Jacksonville, FL	2/2/44	7/29/44	Stm-1	St-3	1	On from S-17, later on Picuda
Piranha	Baker	Wilson		10/13/43	Waterloo, IA	5/31/44	6/11/44	Stm-2	Stm-2	0	Relief duty only
Piranha	Carpenter	James		2/7/44	Nashville, TN	1/30/45	2/5/45	Stm-1	Stm-1	0	Relief duty only
Piranha	Clark, III	Warren		6/8/43	Shreveport, LA	2/5/44	EOW	Stm-1	Ck-3	5	On at PNSY; Made all this boat's WPs
Piranha	Cooper	Hethel	Elisa	3/26/43	Jackson, MS	6/11/44	1/29/45	St-3	St-3	3	Made boat's first 3 WPs
Piranha	Sistrunk	Edward		unk.		2/5/45	5/6/45	Stm-1	Stm-1	1	Off to ns Aegir
Piranha	Smith	Milton		9/24/43	Chicago, IL	4/1/44	5/26/44	Stm-2	Stm-2	0	On from Pike, off to Plunger flag
Piranha	Strickland	Frank	Bernie	9/16/43	Raleigh, NC	2/5/44	3/31/44	Stm-2	Stm-3	1	On at PNSY-CM 2/25/44, reduced in rate
Piranha-389	Williams, Jr.	Earl		1/29/42	Dallas, TX	2/4/45	EOW	Stm-2	Stm-1	2	On Board
Plaice	Carpenter	James		2/7/44	Nashville, TN	5/15/44	1/7/45	Stm-2	Stm-1	3	At USNH #18 from 12/24/1944 to 1/6/1945
Plaice	Cornish	Tyree		7/14/42	Coco Sola, CZ	2/12/44	5/17/44	Ck-3	Ck-3	0	First enlisted 1938, later on Hake
Plaice	Davis	Lewis	P.	9/23/42	Tyler, TX	2/12/44	EOW	Stm-2	Stm-1	6	Comm crew
Plaice-390	Guillory	Alton	P.	unk.		1/4/45	EOW	Stm-1	Stm-1	3	Made boat's final 3 WPs
Plunger	Allen	John	Harvey	9/11/41	Macon, GA	12/13/41	8/2/42	MA-3	MA-3	3	Made boat's first 2 WPs
Plunger	Ashford	Alfred	Cleotha	5/15/43	Raleigh, NC	10/21/43	10/27/43	Stm-2	Stm-2	0	Relief duty only
Plunger	Berger	Otis	L.	unk.		12/1/44	EOW	Ck-2	Ck-2	0	
Plunger	Gilmer	Arthur	Earl	9/6/38	Houston, TX	8/3/42	1/16/43	MA-2	MA-1	2	On from tender Fulton, off to Plunger flag
Plunger	Kimmons	Carl	Eugene	6/4/40	Cincinnati, OH	5/28/42	4/6/43	MA-1	OS-2	4	On from ns Mcfarland, later on Parche
Plunger	Laster	Robert		10/13/42	Dallas, TX	10/31/43	11/5/43	Stm-1	Stm-1	0	On from USNH, relief duty only
Plunger	Lewis	Albert	Sylvester	5/17/43	Richmond, VA	9/21/43	10/27/43	Stm-2	Stm-2	0	Later on Plunger, lost on Trout 3/1944
Plunger	McGuire	James	Thomas	12/6/38	Louisville, KY	1/20/43	9/20/43	MA-1	Ck-2	4	Prior on Permit, off to flag duty

Boat	Last	First	Middle	Birth date	Birthplace	Enlist date	Rate 1	Rate 2	Rate 3	WPs	Notes
Plunger	Murray	Willie	Herriott	5/14/43	Charleston, SC	9/21/43	EOW	Stm-2	Stm-1	5	CM 9/44 (see Murray's story for details)
Plunger	Reid, Jr.	Cicero		1/6/43	Norfolk, VA	2/1/44	12/10/44	Stm-2	Stm-1	2	Off to Pollack flag
Plunger-179	Toler	Otha	Lavada	10/2/41	Little Rock, AR	4/12/43	2/2/44	Stm-1	Ck-3	4	On at PH, later on Spikefish
Pogy	Anderson	Roscoe		11/12/43	Nashville, TN	9/16/44	EOW	Stm-2	Stm-1	4	On from relief duty; Made boat's final 4 WPs
Pogy	Clark	Robert	Lilton	10/12/43	Mare Island, CA	5/31/44	6/8/44	Ck-1	Ck-1	0	Off to MI, NC
Pogy	Harris, Jr.	William	Thomas	7/30/42	Raleigh, NC	3/24/44	9/16/44	Stm-1	Stm-1	1	Made this boat's 6th WP, later on Bugara
Pogy	Johnson, Jr.	Robert		1/4/43	Birmingham, AL	3/24/44	7/27/44	Stm-2	Stm-1	1	Made this boat's 6th WP
Pogy	Morris	Jesse	Thomas	4/3/40	unk.	ca. 6/1943	3/24/44	St-2	St-1	5	Date aboard uncertain
Pogy	Thompson	Willie	Jay	6/23/41	Cleveland, OH	6/20/43	EOW	Stm-1	St-2	9	Prior on Sawfish; Made boat's final 9 Wps
Pogy	Wade	James	Earl	9/7/38	Nashville, TN	5/31/44	6/8/44	Ck-3	Ck-3	0	Off at MI, NC
Pogy-266	Walton	Willie		3/27/43	Birmingham, AL	1/15/44	EOW	Stm-2	Stm-2	6	On from tender Sperry
Pollack	Ashford	Alfred	Cleotha	5/15/43	Raleigh, NC	7/13/43	9/27/43	Stm-2	Stm-2	0	Off to Plunger
Pollack	Brown	Ralph		1/14/43	Jacksonville, FL	2/17/44	2/25/44	Stm-2	Stm-2	0	Relief duty only
Pollack	Coleman	Wallace		7/2/40	New Orleans, LA	9/30/44	8/1/45	Ck-2	Ck-1	0	On from Nautilus flag in Australia
Pollack	Criss	Scott		12/14/41	New Orleans, LA	Pre-war	9/17/42	MA-2	MA-1	3	Off at PH
Pollack	Foster	Russell	Douglas	2/25/42	Denver, CO	2/28/44	EOW	Stm-1	Stm-1	3	Made boat's final 3 WPs
Pollack	Hannah, Jr.	Edmund	Richard	8/7/41	Macon, GA	2/7/42	12/31/43	MA-2	Ck-3	7	On from Plunger flag; Headed "In to dangerous waters"
Pollack	Reese	Lemuel	Lincoln	12/15/41	Richmond, VA	10/31/43	unk.	Stm-1	unk.	0	Transferred from Plunger; "Tried by Deck Court"
Pollack	Roberts	Roy	Lee	unk.		3/31/45	9/21/45	Stm-2	Stm-1	0	On from S-11, off at NL
Pollack	Sanders	John	Edward	1/7/43	Jackson, MS	2/25/44	9/28/44	Stm-1	Stm-2	3	CM 8/44 Failure to stand watch, reduced in rate; off to SRU
Pollack-180	Thompson	Hadwick	Alvin	1/11/39	San Francisco, CA	7/31/42	2/28/44	MA-2	St-3	5	On from destroyer Ramsey, off to USNH MI

Submarine	Last Name	First Name	Middle	D.O.E.	Place of Enlistment	Date on Board	Date Off	Rating On	Rating Off	War Patrols	Notes About Service
Pomfret	Brooks	John	S.	7/5/43	Chicago, IL	4/4/44	4/5/44	Stm-1	Stm-1	0	On from O-4, off as a straggler with King
Pomfret	Derr	Noble	Augustus	7/7/44	Charlotte, NC	4/17/45	EOW	Stm-1	Stm-1	2	Made boat's final 2 WPs
Pomfret	Freeman	Johnny	B.	unk.		9/7/44	4/19/45	Stm-2	Stm-1	2	
Pomfret	Hall	Alfred	Leander	12/3/43	New Haven, CT	4/13/44	EOW	Stm-2	St-2	6	On from O-2 at NL; Made all this boat's WPs
Pomfret	Jones, Jr.	Willie	W.	9/15/43	Macon, GA	2/19/44	4/9/44	Stm-2	Stm-2	0	Comm Crew, off at NY
Pomfret-391	King	James	Ernest	12/4/41	Raleigh, NC	2/19/44	9/3/44	Stm-1	Stm-1	1	Comm Crew, a straggler 4/44, off at USNH Midway
Pompano	Ganious	Sherman		10/22/41	Houston, TX	5/27/43	KIA	Stm-2	Stm-1	2	Lost with boat 9/43, cause unknown
Pompano	Hairston	Lorenzo		10/11/39	Raleigh, NC	12/18/41	2/23/42	MA-2	MA-1	1	Off to Plunger flag
Pompano	Lamb	George		10/14/41	Norfolk, VA	2/24/42	3/30/42	MA-2	MA-2	0	On from, off to Plunger flag; relief duty only
Pompano	Leonard	Wesley	Lewis	10/28/41	Birmingham, AL	3/30/42	KIA	MA-2	Stm-1	6	On from Plunger flag, lost with boat 9/43, cause unknown
Pompon-181	McBride	Lloyd	George	11/13/39	New Orleans, LA	7/6/40	5/23/43	MA-3	Ck-3	2	Pre-war submariner
Pompon	Butler	Clarence		unk.		3/9/45	8/6/45	Stm-2	Stm-2	2	
Pompon	Jonkins	Walter			Texas(?)	4/13/43	3/2/45	Stm-2	Stm-1	7	
Pompon	Lieteau	Joseph	Phillip	9/21/40	New Orleans, LA	8/6/45	EOW	Ck-3	Ck-3	0	Prior on Picuda
Pompon	Love	Alexander				12/23/44	EOW	Stm-2	Stm-1	3	
Pompon	Washington	James		1938	South Carolina	3/17/43	12/23/44	unk.	Ck-1	6	Comm crew at MAN; On from Cuttlefish; Off to NC
Pompon-267	Weaver	Charles		3/16/43		3/16/43	4/4/43	Stm-2	Stm-2	0	Comm crew at MAN
Porpoise	Crawley	William	A.	10/13/43	Camden, NJ	12/30/43	ca. 1945	Stm-2	Stm-2	0	On from Bainbridge
Porpoise	Galbreath	George	A.	10/26/43	Detroit, MI	1/20/44	EOW	Stm-2	Stm-1	0	On from Bainbridge
Porpoise	Lee	Elmer		12/17/41	Detroit, MI	8/12/43	8/31/43	Stm-2	Stm-2	0	CM 8/43 for disrespect and shirking duty

Boat	Last	First	Middle	DOB	Birthplace	Date1	Date2	Rate1	Rate2	#	Notes
Porpoise	Polk	Ben		11/11/43	Tyler, TX	1/28/44	EOW	Stm-2	Stm-2	0	On from Bainbridge
Porpoise	Rogers	Roosevelt		4/2/43	Macon, GA	11/24/43	EOW	Stm-1	Stm-1	0	On from Mackerel
Porpoise	Turner	Edward	A.	11/20/42	Charleston, NC	11/15/43	EOW	Stm-2	Stm-2	0	On at NL
Porpoise	Welch	Namon		8/31/42	Birmingham, AL	9/14/43	12/17/43	Stm-1	Ck-3	0	On at NL, off to same for treatment
Porpoise-172	Wiggins	John	W.	3/17/43	Camden, NJ	10/25/43	11/8/43	Stm-2	Stm-2	0	On from O-10, off at NL-Relief duty only
Puffer	Allen	Carrol	Louden	12/20/43	Columbia, SC	4/19/44	EOW	Stm-1	Ck-1	6	
Puffer	Patton, Jr.	James	Woodley	4/2/40	Kansas City, MO	4/27/43	EOW	Ck-2	Ck-1	9	Comm crew; Made all of this boat's WPs
Puffer-268	Pruitt	John	Alden	8/1/41	New Orleans, LA	4/27/43	3/15/44	Stm-3	Stm-2	3	Comm crew, off to relief duty, later court-martialed and imprisoned
Queenfish	Boulet	William	Joseph	ca. 1943	Houston, TX	3/11/44	ca. 4/1945	Stm-1	St-3	4	Prior on Halibut
Queenfish	Cooper	unk.		3/4/42		ca. 5/1945	EOW	Stm-2	Stm-2	1	Made boat's final WP
Queenfish-393	Debro, Jr.	Jesse		ca. 1944	Knoxville, TN	3/11/44	EOW	Stm-2	Stm-1	5	Made all this boat's WPs
Quillback	Fields	H.	G.			12/29/44	EOW	Stm-2	Stm-2	1	Boat only made 1 WP
Quillback-424	Tuttle	Carlos	A.	5/9/39	Birmingham, AL	12/29/44	EOW	Ck-1	Ck-1	1	Prior on Peto
Rasher	Ball	Dave		2/16/40	Washington, DC	6/6/43	7/31/44	CCK	CCK	4	On at Man; Prior enlist 1936; Re-enlist for 4 years 2/8/44
Rasher	Bolton	Levi		1/31/42	Kansas City, MO	ca. 4/1945	EOW	Stm-1	Stm-1	2	Prior on S-28 and Lizardfish
Rasher	Davis	Waymon		1/26/43	Shreveport, LA	6/6/43	2/7/44	Stm-2	Stm-1	2	On at MAN
Rasher	Heisser	Melvin		5/24/41	New Orleans, LA	7/7/44	4/16/45	Ck-3	Ck-3	2	Prior on Hoe
Rasher	Oliver	James	Dorsey	1/13/43	Omaha, NE	2/7/44	7/17/44	St-3	St-3	2	Later on Bluegill
Rasher	Pennyman	Timothy	Matthew	2/26/43	Cleveland, OH	7/13/44	11/17/44	St-3	St-3	1	Prior on Crevalle, off to ATRC
Rasher-269	Washington	James	C.			11/18/44	EOW	Stm-2	Stm-1	2	
Raton	Gordelle	Eddie		5/17/43	Cincinnati, OH	10/24/43	8/20/43	Stm-2	Stm-2	2	On from TF 72, off to tender Orion
Raton	Jones, Jr.	Dave		1/4/43	Jackson, MS	2/9/44	3/8/45	Stm-2	Ck-3	4	On from Bluefish, off at USNH MI

Submarine	Last Name	First Name	Middle	D.O.E.	Place of Enlistment	Date on Board	Date Off	Rating On	Rating Off	War Patrols	Notes About Service
Raton	Lucas	Richard	Ralph	ca. 1944	Raleigh, NC (?)	6/10/45	EOW	Stm-1	St-3	1	Qualified 10/45
Raton	Matthews	Edward		5/26/43	Camden, NJ	7/25/43	8/20/43	Stm-2	Stm-2	0	On from MAN, off at USNH Balboa, CZ
Raton	McCall	Gus	Armstrong	1/31/42	Columbia, SC	11/12/43	2/9/44	Stm-2	Stm-2	2	On from TF 72, off to Bluefish
Raton	Porter, Jr.	James		5/7/43	Indianapolis, IN	8/30/43	10/24/43	Stm-2	Stm-2	0	On from S-15, off to TF 72
Raton	Sherman	William		4/16/40	Houston, TX	1/26/44 (2nd)	6/8/45	St-3	St-1	6	On from TF 72
Raton	Sherman	William		4/16/40	Houston, TX	7/13/43 (1st)	10/1/43	Stm-1	St-3	0	Comm crew, off to SRU 89 for hospitalization
Raton-270	Smith	Richard	G.	ca. 1944	Raleigh, NC (?)	3/8/45	EOW	Stm-2	Stm-1	1	On at MI, Qualified 7/23/45, off at Brooklyn, NY USNH 10/45
Ray	Hicks	Charlie		10/2/42	Chicago, Ill	7/2/45	9/14/45	St-3	St-3	1	On at Midway for war patrol
Ray	James	Jacob		1/14/42	Columbus, GA	6/28/44	7/9/44	Stm-2	Stm-2	0	On from Puffer flag, relief duty only
Ray	O'Bryant, Jr.	Robert		6/7/42	Indianapolis, IN	7/9/44	9/22/44	Stm-1	Stm-1	1	On from Bluefish, off to Puffer flag
Ray	Pinkney	Solomon	Isiah	5/7/43	Washington, DC	7/27/43	6/28/44	Stm-2	Ck-3	4	Comm crew, 12/8/43 "Qualified for Submarine Torpedo boat duty"
Ray	Pope	Willie	R.	9/22/43	Anniston, AL	9/22/44	7/6/45	Stm-1	St-3	2	Made boat's 6-7 WPs
Ray	Rucker	Emmanuel	Frank	unk.		7/6/45	EOW	Stm-1	Stm-1	1	Made boat's final WP
Ray	Soles	Albert		1/26/42	Dallas, TX	6/28/44	6/17/45	Stm-1	Ck-3	3	3/1945 re-enlisted for 2 years, prior on Cod
Ray-271	Stallworth	Talmon		11/18/42		7/27/43	6/28/44	Stm-2	Ck-2	4	Comm crew, off to Bluefish flag
Razorback	Blue, Jr.	Robert	J.	5/11/42	Nashville, TN	4/3/44	1/20/45	Stm-1	Stm-1	2	On at PNSY; CM 7/44
Razorback	Bryant	Edwin	Benny	unk.		1/20/45	EOW	Stm-1	St-3	3	Qualified 6/45; Made final 3 WPs; Present at Tokyo Bay surrender

Boat	Last	First	Middle	Date	Place	Date	Date	Rating	Rating	#	Notes
Razorback	Hall	Elbert		4/23/43	Cleveland, OH	11/3/44	1/20/45	Stm-2	Stm-2	1	Off to tender Sperry
Razorback	Howard	Berkeley	William	unk.		1/20/45	EOW	Stm-1	St-3	3	Qualified 6/45; Made final 3 WPs; Present at Tokyo Bay surrender
Razorback	Jackson	Fred		12/18/41	Raleigh, NC	6/11/44	11/3/44	Ck-1	Ck-1	1	Made boat's first WP
Razorback-394	Sherrad	Welford		11/16/43	Washington, DC	4/3/44	6/12/44	Stm-2	Stm-2	0	Comm Crew, off at NL
Redfin	Gardner	Slyvester		7/6/39	Richmond, VA	5/16/44	5/16/44	Ck-2	Ck-2	0	Relief duty only
Redfin	Hoyt	Henry	A.	12/16/43	Tyler, TX	5/16/44	EOW	Stm-2	Stm-1	5	
Redfin	LeBeau	Clifton		9/16/40	New Orleans, LA	8/31/43	12/24/43	Stm-3	Stm-2	0	Comm crew, off to Guard-fish flag
Redfin-272	Morgan	Otis		7/3/43	Cincinnati, OH	11/11/43	EOW	Stm-2	St-2	7	Made all this boat's WPs
Redfish	Beeler	Harrison		unk.		10/17/44	EOW	Stm-2	Stm-1	1	Boat retired after 2nd WP due to battle damage 1/1945
Redfish	Bristow	Henry		unk.	Raleigh, NC	10/17/44	EOW	Stm-1	Stm-1	1	Boat retired after 2nd WP due to battle damage 1/1945
Redfish	Jones	Woodrow	Wilson	12/29/41	Louisville, KY	4/12/44	7/23/44	Ck-3	Ck-3	0	Comm crew, on at PNSY, prior on Pike
Redfish	Madison	Lester		4/2/42	Houston, TX	7/23/44	10/3/44	St-3	St-3	1	Prior on Tang
Redfish-395	Stone	William	H.	11/4/42	Philadelphia, PA	4/12/44	10/17/44	St-3	St-3	1	Comm crew, on at PNSY
Robalo	Gleaton, Jr.	Elliott		8/15/40	Charleston, SC (?)	9/28/43	KIA	Ck-3	Ck-2	3	Lost with boat 7/26/44 off Palawan
Robalo-273	Williams	Davie	L.	6/6/43		9/28/43	KIA	Stm-2	Stm-1	3	Lost with boat 7/26/44 off Palawan
Rock	Deavers	Willie		unk.		2/23/45	EOW	Stm-2	Stm-1	1	Made boat's final WP
Rock	McRae	Curtiss		5/11/44	Brooklyn, NY	9/4/44	12/3/44	Stm-2	Stm-2	1	Off to USNH
Rock	Peterson	John	A.	11/18/39	New Orleans, LA	12/4/44	EOW	Ck-2	Ck-2	2	On from tender Euryale; NOK mom Francis Peterson, Pasadena, CA
Rock-274	Thomas, Jr.	William		7/19/43	Detroit, MI	10/26/43	2/23/45	Stm-2	Stm-1	5	Made boat's first 5 WPs
Ronquil	Gray	James		11/8/43	Columbia, SC	4/22/44	8/1/45	Stm-2	Stm-1	5	On at PNSY
Ronquil	Jones	Don	Ginger	unk.		8/26/45	EOW	Stm-2	Stm-2	0	

Submarine	Last Name	First Name	Middle	D.O.E.	Place of Enlistment	Date on Board	Date Off	Rating On	Rating Off	War Patrols	Notes About Service
Ronquil	Sawyer	Curlee		10/9/42	Birmingham, AL	4/22/44	5/14/45	Stm-1	St-3	5	On at PNSY; Made all this boat's WPs
Ronquil-396	Watkins	Raymond		unk.		5/10/45	EOW	Stm-2	Stm-1	1	Made boat's final WP
Runner 1	Hayward	Edward	L.	7/23/41	New Orleans, LA	10/3/42	1/12/43	MA-2	MA-2	0	On at NL, off at PH
Runner 1	Laws	Charles		4/23/42	Baltimore, MD	8/3/42	KIA	MA-3	MA-2	3	On from ns Harry Lee, lost with boat 6/1943 off Japan
Runner 1	Robinson, Jr.	Claude		10/12/42	Houston, TX	1/12/43	3/23/43	MA-2	MA-2	1	On at PH, off to flag duty
Runner 1-275	Songco	Zacarias		9/17/42	New London, CT	Sep. 42	10/31/42	CCK	CCK	0	On from Shad, prior enlist ca. 1934–38; Nationality uncertain
Runner 2	Holt, Jr.	Alexander	Eugene	8/4/44	Houston, TX	2/6/45	EOW	Stm-2	Stm-1	2	Comm Crew; Made both WPs; Present at Tokyo Bay surrender
Runner 2	Theirse	Leroy	Bedy	11/20/42	New York, NY	2/6/45	2/13/45	Ck-3	Ck-3	0	Comm crew; Off at NL for medical treatment
Runner 2	Waddell	Robert	Lee	unk.		8/5/45	EOW	Stm-2	Stm-2	1	On from Moray flag for last WP; Present at Tokyo Bay surrender
Runner 2	Wilson	Edward	Frank	5/27/43	New York, NY	2/13/45	10/1/45	Stm-2	Ck-3	2	On at NL; Made both of this boat's WPs
Runner 2-476	Hewitt, Jr.	Jeff		unk.		4/2/45	4/4/45	Stm-2	Stm-2	0	Relief duty only; Off at NL
S-18	Napier	Edward	Ross	12/22/39	unk.	5/7/40	after 12/43	MA-3	OC-2	8	Made all this boat's WPs; 1 in Atlantic, 7 in Alaska ending 2/43
S-18-123	Conars	Walter		3/26/43	Cincinnati, OH	6/14/43	after 12/43	Stm-2	Stm-2	0	On after final Wps
S-23	Gaines	John	R.	1/10/39	New Orleans, LA	3/1/42	5/18/42	MA-1	MA-1	0	Off at San Diego
S-23	Hadden	Lonnie	B.	6/10/39	Dallas, TX	10/31/41	after 1/44	MA-1	St-2	6	6/43 Re-enlist for 2 years; Made all of this boat's WPs, all in Alaska

Boat	Last	First	Middle	DOB	Hometown	Enlisted	Status Date	Rate1	Rate2	WPs	Notes
S-23-128	Washington	Curtis	Clark	11/22/41	Dallas, TX		after 12/43	MA-3	Ck-3	6	Made all of this boat's WPs, all in Alaskan waters
S-26-131	Johnson	Nathaniel	N.	ca. 1939		Pre-war	Lost	unk.	MA-1	0	Lost with boat 1/24/42, collision in Gulf of Panama
S-28	Bolton	Levi		1/31/42	Kansas City, MO	12/5/42	7/4/44	MA-2	Stm-1	4	Cited as being lost with boat 7/4/44, but incorrect; Made 4 AL WPs
S-28	Brown	Bennie	Lawrence	6/20/39	New Orleans, LA	12/1/41	2/3/43	MA-2	OC-3	4	On from Plunger, off at DH, Alaska; All WPs in AL waters
S-28	Savage	Leodies		11/25/39	Little Rock, AR	11/14/41	5/18/42	MA-2	MA-1	0	On at San Diego, off to flag duty
S-28	Spurlock	Jake		4/24/42	Houston, TX	3/2/43	LOST	MA-1	Ck-2	2	On at DH, Alaska; lost with boat in training accident off PH 7/4/44
S-28	Stewart	James	David	2/3/42	Raleigh, NC	5/18/42	12/9/42	MA-3	MA-2	3	On from flag duty; All Wps from AL
S-28-133	Wisner	Frank		5/10/41	St. Georges, Bermuda	ca 2/1943	3/2/43	MA-1	MA-1	0	Relief duty only, off at DH, Alaska
S-30	Alexander	Joseph		10/16/42	New Orleans, LA	12/26/42	9/6/45	MA-2	Ck-2	4	At USNH San Diego 4/6 to 6/28 1944
S-30	Bolton	Levi		1/31/42	Kansas City, MO	7/28/42	12/5/42	MA-3	MA-2	2	On from Whale, off to S-28, later on Lizardfish, Rasher
S-30	Jackson	Lee	Montgomery	7/31/41	Philadelphia, PA	Pre-war	12/15/43	MA-2	Ck-1	9	Off to USNH, San Diego
S-30-135	Wisner	Frank		5/10/41	St. Georges, Bermuda	7/29/40	7/15/42	MA-2	MA-1	3	On from USNH, Philadelphia, off at San Diego for medical treatment
S-31	Campbell	Charles	Duffy	8/7/40		7/28/41	10/2/42	MA-2	MA-1	4	Duty at DH, Alaska, off to S-35 flag
S-31-136	Carpenter	Savoy		2/3/42	Richmond, VA	8/18/42	10/3/42	MA-2	MA-2	2	Off at DH, Alaska

Submarine	Last Name	First Name	Middle	D.O.E.	Place of Enlistment	Date on Board	Date Off	Rating On	Rating Off	War Patrols	Notes About Service
S-32	Evans	Joe	Caesar	8/8/40	Washington, DC	9/18/40	8/30/43	MA-1	Ck-3	8	Off to SRU, San Diego; Last 6 WPs made in AL waters
S-32	Lewis	Sanders	H.	4/4/40	St. Louis, MO	1/31/42	3/4/42	MA-3	MA-3	1	On from tender Griffin, off to ns Antaeus; WP data uncertain
S-32	Mann	Bernard	Osborn	unk.		3/4/42	7/7/42	MA-3	MA-3	2	On from ns Antaeus, off to S-27; WPs made in Atlantic, dates uncertain
S-32-137	Price	Robert		6/7/34	Raleigh, NC	12/22/41	1/31/42	MA-2	MA-2	0	On from tender Griffin, off to same
S-33	Barber	James	Augustus	10/12/42	San Francisco, CA	7/14/43	8/9/43	Stm-1	Stm-1	1	Made boat's final Alaskan WP; Off at DH
S-33	Freeman	Samuel	Edward	9/13/40	Houston, TX	pre-war	6/2/43	MA-2	OC-3	5	1 Atlantic and 4 Alaskan WPs; Off at NL
S-33	Robinson	Allen	Ray	5/28/41	Nashville, TN	2/27/42	7/12/43	MA-2	Stm-2	5	Reduced by DC from MA-1 3/43; All patrols in Alaska, 1 possible Atlantic
S-33-138	Smith	Napoleon		6/4/41	Houston, TX	11/4/41	2/27/42	MA-3	MA-3	0	Relief duty only; Off to tender Griffin
S-34	Gaston	Isaac		9/9/41	St. Louis, MO	2/28/42	4/11/42	MA-2	MA-2	0	Off at Naval Air Station, Dutch Harbor, Alaska
S-34-139	Higgins	Lloyd		1/22/42	Kansas City, MO	4/11/42	10/15/42	MA-3	MA-3	3	Made boat's first 3 WPs; 7/42 reduced from MA-2; Off at DH
S-35	Baker	James	Lee	4/7/42	Hopkinsville, KY	10/23/42	12/2/42	MA-2	MA-2	1	On and off at S/M Base Dutch Harbor, AK
S-35	Rives	John	Lee	5/17/43	Raleigh, NC	12/27/43	after 2/44	Stm-2	Stm-1	0	
S-35	Savage	Leodies		11/25/39	Little Rock, AR	12/2/42	after 2/44	OS-3	St-1	4	On at DH, Alaska
S-35-140	Wade	James	Earl	ca. 1938		Pre-war	after 12/43	MA-2	Ck-2	8	Re-enlisted for 2 years 8/1/42

Boat	Surname	Given	Middle	Birthplace	Date 1	Date 2	Date 3	Rate 1	Rate 2	#	Notes
S-41-146	Pamusposan	Paul	M.	San Francisco, CA	11/18/42	5/13/43	after 12/43	Stm-2	Stm-2	3	Ethnicity uncertain; Made this boat's final WPs, all in Alaska
S-42	Anthony	Masca	L.	Nashville, TN	7/12/39	9/30/41	6/3/43	MA-1	CK-2	4	Off at NL
S-42	Arder	Milton		Little Rock, AR	4/24/43	10/27/43	2/24/44	Stm-2	Stm-1	0	On at DH, Alaska
S-42	Bonner	Calvin		Houston, TX	5/1/42	8/11/43	8/13/43	Stm-2	Stm-2	0	On at MI, relief duty only
S-42	Colvin	Alfonso		Columbus, OH	7/30/43	5/17/44	EOW	Stm-1	unk.	0	On from tender Euryale
S-42	Feagin	Zebedee		Birmingham, AL	2/10/43	2/22/44	5/17/44	Stm-2	Stm-2	0	Off to tender Euryale
S-42	Freeman	Alfonso			unk.	1/5/45	1/6/45	Ck-1	St-1	0	Off to S-42 flag duty
S-42	Freeman	Archie	L.	Raleigh, NC	8/9/39	7/29/42 (2nd)	EOW	MA-1	Ck-1	3	On from tender Griffin
S-42	Freeman	Archie	L.	Raleigh, NC	8/9/39	ca 9/41 (1st)	6/19/42	MA-1	MA-1	1	Off to tender Griffin for treatment
S-42	Gordon	Charles	Lee	Chicago, IL	4/8/43	8/11/43	10/27/43	Stm-2	Stm-2	1	Off at DH, Alaska
S-42-153	Webster	Antonio			unk.	1/6/45	EOW	St-1	CST	0	On from S-42 flag; Pre-war on Seawolf
S-43	Lile	Matthew	H.	Cleveland, OH	12/18/41	11/7/43	after 1/44	MA-2	Ck-3	3	Made all this boat's WPs, all from Brisbane
S-43-154	McNair	Edward		Macon, GA	2/5/36	6/27/39	EOW	MA-3	OC-2	3	Made all this boat's WPs from Brisbane; Re-enlist CZ 2/5/42
S-44	Campbell	Charles	Duffy		8/7/40	7/31/41	7/31/41	MA-3	MA-3	0	On from Grayback, off to S-31
S-44	Glenn	Curtis		Nashville, TN	7/12/39	Pre-8/41	KIA	MA-2	Ck-2	5	Lost with boat 10/7/43 off Kurile Islands
S-44	Jones	Stanley	S.	Richmond, VA	3/5/41	9/30/41	10/31/42	MA-2	MA-1	4	On from ns Antaeus, off to tender Griffin
S-44	Keith	Leonard	Henshaw	Pensacola, FL	8/9/40	3/31/42	5/31/42	MA-2	MA-2	1	On from tender Griffin, off to same, later on Narwhal
S-44-155	Mitchell	Herman	Mondell	New Orleans, LA	12/17/41	10/31/42	KIA	MA-2	Stm-2	2	On from S-42, lost with boat 10/7/43 off Kurile Islands
S-45	Gardner	Rufus	Louis	Indianapolis, IN	12/4/41	3/15/43	after 12/43	MA-1	Ck-3	0	On at Coco Solo, CZ after last WP

Submarine	Last Name	First Name	Middle	D.O.E.	Place of Enlistment	Date on Board	Date Off	Rating On	Rating Off	War Patrols	Notes About Service
S-45	Harcum	Samuel	E.	9/26/39	Richmond, VA	2/24/42	3/15/43	MA-3	MA-1	4	Made all this boat's WPs, 3 from Brisbane, final 1 in Alaska
S-45-156	Watkins	Oscar	Edward	8/11/38	St. Louis, MO	6/6/40	after 12/43	MA-2	Ck-2	4	Made all this boat's WPs, 3 from Brisbane, final 1 in Alaska
S-46	Brown	Bennie	Lawrence	6/20/39	New Orleans, LA	10/5/43	11/26/43	Ck-3	Ck-3	0	Off at Puget Sound, WA-Prior on S-28, later on Hardhead
S-46	Irving	Tim		9/22/39	Chicago, IL	9/12/41	1/14/42	MA-1	MA-1	0	Relief duty only, off to tender Antaeus
S-46-157	Lee	Willie		1/10/39	New Orleans, LA	1/13/42	9/29/43	MA-1	Ck-3	3	Made all this boat's Pacific-Brisbane WPs
S-47	Hodges, Jr.	Charles		7/10/40	Macon, GA						Details of service not known-Boat made 6 WPs, incl. 2 in Alaska
S-47-158	Lee	Elmer		12/17/41	Detroit, MI						Details of service not known-Boat made 6 WPs, incl. 2 in Alaska
Sailfish	Batts	Allen		1/13/44	Richmond, VA	4/1/44	EOW	Stm-2	Stm-2	2	On at NL, Cm 9/1945, reduced in rate from Stm-1
Sailfish	Deas	Morris		9/20/40	Columbia, SC	10/8/43	3/6/44	Stm-1	Stm-1	1	On from tender Holland, off at MI
Sailfish	Deckard	Earl		9/1/43	San Francisco, CA	3/6/44	4/7/44	Stm-2	Stm-2	0	Relief duty only, at MI
Sailfish	Mosley	Robert	Daniel	1/26/43	Dallas, TX	11/12/43	6/17/44	Stm-1	Stm-2	1	CM 3/1944, reduced in rate, off at MI
Sailfish	Newton, Jr.	Killraine		8/28/43	Richmond, VA	6/17/44	3/30/45	St-3	St-2	2	On at MI, off to NC, Sea Leopard
Sailfish	Rozar	Leonard	Cicero	11/28/39	Macon, GA	2/1/45	9/12/45	St-1	St-1	0	On at NL, prior on Saury, Tuna
Sailfish-192	Whitten	James	Leon	3/16/43	Cleveland, OH	10/8/43	11/12/43	Stm-2	Stm-2	0	Relief duty only

Boat	Last	First	Middle	DOB	Hometown	Enlisted	EOW	Rate 1	Rate 2	Rate 3	Awards	Notes
Salmon	Adams	Floyd		5/7/42	Macon, GA	9/10/43	1/15/45	STM1c	St-3		4	CM 8/16/44-Off to NC Stickleback MI
Salmon	Anthony	Wilbur		5/5/42	Kansas City, KS	12/14/43	1/15/45	St-3	St-3		2	Off to NC Stickleback MI
Salmon	Bivens	Charles	Henry	2/2/37	Baltimore, MD	9/11/43	12/2/43	St-1	St-1		1	Made boat's 8th WP
Salmon	Bowen	Emmitt	Paul	9/28/39		Pre-9/41	12/8/41	MA-2	MA-2		0	Off to tender Holland
Salmon	Clark	Dallas	Clinton	4/2/43	Richmond, VA	12/5/43	12/14/43	Stm-2	Stm-2		0	Relief duty only
Salmon	Clark	Fred		unk.		12/3/43	12/5/43	Stm-2	Stm-2		0	Relief duty only
Salmon	Greene	Joe	William	unk.		3/28/45	6/10/45	St-3	St-3		0	On from Conger, off at PNSY
Salmon	Sharp	Samuel		10/9/42	Atlanta, GA	1/17/45	9/24/45	Stm-1	Stm-1		0	On from Seahorse; 2/7 to 3/19/45 at USNH, Balboa, CZ
Salmon	Stewart	Tommie	Lee	unk.		1/10/45	9/24/45	Stm-2	Stm-1		0	On at NL, off to same
Salmon	Trainer	Leonard		unk.		8/13/45	EOW	Stm-2	Stm-2		0	On at NL
Salmon-182	Willis	Charles	H.	unk.		1/10/45	EOW	Stm-2	Stm-1		0	On at NL
Sand Lance	Craig	Eugene		unk.		1/31/45	EOW	Stm-2	Stm-1		2	On from MI
Sand Lance	Howard, Jr.	Leroy		7/6/43	Greensburg, PA	1/31/44	8/1/44	Stm-2	Stm-1		3	Off to tender Griffin for treatment
Sand Lance	Marable	Earl	Richard	7/16/43	Boston, MA	8/31/44	1/31/45	Stm-1	Stm-1		0	Off as a straggler
Sand Lance-381	Shelton	Leotis	H.	4/4/42		10/9/43	EOW	Ck-1	Ck-1		5	On at PNSY; Made all this boat's WPs
Saury	Bruce	Curtis	Donzell	11/5/38	Little Rock, AR	5/6/43	9/7/44	Stm-1	Stm-1		5	CM 6/1944, reduced from St-3
Saury	Chadwick	Charles	Ardell	1/29/43	Philadelphia, PA	3/21/40	3/31/43	MA-1	MA-1		0	On from MI
Saury	Cosby	William	Henry	3/4/44	Philadelphia, PA	9/7/44	2/28/45	Stm-2	Stm-1		2	Father of comedian/television star Bill Cosby
Saury	Dawson, Jr.	Elijah		7/10/40	Norfolk, Va	5/31/45	EOW	Ck-2	Ck-2		0	Prior on Drum
Saury	Rozar	Leonard	Cicero	11/28/39	Macon, GA	12/22/42	12/31/44	MA-1	St-1		7	Prior on Tuna
Saury-189	Stewart, Jr.	Hayward		6/16/43	Shreveport, LA	2/28/45	5/31/45	Stm-1	Stm-1		0	
Sawfish	Bell	Lawrence	Warren	3/23/43	Washington, DC	11/1/43	12/21/43	Stm-1	Stm-1		1	Transferred from SM Base for duty
Sawfish	Campbell	James		unk.		5/26/44	EOW	Stm-2	Stm-2		4	On from MI

Submarine	Last Name	First Name	Middle	D.O.E.	Place of Enlistment	Date on Board	Date Off	Rating On	Rating Off	War Patrols	Notes About Service
Sawfish	Catlin, Sr.	Albert	Merrit	unk.		11/30/44	EOW	Stm-1	Stm-1	1	Made boat's final WP
Sawfish	Deas	Morris		8/20/40	Georgetown, SC	3/8/44	6/15/45	Stm-1	St-2	4	On from MI, prior on Sailfish
Sawfish	Hairston	Lorenzo		11/10/39	Raleigh, NC	6/30/43	8/10/43	St-2	St-2	1	Made boat's 3rd WP
Sawfish	Harris	Robert		12/6/38	New Orleans, LA	9/1/43	9/7/44	Stm-1	Ck-2	4	Made WPs 4-7
Sawfish	Haywood	William	T.	11/19/43	Pittsburgh, PA	9/7/44	EOW	Stm-2	Stm-1	3	Made boat's final 3 WPs
Sawfish	Jordan, Jr.	Ruben		11/20/42	Birmingham, AL	6/13/44	11/8/44	St-3	St-2	2	Made boat's 7-8 WPs
Sawfish	Robinson	Alfred		1/7/43	Macon, GA	8/12/43	9/14/43	Stm-2	Stm-2	0	Relief duty only
Sawfish	Thompson	Willie	Jay	6/23/41	Cleveland, OH	10/8/42	4/2/43	MA-1	MA-1	1	On at NL; Later on Pogy
Sawfish	Washington, Jr.	Ripley		1/13/42	New York, NY	8/26/42	8/28/43	MA-3	MA-1	7	Comm crew, off to USNH #128, lost on Tullibee 3/26/44
Sawfish-276	Wells	Edward		1/4/43	Jackson, MS	9/2/43	3/24/44	Stm-2	Ck-3	2	Made WPs 4-5
Scabbardfish	Brown	Harold	Weeks	3/31/44	Elizabeth, NJ	10/31/44	6/30/45	Stm-2	Stm-1	4	On from Tambor
Scabbardfish	Greer	James	M.	11/19/43	San Francisco, CA	8/17/44	10/31/44	Stm-3	Stm-3	1	Off to Tambor
Scabbardfish	Jones	Robert	Lawrence	5/17/43	Omaha, NE	4/29/44	8/17/44	Stm-1	Stm-1	0	On at PNSY
Scabbardfish-397	Sims	James	T.	6/12/43	Macon, GA	4/29/44	12/31/44	Stm-2	Stm-1	2	
Scamp	Bass	Odie		5/16/44	New York, NY	8/7/44	KIA	Stm-2	Stm-2	1	On from MI, lost with boat 11/44 off the Bonin Islands
Scamp	Carter	William		1/7/42	Indianapolis, IN	10/16/42	12/14/42	MA-2	MA-2	0	On from Marlin, off to Steelhead
Scamp-277	Johnson	John	Lewis	1/2/43	Tyler, TX	12/15/43	8/8/44	Stm-2	Stm-1	2	On from NRU #89; AOL 6/44 for 5 days
Scorpion	Alston	John	Wesley	12/4/41	Raleigh, NC	2/21/43	7/24/43	MA-1	Stm-1	2	From S-48-Reduced from Ck-3 CM 7/43
Scorpion	Dews	Raymond	Palmer	3/26/43	Camden, NJ	10/11/43	KIA	Stm-1	Stm-1	2	On from Runner, lost with boat ca. 2/1944 in East China Sea
Scorpion	Fergerson	Nearest		8/28/42	Los Angeles, CA	6/2/43	KIA	Stm-1	St-3	3	Lost with boat ca. 2/1944 in East China Sea

Boat	Last	First	Middle	Birthplace	Date 1	Date 2	Rate 1	Rate 2	#	Notes
Scorpion	Hoskins	Walter		Nashville, TN	1/9/41	10/26/42	MA-1	OC-3	0	On at NL
Scorpion	Jones	Joseph	Leo	Macon, GA	8/20/42	10/12/42	1/7/43	MA-3	MA-3	0	On at NL, off to same; AWOL 11/5–11/2 1942
Scorpion	Sharp	Samuel		Atlanta, GA	10/9/42	1/9/43 (1st)	6/2/43	MA-2	Stm-2	1	Declared a straggler on 2/7/43, surrendered on board 2/10/43
Scorpion-278	Sharp	Samuel		Atlanta, GA	10/9/42	7/21/43 (2nd)	10/21/43	Stm-2	Stm-2	0	on from Pickerel, off to Runner
Sculpin	Boyd	Cleo	L.C.	Raleigh, NC	10/20/34	9/27/40	7/20/42	MA-2	MA-1	4	Off to tender Otus; no Black stewards on this boat after 7/1942
Sculpin-191	Newton	A.L.		Dallas, TX	8/6/41	12/1/41	7/20/42	MA-3	MA-2	4	Off to tender Otus; no Black stewards on this boat after 7/1942
Sea Cat	Galbreath	George	A.	Detroit, MI	10/26/43	5/16/44	6/28/44	Stm-1	Stm-1	0	On at PNSY; Off at NY
Sea Cat	Hollingsworth	Yancey	Henry	unk.	4/17/44	4/8/45	EOW	Stm-1	Stm-1	2	Made boat's final 2 WPs; Present at Tokyo Bay surrender
Sea Cat	Ings	Hugo	B.	Columbia, SC	6/21/43	5/16/44	EOW	Stm-1	Stm-1	4	Made all boat's WPs; Present at Tokyo Bay surrender
Sea Cat-399	Zanes	Herbert	Eugene	Columbus, OH	4/29/43	6/26/44	7/1/44	Stm-2	Stm-2	0	Left before 1st WP, off to Spikefish
Sea Devil	Esters	Harry		St. Louis, MO	10/18/43	5/26/44	EOW	Stm-2	Stm-1	5	On from O-3; Made all this boat's WPs; NOK wife Katherine, Humboldt, TN
Sea Devil	Melvin	Paul	Lawrence		unk.	8/2/45	EOW	Stm-2	Stm-2	1	Made boat's final WP
Sea Devil-400	Postell	L.	D.	Columbia, SC	4/29/43	5/24/44	8/19/45	Stm-1	St-3	4	Comm crew, on at PNSY
Sea Dog	Bass	Joe	Willie	Indianapolis, IN	3/20/44	9/17/44	8/26/45	Stm-2	St-3	4	
Sea Dog	Cobb	Washington		Atlanta, GA	1/25/44	6/3/44	6/3/44	Stm-2	Stm-2	0	Off to USNH, Portsmouth, NH
Sea Dog	Cosby	William	Henry	Philadelphia, PA	ca. 1940	9/19/45	8/2/45	St-3	Stm-1	0	CM 8/45, reduced from St-3

Submarine	Last Name	First Name	Middle	D.O.E.	Place of Enlistment	Date on Board	Date Off	Rating On	Rating Off	War Patrols	Notes About Service
Sea Dog	Johnson	Otis	Cleo	3/20/44	Birmingham, AL	6/8/44	2/22/45	Stm-2	Stm-1	2	On from O-6
Sea Dog	Pennington	Roscoe	Cleveland	1/15/43	Dallas, TX	8/25/45	9/19/45	Stm-1	Stm-1	0	Prior on Seadragon
Sea Dog	Singleton	William	Lawrence	5/3/44	Philadelphia, PA	7/21/44	9/17/44	Stm-1	Stm-1	0	On at NL
Sea Dog	Walker	Roosevelt		1/24/42	Birmingham, AL	6/3/44	7/21/44	St-3	St-3	0	
Sea Dog-401	Wilson	Richard	Dorthy	unk.		2/26/45	9/19/45	Stm-1	Stm-1	2	
Sea Fox	Chambers	George		unk.		2/20/45	EOW	Stm-1	Stm-1	2	On from SD 282
Sea Fox	McCants	Jimmie		unk.		2/20/45	EOW	Stm-1	Stm-1	2	On from SD 282
Sea Fox	Smith	Roy	Eugene	3/2/44	Huntington, WVA	6/13/44	2/20/45	Stm-2	Stm-1	2	Comm crew; made first 2 WPs; NOK wife Helen Estelle Smith
Sea Fox-402	Thorpe	Robert	Lee	unk.		5/27/45	EOW	Stm-1	Stm-1	1	Made boat's final WP
Sea Owl	Brown	George	Henry	8/10/43	New York, NY	7/17/44	8/22/44	Stm-1	Stm-1	0	On from PNSY, off to USNH
Sea Owl	Hodges, Jr.	Samuel		4/17/42	Detroit, MI	8/31/44	5/20/45	St-3	St-3	2	On at PNSY, off to ns Aegir
Sea Owl	Richardson	Nathaniel	Hawthorne	3/7/43	New Haven, CT	7/17/44	EOW	Stm-1	St-3	3	On at PNSY; Made all this boat's WPs
Sea Owl	Waller	Robert	Lee	unk.		8/29/45	EOW	Stm-2	Stm-2	0	
Sea Owl-405	Irby	Otis		unk.		5/20/45	8/29/45	Stm-1	Stm-1	1	
Sea Poacher	Carbullido	Edward	C.	unk.		1/31/45	EOW	Stm-3	Stm-1	3	On from tender Sperry; Ethnicity uncertain
Sea Poacher	Cullen	Homer	B.	unk.		1/28/45	1/31/45	Stm-1	Stm-1	0	Relief duty only; On from Drum flag, off to tender Sperry
Sea Poacher	Dimmings	Arthur		9/24/43	Cleveland, OH	7/31/44	1/28/45	Stm-2	Stm-2	1	Comm crew; Off to relief duty
Sea Poacher	Poole	Ivory	L.	unk.		10/6/44	1/11/45	Stm-2	Stm-2	1	On from S-13; Off to tender Sperry
Sea Poacher-406	Rankins, Jr.	Thomas	J.	12/23/41	Cleveland, OH	7/31/44	10/6/44	St-2	St-2	0	On at PNSY, off for flag duty

Boat	Last	First	Middle	Date	City	Date	Date	Rate	Rate	#	Notes
Sea Raven	Bowser, Jr.	Percy	McKinley	ca. 1944	Philadelphia, PA	unk.	unk.	Stm-2	unk.	1	On sailing list for 13th WP; NOK father Percy Bowser, Phil., PA
Sea Raven	Evans	Benjamin	Franklin	unk.	Richmond, VA	unk.	unk.	Stm-1	unk.	1	On sailing list for 13th WP; NOK wife Viola Evans, Richmond, VA; Not same man as was lost on Escolar
Sea Raven	Penn	James	Paul	4/28/44		ca. 8/1945	EOW	Stm-1	Stm-1	0	Dates of service uncertain; Prior on Gurnard
Sea Raven-196	Tadle	Cecil		2/8/40		3/19/42	ca. 8/1943	OC-2		5	Date off uncertain
Sea Robin	Everett	Howard	Elliot	4/7/44	Macon, GA	4/7/44	EOW	Stm-2	Stm-1	3	On at PNSY; Comm crew; Made all this boat's WPs
Sea Robin	Kennon	John	Clarence	unk.		5/30/45	EOW	Stm-2	Stm-2	1	
Sea Robin-407	Davidson	Parkes	Lee	11/12/43	Louisville, KY	8/7/44	2/24/45	Ck-3	Ck-3	1	Comm Crew, on at PNSY; CM 2/1945, fined $150
Seadragon	Butler	Nathaniel	Lewis	unk.		11/23/44	2/18/45	Stm-2	Stm-2	1	
Seadragon	Foust	Theodore	C.	5/8/44	Greensboro, NC	8/1/44	11/16/44	Stm-2	Stm-1	1	
Seadragon	Laster	Robert		10/13/42	Dallas, TX	3/24/44	8/12/44	Stm-1	St-3	1	
Seadragon	Pennington	Roscoe	Cleveland	1/15/43	Dallas, TX	9/16/43	9/10/44	Stm-2	St-3	2	Later on Spikefish
Seadragon	Smith	Charlie	Baker	1/24/42	Nashville, TN	2/18/45	EOW	St-2	St-2	0	
Seadragon-194	Southerland	Neil		4/26/44	New York City, NY	8/12/44	EOW	Stm-2	Stm-1	2	
Seahorse	Adams, Jr.	Culasket		3/27/43	Columbus, GA	5/31/44	3/19/45	OC-3	Ck-2	2	
Seahorse	Bethea	Marcus	Rudolf	6/6/44	Raleigh, NC	4/30/45	5/1/45	Stm-1	Stm-1	0	Relief duty only
Seahorse	Bowman	Gerald	R.	8/14/44	Albany, NY	4/30/45	7/1/45	Stm-2	Stm-2	1	On from Puffer flag
Seahorse	Crawford	J.	C.	1/22/43	Macon, GA	8/3/43	5/31/44	Stm-1	Stm-1	4	Made boat's first 4 WPs
Seahorse	Hall	Elbert		4/23/43	Cleveland, OH	7/16/43	7/30/43	Stm-2	Stm-2	0	On from NL, relief duty only
Seahorse	O'Neal	Harry	C.	11/17/42	Los Angeles, CA	5/31/43	6/30/43	Stm-2	Stm-2	0	On from NL, relief duty only
Seahorse	Sharp	Samuel		10/9/42	Atlanta, GA	3/16/44	8/21/44	Stm-2	Stm-1	2	Off to USNH

Submarine	Last Name	First Name	Middle	D.O.E.	Place of Enlistment	Date on Board	Date Off	Rating On	Rating Off	War Patrols	Notes About Service
Seahorse	Williams	James	Leo	9/6/44	Columbus, OH	1/31/45	EOW	Stm-2	Stm-1	2	On at MI
Seahorse-304	Walker	Roosevelt		1/24/42	Birmingham, AL	5/31/43	3/16/44	Stm-1	St-3	3	On at MI
Seal	Banks, Jr.	George		4/6/44	Columbus, GA	6/26/44	7/15/44	Stm-2	Stm-2	0	On at MI, relief duty only
Seal	Collins	George		2/3/44	Birmingham, AL	7/15/44	9/18/44	Stm-2	Stm-2	1	Made boat's 11th WP
Seal	Cooper	George	Edward	unk.		10/2/44	7/7/45	Stm-1	Stm-1	1	CM 6/23/45 for theft on 2 counts, off at NL to await action of JAG
Seal	Cox	Leroy		8/22/40	Macon, GA	6/18/43	11/7/43	Ck-3	Ck-2	3	On from Pickerel flag
Seal	Moye	Lawrence	Washington	5/26/43	Columbus, GA	10/18/43	5/30/45	Stm-2	Ck-3	4	On from Salmon flag
Seal	Ramsey	Walter	R.	unk.		7/3/45	EOW	Stm-2	Stm-2	0	A straggler 7/27/45, thence AOL, CM 8/7/45, found guilty
Seal-183	Williams, Jr.	Edward		Mar-43	Columbus, GA	11/7/43	12/20/43	Stm-2	Stm-2	0	Relief duty only
Sealion II	Bell	Isaac	5/7/43		Detroit, MI	3/8/44	EOW	Stm-1	Ck-3	6	Made all this boat's Wps
Sealion II	Dance	Samuel	Lee	11/28/38	Philadelphia, PA	3/31/44	ca. 4/1944	Ck-1	Ck-1	0	Relief duty only, on from Shark
Sealion II	Filemon	Montierde		7/19/40	Portsmouth, NH	3/8/44	EOW	St-1	CST	6	Made all this boat's Wps; Probable prior enlistment in 1936 (ethnicity uncertain)
Sealion II-195	Fisher, Jr.	John		7/15/43	New York, NY	7/9/45	EOW	Stm-1	Stm-1	0	Prior on Tambor
Segundo	Castle	Albert		8/3/43	Hartford, CT	5/9/44	6/6/44	Stm-2	Stm-2	0	Comm crew; Deserted 6/6/1944
Segundo	Johnson	Otis	Cleo	3/20/44	Birmingham, AL	4/12/45	EOW	Stm-1	Stm-1	2	Made boat's last 2 WPs; Present at Tokyo Bay surrender
Segundo	Johnson	Peter		1/22/43	New York City, NY	5/9/44	3/29/45	Stm-1	Stm-1	3	Comm crew
Segundo-398	Ross, Jr.	Limous		4/7/44	Atlanta, GA	6/26/44	EOW	Stm-2	Stm-1	5	On at NL; Made all this boat's WPs; Present at Tokyo Bay surrender
Sennet	Blue, Jr.	Robert	J.	5/11/42	Nashville, TN	5/31/45	EOW	Stm-1	Stm-1	2	On from Silversides flag

Boat	Last	First	Middle	Birthplace	Birthdate	Enlisted	Discharged	Rating1	Rating2	WPs	Notes
Sennet	Dildy	Vernon		Richmond, VA		3/31/44	2/6/45	4/3/45	Stm-1	St-3	1	On from Peto, off to tender Apollo
Sennet	Jones	William	Lee	Charlotte, NC	1/15/43		2/6/45	1/9/45	6/2/45	Stm-2	Stm-1	3	From Piranha flag
Sennet	Thompson	Joseph	Floris	Washington, DC	11/4/42	8/22/44	2/6/45	Stm-1	Stm-1	1	Made boat's first WP
Sennet	Webster	James	William		unk.	12/17/44	1/9/45	Stm-2	Stm-2	0	Relief duty only
Sennet-408	Johnson	Issac		Chicago, IL	4/13/44	8/22/44	11/29/44	Stm-2	Stm-1	0	Off to USNH, CZ
Shad	Feagin	James		Birmingham, AL	5/15/42	7/15/42	7/26/42	MA-3	MA-3	0	Off at USNH
Shad	Fitzpatrick	Essex	Lee	Tuskeegee, AL	3/25/43	8/11/43 (1st)	5/3/45	Stm-1	St-3	4	On from NL, off to Redfish flag
Shad	Fitzpatrick	Essex	Lee	Tuskeegee, AL	3/25/43	7/1/1945 (2nd)	EOW	St-3	St-3	1	Back on for boat's final WP
Shad	Gleaton, Jr.	Elliot		Portsmouth, NH	8/15/40	6/12/42	8/11/43	OC-3	OC-2	5	AWOL at sailing from NL, lost on Robalo 7/26/44
Shad	Goode, Jr.	Edward	Franklin	Braddock, PA	9/3/43	7/3/44 (1st)	5/3/45	Stm-1	Stm-1	3	Off to Redfish flag
Shad	Goode, Jr.	Edward	Franklin	Braddock, PA	9/3/43	7/1/1945 (2nd)	EOW	Stm-1	St-3	1	Back on for boat's final WP
Shad	Morris	James			unk.		6/30/45	EOW	Stm-2	Stm-2	1	Made boat's final WP
Shad	Moss	Fred	Lee	St. Louis, MO	1/7/42	8/9/42	7/4/44	MA-2	St-3	6	On at NL, temp. relief duty 9/1 to 9/27 1943
Shad-235	Williams	Clarence			unk.		5/3/45	6/30/45	Stm-1	Stm-1	1	On from Tilefish Flag, off to tender Bushnell
Shark 2	Dance	Samuel	Lee	Philadelphia, PA	11/28/38	2/29/44	3/26/44	Ck-1	Ck-1	0	On from Philadelphia, off to Seal flag
Shark 2	Hooker	Richard	Edward	Columbia, SC	9/9/43	2/14/44	KIA	Stm-2	Stm-1	3	Made all boat's WPs; Lost with boat 11/1944 in Luzon Strait
Shark 2-314	Pittman	George	Washington	Washington, DC	12/2/42	2/14/44	KIA	Ck-3	Ck-2	3	Made all boat's WPs; Lost with boat 11/1944 in Luzon Strait
Silversides	Brown, III	William	H.					Stm-2	Stm-2	1	On for final WP, #14
Silversides	Flewellen	James	E.					Stm-2	Stm-2	1	On for WP 11
Silversides	Ingram	Fred	P.					Stm-2	Stm-1	5	On for WPs 6-10

Submarine	Last Name	First Name	Middle	D.O.E.	Place of Enlistment	Date on Board	Date Off	Rating On	Rating Off	War Patrols	Notes About Service
Silversides	Odom	Herbert	G.	unk.		12/15/41		MA-1	MA-1	1	Comm crew; Off after first WP
Silversides	Rapier	William	Fairfield	1/22/40	Indianapolis, IN	unk.		MA-1	MA-1	2	Later on Tunny
Silversides	Royal	Anderson	Peter	7/2/40	Dallas, TX	ca. 6/1942		MA-1	OS-3	4	On from ns McFarland, later on Dragonet
Silversides	Watson	James	E.	unk.		12/15/41		MA-2	MA-2	1	Comm crew; Off after first WP
Silversides-236	Sharpe, Jr.	Myles						Stm-2	Stm-2	1	On for final WP, #14
Skate	Daniels	James		1/25/43	Shreveport, LA	4/15/43 (1st)	1/23/44	Stm-2	Stm-1	2	Comm crew, on at MI, off to relief duty
Skate	Daniels	James		1/25/43	Shreveport, LA	3/12/45 (2nd)	EOW	Stm-1	Stm-1	1	Back on from MI
Skate	Gober	Charlie		8/16/43	Columbus, GA	8/16/43	2/8/45	Stm-2	St-2	6	Off to USNH #113
Skate	Murphy	Willie		12/4/41	Macon, GA	4/15/43	6/15/43	Stm-2	Stm-2	0	Comm Crew at MI
Skate	Scott	Albert	Lee	unk.	Memphis, TN	11/4/44	2/12/45	St-3	St-3	0	Off to Halibut
Skate	Thomas	Earl		1/29/42	Memphis, TN	6/15/43	8/9/43	OS-3	OS-3	0	On at Coco Solo, CZ, off at USNH San Diego
Skate-305	Thomas	Leroy		7/2/43	Shreveport, LA	1/24/44	EOW	Stm-2	Stm-1	5	Made boat's 3-7 WPs
Skipjack	Bolden	John	Francis	9/20/39	Charleston, SC	5/7/40	12/8/41	MA-3	MA-2	0	Off to tender Holland on second day of war
Skipjack	Butler	Clarence		unk.		12/27/44	1/2/45	Stm-2	Stm-2	0	Relief duty only
Skipjack	Cave, Jr.	Albert		12/18/43	Raleigh, NC	7/11/44	8/10/44	Stm-2	Stm-2	0	Relief duty only
Skipjack	Denson	William	Berkley	9/24/43	Cleveland, OH	9/3/45	EOW	St-3	St-3	0	On at NL
Skipjack	Fisher	Whaylon	O'Neal	2/25/43	Baltimore, MD	5/15/45	9/4/45	St-2	St-2	0	Off at NL
Skipjack	Harris, Jr.	Robert		12/6/38	New Orleans, LA	10/8/44	9/3/45	Ck-2	Ck-2	1	On from ns Litchfield, off at NL
Skipjack	Kendrick	Herman		5/29/43	New York, NY	8/13/44	5/9/45	Stm-1	Stm-1	1	Off for trial by General Court Martial
Skipjack	McRae	John	Wesley	unk.		7/3/45	EOW	Stm-2	Stm-1	0	
Skipjack	Smith, Jr.	Fred		2/7/40	New Orleans, LA	1/22/42	3/16/43	MA-2	MA-1	5	On from tender Holland at Darwin, Australia

Boat	Last Name	First Name	Middle	DOB	Hometown	Date	Status	Rate 1	Rate 2	#	Notes
Skipjack-184	Taylor	Robert		unk.		9/5/45		Stm-1	Stm-1	0	Possibly same man that served on Springer and Tang
Snapper	Carpenter	Richard	Lee	6/5/40	Indianapolis, IN	8/31/44	EOW	Stm-1	Stm-1	1	Made boat's final WP
Snapper	Fenner	Donald	M.	8/15/40	Richmond, VA	10/31/41	EOW	MA-3	MA-2	2	CM 5/42 incapacitated for duty, off to tender Otus, lost on Grampus
Snapper	Gaylor	James	Lewis	11/17/39	Raleigh, NC	5/28/42		MA-2	MA-1	1	Off to tender Holland, later on Dace
Snapper	Higgins	Lloyd		1/22/42	Kansas City, MO	Pre-war		Stm-3	Stm-3	0	On at Bremerton, WA, off to tender Holland
Snapper	Moody	Cubby	E.	8/6/41	Dallas, TX	8/31/43		MA-2	MA-2	1	On from tender Holland, off to same
Snapper	Vall	Edward	George	11/25/42	New Orleans, LA	2/28/42		Stm-1	Stm-1	1	On from Flying Fish, off to tender Holland
Snapper	Walker, Jr.	Marshall		7/22/40	St. Louis, MO	10/31/43		Ck-2	Ck-1	2	Off to Sturgeon
Snapper	Whitten	James	Leon	3/16/43	Cleveland, OH	12/31/43		Stm-2	Stm-1	2	Made boat's final 2 WPs
Snapper	Whitten	James	Leon	3/16/43	Cleveland, OH	5/26/44 (2nd) EOW		Stm-2	Stm-2	0	On from tender Holland, off to Sailfish
Snapper-185	Wisner	Frank		5/10/41	St. Georges, Bermuda	9/30/43 (1st)		Stm-1	Ck-3	0	Off to Flying Fish
Snook	Hall	Elbert		4/23/43	Cleveland, OH	7/31/43		Stm-2	Stm-2	1	Made boat's 6th WP
Snook	Heard	Bernard	Madison	11/2/40	New Orleans, LA	6/28/44		MA-1	St-3	3	On at NL, off to Runner flag
Snook	Rodney	William	James	12/8/43	Minneapolis, MN	1/18/43		Stm-2	Stm-1	4	Lost with boat 4/1945 near Formosa
Snook	Shelton	William	Everett	7/10/43	New York, NY	3/21/44	KIA	Stm-2	St-3	6	On from Tinosa flag, lost with boat 4/1945 near Formosa
Snook	Washington, Jr.	Ripley		1/13/42	New York, NY	10/29/43	KIA	Stm-1	Stm-1	0	On and off from Runner flag, later lost on Tullibee 3/26/44
Snook	Webb	James	Benjamin	6/8/41	Birmingham, AL	10/23/43		MA-1	MA-1	0	On at NL, off to flag duty
Snook-279	Wilder	Thomas		8/31/42	Columbia, SC	11/13/42		MA-3	Stm-1	5	On at PNSY
Spadefish	Brooks, Jr.	Sie		unk.		10/24/42		Stm-1	Stm-1	0	Relief duty only
						12/13/44					

Submarine	Last Name	First Name	Middle	D.O.E.	Place of Enlistment	Date on Board	Date Off	Rating On	Rating Off	War Patrols	Notes About Service
Spadefish	Bynum	William	Thomas	9/16/43	New Haven, CT	3/3/45	EOW	Stm-1	St-3	2	Made boat's final 2 WPs
Spadefish	DeLoney	Adam		3/24/43	Jacksonville, FL	3/28/44	5/27/44	Ck-3	Ck-3	0	
Spadefish	Portwood	William	Marshall	10/20/43	Cincinnati, OH	5/11/44	EOW	Stm-2	Stm-1	5	Made all this boat's WPs
Spadefish	Solomon	Henry	Lewis	11/28/42	Des Moines, IA	4/9/44	2/26/45	Stm-1	Stm-1	3	On from MI-CM 2/1945, reduced from St-3
Spadefish-411	Larkie	Arthur		4/23/43	New Haven, CT	3/9/44	3/28/44	Stm-1	Stm-1	0	On from MI, Comm crew
Spearfish	Beverly	Claude	Cowan	4/30/42	Nashville, TN	1/17/44	3/16/44	Stm-1	Stm-1	0	
Spearfish	Briscoe	John	Henry	3/3/42	Nashville, TN	8/16/43	8/24/43	Stm-1	Stm-1	0	On from Pickerel Flag, relief duty only
Spearfish	Brown	Quincy	Timothy	4/28/43	Oklahoma City, OK	10/23/44	10/30/44	Stm-2	Stm-2	0	Relief duty only
Spearfish	Buttrill	J.	P.	8/6/41	Dallas, TX	6/18/42 (2nd)	1/17/44	MA-2	Ck-3	6	On from Sargo
Spearfish	Buttrill	J.	P.	8/6/41	Dallas, TX	3/16/44 (3rd)	EOW	Ck-3	Ck-2	2	On from Salmon flag
Spearfish	Buttrill	J.	P.	8/6/41	Dallas, TX	11/24/41 (1st)	2/19/42	MA-3	MA-3	1	Off to tender Holland
Spearfish	Harris, Jr.	Robert		12/6/38	New Orleans, LA	5/14/43	8/16/43	Stm-1	Stm-1	1	On from tender Holland
Spearfish	Jones	Robert	Lawrence	5/17/43	Omaha, NE	10/30/44	EOW	Stm-1	St-3	1	Made boat's final WP
Spearfish	McAdoo	Arthur	J.	6/13/39	St. Louis, MO	6/18/42 (2nd)	3/31/43	MA-1	OC-3	3	Off to tender Holland
Spearfish	McAdoo	Arthur	J.	6/13/39	St. Louis, MO	2/27/41 (1st)	3/31/42	MA-1	MA-1	2	Off to tender Holland for medical treatment and duty
Spearfish	Raiford	Rubin	MacNeil	10/13/42	Charleston, WVA	8/16/43	7/21/44	Stm-1	Ck-3	4	Off at MI, later lost on Tang 10/24/44
Spearfish	Reaves	Elijah	Alexander	4/24/44	New Haven, CT	7/31/44	11/12/44	Stm-2	Stm-2	0	On from MI
Spearfish-190	Smith, Jr.	Fred		2/7/40	New Orleans, LA	3/31/43	5/15/43	MA-1	MA-1	0	Off to tender Holland
Spikefish	Pennington	Roscoe	Cleveland	1/15/43	Dallas, TX	10/31/44	6/30/45	St-3	St-3	3	Prior on Seadragon, off to Tilefish flag
Spikefish	Toler	Otha	Lavada	10/2/41	Little Rock, AR	8/16/44	10/31/44	Ck-3	Ck-3	0	On from Sea Owl, prior on Plunger, off to Tilefish flag, later on croaker
Spikefish	Zanes	Herbert	Eugene	4/17/44	Columbus, OH	7/31/44	EOW	Stm-2	St-3	1	On from Seacat

Boat	Last	First	Middle	Birthplace	Date1	Date2	Date3	Rating1	Rating2	#	Notes
Spikefish-404	Bullock	John	Thurston	Raleigh, NC	6/17/43	6/30/44	8/27/44	Stm-1	Stm-1	0	On from PNSY, AWOL 8/7/44, off at Norfolk, VA
Spot	Barrett	Samuel	James	Yonkers, NY	7/11/44	5/19/45	EOW	Stm-2	Stm-1	1	Made boat's final WP
Spot	Battle	Bula	B.		unk.	8/21/45	EOW	Stm-2	Stm-2	0	
Spot	Claxton	Robert	S.	Philadelphia, PA	5/11/44	8/3/44	5/4/45	Stm-2	Stm-2	3	Made all this boat's WPs
Spot	Royal	David	C.		unk.	8/21/45	EOW	Stm-2	Stm-2	0	
Spot-413	Fisher, Jr.	John		New York City, NY	7/15/43	3/7/45	5/19/45	Stm-1	Stm-1	0	
Springer	Alston	Robert	Lee		unk.	10/22/44	EOW	STM-1	Stm-1	3	On from Marlin; Made all this boat's WPs
Springer	Barnes	Warren	G.		unk.	1/6/45	4/10/45	Stm-2	Stm-2	1	On from MI
Springer	Burrell	Christopher Columbus			unk.	4/10/45	EOW	Stm-1	Stm-1	2	On from Guardfish Flag
Springer	Talton	William	Marion		unk.	10/21/44	1/5/45	Stm-2	Stm-2	0	Off at USNH MI, later on Cabrilla
Springer-414	Taylor, Jr.	Robert		New Haven, CT	7/15/43	2/17/45	EOW	Stm-1	Stm-1	3	On from Redfish flag; Made all this boat's WPs
Steelhead	Banks	Ernest			unk.	3/12/45	EOW	St-3	St-3	1	Made boat's final WP
Steelhead	Carter	William		Indianapolis, IN	1/7/42	12/14/42	6/24/43	MA-2	Stm-2	1	On from Scamp; CM 1/1943 for possession of alcohol
Steelhead	Davis	Theodore	Clifton	New York, NY	12/19/41	6/24/43	6/7/44	Stm-1	St-3	4	Off to Tambor flag
Steelhead	Deville	Joseph	Milsted	Houston, TX	10/21/42	9/3/43	11/16/44	Stm-1	St-3	4	On from Tinosa
Steelhead	Jackson	Charlie			unk.	3/12/45	3/14/45	Stm-1	Stm-1	0	Relief duty only
Steelhead	Rankins, Jr.	Thomas	John	Cleveland, OH	12/23/41	6/24/43	12/10/43	St-3	St-2	2	Off to Plunger
Steelhead	Reese	Lemuel	Lincoln	Richmond, VA	12/15/41	12/7/42	6/24/43	MA-2	MA-2	1	On at PNSY, but AWOL prior to coming aboard
Steelhead-280	Turman	Willie		Tyler, TX	10/4/43	6/7/44	EOW	Stm-2	Stm-1	2	On from Tambor
Sterlet	Adams, Jr.	Sylvester			unk.	4/19/45	EOW	Stm-1	Stm-1	2	Made boat's final 2 WPs
Sterlet	Bush	Charles	Wesley		unk.	12/17/44	EOW	Stm-2	Stm-1	3	On from Snapper flag
Sterlet	Cox, Jr.	William	Henry		unk.	12/21/44	12/28/44	Stm-1	Stm-1	0	Relief duty only, off to tender Holland

Submarine	Last Name	First Name	Middle	D.O.E.	Place of Enlistment	Date on Board	Date Off	Rating On	Rating Off	War Patrols	Notes About Service
Sterlet	Davis	Eugene		unk.		1/23/45	4/8/45	Stm-2	Stm-2	1	Made boat's 3rd WP
Sterlet	Flores	William	Henry	7/22/43	Philadelphia, PA	3/4/44	12/28/44	Stm-1	Ck-3	3	On at PNSY
Sterlet	Freeman	Johnny	B.			4/19/45	4/20/45	Stm-1	Stm-1	0	On from Pomfret, relief duty only
Sterlet	Myree	O.	T.	10/5/43	Columbus, GA	3/4/44	5/1/44	Stm-2	Stm-2	0	On at PNSY, AOL 4/27/44, off at NL
Sterlet	Singleton	Early	Lee	unk.		12/29/44	1/9/45	Stm-2	Stm-2	0	Relief duty only, off to USNH #10
Sterlet-392	Finley	Napoleon		12/1/43	Jacksonville, FL	4/28/44	12/17/44	Stm-1	Stm-1	3	On from Pike, off to USNH #10
Stickleback	Adams	Floyd		5/7/42	Macon, GA	4/20/45	EOW	St-3	St-2	1	On from Salmon at MI; Made boat's only WP
Stickleback	Anthony	Wilbur		5/5/42	Kansas City, MO	3/29/45	7/13/45	St-3	St-3	0	On from Salmon at MI; Comm crew only
Stickleback	Clark	Melvin	Ernest	unk.		7/5/45	7/20/45	Stm-2	Stm-2	0	Relief duty only; On from, back to Entemedor flag
Stickleback	Echols	Harold	Eugene	unk.		7/20/45	EOW	Stm-2	Stm-1	1	On from Entemedor flag; Made boat's only WP
Stickleback-415	Palmer	Lether	Eugene	unk.		7/5/45	EOW	Stm-2	Stm-2	1	On from Entemedor flag; Made boat's only WP
Stingray	Baker	James	Lee	4/7/42	Louisville, KY	3/13/45	EOW	Stm-1	Stm-1	0	On from Boarfish, off at NL 10/1945
Stingray-186	Smith	James	Sterling	unk.		5/31/45	EOW	Stm-2	Stm-2	0	This boat had no Black stewards until 1945
Sturgeon	Cromarty	Arthur		3/11/43	Pittsburgh, PA	12/19/43	EOW	St-3	St-2	3	Made boat's final 3 WPs
Sturgeon	Grandy	William	Penn	10/18/39	Raleigh, NC (?)	9/11/40	7/24/42	MA-3	MA-2	2	Off to tender Otus, lost on Swordfish 1/12/45 off Nansei Shoto
Sturgeon	Jackson	Eddie		6/2/38	Nashville, TN	8/15/41	7/24/42	MA-2	MA-1	2	Off to tender Otus, lost on Corvina 11/43
Sturgeon	Thornewell	William	Dempsey	3/6/43	Pittsburgh, PA	11/13/43	12/19/43	Stm-1	Stm-1	0	On from tender Holland, relief duty only

Boat	Last	First	Middle	Date1	Birthplace	Date2	Date3	Rate1	Rate2	#	Notes
Sturgeon	Walker, Jr.	Marshall		7/22/40	St. Louis, MO	8/6/44 (1st)	10/27/44	Ck-1	Ck-1	0	On from Snapper, off to USNH TI
Sturgeon	Williams	Emmett	Jay	3/15/43	Los Angeles, CA	11/19/43	11/29/44	St-3	St-2	3	Off to USNH TI
Sturgeon-187	Walker, Jr.	Marshall		7/22/40	St. Louis, MO	12/5/44 (2nd)	12/26/44	Ck-1	Ck-1	0	Off to Snapper
Sunfish	Adams	Columbus		3/13/43	Columbus, GA	12/29/43	7/14/45	StM2c	Ck-2	6	Made boat's final 6 WPs
Sunfish	Arnold	Edwin		10/21/41	Birmingham, AL	11/17/42	1/30/43	MA-1	MA-1	1	Off to Pike
Sunfish	Bartie	Loundis		ca. 1943		7/14/45	EOW	Stm-1	St-3	0	Prior on Bluegill
Sunfish	Bigbee	Robert	L.	1/19/44	Cleveland, OH	7/16/45	EOW	Stm-1	Stm-1	0	
Sunfish	Carmouche	William	Joseph	8/28/42	Houston, TX	10/14/44	7/16/45	Stm-2	Stm-1	3	On from tender Sperry
Sunfish	Davis	Theodore	G.	12/19/41	New York, NY	9/1/42	11/17/42	MA-2	MA-2	0	On from Carrier service unit, off at PH
Sunfish	Hamilton	Frank	Garret	11/6/40	Norfolk, VA	1/29/43	2/1/43	MA-1	MA-1	0	On from Pickerel flag, off at USNH, Midway
Sunfish	Perry	William	Sidney	7/19/39	Philadelphia, PA	8/11/42	12/29/43	MA-1	Ck-3	5	Pre-war on Narwhal, off to Drum flag
Sunfish	Todd	Archie	Winfield	12/20/40	Washington, DC	10/9/43	8/1/44	OS-1	St-1	3	On from tender Sperry, off to Aspro flag
Sunfish-281	Howze	Comer		9/3/41	Birmingham, AL	2/2/43	ca 10/43(?)	MA-1	OC-3	3	Made WPs 2-4, later on Apogon
Swordfish	Grandy	William	Penn	10/18/39	Norfolk, VA	7/24/44	KIA	Stm-2	Stm-1	1	Prior on Trout, Sturgeon, lost with boat 1/12/45 off Okinawa
Swordfish	Jones	Johnnie		11/7/41	Oklahoma City, OK	5/11/43	6/17/43	Stm-1	Stm-1	0	On from tender Holland; 6/43 a deserter, missed ship on sailing
Swordfish	Kirk	Vernon		10/13/42	Indianapolis, IN	2/22/44	KIA	Stm-1	St-3	3	On from Snapper flag, lost with boat 1/12/45 off Okinawa
Swordfish-193	Murrell	Archie		12/15/41	Los Angeles, CA	4/28/43	5/11/43	Stm-1	Stm-1	0	Relief duty only
Tambor	Carr	Robert	Lee	1/29/44	Columbus, GA	7/4/44	EOW	Stm-2	Stm-1	3	On from Tang flag
Tambor	Coley	Robert		8/21/41	Birmingham, AL	3/13/42	7/19/43	MA-3	OC-3	7	Off to Tambor flag, later on Bugara
Tambor	Fisher, Jr.	John		7/15/43	New York, NY	3/28/44	9/25/44	Stm-1	Stm-1	2	Off to Trepang

Submarine	Last Name	First Name	Middle	D.O.E.	Place of Enlistment	Date on Board	Date Off	Rating On	Rating Off	War Patrols	Notes About Service
Tambor	Leeks	David	Frank	2/26/42	Jacksonville, FL	10/9/42	6/18/44	MA-1	St-2	7	On from Triton, off to flag duty
Tambor	McCoy	James	Davenport	7/15/43	Chicago, IL	6/19/44	7/4/44	Stm-2	Stm-2	0	Relief duty only
Tambor	Morris	Albert	Leon	12/21/41	Des Moines, IA	3/1/44	3/28/44	Ck-1	Ck-1	0	Relief duty only
Tambor	Sanders	Charles	Frederick	8/14/40	Raleigh, NC	12/2/44	EOW	Stm-1	Stm-1	0	
Tambor-198	Walker, Jr.	Luster		5/28/43	Akron, OH	9/26/44	12/2/44	Stm-1	Stm-1	2	On from Trepang, off to same
Tang	Adams	Ralph	Francis	ca. 1944	New Jersey (?)	9/18/44	KIA	Stm-2	Stm-2	1	Lost with boat 10/24/44 near Formosa
Tang	Bussey	Cleon		8/5/40	Houston, TX	10/15/43	3/13/44	Ck-3	Ck-3	1	On at MI
Tang	Chambers	George		2/2/44	Raleigh, NC	7/31/44	9/23/44	Stm-2	Stm-2	0	Off to Tilefish flag
Tang	Kendrick	Herman		5/29/43	Camp Perry, MD	5/30/44	6/6/44	Stm-2	Stm-2	0	Relief duty only
Tang	Madison	Lester		4/2/42	Houston, TX	3/13/44	5/30/44	St-3	St-3	1	Made boat's 2nd WP
Tang	Raiford	Rubin	MacNeil	10/13/42	Charleston, WVA	9/24/44	KIA	Ck-3	Ck-3	1	Prior on Spearfish, lost with boat 10/24/44 near Formosa
Tang	Sutton	Joseph	L.	7/12/43	Newark, NJ	11/10/43	12/8/43	Stm-2	Stm-2	0	On from MI, off at USNH, San Diego
Tang	Walker	Howard	Madison	8/9/43	Cincinnati, OH	1/13/44	KIA	Stm-2	Stm-1	5	Lost with boat 10/24/44 near Formosa; Made all boat's WPs
Tang-306	Taylor, Jr.	Robert		7/15/43	New Haven, CT	6/6/44	9/18/44	Stm-1	Stm-1	2	Off to Plunger flag
Tarpon	Alston	John	Wesley	12/4/41	Raleigh, NC	10/1/43	1/27/44	Stm-1	St-3	2	Made WPs 9-10, incl. one special mission
Tarpon	Barfield	Kenneth		10/23/41	Raleigh, NC	3/18/43	12/4/43	MA-1	Stm-2	3	CM 6/1/43, reduced in grade; later on Baya, Bergall
Tarpon	Houston	Waymon		12/4/42	Houston, TX	1/27/44	ca. 2/1945	Stm-1	Ck-3	2	Made boat's final 2 WPs
Tarpon	Howard	James	Burwin	unk.		4/17/45	EOW	Stm-2	Stm-2	0	On at NL
Tarpon	Laster	Robert		10/13/42	Dallas, TX	12/4/43	2/3/44	Stm-1	Stm-1	1	Off to USNH #10
Tarpon	Nesbitt	Hezekiah		12/19/41	New York, NY	12/21/44	EOW	Stm-2	Stm-1	0	

Boat	Last	First	Middle	Birth	Birthplace	Enlist	Discharge	Rate1	Rate2	WPs	Notes
Tarpon	Polk	Ben		11/11/43	Tyler, TX		2/19/45	3/19/45	Ck-3	Ck-3	0	On from Porpoise flag, off to Carp flag-Relief duty only
Tarpon	Reaves	William		unk.			2/14/45	EOW	Stm-1	Stm-1	0	On from Bonita
Tarpon-175	Stewart, Jr.	Hayward		6/16/43	Shreveport, LA		2/11/44	12/21/44	Stm-2	Stm-2	2	Made boat's final 2 WPs
Tautog	Craig	Jacob	Delbert	8/23/39	Birmingham, AL		4/24/42	6/25/42	MA-2	MA-2	1	On from tender Pelias, off to tender Holland
Tautog	Derr	Noble	Augustus	7/7/44	Charlotte, NC		10/23/44	2/25/45	Stm-2	Stm-2	1	Made boat's final WP
Tautog	Glenn	Fred		11/17/42	Columbia, SC		6/30/44	11/4/44	Stm-2	Stm-2	1	Made boat's 12th WP
Tautog	Gray	John	Andrew	11/18/41	Norfolk, VA		4/9/42	1/31/44	MA-3	MA-2	7	Made boat's 3-9 WPs
Tautog	Hicks	Charles	Morris	10/2/42	Chicago, IL		2/24/44	11/30/44	Stm-1	Ck-2	3	Off to ATRC
Tautog	Majors	Ward	Lunie	7/6/39			6/30/42	4/7/44	MA-1	Ck-1	8	Made boat's 3-10 WPs
Tautog	Neal	Joseph		9/25/41	Louisville, KY		1/31/42	4/30/42	MA-3	MA-2	0	On from tender Pelias, off to same
Tautog	Rives	John	Lee	5/17/43	Raleigh, NC		11/30/44	5/31/45	Ck-3	Ck-3	1	On from S-37
Tautog	Webster	James	William	unk.			2/25/45	EOW	Stm-1	Stm-1	0	
Tautog-199	Knapper	Alex		1/6/44	Shreveport, LA		4/30/44	6/6/44	Stm-3	Stm-2	1	On from Tambor flag
Tench	Majors	Ward	Morris	7/6/39			10/6/44	EOW	Ck-1	Ck-1	3	Comm crew-7/45 re-enlisted for 2 years; prior on Tautog
Tench-417	Demitte	Joseph		unk.			10/6/44	EOW	Stm-2	St-3	3	Comm crew; Made all this boat's WPs
Thornback	Lacy	Arthur	Sinclair	unk.			1/27/45	EOW	Stm-2	Stm-2	1	On at NL for boat's only WP
Thornback	Redmond, Jr.	Thomas	Calvin	8/17/43	Pittsburgh, FA		8/2/44	EOW	Stm-1	Stm-1	1	Comm crew; Made boat's only WP
Thornback	Slayton	Claude	Amos	unk.			3/7/45	3/12/45	Stm-2	Stm-2	0	Relief duty only at NL
Thornback-418	Williams	Paul	Harfield	7/17/42.	Richmond, VA		8/16/44	EOW	Stm-1	Stm-1	1	Comm crew at PNSY; Made this boat's only WP
Threadfin	Hargraves	Issac	Nathaniel	ca.1944			12/9/44	EOW	Stm-2	Stm-1	3	Made all this boat's WPs
Threadfin	Matthews	William	A.	unk.			8/15/45	EOW	Stm-2	Stm-2	0	

Submarine	Last Name	First Name	Middle	D.O.E.	Place of Enlistment	Date on Board	Date Off	Rating On	Rating Off	War Patrols	Notes About Service
Threadfin-410	Rochester	Leon	Virgil	4/25/44	New York, NY	8/30/44	EOW	Stm-2	Stm-1	3	NOK sister Gwendolyn Rochester, NY; Made all this boat's WPs
Thresher	Day	Shirley				12/15/43	3/1/44	Ck-3	Ck-3	1	Made boat's 11th WP
Thresher	Floyd	Alphonse		ca. 1944		ca. 1/1945	EOW	Stm-2	Stm-2	1	Made boat's final WP
Thresher	Green	E.		ca. 1943		3/1/44	ca. 12/1944	Stm-3	Stm-2	3	Made boat's 12-14 Wps
Thresher	Robinson	Eddie	W.	ca. 1943	Birmingham, AL	3/1/44	EOW	Stm-3	St-3	4	Made boat's final 4 WPs
Thresher	Skipper	John	V.	ca. 1943		10/20/43	3/1/44	Stm-2	Stm-2	2	Made boat's 10-11 WPs
Thresher-200	Hamilton	Leslie			Birmingham, AL	ca. 6/1942	ca. 6/1/43	MA-1	OC-1	5	On for boat's 4-8 WP's, later on Billfish and Brill
Tigrone	Catabijan	Peter	C.	unk.		9/9/44	EOW	Stm-1	Stm-1	3	Comm crew; Made all boat's WPs; Ethnicity uncertain
Tigrone-419	English	Reynolds	Lloyd	5/26/44	New York, NY	8/16/44	EOW	Stm-2	Ck-2	3	Comm crew; On at PNSY; Made all this boat's WPs; Present at Tokyo Bay surrender
Tilefish	Heard	Bernard	Madison	11/2/40	New Orleans, LA	12/15/43	1/16/45	St-3	St-2	4	On at MI, prior on Snook
Tilefish	Jordan, Jr.	Samuel	W.	unk.		5/1/45	EOW	Stm-2	Stm-2	1	On from ATRC; Made boat's final WP
Tilefish	Murphy	Darby		9/24/43	Cleveland, OH	8/15/44 (2nd)	4/16/45	St-3	St-3	3	Off to USNH
Tilefish	Murphy	Darby		9/24/43	Cleveland, OH	12/15/43 (1st)	6/21/44	Stm-2	Stm-1	1	On at MI
Tilefish-307	Stallworth	Talmon		11/18/42		1/16/45	EOW	St-2	St-2	2	Made boat's final 2 WPs
Tinosa	Collins	Isaac		9/25/41	Macon, GA	10/22/43	9/4/44	Stm-1	Stm-1	4	On from Silversides flag, off to MI; prior on Tunny
Tinosa	Crawford	J.	C.	1/22/43	Macon, GA	7/29/43	7/30/43	Stm-2	Stm-2	0	Off to Seahorse
Tinosa	Deville	Joseph	Milsted	10/21/42	Houston, TX	1/15/43	9/11/43	MA-2	Stm-1	2	Comm crew, on at MI, off to Steelhead
Tinosa	Jackson	Nathaniel		unk.		10/23/44	EOW	Stm-2	Stm-1	4	On at NL

Boat	Last	First	Middle	Date1	Hometown	Date2	Rate1	Rate2	#	Notes
Tinosa	Kellum	William		5/16/42	Tulsa, OK	8/13/43	Stm-2	Stm-1	1	On from flag duty, off to tender Sperry
Tinosa	Settle	Spaulding	Bedford	7/10/43	Newark, NJ	1/3/44	Stm-1	Ck-3	6	On from Bluefish flag
Tinosa	Turner	John	Clyde	10/23/42	Atlanta, GA	1/15/43	MA-2	Stm-1	5	Comm crew, later lost on Flier 8/13/44 off Palawan
Tinosa-283	Prentiss	James		11/23/43	Hattiesburg, MS	9/7/44	Stm-1	Stm-1	0	On from MI, relief duty only
Tirante	Brown	George	Henry	8/10/43	New York, NY	11/6/44	Stm-1	Stm-1	2	On at PNSY; Made all this boat's WPs
Tirante	Jones, Jr.	Von	Haskell	unk.		1/31/45	Stm-2	Stm-1	2	On at NL; Made all this boat's WPs
Tirante-420	Brown	Roscoe	Munford	unk.		11/6/44	Stm-1	St-3	2	On at PNSY, on until late 1945; Made all this boat's WPs
Torsk	Chambers	George		2/2/44	Raleigh, NC	7/17/45	Stm-1	Stm-1	0	Relief duty only
Torsk	Jefferson	Isaac	Eli	unk.		12/16/44	Stm-2	Stm-2	1	Comm crew
Torsk	Thompson	George	Edward	unk.		12/16/44	Ck-1	Ck-1	2	Comm crew; Made all this boat's WPs
Torsk-423	Chavis	Percy		unk.		7/4/45	Stm-2	Stm-2	1	Made boat's final WP
Trepang	Caldwell	Charles		unk.		8/20/45	St-2	St-2	0	
Trepang	James	Jesse		6/10/43	Jacksonville, FL	6/2/44	Ck-3	Ck-2	5	On from MI-Part of group CM 9/44, 8 men total, incl both stewards
Trepang	Martin	Luke		unk.		1/11/45	Stm-1	Stm-2	0	Relief duty only
Trepang	Smith	Charlie	Baker	1/24/42	Nashville, TN	5/22/44	St-2	St-2	2	On from MI; CM 9/44; Off to USNH #10
Trepang-412	Van Eskringe	James		unk.		1/23/45	Stm-1	Stm-1	3	Off to USNH #10
Trigger	Carter	Andrew	Jordan		New York	2/22/45	Stm-1	Stm-1	1	Lost with boat 3/28/45 off Nansei Shoto
Trigger	Morris	Albert	Leon	12/21/41	Des Moines, IA	5/23/44	Ck-1	Ck-1	0	Off to Shark flag
Trigger	Thompson	Nathaniel	Elton	8/1/40	Georgetown, SC	3/20/44 (2nd) KIA	OC-3	Ck-2	5	Lost with boat 3/28/45 off Nansei Shoto

Submarine	Last Name	First Name	Middle	D.O.E.	Place of Enlistment	Date on Board	Date Off	Rating On	Rating Off	War Patrols	Notes About Service
Trigger	Thompson	Nathaniel	Elton	8/1/40	Georgetown, SC	1/31/42 (1st)	4/21/43	MA-2	OC-3	5	Comm crew at MI, later on Tullibee
Trigger	Vaughn	Willie	Edward	11/25/42		4/20/43	12/23/43	MA-2	Stm-1	3	On from Silversides
Trigger	Wharton, Jr.	Arthur	J.	3/4/41	Louisville, KY	12/23/43	3/21/44	Stm-1	Stm-1	1	On from tender Sperry
Trigger-237	Wilson	Walter	Pye	12/28/38	Pittsburgh, PA	1/31/42	2/22/45	MA-1	CCK	13	Prior enl. 1934-11/16/44 Meritorious advance in rating to CCK
Triton	Bivens	Charles	Henry	2/2/37	Baltimore, MD	4/28/42	10/25/42	MA-1	OC-3	2	On from Grampus, later on Jallao
Triton	Dabney	John	D.	4/3/40	Des Moines, IA	10/28/40	KIA	MA-3	OC-3	6	On from ns Reina Mercedes, lost with boat 3/13/43 in Solomons
Triton	Deas	Morris		8/20/40	Georgetown, SC	1/1/42	1/26/42	MA-3	MA-3	0	On from tender Pelias, off to Grenadier
Triton	Ellis	John	Oscar	12/16/41	Birmingham, AL	10/2/42	10/25/42	MA-1	MA-1	0	On from tender Pelias, relief duty only
Triton	Gordon	Eddie	J.	8/5/40	Jacksonville, FL	2/21/42	3/28/42	MA-2	MA-2	0	On from tender Pelias, off to Tuna
Triton	Harper, Jr.	Moses	E.	12/19/41	Norfolk, VA	4/27/42	5/1/42	MA-2	MA-2	0	On from Tambor flag, off to ns Wharton
Triton	Hicks	Thomas		12/16/41	Nashville, TN	2/27/42	5/1/42	MA-3	MA-3	1	On from tender Pelias, off to ns Wharton
Triton	Jones	Johnnie		11/7/41	Oklahoma City, OK	10/2/42	10/25/42	MA-1	MA-1	0	On from tender Pelias, relief duty only
Triton	Leeks	David	Frank	2/26/42	Jacksonville, FL	5/1/42	10/9/42	MA-3	MA-1	1	On from Wharton, off to Tambor
Triton	McAphee	Homer		2/26/42	Birmingham, AL	5/1/42	5/2/42	MA-3	MA-3	0	Relief duty only
Triton	McCalop	Hermon	T.	10/25/39	Raleigh, NC	2/10/43	KIA	MA-1	MA-1	1	On from tender Fulton, lost with boat 3/13/43 in Solomons
Triton	Stewart	Norman	J.	12/29/39	Chicago, IL	5/6/42	9/24/42	MA-1	OC-3	1	On from ns Hulbert, off to tender Holland

Boat	Last name	First name	Middle name	Date	City/State	Date	Date	Rank1	Rank2	Num	Notes
Triton-201	Mosley, Jr.	Eugene		4/4/40	Nashville, TN	1/1/42	2/18/42	MA-2	MA-2	1	On from tender Pelias, off to Gudgeon
Trout	DeHosnery	Stewart	Alexander	11/10/39	San Diego, CA	9/2/41	8/9/43	MA-2	St-2	9	On from ns Litchfield, off to Tuna flag
Trout	Ewell	John	Edward	9/4/43	New York, NY	12/10/43	KIA	Stm-2	Stm-1	1	Lost with boat 2/29/44 off China
Trout	Grandy	William	Penn	10/18/39	Norfolk, VA	8/7/43	12/8/43	Stm-1	Ck-3	1	A straggler, thence AOL on 12/8/43; Lost on Swordfish 1/12/45
Trout	Jackson	Lonnie	David	6/2/36	Raleigh, NC	11/15/40	3/13/43	MA-1	OC-2	7	3/1942 Meritorious advance to OC-3; Re-enlist for 4 yrs. 3/1942
Trout	Johnson, Jr.	Robert		1/4/43	Birmingham, AL	1/28/44	2/7/44	Stm-2	Stm-2	0	Relief duty only
Trout	Lewis	Albert	Sylvester	5/17/43	Richmond, VA	1/29/44	KIA	Stm-2	Stm-2	1	Prior on Plunger; Lost with boat 2/29/44 off China
Trout	Millner	Calvin	Coolidge	1/7/43	Richmond, VA	8/9/43	KIA	Stm-2	Stm-1	2	On from Tuna; Lost with boat 2/29/44 off China
Trout-202	McAphee	Homer		2/26/42	Birmingham, AL	3/24/42	5/17/42	MA-3	MA-3	1	Off to Grayling
Trutta	Blanchard	William	Ardell	unk.		10/18/44	EOW	Stm-1	St-3	2	Comm crew-Made boat's only WPs
Trutta-421	Moore, Jr.	George	Israel	unk.		11/16/44	EOW	Stm-2	Stm-1	2	Comm crew-Made both of this boat's WPs
Tullibee	Camp	Nathan	Delmas	3/29/43	Little Rock, AR	12/5/43	12/18/43	Stm-2	Stm-2	0	Relief duty only
Tullibee	Chadwick	Charles	Ardell	3/21/40	Philadelphia, PA	5/7/43	6/11/43	Stm-1	Stm-1	0	On from tender Holland, relief duty only
Tullibee	Ellis	Leroy		5/8/43	Coco Sola, C.Z.	2/25/44	KIA	St-1	St-1	1	Possibly first in Navy in 1939; Lost with boat 3/26/44 off Palau
Tullibee	Hill	Walter		11/16/42	Birmingham, AL	2/19/43	5/8/43	MA-2	Stm-1	0	On at Norfolk, VA, deserted on sailing from U.S.
Tullibee	Houston	Waymon		12/4/42	Houston, TX	2/19/43	12/4/43	MA-2	Stm-2	2	On at Norfolk, VA, off to Narwhal

Submarine	Last Name	First Name	Middle	D.O.E.	Place of Enlistment	Date on Board	Date Off	Rating On	Rating Off	War Patrols	Notes About Service
Tullibee	Reid, Jr.	Cicero		1/6/43	Norfolk, VA	6/12/43	9/21/43	Stm-2	Stm-2	1	Off to Drum, later on Plunger
Tullibee	Thompson	Nathaniel	Elton	8/1/40	Georgetown, SC	9/21/43	2/26/44	OC-3	OC-3	2	On from Silversides, lost on Trigger 3/45
Tullibee-284	Washington, Jr.	Ripley		1/13/42	New York, NY	12/18/43	KIA	Stm-1	Stm-1	2	Lost with boat 3/26/44 off Palau
Tuna	Buchanan	Paul		11/16/43	Buffalo, NY	9/20/44	12/14/44	Stm-1	Stm-1	2	On from Snapper, off to ATRC
Tuna	Cooper	Clark	Verlin	4/22/44	Fort Worth, TX	9/1/44	8/17/45	Stm-2	St-3	2	On from flag duty
Tuna	Gordon	Eddie	J.	8/5/40	Jacksonville, FL	3/28/42	9/21/44	MA-2	St-2	9	On from Triton, off to Snapper
Tuna	Kearney	Plummer	Edwin	4/13/40	San Diego, CA	1/6/41	4/3/42	OC-3	OC-3	1	Made boat's 1st WP
Tuna	Rozar	Leonard	Cicero	11/28/39	Macon, GA	1/6/41	11/3/42	MA-2	MA-1	3	Later on Saury and Sailfish
Tuna	Templeton, Jr.	Clarence	Maxi	unk.		8/15/45	EOW	Stm-1	Stm-1	0	
Tuna	Whitfield	Freddie	Lee	11/29/43	Jacksonville, FL	3/24/44	EOW	Stm-2	St-3	4	On from flag duty
Tuna-203	Williams, Jr.	Earl		1/29/42	Dallas, TX	11/3/42	3/18/44	MA-2	Stm-1	6	On from Nautilus, off to USNH, TI
Tunny	Chase	Sheldon	Rupert	unk.		5/27/45	EOW	Stm-1	Stm-1	1	Made final WP
Tunny	Collins	Isaac		9/25/41	Macon, GA	9/1/42	ca. 3/1943	MA-2	MA-2	1	Comm crew; Made boat's first WP, later on Tinosa
Tunny	Hale	Harold	Herbert	10/17/39	Richmond, VA	9/1/42	4/14/44	MA-1	St-3	4	Comm crew, on at MI; On WPs 1-3 and 5th, later on Manta detail
Tunny	Howard	Herman	Jackson	unk.		1/21/45	4/29/45	Stm-2	Stm-2	1	Made boat's 8th WP
Tunny	Rapier	William	Fairfield	1/22/40	Indianapolis, IN	3/8/43	1/21/45	OC-3	CK-1	6	Prior on Silversides
Tunny	Robinson	Lawrence		1/8/43	Charleston, SC	8/3/43	9/11/43	Stm-2	Stm-2	0	Relief duty only
Tunny	Thomas	Beachor		unk.		4/29/45	EOW	Ck-3	Ck-3	2	Records illegible; Appears to have made boat's final WPs

Boat	Last Name	First Name	MI	Enlisted	Hometown	Reported	Detached	Rate In	Rate Out	WPs	Notes
Tunny	Turner	James		9/29/43	New Haven, CT	4/13/44	5/27/45	Stm-1	Stm-1	3	On for WPs 6-8; NOK Edna Turner, wife, Jacksonville, FL
Tunny-282	Washington, Jr.	Booker	T.	5/10/43	Chicago, IL	7/29/43	8/3/43	Stm-2	Stm-2	0	Relief duty only
Wahoo	Smith	C.	J.	9/25/41	Little Rock, AR	5/15/42	8/21/42	MA-2	MA-2	1	Comm crew, on at MI
Wahoo-238	James	Willie		12/17/41	New Orleans, LA	8/21/42	1/11/43	MA-1	MA-1	2	Prior on Drum, off to Drum flag
Whale	Amie	William	Arthur	4/27/44	Little Rock, AR	8/21/44	4/26/45	Stm-2	Stm-2	2	CM Reduced from Stm-1 3/45; Off to MI
Whale	Bolton	Levi		1/31/42	Kansas City, MO	6/1/42	7/31/42	MA-3	MA-3	0	Off to S-30, later on S-28 and Rasher
Whale	Carpenter	James		2/7/44	Nashville, TN	4/26/45	EOW	Stm-1	St-3	1	Transferred from Silversides Flag for duty
Whale	Fields	Alonzo	Emerson	9/6/38	Cincinnati, OH	7/3/42	5/4/43	MA-1	St-2	3	On from Silversides flag; Re-enlisted for 2 years 9/42
Whale	Hairston	Lorenzo		10/11/39	Raleigh, NC	6/1/42	2/16/43	MA-1	OS-3	2	Off to Pickerel
Whale	James	Willie		12/17/41	New Orleans, LA	5/5/43	ca. 8/1944	Stm-1	Ck-1	5	Prior on Drum, Wahoo; Later NC, Cobbler, at NL
Whale	Knight	William	Edward	11/16/39	Norfolk, VA	2/26/43	2/16/44	OC-3	Ck-1	4	On from Pickerel flag, off to Tambor flag
Whale	Slayton	Claude	Amos	unk.		6/15/45	EOW	Stm-2	Stm-2	1	On from Silversides flag
Whale	Thomas	Montell	Francis	2/23/44	Harrisburg, PA	8/21/44	11/21/44	Stm-2	Stm-2	1	Relief duty only, off to Pompano flag
Whale-239	Thomas	Isaiah		4/1/42	New Orleans, LA	2/18/44	5/31/44	Stm-2	Stm-1	1	On from Tambor flag, off to Silversides flag

Bibliography

PUBLISHED WORKS

Allison, William A. *Race, Religion, and Slavery in Providence Township*. Temple Hills, MD: The United Methodist Church of the Redeemer, 1996.
Anderson, William R., with Clay Blair, Jr. *Nautilus 90 North*. Cleveland, OH: The World Publishing Company, 1959.
"Base Pitcher Sets Softball Record." *Submarine Base Gazette*, July 2, 1948, p. 4.
Beach, Edward L. *Around the World Submerged—The Voyage of the Triton*. New York: Holt, Rinehart, and Winston, 1962.
_____. *Salt and Steel:Reflections of a Submariner.*Annapolis, MD: Naval Institute Press, 1999.
Blair, Jr., Clay. *Silent Victory—The U.S. Submarine War against Japan*. Philadelphia: J.B. Lippincott and Company,1975.
Clark, Carl E. *Pieces from My Mind*. Berkeley, CA: Creative Arts Book Company, 2001.
Cope, Harley, and Walter Karig. *Battle Submerged—Submarine Fighters of World War II*. New York: W.W. Norton & Company, 1951.
Copeland, Golda C. *Unit K West, B East Chapter II Stewards and Mess Attendants World War II and Beyond*. N.p.: privately published by the author, 2002.
Davis, John P. (ed.). *The American Negro Reference Book*. Englewood Cliffs, NJ: Prentice-Hall, 1966.
Day, Shirley. "Shirley Day III" in "Palestine's Black World War Two Veterans," *Palestine Herald Press,* Palestine, TX, February 25, 1988, p. C-6.
DuBois, W.E.B. *The Souls of Black Folk*. Mineola, NY: Dover Publications, 1994.
Edgerton, Robert B. *Hidden Heroism—Black Soldiers in America's Wars*. Boulder, CO: Westview Press, 2001.
Fluckey, Eugene. *Thunder Below*. Urbana: University of Illinois Press, 1997.
Foner, Jack D. *Blacks and the Military in American History*. New York: Praeger Publishers, 1974.
Galantin, I.J. *Take Her Deep! A Submarine against Japan in World War II*. New York: Pocket Books, 1988.
Grider, George, with Lydel Sims. *War Fish*. Boston: Little, Brown, and Company, 1958.
Hagendorn, Bill. "Trapped at Thirty Fathoms: Jesse DaSilva's Story," *The Kangaroo Express*, Temecula, CA, October 1998, 18 pages unpaginated.
Holmes, W. J. *Undersea Victory: The Influence of Submarine Operations on the War in the Pacific*. Garden City, New York: Doubleday & Company, Inc., 1966.
Hoyt, Edwin P. *Bowfin*. New York: Van Nostrand-Reinhold, 1983.

Huxley, Elspeth. *Their Shining Eldorado: A Journey through Australia.* New York: William Morrow and Company, 1967.

Liburd, Sondra. "Friends thank him, he thanks the Lord," *The Day,* New London, CT.

Lockwood, Charles A., and Hans Christian Adamson. *Through Hell and Deep Water.* New York: Bantam Books, 1991.

Mills, Ernie. "While Pearl Harbor Slept ... He Was Waking the Admirals," *The Dolphin,* Sub Base New London, CT, February 8, 1985, p. 1.

National Park Service. "Port Chicago Naval Magazine National Memorial — California." Washington, D.C.: National Park Service, U.S. Department of the Interior, undated.

Nelson, Dennis D. *The Integration of the Negro into the U.S. Navy.* New York: Farrar, Straus and Young, 1951.

O'Kane, Richard H. *Clear the Bridge: The War Patrols of the* USS Tang. Chicago: Rand McNally, 1977.

Peters, James S. *The Saga of Black Navy Veterans of World War II.* San Francisco: International Scholars Publications, 1996.

Petway, Rita. "It's a Whole New Ballgame," *Gosport,* Naval Air Station, Pensacola, FL, January 9, 1976, p. 13.

Quarles, Benjamin. *The Negro in the Civil War.* New York: DaCapo Press, 1989.

Reddick, Lawrence D. "The Negro in the United States During World War II." *Journal of Negro History,* vol. xxxii, No. 2, April 1947.

Reynolds, Quentin. "Take 'er Down," *Collier Magazine,* November 4, 1944, pp. 41–44.

Roscoe, Theodore. *United States Destroyer Operations in World War II.* Annapolis, MD., Naval Institute Press, 1966.

Roscoe, Theodore. *United States Submarine Operations in World War II.* Annapolis, MD: Naval Institute Press, 1954.

Ruhe, William J. *War in the Boats: My World War II Submarine Battles.* Washington, DC: Brasseys International, 1996.

Salster, Mike. "Twenty-Five Who Have Made a Difference in Today's Amelia County," *Amelia Bulletin Monitor,* Amelia County, VA, clipped article, 1995.

Schratz, Paul R. *Submarine Commander.* Lexington: University Press of Kentucky, 1988.

Sherlock, Martin H. *United States Submarine Data Book.* Groton, CT: Submarine Force Library & Museum Association, Inc., 1976.

Snapp, Martin. "Hadwick Thompson: A Good Man Who Defines Heroism," *Hills Newspaper,* Oakland, CA, December 1, 2000, p. A-9.

Sontag, Sherry, and Christopher Drew. *Blind Man's Bluff—The Untold Story of American Submarine Espionage.* New York: Harper Paperbacks, 1998.

Submarine Base Gazette. June 2, 1948, p. 4.

Trumbull, Robert. *Silversides.* New York: Henry Holt and Company, 1945.

United States Navy. *Ship's Data U.S. Naval Vessels,* vol. 1. Washington, DC: Government Printing Office, 1945.

_____. *Steward's Mates.* Washington, DC., Government Printing Office, 1946.

_____. *United States Ship Scorpion (SSN-589)—In Memoriam.* N.p., N. pub., 1968.

_____. *United States Ship Thresher (SSN-598)—In Memoriam.* N.p.: N. pub., 1963.

_____. *United States Submarine Losses World War II.* Washington, DC: Government Printing Office, 1963.

Waller, Douglas C. *Big Red—Three Months on Board a Trident Nuclear Submarine.* New York: Harper Collins, 2001.

Winslow, Richard E. *Portsmouth-Built—Submarines of the Portsmouth Naval Shipyard.* Portsmouth, NH: Portsmouth Marine Society Publication Six, Peter E. Randall, 1985.

Wright, Chester A. *Historical Background of the Human Resources Management Problem Implicit in the Recent Amalgamation of the Steward and Commissary Branches of the U.S. Navy.* Monterey, CA: Naval Postgraduate School, Human Resource Management Center, 1975.

Internet Sources

Barron, Pat, and Patrick Meagher. "Loss of the USS *Stickleback SS-415*," www.submarine-sailor.com, December 3, 2002.
Fleming, Thomas C. "Looking Back: Job Discrimination in the 20's," www.abouttimemag.com/lookingback.html, August 14, 2002.
McKenzie (Allen), Jeanine. "The Volunteers of Spritz's Navy," www.home.earthlink.net/~text/spritz_Navy.html, no date.
Truman, Harry S. "Desegregation of the Armed Services — Executive Order 9981," July 26, 1948, WWW.history.navy.mil/faqs/faq59-17.htm.
Zumwalt, Jr., Admiral E.R. "Z-gram #57 (Elimination of Demeaning or Abrasive Regulations)," November 10, 1970, www.history.navy.mil/faqs/faq93-57.htm.
_____. "Z-gram #66 (Equal Opportunity)," December 17, 1970, www.history.navy.mil/faqs/faq93-66.htm.
_____. "Z-gram #117 (Good Order and Discipline)," November 14, 1972, www.history.navy.mil/faqs/faq93-117.htm.

Unpublished Personal Manuscripts, Documents, and Letters

Adams, Captain O.B. Letter to George Lytle, New London, CT, November 21, 1986.
Anderson, Rae. "*Sea Fox* Diary." [A compilation of events in diary form for this boat from the 1944 to 1945 time period by one of her crew.]
Barnes, John. "USS *Thresher SS-200*." Dated August 1992. [A compilation of *Thresher's* war patrol reports with commentary on the crew and patrol events. Barnes served on this boat during the war.]
Carter, Fate, Jr. "Home Going Service" program. Dated December 2000. Agape Fellowship Freewill Baptist Church, Wilmington, Delaware. [Funeral program.]
Fenner, Donald. Enlistment Letter, NRB Form #53, from the U.S. Navy Recruiting Station, Richmond, VA, dated August 10, 1940.
_____. Undated letter written while on the battleship *Tennessee* at Honolulu, Hawaii, to his mother, Cousy Fenner, of Halifax, NC, circa January 1941.
Love, Captain Winifred. Master Chief Petty Officer Evaluation Report of Abraham Mozeak, dated 12/10/72.
McDonald, Craig. "USS *Puffer* (SS-268): From Manitowoc to the Depths of the Makassar Strait — The First War Patrol." [A compilation of eye-witness accounts, with commentary, about this boat's harrowing and nearly fatal first patrol. McDonald's father served on this boat during the war.]
Perry, William Sydney. Letter from Perry to the Chief of Naval Personnel, dated 7/5/52.
Southern Association of Colleges and Schools. Letter to A.P. Royal, June 10, 1975.
Stempf, Charles R. Letter to Mrs. George Lytle, New London, CT, January 22, 1988.
Williams, Edwin E. Letter to Rufus Weaver, dated 9/18/63.
Williams, Captain J. E. Letter of Appreciation from Senior Member, Petty Officer Quality Control Review Board to Abraham Mozeak, Pers-B1604B/dsn/2, dated 3/8/73.
Williams, Melvin G. "Keynote Presentation Unit K-West, B East, 19th Annual Reunion," Norfolk, VA, September 28, 1995.
_____. "Naval Historical Center Interview with Intern Timothy Shives," Washington, DC, August 17, 2001. [I have used a corrected version that was edited by Williams.] Ser/NHC/MU/05862.

Unpublished Government Documents, Citations, and Commendations

Note: Most of the citations and commendations listed here have no document or identifying number other than their date of issue.

Burrell, Donald. "Citation," from Captain C.C. Cole, Commander Submarine Squadron One, for period August 1955 to October 8, 1955 while on *Carp*.
Coleman, Wallace. "Commendation," from Captain Joseph W. Russel, *USS Nathan Hale* (SSBN-623), December 21, 1964.
____. "Meritorious Mast for Superior Performance of Duty," from Captain W. A. Brockett, Boston Naval Shipyard, April 21, 1961.
Fenner, Donald. "Naval Recruiting Board Form 53, Induction Notice," August 10, 1940.
Holloman, Frank. "Commendation," from D.P. Brooks, Commanding Officer, *USS Sam Houston* (SSBN-609), Ser: 134 (B), April 28, 1965.
____. "Navy Achievement Medal Citation," from James B. Wilson, Vice Admiral, Chief of Naval Education and Training, for period September 1969 to August 1975.
Lytle, George. "Bronze Star Citation," from James Forrstal, Secretary of the Navy, Washington, D.C., undated.
Mozeak, Abraham. "Letter of Appreciation."
O'Meally, John. "Citation," from Rear Admiral E.B. Fluckey, Commander Submarine Force, United States Pacific Fleet for period spring 1964 while on *USS Halibut* (SSGN-587).
Pruitt, John Alden. "Case of John Alden Pruitt, Steward's Mate First Class, U.S. Navy, June 2, 1944—Record of Proceedings of a General Court-Martial Convened on Board the U.S.S. *Orion* by order of the Commander U.S. Naval Forces Western Australia," Document #128932. Obtained via the Freedom of Information Act.
Stallings, Jim. "Letter of Commendation," from Commanding Officer J.E. Magee, *USS Grenadier* (SS-525), dated July 28, 1962.
____. "Letter of Recognition for Superior Performance of Duty," Helicopter Anti-Submarine Squadron One, FF12/HS, May 7, 1966.
Weaver, Rufus J. "Memorandum: Transfer of Weaver, R.J., SDCA (SS),USN," from M.W. Huffer, Personnel Officer, Submarine Development Group Two, to Executive Officer, USS *Cavalla* (SS-244), March 21, 1963. [Subject concerns Weaver's transfer to *Thresher*.]

Personal Accounts

The following individuals were interviewed either by phone or in person regarding their submarine experiences or career, or provided information on one of the Black submariners detailed in this book based on first-hand knowledge of the individual in question. Citations in the text to this quoted material consist of the name of the contact person.

Allen, Harold Hurley, email 12/26/03 regarding his father, Carroll Louden Allen.
Allen, Herman, phone interview 12/15/03 regarding his father, Carrol Louden Allen.
Allen, Jesse, phone interview 12/17/03.
Allison, William, phone interview 8/20/02, personal interview 6/27/03 and written account of his career 10/24/03.
Anderson, Bruce, phone interview 9/3/02 with follow-up email correspondence.
Andrews, Dennis, email correspondence 8/02 regarding stewards on *Plunger*.
Baker, Richard, phone interview 9/24/03 regarding Shirley Day on *Grayling*.

Barron, Pat, phone interview 10/25/03.
Brown, Arthur, initial phone interview 9/7/02 and ongoing personal correspondence.
Brown, Dean, phone interview 9/02 regarding the stewards on *Trout*.
Burrell, Donald O., letter to the author October 2003.
Burton, Howard, phone interviews 9/03.
Butcher, Billy, letter to author 8/29/02 about the stewards on *Plaice*.
Caverly, Floyd, *Tang* survivor, phone interview 10/14/03.
Church, Hollis, personal interview with author 8/29/02.
Coleman, Lawrence, phone interviews and correspondence 4/03 regarding the service of his father, Wallace Coleman.
Coley, Robert, phone interview 8/19/02.
Collier, David, phone interview 8/31/02.
Cooper, Clark, phone interviews 9/02.
Curry, Don, email correspondence 11/21/03 regarding *Manta*'s stewards.
Cutter, Captain Slade, phone interview 3/19/03 regarding the stewards on *Seahorse*.
Danford, Earnest, phone interview 8/30/02.
Davis, Alonza, phone interview 8/02.
Davis, Carrie Grooms, phone interview 1/3/03, subsequent email correspondence.
Davis, Mildred, wife of Everett Davis, phone interviews 11/21/02 and 2003 to 2/2004.
Debro, Jesse, phone interview 8/14/02.
Denson, Archie, phone interview 12/21/02 and personal interview 6/27/03.
Drewry, Alexander, phone interview 4/4/03 regarding Joseph Cross on *Tigrone* and Dave Ball on *Rasher*.
Dwyer, Captain Carl, phone interview 1/8/04 regarding stewards on *Puffer*.
Erickson, Floyd "Doc," phone interview 9/12/03 regarding Willie James and Willie Knight on *Whale*.
Fitchpatrick, Curtis, phone interview 9/02.
Foulke, Frank, email correspondence 8/22/02 regarding the stewards on *Gurnard*.
Frazelle, Edgar, series of phone interviews 7/03.
Gauthwaite, Edward, personal interview 8/29/02.
Gentry, Ingram, phone interview 3/25/03.
Goens, Robert, phone interview 8/13/02.
Green, Charlotte, letter to the author 12/23/03 regarding the service of her father William Green.
Groom, Charles, phone interview 7/7/03.
Hale, Harold H., phone interview 1/3/03.
Hall, Alfred, phone interview 9/18/02.
Hall, Harry, email correspondence 8/19/02 regarding the stewards on *Queenfish*.
Hammonds, L.T., phone interview 3/1/03.
Harris, Richard D., email correspondence 8/11/02 regarding a steward on *S-12*.
Harrison, William O., email 1/30/03 regarding steward "Sheriff" John Stone.
Haynes, Arthur, phone interview 8/10/02.
Henderson, Nathan, email correspondence 11/02/03 regarding the stewards on *Pompon*.
Higgins, Jack, email correspondence 9/3/02 regarding the stewards on *Dentuda*.
Hussey, Dave, personal interview 9/20/03 regarding the stewards on *Parche*.
Jackson, William, personal interview at Submarine Veterans Convention, Buffalo, NY, 8/29/02 regarding the stewards on *Scabbardfish*.
Jacobs, Ken, email 8/18/02 regarding Mack Butler on *Queenfish*.
Jameson, Howard, phone interview 8/14/02.
Johnson, Isaac, phone interviews 8/02, 12/26/03, and 1/04.
Jones, Jerry, phone interview 3/9/03 regarding his brother, Curtis Hill.
Jones, Sanfuel, interview 4/9/03 regarding his brother, Curtis Hill.
Joyner, Kenneth, series of phone interviews 7/03 and email correspondence in 12/03.

Kelley, Kane, phone interview 8/02 regarding the stewards of *Hardhead*, with follow-up personal correspondence.
Kimmons, Carl E., on-going email correspondence between 8/02 and 1/04.
Latham, Hugh, phone interview 11/03 regarding the stewards on *Tunny* and postwar *Catfish*.
Lester, Doyle, phone interview 10/02 regarding the stewards on *Sterlet* and *Marlin*.
Lewis, Jim, phone interview 8/24/02 regarding the stewards on *S-28*.
Lomax, Gilbert, phone interview 9/9/02.
Lucas, Richard, phone interview 8/25/02.
Marion, Jim, phone interview 1/10/03 regarding Russell Donan on *Cobia*.
Maurer, Admiral John, phone interview 9/29/02 regarding the stewards on *Atule*.
Mayo, Elvin, personal interview 3/28/03.
Mays, Hosey, personal interview at the Submarine Veterans Convention, Buffalo, NY, 8/29/02.
McDonald, Craig, on-going email correspondence from 9/02 to 3/04.
Milhorn, Glenn, email correspondence 3/03 regarding the stewards of *Gurnard*.
Minor, Bert, phone interview 9/4/02.
Mochio, Steve, phone interview 11/14/03 regarding the stewards on *Lionfish*.
Mosely, R.D., phone interview 9/02.
Mosley, James, letter to the author 10/15/02.
Mozeak, Abraham, letter to the author 1/23/03.
Murray, William H. "Bill," letter to the author 11/12/03.
Nalle, Peter, letter to the author 6/2/03 regarding steward Willie James on *Whale*.
Nash, John, email to the author 8/14/02.
Nash, Norm, phone interview 11/7/03 regarding the stewards on *Tunny*.
Neely, Edward, phone interview 9/02.
Newton, Killraine, phone interview 8/02.
Olmstead, Elmer, email correspondence 10/14/02 regarding the stewards on *Sterlet*.
O'Meally, Arthur, letter to the author 10/03 and subsequent email correspondence.
O'Meally, John, letter to the author 5/12/03 and follow-up correspondence through 12/03.
Owens, James, Jr., letter to the author April 2003.
Patrick, Walter, undated letter to the author 5/03.
Perkins, John, Jr., personal interview at the Submarine Veterans convention, Buffalo, NY, 8/29/02, regarding Steward Joseph Cross on *Halibut*.
Perry, June, phone interview 10/10/02 regarding the navy career of her husband, William Perry.
Pilger, Gerald, phone interview 11/13/03 regarding the stewards on *Jallao*.
Ragland, Letha, phone interview 12/03 regarding the service of her husband, Paul Ragland, with follow-up correspondence.
Richardson, Moyna, phone interviews 1/12/03 and 2/7/03 regarding the service of her husband, Charles Richardson, and conditions in wartime Australia.
Rindskopf, Captain Maurice, phone interview 9/19/02 and subsequent email correspondence regarding George Lytle on *Drum*.
Royal, Anderson Peter, ongoing personal communication from 11/02 to 1/04.
Rozar, Albert, phone interview 9/6/02.
Rozar, Leonard, phone interviews 8/28/02 and 10/23/02.
Rush, Captain Charles, email correspondence 2/14/03 and 2/25/03 regarding the stewards on *Billfish* and postwar *Carbonero*.
Senior, Harry, phone interview 9/10/02.
Shelby, Steve, letter to the author 5/5/03.
Simonds, Steve, email correspondence 8/8/02 regarding the stewards on *Caiman*.
Slaughter, Louis, phone interview 9/10/02 and follow-up letter to the author regarding his service and that of Fate Carter, Jr.
Smith, Mason B., phone interview 7/15/02.
Soles, Albert, phone interviews 8/20/02 and 1/7/04.

Thomas, Don, email 8/6/02 regarding stewards on *Manta*.
Topor, Ladislaus, phone interview July 10, 2003 regarding the steward John Pruitt on *Puffer*.
Vasey, Joe, email correspondence 9/4/02 regarding steward Magnus Wade on *Gunnel*.
Veder, Dave, phone interview 4/15/03 and personal interview 7/26/03 regarding steward Willie James on *Wahoo* and steward Hosie Washington on *Tusk*.
Wallace, Sam, letter to the author 9/02 and ongoing correspondence from 8/02 to 12/03.
Walsh, Mike, email correspondence 8/13/02 regarding the stewards on *Peto*.
Ward, James, email to author 8/10/02.
Washington, Hosea "Hosey," phone interview 9/17/02 and letter to the author 4/5/03.
Washington, James, phone interview 3/7/03.
Weaver, Rufus Jack, phone interview 9/20/03 with follow-up letter to the author.
Whelan, William, email correspondence 11/14/03 regarding the stewards on *Brill*.
White, Carl, phone interview 12/18/02.
Whitehead, John Wesley, phone interview 2/7/03.
Whitehead, Ruby, letter to the author 3/03 regarding the service of her husband, John Whitehead.
Williams, Charles, phone interview 2/10/03.
Williams, Melvin, Sr., phone interview 2/17/03 and personal interview on 6/27/03.
Willis, Avery, phone interview 11/8/03 regarding the stewards on *Tunny*.
Wilson, Donald, phone interview 10/19/02 and ongoing communication from 10/02 to 1/04.
Wilson, Viola, personal interview 4/1/03 regarding the service of her husband, Walter Pye Wilson.

NATIONAL ARCHIVES SOURCE MATERIAL

The following are enlisted man muster rolls for World War II submarines located at the National Archives II facility at College Park, MD. These records are part of Records Group 24 (RG24) and are on microfilm reels. The individual reel numbers for each record consulted are listed below after the name of the submarine in question. Submarine training activity for Portsmouth, New Hampshire, can be found on reels 7881, 7883, and 7890.

Amberjack, 168
Angler, 206
Apogon, 351
Argonaut 2, 408
Aspro, 437
Atule, 516
Balao, 615
Bang, 624
Barb, 632
Barbel, 633
Barbero, 635
Bashaw, 658
Baya, 669
Becuna, 685
Bergall, 708
Besugo, 717
Billfish, 723
Blackfin, 737
Blackfish, 738
Blenny, 745

Bluefish, 756
Boarfish, 759
Bonefish, 772
Bowfin, 793
Bream, 810
Bugara, 854
Bullhead, 855
Bumper, 862
Burrfish, 873
Cabrilla, 889
Caiman, 898
Capelin, 932
Capitaine, 395
Carbonero, 941
Carp, 954
Cavalla, 986
Cero, 995
Chub, 1092
Cisco, 1100
Cobia, 1129

Corvina, 1209
Croaker, 1237
Cutlass, 1268
Dace, 1279
Darter, 1294
Dentuda, 1329
Dragonet, 1387
Entemedor, 1483
Finback, 1550
Flasher, 1562
Flier, 1566
Flounder, 1570
Flying Fish, 1574
Gabilan, 1619
Gar, 1636
Gato, 1622
Golet, 1733
Grampus, 1750
Grayling, 1760
Greenling, 1767

Grenadier, 1774
Grouper, 1783
Growler, 1785
Grunion, 1788
Guardfish, 1792
Guavina, 1794
Gudgeon, 1795
Guitarro, 1800
Gunnel, 1806
Gurnard, 1809
Hackleback, 1826
Haddo, 1827
Haddock, 1828
Hake, 1832
Halibut, 1839
Hammerhead, 1851
Hardhead, 1866
Hawkbill, 1891
Herring, 1931
Hoe, 1956

Icefish, 2254
Jack, 2077
Jallao, 2085
Kete, 2196
Kingfish, 1992
Lagarto, 2232
Lamprey, 2254
Lapon, 2268
Lizardfish, 3496
Loggerhead, 3504
Macabi, 5193
Manta, 5239
Muskallunge, 5475
Narwhal, 5444
Nautilus, 5506
Paddle, 5669
Perch 2, 6178
Permit, 6184
Peto, 6192
Pickerel, 6240
Picuda, 6243
Pilotfish, 6252
Pintado, 6258
Pipefish, 6261
Piranha, 6263
Plaice, 6268
Plunger, 6274
Pogy, 6282
Pollack, 6267
Pomfret, 6290
Pompano, 6292

Porpoise, 6306
Rasher, 6100
Raton, 6427
Ray, 6430
Razorback, 6434
Redfin, 6440
Redfish, 6441
Robalo, 6502
Rock, 6521
Ronquil, 6541
Runner I, 6562
S-18, 6577
S-23, 6582
S-26, 6585
S-28, 6587
S-30, 6589
S-31, 6590
S-32, 6591
S-33, 6592
S-34, 6593
S-35, 6594
S-38, 6597
S-39, 6598
S-41, 6600
S-42, 6601
S-43, 6602
S-44, 6603
S-45, 6604
S-46, 6605
S-47, 6606
Sailfish, 6622

Salmon, 6636
Sandlance, 6659
Sargo, 6670
Saury, 6699
Sawfish, 6704
Scabbardfish, 7147
Scamp, 6400
Scorpion, 7157
Sculpin, 7166
Sea Cat, 7169
Sea Devil, 7170
Sea Dog, 7171
Sea Fox, 7174
Sea Owl, 7181
Sea Poacher, 7182
Sea Robin, 7184
Seahorse, 7176
Seal, 7177
Sealion I, 7179
Sealion II, 7180
Seawolf, 7186
Sennet, 7205
Shark II, 7229
Skate, 7285
Skipjack, 7299
Snook, 7298
Spadefish, 7316
Spearfish, 7320
Spikefish, 7330
Spot, 7333
Springer, 7335

Steelhead, 7362
Sterlet, 7369
Stickleback, 7376
Stingray, 7378
Sturgeon, 7399
Sunfish, 7410
Swordfish, 7434
Tambor, 7460
Tang, 7463
Tarpon, 7472
Tautog, 7483
Tench, 7476
Thornback, 7524
Threadfin, 7527
Tilefish, 7537
Tinosa, 7545
Tirante, 7548
Torsk, 7573
Trepang, 7587
Trigger, 7591
Triton, 7597
Trout, 7599
Trutta, 7604
Tullibee, 7612
Tuna, 7615
Tunny, 7616
Wahoo, 7663
Whale, 7774

Index

Aaron Ward (destroyer) 15
Aborigine population (Australia) 128
Abraham Lincoln (SSBN-602) 320
Acker, Frank 297
Adams, Culasket 65
Adams, O.B. 317
Adams, Ralph 72, 106
Adams, Willie 99
African–Americans: in Civil War 10; drafting of in WWII 21; duty as Chief of Boat (COB) 203–4, 212–13, 218, 233, 234; enlistment halted pre-war 12; enrollment at Naval Academy 211; non-steward ratings held in WWII 16; quotas for enlistment in WWII 19
Alabama (Confederate raider) 10
Albacore (SS-218) 15, 140
Albacore (SS-569) 199, 200, 375
Aleutian Islands 39, 79, 87
Alexander, Joseph 81, 94, 138
Allen, Beecher 177
Allen, Carrol Louden 66, 86, 99, 104, 107, 258–59
Allen, Jesse 58, 61, 67, 97, 145, 240, 260–61
Allen, John 93
Allison, William 58, 103, 127, 138, 154, 261–62, 289
Amberjack (SS-219) 73
Amberjack (SS-522) 266, 272

American Revolution 9
Anderson (transport) 262
Anderson, Aaron 10
Anderson, Bruce 24, 27, 147, 170, 175, 263–64
Anderson, Jack 249
Anderson, William 195–96
Andrews, Charles 286
Andrews, Herb 93
Andrews, Richard 282
Angler (SS-240) 88, 207
Anthony, Masca 79
Antietam (carrier) 198
Apollo (tender) 184
Archerfish (SS-311) 115, 318
Argonaut (SS-166) 15, 45, 46, 59, 87
Argonaut (SS-475) 273, 382
Arleigh Burke Fleet Trophy 232, 234
Armbruster, Stephen 272
Armed Services Police Detachment 186, 340
Ashe, Arthur 155, 288
Asheville (SSN-758) 256
Ashley, James 338
Aspro (SS-309) 361
Astoria (cruiser) 315
Atule (SS-403) 84, 107, 127, 226, 322
Aubert, Lilly 365
Axeman, Minnie 376
Axene, Dean 236
Ayers, R. 96

Bailey, Viola 382

Bainbridge Naval Training Station 22, 24
Baker, Richard 284
Balao (SS-285) 279
Ball, Dave 42, 50, 58, 78, 85, 131, 157, 186–87, 191, 264–66, 297, 332, 355, 371
Baltimore (cruiser) 40
Bang (SS-385) 140, 234, 373
Barb (SS-220) 51, 84, 157, 341–42, 362–63
Barbel (SS-316) 73, 145
Barbel (SS-580) 256, 274
Barley, Lillian 337
Barnes, John 96
Barr, Eric, Jr. 37, 58, 102, 335, 338
Barracuda (SS-163) 302
Barracuda (SSK-3) 318, 367
Bashaw (SS-241) 201, 287
Bass (SS-164) 60
Bass, Raymond 101–2, 311, 328–29, 366
Batfish (SS-310) 34, 47, 298–99
Batfish (SSN-681) 245
Batts, Allen 331, 332
Baya (SS-318) 48, 61, 156, 279
Beach, Edward 72, 106, 139, 226–228, 295, 382, 383
Beaver (tender) 277, 360, 363, 367
Becker, Albert 287
Beckman, Lt. 335
Becuna (SS-319) 331
Bell, David 102, 226, 353
Benham (destroyer) 15

Benitez, Rafael 178, 179
Benjamin Franklin (SSBN-640) 223
Benson, Roy 382
Bergall (SS-320) 206, 207, 295, 324
Bermuda 124
Berthrong, Raymond 364
Besugo (SS-321) 62, 181–82, 201, 273, 322, 333, 360
Bigelow, Reginald 175–76
Billfish (SS-286) 39, 92, 136, 156, 157, 299, 330
Bismarck (German battleship) 296
Bivens, Charles 99
Black, Curtheal 262
Black and Tan Bar 123
Blake, Robert 10
Blakely (destroyer) 276
Blenny (SS-324) 202, 203, 216, 334
Blue, Robert, Jr. 172
Bluefish (SS-222) 138, 145, 153, 266, 316, 343, 355, 356
Bluegill (SS-242) 47, 56, 58, 67, 87, 93, 102, 119–20, 129, 155, 265, 322, 335–37
Boise (light cruiser) 374
Bolton, Levi 80, 81
Bonefish (SS-223) 115, 117–18, 143, 145–46, 157, 325–26
Bonita (SS-165) 302
Boothe, Percy 145
Boston Naval Shipyard 35
Boulet, William 51
Bowe, Julius 157
Bowfin (SS-287) 51, 61, 94–95, 103, 105, 115, 138, 155–56, 321, 330, 373
Boyd, Cleo 59
Boyle, Francis 366
Bracey, George 59, 145, 152, 236, 266
Bracey, Letha 58, 236
Brandon, William 140
Brill (SS-330) 67, 122, 135–36, 157, 279, 299, 357
Brockman, William 361
Bronze Star (military award) 15, 76–77, 187, 198, 210, 239, 264, 277, 317, 327, 361
Brooks, Daniel 212, 213
Brown, Arthur 20, 38, 39, 67, 84, 88, 102–4, 115, 144, 152, 156, 256–57, 266–69
Brown, Benjamin 67, 81
Brown, Dean 34, 303
Brown, Ethel June 339
Brown, Francis 81, 322

Brown, James 268
Brown, Roscoe 147
Brown, William 133
Bryant, George 122, 135
Bryant, Luther 97, 157
Buffington, Bill 138
Bugara (SS-331) 100, 157
Bullhead (SS-332) 16, 73, 145–46
Bumper (SS-333) 344
Bundy, William 256
Burke, Arleigh 265
Burkett, Timothy 120
Burlingame, Creed 43, 58, 61, 102, 104, 190, 346, 348–49
Burrell, Donald 164–65, 201, 203, 204, 209, 211, 214–15
Burrfish (SS-312) 78
Burrows, Albert "Ace" 142, 205, 316
Burton, Howard 186, 188–91, 232
Bush, George H. 89
Bushnell (tender) 176, 181, 355, 360
Butler, Mack 57, 97, 104, 157, 269–70
Butler, Ovid 282
Buttrill, JP 59, 142
Bynum, William 78
Byrd, Richard 61
Byrd Antarctic Expedition 173–74

Cabrilla (SS-288) 326
Caiman (SS-323) 82
Calhoun, John 10
Camden (cruiser) 301
Camp Dealey (Guam) 133, 135
Campbell, Charles 81
Campbell, J.G. 361
Campbell, Nathaniel 120
Capella (auxiliary cargo ship) 364
Capitaine (SS-336) 181
Carbonero (SS-337) 176–77, 190, 192, 284, 307, 346, 348, 367
Career Appraisal School 219–20, 324
Carp (SS-338) 177, 203–5, 214, 216, 221, 287
Carter, Fate, Jr. 215, 240–41
Catfish (SS-339) 165, 193, 274, 380
Cavalla (SS-244) 149, 200, 212, 238, 295, 342, 378, 379
Cavalla (SSN-684) 246
Census population statistics 19
Centennial Seven 256

Cero (SS-225) 78, 157, 363
Chaffee, John 250
Chanticleer (auxiliary sub rescue ship) 201
Charr (SS-328) 284
Chavis, Percy 149
Chewink (auxiliary rescue ship) 300, 326
Chicago (guided missile cruiser) 216, 244, 245
Chivo (SS-341) 164, 295, 338
Chopper (SS-342) 172, 173, 298, 332, 354, 373
Christie, Ralph 12, 118, 146, 300, 326
Chub (SS-329) 66, 89, 90, 301, 380
Churchill, Winston 367
Chuyo (Japanese carrier) 327
Cisco (SS-290) 73
Civil Rights Act (1964) 214
Claggett, Bladen 269
Clamagore (SS-343) 266, 344
Clark, Albert 101
Clark, Carl 15
Clinton, William 17
Club Cosmo 378
Cobbler (SS-344) 147, 164, 171, 175, 187, 306, 312, 353
Cobia (SS-245) 155, 287–88
Cochino (SS-345) 177–79, 185, 195, 318
Cod (SS-224) 102, 154, 358, 360
Cole, Cy 142, 203
Cole, Otis 269
Cole, Shelley 193, 194
Coleman, Emma Martin 129–30, 271
Coleman, Wallace 27, 129–31, 157, 211, 224, 271–72
Coley, Robert 66, 100, 157, 272
Collier, David 21, 58, 67, 150, 156, 273, 276
Collins, Isaac 76
Colston, Sammy 61, 99
Constellation (carrier) 249
Coolangatta (Australia) 128, 336
Cooley, Quintus 146
Cooper, Clark 21, 102, 156, 175, 274–75
Cooper, George 115–16
Corbus, John 103, 321, 330
Cornish, Tyree 151, 273, 276–77
Corporal (SS-346) 326, 361
Correigidor (escort carrier) 260
Corsair (SS-435) 177–78, 190, 265, 272, 320

Corvina (SS-226) 303
Cosby, William, Jr. 205, 354
Cosby, William, Sr. 354
Cox, Charles, Jr. 109–10
Cox, Leroy 116–17
Craig, John 289
Cramp Shipbuilding Company 35
Crawford, Alonza, Jr. 15
Crawford, J.C. 63, 107, 144
Creole Palace 123
Crevalle (SS-291) 47, 58, 59, 61, 66, 87, 102, 103, 104, 105, 127, 128, 137, 138, 155, 157, 321, 325
Croaker (SS-246) 366
Crockett, Barnard 145
Cross, Anna-Mae 239
Cross, Joseph 15, 76, 153, 157, 167, 200, 239, 277–78, 297
Cross, Joseph Fabian 239
Curtis (seaplane tender) 369
Cusk (SS-348) 164, 176, 234–35, 242, 338, 355
Cutlass (SS-478) 265
Cutter, Slade 63, 107, 144
Cuttlefish (SS-171) 58, 76, 103, 374, 375

Dace (SS-247) 57, 97, 105, 140, 157, 269–70, 326
Dace (SSN-607) 232
Danford, Ernest 21, 24, 48, 61, 156, 196, 197, 278–79
Daniel Webster (SSBN-626) 223, 298
Darter (SS-227) 140, 149, 269, 343
Darwin Sub House (Australia) 120, 337
DaSilva, Jesse 71–72
Davenport, Roy 58, 104, 346, 347, 361
David Taylor Model Basin 237
Davis, Alonza 46, 132, 279–80, 352
Davis, Eddie 193, 196
Davis, Everett 155–56, 171, 280–82
Davis, Lewis 282–83
Dawson, Elijah, Jr. 89, 140, 157
Day, Shirley 113, 114, 157, 283–85
Dealey, Samuel 73, 75, 76
Debro, Jesse 51, 61, 85, 92, 102, 154, 285–86
DeHosnery, Stewart 14, 84, 97, 152
Dempsey, James 102, 358

Denson, Archie 2, 62, 180–83, 223, 252, 254–55
Dentuda (SS-335) 97, 137, 368, 369
DeTar, John 103, 337, 353, 354
Devilfish (SS-292) 58, 67, 97, 145–46, 260
Dewey, George 11
Diablo (SS-479) 375
Diodon (SS-349) 175, 274
Dodge, Harry 299
Dogan, Nathan 286–87
Dogfish (SS-350) 232
Dolphin (SS-169) 36
Dolphin (SS-555) 256
Donaho, Glynn 117, 380, 381
Donan, Russell 154, 155, 287–88
Dornin, Robert 382
Dragonet (SS-293) 57, 69, 107, 137, 156, 157, 345, 348
Dropp, Anthony 354
Drum (SS-228) 15, 49, 50, 63, 66, 77, 97, 105, 107, 140, 144, 157, 304, 305, 317
Drum (SSN-677) 246
Drury, Alexander 266
Dubois, W.E.B. 121, 256
Duncan, Arnold 201, 216
Dutch Harbor (Alaska) 79, 360
Dwyer, Carl 99, 104, 107
Dykers, Thomas 43–44, 102, 190, 319, 320

Echo class submarine (Soviet) 243
Eddy, Ian 102, 280, 327, 352, 353
Edge, Lawrence 146
Edwards, John 78
Electric Boat Company 35, 122
Ellis, Arthur 84
Ellis, John 136, 292
Emmanuel, Thomas 194, 196
Enright, Joseph 269
Entemedor (SS-340) 226, 326, 343
Enterprise (carrier) 15
Epps, William, Jr. 146
Erickson, Floyd "Doc" 106, 305, 316
Escolar (SS-294) 140, 142, 307, 347
Ethan Allen (SSBN-608) 183, 223, 295, 357
Eurayle (tender) 120, 337
Evans, Benjamin 142
Evans, Joe 81
Evans, Melton 114
Executive Order 8802 16

Executive Order 9981 168–69

Fahy, Charles 168
Fahy, Edward 111–13, 328, 329
Fahy Committee 168–69, 179
Fairfax (destroyer) 367
Falcon (auxiliary rescue ship) 264
Farr, Horace 149
Fenner, Cousy 41
Fenner, Donald 41–42, 97, 138–39, 262, 289–90
Fenno, Frank 303
Ferguson, Hosea 171
Fernandez, Ambrosio 143
Finback (SS-230) 58, 89, 116, 157
Finley, Napoleon 61, 90–91
Fisher, LC 139, 154, 290, 312
Fitchpatrick, Curtis 60
Flasher (SS-249) 91, 110, 115–16
Fleet Ballistic Missile (FBM) patrols 222–23
Fleet Operations Control Center Pacific (FOCCPAC) 218, 232–33
Flier (SS-250) 70
Floyd, Alphonse 73, 75
Fluckey, Eugene 107, 230, 341, 342
Flying Fish (SS-229) 99–100, 116–17, 188, 308, 354, 379–80
Forrestal (carrier) 324
Forrestal, James 77, 156, 162
Fort Benning (Georgia) 20
Foster, Robert 212, 213
Foulke, Frank 286, 287
Franklin, Sir John 195
Frazelle, Edgar 188–89
Freeman, Archie 79, 81
French, Charles 15
Fuhrman, Albert 320
Fulton (tender) 12, 159, 300, 311, 313
Fyfe, John 47, 300

Galantin, Ignacius "Pete" 277, 341, 374
Galbreath, Woodrow 188
Gallaher, Anton 142
Gallery, Daniel 152
Gamble (minelayer) 60
Gar (SS-206) 111, 115
Garcia, Napoleon 238
Gaylor, James 105, 269
Geer (unknown ship) 302
Gentry, Ingram 87
George Bancroft (SSBN-643) 223, 240

George Washington (carrier) 260
George Washington (SSBN-598) 199, 220, 221, 223, 238, 260, 298, 379
Gilmore, Howard 65–66
Gimber, Stephen 102, 374, 375
Glenn, Curtis 79, 81
Goens, Robert 61, 66, 76, 102, 123, 128, 136, 154, 257, 291–94
Golay, Frank 86
Golden Fleece Award 249
Golet (SS-361) 292
Goode, Claude 109–11
Gordelle, Eddie 109, 110
Gordon, Eddie 353
Grable, Betty 63, 86
Grady, James 305, 316
Grampus (SS-207) 58, 103, 127, 138–39, 154, 261–62, 289
Grampus (SS-523) 189, 375, 383
Grandy, William 59, 76
Gravely, Samuel 218
Gray, John 33, 157, 294, 306
Grayback (SS-208) 73
Grayling (SS-209) 157, 284
Grayling (SSN-646) 231
Great Lakes Naval Training Center 22
Great White Fleet 11, 129
Green, Johnnie 110, 268
Green, Joseph 171
Green, Robert 146
Green, William 206, 207, 226–29, 294–95, 378
Greenfish (SS-351) 353
Greenlet (rescue ship) 207
Gregory, Willie 87–88
Grenadier (SS-210) 70, 73
Grenadier (SS-525) 211–12, 322, 331, 361
Grenfell, Elton 326, 332
Grider, George 85, 91, 365
Gridley (destroyer) 215
Griffin (tender) 140, 176, 266, 318, 355, 356, 371
Griffith, Monroe 127
Griffith, Walter 94, 103, 330
Groom, Charles 189, 198–99, 231
Grooms, Bruce 256
Grouleff, Paul 364
Grouper (SS-214) 309
Growler (SS-215) 65–66, 97, 140, 157
Guadalcanal (escort carrier) 152
Guam 133

Guam Disorders 134–35
Guardfish (SS-217) 156, 301
Guardfish (SSN-612) 242–44
Guavina (SS-362) 208, 342
Gudgeon (SS-211) 45, 66, 73, 114, 136, 143, 157, 326, 339, 352
Gugliotta, Gus 102, 316
Guico, Justiniano 70
Gunn, Frederick 69, 98
Gunnel (SS-253) 72, 137, 367–69
Gurnard (SS-254) 56, 92–93, 148, 286–87

Hackett, Hubert 16, 146
Haddo (SS-255) 19, 97, 150, 157
Haddo (SSN-604) 232, 248
Haddock (SS-231) 31, 97, 144, 157, 204, 210, 214, 361
Hake (SS-256) 58, 67, 150, 156, 157, 273, 276, 277
Hale, Harold 30, 40, 42, 63, 66, 76, 102, 154, 295–97
Halfbeak (SS-352) 218, 318
Halibut (SS-232) 15, 76, 153, 157, 277, 278, 341, 374
Halibut (SSGN-587) 215–17, 230, 239, 240, 264
Hall, Alfred 21, 66, 97, 102, 156, 199, 223, 197–98
Hamilton, Leslie 67, 93, 136, 157, 298–99
Hamman (destroyer) 15
Hammerhead (SS-364) 156, 312, 331
Hammond, Lewis 33, 34, 36, 47, 299–300
Haney, Cecil 256
Hannon, Edward 322
Harder (SS-257) 67, 73, 75, 107, 133, 285, 344, 353
Hardhead (SS-365) 67, 157
Hardin, James 102, 274
Hargreaves, Isaac 145
Harlfinger, Fritz 382
Harmon, Leonard 14
Harper, Ivory 150
Harris, John 12, 300
Harris, Richard 79
Hartford (gunboat) 10
Harvey, Walter 196–97
Hassayampa (oiler) 249
Havanna (Cuba) 124–25
Hawk, Earl 102, 374, 375
Hawkbill (SS-366) 380
Hawkins (destroyer) 344
Haynes, Arthur 21, 24, 33, 66, 89–90, 301

Heard, Bernard 157
Hearn, Marvin 88
Heisser, Melvin 156
Helicopter Anti-Submarine Squadron One 212
Henderson, Charles 343
Henderson, Nathan 84, 375
Henry L. Stimson (SSBN-655) 218
Henson, Matthew 198
Hepburn, Katharine 154, 290
Herbert (auxiliary transport) 264
Herring (SS-233) 120
Hess, Franklin 108–9
Hess, John 102, 297
Higgins, Jack 97
Higgins, Jim 180, 232
Hill, Curtis 301–3
Hines, Andrew 78
Hinman, Gerald 348
Hoe (SS-258) 156
Hogan, Thomas 117, 118, 326
Holland (tender) 128, 245
Holloman, Frank 147, 149, 180–81, 212–14, 252–54, 263
Holman, William 104, 269
Holmes, Jasper 66
Holmes, Joseph 177, 179
Holt, E.R. 146
Holtz, Arnold 354
Honolulu (SSN-7718) 256
Hood (British battleship) 296
Hooper Island (repair ship) 157, 192, 349
Hopkins, Raymond 147
Hoppes, John 177
Horne, Lena 86
Hornet (carrier) 189
Hottell, Martin 103, 374, 375
Houston (SSN-713) 162, 246, 256
Howard W. Gilmore (tender) 87, 265, 274, 304, 361
Hull, Harry 298
Hull, Jesse 116
Humphrey, Hubert 250
Huntley, David 336
Hutchinson, Edward 103
Hydeman, Earl 325

I-28 (Japanese sub) 294
I-41 (Japanese sub) 300
I-42 (Japanese sub) 296
I-351 (Japanese sub) 145
I-373 (Japanese sub) 145
Icefish (SS-367) 61, 66, 76, 102, 123, 128, 136, 137, 154, 291–93, 304
Idaho (battleship) 189

Indianapolis (cruiser) 42, 264
Ingalls Shipbuilding Company 242
Intrepid (carrier) 15
Irex (SS-482) 295, 378

Jack (SS-259) 43–44, 102, 105, 156, 190, 319–20, 372
Jackson, Dallas 79
Jackson, Eddie 60, 76
Jackson, Lee 79, 81
Jackson, Lewis 333
Jackson, Lonnie 14, 97, 114, 157, 303–4
Jackson, Zedell 304
Jacksonville (SSN-699) 256
Jackstadt, Steve 247
Jacobs, Ken 270
Jallao (SS-368) 99, 320
James, Willie 49–50, 66, 89, 106, 126, 143–44, 149, 155, 304–6, 312
James, Willie (second) 306
James K. Polk (SSBN-645) 218, 224, 241, 249
Jameson, Howard 136
Japanese stewards 11
Jarvis, Benjamin 279
Jaycox (steward's mate) 325
John Marshall (SSBN-611) 212, 240, 244–45, 355
Johnson, Isaac 24, 33, 66, 102, 106, 138, 142, 157, 171, 176, 192, 198, 209, 218–19, 222, 247, 294, 306–7, 333, 346, 348, 367
Johnson, Louis 168
Johnson, Lyndon 250
Johnson, Nathaniel 16, 81
Johnson, Percy, Jr. 16, 146
Johnston Island 132
Joint Army-Navy Assessment Committee (JANAC) 258
Jones, Jimmie 148
Jones, Jimmy 378
Jones, Louis 67, 99
Jones, Louis (lost at sea) 120
Jones, Stanley 79
Jones, Woodrow 104, 156, 197–98, 231, 308–9
Jonkins, Walter 84
Jordan, John 11
Jordan, Paul 176, 348
Jordan, Robert 149
Joyner, Kenneth 165, 180, 184, 201–5, 209, 216, 218, 232–34, 241, 247
Jubry, Florence 308

Kako (Japanese cruiser) 79

Kamehameha (SSBN-642) 223
Kearsarge (Civil war ship) 10
Kefauver, Russell 272
Kennedy, Houston, Jr. 157
Kennedy, Marvin 143, 144, 305
Kennedy, Robert F. 246
Kennon, John 172
Kent State University (Ohio) 246
Kete (SS-369) 145
Kimmel, Husband 339
Kimmons, Carl 3, 15, 19, 23–4, 25, 39, 40, 57, 61, 82, 85, 123–26, 136–39, 143–44, 149, 157, 159–60, 162, 164, 171, 175, 209, 239, 256, 290, 306, 309–311, 313–15, 326, 345
King, Ed 167
King, Martin Luther 246, 265
King Edward Hotel (Australia) 109, 127
King Neptune 87
Kingfish (SS-234) 129, 153, 343
Kinsella, William 358, 359
Kirtley, Albert 145
Kittiwake (auxiliary ship) 326
Kittyhawk (carrier) 249
Knapp, Lt. 208
Knight, William 42, 106, 113–14, 142, 191, 315–16, 326
Knox, Frank 125, 156, 162
Kraken (SS-370) 287
Krapf, Arthur 320
Kumano (Japanese cruiser) 359

L-class submarines 12
Lagarto (SS-371) 145, 146, 279
Lapon (SS-260) 78, 274
Larson, Paul 71
Latham, Hugh 61, 166
Latham, Richard 356
Latta, Frank 43, 102, 146, 268, 279
Lawson, John 10
Leary (destroyer) 264
Lemon, B.F. 96
Lent, Willis 326
Lester, Doyle 91
Lewellen, Bafford 365
Lewis, Albert 100–1
Lewis, Jack 57, 348, 382
Lewis, Jim 80, 360–61
Lewis, Thelma Jean 311
Lexington (carrier) 15, 276, 315
Limited Duty Officer (LDO) Program 214, 215, 313
Ling (SS-297) 320
Linthicum, Andrew 268
Lionfish (SS-298) 61, 67, 99, 260

Liscome Bay (Carrier) 14
Little Rock (cruiser) 97, 354
Lizardfish (SS-373) 78, 155, 280, 282
Locust (minelayer) 265
Logan Heights (San Diego, CA) 219
Loggerhead (SS-374) 151
Lomax, Gilbert 24, 171
Lookout (auxiliary ship) 159, 333
Loughlin, Charles 102, 285
Louisville (SSN-724) 255
Love, Alexander 378
Lowe, Paul 307
Lowrance, Vernon 343
Lucas, Frederick 299
Lucas, Richard 20, 33, 36, 61, 96, 126, 154, 316–17
Lynch, Frank 75
Lytle, George 15, 50–51, 52, 63, 66, 77, 97, 105, 107, 144, 157, 204, 264, 317–18

MacArthur, Douglas 303
Mack, Isaac 138
Mackerel (SS-204) 78, 316, 333, 380
Madison, John 102, 104, 357, 372, 380
Madison, Lester 89
Madison Square Garden (New York) 157, 265
Maine (battleship) 176
Major, Sammy 20, 157, 177, 223, 224, 240, 318–19
Majuro Atoll 132
Makin Islands 87
Malone, James 150
Manitowoc Shipbuilding Company (Wisconsin) 35
Mann, Stephen 260
Manta (SS-299) 296
Marblehead (cruiser) 10
Mare Island Naval Shipyard (California) 35
Marion, Jim 286
Marlin (SS-205) 78, 265, 363, 364
Marshall, Elliot 103, 374
Martinez, Electrician's Mate 178
Mason (destroyer) 137
Maurer, John 107
Maury (destroyer) 300
Maya (Japanese heavy cruiser) 269
Mayo, Elvin 36, 43–44, 105, 156, 190, 319–20
Mays, Hosea 21, 24, 31, 36, 46,

61, 66, 105, 127–28, 138, 155, 171, 320–22
McAdoo, Arthur 59
McCain, John, Jr. 367, 368, 369
McCauley, Ed 205
McClintock, David 149
McCormick, Daniel 115, 117–18
McCrory, Woodrow 139, 143, 290, 312
McDaniels, William 216
McFarland (destroyer) 40, 58, 136, 159, 310, 345
McFarland, Henry 177
McGregor, Louis 104, 308
McGuire, James 67
McKay, Claude 105
McMaster, Fitzhugh 67
McMillan, Duncan 284
McNair, Edward 172, 173, 174, 219–20, 322–24
Medal of Honor (military award) 10, 11, 14, 66, 103, 107, 133, 143, 312
Medical Service Corp 215
Medregal (SS-480) 159, 175, 284, 313
Menhaden (SS-377) 147, 149, 181, 212
Merrill, Wayne 300
Merriweather, Eddie 215, 216
Mess Management Specialist rating 252
Mestichelli, Angelo 109, 111
Mestichelli, Lavinia 109
Metz, Thomas 69
Michael, Willard 343
Midway (carrier) 198
Midway Island 131
Milhorn, Glenn 54, 287
Military Sealift Command 282
Miller, Dorie 13–14, 17, 167
Miller, Glen 84, 268
Miller, Herman 333
Miller, "Low Voltage" 322
Millican, William 298
Milne Bay (New Guinea) 132
Mingo (SS-261) 57, 78, 89, 102, 104–5, 126, 128, 139–40, 156, 198, 356, 357, 369–73, 380
Minor, Bert 36, 58, 59, 155, 324–25
Minton, D.C. III 244
Mississippi (battleship) 40, 296
Missouri (battleship) 150
Mitchell, Herman 81
Mocio, Steve 99
Moore, John 79
Moore, Robert 67, 73, 75–76
Moray (SS-300) 342

Morton, Dudley 143, 305
Mosley, Eugene, Jr. 143, 157, 325–26
Mosley, James 164, 165, 198, 205–6, 215, 237
Mosley, Robert 66, 102, 280, 326–27, 331
Mosley, Steve 94–95, 326
Mozeak, Abraham 180, 183–84, 216, 218, 232, 241
Munson, Hank 102, 103, 104, 138, 321
Murphy, John 272
Murray, William 36, 38, 61, 62, 100–2, 111–13, 120, 157, 224–25, 327–30

Nalle, Peter 106, 305, 306
Narwhal (SS-167) 38, 39, 43, 59, 67, 84, 87–88, 102, 104, 110, 115, 144, 152, 156, 185, 187, 257, 267–69, 322, 339, 340, 343, 361
Nash, John 270
Nathan Hale (SSBN-623) 224, 272
National Football League (NFL) 301, 308
Nautilus (SS-168) 59, 87, 153, 343
Nautilus (SSN-571) 185, 188, 192–99, 220, 226, 229, 264, 298
Naval Academy (Annapolis, MD) 105
Naval Enlisted Science Education Program (NESEP) 214, 215, 216, 244
Navy Cross (military award) 92, 103, 104, 118, 167, 321, 361
Navy Training Publication Department 241
Nebraska (SSBN-739) 162, 255, 256
Neely, Edward 39, 61, 103, 155, 156, 170, 330–31
Neurius (tender) 274, 342
Newton, A.L. 59
Newton, Killraine 21, 38, 58, 67, 124, 147, 157–160, 169, 171, 174, 209–11, 240, 263, 304, 331–33, 350–51
Nicholas, Nicholas 338
Nimitz (carrier) 254, 260
Nimitz, Chester, Jr. 109
Nixon, Richard 265
Nokaze (Japanese destroyer) 145
Norfolk (Virginia), description of 24

Normand, William 248
Norrington, Bill 50
Norris (destroyer) 207
Northwest Passage 195
Northwind (Coast Guard cutter) 172, 174

O-2 (SS-63) 263
O-4 (SS-65) 78, 265, 266
O-6 (SS-67) 78, 265, 333, 371
O-9 (SS-70) 78, 370, 371
O-class submarines 78, 370, 371
Oakland (California) Police Department 154
Odax (SS-484) 265, 318
Odom, Herbert 61, 157, 171
O'Kane, Richard 70, 84, 106, 107
Okinawa Island 15
Oklahoma City (guided missile cruiser) 215, 380
Olds, Percy 46
Oliver, Elbert 15
Olmstead, Elmer 84
Olsen, Elliot 284
Olsen, Robert 88
Olympia (cruiser) 10
O'Meally, Arthur 180, 183, 234–35, 241–44
O'Meally, John 180–83, 200–1, 208, 215–17, 230–31, 237, 241–42, 244
O'Neil, Guy 368, 369
Operation Desert Shield 255
Operation Enduring Freedom 260
Operation Highjump 171–72
Operation Kayo 177–78
Orion (tender) 109, 316, 325, 343, 353, 377
Orr, Charles 78
Otus (tender) 128, 138, 262, 289
Owens, James, Jr. 171, 189, 192–93, 194–96, 198, 223, 240

Paddle (SS-263) 380
Page, Clarence 91, 115–16
Palmer, Claude, Jr. 33, 170, 202, 203, 333–34
Palmer, Robie 365
Pampanito (SS-383) 364
Parche (SS-384) 15, 40, 43, 102, 124, 138–39, 143, 154, 157, 159, 290, 312, 332
Pargo (SS-264) 58, 66, 102, 132, 137, 145, 152, 157, 236, 266, 279, 280, 319, 326, 327, 352, 353
Parker, Velton 192

Parks, Rosa 272
Parnell, Charles 11
Patrick, Frank 347
Patrick, Walter 22, 28, 33–34, 37, 47, 56, 57–58, 67, 87, 93, 102, 119–21, 129, 155, 334–38
Patrick Henry (SSBN-599) 223, 224, 319
Patterson, Jones 115
Patton, James 65, 66, 69, 97, 98, 104, 107, 123
PC-479 (patrol craft) 132, 262
Pearson, Ltjg. 111–12
Peary Arctic Expedition 198
Pease, Joachim 10
Peeples, Washington, Jr. 116
Pelias (tender) 109, 111, 176, 272, 326, 343, 355
Penn, Robert 11
Pennington, Roscoe 152–53, 162, 164, 171, 236–37, 247, 338–39
Pennyman, Timothy 46, 104, 321
People's Baptist Church (Portsmouth, NH) 236
Perch (SS-176) 70
Perkins, John, Jr. 76
Perkins, Morris 89, 90, 301
Permit (SS-178) 316
Perry, June 186
Perry, Oliver Hazzard 9
Perry, William 156, 186–87, 191, 339–40
Peterson, Joe 256
Peterson, Joe, Jr. 306
Peterson, Richard 102, 292–93, 304, 339
Peto (SS-265) 99
Phelps, John, Jr. 184, 207
Philadelphia (SSN-690) 245
Philadelphia Navy Yard 35
Philippine Sea (carrier) 172
Phillips, John 341, 374
Pickerel (SS-177) 142, 315, 316
Picuda (SS-382) 157, 224, 306, 318
Piedmont (destroyer tender) 252, 255
Pike (SS-173) 104, 156, 197, 308, 309
Pilger, Gerald 99
Pilotfish (SS-386) 150, 151, 277
Pintado (SSN-672) 246
Piper (SS-409) 309, 361
Plaice (SS-390) 282, 283
Plunger (SS-179) 15, 40, 61, 67, 93, 100–2, 111, 120, 137, 157, 159, 177, 310–11, 313, 328–30, 353, 366
Plunger (SSN-595) 218, 232–34, 241, 247
Polaris Training and Evaluation Program (PTEP) 245
Pollack (SS-180) 59, 85, 116, 154, 157, 271, 353, 365
Pollack (SSN-603) 232
Pomfret (SS-391) 66, 97, 102, 156, 297
Pompano (SS-181) 107, 353
Pompon (SS-267) 84, 102, 264, 332, 374, 375
Port Chicago (California) Incident 16–17
Porter, George 102, 307, 343
Portland (cruiser) 264
Portsmouth Naval Shipyard (New Hampshire) 35
Potomac (presidential yacht) 367
Power (destroyer) 344
Prairie View A&M College (Texas) 211, 215
Presidential Advisory Committee on Universal Military Training 168
Prophet, John 97
Proteus (tender) 325, 373
Proxmire, William 249
Pruitt, John 65, 92, 108–11, 123
Puerto Rico 159
Puffer (SS-268) 63, 65, 66, 69, 86, 92, 97–99, 104, 108, 111, 123, 259, 265, 343
Purple Heart (military award) 15

Qualifying card 55
Queenfish (SS-393) 51, 61, 85, 92, 102, 154, 270, 285, 367
Quirk, P.D. 103

R-1 (SS-78) 152, 377
R-3 (SS-80) 287
R-5 (SS-82) 260, 287, 367
R-7 (SS-84) 186, 287, 339
R-11 (SS-88) 326
R-12 (SS-89) 78
R-14 (SS-91) 78, 343
R-18 (SS-95) 269
R-class submarines 78
Ragland, Herbert 342
Ragland, Paul 51, 84, 107, 157, 191, 200, 341–43
Raiford, Rubin 71–72, 106
Raleigh (cruiser) 40, 374
Raley, James 142
Ramage, Lawson 43, 102, 103, 143, 303, 312
Ramsey (destroyer) 364, 365
Ramsey, Gene 378
Ramsey, Walter 115
Randolph (carrier) 380
Randolph, A. Phillip 16
Ranger (carrier) 266, 381
Rapier, William 61, 68–69, 89
Rasher (SS-269) 50, 78, 81, 103, 131, 156, 157, 187, 265, 266, 321
Raton (SS-270) 61, 96, 102, 109, 126, 154, 316
Ray (SS-271) 226, 358, 359
Razorback (SS-394) 266, 296
Reaves, Reginald 194
Redfin (SS-272) 309, 331
Redfish (SS-395) 104, 156, 197, 308
Reed, Ulysses 19, 109, 157
Regulus I missile system 176, 230, 231
Requin (SS-481) 273
Rhymes, Cassius, Jr. 301
Rice, Robert 50, 51, 304, 317, 380
Richardson, Charles 129, 131, 153–54, 170, 223, 343–44
Richardson, Moyna 129
Rickover, Hyman 193–97, 229
Rigel (auxiliary repair ship) 308
Riley, Henry 177, 179
Rindskopf, Maurice 50, 51, 107, 317
Ring magazine 131
Risser, Robert 380, 381
RO-30 (Japanese sub) 293
RO-112 (Japanese sub) 300
RO-113 (Japanese sub) 300
Roach, John 361
Robalo (SS-273) 70
Robert E. Lee (SSBN-601) 218, 219, 222, 224, 225, 307, 330
Robinson, Dorothy 367, 369
Robinson, Eddie 75, 96
Robinson, John, Jr. 89
Rock (SS-274) 373
Rodney, William 142
Roncador (SS-301) 138, 307
Ronquil (SS-396) 164, 236, 273, 338
Roosevelt, Eleanor 187, 265
Ross, Phillip 277
Royal, Anderson 3, 20, 40, 51–2, 57, 58, 68, 69, 82, 104, 107, 136–37, 156–59, 171, 176, 190, 192, 209, 256, 275, 333, 338, 344–51, 367
Royal, Will 20, 344

Royal Hawaiian Hotel 125–26, 135
Rozar, Albert 46, 66, 67, 97, 137, 157, 280, 319, 352–53
Rozar, Leonard 20, 62, 66, 96, 97, 103, 157, 352–55
Runner (SS-476) 361
Rush, Charles 92, 93, 176, 299
Rusk, Dean 250
Russel, Joseph 224
Rutter, Royal 338

S-1 (SS-105) 12, 300
S-12 (SS-117) 79
S-15 (SS-120) 280, 304
S-22 (SS-127) 60, 264
S-26 (SS-131) 16, 81
S-28 (SS-133) 80, 81, 360
S-29 (SS-134) 326
S-30 (SS-135) 79, 81
S-32 (SS-137) 81
S-35 (SS-140) 81
S-42 (SS-153) 79, 81
S-43 (SS-154) 322
S-44 (SS-155) 79, 81
S-45 (SS-156) 322
S-47 (SS-158) 322
S-48 (SS-159) 367
S-class submarines 78–79, 81
Sabalo (SS-302) 147, 208, 209
Sablefish (SS-303) 175, 340, 383
Sailfish (SS-192) 58, 67, 102, 124, 157, 159, 288, 312, 327, 331, 333, 354, 375
Salmon (SS-182) 59, 284, 333
Salster, Mike 155
Sam Houston (SSBN-609) 212, 213, 219, 223, 224, 240, 324
Sample, Christopher 145
San Francisco (cruiser) 14
Sand Lance (SS-381) 177
Sanders, John 116
Sarda (SS-488) 212, 265, 272, 355
Sargo (SSN-583) 192, 198, 223, 357, 381
Saury (SS-189) 157, 354
Savadkin, Lawrence 106
Savannah (light cruiser) 300
Scabbardfish (SS-397) 66, 69, 83, 98
Scamp (SS-277) 45, 73, 140
Schratz, Paul 91
Scorpion (SS-278) 238
Scorpion (SSN-589) 153, 157, 220, 231, 238–39, 277, 278, 309
Scott (destroyer) 137–38, 311

Scott, John 102, 296
Scott, Lewis 120
Sculpin (SS-191) 59, 327
Sculpin (SSN-590) 232
Sea Cat (SS-399) 185, 260, 324, 361
Sea Devil (SS-400) 273
Sea Dog (SS-401) 338
Sea Fox (SS-402) 134
Sea Leopard (SS-483) 147, 159, 170, 175, 263, 331, 332, 361
Sea Owl (SS-405) 184–85, 375, 376, 377, 378
Sea Pike (troop ship) 355
Sea Poacher (SS-406) 266, 324
Sea Robin (SS-407) 159, 172, 192, 313, 329–30
Seadragon (SS-194) 153, 236, 338, 377
Seadragon (SSN-584) 198–99, 231
Seahorse (SS-304) 63, 64, 65, 144
Seal (SS-183) 115, 381
Sealion (SS-315) 278, 331
Searaven (SS-196) 289
Seawolf (SS-197) 45, 140
Seawolf (SSN-575) 196, 197, 279
Senior, Harry 176, 212, 213, 240, 355
Sennet (SS-408) 66, 102, 138, 172–4, 192, 307, 324
Sequoia (presidential yacht) 225, 250
Settle, Spaulding 61, 66, 355–56
Shark (SS-314) 140
Shark (SSN-591) 239, 278, 353
Sharp, George 364
Sharp, Samuel 65
Shelby, Steve 55, 208–9, 216, 232
Shelton, Leotis 177, 179
Shelton, William 142
Shepard, Evan 318
Siboney (escort carrier) 263
Sieglaff, William 294
Silver Star (military award) 14, 114, 264, 265, 303
Silversides (SS-236) 3, 40, 43, 51, 52, 58, 61, 68, 69, 82, 102, 104, 107, 133, 137, 156, 157, 269, 345–47, 374
Silverstein (destroyer) 207
Sims, Hollis 232, 244, 245
Sims, James 66, 69–70, 98
Singer, Earl 81
Singleton, John 78

Sirago (SS-485) 141, 147, 278, 382, 383
Sisler, Vince 360
Skate (SSN-578) 197, 198, 215, 218, 231, 232, 244, 273, 309
Skipjack (SSN-585) 198, 206, 218–19, 307
Slaughter, Louis 180, 232, 241, 248–9
Sloppy Joe's Bar 124–25
Smith, C.J. 144
Smith, Frank 331
Smith, Henry 92, 93
Smith, Mason 46, 97, 125, 140, 198, 223, 356–57, 372
Smith, R.H. 369, 371
Smith, Richard 316
Snapper (SS-185) 41, 288, 289, 316
Snook (SS-279) 142, 145, 157, 353
Sococco, Peter 5
Soles, Albert 154, 358–59
Soviet class submarines 233
Spadefish (SS-411) 102
Spanish-American War 11
Spaulding, Robert 65
Spearfish (SS-190) 59, 142
Sperry (tender) 201, 273, 287, 305, 342
Sperry Corporation 231
Spikefish (SS-404) 145, 153, 157, 236, 309, 338, 354, 366, 377
Spinax (SS-489) 332, 360, 383
Spriggs, Paul 143
Spritz, Charlie 36
Spurlock, Jake 80, 81, 360–61
Staley, Joseph 102, 357, 371, 380
Stallings, Jim 18, 31, 42, 97, 144, 157, 175, 184, 204, 210–12, 214, 361–62
Stallings, William 207
Steelhead (SS-280) 312
Steffanides, Edward 102, 274
Steinmetz, Everett 325
Sterlet (SS-392) 61, 73, 84, 90, 91, 181, 202, 216, 322
Stevens, Clyde 282
Stevenson, Lacey 157, 362–63, 378–79
stewards: abolishment of 252; association with Aborigine population 127; attendance of ship's parties 136–37; battle-stations of 61–62; conflict between 100–101; conversion to mess management specialist 251; culinary skills of 50–51; flag duty 191; lookout

duty 73, 75–76; marriage to Australians 129; payrates 29, 251; performance of religious service 90, 224; postwar rating changes 313; postwar rating system 168, 252; postwar training 163, 166, 167; power wielded by 31–32; prejudicial incidents against 98–100; pre-war and wartime training 35–39; psychological screening of 36–37; qualifying procedures of 57–59; rating badge 17, 32; as recruiters 219, 237; service on gun crews 66–70, 72, 73, 167; uniform appearance 29–31; war-time rating system 28–30
Stickleback (SS-415) 184, 207, 374
Stingray (SS-186) 5
Stone, Hamilton 288
Stone, Herman 115
Stone, John 223
Strategic Arms Limitation Talks (SALT) 242
Street, George 102, 103, 149
Strong, Ezell "Tommy" 78, 313, 363
Strouther, Elijah 88
Strow, A.L. 361
Sturgeon (SS-187) 59, 263
Submarine Combat Insignia card 275, 278
Sumner, Charles 10
Sunbird (rescue ship) 231
Sunfish (SS-281) 156, 186, 339
Surcouf (Free French sub) 78
Swordfish (SS-193) 145

T-1 (SST-1) 199
Taiyo (Japanese carrier) 296, 308
Talton, William 378
Tambor (SS-198) 59, 66, 100, 157, 272, 278, 284, 316
Tang (SS-306) 15, 70–72, 89, 106, 139
Tautog (SS-199) 59, 157, 294
Taylor, Art 361
Tench (SS-417) 260, 279
Tennessee (battleship) 41, 97, 288
Texas (battleship) 302
Thaxton, O'Neal 78, 363–64
Theodore Roosevelt (SSBN-600) 223, 344
Thomas, Issiah 120
Thomas, William 366, 367

Thomas, Willie 46
Thomas Edison (SSBN-610) 215, 326
Thomas Jefferson (SSBN-618) 209, 221–22, 223, 245
Thompson, George 149
Thompson, Hadwick 85, 154, 363–65
Thornback (SS-418) 266
Threadfin (SS-410) 145
Thresher (SS-200) 59, 73–74, 96, 136, 157, 284
Thresher (SSN-593) 59, 152–53, 236–38, 266, 338, 379
Thunman, Nils 233, 234
Tigrone (SS-419) 89, 200, 278, 342
Tilefish (SS-307) 164, 192, 201, 203, 214, 307, 338, 344, 364
Tinosa (SS-283) 61, 66, 356
Tirante (SS-420) 43, 102, 103, 149
Tiru (SS-416) 235
Titus, Jack 102, 268, 296
Tokyo Rose 84
Toler, Otha 122, 157, 176, 177, 328, 346, 348, 365–67
Toombs, Leroy 156, 301
Toowoomba (Australia) 129
Toper, Ladislaus 65
Toro (SS-422) 177, 178
Trigg, Thomas 70
Trigger (SS-237) 72, 73, 97, 104, 106, 114, 123, 126, 139, 141, 144, 145, 147, 157, 381–83
Trigger (SS-564) 383
Tringa (sub rescue ship) 295
Triton (SS-201) 143, 284
Triton (SSRN-586) 199, 225–30, 238–39, 278, 295, 326
Trout (SS-202) 14, 15, 84, 97, 101, 152, 157, 303, 320
Truman, Harry 306
Trumbull, Robert 344, 345, 346
Trumpetfish (SS-425) 375
Trutta (SS-421) 200, 201, 272
Tuna (SS-203) 62, 96, 102, 103, 156, 157, 274–75, 353–54
Tunny (SS-282) 61, 63, 66, 69, 76, 89, 102, 142, 154, 296
Turner, James 63
Turner, Vernon 299
Tuscaloosa (cruiser) 276, 367
Tusk (SS-426) 177–79, 185, 228, 272, 326, 342, 344, 383

Tuskegee Airmen 13
Tuskegee Institute (Alabama) 253, 254
Tuttle, Carlos 99
Tzomes, Chancellor 162, 211, 244, 245–46, 256

U-183 (German sub) 333
U-505 (German sub) 150, 152, 377
U-530 (German sub) 152, 269
Ulysses S. Grant (SSBN-631) 255
Underwood, Gordon 102, 296
Union Pacific Railroad 320
Unit K West/B East 22, 24
United Service Organization (USO) 124–25, 127, 129
United States Armed Forces Institute (USAFI) 226
United States Supreme Court 10
Unryu (Japanese carrier) 308
Unyo (Japanese carrier) 342, 354

Veder, Dave 126, 177, 305
Ventress, Willa-Mae 366
Vesey, Joe 368
Vietnam War 280
Vincennes (cruiser) 302, 315
Vixen (yacht) 367, 369
Vogelsang (destroyer) 266
Volador (SS-490) 206–7, 215

Waddell, Willie 150, 157
Wade, Hattie 367
Wade, James 81
Wade, Magnus 39, 72, 73, 137, 204, 367–69
Wahoo (SS-238) 126, 144
Walker, Howard 72, 89, 107
Wall, Frank 375
Wallace, Sam 36, 42, 46, 57, 78, 89, 104–5, 122, 126, 128, 129, 139, 140, 156, 169, 172–73, 234, 256, 303, 324, 356, 358, 366, 369–73, 380
Wallace, Strauther 374
Walsh, Mike 99
War of 1812 9
Ward, James 226
Ward, Jim 85
Ward, Robert 93, 102, 327, 331, 332, 333
Warner, John 250
Washington, Daniel 164
Washington, Fred 164
Washington, Hosea 164–65, 171, 177–79, 209, 226–29

Washington, James 40, 58, 76, 113, 199–200, 374–75
Washington, Melvin 164
Waterman, John 341, 362
Watson, Tony 256
Waugh, Richard 354
Weaver, Rufus 150, 152, 184, 185, 212, 221, 237–38, 375–79
Weiss, Donald 356
Wells, Robert 109, 110, 111
West, Thomas, Jr. 48
West Virginia (battleship) 14, 308
Western Pacific (WESTPAC) operations 176–77, 201–7, 214, 222, 232, 234, 235, 260, 307
Whale (SS-239) 49, 50, 89, 106, 142, 155, 305, 309, 316
Whelan, William 122, 299
White, Carl 379–80
White, David 310, 311
White, Walter 16
Whitehead, John 21, 24, 42, 99–100, 117, 380–81
Whitehead, Ruby 381
Will Rogers (SSBN-659) 211, 213, 223, 245, 252, 253, 254
Williams, Charles 40, 171
Williams, Clarence 154
Williams, Edwin 212
Williams, Melvin, Jr. 255, 256
Williams, Melvin, Sr. 2, 180–81, 221–22, 224–25, 250–52, 255–56
Williamson, Delbert 317
Williamson, Robert 216
Willingham, Joseph 294
Willis, Avery 63
Wilson, Donald 19, 24, 184–85, 193–96, 226, 229, 342
Wilson, Harold 242
Wilson, Viola 140–41, 383
Wilson, Walter 72, 97, 104, 106, 114, 123, 126, 139–41, 144, 147, 157, 204, 381–83
Wilson, Woodrow 149
Wogan, Thomas 333
Worthington, Robert 179
Wouldridge, John 180, 183, 226, 238
Wright (unknown ship) 333
Wright, "Bull" 76
Wright, Chester 19
Wyandank (Civil War ship) 10

Yates, Roscoe, Jr. 116–17
Yorktown (carrier) 192
Young, Willie 78
Yubari (Japanese cruiser) 93, 335

Z-Gram 57 246–47
Z-Gram 66 247–48
Zanes, Herbert 145
Zeilen (transport) 198
Zumwalt, Elmo 246–252

www.ingramcontent.com/pod-product-compliance
Lightning Source LLC
Chambersburg PA
CBHW081532300426
44116CB00015B/2599